T0189091

Communications in Computer and Information Science   1363

More information about this series at http://www.springer.com/series/7899

Linqiang Pan · Shangchen Pang ·
Tao Song · Faming Gong (Eds.)

Bio-Inspired Computing: Theories and Applications

15th International Conference, BIC-TA 2020
Qingdao, China, October 23–25, 2020
Revised Selected Papers

 Springer

Editors
Linqiang Pan (iD)
Huazhong University of Science
and Technology
Wuhan, China

Shangchen Pang
China University of Petroleum
Qingdao, China

Tao Song
China University of Petroleum
Qingdao, China

Faming Gong
China University of Petroleum
Qingdao, China

ISSN 1865-0929   ISSN 1865-0937   (electronic)
Communications in Computer and Information Science
ISBN 978-981-16-1353-1   ISBN 978-981-16-1354-8   (eBook)
https://doi.org/10.1007/978-981-16-1354-8

This Springer imprint is published by the registered company Springer Nature Singapore Pte Ltd.
The registered company address is: 152 Beach Road, #21-01/04 Gateway East, Singapore 189721,
Singapore

Preface

Bio-inspired computing is a field of study that abstracts computing ideas (data structures, operations with data, ways to control operations, computing models, artificial intelligence, etc.) from biological systems or living phenomena such as cells, tissues, neural networks, immune systems, ant colonies, and evolution. The areas of bio-inspired computing include neural networks, brain-inspired computing, neuromorphic computing and architectures, cellular automata and cellular neural networks, evolutionary computing, swarm intelligence, fuzzy logic and systems, DNA and molecular computing, membrane computing, and artificial intelligence and their application in other disciplines such as machine learning, image processing, computer science, and cybernetics. Bio-Inspired Computing: Theories and Applications (BIC-TA) is a series of conferences that aims to bring together researchers working in the main areas of bio-inspired computing, to present their recent results, exchange ideas, and cooperate in a friendly framework.

Since 2006, the conference has taken place at Wuhan (2006), Zhengzhou (2007), Adelaide (2008), Beijing (2009), Liverpool and Changsha (2010), Penang (2011), Gwalior (2012), Anhui (2013), Wuhan (2014), Anhui (2015), Xi'an (2016), Harbin (2017), Beijing (2018), and Zhengzhou (2019). Following the success of previous editions, the 15th International Conference on Bio-Inspired Computing: Theories and Applications (BIC-TA 2020) was held in Qingdao, China, during October 23–25, 2020, organized by the China University of Petroleum with the support of the Operations Research Society of Hubei.

We would like to thank the keynote speakers for their excellent presentation: Hao Yan (Arizona State University, USA), Shahid Mumtaz (Instituto de Telecomunicações, Portugal), Mario J. Pérez-Jiménez (University of Seville, Spain), and Guanyu Wang (Southern University of Science and Technology, China). Thanks are given to the tutorial speakers for their inspiring presentation: Qinghua Lu (CSIRO, Australia) and Bosheng Song (Hunan University, China)

A special thankyou is given to professor Jun Yao and professor Jin Xu for their guidance and support to the conference.

We gratefully thank Sicheng He, Wenjian Luo, Fan Meng, Sibo Qiao, Xiaolong Shi, Qingyu Tian, Min Wang, Shaoqiang Wang, Pengfei Xie, and Xue Zhai for their contribution in organizing the conference.

Although BIC-TA 2020 was affected by COVID-19, we still received a wide spectrum of interesting research papers on various aspects of bio-inspired computing; 43 papers were selected for this volume of *Communications in Computer and Information Science*. We are grateful to all the authors for submitting their interesting research work. The warmest thanks should be given to the external referees for their careful and efficient work in the reviewing process.

We thank Lianlang Duan, Fan Meng, Qingyu Tian, and Yi Zhao, et al. for their help in collecting the final files of the papers and editing the volume. We thank Zheng

Zhang and Lianlang Duan for their contribution in maintaining the website of BIC-TA 2020 (http://2020.bicta.org/). We also thank all the other volunteers, whose efforts ensured the smooth running of the conference.

Special thanks are due to Springer Nature for their skilled cooperation in the timely production of this volume.

December 2020

Linqiang Pan
Shangchen Pang
Tao Song
Faming Gong

Organization

Steering Committee

Atulya K. Nagar	Liverpool Hope University, UK
Gheorghe Păun	Romanian Academy, Romania
Giancarlo Mauri	Università di Milano-Bicocca, Italy
Guangzhao Cui	Zhengzhou University of Light Industry, China
Hao Yan	Arizona State University, USA
Jin Xu	Peking University, China
Jiuyong Li	University of South Australia, Australia
Joshua Knowles	University of Manchester, UK
K. G. Subramanian	Liverpool Hope University, UK
Kalyanmoy Deb	Michigan State University, USA
Kenli Li	Hunan University, China
Linqiang Pan (Chair)	Huazhong University of Science and Technology, China
Mario J. Pérez-Jiménez	University of Seville, Spain
Miki Hirabayashi	National Institute of Information and Communications Technology, Japan
Robinson Thamburaj	Madras Christian College, India
Thom LaBean	North Carolina State University, USA
Yongli Mi	Hong Kong University of Science and Technology, Hong Kong

Honorary Chair

Jun Yao	China University of Petroleum, China

General Chair

Jin Xu	Peking University, China

Program Committee Chairs

Linqiang Pan	Huazhong University of Science and Technology, China
Shanchen Pang	China University of Petroleum, China
Tao Song	China University of Petroleum, China

Special Session Chair

Bosheng Song	Hunan University, China

Tutorial Chair

Xiaolong Shi   Guangzhou University, China

Publicity Chairs

Fan Meng	China University of Petroleum, China
Wenjian Luo	Harbin Institute of Technology, China
Pengfei Xie	China University of Petroleum, China

Local Chairs

Sicheng He	China University of Petroleum, China
Qingyu Tian	China University of Petroleum, China

Publication Chairs

Min Wang	China University of Petroleum, China
Xue Zhai	China University of Petroleum, China

Registration Chairs

Sibo Qiao	China University of Petroleum, China
Shaoqiang Wang	China University of Petroleum, China

Program Committee

Muhammad Abulaish	South Asian University, India
Chang Wook Ahn	Gwangju Institute of Science and Technology, Republic of Korea
Adel Al-Jumaily	University of Technology Sydney, Australia
Bin Cao	Hebei University of Technology, China
Junfeng Chen	Hohai University, China
Wei-Neng Chen	Sun Yat-sen University, China
Shi Cheng	Shaanxi Normal University, China
Tsung-Che Chiang	National Taiwan Normal University, China
Kejie Dai	Pingdingshan University, Zhengzhou, China
Bei Dong	Shaanxi Normal University, China
Xin Du	Fujian Normal University, China
Carlos Fernández-Llatas	Universitat Politècnica de València, Spain
Shangce Gao	University of Toyama, Japan
Wenyin Gong	China University of Geosciences, China
Shivaprasad Gundibail	Manipal Institute of Technology, India
Ping Guo	Beijing Normal University, China
Yinan Guo	China University of Mining and Technology, China
Guosheng Hao	Jiangsu Normal University, China

Zhou Wu	Chongqing University, China
Xiuli Wu	University of Science and Technology Beijing, China
Bin Xin	Beijing Institute of Technology, China
Gang Xu	Nanchang University, China
Yingjie Yang	De Montfort University, UK
Zhile Yang	Shenzhen Institute of Advanced Technology, Chinese Academy of Sciences, China
Kunjie Yu	Zhengzhou University, China
Xiaowei Zhang	University of Science and Technology of China, China
Jie Zhang	Newcastle University, UK
Gexiang Zhang	Chengdu University of Technology, China
Defu Zhang	Xiamen University, China
Peng Zhang	Beijing University of Posts and Telecommunications, China
Weiwei Zhang	Zhengzhou University of Light Industry, China
Yong Zhang	China University of Mining and Technology, China
Xinchao Zhao	Beijing University of Posts and Telecommunications, China
Yujun Zheng	Zhejiang University of Technology, China
Aimin Zhou	East China Normal University, China
Fengqun Zhou	Pingdingshan University, China
Xinjian Zhuo	Beijing University of Posts and Telecommunications, China
Shang-Ming Zhou	University of Plymouth, UK
Dexuan Zou	Jiangsu Normal University, China
Xingquan Zuo	Beijing University of Posts and Telecommunications, China

Contents

Neural Network and Machine Learning

DNA Computing and Membrane Computing

Evolutionary Computation and Swarm Intelligence

Wingsuit Flying Search Enhanced by Spherical Evolution

Jiaru Yang[1], Yu Zhang[1], Ziqian Wang[1], Yuki Todo[2], and Shangce Gao[1(✉)]

[1] Faculty of Engineering, University of Toyama, Toyama 930-8555, Japan
gaosc@eng.u-toyama.ac.jp
[2] Faculty of Electrical, Information and Communication Engineering,
Kanazawa University, Kanazawa-shi 9201192, Japan
yktodo@ec.t.kanazawa-u.ac.jp

Abstract. Wingsuit flying search (WFS) is a novel metaheuristic search algorithm that mimics the process of a flier to land on the earth's surface within their range, i.e., a global minimum of the search space. The main advantage of this algorithm is parameter-free except for the population size and the maximal number of iterations. Spherical evolution (SE) uses a spherical search style which possesses a strong exploring ability especially for multimodal optimization problems. This paper proposes a novel mechanism to incorporate SE into WFS for considerably exploiting the search space while maintaining the strong exploration capability. The resultant hybrid algorithm WFSSE is tested on 30 classical benchmark functions. Experimental results in comparison with other state-of-the art algorithms verify the superior performance of WFSSE in terms of robustness and effectiveness.

Keywords: Spherical evolution · Wingsuit flying search · Global optimization · Metaheuristic · Evolutionary algorithms · Bio-inspired algorithms

1 Introduction

Throughout human history, many problem-solving procedures have tended to be heuristic. However, heuristics as a scientific method of optimization is a modern phenomenon. Heuristics have been used in a variety of applications from the 1940s to the 1960s, but the first milestone was the advent of evolutionary algorithms. Evolutionary algorithms (EAs) [1,2] as population-based computational intelligence are widely applied to various optimization problems, which show tremendous potential and make great effort in the field of optimization.

Recently, nature-inspired meta-heuristic (NMH) [3,4] algorithms are good at promising results in combinatorial optimization. Nakrani and Tovey [5] proposed a honey bee algorithm and its application for optimizing Internet hosting centers. Then, the development of a novel bee algorithm by Pham et al. [6] was accomplished. The artificial bee colony (ABC) [7,8] simulates the intelligent foraging behaviour of a honeybee swarm. Gravitational search algorithm (GSA) [9–12] is an adaptive search technology based on Newtonian gravity. Particle swarm

© Springer Nature Singapore Pte Ltd. 2021
L. Pan et al. (Eds.): BIC-TA 2020, CCIS 1363, pp. 3–16, 2021.
https://doi.org/10.1007/978-981-16-1354-8_1

optimization (PSO) [13,14] is well-known for simulating social behaviors of wild animals such as birds' flocking and fishes' schooling. Specially, Tian et al. have successfully combined PSO with DE [15,16] to arrange rescue vehicles to extinguish forest fire problem. Brain storm optimization (BSO) [17–19] is inspired by the human brainstorming process. Most recently, more and more bio-inspired algorithms with promising search performance have been developed, and they have also been successfully applied on various real-world optimization problems.

In computer science and mathematical optimization, a meta-heuristic algorithm is an appropriate process or heuristic method designed to find, generate, or select heuristics that provide a good enough solution to an optimization problem. In general, an optimization problem can be written as

$$minimize \ \ f_1(x), ..., f_i(x), ..., f_I(x), x = (x_1, ..., x_d), \tag{1}$$

subject to

$$h_j(x) = 0, (j = 1, 2, ..., J);$$
$$g_k(x) \leq 0, (k = 1, 2, ..., K).$$

where $f_1, ..., f_I$ are the objectives, while h_j and g_k are the equality and inequality constraints, respectively. In the case when $I = 1$, it is called single-objective optimization. When $I \geq 2$, it becomes a multiobjective problem [20] whose solution strategy is different from those for a single objective. In general, all the functions f_i, h_j and g_k are nonlinear.

Compared to optimization algorithms and iterative methods, meta-heuristics are not guaranteed to find global optimal solutions to certain problems. The basic principle of meta-heuristic strategies is reinforcement, which is based on the idea of the closest to the principle of optimality, while diversification is to avoid invalid operations and requires the generation of solutions with different structures. In optimization, by searching for a large number of feasible solutions, meta-heuristic algorithms can often find good solutions with less computational effort than heuristic, iterative or simple heuristic algorithms [21]. Meta-heuristics can make few assumptions about the optimization problem to be solved, so they can be used for a variety of problems.

In this paper, we propose a new algorithm called WFSSE which combines wingsuit flying search (WFS) [22] and spherical evolution (SE) [23]. We take advantage of them to implement more sufficient and effective search by incorporating the spherical evolution search into the wingsuit flying search algorithm. As the spherical search has a strong exploitation capacity of search, while wingsuit flying search has inherent exploration ability, such hybridization of both search dynamics is capable of balancing the exploration and exploitation of the search, thus achieving a better search efficiency. The performance of the resultant WFSSE is verified on a number of thirty complex classic numerical optimization problems. The experimental results demonstrate its superiority in terms of search efficiency and robustness. Moreover, the statistical analysis based on Wilcoxon rank-sum test shows that WFSSE is significantly better than its peers.

The contribution of this work can be summarized as follows: 1) we innovatively proposed a novel hybrid algorithm by incorporating a spherical evolution that pays main attain on the local exploitation of the search space into the wingsuit flying search algorithm which has a strong global exploration capacity. 2) The two distinct search dynamics inherited from the two search algorithms were performed in a co-evolutionary manner, thus achieving a better balance of the global and local search and a better population diversity as well. 3) Extensive experimental results demonstrated the effectiveness of such hybridization, which gives more insights into the key scientific problem that how to co-evolution two or more different algorithm to construct an efficient problem-solving algorithm.

The rest part is organized as follows: Sect. 2 and Sect. 3 introduce the basic algorithm WFS and SE, respectively. Section 4 gives the work of the hybrid algorithm WFSSE and its pseudo-code. In Sect. 5, the experimental results are given and the comparative results is discussed. Finally, Sect. 6 shows the conclusions and vision of future.

2 Wingsuit Flying Search

Wingsuit flying search is actually an algorithm which functions like a global minimum of the search space. This is achieved by probing the search space at each iteration with a carefully picked population of points. Iterative update of the population corresponds to the flier progressively getting a sharper image of the surface, thus shifting the focus to lower regions.

The algorithm is essentially a population-based search that iteratively updates the set of candidate solution points. In the following, we describe the proposed approach briefly. First, we need to determine how initial set of points is generated.

2.1 Generating Initial Points

Let N^* be the number of points in population size of the algorithm and let

$$N = N^* - 2 \tag{2}$$

be the number of initial points in a search space defined as

$$\left\{ x = [x_1, x_2, ..., x_n]^T \in R^n : x_{min} \le x \le x_{max} \right\}. \tag{3}$$

In the first iteration ($m = 1$), each point $x_i, i \in 1, 2, ..., N$, may be located in a node in n-dimensional grid. The point $x^{(1)}$ is located randomly into the box constrained with $x_{\min}$ and $x_{\min} + \Delta x^{(1)}$, where $\Delta x^{(1)} = \left[\Delta x_1^{(1)} \Delta x_2^{(1)} ... \Delta x_n^{(1)} \right]^T$ is referred to as initial discretization step, which is defined as

$$\Delta x^{(1)} = \frac{x_{\max} - x_{\min}}{N_0}. \tag{4}$$

Locate other points according to x_1 in order to form a grid (full or incomplete). The cost function is then evaluated at each point and a minimum is selected. This is the end of the first iteration.

2.2 Determining Neighborhood Size for Each Point

The first point is the *gbest* one which is assigned a neighborhood with the largest number of points $P_{max}^{(m)}$. The second point will be assigned a neighborhood with less points. The $N^{(m)}$-th point is assigned zero neighborhood points. Note that $N^{(1)} = 0$.

In general, only the first $N^{(m)}$ points are assigned with neighborhood points. Moreover, $\sum_{i=1}^{N^{(m)}} P(m)$ "new" points will be passed to the next iteration. This number is kept equal to N in order to maintain the constant number of cost function evaluations at each iteration. The linear dependence of the function $P^{(m)}(i)$ can be represented as

$$P^{(m)}(i) = \left\lceil P_{max}^{(m)} \left(1 - \frac{i-1}{N(m)-1} \right) \right\rceil \tag{5}$$

2.3 Generating Neighborhood Points

After assigning neighborhood size to each point, the question is how to generate N new points. The flier's "altitude" decreases with the number of iterations, resulting in a higher resolution of the search space. The discretization step consequently gets smaller as:

$$\Delta \boldsymbol{x}^{(m)} = \left(1 - \alpha^{(m)} \right) \Delta \boldsymbol{x}^{(1)}, \quad m \geq 2 \tag{6}$$

Thus, WFS refers to parameter $\alpha^{(m)}$ as search sharpness in mth iteration.

Afterwards, N new points, i.e., neighborhood points denoted $y_j \left(x_i^{(m)} \right) j \in \{1, 2, \ldots, P^{(m)}(i)\}$, are generated. After generating all neighborhoods, the cost function is evaluated at each of N new points and the minimum is selected from $N^{(m)} + N$ points. Before the end of the mth iteration, two more points will be generated and added to the population.

2.4 Generating Centroid and Random Point

In reality, at the beginning, the flier tends to be located above the middle of the Earth surface of interest, since it is a priori the best way to deal with unknown surrounding. It proves beneficial to have a point which plays a role of the flier's current location. WFS refers to this point as centroid, and it is determined as:

$$z_1^{(m)} = \frac{\sum_{i=1}^{N^{(m)}+N} \boldsymbol{W}^{(m)}(i) \cdot \gamma \left(\boldsymbol{W}^{(m)}(i) \right)}{\sum_{i=1}^{N^{(m)}+N} \gamma \left(\boldsymbol{W}^{(m)}(i) \right)}, \tag{7}$$

where $\boldsymbol{W}^{(m)}$ is the pattern matrix containing all points, $\boldsymbol{x}_i^{(m)}$ and $\boldsymbol{y}_j \left(\boldsymbol{x}_i^{(m)} \right)$, represented as columns. Its dimensions are $n \times \left(N^{(m)} + N \right)$ and $W^{(m)}(i)$ denotes its ith column.

WFS is suitable for parallelized computation since it can optimize different parts of the search space [24] independently, which differs it from most concurrent algorithms. One more advantage that should be highlighted, is that WFS is able to rapidly converge to the global optimum solution of the related objective function. The numerical results indicate that WFS algorithm provides considerable performance improvements (mean solution values, standard deviation of solution values, runtime and convergence rate).

3 Spherical Evolution

Spherical evolution is actually a search pattern and a search style represented by a mathematical model. At the same time, it can also be understood as a new search style, namely a spherical search style, inspired by the traditional hypercube search style. Furthermore, a spherical evolution algorithm is proposed based on the search pattern and spherical search style. Thus, search pattern can be represented as:

$$X_{i,d}^{new} = X_{\gamma,d} + \Sigma_{k=1}^{n} S\left(X_{\alpha,d}^{k}, X_{\beta,d}^{k}\right) \qquad (8)$$

where $X_{i,d}^{new}$ indicates the new i th solution in the d th dimension. X_{α}, X_{β} and X_{γ} are three definite solutions selected by a certain strategy. $S()$ represents updating units in the search operator and n is the number of updating units.

In one-dimension, two-dimension and high-dimension, spherical search can be represented as Eqs. (9)–(11).

$$SS_1\left(X_{\alpha,d}, X_{\beta,d}\right) = SF() \cdot |X_{\alpha,d} - X_{\beta,d}| \cdot \cos\left(\theta\right) \qquad (9)$$

$$SS_2\left(X_{\alpha,d}, X_{\beta,d}\right) = SF() \cdot |X_{\alpha,*} - X_{\beta,*}| \cdot \sin\left(\theta\right)$$
$$SS_2\left(X_{\alpha,d}, X_{\beta,d}\right) = SF() \cdot |X_{\alpha,*} - X_{\beta,*}| \cdot \cos(\theta) \qquad (10)$$

$$SS_{\geq 3}\left(X_{\alpha,d}, X_{\beta,d}\right) = SF() \cdot ||X_{\alpha,*} - X_{\beta,*})||_2 \cdot \prod_{k=d}^{dim-1} \sin(\theta), d = 1$$

$$SS_{\geq 3}\left(X_{\alpha,d}, X_{\beta,d}\right) = SF() \cdot ||X_{\alpha,*} - X_{\beta,*})||_2 \cdot \cos(\theta_{d-1}) \cdot \prod_{k=d}^{dim-1} \sin(\theta), 1 < d \leq dim - 1$$

$$SS_{\geq 3}\left(X_{\alpha,d}, X_{\beta,d}\right) = SF() \cdot ||X_{\alpha,*} - X_{\beta,*})||_2 \cdot \cos(\theta_{d-1}), d = dim \qquad (11)$$

where $|X_{\alpha,d} - X_{\beta,d}|$ represents the absolute value of distance between $X_{\alpha,d}$ and $X_{\beta,d}$ in one dimension. $||X_{\alpha,*} - X_{\beta,*}||_2$ indicates the Euclidean distance between $X_{\alpha,*}$ and $X_{\beta,*}$ in high dimensions. θ is a random number in $[0, 2\pi]$ and denotes the angle between $X_{\alpha,*}$ and $X_{\beta,*}$.

SE is an effective heuristic due to its simple mechanism and large search scope. Its search angle is distributed in $[0, 2\pi]$, so its search trajectory is directionless, providing a more diverse evolutionary path [25], it may produce the opposite direction, which leads to slow convergence.

Algorithm 1: Pseudocode of WFSSE

---

1 **begin**
2   /*Initialize parameter */
3     $v = rand(10, 100)$
4     $N = N^* - 2$
5     $N_0 = Ceil(N^{(1/n)})$
6     $\triangle x = (x_{max} - x_{min}) * N_0$
7     $X \leftarrow$ generate population through $N, N_0, \triangle x$
8     $f(X) = evaluate(X)$
9   Generate extract point,then update population X
10   **while** *Terminal Condition* **do**
11   /*WFS process*/
12       $\alpha = 1 - v^{-(m-1)/(M-1)}$
13       $P_{max} = Ceil(\alpha * N)$
14       $N = Ceil(2 * N/P_{max})$
15       $X \leftarrow$ sort X and select N_{th} point
16       $P \leftarrow$ generate neighborhood size
17   /*Spherical evolution*/
18   **for** $i = 1$ *to* N **do**
19   **for** $j = 1$ *to* P **do**
20   **if** $mod(j) == 0$ **then**
21                $x =$ generate neighborhood point
22   **end**
23   **else**
24   Randomly choose two individual X_1, X_2 from X
25   dim$\leftarrow$ selected dimension
26                $x = SS(X_1, X_2, dim)$
27   **end**
28             $X = [X; x]$
29   **end**
30   Generate centroid and random point, update X
31   **end**
32   **end**
33 **end**

---

4   Wingsuit Flying Search Enhanced by Spherical Evolution

Two major components of any metaheuristic algorithms are: intensification and diversification, or exploitation and exploration. Diversification means to generate diverse solutions so as to explore the search space on a global scale [26], while intensification means to focus the search in a local region knowing that a current good solution is found in this region. A good balance between intensification and diversification should be found during the selection of the best solutions to improve the rate of algorithm convergence. The selection of the best ensures that solutions will converge to the optimum [27], while diversification via randomization allows the search to escape from local optima and, at the same time, increases the diversity of solutions [28]. A good combination of these two major components will usually ensure that global optimal is achievable.

Based on the inherent characteristics of the WFS and SE, a novel hybrid algorithm is presented in this paper. Actually, WFS is suitable for parallelized computation since it can optimize different parts of the search space independently, which differs it from most concurrent algorithms. The opposite is its relatively weak exploration ability. But at the same time, SE has extremely powerful search capabilities while its convergence speed is unsatisfying. Therefore, we try to use SE ideas in the process of finding neighborhood points in WFS, in order to enhance the exploration ability and achieve the unity of the two aspects.

In WFS, clearly, $\delta X = \Delta x^{(1)}$ and $s = \left(1 - \alpha^{(m)}\right)$ according to Eq. (8), are always used when generating neighborhood around each $X_i \left(= x_i^{(m)} \right)$. Meanwhile, SE adopts a spherical search style whereas others use a hypercube search style. When algorithms are limited to two dimensions, SE presents a circular search style whereas others conduct a rectangular one. Therefore, combining "parallelized computation" and rapidly convergence helps this algorithm to make a good balance between exploration and exploitation of the search space. The mentioned balance turns out to be the inherent feature of the algorithm due to the fact that WFSSE is essentially parameter-free. The hybridization WFSSE whose prime steps can be described as follows:

(1) Firstly, algorithm generate initial population by some mechanism.
(2) Set the height of pilot (threshold) and select suitable point by sorting.
(3) Generate neighbor point through selected point by vector difference and spherical evolution strategy, and add them to population.
(4) Add random point and centroid point to population.
(5) Repeat steps (2)–(4) until terminal condition.

The pseudo-code of WFSSE is shown as in Algorithm 1. From the line 11 to 16 is the part that sort X and select suitable point. Then, it is time to generate neighborhood point. From the line 18 to 31, we use vector difference to choose random point and add random point and centroid point to population. Due to the large search space of spherical search, WFS uses δ to search for neighborhood points that in some cases will enter the local optimum, but proper spherical search enhances the algorithm's exploratory capabilities and balances the algorithm's exploration and search capabilities.

Table 1. The function and real optimal value of classic benchmark functions.

Fnum	Function name	Dimension	Real value	Fnum	Function name	Dimension	Real value
1	Step	30	0	16	Michalewicz2	2	−1.8013
2	Sphere	30	0	17	Michalewicz5	5	−4.6877
3	SumSquares	30	0	18	Michalewicz10	10	−9.6602
4	Quartic	30	0	19	Rastrigin	30	0
5	Beale	2	0	20	Schaffer2	2	0
6	Easom	2	−1	21	Schaffer4	2	0.29258
7	Matyas	2	0	22	Schaffer6	30	0
8	Colville	4	0	23	SixHumpCamelBack	2	−1.0316
9	Zakharov	30	0	24	Bohachevsky2	2	0
10	Schwefel2_22	30	0	25	Bohachevsky3	2	0
11	Schwefel1_2	30	0	26	Shubert	2	−186.73
12	DixonPrice	30	0	27	DropWave	2	−1
13	Bohachevsky1	2	0	28	Rosenbrock	30	0
14	Booth	2	0	29	Griewank	30	0
15	HolderTable	2	−19.209	30	Ackley	30	8.88E−16

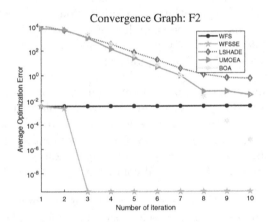

Fig. 1. Convergence graph of F2.

5   Experimental Results

In this section, to verity the performance of the proposed WFSSE algorithm, 30 classical benchmark functions composed of Unimodal and separable benchmark functions (F1–F4), unimodal and non-separable benchmark functions (F5–F12), multimodal and separable benchmark functions (F13–F19), multimodal and non-separable benchmark functions (F20–F30). All algorithms are implemented 30 times with 200 iterations. Besides WFS, WFSSE is compared with three state-of-the-art algorithms including linear population size reduction technique of success history based adaptive differential evolution (LSHADE) [29,30], united multi-

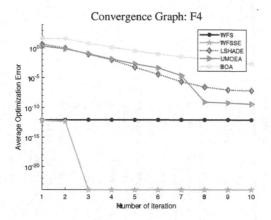

Fig. 2. Convergence graph of F4.

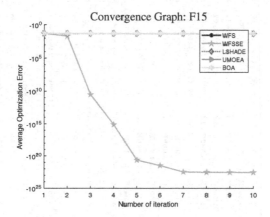

Fig. 3. Convergence graph of F15.

operator evolutionary algorithms (UMOEA) [31], and brain storm optimization (BOA) [32].

Table 1 shows the function and real value of classical algorithms. The experiment results on classical algorithm are listed in Table 2. W/T/L in the last row represents WFSSE performs significantly better/tied/worse than its competitor under a significance level 5%, respectively. The highlighted ones are the best, and the last line shows the number of the winner, tie or loser of WFSSE as 18/4/8, 22/0/8, 22/0/8, 30/0/0 with WFS, UMOEA, LSHADE and BOA, respectively. The result shows WFSSE performs particularly well on separable benchmark functions, multimodal and separable benchmark functions, multimodal and non-separable benchmark functions. From the Table 2, we can find that WFSSE performs significantly better than those state-of-the-art algorithms.

Figures 1, 2 and 3 show convergence graphs for three typical functions F2, F4, F15. From these results, we can find that in the initial stage of convergence

Table 2. Experimental results on classic algorithm.

	WFSSE		WFS		UMOEA		LSHADE		BOA	
	Mean	Std	Mean	std	Mean	Std	Mean	Std	Mean	Std
F1	6.983E−01	5.701E−01	1.841E−01	9.584E−02	**1.128E−13**	2.049E−13	1.347E−03	2.818E−04	2.576E+00	3.466E−01
F2	**0.000E+00**	0.000E+00	3.308E−03	1.069E−03	2.635E−02	1.443E−01	5.200E−01	1.779E−01	5.479E−06	7.688E−06
F3	**0.000E+00**	0.000E+00	9.763E−04	3.026E−04	1.671E−14	1.334E−14	8.094E−02	2.280E−02	1.657E−01	1.427E−02
F4	**0.000E+00**	0.000E+00	8.057E−13	4.862E−13	3.745E−10	7.633E−10	6.341E−08	4.429E−08	2.097E−03	2.103E−04
F5	1.015E−09	1.112E−09	2.452E−08	7.611E−08	**1.156E−14**	1.859E−14	3.401E−10	9.246E−10	3.711E−03	3.605E−03
F6	−**1.000E+00**	2.787E−07	−9.999E−01	2.362E−05	−1.000E+00	3.242E−06	−1.000E+00	2.371E−06	−1.589E−01	3.017E−01
F7	1.815E−10	5.426E−10	2.164E−09	3.189E−09	**1.896E−13**	8.773E−13	2.235E−11	4.471E−11	3.155E−04	2.976E−04
F8	1.838E−02	3.270E−02	9.923E−03	1.560E−02	**4.709E−13**	1.851E−13	5.921E−02	5.786E−02	2.200E+00	1.544E+00
F9	3.000E−02	4.332E−02	2.244E−02	3.374E−02	**8.382E−14**	9.330E−14	4.970E−03	2.531E−03	1.039E−08	1.225E−08
F10	**0.000E+00**	0.000E+00	1.171E−02	2.157E−03	6.667E−04	3.651E−03	1.441E+00	3.029E−01	8.495E−04	7.069E−04
F11	**0.000E+00**	0.000E+00	1.353E−01	2.049E−01	8.075E−02	4.423E−01	1.730E+01	4.977E+00	3.527E−09	4.452E−09
F12	7.540E−01	8.398E−02	1.159E+00	2.229E−02	**6.666E−01**	1.376E−14	1.011E+00	1.253E−01	9.605E−01	6.787E−03
F13	4.196E−08	1.679E−07	9.188E−05	1.502E−04	**4.774E−16**	7.867E−16	6.142E−08	1.011E−07	2.227E−01	1.211E−01
F14	2.648E−09	9.879E−09	1.401E−07	3.576E−07	**2.815E−15**	4.578E−15	9.477E−10	1.697E−09	9.623E−03	1.152E−02
F15	−**3.340E+22**	1.767E+23	−1.920E+01	6.040E−07	−1.920E+01	2.652E−14	−1.920E+01	3.358E−05	−1.911E+01	9.856E−02
F16	−**1.801E+00**	6.295E−09	−1.801E+00	4.561E−08	−1.801E+00	3.764E−15	−1.801E+00	3.991E−11	−1.790E+00	1.101E−02
F17	−**4.458E+00**	2.409E−01	−4.422E+00	2.716E−01	−4.677E+00	1.744E−02	−4.678E+00	1.036E−02	−3.464E+00	1.728E−01
F18	−7.671E+00	7.370E+00	−7.737E+00	8.691E−01	−**8.871E+00**	4.147E−01	−8.576E+00	3.058E−01	−5.317E+00	2.949E−01
F19	**0.000E+00**	0.000E+00	4.335E−03	1.449E−03	2.468E−01	1.279E+01	1.307E+02	9.754E+00	1.575E+00	1.099E−01
F20	**1.051E−11**	3.995E−11	5.159E−09	8.181E−09	7.495E−10	4.105E−09	2.305E−06	6.006E−06	5.142E−03	5.011E−03
F21	**2.925E−01**	2.061E−07	2.925E−01	4.269E−07	2.925E−01	3.594E−06	2.926E−01	9.029E−05	2.971E−01	2.844E−03
F22	**0.000E+00**	0.000E+00	2.060E−01	6.765E−02	6.755E+00	9.172E−01	1.036E+01	2.783E−01	8.602E+00	5.426E−01
F23	−**1.031E+00**	3.523E−09	−1.031E+00	5.539E−07	−1.031E+00	8.881E−16	−1.031E+00	4.116E−07	−1.031E+00	6.614E−04
F24	1.008E−06	3.595E−06	6.405E−05	2.171E−04	**6.365E−16**	1.429E−15	7.497E−08	1.447E−07	1.520E−01	7.294E−02
F25	1.017E−06	2.360E−06	1.241E−06	2.282E−05	**3.908E−15**	8.735E−15	1.406E−07	2.449E−07	7.376E−02	5.355E−02
F26	−**1.867E+02**	2.905E−05	−1.867E+02	1.381E−04	−1.867E+02	3.264E−12	−1.866E+02	4.832E−02	−1.852E+02	1.317E+00
F27	−9.978E−01	1.164E−02	−9.978E−01	1.164E−02	−**1.000E+00**	5.946E−16	−9.999E−01	1.964E−05	−9.632E−01	2.585E−02
F28	2.850E+01	1.086E−01	3.011E+01	2.793E−01	**7.973E−01**	1.621E+00	5.073E+01	1.048E+01	2.891E+01	2.740E−02
F29	**0.000E+00**	0.000E+00	4.640E−03	1.304E−03	4.293E−12	2.733E−12	5.962E−01	1.247E−01	1.170E+00	8.031E−03
F30	**8.881E−16**	0.000E+00	9.230E−02	1.748E−02	2.088E−01	2.873E−02	3.091E−01	7.740E−02	2.876E+00	8.791E−02
W/T/L	−/−/−		18/4/8		22/0/8		22/0/8		30/0/0	

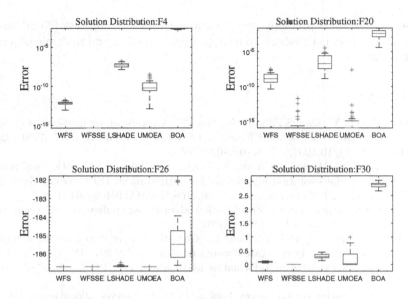

Fig. 4. Box-and-whisker graphs of F4, F20, F26 and F30.

graph, the overall slope of the curve of WFSSE is roughly smaller than other four algorithms. Meanwhile, the convergence curve of WFSSE is lower than other curves. Initially, WFSSE has a clear tendency to converge, after which it rapidly converges to the global optimum, while other algorithms compare poorly with it. These characteristics reveal that WFSSE can not only converge quickly and get rid of the local optimum, but also provide the best solutions.

Figures 4 depicts box-and-whisker graphs. The top and bottom line in the figure represents the maximum and minimum value in fitness except for outliers, respectively. The upper and lower borderline of the rectangle represents the upper and lower quantiles, respectively. The line in the middle of a rectangle represents the median. The results show that the values of all types of lines of WFSSE are smaller than those of other algorithms. It proves that WFSSE has smaller value in fitness than other algorithms.

Above all, we can conclude that the experimental results demonstrate that combining the advantages of wingsuit flying search and the spherical search style of SE is effective.

6   Conclusion

In this article, we proposed a hybrid algorithm by combining WFS and SE, namely WFSSE, to achieve the balance and optimization of exploitation and exploration. To prove the performance of the hybrid algorithm, we compare with WFS, UMOEA, LSHADE and BOA on benchmark functions in classical algorithm. Experiment results prove the superior of WFSSE in terms of effectiveness and robustness. In the near future, we can employ this hybrid algorithm to solve some real-world problems, e.g., neural network learning task [33], dynamic clustering question [34], vehicle routing problems [35, 36], and multiple objective optimization.

References

1. Wang, Y., Yu, Y., Cao, S., Zhang, X., Gao, S.: A review of applications of artificial intelligent algorithms in wind farms. Artif. Intell. Rev. **53**(5), 3447–3500 (2019). https://doi.org/10.1007/s10462-019-09768-7
2. Gao, S., Yu, Y., Wang, Y., Wang, J., Cheng, J., Zhou, M.: Chaotic local search-based differential evolution algorithms for optimization. IEEE Trans. Syst. Man Cybern. Syst. (2019). https://doi.org/10.1109/TSMC.2019.2956121
3. Yang, X.S.: Nature-inspired optimization algorithms: challenges and open problems. J. Comput. Sci. **46**, 101104 (2020)
4. Wang, S., Yang, X., Cai, Z., Zou, L., Gao, S.: An improved firefly algorithm enhanced by negatively correlated search mechanism. In: 2018 IEEE International Conference on Progress in Informatics and Computing (PIC), pp. 67–72. IEEE (2018)
5. Nakrani, S., Tovey, C.: On honey bees and dynamic server allocation in internet hosting centers. Adapt. Behav. **12**(3–4), 223–240 (2004)
6. Pham, D.T., Ghanbarzadeh, A., Koç, E., Otri, S., Rahim, S., Zaidi, M.: The bees algorithm–a novel tool for complex optimisation problems. In: Intelligent Production Machines and Systems, pp. 454–459. Elsevier (2006)
7. Karaboga, D., Akay, B.: A comparative study of artificial bee colony algorithm. Appl. Math. Comput. **214**(1), 108–132 (2009)
8. Ji, J., Song, S., Tang, C., Gao, S., Tang, Z., Todo, Y.: An artificial bee colony algorithm search guided by scale-free networks. Inf. Sci. **473**, 142–165 (2019)
9. Wang, Y., Yu, Y., Gao, S., Pan, H., Yang, G.: A hierarchical gravitational search algorithm with an effective gravitational constant. Swarm Evol. Comput. **46**, 118–139 (2019)
10. Lei, Z., Gao, S., Gupta, S., Cheng, J., Yang, G.: An aggregative learning gravitational search algorithm with self-adaptive gravitational constants. Expert Syst. Appl. **152**, 113396 (2020)
11. Wang, Y., Gao, S., Yu, Y., Wang, Z., Cheng, J., Yuki, T.: A gravitational search algorithm with chaotic neural oscillators. IEEE Access **8**, 25938–25948 (2020)
12. Wang, Y., Gao, S., Zhou, M., Yu, Y.: A multi-layered gravitational search algorithm for function optimization and real-world problems. IEEE/CAA J. Automatica Sin. **8**, 94–109 (2020)
13. Yu, H., Xu, Z., Gao, S., Wang, Y., Todo, Y.: PMPSO: a near-optimal graph planarization algorithm using probability model based particle swarm optimization. In: 2015 IEEE International Conference on Progress in Informatics and Computing (PIC), pp. 15–19. IEEE (2015)
14. Gong, Y.J., et al.: Genetic learning particle swarm optimization. IEEE Trans. Cybern. **46**(10), 2277–2290 (2015)
15. Sun, J., Gao, S., Dai, H., Cheng, J., Zhou, M., Wang, J.: Bi-objective elite differential evolution for multivalued logic networks. IEEE Trans. Cybern. **50**(1), 233–246 (2020)
16. Tang, Y., Ji, J., Zhu, Y., Gao, S., Tang, Z., Todo, Y.: A differential evolution-oriented pruning neural network model for bankruptcy prediction. Complexity **2019**, Article ID 8682124 (2019)

17. Yu, Y., Yang, L., Wang, Y., Gao, S.: Brain storm algorithm combined with covariance matrix adaptation evolution strategy for optimization. In: Cheng, S., Shi, Y. (eds.) Brain Storm Optimization Algorithms. ALO, vol. 23, pp. 123–154. Springer, Cham (2019). https://doi.org/10.1007/978-3-030-15070-9_6

18. Wang, Y., Gao, S., Yu, Y., Xu, Z.: The discovery of population interaction with a power law distribution in brain storm optimization. Memetic Comput. 11(1), 65–87 (2017). https://doi.org/10.1007/s12293-017-0248-z

19. Yu, Y., Gao, S., Wang, Y., Lei, Z., Cheng, J., Todo, Y.: A multiple diversity-driven brain storm optimization algorithm with adaptive parameters. IEEE Access 7, 126871–126888 (2019)

20. Wang, J., Yuan, L., Zhang, Z., Gao, S., Sun, Y., Zhou, Y.: Multiobjective multiple neighborhood search algorithms for multiobjective fleet size and mix location-routing problem with time windows. IEEE Trans. Syst. Man Cybern. Syst. (2019)

21. Jia, D., Tong, Y., Yu, Y., Cai, Z., Gao, S.: A novel backtracking search with grey wolf algorithm for optimization. In: 2018 10th International Conference on Intelligent Human-Machine Systems and Cybernetics (IHMSC), vol. 1, pp. 73–76. IEEE (2018)

22. Covic, N., Lacevic, B.: Wingsuit flying searcha novel global optimization algorithm. IEEE Access 8, 53883–53900 (2020)

23. Tang, D.: Spherical evolution for solving continuous optimization problems. Applied Soft Computing 81, 105499 (2019)

24. Gao, S., Yu, Y., Wang, Y., Wang, J., Cheng, J., Zhou, M.: Chaotic local search-based differential evolution algorithms for optimization. IEEE Trans. Syst. Man Cybern. Syst. (2019)

25. Wang, J., Cen, B., Gao, S., Zhang, Z., Zhou, Y.: Cooperative evolutionary framework with focused search for many-objective optimization. IEEE Trans. Emer. Topics Comput. Intell. 4, 398–412 (2018)

26. Gao, S., Wang, R.L., Ishii, M., Tang, Z.: An artificial immune system with feedback mechanisms for effective handling of population size. IEICE transactions on fundamentals of electronics, communications and computer sciences 93(2), 532–541 (2010)

27. Gao, S., Wang, W., Dai, H., Li, F., Tang, Z.: Improved clonal selection algorithm combined with ant colony optimization. IEICE Trans. Inf. Syst. 91(6), 1813–1823 (2008)

28. Yang, Y., Dai, H., Gao, S., Wang, Y., Jia, D., Tang, Z.: Complete receptor editing operation based on quantum clonal selection algorithm for optimization problems. IEEJ Trans. Electr. Electron. Eng. 14(3), 411–421 (2019)

29. Mohamed, A.W., Hadi, A.A., Fattouh, A.M., Jambi, K.M.: LSHADE with semi-parameter adaptation hybrid with CMA-ES for solving CEC 2017 benchmark problems. In: 2017 IEEE Congress on Evolutionary Computation (CEC), pp. 145–152. IEEE (2017)

30. Awad, N.H., Ali, M.Z., Suganthan, P.N., Reynolds, R.G.: An ensemble sinusoidal parameter adaptation incorporated with L-SHADE for solving CEC2014 benchmark problems. In: 2016 IEEE Congress on Evolutionary Computation (CEC), pp. 2958–2965. IEEE (2016)

31. Elsayed, S.M., Sarker, R.A., Essam, D.L.: United multi-operator evolutionary algorithms. In: IEEE Congress on Evolutionary Computation (CEC), pp. 1006–1013. IEEE (2014)

32. Yu, Y., Gao, S., Cheng, S., Wang, Y., Song, S., Yuan, F.: CBSO: a memetic brain storm optimization with chaotic local search. Memetic Comput. 10(4), 353–367 (2017). https://doi.org/10.1007/s12293-017-0247-0

33. Gao, S., Zhou, M., Wang, Y., Cheng, J., Yachi, H., Wang, J.: Dendritic neural model with effective learning algorithms for classification, approximation, and prediaaction. IEEE Trans. Neural Netw. Learn. Syst. **30**(2), 601–604 (2019)
34. Cheng, J.J., Yuan, G.Y., Zhou, M.C., Gao, S.C., Huang, Z.H., Liu, C.: A connectivity prediction-based dynamic clustering model for VANET in an urban scene. IEEE Internet Things J. **7**, 8410–8418 (2020)
35. Cheng, J., Cheng, J., Zhou, M., Liu, F., Gao, S., Liu, C.: Routing in internet of vehicles: a review. IEEE Trans. Intell. Transp. Syst. **16**(5), 2339–2352 (2015)
36. Cheng, J., Yuan, G., Zhou, M., Gao, S., Liu, C., Duan, H.: A fluid mechanics-based data flow model to estimate VANET capacity. IEEE Trans. Intell. Transp. Syst. **21**, 2603–2614 (2019)

Adaptive Total Variation Constraint Hypergraph Regularized NMF and Its Application on Single-Cell RNA-Seq Data

Ya-Li Zhu, Ming-Juan Wu, Chuan-Yuan Wang, Yue Hu,
and Jin-Xing Liu(✉)

School of Computer Science, Qufu Normal University, Rizhao, China
sdcavell@126.com

Abstract. Single-cell RNA sequencing (scRNA-seq) data provides a whole new view to study the development of disease and cell differentiation. As the explosive increment of scRNA-seq data, effective models are demanded to mining the intrinsic biological information. In this paper, we propose a novel nonnegative matrix factorization (NMF) method for clustering and gene co-expression network analysis, termed Adaptive Total Variation Constraint Hypergraph Regularized NMF (ATV-HNMF). Based on the gradient information, ATV-HNMF can adaptively select the different schemes to denoise in the cluster or preserve the cluster boundary information between clusters. Besides, ATV-HNMF incorporates hypergraph regularization which can consider high-order relationships between cells, which is helpful to reserve the intrinsic structure of the original data space. Experiments show that the performance on clustering outperforms other compared methods. And the related genes mined by co-expression network construction are consistent with the previous research, which illustrates that our model is effective and useful.

Keywords: Adaptive total variation · Single-cell RNA sequencing · Network analysis · Nonnegative matrix factorization · Hypergraph

1 Introduction

With the advancement of scRNA-seq technology, researchers can separate individual cells from each other and sequence the transcriptome data at the level of the individual cell, which can provide a deeper insight into the biological process [1]. ScRNA-seq technology has a profound influence on us to understand the complexity, variety and irregularity of cellular biological activity. While the technology has great potential to explore the gene expression of cells, they also present new challenges that require advanced algorithm tools to extract potential biological information.

There are many methods to analyze single-cell sequencing data. T-distributed stochastic neighbor embedding (t-SNE) [2] is based on the local similarity that places the similar cells cluster together and separate different cells from each other, however, the relative position used is not always meaningful. Spectral clustering (SC) [3] uses the similarity graph to cluster single-cells. Wang et al. [4] propose the multi-kernel learning

© Springer Nature Singapore Pte Ltd. 2021
L. Pan et al. (Eds.): BIC-TA 2020, CCIS 1363, pp. 17–24, 2021.
https://doi.org/10.1007/978-981-16-1354-8_2

method for single-cell interpretation called SIMLR, which can learn from 55 Gaussian kernels to get the final results.

NMF has been widely used in the field of bioinformatics in recent years [5–7]. Cai et al. [8] propose graph regularized NMF (GNMF) that considers the intrinsic manifold of the data space, which is practical to real applications. Zeng et al. [9] propose hypergraph regularized NMF (HNMF) which extends the simple graph on two samples to higher-order relationships, considering multiple samples interactions. However, these methods do not deal with noise and outliers very well. Recently, Leng et al. [10] present an adaptive total variation constrained nonnegative matrix factorization on manifold (ATV-NMF), which considers the total variation and simple pairwise relationships between samples.

Based on the above problems, we consider introducing adaptive total variation (ATV) and hypergraph regularization into NMF model, named ATV-HNMF. The ATV term can adaptively select different scheme to deal with data noise, the hypergraph regularization can retain the inherent high-order geometric structure.

The rest of the paper is organized as follows: we present a brief review about adaptive total variation and hypergraph theory in Sect. 2; in Sect. 3, we give the algorithm of ATV-HNMF and its details; experimental results about clustering and network analysis are presented in Sect. 4; and finally, we conclude the paper in Sect. 5.

2 Related Work

2.1 Adaptive Total Variation

ATV-HNMF is based on the idea of ATV which is first proposed by Stacey Levine et al. [11]. Based on the gradient information, the data can adaptively select an anisotropic scheme so as to preserve the cluster boundary information or denoise. The term is defined as follows:

$$E(\mathbf{F}) = \|\mathbf{F}\|_{ATV}, \tag{1}$$

where E is the function of energy, and the size of $\mathbf{F}$ is $k \times n$. The ATV regularization scheme $\|\mathbf{F}\|_{ATV}$ is defined as $\int_{\Omega} (1/p(\text{x,y}))|\nabla F|^{p(x,y)} dxdy$, $p(x, y) = 1 + 1/(1 + |\nabla F|^2)$, $1 < p(x, y) < 2$, where $\Omega \subset R^n$ denotes the data space.

The adaptive total variation regularization term contains a parameter expressed as $1/|\nabla F|^{2-p}$ in Eq. (11) to control the diffusion speed of the different direction. In the boundary part of the cluster, the value of $|\nabla F|^{2-p}$ is large, and the diffusion coefficient is small, so the diffusion speed is slow, so that can keep the difference from cluster to cluster. Between clusters, based on the small change of gradient information, the value of $1/|\nabla F|^{2-p}$ is large so that the diffusion is strong, which helps in denoising and keeps samples between clusters tighter.

2.2 Hypergraph Theory

In a hypergraph, the relationship is between two or more vertices, so the hypergraph is composed of many hyperedges and one hyperedge is composed of many vertices. In reality, interactions between more than two samples are more critical to preserve the geometrical structure.

The hypergraph is denoted as $G = (V, E, W)$, where V denotes all the samples, E is the family of e that $\cup_{e \in E} = V$, W is a diagonal matrix with hyperedge weights elements $w(e)$. The incidence matrix is defined as follows:

$$\mathbf{H}(v, e) = \begin{cases} 1, & if\ v \in e \\ 0, & if\ v \notin e \end{cases}. \tag{2}$$

Based on $\mathbf{H}$, the degree of each vertex is defined as

$$d(v) = \sum_{e \in E} w(e)\mathbf{H}(v, e). \tag{3}$$

And the degree of each hyperedge is given by

$$\delta(e) = \sum_{v \in V} \mathbf{H}(v, e). \tag{4}$$

We use the diagonal matrices $\mathbf{D}_e$ and $\mathbf{D}_v$ to denote the vertices degree and hyperedges degree respectively. As for the hypergraph Laplacian matrix, it is denoted as

$$L = \mathbf{D}_v - \mathbf{A}, \tag{5}$$

where $\mathbf{A} = \mathbf{HWD}_e^{-1}\mathbf{H}^T$.

The affinity matrix of vertices is defined as

$$\mathbf{S}_{ij} = \exp\left(-\frac{\|\mathbf{v}_i - \mathbf{v}_j\|^2}{\sigma}\right), \tag{6}$$

and the weight of each hyperedge is given by

$$w(e_j) = \sum_{v_i \in e_j} \mathbf{S}_{ij}. \tag{7}$$

3 Method

3.1 ATV-HNMF

Assuming that the input matrix $\mathbf{X} = (\mathbf{x}_1, \mathbf{x}_2, \dots \infty, \mathbf{x}_n) \in \mathbb{R}^{m \times n}$, each row of $\mathbf{X}$ indicates the expression level of a gene among all single-cells, each column of $\mathbf{X}$ indicates the all gene expression level in a single-cell. The task of ATV-HNMF aims to factorize the original data into two matrixes $\mathbf{U} = (\mathbf{u}_1, \mathbf{u}_2, \dots, \mathbf{u}_k) \in \mathbb{R}^{m \times k}$ and $\mathbf{F} = (\mathbf{f}_1, \mathbf{f}_2, \dots, \mathbf{f}_n) \in \mathbb{R}^{k \times n}$, so that get the approximation $\mathbf{X} \simeq \mathbf{UF}$. The objective function is designed as follows:

$$\min_{\mathbf{U},\mathbf{F}} O = \|\mathbf{X} - \mathbf{UF}\|_F^2 + \lambda Tr(\mathbf{FLF}^T) + 2\|\mathbf{F}\|_{ATV}\ s.t.\ \mathbf{U} \geq 0, \mathbf{F} \geq 0, \tag{8}$$

where $\|\cdot\|_F$ denotes the Frobenius norm to indicate the error term, $Tr(\cdot)$ represents the trace of the matrix, λ is the parameter of hypergraph regularization term ($\lambda > 0$).

The original data matrix is decomposed into two matrices, then we use the basis matrix $\mathbf{U}$ to mining the related genes by network construction and use the coefficient matrix $\mathbf{F}$ to process sample clustering.

3.2 Optimization

Note that $\|\mathbf{A}\|_F^2 = Tr(\mathbf{A}\mathbf{A}^T)$. Equation (8) can be rewritten as follows:

$$\min_{\mathbf{U},\mathbf{F}} O = Tr\left((\mathbf{X} - \mathbf{U}\mathbf{F})(\mathbf{X} - \mathbf{U}\mathbf{F})^T\right) + \lambda Tr(\mathbf{F}\mathbf{L}\mathbf{F}^T) + 2\|\mathbf{F}\|_{ATV} \; s.t. \, \mathbf{U} \geq 0, \mathbf{F} \geq 0. \quad (9)$$

The multiplicative iterative updating rules of $\mathbf{U}$ and $\mathbf{F}$ are obtained as follows:

$$\mathbf{U}_{i,r} \leftarrow \mathbf{U}_{i,r} \frac{(\mathbf{X}\mathbf{F}^T)_{i,r}}{(\mathbf{U}\mathbf{F}\mathbf{F}^T)_{i,r}}, \quad (10)$$

$$\mathbf{F}_{r,j} \leftarrow \mathbf{F}_{r,j} \frac{\left(\mathbf{U}^T\mathbf{X} + \lambda \mathbf{F}\mathbf{A} + div\left(\frac{\nabla \mathbf{F}}{|\nabla \mathbf{F}|^{2-p}}\right)\right)_{r,j}}{\left(\mathbf{U}^T\mathbf{U}\mathbf{F} + \lambda \mathbf{F}\mathbf{L}\right)_{r,j}}, \quad (11)$$

where $div = \left(\frac{\partial}{\partial_x}, \frac{\partial}{\partial_y}\right)$ denotes divergence. $\nabla \mathbf{F} = (\partial_x \mathbf{F}, \partial_y \mathbf{F})$ indicates the gradient information, and $|\nabla \mathbf{F}| = \sqrt{(\partial_x \mathbf{F})^2 + (\partial_y \mathbf{F})^2}$ is the gradient norm.

4 Experimental Results and Discussion

4.1 Datasets

The two involved single-cell datasets are downloaded from the Gene Expression Omnibus (GEO) database. The statistics for datasets are summarized in Table 1.

Table 1. Data information about single-cell datasets.

Datasets	The number of genes	The number of cells	Cell types
Islet [12]	39851	1600	4
Darmanis [13]	22085	420	8

In ATV-HNMF, we filter the gene and normalize the data matrix as preprocessing steps. For the gene filter step, we delete genes whose expression (gene expression value is non-zero) less than 5% of all cells. In the normalize step, the L_2-norm is used to eliminate scale differences between samples.

4.2 Performance Evaluation and Comparisons

Evaluation Metrics
To prove the effectiveness of our method, we introduce two evaluation metrics to make

a fair comparison. Adjusted Rand Index (ARI) is one of the most popular metrics to reflect the clustering results, which is defined as

$$\text{ARI}(L_E, L_T) = \frac{\sum_{ij}\binom{n_{ij}}{2} - \left[\sum_{ij}\binom{n_{ij}}{2}\sum_{ij}\binom{n_{ij}}{2}\right]\Big/\binom{n}{2}}{\frac{1}{2}\left[\sum_i\binom{e_i}{2} + \sum_j\binom{t_j}{2}\right] - \left[\sum_i\binom{e_i}{2}\sum_j\binom{t_j}{2}\right]\Big/\binom{n}{2}} \tag{12}$$

where L_p denotes the predicted labels obtained from the method, and L_T are the true labels from the original data, respectively.

Normalized Mutual Information (NMI) is defined as follows:

$$\text{NMI}(L_p, L_t) = \frac{M\left(L_p, L_t\right)}{\left[H\left(L_p\right) + H\left(L_t\right)\right]\big/2} \tag{13}$$

where H denotes the entropy and $M\left(L_p, L_t\right)$ denotes the mutual information between L_p and L_t. The value range of ARI is $[-1,1]$, the value range of NMI is $[0, 1]$. The larger the value is, the more consistent the clustering result is with the real situation.

Parameter Settings
For all methods, we set the dimensionality reduction parameter k equals to the number of cell types. We vary the parameter λ from 0.01, 0.1, 1, 10, 100, 1000, the results shown in Fig. 1. From Fig. 1, we can discover that when λ is too large, the accuracy is extremely low. Therefore, we do not recommend setting it to a larger value.

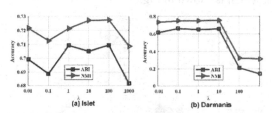

Fig. 1. The impact of parameter λ on two datasets. The red curve denotes the NMI value, the blue curve denotes the ARI value. The higher accuracy denotes the better clustering performance.

Clustering Results and Analysis
Since t-SNE, SC, NMF, ATV-NMF and our proposed method ATV-HNMF have unstable clustering results, we take their average value of 30 times as the final result. Table 2 list the clustering results about eight comparative methods, and we can discover that:

1. Obviously, our proposed method is better than ATV-NMF. Since hypergraph regularization scheme in ATV-HNMF considers the complex relationship between multiple data points, it retains the high-order geometric structure. Therefore, it performs better than simple graph in the experiment.

Table 2. Clustering results on single-cell datasets.

Methods	NMI		ARI	
	Islet	Darmanis	Islet	Darmanis
t-SNE	0.6342 ± 0.0067	$0.6959 \pm 7.4E - 4$	0.4427 ± 0.0067	$0.5237 \pm 3.7E - 4$
PCA	0.6008 ± 0.0000	0.5835 ± 0.0000	0.3864 ± 0.0000	0.3388 ± 0.0000
SC	0.7081 ± 0.0000	$0.6356 \pm 2.1E - 6$	0.5592 ± 0.0000	$0.4503 \pm 3.8E - 6$
SIMLR	0.0678 ± 0.0000	0.5693 ± 0.0000	0.0534 ± 0.0000	0.2991 ± 0.0000
NMF	0.6948 ± 0.0022	$0.7030 \pm 8.5E - 4$	0.6723 ± 0.0111	0.5703 ± 0.0039
ATV-NMF	0.7136 ± 0.0026	$0.6944 \pm 5.8E - 4$	0.6951 ± 0.0135	0.5712 ± 0.0024
ATV-HNMF	$\mathbf{0.7296 \pm 0.0050}$	$\mathbf{0.7950 \pm 0.0231}$	$\mathbf{0.7170 \pm 0.0163}$	$\mathbf{0.7617 \pm 0.0040}$

2. T-SNE and SC directly cluster the samples without dimension reduction, so their performance is not as good as NMF. SIMLR considers the similarity between cells, however, it cannot retain the inner local geometric structure hidden in data. ATV-HNMF not only incorporates hypergraph regularization, but also considers the ATV scheme, which can adaptively choose the different schemes to denoise in the cluster or preserve the cluster boundary information between clusters, so it has better clustering performance.

In order to observe the clustering results more intuitively, we further use t-SNE to visualize the results, which is shown in Fig. 2.

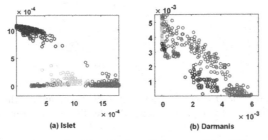

Fig. 2. The clustering result graph of the single-cell datasets. The different color represents the different cell types.

Network Construction and Mining

To illustrate the effectiveness of the ATV-HNMF method, we use the selected 1000 genes to construct the network and mining the gene information. Betweenness indicates the role of the node in the interconnection of others, so we select betweenness as the metric to evaluate the importance of gene nodes.

Due to space limitations, we select Islet dataset as instance to show the network construction results. We set 20 nodes as the baseline to reserve 4 modules for the dataset. Figure 3 (visualized by Cytoscape [14]) show the network constructed by ATV-HNMF.

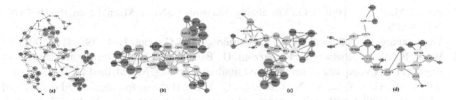

Fig. 3. Network Construction based on Human Islet Cells. A larger size indicates a greater degree of node, while a darker node indicates a greater betweenness. The nodes with higher betweenness scores are more important genes and are worth mining.

The genes with higher scores can be considered as suspicious genes. HIF1A is related to type 2 diabetes (T2D), and it keeps a consistently high expression level in transcriptional activity [15]. GPX1 plays a dual role in insulin synthesis, secretion and signal transduction by regulating redox homeostasis, the overexpression of GPX1 is associated with the elevated protein level of SELENOT, which may partially affect the T2D phenotype [16]. The expression of EIF6 regulates the amount of histone acetylation and fatty acid synthase mRNA, so EIF6 may be a therapeutic target to the fasn-driven lipogenesis in T2D [17]. ATP6V1H is down-regulated in islet of T2D [18], it plays a significant role in the regulation of vacuolar-ATPase activity and may be involved in the development important molecular mechanism of T2D [19].

5 Conclusion

In this paper, we propose a nonnegative matrix factorization model for clustering and network analysis, called ATV-HNMF. On the one hand, this model introduces the high-order relationships between cells that can keep the intrinsic structure in high-dimensional. On the other hand, adaptive total variation is used for reducing the noise interference. From the clustering results, we can see that ATV-HNMF outperforms other methods. From the constructed network, we can discover many disease-related genes, and some are worthy of further clinical exploration. In the future, we will consider reducing the loss of error terms to make the model more robust.

Acknowledgment. This work was supported in part by the grants provided by the National Science Foundation of China, No. 61872220.

References

1. Villani, A.C., et al.: Single-cell RNA-seq reveals new types of human blood dendritic cells, monocytes, and progenitors. Science **356**(6335), eaah4573 (2017)

2. van der Maaten, L., Hinton, G.: Visualizing data using t-SNE. J. Mach. Learn. Res. **9**, 2579–2605 (2008)
3. Von Luxburg, U.: A tutorial on spectral clustering. Stat. Comput. **17**(4), 395–416 (2007)
4. Wang, B., Zhu, J., Pierson, E., Ramazzotti, D., Batzoglou, S.: Visualization and analysis of single-cell RNA-seq data by kernel-based similarity learning. Nat. Method **14**(4), 414 (2017)
5. Jiao, C.-N., Gao, Y.-L., Yu, N., Liu, J.-X., Qi, L.-Y.: Hyper-graph regularized constrained NMF for selecting differentially expressed genes and tumor classification. IEEE J. Biomed. Health Inf. **24**(10), 3002–3011 (2020)
6. Lin, X., Boutros, P.C.: Optimization and expansion of non-negative matrix factorization. BMC Bioinform. **21**(1), 7 (2020)
7. Yu, N., Wu, M., Liu, J., Zheng, C., Xu, Y.: Correntropy-based hypergraph regularized NMF for clustering and feature selection on multi-cancer integrated data. IEEE Trans. Cybernet. 1–12 (2020)
8. Cai, D., He, X., Han, J., Huang, T.S.: Graph regularized nonnegative matrix factorization for data representation. IEEE Trans. Pattern Anal. Mach. Intell. **33**(8), 1548–1560 (2011)
9. Zeng, K., Yu, J., Li, C., You, J., Jin, T.: Image clustering by hyper-graph regularized non-negative matrix factorization. Neurocomputing **138**, 209–217 (2014)
10. Leng, C., Cai, G., Yu, D., Wang, Z.: Adaptive total-variation for non-negative matrix factorization on manifold. Pattern Recogn. Lett. **98**, 68–74 (2017)
11. Levine, S., Chen, Y., Stanich, J.: Image restoration via nonstandard diffusion, Duquesne University, Department of Mathematics and Computer Science Technical report, 04–01 (2004)
12. Xin, Y., et al.: RNA sequencing of single human islet cells reveals type 2 diabetes genes. Cell Metab. **24**(4), 608–615 (2016)
13. Darmanis, S., et al.: A survey of human brain transcriptome diversity at the single cell level. Proc. Natl. Acad. Sci. **112**(23), 7285–7290 (2015)
14. Shannon, P., et al.: Cytoscape: a software environment for integrated models of biomolecular interaction networks. Genome Res. **13**(11), 2498–2504 (2003)
15. Yamada, N., et al.: Genetic variation in the hypoxia-inducible factor-1α gene is associated with type 2 diabetes in Japanese. J. Clin. Endocrinol. Metab. **90**(10), 5841–5847 (2005)
16. Zhou, J.-C., Zhou, J., Su, L., Huang, K., Lei, X.G.: Selenium and diabetes. In: Michalke, B., (ed.) Selenium, pp. 317–344. Springer International Publishing, Cham (2018)
17. Brina, D., et al.: eIF6 coordinates insulin sensitivity and lipid metabolism by coupling translation to transcription. Nat. Commun. **6**, 8261 (2015)
18. Olsson, A.H., et al.: Decreased expression of genes involved in oxidative phosphorylation in human pancreatic islets from patients with type 2 diabetes. Eur. J. Endocrinol. **165**(4), 589–595 (2011)
19. Molina, M.F., et al.: Decreased expression of ATP6V1H in type 2 diabetes: a pilot report on the diabetes risk study in Mexican Americans. Biochem. Biophys. Res. Commun. **412**(4), 728–731 (2011)

Covariance Matrix Adaptation Evolutionary Algorithm for Multi-task Optimization

Wei Li[1,2(✉)], Zhou Lei[1], Junqing Yuan[1], Haonan Luo[1], Qiaoyong Jiang[1,2], and Jinbo Li[1]

[1] School of Computer Science and Engineering,
Xi'an University of Technology, Xi'an 710048, China
liwei@xaut.edu.cn
[2] Shaanxi Key Laboratory for Network Computing and Security Technology,
Xi'an 710048, China

Abstract. Multifactorial evolution is a relatively new evolutionary multitasking paradigm which aims to solve multiple optimization problems simultaneously. In order to make a further contribution to multifactorial optimization, this paper introduced a covariance matrix adaptation evolutionary strategy to explore the generality of the multitasking paradigm. A novel encoding and decoding method is employed so that each component problem is solved by a unique population. Further, a mating approach is proposed to transfer implicit knowledge among tasks for generating offspring. Experimental and statistical analyses are performed on CEC2017 evolutionary multitask optimization competition. Results show that the proposed algorithm has a superior performance in comparison with other state-of-the-art multifactorial optimization algorithms.

Keywords: Multi-task optimization · Covariance matrix adaptation · Evolution strategy

1 Introduction

Multifactorial optimization (MFO) [1], which is also called multi-task optimization (MTO) [2], is a newly emerging evolutionary multitasking paradigm. MFO aims to study on how to solve multiple optimization problems simultaneously using evolutionary algorithms. In recent years, evolutionary algorithms (EAs) have been successfully applied to solve many optimization problems including single-objective optimization (SOO) and multiobjective optimization (MOO). Multifactorial optimization can be considered as a third category of problems, which is characterized by solving multiple optimization problems during one optimization process. MFO is different from MOO. MFO aims to optimize multiple tasks at the same time. These tasks may come from completely different fields and have different characteristics. MOO aims to solve conflicts among competing objectives of the same task [1].

© Springer Nature Singapore Pte Ltd. 2021
L. Pan et al. (Eds.): BIC-TA 2020, CCIS 1363, pp. 25–36, 2021.
https://doi.org/10.1007/978-981-16-1354-8_3

A strong motivation for the MFO paradigm is derived from the fact that many real-world problems possess the high degree of similarity. Then, their optimal solutions may possess certain commonality which can be utilized to improve their optimization processes. In particular, the promising solutions found in solving one optimization problem can be transferred to help another relevant problem. Ever since the idea of MTO is proposed, many researchers show great interest in designing and developing more MTO methods. For example, Feng *et al.* proposed multifactorial particle swarm optimization (MFPSO) paradigm and multifactorial differential evolution (MFDE) paradigm [3]. New assortative mating schemes are developed in MFPSO and MFDE, respectively. Zheng *et al.* presented differential evolutionary multitask optimization (DEMTO) which using differential evolution as the optimizer [2]. In DEMTO, an effective light-weight knowledge transfer strategy is implemented to realize a multi-task optimization during the optimization process. Chen *et al.* proposed a multifactorial memetic algorithm to solve the shortcomings of MTO [4]. More specifically, a local search method based on quasi-Newton, reinitialize technology and a self-adapt parent selection strategy are introduced into MTO to improve the performance of the proposed algorithm. Inspired by domain adaptation in machine learning, Bali *et al.* proposed a novel idea of linearized domain adaptation (LDA) to solve evolutionary multitasking [5]. More specifically, LDA strategy transforms the search space into the search space similar to its complex task composition. Zheng et al. proposed a multifactorial brain storm optimization algorithm (MFBSA) which employed clustering technique into multitasking [6].

In this paper, we make a study on multitasking with covariance matrix adaptation evolutionary strategy (CMA-ES) to further contribute to multifactorial optimization. The aim of this paper is to explore the generality of the MFO paradigm proposed in [1]. To the best of our knowledge, this is the first attempt in the literature to implement multitask optimization by using covariance matrix adaptation evolutionary strategy as the optimizer, and propose a covariance matrix adaptation evolutionary multitask optimization (CMAMTO) algorithm. In particular, we present a novel encoding and decoding method which suitable for covariance matrix adaptation evolution. Subsequently, we present a mating approach for multitask optimization in CMAMTO to exploit the search mechanism of CMA-ES. Finally, nine single objective MFO benchmarks reported in [7] are used to evaluate the performance of CMAMTO.

The rest of this paper is organized as follows. Section 2 reviews the brief introduction of the concept of multifactorial optimization and covariance matrix adaptation evolutionary strategy. Section 3 introduced the proposed covariance matrix adaptation evolutionary multitask optimization (CMAMTO) algorithm. Section 4 reports and discusses the experimental results while Sect. 5 draws the concluding remarks of this paper.

2   Background

In this section, the multifactorial optimization (MFO) paradigm proposed in [1] is simply introduced and the background of the covariance matrix adaptation evolutionary strategy is also presented.

2.1   Multifactorial Optimization

Classical optimization methods (e.g., differential evolution, particle swarm optimization, etc.) find the optimal solution for an optimization task in one optimization process. However, the aim of MFO is to simultaneously optimize multiple optimization problems and find the optimal solution for each optimization problem. To deal with multiple tasks, a unique problem specific representation for each task is built by encoding and decoding. More specifically, a random key scheme is used to encode and linear map is used to decode. Moreover, some properties for each individual are given as follows [1].

Definition 1. (Factorial Cost): For a given task T_j, the ith individual p_i's factorial cost is recorded as $\Psi_j^i = \lambda \cdot \delta_j^i + f_j^i$, where parameter λ is a penalizing multiplier, f_j^i and δ_j^i are the objective value and the total constraint violation of the ith individual on task T_j.

Definition 2. (Factorial Rank): The ith individual p_i's factorial rank on task T_j, recorded as r_j, is defined as the index of p_i's in the list of population sorted in ascending order according to the factorial cost Ψ_j.

Definition 3. (Scalar Fitness): The ith individual p_i's scalar fitness is defined as $\varphi_i = 1/ \min_{j \in \{1,...,k\}} \{r_j^i\}$.

Definition 4. (Skill Factor): The ith individual p_i's skill factor τ_i is the one task on which the individual p_i performs the best amongst all other tasks. $\tau_i = \mathrm{argmin}_j \{r_j^i\}$, where $j \in \{1, 2, ..., k\}$.

Similar to other EA paradigms, multifactorial evolutionary algorithm (MFEA) starts with population initialization. In view of K optimization tasks to be performed simultaneously, a unified search space with $\max_j \{D_j\}$, denoted as $D_{multitask}$, is defined. Each individual is encoded with a vector of random variables. More specifically, the ith dimension of the unified search space is represented by a random key y_i.

At each generation, a pair of genetic operators, namely crossover and mutation [8,9], are employed on current population to generate an offspring population. Two parent candidates are randomly selected to undergo crossover if they have the same skill factor. On the contrary, if their skill factors differ, whether crossover or mutation occurs will be determined by random mating probability rmp. It is computationally expensive for each individual to be evaluated for every task. Then, after genetic operators, every individual in offspring is evaluated for only selected tasks on which it is most likely to perform well. To realize this feature, vertical cultural transmission is employed so that the offspring imitates the cultural trait of any one of their parents. After evaluation, an elitist strategy is used to ensure that the best individuals survive through the generations.

2.2   Covariance Matrix Adaptation Evolutionary Strategy

CMA-ES, proposed by Hansen and Ostermeier [10], is one of the state-of-the-art evolution algorithm paradigm. Two evolution paths are used in CMA-ES to realize exploitation and exploration during the search process, namely the update of the covariance matrix and the learning of the covariance matrix, respectively. The main operations of CMA-ES include sampling and recombination, covariance matrix adaptation, path evolution and global step size adaptation.

1) *Sampling and recombination*

   At generation $g+1$, λ candidate solutions are generated according to the Gaussian distribution

$$x_i^{g+1} \sim \mathcal{N}(\mathbf{m}^g, (\sigma^g)^2 \mathbf{C}^g) i = 1, ..., \lambda \tag{1}$$

where $\mathbf{m}^g$ is the weighted mean value, $\mathbf{C}^g$ is the covariance matrix and σ^g is the step size. The weighted mean value of the selected candidate solutions can be expressed as follows:

$$\mathbf{m}^g = \langle x \rangle_w^g = \sum_{i=1}^{\mu} w_i x_{i \cdot \lambda}^g \tag{2}$$

$$\sum_{i=1}^{\mu} w_i = 1, w_1 \geq w_2 \geq ... w_\mu > 0 \tag{3}$$

where $x_{i \cdot \lambda}^g$ is the ith best individual in the whole population, μ is the number of selected candidate solutions, and $w_i > 0$ for all $i = 1, ..., \mu$.

2) *Covariance matrix adaptation*

   The covariance matrix is updated by the evolution path $\mathbf{p}_c^{g+1}$ and the μ weighted difference vectors between the recent parents and $\mathbf{m}^g$ [11]:

$$\mathbf{p}_c^{g+1} = (1 - c_c)\mathbf{p}_c^g + \sqrt{\mu_{eff} c_c (2 - c_c)} \tilde{\mathbf{d}}_{m:\lambda}^g \tag{4}$$

$$\tilde{\mathbf{d}}_{m:\lambda}^g = \frac{\mathbf{m}^{g+1} - \mathbf{m}^g}{\sigma^g} \tag{5}$$

where $c_c = \frac{4}{D+4}$, D is the dimension of search space, and μ_{eff} represents the variance effective selection mass [11], which is calculated as follows [12]:

$$\mu_{eff} = \frac{1}{\sum_{m=1}^{\mu} w_m^2} \tag{6}$$

where $\mu = \lfloor \frac{\lambda}{2} \rfloor$, $\lambda = 4 + \lfloor 3 ln D \rfloor$, $w_m = \frac{1}{\mu}$.

The covariance matrix C is updated according to the following equation [11,12] (Table 1):

$$\mathbf{C}^{g+1} = (1 - c_1 - c_w)\mathbf{C}^g + c_1 \boldsymbol{p}_c^{g+1}(\boldsymbol{p}_c^{g+1})^T + c_w \langle \widetilde{\mathbf{d}^g}(\widetilde{\mathbf{d}^g})^T \rangle_w \qquad (7)$$

$$\langle \widetilde{\mathbf{d}^g}(\widetilde{\mathbf{d}^g})^T \rangle_w = \sum_{m=1}^{\mu} w_m \widetilde{\mathbf{d}}_{m:\lambda}^g (\widetilde{\mathbf{d}}_{m:\lambda}^g)^T \qquad (8)$$

where $c_w = \min\left(1 - c_1, \alpha_{cov}\dfrac{\mu_{eff} + \frac{1}{\mu_{eff}} - 2}{(D+2)^2 + \frac{\alpha_{cov} \times \mu_{eff}}{2}}\right)$, $c_1 = \dfrac{\alpha_{cov}}{(D+1.3)^2 + \mu_{eff}}$ and $\alpha_{cov} = 2$.

3) *Path evolution and global step size adaptation*

The path cumulation p_σ^{g+1} can be detailed as follows:

$$p_\sigma^{g+1} = (1 - c_\sigma)p_\sigma^g + \sqrt{\mu_{eff}c_\sigma(2 - c_s)}(\mathbf{C}^g)^{-\frac{1}{2}}\frac{(\mathbf{m}^{g+1} - \mathbf{m}^g)}{\sigma^g} \qquad (9)$$

$$c_\sigma = \frac{\mu_{eff} + 2}{\mu_{eff} + D + 3} \qquad (10)$$

The global step size σ^{g+1} is updated according to the following equation [11]:

$$\sigma^{g+1} = \sigma^g exp\left(\frac{c_\sigma}{d_\sigma}\left(\frac{\|p_\sigma^{g+1}\|}{E[\|\mathcal{N}(0,\mathbf{I})\|]} - 1\right)\right) \qquad (11)$$

where $E[\|\mathcal{N}(0,\mathbf{I})\|] = \sqrt{2}\Gamma(\frac{D+1}{2})/\Gamma(\frac{D}{2})$, $d_\sigma = 1 + c_\sigma + 2\max(0, \sqrt{\frac{\mu_{eff}-1}{D+1}} - 1)$

Table 1. Pseudo-code of the CMA-ES algorithm [12] (Algorithm 1).

1:	Initialize ($x^{(0)}$, $\sigma^{(0)}$, g = 0, $p_\sigma^{(0)}$= 0, $p_c^{(0)}$ = 0, $C^{(0)}$ = I)
2:	**while** termination condition(s) is not fulfilled
3:	**for** l = 1 to λ do
4:	$\widetilde{\mathbf{z}}_l^{(g)} = \mathcal{N}_l(0,\mathbf{I})$
5:	$\widetilde{\mathbf{d}}_l^{(g)} = \sqrt{\mathbf{C}^{(g)}}\widetilde{\mathbf{z}}_l^{(g)}$
6:	Update $\mathbf{x}_l^{(g)}$ according to (1)
7:	Evaluate $\mathbf{x}_l^{(g)}$
8:	**end for**
9:	SortOffspringPopulation
10:	Update $\mathbf{x}^{(g+1)}$ according to (1)
11:	Update $p_\sigma^{(g+1)}$ according to (9)
12:	Update $p_c^{(g+1)}$ according to (4)
13:	Update $C^{(g+1)}$ according to (7)
14:	Update $\sigma^{(g+1)}$ according to (11)
15:	g = g + 1
16:	**end while**

3 Covariance Matrix Adaptation Evolutionary Multitask Optimization

In this section, we propose a covariance matrix adaptation evolutionary multi-task optimization (CMAMTO) algorithm characterized by a new encoding and decoding method and assortative mating scheme. The assortative mating scheme can be considered as the new cultural reproduction operator, which promotes implicit knowledge transfer among tasks for offspring generation.

1) *Encoding and decoding for CMAMTO*

   At each generation g, the corresponding random key $\mathbf{y} = \{y_1, y_2, ..., y_D\}$ of an individual is calculated as follows.

$$\mathbf{y} = \sum\nolimits_{i=1}^{\mu} \mathbf{w}_i \mathbf{x}_i^g \tag{12}$$

   where $\mathbf{x}_i^g$ is the ith best individual in the whole population, μ is the number of selected candidate solutions, and $\mathbf{w}$ is the weight vector. The decoding operator for each individual is defined as follows.

$$\mathbf{x} = \mathbf{y} + \sigma \boldsymbol{B}\boldsymbol{D}\mathcal{N}(0, 1) \tag{13}$$

   where σ is step size; $\boldsymbol{B}$ is the orthogonal matrix and $\boldsymbol{D}$ is the diagonal matrix; $\boldsymbol{C}$ is covariance matrix. Moreover, $\boldsymbol{B}$ and $\boldsymbol{D}$ are obtained according to $\boldsymbol{C} = \boldsymbol{B}\boldsymbol{D}^2\boldsymbol{B}^T$ [13].

2) *Assortative Mating for CMAMTO*

   The assortative mating is employed to select best candidate individual for updating the search distribution. The pseudo code of the assortative mating in CMAMTO is given in Algorithm 2. $pbest_{T1}(k_1)$ and $pbest_{T2}(k_2)$ denote the k_1th best individual on task T_1 and the k_2th best individual on task T_2, respectively. $gbest_{T2}$ denotes the best individual on task T_2.

The pseudo-code of CMAMTO is given in Algorithm 3.

4 Experiments

In this section, the CMAMTO algorithm is compared with the original MFEA, the MFPSO and the MFDE in terms of the performance on the 9 problems from [7] to show the superiority of the proposed algorithm (Tables 2 and 3).

4.1 Experimental Setup

The aforementioned 9 benchmark problems from CEC2017 Evolutionary Multi-Task Optimization Competition is given in Table 4. The benchmark problems are composed of pairing classical single objective functions, such as *Griewank*, *Rastrigin* and *Schwefel*, etc. The details of these benchmark problems can be found in [7].

Table 2. Pseudo-code of the assortative mating in CMAMTO (Algorithm 2).

1: xmean = [ ];
2: $k_1 = 0$; $k_2 = 0$
3: **for** $i = 1$ to μ **do**
4:      Generate a random number $rand$ between 0 and 1
5:      **if** $rand < rmp$ **then**
6:          Generate a random number r between 0 and 1
7:          $k_1 = k_1 + 1$
8:          $P = r \times pbest_{T1}(k_1) + (1 - r) \times gbest_{T2}$
9:      **else**
10:         $k_2 = k_2 + 1$
11:         $P = pbest_{T2}(k_2)$
12:     **end if**
13:     xmean = xmean $\cup$ P
14: **end for**

Table 3. Pseudo-code of CMAMTO (Algorithm 3).

1: Initialize ($x^{(0)}$, $\sigma^{(0)}$, g = 0, $p_\sigma^{(0)} = 0$, $p_c^{(0)} = 0$, $C^{(0)} = I$)
    Evaluate the individuals on every tasks and obtain the skill factor of each individual
2: **while** termination condition(s) is not fulfilled
3:      Sort the population according to factorial cost
4:      Update $\mathbf{x}^{(g+1)}$ of task T_1 according to (1)
5:      Update $p_\sigma^{(g+1)}$ of task T_1 according to (9)
6:      Update $p_c^{(g+1)}$ of task T_1 according to (4)
7:      Update $C^{(g+1)}$ of task T_1 according to (7)
8:      Update $\sigma^{(g+1)}$ of task T_1 according to (11)
9:      Update $\mathbf{x}^{(g+1)}$ of task T_2 according to Algorithm2 and (1)
10:     Update $p_\sigma^{(g+1)}$ of task T_2 according to (9)
11:     Update $p_c^{(g+1)}$ of task T_2 according to (4)
12:     Update $C^{(g+1)}$ of task T_2 according to (7)
13:     Update $\sigma^{(g+1)}$ of task T_2 according to (11)
14:     Update the scalar fitness and skill factor of all the offspring individuals
15:     g = g + 1
16: **end while**

The parameters in MFEA, MFPSO, MFDE and CMAMTO used in this study are summarized as follows:

1) Parameter settings in MFEA:
   - population size : $n = 100$; random mating probability $rmp = 0.3$
   - distribution index of SBX : 2; distribution index of PM: 5
2) Parameter settings in MFPSO:
   - population size : $n = 100$; random mating probability $rmp = 0.3$
   - inertia weight: $\omega_G = \omega_{max} - \frac{\omega_{max} - \omega_{min}}{MaxGen} G$; $\omega_{max} = 0.9$; $\omega_{min} = 0.4$
     G is the current generation. $MaxGen$ is the maximum generation.
   - $c_1 = c_2 = c_3 = 0.2$
3) Parameter settings in MFDE:
   - population size : $n = 100$; random mating probability $rmp = 0.3$
   - scaling factor : $F = 0.5$; crossover rate: $CR = 0.9$
4) Parameter settings in CMAMTO:
   - population size : $n = 4 + \lfloor 3 ln D \rfloor$; random mating probability $rmp = 0.3$
     D is the dimension of the search space.

To obtain an unbiased comparison, all the experiments are carried out on the same machine with an Intel Core i7-5500 2.40 GHz CPU and 8 GB memory.

Table 4. Properties of problem pairs for evolutionary multitasking.

Problem	Component tasks	Dimension	Optimal values	Search ranges	Inter-task similarity
1	T1:Griewank	50	0	$[-100, 100]$	1.00
	T2:Rastrigin		0	$[-50, 50]$	
2	T1:Ackley	50	0	$[-50, 50]$	0.22
	T2:Rastrigin		0	$[-50, 50]$	
3	T1:Ackley	50	0	$[-50, 50]$	0.00
	T2:Schwefel		0	$[-500, 500]$	
4	T1:Rastrigin	50	0	$[-50, 50]$	0.86
	T2:Sphere		0	$[-100, 100]$	
5	T1:Ackley	50	0	$[-50, 50]$	0.21
	T2:Rosenbrock		0	$[-50, 50]$	
6	T1:Ackley	50	0	$[-50, 50]$	0.07
	T2:Weierstrass	(T2:25)	0	$[-0.5, 0.5]$	
7	T1:Rosenbrock	50	0	$[-50, 50]$	0.94
	T2:Rastrigin		0	$[-50, 50]$	
8	T1:Griewank	50	0	$[-100, 100]$	0.36
	T2:Weierstrass		0	$[-50, 50]$	
9	T1:Rastrigin	50	0	$[-50, 50]$	0.00
	T2:Schwefel		0	$[-500, 500]$	

All experiments are run 25 times, and the codes are implemented in Matlab R2016a, and conducted with the maximum number of function evaluations *(MaxFES)* as the termination criterion, which is set to 100,000.

4.2   Experimental Results and Discussion

Table 5 shows the achieved mean fitness values over 25 runs by all the compared algorithms. The best values are shown in bold. As can be observed in Table 5, CMAMTO performs better than MFEA, MFPSO and MFDE in 14 out of 18 tasks, which indicates that the improvement strategies employed in the proposed algorithm work effectively and efficiently. More specifically, CMAMTO performs best on T_1 and T_2 of problem 1, 2, 6, 7 and 8. For problem 3, 4, 5 and 9, CMAMTO performs best on T_1.

Figure 1 shows the average convergence curves of CMAMTO versus MFEA, MFPSO, MFDE on problem 1, 3, 6 and 7. From these curves, we can verify that CMAMTO performs better on the problems which have high inter-task similarity or lower inter-task similarity.

Table 5. Average fitness values (mean) of CMAMTO and other algorithms.

Problem	Tasks	MFEA	MFPSO	MFDE	CMAMTO
1	T1	1.7264e−01	9.1465e−01	1.1233e−03	**0**
	T2	1.7308e+02	3.7209e+02	3.5107e+00	**3.9869e−13**
2	T1	8.7476e+00	7.7607e+00	1.6009e−01	**1.4388e−14**
	T2	4.9117e+02	5.6034e+02	1.9504e+00	**0**
3	T1	2.0514e+01	2.1288e+01	2.1206e+01	**2.0095e+01**
	T2	**9.1492e+03**	1.5758e+04	1.1569e+04	1.3386e+04
4	T1	7.6775e+02	9.7287e+02	8.0360e+01	**7.4343e+01**
	T2	3.3673e+00	4.8124e+03	**1.8533e−05**	1.6897e+03
5	T1	4.1821e+00	6.0680e+00	1.5716e−03	**1.4104e−14**
	T2	5.5390e+02	8.4799e+04	**7.9646e+01**	9.3289e+01
6	T1	2.0370e+01	1.3406e+01	2.8489e−01	**1.3394e−14**
	T2	2.3871e+01	1.1621e+01	2.2439e−01	**1.1935e−14**
7	T1	4.7257e+02	5.3685e+05	9.2303e+01	**2.2514e+01**
	T2	2.2944e+02	5.9887e+02	2.2979e+01	**2.1307e+01**
8	T1	2.4287e−01	1.1351e+00	6.5713e−04	**2.9584e−04**
	T2	2.8319e+01	3.2034e+01	3.5746e+00	**3.2906e+00**
9	T1	7.5207e+02	3.4581e+03	1.0256e+02	**7.4065e+01**
	T2	8.7888e+03	1.5900e+04	**4.0978e+03**	1.1211e+04

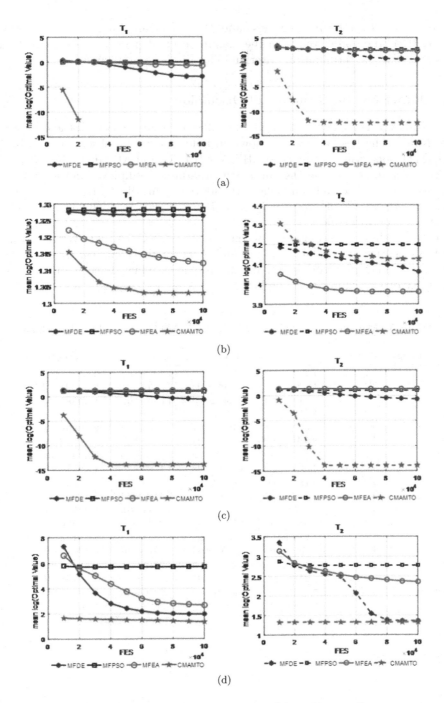

Fig. 1. (a) problem 1; (b) problem 3; (c) problem 6; (d) problem 7; Convergence traces of CMAMTO versus MFDE, MFPSO and MFEA on representative multitasking benchmarks. X-axis denotes the number of function evaluations (*FES*).

5   Conclusions

In this paper, a covariance matrix adaptation evolutionary algorithm is modified to solve different component tasks. Two improvement strategies are introduced to improve the performance of the algorithm: 1) a new encoding and decoding method; and 2) assortative mating scheme. Furthermore, experiments are conducted on the CEC2017 competition test problems to compare CMAMTO with three state-of-the-art evolutionary multitask optimization algorithms. The experimental results shows the effectiveness of CMAMTO for problem solving.

Acknowledgement. This research is partly supported by the Doctoral Foundation of Xi'an University of Technology (112-451116017), National Natural Science Foundation of China under Project Code (61803301, 61773314).

References

1. Gupta, A., Ong,, Y.S., Feng, L.: Multifactorial evolution: toward evolutionary multitasking. IEEE Trans. Evol. Comput. **20**(3), 343C357 (2016)
2. Zheng, X., Lei, Y., Qin, A.K., et al.: Differential evolutionary multi-task optimization. In: 2019 IEEE Congress on Evolutionary Computation (CEC), pp. 1914–1921. IEEE, Wellington, New Zealand (2019)
3. Feng,, L., Zhou, W., Zhou, L., et al.: An empirical study of multifactorial PSO and multifactorial DE. In: 2017 IEEE Congress on Evolutionary Computation (CEC), pp. 921–928. IEEE, San Sebastian, Spain (2017)
4. Chen, Q., Ma, X., Sun, Y., et al.: Adaptive memetic algorithm based evolutionary multi-tasking single-objective optimization. In: Proceedings of Asia-Pacific Conference on Simulated Evolution and Learning, pp. 462–472. Springer, Cham, Shenzhen, China (2017)
5. Bali, K.K., Gupta, A., Feng, L., et al.: Linearized domain adaptation in evolutionary multitasking. In: 2017 IEEE Congress on Evolutionary Computation (CEC), pp. 1295–1302. IEEE, San Sebastian, Spain (2017)
6. Zheng,, X.L., Lei, Y., Gong, M.G., et al.: Multifactorial brain storm optimization algorithm. In: Proceedings of International Conference on Bio-inspired Computing Theories and Applications, pp. 47–53. Springer, Singapore, Xi'an, China (2016)
7. Da, B.S., Ong, Y.S., Feng, L., et al.: Evolutionary multitasking for single-objective continuous optimization: benchmark problems, performance metrics and baseline results. Technical Report, Nanyang Technological University (2016)
8. Goldberg, D.E.: Genetic Algorithms in Search Optimization and Machine Learning. Addison Wesley, MA, USA (1989)
9. Srinivas, M., Patnaik, L. M.: Genetic algorithms: a survey. Computer **27**(6), 17C26 (1994)
10. Hansen, N., Mller, S.D., Koumoutsakos, P.: Reducing the time complexity of the derandomized evolution strategy with covariance matrix adaptation (CMA-ES). Evol. Comput. **11**(1), 1–18 (2003)

11. Hansen, N., Kern, S.: Evaluating the CMA Evolution Strategy on Multimodal Test Functions. In: Yao, X., et al. (eds.) PPSN 2004. LNCS, vol. 3242, pp. 282–291. Springer, Heidelberg (2004). https://doi.org/10.1007/978-3-540-30217-9_29
12. Beyer, H.G., Sendhoff, B.: simplify your covariance matrix adaptation evolution strategy. IEEE Trans. Evol. Comput. **21**(5), 746–759 (2017)
13. Hansen, N., Ostermeier, A.: Completely derandomized self-adaptation in evolution strategies. Evol. Comput. **9**(2), 159–195 (2001)

Short Text Similarity Calculation Based on Jaccard and Semantic Mixture

Shushu Wu[1](✉), Fang Liu[1], and Kai Zhang[1,2]

[1] School of Computer Science, Wuhan University of Science and Technology, Wuhan 430081, China
[2] Hubei Province Key Laboratory of Intelligent Information Processing and Real-time Industrial System, Wuhan 430081, China

Abstract. For the sake of enhancing the accuracy of short text similarity calculation, a short text similarity calculation method on account of Jaccard and semantic mixture is proposed. Jaccard is a traditional similarity algorithm based on literal matching. It only considers word form, and its semantic calculation has certain limitations. The word vector can represent the semantic similarity by computing the cosine similarity of two terms in the vector space, and the semantic similarity is obtained by adding and averaging the word similarity of two sentences according to a certain method. The two methods are now weighted to compute the final text similarity. Experiments show that the algorithm improves the recall rate and F value of short text calculation to some extent.

Keywords: Short text similarity · Jaccard · Word vector · Semantic similarity

1 Introduction

In the wake of the development of computer technology and the Internet, more and more information is presented in short texts. How to correctly compute the similarity of short texts has become particularly important, and it has also become a hot spot in natural language processing. Text similarity refers to the degree of semantic similarity of text. It can not only be applied to search engines, document duplicate checking, and automatic question and answer systems, but also can be applied to document classification and clustering and accurate document push [1]. We have brought great convenience. Compared with long texts, short texts have shorter content and sparse words, which makes calculations more difficult. For example, the same words can express different meanings, and different words can also express the same meaning, that is, the so-called polysemous and multi-sense words. And even if the word composition of the two sentences is exactly the same, but their combined structure is different, the meanings expressed are also different. According to the characteristics of similarity calculation methods, text similarity can be divided into literal matching similarity, semantic similarity and structural similarity. The calculation method of literal matching only considers the similarity of the text from the morphology,

© Springer Nature Singapore Pte Ltd. 2021
L. Pan et al. (Eds.): BIC-TA 2020, CCIS 1363, pp. 37–45, 2021.
https://doi.org/10.1007/978-981-16-1354-8_4

which has great limitations; the semantic similarity method solves the semantic matching of words, but it needs to rely on the corpus; the structural similarity can analyze the grammatical structure of the text, But the accuracy will decrease with the increase of sentence length [2]. The three calculation methods have their own advantages and disadvantages, and they all need certain optimization.

For the study of short text similarity, Huang Xianying et al. added word order to the term, and combined the overlap similarity algorithm with the word order similarity algorithm between common word blocks to calculate the short text similarity [3]. Gu Zhixiang et al. used part of speech and word frequency weighting to improve the simhash algorithm [4]. Li Lian et al. optimized the vector space model algorithm by considering the influence of the same feature words between texts on the text similarity [5]. These methods all consider other features of the term on the basis of the word shape, and improve the text similarity algorithm to a certain extent, but do not involve the semantic level of the sentence. The realization of sentence semantics can use corpus, such as HowNet, WordNet, etc. Yuan Xiaofeng uses HowNet to calculate the semantic similarity of words, and uses the TF/IDF values of a small number of feature words to assign weights to the vectors in the VSM, and then computes the similarity between texts [6]. On the basis of improving the edit distance, Che Wanxiang et al. used two semantic resources HowNet and synonym cilin to calculate the semantic distance between words, and obtained better results on the basis of taking into account word order and semantics [7]. Zhang Jinpeng et al. studied text similarity based on the vector space model and semantic dictionary, and discussed the semantic similarity of texts of different lengths and their applications [8]. Liao Zhifang et al. proposed a short text similarity algorithm based on syntax and semantics. By calculating the similarity of short texts with the same syntactic structure and considering the contribution of sentence phrase order to the similarity, the similarity of Chinese short texts was calculated [9]. These methods consider the part of speech and semantics of the sentence, but the semantics need to rely on an external dictionary, which cannot calculate the semantic similarity of words between different parts of speech. The word vector makes up for this shortcoming. It can also be used for extended training based on the corpus and the one-hot vector can be converted into a low-dimensional word vector. Therefore, Jaccard is combined with a semantic algorithm based on word vectors to find text similarity. Jaccard is an algorithm based on literal matching, which takes into account the morphology of the text. It is suitable for calculating two sentences with more co-occurring words, but for two sentences that do not overlap at all, the calculated similarity is 0 and cannot be calculated Similarity of similar words. The word vector can calculate the semantic similarity of words, which makes up for the shortcomings of the Jaccard algorithm, so the two are combined to find the short text similarity.

The first part of this article mainly introduces the short text and some related research content, the second part describes the algorithm used in detail, the third part is the experimental results and comparative analysis, and the fourth part gives the conclusion.

2 Related Algorithms

2.1 Jaccard Algorithm

Jaccard ratio is an indicator which is used to weigh the similarity of two musters. It is defined as the intersection of two musters divided by the union of two musters. The Jaccard ratio only focuses on words with the same characteristics. The more feature words in the two sentences, the greater the value of the jacard ratio. For the two sentences S1 and S2, their Jaccard similarity is:

$$Sim(S1, S2) = \frac{|S1 \cap S2|}{|S1 \cup S2|} \tag{1}$$

The numerator is a quantity of identical terms in two sentences, and the denominator is a quantity of total terms.

2.2 Semantic Algorithm Based on Word Vector

Word2vec. Along with the popularization of deep learning in natural language processing, word vectors have also been proposed Word embedding refers to vectors that map words or phrases in the word list to the actual number through some method. The traditional One-Hot encoding converts words into discrete individual symbols, which can simply represent word vectors, but the vocabulary is often very large, which causes the vectors to be high-dimensional and sparse. Word2vec [10] can transform high-dimensional sparse vector into low-dimensional dense vector, and the position of synonyms in vector space is also close. Word2vec was released by Google in 2013 and can be used to generate and calculate word vectors. It can be effectively trained on the data set, and the training word vector can well weigh the similarity between words.

At the back of word2vec is a superficial neural network, which includes two models, one is CBOW model, and the other is Skip-gram model. Both models include input layer, hidden layer and output layer, as shown in Fig. 1. But CBOW forecasts the present word according to the context, while Skip-gram forecasts the context according to the present word. This paper is on account of the CBOW model to train word vectors. Input layer: the input is the context one hot encoding vector of the word of the selected window size; hidden layer: simple summation and average of the word vectors of the context words; output layer: this layer corresponds to a Huffman tree. The leaf nodes of the tree are the words that appear in the corpus. The non-leaf nodes are generally a two-classifier, along the left subtree is the negative class, and the right subtree is the positive class, thus calculating the probability of each word. For the sake of simplifying the complexity of the model, in comparision with the neural probabilistic language model, the CBOW model changes the stitching method to the cumulative summation method in the hidden layer, and changes the linear structure of the output layer to a tree structure.

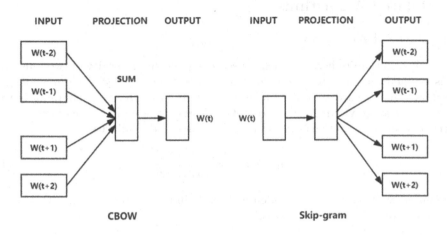

Fig. 1. word2vec model

Semantic Algorithm. The traditional Jaccard algorithm does not involve the similarity calculation at the semantic level, while the word vector can calculate the similarity of synonyms, and the sentences S1 and S2 are used to illustrate the specific algorithm steps:

Step 1: Use word2vec to train the corpus to generate model and word vectors of each vocabulary;

Step 2: Segment the sentences S1 and S2 and remove the stop words. The words in S1 are ai (i = 1,2,3, ..., m), and the words in S2 are bj (j = 1,2,3, i, n);

Step 3: Compute the semantic similarity of each word in S1 and each word in S2 through the word vector to form a two-dimensional matrix M. The formula is:

$$cos(ai, bj) = \frac{ai \cdot bj}{|ai| \times |bj|} \tag{2}$$

Step 4: Find the largest value in the matrix M, add it to the set P, and assign the value of the row and column corresponding to the value to -1, repeat this step until all the values in the matrix are -1;

Step 5: Add all the values in the set P and divide by the average similarity obtained by the set length n, as the final semantic similarity of the two sentences. The formula is:

$$Sim(S1, S2) = \frac{\sum_{i=0}^{n-1} P(i)}{n} \tag{3}$$

2.3 Algorithm Based on Jaccard and Semantics

Calculate the Jaccard similarity and semantic similarity for sentences S1 and S2, and record them as Sim1 (S1, S2) and Sim2 (S1, S2), and mix the two with a certain weight to get the final similarity. The formula is:

$$Sim(S1, S2) = \alpha \cdot Sim1(S1, S2) + (1 - \alpha) \cdot Sim2(S1, S2) \qquad (4)$$

Among them, α is the weight adjustment factor, and the specific value is analyzed in the experiment. The obtained sentence similarity Sim (S1, S2) needs to be compared with the similarity threshold β, if it is greater, it is determined to be similar, otherwise it is not similar.

3 Experiment Design and Result Analysis

3.1 Experimental Details

In this article, three data sets are used to verify the algorithm. Each data set has human annotations. Two sentence labels with the same semantics are 1, and the other is 0. Data set I is a MSRP data set [11] which is provided by the Microsoft Research Interpretation Corpus. It has many positive categories and comes from news sources on the Web. Data set II is the STS data set [12], which can be used to measure the similarity of the meaning of sentences and has more negative categories than positive categories. Data set III selects 2000 data from Quora data set, and the positive-negative ratio is 1:1.

In order to reduce experimental errors and improve accuracy, all text is pre-processed, uppercase is converted to lowercase, and useless information such as punctuation marks and extra spaces is removed. Use the tf-idf method to extract keywords in the text during testing. After the above processing, all sentences are segmented and trained with word2vec to generate the model and the word vector corresponding to the word. The CBOW model is used during training, and the vector is 200-dimensional. The training corpus consists of two parts, one is the English Wikipedia corpus, the size is about 500M, and the other is the data used. This is to prevent the data of the data set from being included in the word vector model and unable to calculate the semantic similarity. The semantic similarity between words and expressions can be computed by loading the model.

The evaluation standard uses the precision rate P, recall rate R and F score commonly used in the field of information retrieval to estimate the performance of the algorithm. Precision rate P = correct prediction is positive/all predictions are positive, recall rate R = correct prediction is positive/all actual is positive, precision and recall rate affect each other, ideally both are high, but the general case if the precision rate is high, the recall rate is low, and the recall rate is low while the precision rate is high. Therefore, in the case where both require high, the F value can be used to measure. The definition of F is:

$$F = \frac{2 \times P \times R}{P + R} \qquad (5)$$

This article includes two experiments. One experiment is how to ascertain the similarity threshold of two sentences and the respective weights of the two algorithms. Another experiment is to prove the validity of the short text similarity algorithm put forward in this article, using the weighting factors obtained in the first experiment to mix Jaccard and semantic algorithms, and compare with other algorithms.

3.2   Experimental Results and Analysis

Value of Similarity Threshold β **and Weighting Factor** α: To determine whether two sentences are similar, a similarity threshold must be set. A smaller similarity threshold will determine that two dissimilar sentences are similar, and a larger similarity threshold will also cause a judgment error, so it is necessary to select a suitable similarity Degree threshold. The specific method is as follows:

1) Divide the interval according to the similarity value. Set an integer m and divide the interval [0, 1] into[0, 1/m), [1/m, 2/m)...[(m −1)/m,1];
2) Select the minimum and maximum values of each interval and generate a series of values evenly distributed between them;
3) Find the threshold with the lowest error rate and its corresponding accuracy rate in each interval, and record it;
4) Screen the threshold, the array Z1 and Z2 record the threshold and accuracy after screening respectively;
5) The normalized accuracy is weighted and summed with the similarity threshold to obtain the final similarity threshold

In the experiment, the data set I and the data set II are combined to find the similarity threshold and weight factor, m is set to 10, and finally the similarity is 0.58. The weighting factor is calculated according to the determined similarity threshold, and take different values of α in 0.05 steps. The result is shown in Fig. 2:

It can be found from Fig. 2 that with the α increases, the precision rate gradually increases, while the recall rate gradually decreases, and the F value increases first and then decreases. Taking the F value as the selection criterion, when α is 0.35, the maximum F value is 0.734, at this time the precision rate is 0.651, and the recall rate is 0.842. Therefore, this paper takes a weighting factor of 0.35 for subsequent performance evaluation.

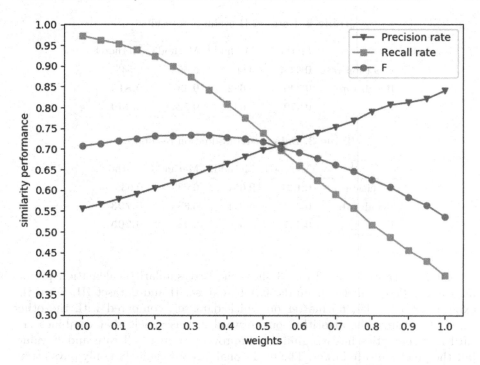

Fig. 2. Comparison of experimental results with different weighting factors

Similarity Algorithm Performance Evaluation. For the sake of proving the performance of the algorithm put forward in this article, the algorithm of this paper is now compared with several classic algorithms. The experiments are conducted in Data Set I, Data Set II and Data Set III. The classic algorithms are as follows:

Method 1: Traditional Jaccard algorithm;
Method 2: Vector-based cosine similarity algorithm;
Method 3: Edit distance algorithm based on terms;
Method 4: This article is based on a hybrid algorithm of Jaccard and semantics.

The results of the experiment are shown in the following table:

Table 1. Data set-I evaluation results.

	Method1	Method2	Method3	Method4
Precision rate	**0.892**	0.781	0.878	0.756
Recall rate	0.428	0.763	0.427	**0.867**
F	0.579	0.772	0.575	**0.807**

Table 2. Data set-II evaluation results.

	Method1	Method2	Method3	Method4
Precision rate	**0.764**	0.605	0.653	0.542
Recall rate	0.349	0.682	0.437	**0.810**
F	0.479	0.641	0.524	**0.649**

Table 3. Data set-III evaluation results.

	Method1	Method2	Method3	Method4
Precision rate	**0.667**	0.651	0.639	0.635
Recall rate	0.334	0.641	0.389	**0.793**
F	0.445	0.646	0.484	**0.705**

Table 1, Table 2 and Table 3 show the text similarity calculation performance of different methods on dataset I , dataset II and dataset III. From the experimental results, no matter on which data set, compared with the other three algorithms, the algorithm put forward in this article that combines jaccard and semantics has a significant improvement in recall rate and F value, but the precision rate Lower. The traditional jaccard algorithm only pays attention to the word form, without considering the semantics of the term, and its recall and F value are low. The vector-based cosine similarity algorithm which concentrates on the word form and its number is more stable, the accuracy and recall are not much different, and the F value is also higher. The word-based edit distance algorithm considers the word order to a certain extent, but also does not consider the semantics of the sentence. The evaluation results are similar to the jaccard algorithm. The algorithm in this paper not only considers the item information of co-occurrence terms, but also considers the semantic information of non-co-occurrence terms, and obtains good results. Comparing the evaluation results of the three data sets, the algorithm proposed in this paper, in terms of F value, data set I > data set III > data set II, which may be related to the characteristics of the data set. Data set I has more positive classes than negative classes, and data set II has more negative classes than positive classes, and the positive class is equal to the negative class in Data Set III. And the data set III has not been used to find the similarity threshold and weighting factor, but when the weighting factor is 0.35, good experimental results are also obtained.

4   Conclusion

This article puts forward a text similarity algorithm based on a mixture of Jaccard and semantics. This algorithm first considers the effect of co-occurrence words on text similarity, and uses the traditional Jaccard algorithm to compute the similarity of two sentences. Secondly, the word vectors are acquired by training the external corpus, then the corresponding values between the word vectors in the two sentences are calculated, the maximum value is taken out and the word vectors in the corresponding two sentences are deleted, then average all the maximum values as the semantic similarity of these two short sentences. Finally, the weighted Jaccard similarity and semantic similarity are combined to compute the final similarity of the two sentences. In this paper, experiments were carried out on three data sets, and the algorithm was compared with the conventional Jaccard algorithm, cosine similarity algorithm, editing distance algorithm, etc. The results show that the algorithm of this paper is higher than other methods in the recall rate R and F of the text similarity calculation, thus proving the effectiveness of the algorithm. However, the effect of this algorithm in text similarity calculation is not very significant, which is related to the linguistic features such as word vectors obtained by training, sentence syntax, and word order. Because the larger the training corpus, the better the word vectors obtained by training, but the training corpus in this article is only a medium size, and the algorithm does not consider the semantic impact of the order of words in the sentence and the composition of the sentence on the sentence.

References

1. Erjing, C., Enbo, J.: A review of text similarity calculation methods. Data Anal. Knowl. Discov. **1**(6), 1–11 (2017)
2. Hanru, W., Yangsen, Z.: A review of research progress in text similarity calculation. J. Beijing Inf. Sci. Technol. Univ. (Nat. Sci. Edn.) **34**(01), 68–74 (2019)
3. Xianying, H., Yingtao, L., Qinfei, R.: An English short text similarity algorithm based on common chunks. J. Chongqing Univ. Technol. (Nat. Sci.) **29**(08), 88–93 (2015)
4. Zhixiang, G., Xie Longen, D.Y.: Implementation and improvement of SimHash algorithm for text similarity calculation. Inf. Commun. **01**, 27–29 (2020)
5. Li, L., Zhu, A., Su, T.: Research and implementation of an improved text similarity algorithm based on vector space. Comput. Appl. Softw. (02), 282–284 (2012)
6. Yuan, X.: Research on text similarity based on HowNet. J. Chengdu Univ. (Nat. Sci. Edn.) **33**(3), 251–253 (2014). https://doi.org/10.3969/j.issn.1004-5422.2014.03.015
7. Wanxiang, C., Ting, L., Bing, Q., et al.: Chinese similar sentence retrieval based on improved edit distance. High-Tech Commun. **14**(7),15–19 (2004). https://doi.org/10.3321/j.issn:1002-0470.2004.07.004
8. Jinpeng, Z.: Research and application of text similarity algorithm based on semantics. Chongqing University of Technology (2014)
9. Zhifang, L., Guoen, Z., Junfeng, L., Fei, L., Fei, C.: Chinese short text grammar semantic similarity algorithm. J. Hunan Univ. (Nat. Sci. Edn.) **43**(02), 135–140 (2016)
10. Mikolov, T., Chen, K., Corrado, G., et al.: Efficient estimation of word representations in vector space (2013). arXiv preprint arXiv:1301.3781
11. Dolan, W., Quirk, C., Brockett, C., et al.: Unsupervised construction of large paraphrase corpora: exploiting massively parallel news sources (2004)
12. Cer, D.M., Diab, M.T., Agirre, E., et al.: SemEval-2017 Task 1: semantic textual similarity multilingual and crosslingual focused evaluation. In: Meeting of the Association for Computational Linguistics, pp. 1–14 (2017)

Density-Based Population Initialization Strategy for Continuous Optimization

Peilan Xu[1], Wenjian Luo[2(✉)], Jiafei Xu[1], Yingying Qiao[1], and Jiajia Zhang[2]

[1] School of Computer Science and Technology,
University of Science and Technology of China, Hefei 230027, Anhui, China
{xpl,xujiafei,bonsur}@mail.ustc.edu.cn
[2] School of Computer Science and Technology, Harbin Institute of Technology,
Shenzhen 518000, Guangdong, China
{luowenjian,zhangjiajia}@hit.edu.cn

Abstract. The population initialization is the first and crucial step in many swarm intelligence and evolutionary algorithms. In this paper, we propose a new density-based population initialization strategy, which is concerned about both uniformity and randomness of the initial population. In experiments, first, the empty space statistic is adopted to indicate its favorable uniformity. Then, the proposed strategy is used to generate an initial population for CMA-ES, and compared with typical initialization strategies over the CEC-2013 multimodal optimization benchmark. The experimental results demonstrate that the density-based initialization strategy could generate more uniform distribution than the random strategy, and such a strategy is beneficial to evolutionary multimodal optimization.

Keywords: Population initialization · Density estimation ·
Evolutionary algorithm · Swarm intelligence

1 Introduction

Swarm intelligence (SI) and evolutionary algorithms (EAs) are population-based search algorithms [1,24,28], and they could achieve satisfactory results when dealing with the complex black-box optimization problems. The first step of both SI and EAs is population initialization, which determines the initial distribution of the candidate solutions. Generally speaking, a well-distribution initial population could promote the efficiency of exploration and the quality of the solution [19], whereas a poor-distribution initial population may deteriorate the performance of SI [13].

Although a well-distributed initial population could be considered to be closer to the optimal solution, it is difficult to define and obtain a *well-distributed* initial population. In most studies of SI and EAs, the distribution of initial population is

This work is partly supported by the National Natural Science Foundation of China (No. 61573327).

routinely not cared for, and the pseudo-random number generators (PRNGs) are widely used to construct a pseudo-random initial population. Although PRNG has the advantages of simplicity, convenience and powerful adaptability, the population formed by it is not uniform enough [13]. Therefore, in the face of complex and large-scale optimization problems, this issue will make the algorithm performance very unstable [8].

Besides PRNGs, other population initialization strategies have been proposed for improving the distribution of the initial population [9]. In [4], Gao *et al.* used chaotic mappings to form the initial population. Compared with the pseudo-random initial population, the former could bring with better results. In [21], Richards *et al.* used centroidal Voronoi tessellations (CVT) to generate the starting points as the initial population, but the time cost of CVT is expensive.

Different from the above random methods, Refs. [13,25] use quasi-random numbers instead of pseudo-random numbers to generate the initial population, while Ref. [17] adopted uniform design (UD) and Refs. [5,10] adopted orthogonal design (OD). In addition, opposition based learning (OBL) is adopted in [18–20], where the worse half of the population is replaced by their oppositions, and this strategy could be adopted in the initial step as well as the evolutionary search process.

In this paper, we propose a density-based population initialization strategy, which tends to generate a uniform initial population with a certain degree of randomness. The proposed strategy balances the distribution of the population by the density function of the population, and generates new individuals in areas with lower density as far as possible. In the experiments, first, the empty space statistic is adopted to measure the uniformity of initial populations. Furthermore, the proposed strategy is embedded into covariance matrix adaptation evolution strategy (CMA-ES), and then tested on the CEC-2013 multimodal optimization benchmark. Experimental results demonstrate that the density-based initial population initialization strategy could achieve better results than other initialization strategies.

The rest of this paper is organized as follows. In Sect. 2, some typical population initialization strategies and kernel density estimation (KDE) are reviewed. Section 3 describes the proposed density-based population initialization strategy. In Sect. 4, the uniformity of the initial population is analyzed, and the experimental results on CEC-2013 multimodal optimization benchmark problems are given. Finally, Sect. 5 summarizes the work in this paper briefly.

2   Related Work

In this section, first, some typical population initialization strategies are briefly reviewed. Then, the kernel density estimation is reviewed.

2.1   Population Initialization Strategies

Population initialization is one of the crucial steps of SI and EAs. The distribution of the initial population will affect the performance of the algorithms. In this section, several typical population initialization strategies are reviewed.

Chaotically Initializing Population. The chaotic system has been employed to generate the initial population, because it is unique in ergodic, randomness, regularity, and sensitivity to initial conditions [2–4]. Formula (1) is a logistic mapping used to generate a set of chaotic numbers $c_i, i = 0, 1, ..., D - 1$, where μ is control parameter, D is the problem dimension, and $c_0 \notin \{0, 0.25, 0.5, 0.75, 1\}$. Taking the logistic mapping as an example, the generation of each individual in the chaotic initial population is as follows [4].

$$c_{i+1} = \mu c_i (1 - c_i), \ c_i \in [0, 1], \ i = 0, 1, \ldots, D - 1. \tag{1}$$

First, generate a D-dimensional chaotic vector $\mathbf{c} = (c_0, c_1, ..., c_{D-1})$, where c_0 is randomly generated by the PRNG, and $c_1, ..., c_{D-1}$ are generated according to Formula (1). Then, map the chaotic vector $\mathbf{c} = (c_0, c_1, ...c_{D-1})$ to search space $[lb, ub]^D$ by formula $x_i = lb_i + c_i(ub_i - lb_i), i = 0, 1, ..., D - 1$ to generate an individual $\mathbf{x} = (x_0, x_1, ..., x_{D-1})$, where lb_i and ub_i are the upper and lower bounds of the ith dimension of the search space, respectively. Finally, generated individual x is added to the chaotic initial population.

Centroidal Voronoi Tessellation. Voronoi tessellation is a partition of the space, which constructs Voronoi cells around a given point set. Each Voronoi cell includes a point (called generator), and the distance from the points inside a Voronoi cell to the corresponding generator is less than other generators. Centroidal Voronoi tessellation (CVT) is a special case of Voronoi tessellation, where each generator is the centroid of its Voronoi cell. In [21,23], CVT has been used to obtain more uniform sampling points in the hypercube.

The main steps to form an initial population by CVT are as follows [21]. First, randomly generate a set of samples and construct the corresponding Voronoi diagram. Then, use the algorithm for computing CVT [7] to get the approximate CVT. Finally, the generators of all Voronoi cells are employed as an initial population.

Orthogonal Design. The orthogonal design (OD) has been used to generate the initial population in some studies [5,10]. The main idea of OD is as follows [10]. First, equidistantly select Q points from each dimension. Then, based on Q^N points in N dimensions, a series of orthogonal arrays are constructed to generate sample points, and these sample points form an initial population. Here, Q is the number of levels at each dimension, N is the problem dimension. In addition, when the search space is large, the search space could be divided into multiple subspaces, and the above operations will be performed in each subspace.

The initial population generated by OD depends on the orthogonal arrays. The distribution of population has satisfactory uniformity in low-dimensional space. However, as the dimension increases, or the size of the population decreases, it is difficult to ensure the quality of the population.

2.2 Kernel Density Estimation

Kernel density estimation (KDE) [12,15,26,29] is a non-parametric method, which is carried to estimate the unknown probability density function of a variable under a given sample set. Assuming the sample set $P = \{x_1, x_2, \ldots, x_k\}$, the density function ρ of a point x_j in the problem space S is estimated as

$$\rho_{x_j} = \frac{1}{k} \sum_{i=1}^{k} K(x_j - x_i). \tag{2}$$

Formula (3) is a further description of the kernel function in Formula (2), which is called the Gaussian kernel function.

$$K(x) = \exp(-\frac{\|x\|^2}{2h^2}), \tag{3}$$

where h is a smoothing parameter, and is known as bandwidth. Although there are many different kernel functions, the Gaussian kernel function is used in this paper.

3 Proposed Algorithm

A well-distributed initial population could improve exploration performance of the population-based algorithms. Without prior knowledge, the uniform initial population could learn more landscape information of the problem. Moreover, as the beginning of the stochastic algorithm, the random initial population has an opportunity to bring unexpected harvest. Therefore, the population initialization strategy needs to cope with the balance between uniformity and randomness of the initial population, which is also the major consideration of the density-based population initialization strategy proposed in this paper.

The density-based population initialization strategy controls the population distribution from the perspective of the density space, and each new individual tends to appear in the areas with lower density. In order to obtain a relatively uniform population, KDE is employed to estimate the density of sample location. Algorithm 1 shows the pseudocode of the proposed algorithm, and the details are described as follows.

The proposed algorithm could be carried to generate the initial population, or add new individuals into the current population to maintain diversity during evolutionary search. Before generating the first individual, whether the population is empty needs to be checked. If the current population is empty, the first

---

Algorithm 1. Density-based population initialization strategy

---
1: **for** $i \leftarrow 1$ **to** N **do**
2:     **if** $i = 1$ **and** the current population is empty **then**
3:         Generate the first individual x_1 by PRNG;
4:     **end if**
5:     Select m positions by PRNG;
6:     Estimate the densities of m positions according to Formula (2);
7:     Select the position x_i with the lowest density from m positions;
8:     Put x_i into current population;
9: **end for**

---

individual is directly generated by PRNG, and when the population P is not empty, new individuals are sequentially generated in the following manner.

First, m positions are randomly selected by PRNG in the search space S. Then, the densities of m positions under current population P are estimated by Formula (2). Finally, the position with the lowest density is selected as a new individual x_i to be added into the population P. The above steps are repeated until N individuals are generated.

There are two parameters in Algorithm 1, namely the number of detection positions m and the bandwidth h. The parameter m is related to the expected effect and time cost of the algorithm. The bandwidth h determines the range affects by each individual, and the h-neighborhood of each individual could be regarded as the high-density region. Ideally, the hypersphere enclosed by the h-neighborhood of each individual should not overlap. Thus, the bandwidth h is estimated as follows.

Assuming that the volume of each hypersphere is V_h, then V_h could be approximated as V/N, where V the volume of the search space S, N is the population size. Thus, the bandwidth h could be estimated by Formula (4), where d is the problem dimension.

$$V_h = C R^d$$
$$\Rightarrow h = R = \sqrt[d]{\frac{V_h}{C}} = \sqrt[d]{\frac{V}{NC}}, \tag{4}$$

where R is the radius of the hypersphere, and C is described by the gamma function.

$$C = \frac{\pi^{d/2}}{\Gamma(d/2 + 1)}. \tag{5}$$

Expand the function $\Gamma(d/2 + 1)$, and h is calculated as follows.

$$h = \begin{cases} \sqrt[d]{\frac{V}{N} \cdot \frac{k!}{\pi^k}} & , \text{if } d = 2k \\ \sqrt[d]{\frac{V}{N} \cdot \frac{(2k+1)!}{2^{2k+1}k!\pi^k}} & , \text{if } d = 2k + 1. \end{cases} \tag{6}$$

Consequently, we only need to consider the parameter m, which is set to 30 for subsequent experiments.

For the sake of intuition, Figs. 1 and 2 display comparisons of the distributions of two populations, which are generated by the density-based population initialization strategy and the PRNG, with the population sizes of 500 and 2000, respectively. Obviously, the population generated by the density-based population initialization strategy looks more uniform.

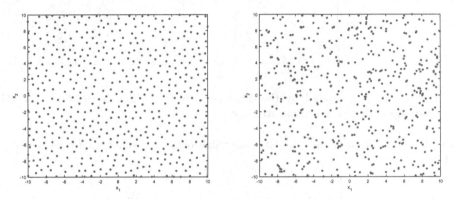

(a) Population generated by the density-based population initialization strategy

(b) Population generated by PRNG

Fig. 1. Comparison of the population distributions in 2-D space with population size of 500

4   Experiments

In this section, we first use the empty space statistic to measure the uniformity of the populations. Second, the experimental setting and results on the CEC-2013 multimodal optimization benchmark problems are provided.

4.1   Experiments on Uniformity Analysis

In this subsection, the empty space statistic (ESS) [22] is used as a uniformity metric to measure the population distribution. Given a population P in the search space S, the ESS function is defined as follows.

$$\text{ESS}(r) = 1 - Pr(B(x,r) \cap P = \emptyset), \tag{7}$$

where x is a point randomly selected from the search space S, $B(x,r)$ is a hypersphere with x as the center and r as the radius, and Pr represents the probability that the hyperball $B(x,r)$ does not intersect the population P.

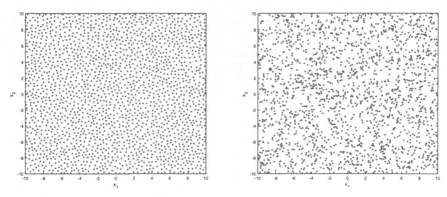

(a) Population generated by the density-based population initialization strategy

(b) Population generated by PRNG

Fig. 2. Comparison of the population distribution in 2-D space with population size of 2000

In experiments, the density-based population initialization strategy is compared with pseudo-random, chaotic, CVT, and OD initialization strategy. The space dimension D is set to four different values, i.e., 2, 3, 5 and 10, respectively, and S is set to $[0, 1]^D$. The population size is set to 256 for the 2-D, 3-D, and 5-D search spaces, and set to 512 for 10-D space. Finally, 10,000 pseudo-random auxiliary points are used to estimate the empirical empty space statistic.

The steepness of the function curve could reveal the uniformity of the population [14]. The steeper the curve, the greater the influence of the radius, that is, whether the ball $B(x, r)$ is empty depends on the radius of the ball rather than the position of auxiliary points.

Figure 3 shows the empirical empty space statistic values in 2-D, 3-D, 5-D and 10-D spaces. It can be observed that the curve corresponding to the density-based population rises faster than the curve corresponding to the pseudo-random population in different dimensional spaces, which means the density-based population is more uniform. Also, the experimental results is in line with the intuitive conclusions obtained from Figs. 1 and 2. On the other hand, the uniformity of the density-based initial population is moderate because it balances randomness and uniformity, and the population constructed by CVT is considered to be the most uniform distribution among the compared algorithms from the trends in ESS values. Nonetheless, considering the time cost of CVT is relatively expensive, the density-based initialization strategy is promising to enhance the uniformity of the initial population with less cost in a higher dimensional space.

There is an another finding in Fig. 3. In the 2-D space, OD is the optimal space filling scheme [27]. However, the uniformity of OD rapidly deteriorates with increasing of dimensions.

In addition, the chaotic initialization strategy uses stochastic properties of chaotic systems to construct the initial population instead of uniformity, so the uniformity is the worst in this comparison.

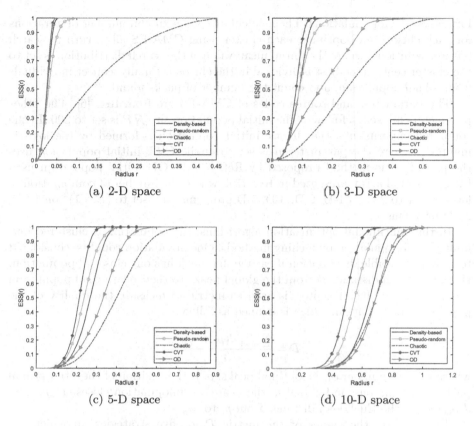

(a) 2-D space   (b) 3-D space

(c) 5-D space   (d) 10-D space

Fig. 3. Empirical empty space statistic values

4.2 Experiments on CEC2013 Multimodal Optimization Benchmark

Compared with the global optimization problems, multimodal optimization problems (MMOPs) often have a higher demand for a well-distribution initial population, and an initial population with poor uniformity are more likely to lose some global optimal solutions. In this subsection, all 20 functions from the CEC2013 multimodal optimization competition [11] are employed as the benchmark to demonstrate the effect of the initialization strategy on the performance of optimization algorithms. Five population initialization strategies, namely density-based, pseudo-random, chaotic, CVT, and OD initialization strategy, are used to generate the initial population for the optimization algorithm, and tested on the CEC2013 MMOPs.

The optimization algorithms for MMOPs pay attention to the niching method and the optimizer. In this paper, the classic niching method, speciation [16], and the classic optimizer, CMA-ES [6], are combined to form the multimodal optimization algorithm. The process of the algorithm is given as follows. First, generate the initial population with size of NP by the initialization strategy. Second, cluster the initial population using the speciation strategy in [16] to form several subpopulations. Then, calculate the maximum number of iterations for each cluster, and optimize each cluster using CMA-ES [6] in turn to search optimal solutions, where the initial mean value of the search distribution is set to the cluster center (the best individual in the cluster). Finally, collect individuals from all subpopulation, and count the number of peaks found.

The parameters and source codes of CMA-ES are from Ref. [6]. The other parameters are set as follows. The initial population size NP is set to 200. In the compared experiments, the chaotic initial population is formed by the logistic mapping, where the parameter μ is set to 4; the CVT initial population uses the probabilistic method proposed by Ref. [7]; the OD initial population used the orthogonal array presented in Ref. [10], where the number of combination of levels is set to 256 on 1-D, 2-D, 3-D, 5-D problems, and set to $(D-1)^3$ on 10-D, 20-D problems.

In the multimodal optimization algorithms, the population is clustered into multiple subpopulation by niching methods. One population could be considered to have a favorable distribution if each global peak has one close subpopulation. Here, the mean distance $\mathcal{D}$ from the global peaks to their nearest subpopulation center, i.e., the cluster center, is used as metric to measure the quality of the population distribution, which is defined as follow.

$$\mathcal{D} = \frac{\sum_{i=1}^{n} d(p_i, ns_i)}{n}, \tag{8}$$

where n is the number of the optimal peaks, p_i is the position of the i-th optimal peak, ns_i is the best individual in the nearest subpopulation closest to p_i, and $d(p_i, ns_i)$ is the Euclidean distance from p_i to ns_i.

Table 1 lists the values of the metric $\mathcal{D}$ for five strategies, in which the stochastic algorithms (except for OD, the rest are stochastic algorithms) use the mean values of $\mathcal{D}$ from 50 independent runs as the final results. As shown in Table 1, OD has best performance on functions 1, 3–7 and 11, and the metric $\mathcal{D}$ of CVT is smallest on functions 3, 8, 10, 12–20. Additionally, the density-based initialization strategy has competitive results on functions 2, 3 and 9. In contrast, the results of pseudo-random and chaotic populations are poor.

Combined with the first experiment, the presented results reveal a significant correlation between the uniformity and the population quality. The more uniform the population, the closer the subpopulation is to the optimal peak. For example, the population obtained by OD has the best ESS values in 1-D and 2-D spaces, and OD also has the best $\mathcal{D}$ values on most 1-D and 2-D functions. Moreover, except for function 9, the $\mathcal{D}$ values of CVT are best on 3-D, 5-D and 10-D functions, and Fig. 3 also shows that the uniformity of the population constructed by CVT in these dimensions is the best.

Further, Fig. 4 shows the distribution of population and the positions of clusters of the density-based and pseudo-random initialization strategies on functions 5, 6, and 12. The blue dots indicate the individuals within the initial population, the red asterisks indicate the global peaks, and the black dash line circles indicate the cluster that are closest to the optimal peaks. Moreover, a colorbar is

Table 1. The mean distance of five initial populations on CEC-2013 multimodal optimization benchmark

Function index		Density-based	Pseudo-random	Chaotical	CVT	OD
1	F_1(1D)	0.037	0.179	0.179	0.090	**0.000**
2	F_2(1D)	**0.001**	0.003	0.003	0.002	0.002
3	F_3(1D)	**0.001**	0.012	0.012	**0.001**	**0.001**
4	F_4(2D)	0.405	0.444	0.869	0.356	**0.262**
5	F_5(2D)	0.096	0.104	0.997	0.082	**0.064**
6	F_6(2D)	0.918	1.037	3.284	0.920	**0.820**
7	F_7(2D)	0.298	0.429	1.348	0.291	**0.262**
8	F_6(3D)	2.117	2.039	5.407	**1.598**	3.743
9	F_7(3D)	**0.843**	1.111	2.391	0.871	1.818
10	F_8(2D)	0.030	0.035	0.165	**0.027**	0.038
11	F_9(2D)	0.339	0.383	1.521	0.282	**0.235**
12	F_{10}(2D)	0.487	0.547	1.362	**0.443**	0.536
13	F_{11}(2D)	0.414	0.462	1.556	**0.357**	0.387
14	F_{11}(3D)	1.139	1.241	2.512	**1.119**	2.745
15	F_{12}(3D)	1.110	1.259	2.525	**1.103**	2.467
16	F_{11}(5D)	2.792	2.758	3.965	**2.394**	4.304
17	F_{12}(5D)	2.708	2.780	4.014	**2.493**	3.857
18	F_{11}(10D)	6.989	6.268	7.829	**5.638**	7.496
19	F_{12}(10D)	6.960	6.395	7.838	**5.795**	7.691
20	F_{12}(20D)	12.856	11.676	13.205	**11.647**	11.964
		3	0	0	12	7

added to the right side of figures to indicate the fitness corresponding to different color contours.

For the function 5, the positions of the clusters of two different populations are similar, and it could be considered that the optimal peaks are located. However, there are differences in the positions of the clusters of two different populations on the functions 6 and 12. On function 6, some global peaks are not included in the clusters from pseudo-random initial population. Also, on function 12, the density-based initial population covered more global peaks. Compared to the pseudo-random initial population, the density-based initial population has a more favorable distribution, which lies a solid foundation for the subsequent evolutionary search.

However, it is unnecessary that the initial population with better distribution will lead to better results. In the following experiments, *Peak Ratio* (PR) and *Success Rate* (SR) are used to measure the performance of optimization algorithms [11], and the final results will be used to check the relationship between the distribution of the initial population and the performance of optimization algorithms. PR represents the average ratio of the peaks found per run, and SR is the ratio of the number of runs where all peaks are found to the total number of runs.

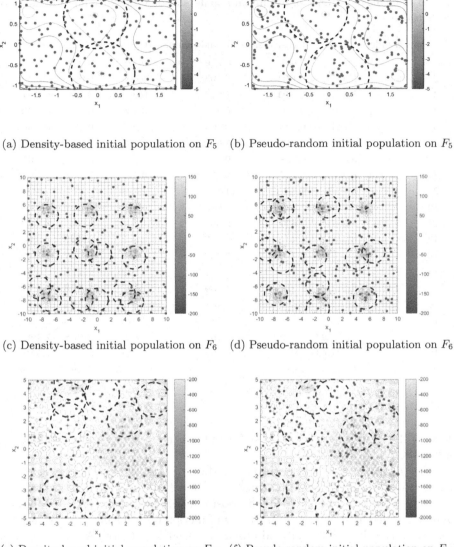

(a) Density-based initial population on F_5 (b) Pseudo-random initial population on F_5

(c) Density-based initial population on F_6 (d) Pseudo-random initial population on F_6

(e) Density-based initial population on F_{12} (f) Pseudo-random initial population on F_{12}

Fig. 4. The distribution of population and the positions of clusters of density-based and pseudo-random initial populations. The black dash line circles indicate the cluster that are closest to the optimal peaks, and other clusters are not shown in the figure. (Color figure online)

Table 2 lists the experimental results on CEC2013 MMOPs at accuracy level $\epsilon = 10^{-4}$. The best result in each pair of comparisons is bold, and the number of the best PR results from these strategies is listed in the last row of the Table 2.

Table 2. Experimental results of five initialization strategies on CEC-2013 multimodal optimization benchmark at the accuracy level $\epsilon = 10^{-4}$

Function index	Density-based		Pseuo-random		Chaotic		CVT		OD	
	PR	SR	PR	SR	PR	SR	PR	SR	PR	SR
1	**1.000**	**1.000**	**1.000**	**1.000**	**1.000**	**1.000**	**1.000**	**1.000**	**1.000**	**1.000**
2	0.860	0.440	0.880	0.440	0.880	0.440	0.868	0.420	**0.892**	**0.520**
3	0.180	0.180	**0.200**	**0.200**	**0.200**	**0.200**	0.120	0.120	0.140	0.140
4	**1.000**	**1.000**	**1.000**	**1.000**	0.995	0.980	**1.000**	**1.000**	**1.000**	**1.000**
5	**1.000**	**1.000**	**1.000**	**1.000**	0.990	0.980	**1.000**	**1.000**	**1.000**	**1.000**
6	0.627	0.000	0.534	0.000	0.206	0.000	0.567	0.000	**0.652**	0.000
7	0.562	0.000	0.501	0.000	0.299	0.000	**0.567**	0.000	0.541	0.000
8	0.224	0.000	0.195	0.000	0.038	0.000	**0.259**	0.000	0.033	0.000
9	**0.303**	0.000	0.253	0.000	0.101	0.000	0.279	0.000	0.073	0.000
10	**0.930**	**0.380**	0.923	0.300	0.628	0.000	0.898	0.280	0.858	0.140
11	0.983	0.900	0.980	0.880	0.750	0.020	0.990	0.940	**0.997**	**0.980**
12	**0.675**	0.000	0.643	0.000	0.445	0.000	0.658	0.000	0.640	0.000
13	**0.863**	**0.200**	0.820	0.160	0.537	0.000	0.833	0.140	0.823	0.000
14	**0.737**	0.000	0.720	0.000	0.663	0.000	0.697	0.000	0.650	0.000
15	**0.685**	0.000	0.638	0.000	0.503	0.000	0.655	0.000	0.330	0.000
16	**0.677**	0.000	0.670	0.000	0.667	0.000	0.667	0.000	0.593	0.000
17	**0.720**	0.000	0.665	0.000	0.585	0.000	0.688	0.000	0.438	0.000
18	**0.623**	0.000	0.600	0.000	0.537	0.000	0.580	0.000	0.493	0.000
19	**0.555**	0.000	0.523	0.000	0.463	0.000	0.510	0.000	0.395	0.000
20	0.175	0.000	**0.220**	0.000	0.148	0.000	0.125	0.000	0.210	0.000
	14		5		2		5		6	

The experimental results suggest that the initial populations with different distributions interfere with the performance of the optimization algorithm. Among these strategies, the density-based initialization strategy achieves the best results, and obtain the best results in 14 functions, especially on complex functions, i.e., functions 9, 10, 12–19. Moreover, compared with the pseudo-random and chaotic initialization strategies, the density-based, CVT, and OD initialization strategies are more competitive. Thus, these results support that the more uniform initial population is promising to achieve better results.

However, the correlation between results in Table 1 and Table 2 is not significant enough. For example, although the density-based initialization strategy is considered to be moderate in terms of metric $\mathcal{D}$, it achieve the best final results. Experimental results indicate that a uniform initial population with a degree of randomness is beneficial to search for the optimal solution.

5   Conclusion

In this paper, we propose a novel population initialization strategy, i.e., the density-based population initialization strategy. The proposed strategy constructs a well-distributed initial population and satisfies the needs of the initial population for uniformity and randomness. The empty space statistic is used to measure the uniformity of the initial population, and the experimental results demonstrate that the density-based initial population has favorable uniform than the pseudo-random initial population, and it could still work when the dimension increases. Moreover, the proposed strategy is embedded into CMA-ES, and tested on the problems of the CEC2013 multimodal optimization competition. Compared with typical initialization strategies, the uniformity of the density-based initial population is moderate, but the final results are competitive.

In future work, we will further study the parameters settings of the density-based population initialization strategy, and try to use the density-based population initialization strategy to maintain the diversity of the population during evolution.

References

1. Bu, C., Luo, W., Yue, L.: Continuous dynamic constrained optimization with ensemble of locating and tracking feasible regions strategies. IEEE Trans. Evol. Comput. **21**(1), 14–33 (2016)
2. Gao, W.F., Liu, S.Y.: A modified artificial bee colony algorithm. Comput. Oper. Res. **39**(3), 687–697 (2012)
3. Gao, W.F., Liu, S.Y., Huang, L.L.: Particle swarm optimization with chaotic opposition-based population initialization and stochastic search technique. Commun. Nonlinear Sci. Numer. Simul. **17**(11), 4316–4327 (2012)
4. Gao, Y., Wang, Y.J.: A memetic differential evolutionary algorithm for high dimensional functions' optimization. In: Proceedings of the Third International Conference on Natural Computation (ICNC 2007), vol. 4, pp. 188–192. IEEE (2007)
5. Gong, M., Jiao, L., Liu, F., Ma, W.: Immune algorithm with orthogonal design based initialization, cloning, and selection for global optimization. Knowl. Inf. Syst. **25**(3), 523–549 (2010)
6. Hansen, N.: The CMA evolution strategy: a tutorial. arXiv e-prints arXiv:1604.00772 (2016)
7. Ju, L., Du, Q., Gunzburger, M.: Probabilistic methods for centroidal Voronoi tessellations and their parallel implementations. Parallel Comput. **28**(10), 1477–1500 (2002)
8. Kazimipour, B., Li, X., Qin, A.K.: Initialization methods for large scale global optimization. In: Proceedings of the 2013 IEEE Congress on Evolutionary Computation (CEC), pp. 2750–2757. IEEE (2013)
9. Kazimipour, B., Li, X., Qin, A.K.: A review of population initialization techniques for evolutionary algorithms. In: Proceedings of the 2014 IEEE Congress on Evolutionary Computation (CEC), pp. 2585–2592. IEEE (2014)
10. Leung, Y.W., Wang, Y.: An orthogonal genetic algorithm with quantization for global numerical optimization. IEEE Trans. Evol. Comput. **5**(1), 41–53 (2001)
11. Li, X., Engelbrecht, A., Epitropakis, M.G.: Benchmark functions for CEC'2013 special session and competition on niching methods for multimodal function optimization. RMIT University, Evolutionary Computation and Machine Learning Group, Australia, Technical report (2013)

12. Luo, W., Zhu, W., Ni, L., Qiao, Y., Yuan, Y.: SCA2: novel efficient swarm clustering algorithm. IEEE Trans. Emerg. Top. Comput. Intell. (2020). https://doi.org/10.1109/TETCI.2019.2961190

13. Maaranen, H., Miettinen, K., Mäkelä, M.M.: Quasi-random initial population for genetic algorithms. Comput. Math. Appl. **47**(12), 1885–1895 (2004)

14. Maaranen, H., Miettinen, K., Penttinen, A.: On initial populations of a genetic algorithm for continuous optimization problems. J. Global Optim. **37**(3), 405 (2007)

15. Ni, L., Luo, W., Zhu, W., Liu, W.: Clustering by finding prominent peaks in density space. Eng. Appl. Artif. Intell. **85**, 727–739 (2019)

16. Parrott, D., Li, X.: Locating and tracking multiple dynamic optima by a particle swarm model using speciation. IEEE Trans. Evol. Comput. **10**(4), 440–458 (2006)

17. Peng, L., Wang, Y., Dai, G., Cao, Z.: A novel differential evolution with uniform design for continuous global optimization. J. Comput. **7**(1), 3–10 (2012)

18. Rahnamayan, S., Tizhoosh, H.R., Salama, M.M.: Opposition-based differential evolution for optimization of noisy problems. In: Proceedings of the 2006 IEEE International Conference on Evolutionary Computation (CEC), pp. 1865–1872. IEEE (2006)

19. Rahnamayan, S., Tizhoosh, H.R., Salama, M.M.: A novel population initialization method for accelerating evolutionary algorithms. Comput. Math. Appl. **53**(10), 1605–1614 (2007)

20. Rahnamayan, S., Tizhoosh, H.R., Salama, M.M.: Opposition versus randomness in soft computing techniques. Appl. Soft Comput. **8**(2), 906–918 (2008)

21. Richards, M., Ventura, D.: Choosing a starting configuration for particle swarm optimization. In: Proceedings of the 2004 IEEE International Joint Conference on Neural Networks, pp. 2309–2312. IEEE (2004)

22. Ripley, B.D.: Spatial Statistics, vol. 575. Wiley, Hoboken (2005)

23. Saka, Y., Gunzburger, M., Burkardt, J.: Latinized, improved LHS, and CVT point sets in hypercubes. Int. J. Numer. Anal. Model. **4**(3–4), 729–743 (2007)

24. Shi, Y.: Brain storm optimization algorithm. In: Tan, Y., Shi, Y., Chai, Y., Wang, G. (eds.) ICSI 2011. LNCS, vol. 6728, pp. 303–309. Springer, Heidelberg (2011). https://doi.org/10.1007/978-3-642-21515-5_36

25. Uy, N.Q., Hoai, N.X., McKay, R.I., Tuan, P.M.: Initialising PSO with randomised low-discrepancy sequences: the comparative results. In: Proceedings of the 2007 IEEE Congress on Evolutionary Computation (CEC), pp. 1985–1992. IEEE (2007)

26. Wand, M.P., Jones, M.C.: Kernel Smoothing. CRC Press, Boca Raton (1994)

27. Wu, Q.: On the optimality of orthogonal experimental design. Acta Mathematicae Applacatae Sinica **1**(4), 283–299 (1978)

28. Xu, P., Luo, W., Lin, X., Qiao, Y., Zhu, T.: Hybrid of PSO and CMA-ES for global optimization. In: Proceeding of the 2019 IEEE Congress on Evolutionary Computation (CEC), pp. 27–33. IEEE (2019)

29. Zhu, W., Luo, W., Ni, L., Lu, N.: Swarm clustering algorithm: Let the particles fly for a while. In: 2018 IEEE Symposium Series on Computational Intelligence (SSCI), pp. 1242–1249. IEEE (2018)

Intelligent Prediction and Optimization of Extraction Process Parameters for Paper-Making Reconstituted Tobacco

Wei Gang[1,2], Wen Shuangshuang[1,2], Zhang Huaicheng[1,2], Li Yichen[1,2(✉)], Zhan Yiming[1,2], and Zeng Wei[3]

[1] China Tobacco Hubei Industrial Co., Ltd., Wuhan 430040, China
{Weigang,wenss,zhanghc,liyichen,zhanyiming}@hbtobacco.cn
[2] Huhei Xinye Reconstituted Tobacco Development Co., Ltd., Wuhan 430056, China
[3] School of Artificial Intelligence and Automation,
Huazhong University of Science and Technology, Wuhan 430074, China
zengwei@hust.edu.cn

Abstract. To study the impact of extraction process parameters on Baume and solid content of extraction solution in paper-process reconstituted tobacco production, artificial neural network and ensemble learning methods are utilized to build the prediction models for the extraction process in the paper. The prediction models describe the influencing factors such as amount of adding water, extraction water temperature, feed mixing time, squeezing time, centrifuge frequency, squeezing dryness and screw pump frequency on Baume and solid content of extraction solution. It is found that the ensemble learning model is better than the artificial neural network model by the comparison of the prediction results of these two models. The influencing parameters of the solid content and Baume are optimized by genetic algorithm based on the ensemble learning model to improve the product quality of the extraction solution. The experimental results show that the proposed models are helpful to improve the product quality of the paper-making reconstituted tobacco.

Keywords: Reconstituted tobacco · Extraction process · ANN · Ensemble learning · Genetic algorithm

1 Introduction

Tobacco sheet is a kind of reconstituted tobacco leaf, which is made from tobacco waste such as tobacco powder, tobacco stem, tobacco fragment and so on. The reproduction technology of tobacco sheet can reuse the originally useless tobacco, save tobacco raw materials to the maximum extent, improve its physical properties and chemical components, and effectively reduce harmful substances such as tar, nicotine and phenol in cigarette. The main manufacturing methods of

This work was partially supported by the National Natural Science Foundation of China (Grant No. 71871100).

L. Pan et al. (Eds.): BIC-TA 2020, CCIS 1363, pp. 60–68, 2021.
https://doi.org/10.1007/978-981-16-1354-8_6

tobacco sheet include rolling method, thick pulp method and paper-making method. The paper-making method not only produces thin sheet with low density and filling rate greater than about 10% of tobacco leaf, but also has the advantages of high tobacco yield and low crushing rate [1]. Therefore, paper-making method has been widely used in the reconstituted tobacco production.

Extraction process is one important step of paper-making reconstituted tobacco production. The output of this process is extraction solution, which is qualified by indicators such as solid content and Baume. In the extraction process, the factors such as squeezing dryness, screw pump frequency, extraction water temperature and so on have complex impacts on Baume and solid content of extraction solution. In order to improve the production efficiency and product quality of the extraction process, the extraction process parameters need to be optimized. In recent years, artificial intelligence and machine learning methods have been gradually popularized and applied in the field of production process parameter analysis and optimization. For example, based on experimental data of alkaloid extraction from lotus leaf, an artificial neural network (ANN) model is proposed to describe the relationship between extraction effect of alkaloids from lotus leaf with its influencing factors is established. Furthermore, the process parameters are simulated and evaluated based on the ANN model [2]. Similarly, Hosu et al. build a correlation model between antioxidant activity of red wine with polyphenols by ANN [3]. Jiang proposes an ANN model to investigate the correlation between microwave extraction rate of VE from wheat germ with technological parameters [4]. Based on ANN model of production process parameters, intelligent optimization algorithm is used to optimize production process parameters. For example, the authors propose a GA-ANN method that is combination of ANN model with genetic algorithm (GA), i.e., an ANN model is used to describe the influence of formula components on Blueberry cyanidin extraction, and genetic algorithm is used to optimize the formula components based on the ANN model [5,6]. Chen et al. use orthogonal design, BP neural network and genetic algorithm to carry out multi-attribute comprehensive optimization of tea extraction process [7].

The basic idea of combining ANN model with GA algorithm to optimize process parameters is to train neural network with existing data to get an ANN model which meets the accuracy requirements, then genetic algorithm is used to find the optimal solution on the basis of ANN model. However, the establishment of ANN model is lack of theoretical guidance and there exists the over-fitting problem. Moreover, the prediction model by using a single ANN method often suffers from shortcomings such as insufficient generalization ability and weak robustness. To overcome the above problems, the method of ensemble learning is proposed to improve the performance of prediction model through the integration of multiple models [8]. Specifically, ensemble learning is to combine multiple weak supervised models in order to obtain a better and more comprehensive strong supervised model. It combines a set of base classifiers from training data, and then classifies by voting on the prediction of each base classifier. If a single prediction model is compared to a decision-maker, the ensemble learning method is equivalent to multiple decision-makers making a decision together. Compared with ANN model, ensemble learning model has better generalization ability.

In order to better explore the optimization problem of extraction process parameters in paper-making reconstituted tobacco, the impact of adding water amount, extraction water temperature, feed mixing time, squeezing time, centrifuge frequency, squeezing dryness and screw pump frequency on solid content and Baume of extraction solution are mainly considered in this paper. Compared with ANN prediction model, the prediction models of the solid content and Baume based on ensemble learning method are selected to establish the optimization model of extraction process parameters. Genetic algorithm is used to obtain the optimal extract process parameters.

2   Prediction Models of Extraction Process

2.1   Test Data and Processing

In this study, the actual production sample data from a reconstituted tobacco factory are used as training data and test data. Several variables including amount of adding water, extraction water temperature, feed mixing time, squeezing time, centrifuge frequency, squeezing dryness and screw pump frequency are selected as the input variables of prediction model, and the solid content and Baume of the extraction solution are taken as the output variables of the model. Considering the actual production conditions, the range of water addition amount is 6000 ml–6500 ml, the extraction water temperature is 60 °C–120 °C, the feed mixing time is 30 min–60 min, the squeezing time is 60 min–90 min; the centrifuge frequency 30 Hz–40 Hz, the screw pump frequency 30 Hz–50 Hz, the squeezing dryness is 25%–40%. The output value of the solid content and Baume are both indicators of the concentration of the extract solution. Table 1 is a sample of experimental data.

Table 1. Parts of production sample data.

Amount of adding water (ml)	Extraction temperature (°C)	Feed mixing time (min)	Squeezing time (min)	Centrifuge frequency (Hz)	Screw pump frequency (Hz)	Squeezing dryness (%)	Solid content (%)	Baume (°Be)
6000	60	30	60	30.0	50	40.0	3.8	2.8
6300	70	56	85	38.0	35	31.2	7.3	6.2
6000	72	50	85	38.0	44	34.0	6.4	5.6
6100	92	43	70	35.4	40	32.0	6.7	5.7
6200	86	45	80	33.8	41	31.0	6.9	5.5
6350	74	44	75	38.7	36	30.9	5.9	4.8
6400	85	35	86	38.0	32	28.0	6.4	5.1

The training set data and test set data are standardized by the following formula:

$$x = (x_i - \mu)/\sigma \tag{1}$$

where μ is the average value and σ is the variance.

2.2   Artificial Neural Network Model of Extraction Process

Artificial neural network is a network structure composed of neurons in input layer, hidden layer and output layer. For the prediction of extraction process of the reconstituted tobacco production, an ANN model with network topology of 7-40-1-2 is established, as shown in Fig. 1. In detail, amount of adding water, extraction water temperature, feed mixing time, squeezing time, centrifuge frequency, squeezing dryness and screw pump frequency are taken as the input layer nodes of the network, and the number of nodes in each layer of the two hidden layers are 40 and 1, respectively. Baume and solid content are the two nodes of the output layer. The activation function is $f(x) = tanh(x)$.

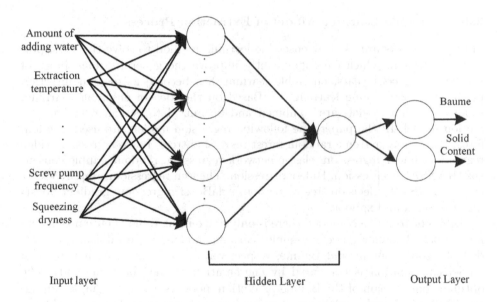

Fig. 1. Artificial neural network of the prediction model of extraction process.

The final prediction model is tested on the test data set, and the of comparisons between the actual data and the ANN model-predicted data are shown in Fig. 2. According to computational analysis, the mean absolute error (MAE) of the solid content and Baume are 0.17 and 0.25, respectively. The mean square error (MSE) is 0.11 and 0.12, respectively. The determination coefficient R^2 is 0.87 and 0.86, respectively.

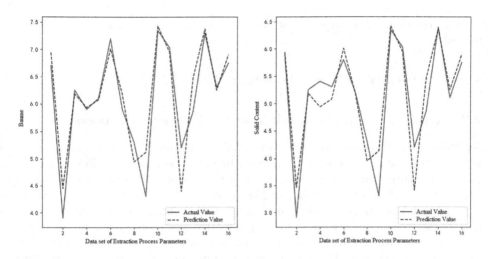

Fig. 2. Comparisons of ANN model-predicted data and actual data.

2.3   Ensemble Learning Model of Extraction Process

Multiple learners are used by ensemble learning method to solve the same prediction problem, which can significantly improve the generalization ability of learners. In recent years, ensemble learning has become a research direction in the field of machine learning [8]. Based on the idea of ensemble learning, some regression models are combined and optimized to get an effective prediction model. In the paper, the following regression models are used: random forest regression, extreme random forest regression trees, Lasso regression, ridge regression, linear regression, elastic network regression, random sample consensus (RANSAC) regression, Huber regression, Theilsen regression, support vector regression (SVR), decision tree regression, AdaBoost regression, gradient boosting regression and xgboot.

Different from ANN model, there is only one output value of ensemble learning model. Therefore, two ensemble learning models are established to predict the solid content and Baume, respectively. The MAE of each regression model combination is compared by enumeration of the above methods. The optimal combination of the Baume prediction model is: random sample consensus (RANSAC) and random forest regression, the mean absolute error (MAE) is about 0.07, the mean square error (MSE) is about 0.012, and the determination coefficient R^2 is about 0.97. The optimal combination of the solid content prediction model includes Thilsen regression, decision tree regression, extreme random forest regression, and gradient boosting regression. The mean absolute error (MAE) is about 0.16, the mean square error (MSE) is about 0.074, and the determination coefficient R^2 is about 0.92. Figure 3 shows the comparisons between the actual data and the ensemble learning model-predicted data.

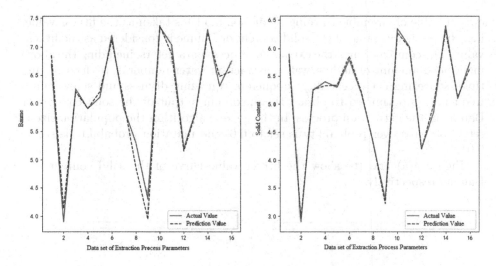

Fig. 3. Comparisons of Ensemble learning model-predicted data and actual data.

2.4 Comparison of Two Prediction Models

ANN model and ensemble learning model have their own advantages. The mean absolute error (MAE), the mean square error (MSE) and the determination coefficient R^2 are used to compare these two models in this paper. For the prediction of the solid content and Baume, the mean absolute error (MAE) and the mean square error (MSE) of the ensemble learning models are lower than those of the ANN model correspondingly, and the determination coefficient R^2 is higher than those of the ANN model correspondingly. Therefore, compared with the ANN prediction model, the ensemble learning prediction models have higher fitting degree and higher prediction accuracy for the solid content and Baume in the extraction process of paper-making reconstituted tobacco.

3 Optimization of Process Parameters

The solid content and Baume are two key indicators of quality level of the extraction process. The higher the solid content or Baume, the higher the quality of the extraction process. Because the solid content and Baume are two indicators to represent solution concentration by different test methods, we take the Baume and solid content as the optimization objective of extraction process, respectively. The optimization of extraction process is to investigate the combination of the extraction process parameters for the goal of maximizing the solid content or Baume. This is a classic combination optimization problem. In the paper, genetic algorithm is used to solve the optimal problem.

Genetic algorithm is an adaptive global optimization algorithm that imitates the genetic and evolutionary process of organisms in the natural environment [9]. In this paper, the initial population is generated by random function, the output value of ensemble learning prediction model is taken as the fitness value, i.e., the predicted value of the solid content or Baume is considered as the fitness value. The combination of the extraction process parameters, including the above mentioned amount of adding water, extraction water temperature, feed mixing time, squeezing time, centrifuge frequency, squeezing dryness and screw pump frequency, is optimized to obtain the maximum output of the solid content or Baume in the extraction process. In the genetic algorithm the population size is set to 50, crossover probability is set to 0.6, and mutation probability is set to 0.01.

Figure 4(a) and (b) show the fitness value curve of the solid content and Baume, respectively.

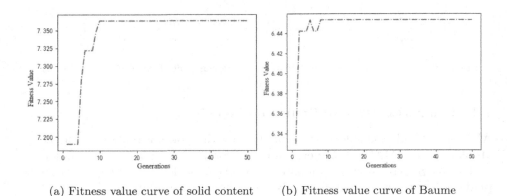

(a) Fitness value curve of solid content   (b) Fitness value curve of Baume

Fig. 4. Fitness value curve of genetic algorithm based on ensemble learning prediction model.

By observing the fitness value curve of the solid content of extraction solution in Fig. 4(a), the maximum prediction value of solid content after 10 generations is about 7.36% by taking ensemble learning prediction value as fitness. The corresponding process parameters are listed as follows: the amount of adding water of 6104 ml, the extraction water temperature of about 97.8 °C, the feed mixing time of 53 min, the squeezing time of 84 min, the centrifuge frequency of 37.2 Hz, the screw pump frequency of 31.7 Hz, and the squeezing dryness of 26.68%. Under these conditions, the Baume value of the extraction solution is about 6.09 °Be.

By observing the fitness value curve of solid content of extraction solution in Fig. 4(b), the maximum prediction value of the Baume after 10 generations is about 6.45 °Be by taking the ensemble learning prediction value as fitness. The corresponding process parameters are listed as follows: the amount of adding water of 6311 ml, the extraction water temperature of 74.38 °C, the feed mixing time of about 55.9 min, the squeezing time of 102.9 min, the centrifuge frequency of 39.5 Hz, the screw pump frequency of 32.15 Hz, and the squeezing dryness of

35.37%. Under these conditions, the solid content value of the extraction solution is about 6.88%.

Based on the porposed prediction and optimization models of the extraction process, an intelligent control module is developed and embed in production control system. This control module can work in online and offline mode, and the prediction data of the solid content and Baume and the optimized process parameters are used to adjust the process control parameters. Experiment results show that the proposed prediction models and optimization model are helpful to improve the quality of extraction solution.

4 Conclusion

Aiming to the problem of prediction and optimization of extraction process parameters for paper-making reconstituted tobacco, ANN prediction model and ensemble learning prediction models are proposed in the paper. It is found that the prediction accuracy of the ensemble learning prediction model is better than those of ANN model. On the basis of the ensemble learning prediction models, genetic algorithm is used to optimize the extraction process parameters, i.e., the optimal combination of extraction process parameters, including amount of adding water, extraction water temperature, feed mixing time, squeezing time, centrifuge frequency, squeezing dryness and screw pump frequency. The experimental results show that the proposed prediction and optimization model are useful to improve the product quality of extraction process.

References

1. Sannino, M., del Piano, L., Abet, M. et al.: Effect of mechanical extraction parameters on the yield and quality of tobacco (Nicotiana tabacum L.) seed oil. J. Food Sci. Technol. **54**, 4009–4015 (2019)
2. Jiang, Y.: Study on optimization of technology for extracting alkaloids from lotus leaf. J. Zhejiang Univ. (Agric. Life Sci.) **30**(5), 519–523 (2004)
3. Hosu, A., Cristea, V.M., Cimpoiu, C.: Analysis of total phenolic, flavonoids, anthocyanins and tannins content in Romanian red wines: prediction of antioxidant activities and classification of wines using artificial neural networks. Food Chem. **150**(4), 113–118 (2014)
4. Jiang, S., Shao, P., Zhao, Y.: Study on microwave-assisted extraction of vitamin E from wheat germ and neural network model. Food Chem. **26**(2), 25–28 (2005)
5. Zheng, X., Xu, X., Liu, C., et al.: Extraction characteristics and optimal parameters of anthocyanin from blueberry powder under microwave-assisted extraction conditions. Sep. Purif. Technol. **104**, 17–25 (2013)
6. Tao, Y., Wang, P., Wang, J., et al.: Combining various wall materials for encapsulation of blueberry anthocyanin extracts: optimization by artificial neural network and genetic algorithm and a comprehensive analysis of anthocyanin powder properties. Powder Technol. **311**, 77–78 (2017)
7. Chen, B., Lv, G., Jin, W., et al.: Study on multi-index comprehensive optimization of tea extraction process based on orthogonal design and BP neural network genetic algorithm. Chin. J. Mod. Appl. Pharm. **36**(10), 1223–1228 (2019)

8. João, M., Carlos, S., Alípio, M., et al.: Ensemble approaches for regression. ACM Comput. Surv. **45**(1), 1–40 (2012)
9. Goldberg, D.E.: Genetic algorithms as a computational theory of conceptual design. In: Rzevski, G., Adey, R.A. (eds.) Appl. Artif. Intell. Eng. VI. Springer, Dordrecht (1991)

Point Cloud Registration Using Evolutionary Algorithm

Gewei Zhang, Zihong Gao, Junbo Huo, and Liangjun Ke[✉]

State Key Laboratory for Manufacturing Systems Engineering, School of Automation
Science and Engineering, Xi'an Jiaotong University, Xi'an 710049, Shaanxi, China
keljxjtu@xjtu.edu.cn

Abstract. Point cloud registration is a hot research topic in computer
vision and related areas. In this paper, inspired by Iterative Closest Point
(ICP), two evolutionary algorithms, that is, Genetic Algorithm (GA) and
Estimation of Distribution Algorithm (EDA), are designed to deal with
the problem of registration. Our study shows that evolutionary algorithm
is potential to be applied to this problem, it can obtain better results
than ICP on the tested real-world datum. Moreover, EDA can provide
better results than GA.

Keywords: Point cloud registration · Evolutionary algorithm ·
Genetic algorithm · Estimation of distribution algorithm

1 Introduction

Point cloud registration is a classical problem in computer vision. In three dimensional space, the information of an object or a scene can usually be collected using radar [15] or vision sensor [18] and the collected data will be stored in the computer in the form of point cloud. Limited by the position and angle of acquisition, point cloud data is often required to acquire from multiple observation points so as to complete the 3D information modeling of the object or the scene. The process of combining these point cloud data is called point cloud registration. For two point clouds, the registration transformation can be represented by a rotation matrix and a translation vector. Point cloud registration is widely used in many areas, such as human organ modeling [8,14], structure from motion [6,20], reverse engineering [16,25]. In practice, the scale and shape of the two point clouds may be different, it is almost impossible to align them completely. Moreover, real-world data is often contaminated by measurement errors, which makes point cloud registration very difficult [6].

More formally, we can describe this problem in the following way. Let $S = \{s_i \in \mathbb{R}^3 | i = 1 : N_s\}$ and $D = \{d_j \in \mathbb{R}^3 | j = 1 : N_D\}$ be two sets of 3D point clouds in different coordinate systems, where S and D are called source and destination respectively. The goal of point cloud registration is to find an

Supported by the National Natural Science Foundation of China (No. 61973244,
61573277).

optimal solution $(\mathbf{R}^*, \mathbf{t}^*)$ where $\mathbf{R}^* \in SO(3)$ and $\mathbf{t}^* \in \mathbb{R}^3$. Then the problem of point cloud registration is to find an optimal (R, t) such that the following value is maximized:

$$\sum_{i=1}^{N_s} r(||\mathbf{R}s_i + \mathbf{t} - d_i||) \tag{1}$$

where the notation $||\cdot||$ is the ℓ_2 norm, d_i is a point in set D which is the nearest point to the transformed point $\mathbf{R}s_i + \mathbf{t}$, that is,

$$d_i = \arg\min_{d_j \in D} ||\mathbf{R}s_i + \mathbf{t} - d_j|| \tag{2}$$

and $r(\cdot)$ is a judge function to determine whether two points are registered, which is defined as:

$$r(x) = \begin{cases} 1 & if \ x < \epsilon \\ 0 & otherwise \end{cases} \tag{3}$$

where ϵ is a sufficiently small positive number which is adjustable for different practical problems. In this way, the problem of point cloud registration is formulated into an optimization problem.

Point cloud registration can be regarded as two subproblems. The one is to establish the correspondence of the coincidence parts of S and D, and the other is to estimate $(\mathbf{R}, \mathbf{t})$ by the correspondence [9]. Inspired by 2D image mosaic, there are many methods to extract feature points of point cloud for matching to establish the correspondence. However, the method of using feature points is limited to dense point clouds, and requires a large overlap between source point cloud and target point cloud. Moreover, in extreme cases, the effect is weaker than using the original data directly. Iterative closest point (ICP) [1] is the most famous algorithm for point cloud registration. Because the effect of ICP depends on the initial solution, it is usually used after the rough matching has been achieved [2,7]. The idea is to find the nearest point of each point in the current point cloud iteratively to establish a correspondence, and then use the correspondence to estimate the transformation. So far, there are many strategies of improvement for ICP. It includes selecting a part of the original point cloud to participate in the operation [19], accelerating the corresponding point search [11,13,24], weighting the corresponding point pairs [3,5], and removing the wrong point pairs [10,17].

It is known that random sampling is an important method to improve ICP [12]. One can randomly sample two population of points P and Q from the source and target point clouds respectively. Due to randomness, the best individual in P and Q may be unsatisfactory. A possible way is to iteratively update the population. This motivates us to consider evolutionary algorithm.

Evolutionary algorithm has been recognized as an important method to deal with hard optimization problems [21]. It evolves a colony of individuals. At each iteration, it learns and guides the search to the promising region. At present, there are many different evolutionary algorithms in the literature. Among them genetic algorithm (GA) [4] and estimation of distribution algorithm (EDA) [21] are two famous representatives. The goal of this paper is to study the effectiveness of these two evolutionary algorithms on point cloud registration. Note that some EA-based point cloud registration have been proposed, which encodes the point cloud registration problem and searches directly in the space of rotation and translate transformations [22,23].

The rest of the paper is organized as follows. Section 2 presents the basic idea of ICP. Section 3 presents the details of our proposed algorithms, the conclusion is drawn in Sect. 5.

2 Background

ICP requires that the two point clouds to be registered have a good initial alignment, that is to say, the two point clouds should be roughly aligned. Its basic idea is to select the nearest point in the two point clouds as the corresponding points and update correspondence. In turn, the alignment is updated by using the new correspondence. The alignment error between the two point clouds is smaller and smaller until the point cloud is sufficiently meet a pre-set threshold requirement or time limit.

Given the source and target point clouds S and D, the algorithm mainly consists of the two alternative steps [24]:

– Correspondence step: let the current rotation and translation transformation are $\mathbf{R}$ and $\mathbf{t}$, for each point $p \in S$, find its closest point $q \in D$:

$$q = \underset{q' \in D}{\arg\min} \|\mathbf{R}p + \mathbf{t} - q'\| \tag{4}$$

– Alignment step: update the transformation $\mathbf{R}$ and $\mathbf{t}$ so as to minimize the distance between the corresponding points:

$$(\mathbf{R}, \mathbf{t}) = ICP(S, D) \tag{5}$$

where $ICP(S, D)$ is the function to determine the transformations using the current correspondence. More details on ICP can be found in [24].

3 The Proposed EAs

In this section, we first present how to compute the fitness of an individual, then describe the details of GA and EDA.

In our algorithms, we first initialize two populations P and Q randomly sampled from the source and target point clouds respectively. Let the population size be M. In population P and Q, each individual consist of n points and can be represented as follows:

$$P_a = \{P_{ai} \in S | i = 1 : n\}, a = 1 : M \tag{6}$$

$$Q_b = \{Q_{bj} \in S | j = 1 : n\}, b = 1 : M \tag{7}$$

We hope to get a pair of sampling sets $(\widetilde{P}, \widetilde{Q})$ which are as coincident as possible, so that the $(\mathbf{R}, \mathbf{t})$ obtained by formula 5 can maximize the value of formula 1. Accordingly, each individual is associated with a fitness value as follows: for each individual $P_a \in P$, put P_a and Q_1 into formula 5 to determine the transformation $(\mathbf{R}, \mathbf{t})$ then put it into formula 1 to obtain a value Ω_a. The fitness value of P_a is then set to Ω_a. After that, the M individuals in P are sorted according to their fitness values in descending order. Similarly, for each individual $Q_b \in Q$, put Q_b and P_1 into formula 5 to determine the transformation $(\mathbf{R}, \mathbf{t})$ then put it into formula 1 to obtain a value Ω_b. The fitness value of Q_b is set to Ω_b. After that, the M individuals in Q are sorted according to their fitness values in descending order. In this way, P_1 and Q_1 are regarded as the best in P and Q respectively.

Because each individual is initialized by random sampling from the original point cloud, it is almost impossible to make P_1 and Q_1 achieve shape similarity. An alternative way is to get better individuals through population evolution, and expand the search space from the initial population. In the following, we will present a GA-based algorithm and an EDA-based algorithm for this purpose. It should be highlighted that the same algorithm is performed on P and Q. For simplicity, we only present the details on P (or the source point cloud).

3.1   The GA-Based Algorithm

In this algorithm, GA runs at the point level, rather than directly carrying out on the solution space of transformation. The main procedure of GA is:

- step 0: initialize the population.
- step 1: generate offsprings by the crossover and mutation operators.
- step 2: update the population.
- step 3: if the stopping condition is satisfied, then output the best individual, otherwise return to step 1.

Note that each individual is a subset of points which are randomly selected from the point cloud at step 0.

The crossover operator and mutation operator are described as follows.

It is expected that the new generation of population can preserve the excellent results of the previous generation as much as possible. Therefore, in the crossover operator, the roulette selection method is used to choose two individuals. Formally, the probability of individual P_a to be selected is:

$$\frac{\Omega_a}{\sum_{i=1}^{M} \Omega_i} \tag{8}$$

where Ω_i is the fitness value of individual P_i. The crossover operator works on two selected individuals P_{i_1} and P_{i_2} in the following way: from $\{1, \cdots, n\}$, two numbers, say k and l, are selected. Then the offspring is obtained by exchange parts of the points:

$$C_1 = \{P_{i_1 1}, \cdots, P_{i_1 k-1}, \underbrace{P_{i_2 k}, \cdots, P_{i_2 l-1}}, P_{i_1 l}, \cdots, P_{i_1 n}\} \tag{9}$$

$$C_2 = \{P_{i_2 1}, \cdots, P_{i_2 k-1}, \underbrace{P_{i_1 k}, \cdots, P_{i_1 l-1}}, P_{i_2 l}, \cdots, P_{i_2 n}\} \tag{10}$$

Given individual P_a, the mutation operator works as follows: randomly select point from P_a and replace it by a point randomly chosen from $S \setminus P_a$.

In the GA-based algorithm, the steady population update rule is applied: once an offspring is obtained after mutation, the fitness value is evaluated and then the worst individual in the population is replaced by the offspring. The algorithm stops when a pre-specified iteration number is achieved.

3.2 The EDA-Based Algorithm

EDA is a very simple evolutionary algorithm [21]. The basic idea of EDA is to construct a probability model by using a set of selected individuals and sample the probability model to obtain the new population of offsprings. The main procedure of EDA is:

- step 0: initialize the population.
- step 1: generate offsprings by the probability model.
- step 2: update the probability model.
- step 3: if the stopping condition is satisfied, then output the best individual, otherwise return to step 1.

Step 0 and 3 is the same as the one of GA. In our EDA, the probability model is formulated as follows: each point k is associated with a desired degree δ_k, and its probability to be selected is

$$\frac{\delta_k}{\sum_{l \in S} \delta_l} \tag{11}$$

If point k does not belong to any selected individuals, then its desired degree is updated as follows:

$$\delta_k = \alpha \delta_k \tag{12}$$

where $\alpha \in [0, 1]$ is a parameter. Suppose that point k belongs to at least one selected individuals. Let Λ be the set of selected individuals which contain point k. The desired degree of point k is updated as follows:

$$\delta_k = \alpha \delta_k + \Omega \tag{13}$$

where Ω is the fitness value of the best individual in Λ.

4 Experimental Study

To verify the proposed algorithms, we compare them with ICP on two datum which are acquired by using Intel realsense d435i. According to the preliminary test, the parameters of these algorithms are set as follows: $\epsilon = 0.5$, $M = 50$, $n = 200$. EDA and GA are stopped when the maximum number of iterations achieves 200. In EDA, the desired degree of each point is initialized to 1 and $\alpha = 0.9$.

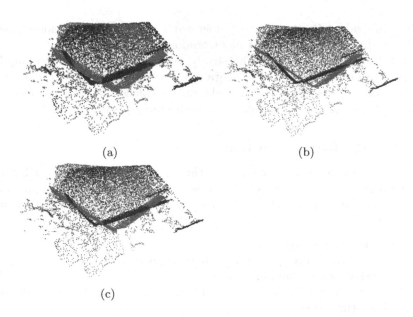

(a)   (b)

(c)

Fig. 1. The results obtained on the first data. The red one is the transformed source point cloud S, and the blue one is the target point cloud D. This scene is composed of two screens on a desk. (a) ICP, (b) GA, (c) EDA. (Color figure online)

Figures 1 and 2 show the results obtained on the first and second data respectively. One can notice that EDA works the best. It almost can make the source and target point cloud overlap. GA performs better than ICP. As seen form Table 1, with respect to the number of matched points, EDA achieves the highest scores for both datum, while GA can obtain better scores than ICP.

Table 1. Comparison among ICP, GA, and EDA in terms of the number of matched points.

Data	ICP	GA	EDA
Data1	7570	7735	7790
Data2	5123	6110	6840

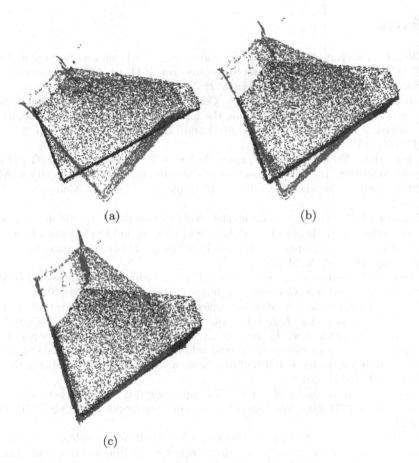

(a)   (b)

(c)

Fig. 2. The results obtained on the second data. The red one is the transformed source point cloud S, and the blue one is the target point cloud D. This scene is a corner under a desk. (a) ICP, (b) GA, (c) EDA. (Color figure online)

5 Conclusion

This paper considers the problem of point cloud registration. Iterative closest point (ICP) is a classical algorithm for this problem. So far, a great number of variants have been proposed to make the original ICP more powerful. In this paper, we adopt some basic ideas of ICP and the characteristics of EA to propose two algorithms. The one is GA-based and the other is EDA-based. According to the results obtained from two real-world datum, our proposed EAs can find better results than ICP. Moreover, EDA seems to be more encouraging.

However, we notice that our algorithms is slow, making it only applicable to offline registration. One main reason is that computing the fitness of an individual is time-consuming. It is interesting to study how to make our algorithm fast. Moreover, our algorithms can be further improved by taking account of more knowledge learnt during the process.

References

1. Besl, P.J., McKay, N.D.: Method for registration of 3-D shapes. In: Sensor Fusion IV: Control Paradigms and Data Structures, vol. 1611, pp. 586–606. International Society for Optics and Photonics (1992)
2. Burlacu, A., Cohal, A., Caraiman, S., Condurache, D.: Iterative closest point problem: a tensorial approach to finding the initial guess. In: 2016 20th International Conference on System Theory, Control and Computing (ICSTCC), pp. 508–513. IEEE (2016)
3. Chetverikov, D., Svirko, D., Stepanov, D., Krsek, P.: The trimmed iterative closest point algorithm. In: 16th International Conference on Pattern Recognition, ICPR 2002, Quebec, Canada, 11–15 August 2002, pp. 545–548. IEEE Computer Society (2002)
4. Chicotay, S., David, E.O., Netanyahu, N.S.: A two-phase genetic algorithm for image registration. In: Bosman, P.A.N. (ed.) Genetic and Evolutionary Computation Conference, Companion Material Proceedings, Berlin, Germany, 15–19 July 2017, pp. 189–190. ACM (2017)
5. Combès, B., Prima, S.: An efficient EM-ICP algorithm for non-linear registration of large 3D point sets. Comput. Vis. Image Underst. **191**, 102854 (2020)
6. Cook, K.L.: An evaluation of the effectiveness of low-cost UAVs and structure from motion for geomorphic change detection. Geomorphology **278**, 195–208 (2017)
7. Haddad, O., Leboucher, J., Troccaz, J., Stindel, E.: Initialized iterative closest point for bone recognition in ultrasound volumes. In: 23rd International Conference on Pattern Recognition, ICPR 2016, Cancún, Mexico, 4–8 December 2016, pp. 2801–2806. IEEE (2016)
8. Huang, S., Wu, K., Meng, X., Li, C.: Non-rigid registration method between 3D CT liver data and 2D ultrasonic images based on demons model. CoRR abs/2001.00035 (2020)
9. Le, H.M., Do, T.T., Hoang, T., Cheung, N.M.: SDRSAC: semidefinite-based randomized approach for robust point cloud registration without correspondences. In: Proceedings of the IEEE Conference on Computer Vision and Pattern Recognition, pp. 124–133 (2019)
10. Liang, L.: Precise iterative closest point algorithm for RGB-D data registration with noise and outliers. Neurocomputing **399**, 361–368 (2020)
11. Maken, F.A., Ramos, F., Ott, L.: Speeding up iterative closest point using stochastic gradient descent. In: 2019 International Conference on Robotics and Automation (ICRA), pp. 6395–6401. IEEE (2019)
12. Neto, P.S.S., Pereira, N.S., Thé, G.A.P.: Improved cloud partitioning sampling for iterative closest point: qualitative and quantitative comparison study. In: Madani, K., Gusikhin, O. (eds.) Proceedings of the 15th International Conference on Informatics in Control, Automation and Robotics, ICINCO 2018 - Volume 2, Porto, Portugal, 29–31 July 2018, pp. 59–70. SciTePress (2018)
13. Pavlov, A.L., Ovchinnikov, G.W., Derbyshev, D.Y., Tsetserukou, D., Oseledets, I.V.: AA-ICP: iterative closest point with Anderson acceleration. In: 2018 IEEE International Conference on Robotics and Automation (ICRA), pp. 1–6. IEEE (2018)
14. Plantefève, R., Peterlik, I., Haouchine, N., Cotin, S.: Patient-specific biomechanical modeling for guidance during minimally-invasive hepatic surgery. Ann. Biomed. Eng. **44**(1), 139–153 (2016)

15. Schumann, O., Hahn, M., Dickmann, J., Wöhler, C.: Semantic segmentation on radar point clouds. In: 2018 21st International Conference on Information Fusion (FUSION), pp. 2179–2186. IEEE (2018)
16. Shah, G.A., Giannini, F., Monti, M., Polette, A., Pernot, J.: Towards the fitting of parametric 2D sketches and 3D CAD models to point clouds of digitized assemblies for reverse engineering. In: Fusiello, A., Bimber, O. (eds.) 40th Annual Conference of the European Association for Computer Graphics, Eurographics 2019 - Posters, Genoa, Italy, 6–10 May 2019, pp. 11–12. Eurographics Association (2019)
17. Sorkine-Hornung, O., Rabinovich, M.: Least-squares rigid motion using SVD. Computing $1(1)$, 1–5 (2017)
18. Takimoto, R.Y., et al.: Shape reconstruction from multiple RGB-D point cloud registration. In: 2014 12th IEEE International Conference on Industrial Informatics (INDIN), pp. 349–352. IEEE (2014)
19. Tazir, M.L., Gokhool, T., Checchin, P., Malaterre, L., Trassoudaine, L.: CICP: cluster iterative closest point for sparse–dense point cloud registration. Robot. Auton. Syst. **108**, 66–86 (2018)
20. Truong, T.P., Yamaguchi, M., Mori, S., Nozick, V., Saito, H.: Registration of RGB and thermal point clouds generated by structure from motion. In: 2017 IEEE International Conference on Computer Vision Workshops, ICCV Workshops 2017, Venice, Italy, 22–29 October 2017, pp. 419–427. IEEE Computer Society (2017)
21. Wang, F., Li, Y., Zhou, A., Tang, K.: An estimation of distribution algorithm for mixed-variable newsvendor problems. IEEE Trans. Evol. Comput. **24**(3), 479–493 (2020)
22. Yan, L., Tan, J., Liu, H., Xie, H., Chen, C.: Automatic registration of TLS-TLS and TLS-MLS point clouds using a genetic algorithm. Sensors **17**(9), 1979 (2017)
23. Zhan, X., Cai, Y., Li, H., Li, Y., He, P.: A point cloud registration algorithm based on normal vector and particle swarm optimization. Meas. Control **53**(3–4), 265–275 (2020)
24. Zhang, J., Yao, Y., Deng, B.: Fast and robust iterative closet point (2020)
25. Zhao, X., Zhang, C., Xu, L., Yang, B., Feng, Z.: IGA-based point cloud fitting using B-spline surfaces for reverse engineering. Inf. Sci. **245**, 276–289 (2013)

Heterogeneous Distributed Flow Shop Scheduling and Reentrant Hybrid Flow Shop Scheduling in Seamless Steel Tube Manufacturing

Xiuli Wu[✉] and Zirun Xie[✉]

College of Mechanical Engineering, University of Science and Technology Beijing, Beijing, China
wuxiuli@ustb.edu.cn

Abstract. In the actual manufacturing process of seamless steel tubes, the scheduling of ordinary production workshops and cold drawing workshops is a problem with NP-hard characteristics. Aiming at ordinary production workshops and cold drawing workshops, distributed flow shop scheduling models and reentrant scheduling models are established. The two are heterogeneously distributed in space and have a sequential relationship in time. For the distributed flow shop scheduling, the fruit fly optimization method is used to solve the problem, and the NEH (Nawaz, Enscore, &Ham) heuristic is used to improve the quality of the initial solution in the initialization phase, and the load distribution in the factory is considered. Simulated annealing algorithm is used to optimize reentrant scheduling, which is of great significance to the actual production of seamless steel tubes.

Keywords: Distributed flow shop · Reentrant scheduling · Heterogeneous · Seamless steel tube

1 Introduction

The development of the manufacturing industry and the deepening of economic globalization have promoted the transformation and upgrading of the steel industry. The fierce competition makes the traditional single-factory production mode of the steel industry no longer meet the needs of enterprises to increase output and enhance their own competitiveness. Seeking a more reasonable and effective scheduling method is currently the key to improving the level of production management, saving costs, and improving the competitiveness of enterprises. Simultaneously, enterprises need to transform from single-factory production to multi-factory collaborative production.

Among a wide variety of steel products, seamless steel tube is a type of products with a wide range of applications. Its main applications include the

Supported by the Beijing Municipal Natural Science Foundation under Grant L191011.

L. Pan et al. (Eds.): BIC-TA 2020, CCIS 1363, pp. 78–89, 2021.
https://doi.org/10.1007/978-981-16-1354-8_8

manufacture of structural and mechanical parts, such as oil drill pipes, automobile drive shafts, bicycle racks, and steel scaffolds. Therefore, the production of seamless steel pipes is becoming more and more important. At the same time, it is also facing many pressures such as delivery time and increasing production capacity. As a bottleneck process in the seamless steel pipe production process, the cold drawing section has many reentrant processes. Long process time and other characteristics that affect production efficiency, so it is of great significance to make scheduling optimization for the production of seamless steel tubes. Subsequent paragraphs, however, are indented.

In recent years, scholars have made sufficient research on the distributed scheduling problem. For the distributed permutation flow shop, Meng et al. [1] have studied the distributed permutation flow shop scheduling problem with customer order constraints, and its optimization goal is Minimizing the makespan, the article optimizes the allocation and processing sequence of orders. Fu et al. [2] used a random multi-objective brain storm optimization algorithm to solve the distributed permutation flow shop scheduling problem. Experimental results demonstrate that the algorithm is very competitive. Bargaoui et al. [3] used the chemical reaction algorithm to solve the distributed permutation flow shop scheduling problem, and the NEH2 method was used for initialization. Inspired by the genetic algorithm, the author designed a single-point crossover operation. The ineffective collision between molecules uses a greedy strategy to make the algorithm converge quickly.

Considering the buffer capacity constraints of the flow shop, Shao et al. [4] proposed a hybrid enhanced discrete fruit fly optimization algorithm for the blocked flow shop in a distributed environment. In order to make the exploration more efficient, insertion-based improvement procedure are used, and local search is enhanced. Zhang et al. [5] first studied the scheduling problem of distributed limited-buffer flow shop scheduling problem (DLBFSP), and combined the DPFSP and PFSP-LB problems to fill the gaps in the research. The author proposed a local search method based on critical factories to further improve the performance of the algorithm.

For distributed hybrid flow shop scheduling problem, Li et al. [6] proposed an improved discrete artificial bee colony (DABC) algorithm. Two neighborhood search methods based on swap and insertion neighborhood structures are proposed, aiming to minimize the makespan. Ying et al. [7] proposed a self-tuning iterated greedy algorithm that incorporates an adaptive cocktail decoding mechanism to dynamically adjust the probability of selecting coding rules (LS, PS, FF). Numerical experiments show that SIG performs better than other algorithms.

Chen et al. [8] addressed the energy-efficient distributed no-idle permutation flow shop scheduling problem, and simultaneously considered two objectives including minimizing makespan and total energy consumption. Proposed a collaborative optimization algorithm (COA) for this problem.

For the heterogeneous distributed scheduling problem, Zhang et al. [9] considered production and assembly, and proposed a novel memetic algorithm (MA) based on the recently developed social spider optimization (SSO). In the proposed MSSO algorithm, the SSO was modified to adapt to the distributed problem, and then local search and adaptive strategy were adopted in the MA framework.

For the reentrant scheduling problem, Lin et al. [10] considered the situation of limited buffer capacity. Due to the limited buffer capacity, the author considered a storage area to temporarily store WIP. The optimization goal is to minimize Maximum processing time and minimized mean flow time. The author designed an algorithm (HHSGA) that combines the harmony search algorithm and the genetic algorithm for optimization. Rifai et al. [11] handled reentrant replacement flow shop scheduling problem by using the multiobjective adaptive large neighborhood search algorithm. For non-single production lines, there are two sub-problems of determining the number of factories to be used and allocating jobs to the factories. Cho et al. [12] proposed a Pareto genetic algorithm for reentrant hybrid flow shop scheduling problem with the optimization goal of minimizing makespan and total tardiness. They compared the proposed algorithm with NSGA2 in three ways, including the convergence, the diversity of solutions and the dominance of solutions. The results proved that the algorithm is feasible.

In summary, domestic and foreign scholars' research on distributed scheduling problem mainly focuses on homogeneous factories, that is, several factories have the same structure and processing characteristics. Research on heterogeneous factories focuses on production and assembly issues, Heterogeneous distributed scheduling problem is worthy of further study. For reentrant scheduling, existing studies are mostly related to the TFT-LCD and semiconductor industries. Therefore, scheduling optimization of seamless steel pipe production in the steel industry can enrich this research field.

In this paper, the heat treatment section and the cold drawing section of the seamless steel pipe production process are studied, and they are summarized as a distributed flow shop scheduling problem (DFSP) and a reentrant hybrid flow shop scheduling problem (RHFSP). The fruit fly optimization algorithm and simulated annealing algorithm are used for optimization. The optimization goal is to minimize the makespan.

The content of this article is set as follows. In Sect. 1, we formulate the problem under study. In Sect. 2, we detailed the fruit fly optimization algorithm and simulated annealing algorithm. The numerical experiments are arranged in Sect. 3. Finally, Sect. 4 concludes the paper and summarizes the future study.

2   Problem Description

The production of seamless steel pipes can be summarized as heat treatment section, cold drawing section and finishing section. The cold drawing section has the characteristics of multiple cycles, limited by deformation conditions and metal strength, small diameter reduction per pass, many intermediate procedures, and many corresponding equipment requirements. There are many cold-drawn production processes of seamless steel pipes.

2.1 Description of RHFSP

The cold drawing process is currently the bottleneck process in the production of seamless steel pipes, which has the characteristics of long processing time and multiple reentrant passes. In view of the characteristics of the problem, it can be simplified into a reentrant hybrid flow shop model. It can be described as having n jobs to be processed, and each process has M_j parallel machines. This scheduling problem has two sub-problems: (1) select a parallel machine for the jobs, (2) determine the processing order of the jobs. An example of RHFSP is shown in the Fig. 1.

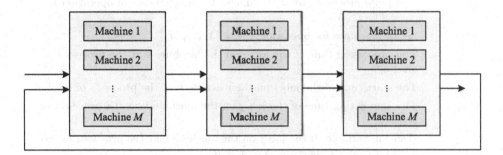

Fig. 1. An example of RHFSP

2.2 Formulation of RHFSP

The indices and notations used about RHFSP are expressed as follows.

Besides the classical assumption, a series of additional properties are adopted to conform the reentrant characteristics.

- All jobs and machines are available at the beginning.
- Each operation of each job can be processed on any parallel machine.
- Each operation of each job can be processed on any parallel machine.
- The transportation time and setup time are not considered.
- The operations of each job follow the sequential constraints.
- The jobs are independent of each other, and there is no sequential restriction between the processes of different jobs.
- Each operation of the job can only be processed by one machine at the same time, and it is not allowed to preempt.
- Each machine can only handle one job at a time.
- Regardless of machine failure and maintenance, and the buffer capacity is unlimited (Table 1).

MILP model is given as follows:

$$\min C_{\max} = \min \left(\max \left(S_{jig_jk} \right) \right) \tag{1}$$

Table 1. Indices and notations

Notations	Descriptions
J	Set of jobs, $J = \{1, \ldots, j, \ldots, n\}$
p	The total number of operations per level, $i = \{1, \ldots, p\}$
l_j	The number of levels for job j
M_i	Set of machines for operation i, $k = \{1, \ldots, M_i\}$
g_i	The current reentrant level of job j, $g_i = \{1, 2, \ldots, l_j\}$
N_{ik}	The total number of jobs processed by k machines in the machine set of operation i
q_{ik}	The job q processed by k machine in the machine set of operation i, $q_{ik} = \{1, \ldots, N_{ik}\}$
M_i	Set of machines for operation i, $k = \{1, \ldots, M_i\}$
T_{jig_jk}	The processing time of the job j on the machine k at the process i of level g_i
S_{jig_jk}	The start time of the job j on the machine k at the process i of level g_i
C_{jig_jk}	The completing time of the job j on the machine k at the process i of level g_i
X_{jig_jk}	Decision variable. If the job j on the machine k at the process i of level g_i, $X_{jig_jk} = 1$. Otherwise, $X_{jig_jk} = 0$

$$\sum_{k=1}^{M_i} X_{jig_jk} = 1 \quad \forall j, \forall g_j, k \in M_i \tag{2}$$

$$\sum_{k=1}^{M_i} N_{ik} = \sum_{j=1}^{n} l_j \quad \forall i, k \in M_i \tag{3}$$

$$S_{j(i+1)g_jk_2} \geq C_{jig_jk_1} \quad \forall j, \forall g_j, i = 1, 2, \ldots, p-1, k_1 \in M_i, k_2 \in M_{i+1} \tag{4}$$

$$S_{ji(g_j+1)k_1} \geq C_{ji_1g_jk_1} \quad \forall j, \forall i, i_1 = n, g_j = 1, 2, \ldots, l_j - 1, k \in M_i, k_2 \in M_{i_1} \tag{5}$$

$$S_{(q+1)_{ik}ig_jk} \geq C_{q_{ik}ig_jk} \quad \forall j, \forall g_j, k \in M_i, q_{ik} = 1, 2, \ldots, N_{ik} - 1 \tag{6}$$

$$S_{jig_jk} + T_{jig_jk} = C_{jig_jk} \quad \forall j, \forall i, \forall g_j, k \in M_i \tag{7}$$

$$X_{jig_jk} \in \{0, 1\} \quad \forall j, \forall i, \forall g_j, k \in M_i \tag{8}$$

$$S_{jig_jk} \geq 0, \quad \forall j, \forall i, \forall g_j, k \in M_i \tag{9}$$

$$T_{jig_jk} \geq 0, \quad \forall j, \forall i, \forall g_j, k \in M_i \tag{10}$$

The objective function (1) is used to minimize the maximum completion time (makespan). Constraint (2) expresses that each job is assigned to only one parallel machine. Constraint (3) represents the total number of jobs that can be processed by all available machines allocated to any process, which is equal to the total number of times all jobs enter the production system. Constraint (4) indicates that each job must complete the previous operation before the next operation can be processed. Constraint (5) means that each job must complete all the operations of the previous level before the processing of the next level can be started. Constraint (6) is machine restriction, which guarantee a job can be started after the preceding job completed when the two jobs are processed on the same machine. Constraints (7) means that the completion time of any job depends on the start time and processing time of its operation on a certain machine. Constraints (8) is decision variable. Constraint (9) and (10) are the time constraints, which assure the starting time and processing time of a job are greater than (or equal to) 0.

3   Algorithms for DFSP and RHFSP

3.1   The Discrete Fruit Fly Optimization Algorithm for DFSP

The discrete fruit fly optimization algorithm [13] is a simulation of the foraging process of fruit fly. Fruit fly relies on the smell system to perceive things during the foraging process. The process of searching for food is the process of moving from a location with low food concentration to a location with high food concentration. Fruit fly corresponds to the solution of the problem, and the fitness corresponds to the food concentration. The optimization process of the algorithm is that the fruit flies continuously search for food to reach the target position. The algorithm mainly includes three stages: initialization, smell-based foraging, and vision-based foraging.

Solution Encoding and Decoding. We adopted the job-based encoding method. The solution matrix has f rows, each row represents the processing sequence of a factory, and the number represents the job assigned to the factory. For example, the meaning of the encoding $\begin{pmatrix} 4\ 3\ 2\ 5 \\ 6\ 1\ 7 \end{pmatrix}$ is as follows. There are two factories: factory 1 and factory 2, and there are 7 jobs to be processed, among which, job 4, job 3, job 2, and job 5 are allocated to factory 1, and the processing sequence is $4 \rightarrow 3 \rightarrow 2 \rightarrow 5$. Job 6, job 1, and job 7 are allocated to factory 2, and the processing sequence is $6 \rightarrow 1 \rightarrow 7$.

Initialization. Constructive heuristics provide high-quality initial solutions. The job sequence assigned to each factory is improved by an insertion procedure of the NEH heuristic [14].

- Sort the n jobs by decreasing total processing time, and the first f jobs are assigned to the f factories.
- When the remaining jobs are assigned to the factory, the makespan value of the partial solution is calculated, and the job is allocated to the position with the minimum makespan.
- The load of the factory is considered to meet the condition that the current factory load is close to the average load.

Algorithm 1. Initialization

1: Sort the n jobs by decreasing total processing time as sequence α.
2: Assign the first f jobs to each factory.
3: $\alpha \leftarrow \alpha \backslash f$.
4: **for** each $\alpha(i) \in sequence\ \alpha$ **do**
5:    **for** factory $k = 1$ to n **do**
6:       Insert the current job into the end of the partial sequence $\pi(k)$, and calculate the C_{max}.
7:    **end for**
8:    Select the factory with the minimum C_{max} as F.
9:    **if** the load of $F \leq$ average load **then**
10:      $\pi(F) \leftarrow \alpha(i)$.
11:    **else if** | average load - load of $F| \leq$ | average load - load of F without $\alpha(i)|$ **then**
12:      $\pi(F) \leftarrow \alpha(i)$.
13:    **else if then**
14:      $\pi(F + 1) \leftarrow \alpha(i)$.
15:    **end if**
16: **end for**

In order to ensure the quality and diversity of the solutions, among the generated N initial solutions, $(N - 1)$ initial solutions are constructed by the above rules, and the remaining one is randomly generated.

Smell-Based Foraging. Smell-based foraging determines the potential search position of fruit flies. In order to conduct a sufficient search, fruit flies in each swarm would explore SF neighboring locations. Since N fruit flies swarms are generated during initialization, the Smell-based foraging will generate $N * SF$ neighborhood solutions. The process of smell-based foraging is described below.

- For a solution, a position is randomly generated for each factory processing sequence, and the processing sequence of each factory is divided into two parts.
- Record the job sequence on the right as R, take a job in R and insert it into all possible positions of the remaining sequences in all factories on the left to get the corresponding makespan, and the final insertion position is the position corresponding to the minimum makespan.
- Repeat the above steps until all the jobs in R have completed the insertion operation, and the solution after smell-based foraging is obtained.

Vision-Based Foraging. Sort the $N * SF$ solutions produced by smell-based foraging in ascending order of makespan, and select the first N high-quality solutions for vision-based foraging. In the vision-based foraging, set the neighborhood structure selection probabilities $P_1 < P_2 < P_3 < P_4$, and generate a random probability P_n for each solution. The vision-based foraging operator uses

---

Algorithm 2. Smell-based foraging

1: **for** $i = 1$ to N **do**
2:     **for** $j = 1$ to SF **do**
3:         $R \leftarrow \emptyset$.
4:         **for** $k = 1$ to f **do**
5:             $R_k \leftarrow \emptyset$.
6:             Randomly generate a position, and the sequence of each factory k is divided into two parts.
7:             Record the job sequence on the right as R_k.
8:         **end for**
9:         **for** $R(l)$ in sequence R **do**
10:             Insert $R(l)$ into the position in Π' results in the lowest C_{max}.
11:             $\Pi' \leftarrow R(l)$.
12:         **end for**
13:     **end for**
14: **end for**

---

the four neighborhood structures proposed by Cai et al. [15]. According to the interval position of the random probability P_n, the corresponding neighborhood structure is selected. The settings of the four neighborhood structures are as follows.

- $\mathcal{N}_1$: Determine the factory f_c with the maximum makespan, and randomly select a factory $f_v(f_c \neq f_v)$. Randomly select a job J_e from factory f_c. Insert J_c into the processing sequence of factory f_v, the final sequence is the sequence corresponding to the minimum makespan after insertion.
- $\mathcal{N}_2$: Determine the factory f_c with the maximum makespan, and randomly select a factory $f_v(f_c \neq f_v)$. Randomly select a job J_c from the factory f_c. Randomly select a job J_v from the factory f_v, and swap J_c and J_v.
- $\mathcal{N}_3$: Determine the factory f_c with the maximum makespan, randomly select one of the jobs and insert it into all locations in all factories to obtain the corresponding makespan, and the final insertion position is the position with the minimum makespan.
- $\mathcal{N}_4$: Determine the factory f_c with the maximum makespan, randomly select two of the jobs, and swap the two jobs.

3.2 The Simulated Annealing Algorithm for RHFSP

The simulated annealing algorithm [16] consists of two parts: Metropolis criterion and annealing process. The Metropolis criterion guarantees that the algorithm will jump out when it traps into local optimum, that is, accept the new state with probability instead of using completely deterministic rules. The annealing process ensures that the algorithm converges in a finite time and thus converges to the global optimum. The procedure of the SA algorithm is outlined in Algorithm 4.

Algorithm 3. Vision-based foraging

1: **for** $n = 1$ to N **do**
2:    Determine the factory f_c with the maximum makespan, and the sequence of f_c is Ω_c.
3:    Generate a random probability P_n for each solution.
4:    **if** $0 \leq P_n \leq P_1$, and $|\Omega_c| ¿ 1$ **then**
5:       Randomly select a factory $f_v(f_c \neq f_v)$, and the sequence of f_v is Ω_v.
6:       Randomly select a job J_c from factory f_c.
7:       Insert J_c into the position in Ω_v results in the lowest C_{max}.
8:       $\Omega_c = \Omega_c \setminus J_c$.
9:       $\Gamma \leftarrow$ update(Π').
10:    **else if** $P_1 < P_n < P_2$, or $|\Omega_c| = 1$ **then**
11:       Randomly select a factory $f_v(f_c \leq f_v)$, and the sequence of f_v is Ω_v.
12:       Randomly select a job J_c from the factory f_c.
13:       Randomly select a job J_v from the factory f_v.
14:       Swap J_c and J_v.
15:       $\Gamma \leftarrow$ update(Π').
16:    **else if** $P_2 < P_n < P_3$, and $|\Omega_c| > 1$ **then**
17:       Randomly select a job J_c from factory f_c.
18:       Insert J_c into the position in Π' results in the lowest C_{max}.
19:       $\Gamma \leftarrow$ update(Π').
20:    **else if** $P_3 < P_n < P_4$, and $|\Omega_c| > 1$ **then**
21:       Randomly select two jobs from factory f_c, and swap the two jobs.
22:       $\Gamma \leftarrow$ update(Π').
23:    **end if**
24: **end for**

Solution Encoding and Decoding. We adopt a job-based encoding method, that is, the number in the solution represents the job to be scheduled. The next job is not scheduled until the current job is scheduled.

Initialization. In order to ensure the diversity of solutions, initialization is performed in a random way.

4   Computational Results

The experiment is carried out by randomly generating calculation examples. For the distributed flow shop scheduling problem, the generated example includes 5 jobs and 5 machines. For the reentrant hybrid flow shop scheduling problem, the randomly generated example is 5 jobs. Whether they are reentrant and the reentry time are shown in the Table 3. Number 0 means that this process of the job is not reentrant. Since the cold drawing process is the bottleneck process in the manufacture of seamless steel pipes, the processing time of the reentrant hybrid flow shop scheduling is set to be longer than the distributed flow shop scheduling. The Gantt chart obtained from the example is shown in the Fig. 2.

Algorithm 4. SA for RHFSP

1: $t_{now} = t_0$.
2: **while** $t_{now} > t_f$ **do**
3:     Calculate the makespan $f(\Phi)$.
4:     Randomly swap the two jobs in the current solution, and denoted as Φ'.
5:     Calculate the makespan $f(\Phi')$.
6:     $\Delta f = f(\Phi') - f(\Phi)$.
7:     **if** $\Delta f \leq 0$ **then**
8:         $\Psi \leftarrow \Phi'$, $f(\Psi) \leftarrow f(\Phi')$.
9:     **else**
10:         Randomly generate a probability value P.
11:         **if** $P \leq P_{accept}$ **then**
12:             $\Psi \leftarrow \Phi'$, $f(\Psi) \leftarrow f(\Phi')$.
13:         **else**
14:             $\Psi \leftarrow \Phi$, $f(\Psi) \leftarrow f(\Phi)$.
15:         **end if**
16:     **end if**
17:     $t_{now} = t_{now} * \alpha..$
18: **end while**

In the Gantt chart, the first three factories are distributed flow shops of the heat treatment section. Factory 4 represents the reentrant hybrid flow shop corresponding to the cold drawing section. The labels on the Gantt chart color blocks describe the processed jobs and operations. For example, job 1 is assigned to factory 2, and the five operations of job 1 are processed in factory 2. The label "1–2" represents the second operation of job 1, and the starting point of the color block represents the current processing start time, the end point of the color block indicates the completion time of the corresponding operation, and its length corresponds to the processing time of the operation. In the reentrant factories, the non-reentrant operations are not marked, and the corresponding operation numbers are postponed (Table 2).

Table 2. Example for DFSP

Job	Process time				
1	7	3	5	5	6
2	6	4	5	4	4
3	3	3	4	6	3
4	3	5	2	4	2
5	6	4	3	4	2

Table 3. Example for RHFSP

Process	Job					
Level	Stage	1	2	3	4	5
Level 1	1	7	8	9	6	9
	2	10	11	12	9	10
	3	6	0	12	10	11
Level 2	1	0	8	0	12	13
	2	12	9	12	0	15
	3	8	10	0	11	9
Level 3	1	0	0	9	11	10
	2	11	11	10	9	11
	3	8	10	0	8	15

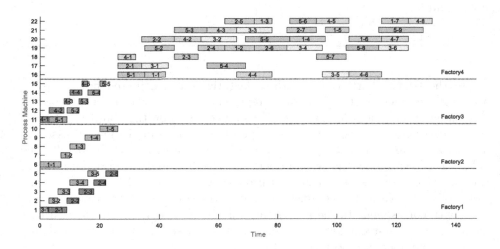

Fig. 2. Gantt chart of the example (Color figure online)

5 Conclusion

In this paper, the heat treatment section and the cold drawing section in the production of seamless steel pipes are studied. To solve the distributed flow shop problem, we proposed the enhanced fruit fly optimization algorithm and the simulated annealing algorithm. In the initialization, we improved initial solutions by an insertion procedure of the NEH heuristic. An insertion-based neighborhood operator was developed to implement the smell-based foraging. We embedded four neighborhood structures to enhance the vision-based foraging. Then, we used the simulated annealing algorithm to solve the reentrant hybrid flowshop scheduling problem. Ultimately, we generated a random instance that was consistent with the problem for testing, and got the final Gantt chart.

In future research, the finishing section will be added, and single goal will be replaced with multiple goals, such as minimum total tardiness, minimum energy consumption and other goals that meet actual production needs.

References

1. Meng, T., Pan, Q.-K., Wang, L.: A distributed permutation flow shop scheduling problem with the customer order constraint. Knowl.-Based Syst. **184**, 104894 (2019)
2. Fu, Y., Tian, G., Fathollahi-Fard, A.M., Ahmadi, A., Zhang, C.: Stochastic multi-objective modelling and optimization of an energy-conscious distributed permutation flow shop scheduling problem with the total tardiness constraint. J. Clean. Prod. **226**, 515–525 (2019)
3. Bargaoui, H., Driss, O.B., Ghédira, K.: A novel chemical reaction optimization for the distributed permutation flow shop scheduling problem with makespan criterion. Comput. Ind. Eng. **111**, 239–250 (2017)
4. Shao, Z., Pi, D., Shao, W.: Hybrid enhanced discrete fruit fly optimization algorithm for scheduling blocking flowshop in distributed environment. Expert Syst. Appl. **145**, 113147 (2020)
5. Zhang, G., Xing, K.: Differential evolution metaheuristics for distributed limited-buffer flow shop scheduling with makespan criterion[J]. Comput. Oper. Res. **108**, 33–43 (2019)
6. Li, Y., Li, F., Pan, Q.-K., Gao, L., Tasgetiren, M.F.: An artificial bee colony algorithm for the distributed hybrid flow shop scheduling problem. Proc. Manuf. **39**, 1158–1166 (2019)
7. Ying, K.-C., Lin, S.-W.: Minimizing makespan for the distributed hybrid flow shop scheduling problem with multiprocessor tasks. Expert Syst. Appl. **92**, 132–141 (2018)
8. Chen, J., Wang, L., Peng, Z.: A collaborative optimization algorithm for energy-efficient multi-objective distributed no-idle flow shop scheduling. Swarm Evol. Comput. **50**, 100557 (2019)
9. Zhang, G., Xing, K.: Memetic social spider optimization algorithm for scheduling two-stage assembly flow shop in a distributed environment. Comput. Ind. Eng. **125**, 423–433 (2018)
10. Lin, C.-C., Liu, W.-Y., Chen, Y.-H.: Considering stockers in reentrant hybrid flow shop scheduling with limited buffer capacity. Comput. Ind. Eng. **139**, 106154 (2020)
11. Rifai, A.P., Nguyen, H.-T., Dawal, S.Z.M.: Multi-objective adaptive large neighborhood search for distributed reentrant permutation flow shop scheduling. Appl. Soft Comput. **40**, 42–57 (2016)
12. Cho, H.-M., Bae, S.-J., Kim, J., Jeong, I.-J.: Bi-objective scheduling for reentrant hybrid flow shop using Pareto genetic algorithm. Comput. Ind. Eng. **61**(3), 529–541 (2011)
13. Pan, W.-T.: A new Fruit Fly Optimization Algorithm: taking the financial distress model as an example. Knowl.-Based Syst. **26**, 69–74 (2012)
14. Nawaz, M., Enscore, E.E., Ham, I.: A heuristic algorithm for the m-machine, n-job flow shop sequencing problem. Omega **11**(1), 91–95 (1983)
15. Cai, J., Zhou, R., Lei, D.: Dynamic shuffled frog-leaping algorithm for distributed hybrid flow shop scheduling with multiprocessor tasks. Eng. Appl. Artif. Intell. **90**, 103540 (2020)
16. Kirkpatrick, S., Gelatt Jr., C.D., Vecchi, M.P.: Optimization by simulated annealing. Science **220**, 671–680 (1993)

Hyperchaotic Encryption Algorithm Based on Joseph Traversal and Bit Plane Reconstruction

Tao Wu, Shida Wang, Kai Zhao, Xuncai Zhang[(✉)], Heng Zhang, and Yanfeng Wang

School of Electrical and Information Engineering, Zhengzhou University of Light Industry, Zhengzhou 450002, China
zhangxuncai@163.com

Abstract. Image encryption is an effective technology to protect digital image security. This paper designs an image encryption algorithm based on Joseph problem and bit plane reconstruction. The encryption algorithm adopts the classical scrambling diffusion structure. By using the principle of Joseph problem, pixel points of encrypted image are moved to different positions to realize pixel scrambling of the image. The pseudo-random sequence generated by hyperchaos is used to scramble the different bit-planes of the encrypted image. Finally, DNA is used to encode the image and cipher feedback is used for diffusion. The simulation results show that the algorithm can encrypt different types of images into evenly distributed encrypted images. The security analysis shows that the algorithm has high key sensitivity and can resist various attacks.

Keywords: Image encryption · Joseph problem · Bit plane reconstruction · DNA

1 Introduction

With the rapid development of modern communication technology, more and more image information is transmitted on social networks. Many of these digital images carry personal information. How to protect these private information has become a hot research topic [5]. Due to digital image has a strong correlation between adjacent pixels and some intrinsic characteristics of high redundancy and so on, some traditional encryption methods such as data encryption standard (DES) or advanced encryption standard (AES) is not suitable for digital image encryption, because the traditional encryption algorithm for digital image encryption had a disadvantage of low efficiency [7].

The advantages of chaotic systems, such as pseudo-randomness, initial value sensitivity, ergodicity and unpredictability [17], have attracted much attention and are widely used in image encryption schemes [6,18,21]. Chaotic systems can

L. Pan et al. (Eds.): BIC-TA 2020, CCIS 1363, pp. 90–105, 2021.
https://doi.org/10.1007/978-981-16-1354-8_9

be divided into high-dimensional (HD) and one-dimensional (1D) chaotic systems [9]. Due to the simple structure of one-dimensional chaotic systems, some chaotic image encryption algorithms based on low-dimensional chaotic systems are vulnerable to attacks, and these algorithms often have disadvantages such as small key space. In contrast, the encryption algorithm of high-dimensional chaotic systems has large key space, high dynamic system behavior and high ergodicity, and is more secure than that of one-dimensional chaotic encryption systems. Therefore, many image encryption algorithms based on hyperchaotic systems have been proposed [3,10,15,19,20]. In [11], Gao and Chen proposed a pixel-level permutation image encryption algorithm based on hyperchaos. Although this algorithm has a large key space, it cannot resist cipher attack. In the current image scrambling methods, many algorithms [4,8,12,22] obtain index vectors by sorting the generated chaotic sequence, and then use these index vectors to scramble the pixels of the image. The security of the scrambling method mentioned above depends on the index vector. The attacker can obtain the index vector by analyzing the relationship between the cipher image and clear image, which may make the scrambling operation invalid.

This paper proposes a hyperchaotic image encryption scheme based on Joseph problem and bit-plane reconstruction. The algorithm adopts the classic confusion structure and generates pseudo-random sequence from the hyperchaotic Lorenz system. In the scrambling stage, Joseph problem [16] is used to traverse the pixel points of the plain image, and the step size increased each time during traversal is controlled by the chaotic sequence, which makes the pixels of the cipher image more random after scrambling and can effectively break the correlation between adjacent pixels. Then the image is decomposed into bit planes, the generated chaotic sequence is sorted by the chaotic sequence to obtain an index vector, and the index vector is used to scramble the bits between the bit planes to reconstruct the bit plane. Different from directly using the index vector to scramble the pixels of the image, the scrambling of the bits between the bit planes can not only make the bits between the various bit planes more disordered, but also change the pixel value analyze the relationship between the cipher image and the clear image to obtain the index vector, which improves the security of the algorithm. After DNA coding of encrypted images, cipher feedback was used for diffusion. Finally, we used SHA-256 to generate the key, which further improves the key space. Experimental analysis shows that the algorithm can basically achieve more than 7.99 information entropy after image encryption, and can effectively resist statistical attacks.

2   Basic Theory

2.1   Hyperchaotic Lorenz System

Because of the disadvantages of the low-dimensional chaotic system such as too simple structure, small key space and fewer parameters, the hyperchaotic system can produce more complex chaotic sequences. Hyperchaos has multiple positive Lyapunov indexes, and has a high key space, which facilitates scrambling and diffusion in a larger space, reduces the correlation between adjacent pixels and improves the overall security of cipher images. The dynamic formula of hyperchaotic Lorenz:

$$\begin{cases} \dot{x} = -a(y - x) + w \\ \dot{y} = cx - y - xz \\ \dot{z} = xy - bz \\ \dot{w} = -yz + rw \end{cases} \tag{1}$$

where, when $a = 10, b = 8/3, c = 28, -1.52 \leq r \leq -0.06$, formula (1) is in a hyperchaotic state. When $r = -1$, the four Lyapunov indexes in Lorenz are: $\lambda_1 = 0.3381, \lambda_2 = 0.1586, \lambda_3 = 0, \lambda_4 = -15.1752$. Figure 1 shows the phase diagram of hyperchaotic Lorenz system.

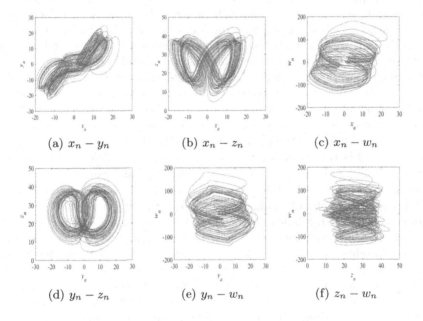

(a) $x_n - y_n$ (b) $x_n - z_n$ (c) $x_n - w_n$

(d) $y_n - z_n$ (e) $y_n - w_n$ (f) $z_n - w_n$

Fig. 1. The hyperchaotic Lorenz system phase diagram with parameters of $a = 10$, $b = 8/3$, $c = 28$, $r = -1$

2.2   Joseph Problem

The Joseph problem occurred during the Roman-Jewish war, when Thirty-nine Jews took refuge in a cave with Joseph and his friends after the Romans occupied Chotapat. 39 Jews decided that they would rather die than surrender, they decided on a method of suicide. 41 people formed a circle and counted off, the first person counted off until the third person killed himself, reluctant to commit suicide, Joseph calculated that he and his friend would be placed in the 16th and 31th positions, and finally he and his friend became the last survivors. In mathematics, the Joseph sequence can be expressed as:

$$D = JS(n, s, j) \tag{2}$$

where n represents the total number of elements, s represents the starting position, j represents the number of shifts, $D = \{d_1, d_2, d_3, ..., d_n\}$ is Joseph sequence.

2.3 DNA Coding

A DNA strand consists of four deoxynucleotides, adenine (A), cytosine (C), guanine (G), and thymine (T). In the case of two single-stranded DNA molecules, these four nucleotides can bind together to form a long sequence that pairs A with T and C with G. This natural quaternary combination is just like the binary system formed by semiconductor on and off. Therefore, the permutation and combination of bases can be used for information storage and calculation.

Coding rules: If $A \rightarrow 00$, $C \rightarrow 01$, $G \rightarrow 10$, $T \rightarrow 11$ for corresponding coding. At the end, the complementary figures can be at $00 \rightarrow 11$ and $01 \rightarrow 10$, and it can be matched with the complementary pair of A $01 \rightarrow 10$ T and C $01 \rightarrow 10$ G. There are 24 such encoding schemes, but only eight of them satisfy the Watson-Crick rule, as shown in Table 1. According to the complementary pairing rule. For the code of rule 1 in Table 1, as shown in Table 2, an xor operation rule between bases is given. For other codes, similar operation rules can also be established [2].

Table 1. Eight encoding/decoding mapping rules for DNA sequences

+	1	2	3	4	5	6	7	8
00	A	A	C	G	C	G	T	T
01	C	G	A	A	T	T	C	G
10	G	C	T	T	A	A	G	C
11	T	T	G	C	G	C	A	T

Table 2. XOR operation rule

XOR	A	C	G	T
A	A	C	G	T
C	C	A	A	G
G	G	T	T	C
T	T	G	C	T

3   Encryption Scheme

Suppose the size of the input plain image P is $M \times N$, the encryption algorithm consists of four parts: key generation, pixel position scrambling, bit plane reconstruction and diffusion algorithm.

3.1   Key Generation

Input the plain image P into SHA-256 algorithm to generate the 256-bit hash key k, then divide every 8 bits into groups, divide k into 32 groups, and then convert each group into decimal values $k_1, k_2, k_3, ..., k_{32}$; Through Formula (3), H_1, H_2, H_3, and H_4 are obtained, where $x \oplus y$ is the bit xor operation between x and y. Formula (4) is used to calculate H_1, H_2, H_3 and H_4, and the initial parameters x_0, y_0, z_0 and w_0 are obtained as the initial values of 4-D hyperchaotic system Lorenz.

$$\begin{cases} H_1 = k_1 \oplus k_2 \oplus k_3 \oplus k_4 \oplus k_5 \oplus k_6 \oplus k_7 \oplus k_8 \\ H_2 = k_9 \oplus k_{10} \oplus k_{11} \oplus k_{12} \oplus k_{13} \oplus k_{14} \oplus k_{15} \oplus k_{16} \\ H_3 = k_{17} \oplus k_{18} \oplus k_{19} \oplus k_{20} \oplus k_{21} \oplus k_{22} \oplus k_{23} \oplus k_{24} \\ H_3 = k_{25} \oplus k_{26} \oplus k_{27} \oplus k_{28} \oplus k_{29} \oplus k_{30} \oplus k_{31} \oplus k_{32} \end{cases} \quad (3)$$

$$\begin{cases} x_0 = \frac{1}{256} mod\,(H_1 + H_2, 256) \\ y_0 = \frac{1}{256} mod\,(H_2 + H_3, 256) \\ z_0 = \frac{1}{256} mod\,(H_3 + H_4, 256) \\ w_0 = \frac{1}{256} mod\,(H_4 + H_1, 256) \end{cases} \quad (4)$$

3.2   Pixel Position Scrambling

Joseph sequence can effectively use the clear image scrambling, break the correlation between adjacent pixels, through after Joseph sequence traversal of pixel scrambling security is not high, because the starting position and traversal fixed step length, an attacker might after scrambling through the analysis of the statistical properties of Joseph traversal sequence can crack the starting position and traverse step, make the scrambling of the operation. Therefore, using chaotic sequence to improve the starting position of Joseph traversal and the step length of each traversal can effectively resist cipher-only attacks. The formula of Joseph sequence is improved. As shown in Formula (5), the mathematical expression of the improved Joseph sequence is:

$$D = JS(n, s, j, Z) \quad (5)$$

where n represents the total number of pixels in the plain image P and s represents the starting position, $j = \{j_1, j_2, j_3, ..., j_n\}$ represents the number of shifts, $Z = \{z_1, z_2, z_3, ..., z_n\}$ represents the variable step size sequence generated by Lorenz chaotic system. order $s = z_1$, while $i \geq 1$, $j_i = z_i + j_{i-1}$.

The specific scrambling methods are as follows:

Use the Lorenz system iterate $M \times N + 1000$ times and the first 1000 times are omitted to produce the sequence $X = \{x_1, x_2, x_3, ..., x_M \times N\}$, after processing the sequence X in accordance with Formula (6), the variable step size sequence Z is obtained;

$$z_i = floor(mod(x_i \times 2^{32}, 8) - 3) \tag{6}$$

Convert P to a one-dimensional sequence U, starting at $S = z_1 = j_1$, remove the element whose position index is u_{j1} and place it in the sequence u', which is $u'_1 = u_{j_1}$. Recycle j_2 elements and remove $u'_2 = u_{j_2}$. Repeat this operation until the last element, and you end up with the Joseph sequence $U' = \left\{u'_1, u'_2, u'_3, ..., u'_n\right\}$. To illustrate the scrambling process in detail, we give a 1×8 one-dimensional sequence $U = \{178, 123, 157, 160, 147, 56, 24, 89\}$ and variable step size sequence $Z = \{4, 1, -3, 1, 1, 0, -1, 0\}$. Figure 2 shows the generation process of Joseph scrambling sequence, and the index vector $O = \{4, 1, 3, 7, 6, 8, 2, 5\}$ generated after Joseph's variable step size traversal. The index vector O is used to scramble the sequence U, and the scrambling sequence $U' = \{160, 178, 157, 24, 56, 89, 123, 147\}$ is generated.

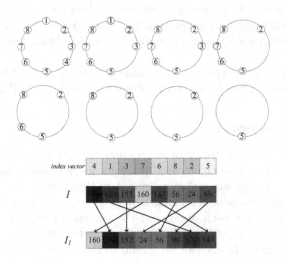

Fig. 2. Flow chart of bit-plane reconstructions

3.3   Bit Plane Reconstruction

Because the bit-plane in the image plane is not uniform, the encryption effect may not be ideal without processing. Therefore, in order to enhance the encryption effect and reduce the algorithm overhead, the algorithm should focus on changing the distribution of image bit plane. To solve these problems, a bit plane reconstruction method based on chaotic sequence is proposed. By changing the bit distribution between the bit-bit planes, the bit-bit planes of encrypted images can reach the state of uniform distribution. The method of bit plane reconstruction will be described in detail below:

Step1: Use the Lorenz system iterate for $8 \times N + 1000$, $8 \times N + 1000$, $8 \times M \times N + 1000$ times, and the first 1000 times were omitted, Generate chaotic sequence $Y = \{y_1, y_2, y_3, ...y_{8 \times M}\}$, chaotic sequence $Z = \{z_1, z_2, z_3, ..., z_{8 \times N}\}$, chaotic sequence $W = \{w_1, w_2, w_3, ..., w_{8 \times M \times N}\}$. Sequence Y, Z and W are sorted in descending order respectively, and their index values are returned to generate index vectors Y', Z', W';

Step2: The plain image is decomposed into eight bit planes of A_1, A_2, A_3, A_4, A_5, A_6, A_7 and A_8, and the bit planes of $A_8 \sim A_1$ are arranged from top to bottom into a two-dimensional bit matrix P_1 of $M \times 8N$, the index vector Y' is used to scramble each row of two-dimensional bit matrix P_1 to generate row scrambling matrix P_2;

Step3: The row-scrambled matrix P_2 was divided into eight $M \times N$ bit planes and rearranged from left to right into a two-dimensional $M \times 8N$ bit matrix P_3. The index vector Y' is used to scramble each column of two-dimensional bit matrix P_3 to generate row scrambling matrix P_4;

Step4: Arrange P_4 from left to right, top to bottom, into a one-dimensional sequence T of $8 \times M \times N$, The index vector W' is used to scramble the one-dimensional sequence T to generate row scrambling vector T_1. The scrambled vector T_1 was rearranged to generate a bit plane $A_1' \sim A_8'$, and the bit plane $A_1' \sim A_8'$ was fused into a two-dimensional matrix to obtain the final encrypted image P_5.

In order to better illustrate the scrambling process, a 2×2 bit-plane reconstruction flow chart of image matrix is presented as shown in Fig. 3 below.

3.4 Diffusion Algorithm

In order to improve the security of encryption algorithm, ordinary pixel information is hidden in as many encrypted pixel points as possible and the ordinary image is diffused. In the algorithm proposed in this paper, the image is transformed into a one-dimensional sequence $R = \{r_1, r_2, r_3, ..., r_{M \times N}\}$, then DNA coding is carried out for each pixel, and the current pixel value is changed by XOR operation with the DNA coding of the first two pixels, so that the small changes in the ordinary image can be spread to the whole encrypted image. The diffusion method is:

$$\begin{cases} r_1' = r_{M \times N-1} \bigoplus r_{M \times N} \bigoplus r_1 & if \quad i = 1; \\ r_2' = r_{M \times N} \bigoplus r_1' \bigoplus r_2 & if \quad i = 2; \\ r_i' = r_{i-1}' \bigoplus r_{i-2}' \bigoplus r_i & if \quad i \geq 3; \end{cases} \qquad (7)$$

where r_i is represents the DNA code of a pixelthe diffusion during decryption is the opposite of the forward operation.

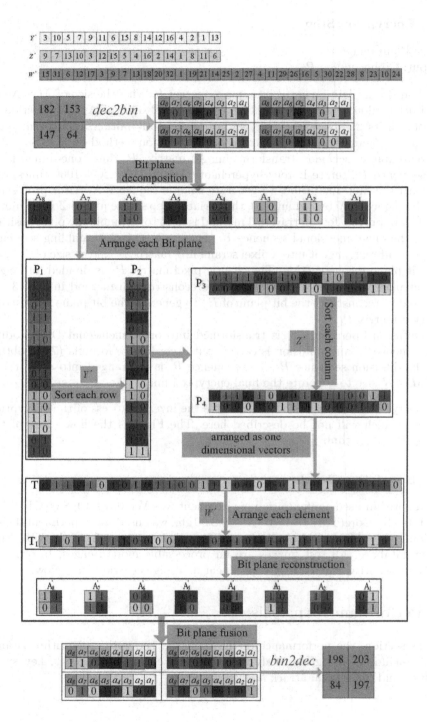

Fig. 3. Flow chart of bit-plane reconstructions

3.5 Encryption Step

Input: Plain image P;
Output: Cipher image P_2.

(1) Transform plain image P into image matrix P' with the size of $M \times N$;
(2) Initial value generation: input image matrix P' into SHA-256 function to obtain its 256-bit hash value, and obtain chaotic initialization parameters x_0, y_0, Z_0 and W_0 according to the key generation method given in Sect. 3.1;
(3) Scrambling scheme: transform image matrix P' into one-dimensional sequence U, iterate Lorenz hyperchaotic system $M \times N + 1000$ times, discard the first 1000 times to generate chaotic sequence X. After processing the sequence X by formula (5), the variable step size sequence Z is obtained. The improved Joseph traversal method is used to scramble the pixel position of the one-dimensional sequence U, generate the pixel scrambling sequence U', and rearrange it into a pixel scrambling matrix P'' in the size of $M \times N$;
(4) Bit plane reconstruction: The chaotic pixel matrix P'' is divided into eight bit planes of $A_8 \sim A_1$. The bit plane reconstruction method in Sect. 3.3 is used to reconstruct the bit plane of P'' to generate the bit plane reconstruction matrix P_1;
(5) Diffusion operation: P_1 is transformed into one-dimensional DNA coding sequence R, and diffusion is carried out according to formula (7) to obtain the diffusion sequence R'. The sequence R' is rearranged into a matrix of $M \times N$ size to generate the final encrypted image P_2;

The decryption process of the algorithm is the inverse process of the encryption process, which will not be described here. The Fig. 4 is the flow chart of the encryption algorithm.

3.6 Simulation Result

The algorithm used configuration environment was Windows 10, 8.00 GB RAM and Intel(R) Core(TM) I7-4510 CPU @2.00 ghz was used for experimental simulation on the Matlab2019A platform. The test images are from the USC-SIPI image database. All test images are un processable mode images, In order to verify its security, the security experiment analysis is carried out below.

4 Performance Analysis

In this section, the performance of the proposed encryption algorithm is analyzed, including histogram analysis, correlation coefficient analysis, key space analysis and differential attack analysis.

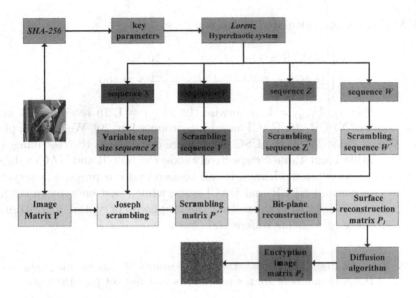

Fig. 4. Flow chart of bit-plane reconstructions

4.1 Key Space Analysis

The key is the most important component of the encryption scheme. The larger the key space is, the stronger its ability to resist the attack of violent cracking. When the key space is greater than 2^{100}, the key is secure enough to withstand brute force attacks. The algorithm proposed in this paper uses SHA-256 to generate the key generated by the 256-bit hash value, so its key space size is 2^{128}, and the calculation precision of x_0, y_0, z_0 and w_0 is 10^{-10}, so the total key space is 3.4028×10^{82}. In the proposed algorithm, the key space is large enough to resist all types of violent attacks.

4.2 Differential Attack Analysis

Differential attack is a common and effective attack method. Differential attack is to study the influence of the difference between the plain images on the cipher images in order to establish the relationship between the plain images and their corresponding cipher images. Diffusion properties show that small changes in the plain image can be propagated to the whole cipher image. If the image encryption algorithm has diffusion property, it can resist differential attack more effectively. Pixel change rate (NPCR) and pixel average change intensity (UACI) are two methods to test whether encryption algorithm can resist differential attack [13]. NPCR calculates the number of different pixels, while UACI calculates the average rate of pixel change between the two images. Assuming that P_1 and P_2 are two cipher images whose plain image has only one bit difference, their NPCR and UACI values are calculated as follows:

$$\begin{cases} NPCR = \frac{\sum_{i=1}^{M} \sum_{i=j}^{N} D_{(i,j)}}{M \times N} \times 100\% \\ UACI = \frac{\sum_{i=1}^{M} \sum_{i=j}^{N} |P_{1(i,j)} - P_{2(i,j)}|}{255 \times M \times N} \times 100\% \end{cases} \tag{8}$$

If $P_{1(i,j)} \neq P_2(i,j)$, $D_{(i,j)} = 1$, otherwise the $D_{(i,j)} = 1$. In recent years, strict critical values of NPCR and UACI have been proposed in [20]. We used six plains images of size 256×256 in the USC-SIPI image database as the test images for simulation. Table 3 and Table 4 respectively show the NPCR and UACI values of different image encryption schemes. It can be seen that our proposed encryption algorithm can pass all NPCR and UACI tests, while other encryption schemes cannot pass some tests. This shows that the proposed encryption algorithm has high performance in resisting differential attack.

Table 3. From "5.1.09" to "5.1.14", the NPCR results of various image encryption schemes and the bold numbers are the test results that did not pass the test.

File name	ZBC [23]	WZNS [14]	CKW [1]	Ours
5.1.09	**99.5575**	99.6506	99.6140	99.5789
5.1.10	**99.5544**	99.6063	99.5880	99.5941
5.1.11	99.8123	99.6490	99.6033	99.5926
5.1.12	99.6109	99.6170	**99.5651**	99.6475
5.1.13	99.7421	**99.5605**	99.5789	99.5804
5.1.14	99.6933	99.6216	99.6765	99.6140

Table 4. From "5.1.09" to "5.1.14", the UACI results of various image encryption schemes and the bold numbers are the test results that did not pass the test.

File name	ZBC [23]	WZNS [14]	CKW [1]	Ours
5.1.09	**33.7574**	33.4387	33.4032	33.4017
5.1.10	**33.1739**	33.4701	33.3557	33.4746
5.1.11	33.3198	33.4150	33.4696	33.4991
5.1.12	**33.6656**	33.5082	33.4634	33.4113
5.1.13	**34.3306**	33.4939	**33.3046**	33.5042
5.1.14	**33.1888**	**33.7240**	33.4796	33.4621

4.3   Key Sensitivity Analysis

In order to ensure the security of encryption algorithm, encryption algorithm should be highly sensitive to the input key. When the wrong key is entered to decrypt the ciphertext image, the output is an image that does not recognize any information. We use the original key to encrypt the Lena image, change the x_0, y_0, z_0, and w_0 to the 10^{-10} power, and use the modified key to decrypt the cipher image. The Lena ciphertext image is displayed in Fig. 5(a), and the decryption image of the correct decryption key is displayed in Fig. 5(b). The decryption image using the wrong decryption key is shown in Fig. 5(c), Fig. 5(d), Fig. 5(e), Fig. 5(f). Obviously, the slightly altered decryption key cannot decrypt the password image.

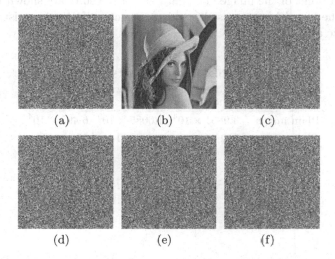

Fig. 5. Decryption images and parameters changed Decrypted images (a)Lena cipher image, (b)Lena decrypted image, (c) x_0 changed 10^{-10} decrypted image, (d)y_0 changed 10^{-10} decrypted image, (e) z_0 changed 10^{-10} decrypted image, (f)w_0 changed 10^{-10} decrypted image

4.4   Histogram Analysis

The histogram of pixel distribution can intuitively reveal the distribution rule of pixel value in the plain image, and the pixel value of the plain image is generally distributed unevenly. The attacker can use the statistical characteristic attack to obtain the effective information in the image. Cipher image makes it difficult for the attacker to obtain valuable information. The more uniform the image distribution in cipher image is, the more difficult it is for the attacker to obtain valuable information, and the better the encryption algorithm is. A good encryption system can make the encrypted image have a histogram with

uniform pixel distribution, which can resist any statistical attack. As shown in
Fig. 6(a) and Fig. 6(c). The pixel values of the plain image are not uniformly
distributed. However, Fig. 6(b)and Fig. 6(d) of the cipher image corresponding
to the plain image show that the pixel value distribution of the cipher image
corresponding to the plain image presents a flat and uniform characteristic. We
verified whether the pixels of the encrypted images Lena, Boat and Face were
evenly distributed, and calculated according to the following formula:

$$x^2 = \sum_{i=1}^{255} \frac{(V_i - V_0)^2}{V_0} \tag{9}$$

where, $V_0 = (M \times N)/256$, $M \times N$ is the size of the image, and V_i is the pixel
value of each point of the image. The data analysis results are shown in Table 5.
Therefore, the algorithm proposed in this paper can effectively resist statistical
characteristic attacks.

Table 5. x^2 test results.

Picture	Lena	Boat	Face
Plain image	3.9851×10^4	1.0085×10^5	6.493×10^4
Cipher image	232.6484	212.6250	228.9688

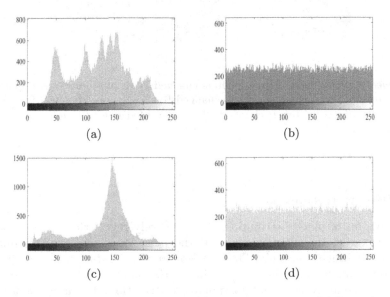

(a)

(b)

(c)

(d)

Fig. 6. (a) Histogram of Lena plain image, (b) Lena cipher image, (c) Boat plain image,
(d) Boat cipher image

4.5 Correlation Analysis

The adjacent pixels of a plain image have a high correlation in the horizontal, vertical and diagonal directions. The ideal encryption algorithm can make the correlation coefficient of the pixels in the cipher image low enough to resist statistical attack. The correlation coefficient is calculated as follows:

$$
\begin{cases}
E_{(x)} = \frac{1}{N} \sum_{i=1}^{N} x_i \\
D_{(x)} = \frac{1}{N} \sum_{i=1}^{N} (x_i - E_{(X)})^2 \\
cov_{(x,y)} = \frac{1}{N} \sum_{i=1}^{N} (x_i - E_{(x)})(y_i - E_{(x)}) \\
\rho_{xy} = \frac{cov_{(x,y)}}{\sqrt{D_x} \times \sqrt{D_y}}
\end{cases}
\tag{10}
$$

where x and y are pixel values, $cov_{(x,y)}$ is the covariance, $D_{(x)}$ is the variance, $E_{(x)}$ is the mean, and ρ_{xy} is the correlation coefficient. In order to analyze and compare the correlation between adjacent pixels in the plain image and the cipher image, we used six gray images and the size is 256×256 in the USC-SIPI image database were used as test images. 5000 pairs of adjacent pixels were randomly selected from the plain image and cipher image, and the correlation distribution of two adjacent pixels was displayed in three directions.

As shown in Table 6, the distribution of adjacent pixels in the plain image is highly concentrated, which means that the adjacent pixels in the plain image have a high correlation. However, the distribution of adjacent pixels in cipher images is random, which means that the correlation of adjacent pixels in encrypted images is low.

Table 6. From "5.1.09" to "5.1.14", correlation analysis of adjacent pixels in plain image and cipher image.

File name	Plain image			Cipher image		
	Horizontal	Vertical	Diagonal	Horizontal	Vertical	Diagonal
5.1.09	0.9406	0.8950	0.8997	0.0037	0.0018	0.0024
5.1.10	0.8539	0.9033	0.8260	0.0011	0.0054	0.0056
5.1.11	0.9423	0.9554	0.8997	−0.0056	0.0002	0.0040
5.1.12	0.9766	0.9596	0.9341	0.0010	0.0060	0.0088
5.1.13	0.8857	0.8834	0.7520	0.0020	0.0013	0.0320
5.1.14	0.8975	0.9507	0.8555	−0.0021	−0.0024	0.0086

4.6 Information Entropy Analysis

Information entropy refers to the average information with redundant parts removed and is the most important feature of randomness. The calculation formula of information entropy is:

$$
H_{(m)} = \sum_{i=1}^{N} P_{(m_i)} \log_2 P_{(m_i)}
\tag{11}
$$

where, n is the gray level of the image, m_i is the ith gray value on the image, and $P_{(m_i)}$ is the probability of the occurrence of m_i. For grayscale images, the theoretical value of information entropy is 8. We used six plain images and the size is 256×256 in the USC-SIPI image database were used as test images, the test results are shown in Table 7. The entropy value of cipher images encrypted by the algorithm is very close to the ideal value.

Table 7. From "5.1.09" to "5.1.14", the information entropy of plain image and cipher image

File name	Plain image	Cipher image
5.1.09	6.7093	7.9971
5.1.10	7.3318	7.9971
5.1.11	6.4523	7.9970
5.1.12	6.7057	7.9973
5.1.13	1.5483	7.9957
5.1.14	7.3424	7.9973

5   Conclusion

In this paper, an image encryption scheme based on hyperchaotic system is proposed based on Joseph problem principle and bit-plane reconstruction. Joseph scrambling is derived from Joseph problem, and the improved Joseph traversal is used to scramble the image to get better scrambling effect. The bit-plane reconstruction method reconstructed the bit-plane of the plain image, made the bit-plane distribution random, and combined with the diffusion algorithm, the pixel distribution histogram of the cipher image obtained was more uniform, which could effectively resist differential attack. Simulation results show that the algorithm can encrypt different types of images into unrecognized cipher images. The key sensitivity, defense ability of differential attack, correlation of adjacent pixels, information entropy and histogram were analyzed, and excellent results were obtained. The analysis results show that the algorithm has good safety performance.

References

1. Cao, C., Sun, K., Liu, W.: A novel bit-level image encryption algorithm based on 2d-licm hyperchaotic map. Signal Process. **143**, 122–133 (2018)
2. Chai, X., Chen, Y., Broyde, L.: A novel chaos-based image encryption algorithm using DNA sequence operations. Opt. Lasers Eng. **88**, 197–213 (2017)
3. Chen, Y.: Optimal windows of rewiring period in randomly coupled chaotic maps. Phys. Lett. A **374**(31), 3185–3189 (2010)

4. Gong, L., Qiu, K., Deng, C.: An image compression and encryption algorithm based on chaotic system and compressive sensing. Opt. Laser Technol. **115**, 257–267 (2019)

5. Li, C., Zhang, Y.: When an attacker meets a cipher-image in 2018: a year in review. J. Inf. Secur. Appl. **48**, 102361 (2019)

6. Lin, H.: Influences of electromagnetic radiation distribution on chaotic dynamics of a neural network. Appl. Math. Comput. **369**, 124048 (2020)

7. Liu, Q., Li, P., Zhang, M., Sui, Y.: A novel image encryption algorithm based on chaos maps with Markov properties. Commun. Nonlinear Sci. Numer. Simul. **20**(2), 506–515 (2015)

8. Pak, C., Huang, L.: A new color image encryption using combination of the 1d chaotic map. Signal Process. **138**, 129–137 (2017)

9. Radwan, A.G., AbdElHaleem, S.H.: Symmetric encryption algorithms using chaotic and non-chaotic generators: a review. J. Adv. Res. **7**(2), 193–208 (2016)

10. Wang, X., Teng, L.: An image blocks encryption algorithm based on spatiotemporal chaos. Nonlinear Dyn. **67**(1), 365–371 (2012)

11. Wang, Y., Wong, K.W., Liao, X., Xiang, T.: A chaos-based image encryption algorithm with variable control parameters. Chaos, Solitons Fractals **41**(4), 1773–1783 (2009)

12. Wu, J., Liao, X., Yang, B.: Cryptanalysis and enhancements of image encryption based on three-dimensional bit matrix permutation. Signal Process. **142**, 292–300 (2018)

13. Wu, Y., Noonan, J.P., Agaian, S.: NPCR and UACI randomness tests for image encryption. Cyber J. Multidiscipl. J. Sci. Technol. J. Sel. Areas in Telecommunications **2**, 31–38 (2011)

14. Wu, Y., Zhou, Y., Noonan, J.P., Agaian, S.: Design of image cipher using Latin squares. Inf. Sci. **264**, 317–339 (2014)

15. Wu, Y., Zhou, Y., Saveriades, G., Agaian, S., Noonan, J.P., Natarajan, P.: Local Shannon entropy measure with statistical tests for image randomness. Inf. Sci. **222**, 323–342 (2013)

16. Xiang, D., Xiong, Y.: Digital image scrambling based on Josephus traversing. Comput. Eng. Appl. **41**(10), 44–46 (2005)

17. Zhang, H., Huang, W., Wang, Z., Chai, T.: Adaptive synchronization between two different chaotic systems with unknown parameters. Phys. Lett. A **350**(5), 363–366 (2006)

18. Zhang, X., Wang, C., Yao, W., Lin, H.: Chaotic system with Bondorbital attractors. Nonlinear Dyn. **97**(4), 2159–2174 (2019). https://doi.org/10.1007/s11071-019-05113-3

19. Zhang, Y.: Spatiotemporal chaos of fractional order logistic equation in nonlinear coupled lattices. Commun. Nonlinear Sci. Numer. Simul. **52**(52), 52–61 (2017)

20. Zhang, Y., Wang, X.: A new image encryption algorithm based on non-adjacent coupled map lattices. Appl. Soft Comput. **26**, 10–20 (2015)

21. Zhao, Q., Wang, C., Zhang, X.: A universal emulator for memristor, memcapacitor, and meminductor and its chaotic circuit. Chaos **29**(1), 13141 (2019)

22. Gan, Z., Chai, X., Han, D., Chen, Y.: A chaotic image encryption algorithm based on 3-D bit-plane permutation. Neural Comput. Appl. **31**(11), 7111–7130 (2018). https://doi.org/10.1007/s00521-018-3541-y

23. Zhou, Y., Bao, L.: A new 1d chaotic system for image encryption. Signal Process. **97**, 172–182 (2014)

Trimmed Data-Driven Evolutionary Optimization Using Selective Surrogate Ensembles

Yawen Shan, Yongjin Hou, Mengzhen Wang, and Fei Xu[✉]

Key Laboratory of Image Processing and Intelligent Control of Education Ministry of China, School of Artificial Intelligence and Automation, Huazhong University of Science and Technology, Wuhan 430074, China
fxu@hust.edu.cn

Abstract. Data-driven evolutionary algorithms (DDEAs) have attracted much attention in recent years, due to their effectiveness and advantages in solving expensive and complex optimization problems. In an offline data-driven evolutionary algorithm, no additional information is available to update surrogate models, so we need to ensure the quality of the surrogate models built before optimization. Based on the offline data-driven evolutionary algorithm using selective surrogate ensembles (DDEA-SE), we propose a trimmed bagging based DDEA-SE (TDDEA-SE) to construct a more accurate model pool. To this end, we use trimmed bagging to prune models with large errors calculated by out-of-bag samples, thus improving the accuracy of the selective surrogate ensembles and promoting the optimization. The experimental results on benchmark problems show that the proposed algorithm can strike a balance between diversity and accuracy of models, and its competitiveness on solving offline data-driven optimization problems.

Keywords: Offline data-driven evolutionary algorithms · Trimmed bagging · Accuracy · Diversity

1 Introduction

Many real-world optimization problems need physical simulations or physical expensive computer to evaluate their candidate solutions [1]. The traditional evolutionary algorithms (EA) evaluates solutions based on fitness evaluations (FEs) [2–4]. However, when the FEs are too expensive, or the fitness cannot be evaluated during the optimization, it cannot solve these optimization problems directly. Surrogate assisted evolutionary algorithms (SAEAs) are a promising way to deal with these optimization problems. SAEAs use cheap surrogates to replace the expensive real fitness functions [5], which can significantly reduce computational costs and speed up the optimization process.

SAEAs have become a prevalent method to solve expensive and complex real-world problems [6]. Many advanced regression models have been used as

© Springer Nature Singapore Pte Ltd. 2021
L. Pan et al. (Eds.): BIC-TA 2020, CCIS 1363, pp. 106–116, 2021.
https://doi.org/10.1007/978-981-16-1354-8_10

surrogates, such as nverse distance weighting (IDW) interpolation [7], polynomial regression(PR) [8,9], gaussian processes [10], radial basis function (RBF) [7,11,12], and artificial neural networks [13,14]. The surrogate ensemble [5,11] has also been used because of its advantages in improving data-driven algorithm robustness.

To ensure that the EA can find the best solution, most existing SAEAs focus on solving online data-driven optimization, selecting appropriate surrogates, and model management strategies. In contrast, only a few SAEAs focus on expensive offline data-driven optimization problems. In offline data-driven optimization, we cannot get any external information to verify the optimal solution in the optimization process, which makes offline SAEAs more challenging than online SAEAs. When optimizing fused magnesium furnaces [8], it builds a smooth global PR model with historical data before optimization and uses this model as a fitness function to manage local surrogates during optimization. In [11], a large model pool with many models is built before the optimization begins, in which a small subset of models are adaptively selected as surrogate ensembles to achieve the best local approximate accuracy. [15] uses boosting strategy (BS) to build a suitable surrogate model for different problems and localized data generation (LDG) to alleviate data shortages, then combine LDG to work with BS to solve offline optimization problems. [16] proposes an EA assisted by a coarse surrogate (CS) and a fine surrogate (FS), then transfers knowledge from CS to FS to enhance the convergence of the FS-assisted optimization process. On this basis, a final solution set generation strategy based on reference vector is proposed to generate high-quality solutions to solve offline multiobjective optimization.

Trimmed bagging [17], as a method of machine learning, only chooses a few good base learners, and trims the base learners whose performance is not good, thus improving prediction accuracy and efficiency of ensemble learning. In [17], the base classifiers are trained by bootstrap samples, then use the out-of-bag samples to predict the estimation errors, and then eliminate bad classifiers to yields better results. [18] proposes two stage pruning method to trim the base learners, which reduces the ensemble scale and improves the classification accuracy.

The DDEA-SE proposed in [11] generates a large number of surrogates offline using bagging technology, and selects a subset of them adaptively during optimization which is called selective surrogate ensembles. Generating a large number of surrogate models ensures the diversity of surrogate ensembles, but there are a lot of models with large prediction errors, which reduce the accuracy of surrogate ensembles and mislead the search. In this paper, our goal is to engage high-accuracy models to participate in optimization thus generating high-accuracy surrogate ensembles. To this end, trimmed bagging technique is used to trim off some models with large errors from the model pool and get a good model pool with smaller errors, then a subset of accurate surrogates is selected adaptively from this new model pool to be taken as the surrogate ensemble to predict the fitness.

The rest of this article is organized as follows. Section 2 introduces the proposed algorithm TDDEA-SE and the trimmed bagging. To further analyze the performance of the proposed algorithm, experimental results on the benchmark problems are provided in Sect. 3. Finally, in Sect. 4, we conclude the algorithm proposed in this paper.

2   The Proposed TDDEA-SE Algorithm

Different from online DDEAs, offline DDEAs cannot get any external information during optimization, so high-quality surrogates must be trained before optimization. Trimmed bagging can strik a good balance between accuracy and diversity of ensemble. In order to improve the quality of models in the model pool established in DDEA-SE, in this section, the offline data-driven evolutionary algorithm TDDEA-SE based on DDEA-SE and trimmed bagging is proposed.

2.1   The Framework

The diagram of TDDEA-SE is shown in Fig. 1. The algorithm consists of evolutionary optimization algorithm and model construction. The optimization part is consistent with traditional EA, including crossover, mutation, fitness evaluations and so on.

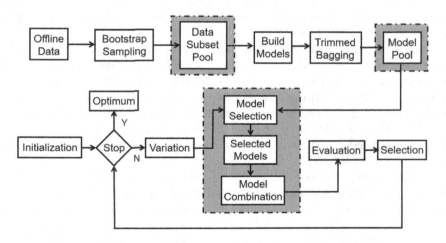

Fig. 1. The diagram of TDDEA-SE.

Before running the optimizer, $11D$ (D is the problem dimension) offline data (including the value of each dimension and the objective function value) is created by using the Latin hypercube sampling (LHS) and real objective function. Then T subsets $(S_1, S_2, \cdots, S_T)$ are generated by performing T independent times bootstrap sampling from the data pool, and T models $(M_1, M_2, \cdots, M_T)$

Algorithm 1. Pseudo code of the TDDEA-SE.

Input: $D_{offline}$-the offline data, d-the dimension of x, T-the size of the model pool, Q: the ensemble size after model selection, r:the ratio of models to be trimmed $(r < 1)$.

1: Use $D_{offline}$ to build models $(M_1, M_2, \cdots, M_T)$ and save the out-of-bag samples of each model.
2: Run **trimmed bagging** to trim off $r \times T$ models and get the model pool $(M_1, M_2, \cdots, M_N)$.
3: **for** each generation **do**
4:    **if** it is the first generation **then**
5:        Randomly choose Q models from the pool.
6:    **else**
7:        Using $(M_1, M_2, \cdots, M_N)$ to predict xb.
8:        Sort N RBF models based on their predictions on xb.
9:        Equally divide N sorted RBF models into Q groups.
10:       **for** each group **do**
11:           One random model is selected to construct the ensemble.
12:       **end for**
13:    **end if**
14:    variation.
15:    Use Q selected models to predict individuals to find the best individual xb.
16: **end for**
Output: Obtained optimum xb

---

are built based on the T subsets. The generalization error of each model is calculated according to the out-of-bag samples of each subset, and then the model pool is composed of N "better" models by trimming off some "bad" models. In the optimization process, TDDEA-SE uses optimal solution xb (estimated by surrogate ensemble) as reference to select Q models from N models, and combined this Q models to predict the fitness value. When stop condition is met, the whole algorithm terminates and outputs the obtained optimal solution. The whole process is detailed in Algorithm 1.

The model selection strategy of TDDEA-SE is the same as [11]. Let xb be the optimal individual according to the ensemble of Q models, then use each RBF models to predict the fitness value of xb. Sort T models according to the estimated fitness and equally divide T models into Q groups, then randomly select one RBF model from each Q groups to form a new surrogate ensemble for next generation to estimate fitness. Because there is no xb for the first generation to select models, so Q models are randomly selected in the first generation.

2.2 Trimmed Bagging

Ensemble learning [19] completes learning tasks by building multiple base learners and combining them into a powerful learner, which is superior to a single learner in terms of diversity and accuracy. Bagging as a popular ensemble generation method, can reduce the prediction bias.

Each bootstrap sample includes some random samples extracted from the training set. Those data that left out of each data subset are called out-of-bag samples, resulting in the diversity of models. Out-of-bag samples are widely used in ensemble learning [20], such as estimating the generalization error of base learners [21] and selecting base learners [22].

As discussed in [17], the number of trimmed bagging may be problem-dependent, generally we use ratio r to denote the ratio of the number of trimmed models to original models. If r is too small, it cannot reflect the advantages of trimmed bagging, if r is too large, it reduces the diversity of models, degrading the ensemble performance. In this work, we trim off models with large error by the ratio of $r = 0.1$, and use the remaining $N = 0.9 \times T$ RBF models as model pool.

The advantage of out-of-bag error is that it can be seen as an unbiased estimate of true error. Thus, after generating T models, we use each model to calculate fitness values of its out-of-bag samples, and then calculate the root mean square error (RMSE) between the predicted fitness values and true fitness values (included in $11D$ offline data). Then sort these models in an ascending order according to theirs RMSEs. Finally, $r \times T$ models with large error (larger RMSEs ranking model) are eliminated, and the remaining N better models are taken as a new model pool, which has a higher accuracy than the previous model pool. The whole process is shown in Algorithm 2.

Algorithm 2. Pseudo code of the Trimmed Bagging.

Input: $(M_1, M_2, ..., M_T)$: T models, *Out*: the out-of-bag samples of models, r: the proportion of models to be trimmed.
1: Use *Out* to calculate the RMSE of each model.
2: Sort T RBF models based on their RMSE.
3: Trim off $r \times T$ models form the model pool.
4: Use the remaining models as model pool $(M_1, M_2, ..., M_N)$
Output: N remaining RBF models

---

3 Experiments

In order to verify the effectiveness of TDDEA-SE, we carry out experiments on five benchmark problems, as shown in Table 1, and compare TDDEA-SE with two state-of-the-art offline DDEAs.

3.1 Comparison of the Trim Ratio r

Since the ratio r in trimmed bagging plays an important role, in this subsection, we study the performance of TDDEA-SE with different trimmed ratio r (0.1, 0.3, 0.5, 0.7, and 0.9).

Table 1. Five benchmark problems.

Problem	D	Global Optimun	Characteristics
Ellipsoid	10,30,50,100	0.0	Uni-modal
Ackley	10,30,50,100	0.0	Multi-modal
Griewank	10,30,50,100	0.0	Multi-modal
Rosenbrock	10,30,50,100	0.0	Multi-modal
Rastrigin	10,30,50,100	0.0	Multi-modal

Since TDDEA-SE is based on DDEA-SE, the parameter settings of TDDEA is the same as [11]. The offline data size is $11D$, the number of offline model T is 2000. During optimization, population size is 100, crossover probability is 1, mutation probability is $1/D$, the number of selected subsets Q is 100, and termination generation is 100. We test these five comparison algorithms on two benchmark problems: Ellipsoid and Rastrigin functions ($D = 10, 30, 50, 100$). Each instance is repeated 20 times to increase data credibility. Since calculating the RMSE of each model and trimming models takes less than 0.1 s, so we ignore this time.

Table 2. Obtained optimum of TDDEA-SE variants on Ellipsoid and Rastrigin.

11D LHS		Obtained optimum				
		0.1	0.3	0.5	0.7	0.9
E	10	0.95 ± 0.55	0.94 ± 0.48	1.10 ± 0.52	1.07 ± 0.50	1.27 ± 0.58
	30	4.01 ± 0.92	4.43 ± 1.31	4.79 ± 1.32	5.38 ± 1.66	4.91 ± 1.27
	50	14.72 ± 4.44	15.27 ± 4.45	15.36 ± 3.21	16.39 ± 3.07	16.18 ± 3.91
	100	319.08 ± 83.62	314.9 ± 96.72	325.9 ± 59.29	327.73 ± 73.46	352.2 ± 86.4
R	10	62.04 ± 21.22	67.22 ± 21.6	64.73 ± 29.21	69.21 ± 19.14	74.20 ± 28.54
	30	116.04 ± 32.05	120.77 ± 32.74	122.30 ± 30.59	117.53 ± 31.21	155.34 ± 33.03
	50	185.19 ± 34.38	178.49 ± 32.41	218.46 ± 48.46	197.62 ± 44.55	196.84 ± 46.14
	100	793.35 ± 115.55	798.63 ± 95.94	832.07 ± 91.83	837.23 ± 86.52	854.82 ± 99.67
Average rank		1.375	1.875	3.375	3.875	4.5
p-value		NA	0.48	**0.0047**	**0.0047**	**0.0047**

The average obtained optimum and executive time of five TDDEA-SE variants are shown in Table 2 and Table 3, and the convergence curves are shown in Fig. 2 and Fig. 3. The results in Table 2 is analyzed by Friedman test [23], where significance level is 0.05 and TDDEA-SE with $r = 0.1$ is the control method. In general, the performance of TDDEA-SE with $r = 0.1$ is significantly superior to that of $r = 0.5, 0.7, 0.9$, and its average rank is better than that of $r = 0.3$. The results in Table 3 show that, with the increase of trim ratio r, algorithm's executive time will decrease.

Table 3. Executive time of TDDEA-SE variants on Ellipsoid and Rastrigin.

11D LHS		Execution time (s)				
		0.1	0.3	0.5	0.7	0.9
E	10	22.76 ± 0.3	21.71 ± 0.3	20.38 ± 0.21	18.28 ± 0.33	16.86 ± 0.6
	30	40.12 ± 0.63	39.10 ± 0.4	37.41 ± 0.7	36.23 ± 0.8	34.36 ± 1.20
	50	71.3 ± 1.93	69.15 ± 2.1	66.78 ± 2.7	63.51 ± 2.3	61.6 ± 1.83
	100	200.39 ± 3.66	193.70 ± 3.44	180.24 ± 2.94	174.37 ± 3.55	162.36 ± 2.47
R	10	41.8 ± 0.7	40.23 ± 0.19	38.9 ± 0.39	38.1 ± 0.32	36.35 ± 0.23
	30	65.47 ± 1.26	63.9 ± 2.17	63.33 ± 2.46	61.85 ± 1.63	60.55 ± 1.74
	50	84.25 ± 6.26	81.58 ± 7.21	76.2 ± 7.2	72.3 ± 5.85	68.18 ± 6.72
	100	222.37 ± 14.6	213.66 ± 13.43	206.27 ± 11.49	195.43 ± 16.85	187.31 ± 10.98

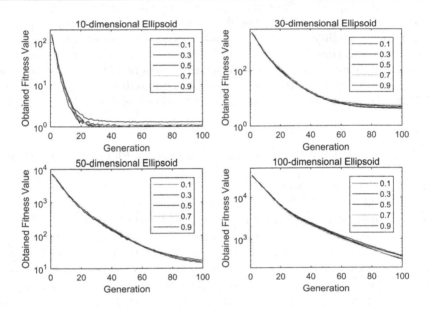

Fig. 2. Convergence profiles of TDDEA-SE variants on the Ellipsoid function.

The convergence profiles of TDDEA-SE with different ratio r (0.1, 0.3, 0.5, 0.7, and 0.9) on $D = 10, 30, 50$, and 100 dimensional Ellipsoid function are shown in Fig. 2. When r is 0.1, TDDEA-SE performs better than other ratio, but when the dimension of decision space D increases, the improvement becomes minor. In general, with the increase of the trim ratio r, the performance of TDDEA-SE will degrade.

Then, we study the performance of TDDEA-SE variants on the multi-modal Rastrigin function. Figure 3 shows the convergence curves of all the compared algorithms on the Rastrigin function with dimensions $D = 10, 30, 50$, and 100. Among the five trimmed-based variants, $r = 0.1, 0.3$ outperforms $r = 0.5, 0.7, 0.9$, and when $r = 0.1$, TDDEA-SE performs the best for $D = 10, 30, 100$.

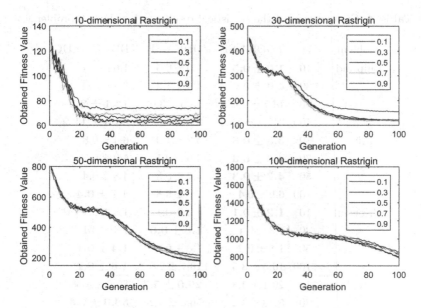

Fig. 3. Convergence profiles of TDDEA-SE variants on the Rastrigin function.

These results indicate that trimmed bagging technique is helpful for mutil-modal optimization problems.

From the above results, we can know that when r is 0.1, the performance of TDDEA-SE is significantly better than that of $r = 0.5$, 0.7, and 0.9, although its executive time is relatively long. The reason is that r of 0.1 can increase the accuracy of models without damaging its diversity, so the bagging subset with higher accuracy can be selected for optimization. When r is bigger than 0.1, the diversity of models is reduced, leading to worse performance. As the ratio r decreases, the execution time of TDDEA-SE becomes longer. Since when $r = 0$, TDDEA-SE becomes DDEA-SE, we can know that the execution time of TDDEA-SE is shorter than that of DDEA-SE. These results show that the ratio r of trimmed bagging seriously affects the optimization performance. In next experiment, we set r in TDDEA-SE to be 0.1.

3.2 Comparison with Offline Data-Driven EAs

In this subsection, we choose two offline data-driven evolutionary algorithms DDEA-SE and BDDEA-LDG to compare with the proposed algorithm. We choose them for the following reasons. Since the TDDEA-SE is proposed based on DDEA-SE, comparing with DDEA-SE can observe the effectiveness of trimmed bagging. As an advanced offline algorithm, BDDEA-LDG is suitable for comparing with offline data-driven optimization algorithms. Parameter settings of DDEA-SE is the same as [11] and those of BDDEA-LDG are taken from [15]. Each algorithm runs 20 times and is averaged as the final result.

Table 4. Comparisons of the statistical results on benchmark problems.

Problem	D	TDDEA-SE	DDEA-SE	BDDEA-LDG
Ellipsoid	10	**1.0 ± 0.5**	1.0 ± 0.5	1.0 ± 0.4
	30	**4.0 ± 0.9**	4.3 ± 1.3	6.7 ± 2.0
	50	14.7 ± 4.4	13.6 ± 3.6	**13.1 ± 3.2**
	100	319.1 ± 83.6	321.9 ± 68.8	**55.5 ± 11.2**
Ackley	10	**5.8 ± 0.8**	5.9 ± 1.0	6.4 ± 0.8
	30	**4.8 ± 0.3**	4.9 ± 0.5	5.0 ± 0.7
	50	**4.7 ± 0.3**	4.7 ± 0.3	4.8 ± 0.4
	100	6.9 ± 0.4	7.0 ± 0.6	**4.7 ± 0.4**
Griewank	10	**1.2 ± 0.1**	1.3 ± 0.1	1.3 ± 0.1
	30	1.3 ± 0.1	**1.3 ± 0.0**	1.4 ± 0.1
	50	1.8 ± 0.2	1.8 ± 0.2	**1.4 ± 0.1**
	100	16.5 ± 3.5	18.7 ± 2.8	**1.8 ± 0.2**
Rosenbrock	10	29.1 ± 4.8	**29.0 ± 5.7**	35.2 ± 8.58
	30	57.5 ± 4.2	56.3 ± 5.2	**50.0 ± 7.3**
	50	**84.7 ± 5.3**	85.8 ± 6.7	98.1 ± 9.0
	100	255.8 ± 45.9	242.8 ± 28.6	**193.0 ± 22.6**
Rastrigin	10	**62.0 ± 21.2**	68.5 ± 27.2	65.1 ± 29.6
	30	**116.0 ± 32.0**	124.9 ± 35.9	146.0 ± 4.3
	50	**185.2 ± 34.4**	189.9 ± 37.0	190.1 ± 30.2
	100	793.3 ± 115.5	825.5 ± 81.0	**405.0 ± 144**
Average rank		1.65	1.9	2
p-value		NA	**0.045**	0.37

Table 4 records the results obtained by TDDEA-SE, DDEA-SE and BDDEA-LDG on 10, 30, 50, and 100 dimensional problems. TDDEA-SE achieves good results on 10 of the 20 problems (marked in **bold**). According to the Friedman test (significance level is 0.05 and TDDEA-SE is the control method), the average rank of TDDEA-SE is smaller than DDEA-SE (p-value = 0.045). In addition to Rosenbrock problem, TDDEA-SE achieves better results on other four problems than DDEA-SE. This is because that Rosenbrock has a narrow valley, where the value does not change much, thus DDEA-SE with more diverse models is easier to find the global optimum. From the Friedman test, we can see that the average rank of TDDEA-SE is smaller than that of BDDEA-LDG, and p-value indicates TDDEA-SE performs similar to BDDEA-LDG. BDDEA-LDG has good results on many high-dimensional problems, which is because $11D$ data is not sufficient for TDDEA-SE to train good models on high-dimensional problems, while BDDEA-LDG uses a localized data generation (LDG) method to alleviate data shortages, thus finding better solutions. The above results show the effectiveness of TDDEA-SE. Its good performance is brought by trimmed bagging technique, which can trim off "worse" models to improve the performance of surrogate ensembles.

4 Conclusion

The data-driven evolutionary algorithms are more effective than traditional EA in solving real-world optimization problems. In this paper, a new algorithm TDDEA-SE is proposed inspired by DDEA-SE and trimmed bagging. Before optimization starts, trimmed bagging is used on the basis of ratio to trim off some models with large error from the model pool of DDEA-SE, so that we can adaptively select a subset of models which has higher accuracy as surrogate ensemble to promote optimization. The experimental results on benchmark problems show that TDDEA-SE can strike a balance between diversity and accuracy of models and it is a competitive algorithm which can handle offline optimization problems with up to 100 decision variables.

Acknowledgements. This work is supported by the National Key R and D Program of China for International S and T Cooperation Projects (2017YFE0103900), China Postdoctoral Science Foundation (2020M672359) and the Fundamental Research Funds for the Central Universities (HUST: 2019kfyXMBZ056).

References

1. Jin, Y.C.: Surrogate-assisted evolutionary computation: recent advances and future challenges. Swarm Evol. Comput. **1**(2), 61–70 (2011)
2. Vikhar, P.A.: Evolutionary algorithms: A critical review and its future prospects. In: International Conference on Global Trends in Signal Processing, Information Computing and Communication, ICGTSPICC 2016, 22–24 December, Jalgaon, India, pp. 261–265 (2016)
3. Pan, L.Q., Li, L.H., He, C., et al.: A subregion division-based evolutionary algorithm with effective mating selection for many-objective optimization. IEEE Trans. Cybern. **50**(8), 3477–3490 (2020)
4. Pan, L.Q., Li, L.H., He, C., et al.: Manifold learning-inspired mating restriction for evolutionary multiobjective optimization with complicated pareto sets. IEEE Trans. Cybern. **1–13** (2019). https://doi.org/10.1109/TCYB.2019.2952881
5. Wang, H.D., Jin, Y.C., Doherty, J.: Committee-based active learning for surrogate-assisted particle swarm optimization of expensive problems. IEEE Trans. Cybern. **47**(9), 2664–2677 (2017)
6. Nguyen, S., Zhang, M.J., Johnston, M., et al.: Automatic programming via iterated local search for dynamic job shop scheduling. IEEE Trans. Cybern. **45**(1), 1–14 (2015)
7. Wang, S., Liu, J., Jin, Y.C.: Surrogate-assisted robust optimization of large-scale networks based on graph embedding. IEEE Trans. Evol. Comput. **24**(4), 735–749 (2020)

8. Guo, D., Chai, T.Y., Ding, J., et al.: Small data driven evolutionary multi-objective optimization of fused magnesium furnaces. In: IEEE Symposium Series on Computational Intelligence, IEEE SSCI 2016, 6–9 December, Athens, Greece, pp. 1–8 (2016)
9. Lian, Y.S., Liou, M.S.: Multiobiective optimization using coupled response surface model and evolutionary algorithm. AIAA J. **43**(6), 1316–1325 (2005)
10. Liu, B., Zhang, Q.F., Gielen, G., et al.: A gaussian process surrogate model assisted evolutionary algorithm for medium scale expensive optimization problems. IEEE Trans. Evol. Comput. **18**(2), 180–192 (2014)
11. Wang, H.D., Jin, Y.C., Sun, C.L., et al.: Offline data-driven evolutionary optimization using selective surrogate ensembles. IEEE Trans. Evol. Comput. **23**(2), 203–216 (2019)
12. Sun, C.L., Jin, Y.C., Cheng, R., et al.: Surrogate-assisted cooperative swarm optimization of high-dimensional expensive problems. IEEE Trans. Evol. Comput. **21**(4), 644–660 (2017)
13. Pan, L.Q., He, C., Tian, Y., et al.: A classification-based surrogate-assisted evolutionary algorithm for expensive many-objective optimization. IEEE Trans. Evol. Comput. **23**(1), 74–88 (2019)
14. Jin, Y.C., Olhofer, M., Sendhoff, B.: A framework for evolutionary optimization with approximate fitness functions. IEEE Trans. Evol. Comput. **6**(5), 481–494 (2002)
15. Li, J.Y., Zhan, Z.H., Wang, C., et al.: Boosting data-driven evolutionary algorithm with localized data generation. IEEE Trans. Evol. Comput. (2020, to be published). https://doi.org/10.1109/TEVC.2020.2979740
16. Yang, C.E., Ding, J.L., Jin, Y.C., et al.: Offline data-driven multiobjective optimization: knowledge transfer between surrogates and generation of final solutions. IEEE Trans. Evol. Comput. **24**(3), 409–423 (2020)
17. Croux, C., Jooseens, K., Lemmensb, A.: Trimmed bagging. Comput. Stat. Data Anal. **52**(1), 362–368 (2007)
18. Zhang, H., Song, Y.J., Jiang, B., et al.: Two-stage bagging pruning for reducing the ensemble size and improving the classification performance. Math. Prob. Eng. **5**(3), 1–17 (2019)
19. Moreira, J.M., Soares, C., Jorge, A.M., et al.: Ensemble approaches for regression: a survey. ACM Comput. Surv. **45**(1), 1–40 (2012)
20. Zhang, C.X., Guo, G.: Research of the applications of out-of-bag sample. Software **32**(3), 1–4 (2011)
21. Bylander, T.: Estimating generalization error on two class datasets using out-of-bag estimates. Mach. Learn. **48**(1), 287–297 (2002)
22. Rao, J.S., Tibshirant, R.: The out-of-bootstrap method for model averaging and selection. Technical report, Cleveland Clinic and University of Toronto (997)
23. Derrac, J., Garcia, S., Herrera, F.: A practical tutorial on the use of nonparametric statistical tests as a methodology for comparing evolutionary and swarm intelligence algorithms. Swarm Evol. Comput. **1**(1), 3–18 (2011)

Research and Application of the Standard Formulation Technology for Three Kinds of Specialized Raw Materials

Shengling Zhou[1], Jiangrong Liu[1(✉)], Kang Zhou[1], Jian Zhou[2],
and Guangbin Li[3]

[1] College of Mathematics and Computer Science, Wuhan Polytechnic University,
Wuhan 430023, China
[2] College of Food Science and Engineering, Wuhan Polytechnic University,
Wuhan 430023, China
[3] Enterprise School Joint Innovation Center, Qianjiang Jujin Rice Industry Co., Ltd.,
Hubei, China

Abstract. There are many raw materials for the production of rice wine, rice flour and glutinous rice products, It is one of the problems to be solved at present to select the appropriate proportion of raw materials for the production of these three products. In order to solve this problem, this paper finds out the specialized raw material index standard of the above three products through data analysis method and multi-objective optimization under the condition of meeting the various characteristic demands of the three products, so as to guide the production of enterprises. Based on the index data of three raw materials and products obtained from experimental tests, firstly, the data was standardized, and the noise of sample data was eliminated through residual analysis. Secondly, the optimal prediction equation was found by comparing various prediction methods, so as to make the formulation of raw materials more effective. Finally, a multi-objective optimization model is established. According to the contribution rate of the raw material index of the three products, the information entropy method is used to calculate the weight of the raw material index corresponding to the three products, so that the final solution of the specific raw material index range is more accurate, effective and reasonable.

Keywords: Specialized raw material · Residual analysis · Prediction equations · Multi-objective optimization model · Information entropy theory

1 Introduction

High quality raw materials are the basic conditions for the production of various high quality products. At present, glutinous rice, japonica rice and indica rice are the main raw materials used in the production of rice wine, rice flour and

L. Pan et al. (Eds.): BIC-TA 2020, CCIS 1363, pp. 117–150, 2021.
https://doi.org/10.1007/978-981-16-1354-8_11

glutinous rice products. Studies have shown that there is a certain relationship between the quality of yellow rice wine and the type of rice used as raw material [1], and the products produced with glutinous rice as raw material have the best quality. Xueqin Gao et al. [2] added glutinous rice flour to affect the quality of minced meat pie, and concluded that glutinous rice flour might be an effective functional ingredient of minced meat pie. Hongwei Wang et al. [3] added appropriate pre-gelatinized starch to improve the storage effect of dumplings, and then improved the texture and nutritional characteristics of tangyuan by complexing with polysaccharides. Li Chunhong et al. [4] studied the effects of different varieties of raw materials on the processing characteristics of corn, and concluded that different varieties of raw materials used in the production of products have great differences. Wang Jianguo [5] analyzed and studied the flavor of yellow rice wine, and found that in the brewing process of yellow rice wine, different technologies, different raw materials, and different proportions would also have different effects on the flavor quality of yellow rice wine. Enbo Xu et al. [6] concluded that the advantages of extrusion and enzymatic hydrolysis could be further reflected in Chinese rice wine products through fermentation and processing. Shuang Chen et al. [7] concluded that the sensory characteristics of the two yellow rice wines are different, mainly due to the large difference in the content of indicators such as benzaldehyde, vanillin, sotalone, geosmin and phenolic compounds. Gao Xiaoxu et al. [8,9] took the sensory quality of rice flour as the reference index, determined the rice raw material index affecting rice flour and obtained the optimal raw material index range of this index, which provided the basis for raw material selection in the production of rice flour. Li Lin et al. [10] combined the texture and sensory evaluation results of rice flour to select suitable rice raw materials for fresh and wet rice flour. Srikaeo et al. [11] concluded that gum could improve the texture and cooking quality of natural fermented dry powder. Fan Zhu [12] studied the effects of different wheat flour raw materials and additives, such as different baking powders, on steamed bread products, and concluded that the selection of appropriate yeast or yeast agent could improve the quality of steamed bread, while the protein composition of flour was crucial to the quality of flour. Bharathi Avula et al. [13] studied the chemical composition of red yeast produced by rice fermentation by adding different strains of Red yeast in aspergillus family, and concluded that adding different strains was closely related to the quality of red yeast produced. Sorada Yoenyong Buddhagal et al. [14] obtained that grinding methods affected the chemical composition and all physicochemical properties of flour. To sum up, different raw materials, additives and processing methods have a great impact on the quality of products. Therefore, it is extremely important to set specific raw material indexes and standards for different products. At present, most of the research of scholars mainly focuses on the prediction of product quality through raw material indicators. Zhang Biao et al. [15] used BP artificial neural network algorithm to predict the quality of dry products by using apple raw material index, providing a basis for the selection of dried apple specialized raw materials. Yang Bingnan et al. [16] predicted the characteristic indexes of potato raw material varieties through stepstep regression model. Wang Zhiming [17] achieved good results in regression prediction by using ridge regression and SVM in the modeling of quantitative structure-activity relationship between high-dimensional peptides and proteins. Huang Meiting [18] studied the correlation between the physical and chemical indexes and gelatinization characteristics of rice raw materials, and concluded that the glue consistency can be used to reflect the amylopectin content and gel performance of rice raw materials, which can be used as the main index for the selection of rice flour raw materials. Khakimov et al. [19] conducted fingerprint identification of the incoming raw materials and components through near-infrared spectroscopy, so as to select the appropriate raw materials. Jianyi Yang et al. [20] used the hierarchical protocol (I-TASSER) to predict protein structure and function using automatic prediction of protein structure and structure-based functional annotation. Secondly, in terms of food storage and processing, Gracheva et al. [21] use radiation technology to improve the storage and processing efficiency of food raw materials, increase the storage time of food raw materials, and meanwhile reduce the waste of resources. Gui-fang Deng et al. [22] used icP-MS to provide new information on the aluminum content of Processed food, raw materials and food additives in China. Ropodi et al. [23] concluded that rapid technology combined with data analysis method achieved good results in several foods with different sensors.

In different areas of research, By comparing the bacterial structure of seven different compost, Xueqin Wang et al. [24] determined the main environmental factors affecting the bacterial species, and concluded that the optimal range of carbon-nitrogen ratio in the environmental index was 14–27. Ghani et al. [25] predicted the selection of appropriate control variables in the process of fish landing through multiple stepstep regression method. Rahimi-ajdadi et al. [26] used artificial neural network to predict tractor fuel consumption, which was used to guide the selection of the best protection measures for agricultural equipment. Yanni Xuan et al. [27] used the improved IPAT model to predict China's steel output from 2010 to 2030. At the same time, improving the use of scrap steel will reduce the demand for natural resources and reduce the overall impact on the environment. Yang Xiujuan et al. [28] selected the optimal raw material through the grey correlation degree evaluation method in the selection of artificial feed for Leechi cattle. Yao Yisa et al. [29] could significantly reduce the content of soybean trypsin inhibitor and antigen protein that caused adverse reactions in animals through extrusion technology, so as to optimize the raw materials. Mingyang Chen et al. [30] obtained the optimal mix ratio of reactive powder concrete, which was used to guide the selection of appropriate raw materials and mix ratios under different strength values. Ya Wang et al. [31] studied the effect of thio-nickel ratio on the performance of NixSy electrocatalyst in raw materials. However, there is no research on using the data analysis method to predict the raw material index standard through the product index.

In order to solve the above problems, the index data of rice wine, rice flour and glutinous rice products as well as the corresponding raw material index data will be studied. According to the data characteristics of the above three products, the data is first standardized to eliminate the dimensionality between indexes, and the index data of the three products are preprocessed by using residual analysis method. Secondly, multiple stepwise regression, principal component regression, ridge regression and other classical prediction methods were used to predict the above three products respectively, and the prediction accuracy of the three products was compared to select the most appropriate prediction method, so as to make the prediction of the three products more accurate and effective. Finally, the standard model of specialized raw materials for three kinds of products is established, and the model is optimized by introducing diffusion factors and floating variables, and the weight of each index is solved by information entropy method. Then the optimal raw material index standard corresponding to the three kinds of products is solved, and the raw material index standard is obtained by anti-standardization treatment, and the standard has certain reference significance for processing enterprises.

2   Establishment and Optimization of the Standard Model of Three Kinds of Specialized Raw Materials

This chapter mainly introduces the solution model and model optimization of specialized raw material index standard. In order to solve the standard range of three kinds of product specific raw material index, firstly, it is necessary to establish the prediction model between the product and the raw material, secondly, to establish the objective model to constrain the raw material and product index, so as to make the solution result more reliable. Finally, the model needs to be optimized to improve the accuracy of the model, so that the range of raw material index solved can provide help for the production of enterprises. The multi-objective model is also introduced briefly, which is convenient for the author to use directly when calculating the standard range of three kinds of products in the following chapters.

2.1   The Model of Specialized Raw Material for Three Kinds of Products Was Established

The purpose of this section is to find out the more accurate range of raw material indicators, so that the products produced under the raw material must meet the standard. First of all, in order to find out the appropriate raw material index range, an optimization model needs to be established. Secondly, in order to find out the change range of the raw material index, it is necessary to restrict the range of the raw material index and the product index.

Establish constraints as follows:

$$x_{ij}^{\min} \leq x_{i1}, x_{i2}, \cdots, x_{ij} \leq x_{ij}^{\max}, i = 1, 2, \cdots, k \tag{1}$$

$$\begin{cases} y_1^{low} \leq y_1 = f(x_1, x_2, \cdots, x_\alpha) \leq y_1^{up} \\ y_2^{low} \leq y_2 = f(x_1, x_2, \cdots, x_\alpha) \leq y_2^{up} \\ \qquad \cdots\cdots\cdots \\ y_k^{low} \leq y_k = f(x_1, x_2, \cdots, x_\alpha) \leq y_k^{up} \end{cases} \tag{2}$$

Where, in Eq. (1) x_{ij} is the raw material index, Represents the j raw material index data corresponding to the i raw material index, $x_{ij}^{\min}$, $x_{ij}^{\max}$ respectively represent the minimum and maximum values of the data set corresponding to the first raw material index. In Eq. (2), $x_1, x_2, \cdots, x_\alpha$ is the raw material index, y_k is the index standard of the k product, y_k^{low} and y_k^{up} respectively represent the maximum and minimum values in the index range of the k product.

Objective function (3) needs to satisfy the constraint conditions of Eq. (1) and (2) above, so as to obtain a wide range of raw material quality index. Objective functions (4) and (5) also need to meet the constraints of Eqs. (1) and (2) above, and the maximum value of the raw material index range obtained by the final solution should not be greater than the maximum value of the raw material index, and the minimum value of the raw material index range obtained by the solution should not be less than the minimum value of the raw material index.

$$\max f_1 = \delta \tag{3}$$

$$\min \ f_2 = \sum_\alpha x_\alpha^{low}, \alpha = 1, 2, \cdots, k \tag{4}$$

$$\min \ f_3 = \sum_\alpha x_\alpha^{up}, \alpha = 1, 2, \cdots, k \tag{5}$$

Where δ represents the index range of raw material quality, namely the diffusion factor, x_α^{low} and x_α^{up} respectively represent the minimum and maximum values of the n index standard that is finally solved.

According to the above Eqs. (1), (2), (3), (4) and (5), the multi-objective optimization model can be obtained as follows:

$$
\begin{aligned}
&P1 \quad \max f_1 = \delta \\
&P2 \quad \min \ f_2 = \sum_\alpha x_\alpha^{low}, \max \ f_3 = \sum_\alpha x_\alpha^{up} \ \ \alpha = 1, 2, \cdots, k \\
&s.t. \ \begin{cases} y_m^{low} \le y_m = f(x_1, x_2, ..., x_n) \le y_m^{up} & m = 1, 2, \cdots, k \\ x_{ij}^{low} \le x_\alpha^{low}, x_\alpha^{up} \le x_{ij}^{up} & \alpha = 1, 2, ..., n \\ x_\alpha^{low} + \delta \le x_\alpha^{up} \end{cases} \quad (A)
\end{aligned}
$$

2.2 Optimize the Raw Material Model for Three Kinds of Products

After the model is established, the above multi-objective model is firstly solved. In this paper, linear weighting method is mainly used to transform multi-objective into single objective. There are many ways to solve the weight. Since the information entropy method calculates the weight according to the relationship between the data of each index and can fully reflect the difference between the data, this paper will use the information entropy method to solve the weight of each index.

$$max \left\{ \beta\delta + \sum_\alpha^m \left[\beta_\alpha * (x_\alpha^{up} - x_\alpha^{low}) \right] \right\} \tag{6}$$

where β_α is the weight of each indicator, and β is the weight of diffusion factor.

The calculation of information entropy weight is divided into the following four steps:

1) First, according to the data characteristics of the three products in this paper, the original data are non-negated and normalized, so that the value of the three products is between 1–2. Suppose there are m raw material indexes and n samples, then x_{ij} is the value of the j sample of the i raw material indexes.

$$y_{ij} = \frac{x_{ij} - \min x_j}{\max x_j - \min x_j} + 1 \quad i = 1, 2, \ldots, n; j = 1, 2, \ldots, m \tag{7}$$

where $\max x_j$ and $\min x_j$ respectively represent the maximum and minimum values of column j of the data set.

2) Calculating entropy. The entropy of the i index is:

$$H_i = -\frac{1}{\ln n} \sum_{j=1}^{n} a_{ij} \ln a_{ij} \tag{8}$$

$$a_{ij} = \frac{x_{ij}}{\sum\limits_{j=1}^{n} x_{ij}}, i = 1, 2, \cdots, m \quad j = 1, 2, \cdots, n \tag{9}$$

3) Calculate information entropy redundancy.

$$D_i = 1 - H_i, \quad i = 1, 2, \cdots, m \tag{10}$$

4) Calculate the weight of each product index.

$$w_i = \frac{D_i}{\sum\limits_{i=1}^{m} D_i}, \quad i = 1, 2, \cdots, m \tag{11}$$

Finally, the diffusion factor constraint $x_\alpha^{low} + \delta \leq x_\alpha^{up}$ solved by the above multi-objective optimization model (A) is adjusted, change it to $x_\alpha^{low} + \delta_0 * (1 - \rho) + \beta_\alpha * \gamma \leq x_\alpha^{up}$, Where ρ is the "relaxation factor", which reduces the obtained diffusion factor and can be adjusted and changed. γ is the "floating variable", which is used to control the final solution of each index to float according to the discrete characteristics of each quality index of actual raw materials, so as to obtain different solution ranges. According to the above adjustment, the final multi-objective optimization model is as follows:

$$
\begin{aligned}
&P1 \quad \max f_1 = r \\
&P2 \quad \min f_2 = \sum_\alpha x_\alpha^{low}, \max f_3 = \sum_\alpha x_\alpha^{up} \quad \alpha = 1, 2, \cdots, n \\
&s.t. \quad \begin{cases} y_m^{low} \leq y_m = f(x_1, x_2, ..., x_n) \leq y_m^{up} \quad m = 1, 2, \cdots, k \\ x_{ij}^{low} \leq x_\alpha^{low}, x_\alpha^{up} \leq x_{ij}^{up} \\ x_\alpha^{low} + \delta_o * (1 - \rho) + \beta_\alpha * r \leq x_\alpha^{up} \end{cases}
\end{aligned} \tag{B}
$$

Again, the linear weighting method is used to solve the problem, and the multi-objective is converted into a single objective.

$$\max\left\{\beta\delta + \sum_{\alpha}^{m}\left[\beta_{\alpha} * (x_{\alpha}^{up} - x_{\alpha}^{low})\right]\right\} \tag{12}$$

Finally, the final results obtained by the above multi-objective optimization model are de-normalized. The anti-standardization formula is as follows:

$$\overline{x_i^{low}} = x_{\alpha}^{low} * \sigma_i + \overline{x_i} \tag{13}$$

$$\overline{x_i^{up}} = x_{\alpha}^{up} * \sigma_i + \overline{x_i} \tag{14}$$

Where x_{α}^{low} and x_{α}^{up} are the results solved by the above optimization model, σ_i is the standard deviation, $\overline{x_i}$ is the mean value, i is the number of raw material quality indexes, and the optimization range of each raw material index is obtained $[\overline{x^{low}}, \overline{x^{up}}]$, $\overline{x^{low}} = (x_1^{low}, x_2^{low}, \cdots, x_k^{low})$, $\overline{x^{up}} = (x_1^{up}, x_2^{up}, \cdots, x_k^{up})$.

3 Improvement of Quality Standard Method for Three Kinds of Specialized Raw Materials

This chapter mainly improves the prediction model in the specialized raw material index standard. By comparing the three regression prediction methods, the optimal prediction model was obtained. The standard model of specialized raw materials introduced in the second chapter is applied to rice wine, rice flour and glutinous rice products.

3.1 The Residual Analysis Method Preprocesses the Data

The quality of data itself has an important influence on the formulation of standards for specialized raw materials, the data quality will cause obvious difference to the final result of this standard, As a result, the standard is not accurate. Data entry errors and non-standardized data can affect the quality of the data itself. In the process of data entry, it is hard to avoid errors in the data entry caused by errors. Before analyzing the data, the inspectors are also required to check the data and correct the data with logical errors to further ensure the quality of the data. The data source used in this paper is a targeted experiment designed according to the indicator set with the national standard method, after measurement, the high-dimensional sample sets for the three product indexes are obtained. It is necessary to preprocess the index data of three kinds of products to ensure the reliability of the index data of products and avoid other interference. In this paper, the residual analysis method is mainly used to preprocess the data and eliminate the abnormal data. Abnormal data refers to the data with a few sample values in the data set of three product indicators that are significantly inconsistent with the rest of the data. For the test of abnormal data, according to the data characteristics of the three products, this paper will combine the residual analysis method of boxplot and residual graph to remove the abnormal sample data, improve the data quality, and make the results obtained by using the data analysis method more reliable. For the boxplot, you need to know the minimum, lower quartile, median, upper quartile, and maximum values of the sample data. The names and locations of the various components of the boxplot are shown in Fig. 1 below:

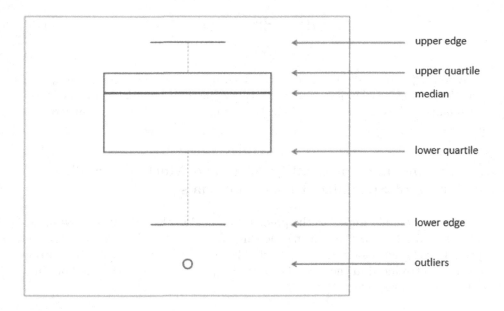

Fig. 1. Box plots.

Quartile refers to the statistics in which all the values are first sorted according to the law from small to large, and then the values are divided into four equal parts. The values at the three segmentation points are the quartiles. Assuming that there are 100 values in the sorted order, the values in the 25th, 50th, and 75th positions are quartile, the values in the 25th position are upper quartile, and the values in the 75th position are lower quartile.

As shown in Fig. 2 below, For the regression method involved in this paper, the data will be outliers processed using the residual graph. Whether a regression model satisfies the hypothesis is mainly seen in the following two points:

1) As shown in the 2 residual figure above, try to satisfy that all the residual areas pass through 0, and the data that does not pass through 0 are outliers, which should be removed.

2) The residuals should all fall in the belt with small residuals to ensure the accuracy of the regression model.

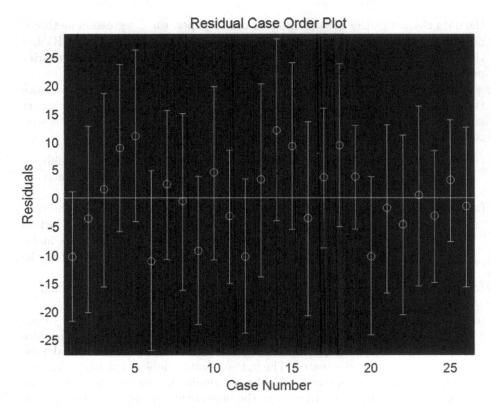

Fig. 2. Residual plots.

According to the boxplot, some abnormal data can be obtained, but this part of data may be normal in the whole product index. Therefore, this paper will combine the residual graph to remove the abnormal data. Combining the two kinds of abnormal data will improve the accuracy of the following regression prediction.

3.2 Comparison and Analysis of Three Forecasting Methods of Product Index

In the actual modeling, there is often a correlation between variables, that is, the variables may have multicollinearity, resulting in the deviation of the prediction results. The reasons for multicollinearity are mainly as follows: first, the variables are highly correlated, resulting in the instability of the estimated regression parameters; Second, the data for analysis is small sample data, that is, the number of variables is greater than the sample content. For testing multicollinearity between small sample data, it is usually based on the variance inflation factor (VIF) method proposed by Chatterjee et al. [5] in 1977. Where $VIF \geq 5$ or $VIF \geq 10$ indicates that there is multicollinearity between independent variables, and the larger VIF is, the stronger the multicollinearity is. According to the data characteristics of small samples in this paper, three regression methods, namely multiple stepwise regression, principal component regression (PCR) and ridge regression (RR), can be used to deal with the possible multicollinearity problems of small samples.

Among them, the idea of multiple gradual regression is: In order to improve the accuracy of prediction and select the optimal model, appropriate indexes are added to the regression model from the original index variables. The stepwise regression process is as follows:

(a) Under the given selection criteria, the variable with the most significant influence on the dependent variable y is selected from all independent variables $\{x_1, x_2, \cdots, x_k\}$ to establish the model.

(b) Every time a variable is selected or eliminated, it is necessary to test the variables in and out of the model, and to reconsider the elimination or selection of variables that are lower than the exclusion criteria or meet the inclusion criteria, so as to ensure that significance variables are included in the regression equation before each introduction of variables.

(c) Repeat step (b) until no variables in the equation can be eliminated and no variables outside the equation can be introduced.

(d) The correlation coefficient matrix between variables can be used to see whether there is a correlation between variables. Highly correlated variables are compared and independent variables that have little influence on dependent variables are eliminated. The independent variables that have a greater influence on the dependent variables are retained. The explanations of the excluded independent variables to the dependent variables are assumed by other independent variables highly related to them, in order to eliminate the multicollinearity problem and then the regression equation obtained is the optimal regression equation.

The idea of principal component regression (PCR) is: by reducing the dimension of the data, the original indicators are reduced, and the relevant indicators are recombined. Finally, a new set of completely unrelated indicators is obtained, and these comprehensive indicators are used to replace the previous numerous indicators. Finally, comprehensive indicators are used as independent variables for regression. For the principal component selection problem, the first principal component F1 should be the value with the largest variance. If the first principal component is insufficient to represent the information of the original P variables, then F2, the second linear combination, should be selected. In order to effectively reflect the original information, the information in F1 does not need to appear in F2 again. The mathematical expression is as follows:

$$\text{cov}(F_1, F_2) = 0 \tag{15}$$

Enter sample set $X = \{x_1, x_2, \ldots, x_m\}$, principal component regression can be calculated according to the following steps:

(1) Calculate the correlation coefficient matrix $R = XX^T$ of the original variables.

(2) Calculate the eigenvalues of correlation coefficient matrix R, and arrange them in order from large to small, denoted as:

$$\lambda_1 \geq \lambda_2 \geq \ldots \geq \lambda_p \tag{16}$$

(3) The eigenvectors corresponding to the eigenvalues are calculated, and the eigenvectors corresponding to the first eigenvalues are formed.

$$W = \{w1, w2, \ldots, wpl\} \tag{17}$$

(4) According to the cumulative contribution rate of principal component, the number of principal component is determined to make the cumulative contribution rate >85%. For the k principal component, the contribution rate of the other side difference is:

$$\frac{\lambda k}{\sum\limits_{i=1}^{p} \lambda i} \tag{18}$$

(5) With the selection of principal components, the cumulative contribution reaches a high percentage (80%–90%). In this case, the principal components F1, F2, F3 and F4 are used to replace the raw material indicators, so as to achieve the purpose of dimensionality reduction, while the loss of information is not much.

(6) Finally, F1, F2, F3 and F4 obtained by principal component analysis were used as independent variables for regression with product indexes.

The idea of ridge regression (RR) is: a data analysis regression method to solve the problem of multicollinearity between raw material indexes is an improved version of least square method. By discarding the unbiased method of least square method, discarding part of the information at the cost of reducing accuracy, a more practical and reliable regression method can be obtained.

All the above three regression forecasting methods can eliminate the multi-collinearity between independent variables, among which the advantage of multiple stepwise regression lies in that the most significant raw material index is selected as the dependent variable y_1 as the most significant raw material index combination such as $\{x_1, x_2, x_6\}$ or $\{x_1, x_2, x_7\}$, the independent variable of the regression equation.

Principal component regression combines multiple raw material indicators or independent variables into one. The raw material index of ridge regression is still the original raw material index, and some useless information is discarded. According to the above three regression prediction methods, And combined with the data characteristics of rice wine, rice flour and glutinous rice products, the significance of R square and prediction equation was taken as the basis, the most appropriate regression method was selected to solve the index standard of specialized raw materials for three kinds of products by comparing the above three regression methods.

4   Simulation Application of Three Kinds of Specialized Raw Material Model

According to the above three product data analysis methods, combined with the characteristics of the data and the theory of multi-objective optimization model, this paper takes solving the special raw material index standard of three products as an example to carry out the application of the model. The data source of the simulation object is a targeted experiment designed according to the index set by adopting the national standard method. After measurement, the high-dimensional sample set about the index of yellow rice wine is obtained.

4.1   The Standard Forecasting Model of Three Kinds of Specialized Raw Materials is Solved

In this paper, rice wine, rice, glutinous rice products, for example, by residual analysis to remove samples of abnormal value, and then compare the multiple stepwise regression, ridge regression, principal component regression three forecasting methods, select the most appropriate method for the above three kinds of standard products specialty materials indicators, improve forecasting precision of the product.

The Standard Forecasting Model of the Index of Specialized Yellow Rice Wine Raw Materials. In this paper, the data of three kinds of products were collected according to the experiment. The first set is a 32-piece sample set of yellow rice wine. According to its characteristics, the following data were analyzed using SPSS 24.0 software. Table 1 is the sample set of actual measured raw materials of yellow rice wine, Table 2 is the indicator sample set of yellow rice wine products.

Step 1: Clean the data of the initial sample set of glutinous rice raw materials and yellow rice wine products measured above. The method of combining boxplot and residual plot introduced in the third chapter is used to eliminate abnormal

Table 1. Sample set of yellow rice wine raw materials.

Number	Indicators of rice wine raw materials								
	Rice	Protein moisture	Fat	Crude	Amylose starch	Lowest	Pad viscosity	Setback value	Gelatinization point
1	11.52	9.1114	0.893	38.27	2.52	1847.67	670.67	271.67	82.43
2	13.35	8.5145	0.952	39.54	2.47	924.33	659.67	197.33	70.97
3	12.46	7.8507	0.777	41.13	3.1	1356	1176	365.33	80.52
					......				
30	13.95	6.2	1.254	35.86	23.4	1824	860	1161	69.15
31	12.52	7.66	1.278	40.34	20	1956.5	1807	1549	87.5
32	13.43	7.35	0.896	34.76	19.9	1799	1157.5	1493.5	87.025

Table 2. Sample set of yellow rice wine products.

Number	Indicators of yellow rice wine products						
	Total sugar	PH	Total acid	CaO	Alcohol	Non-sugar solids	Total score
1	18.4	3.71	4.01	0.17	5.65	114.16	75
2	74.75	3.62	3.26	0.59	10.6	175.28	78
3	59.25	3.63	3.55	0.31	8.9	135.32	58
			......				
30	56.65	3.69	3.96	0.14	9.4	210.08	80
31	45.47	3.69	4.46	0.1	8.4	112.12	54
32	47.66	3.73	4.1	0.41	8.45	178.48	63

Table 3. Correlation between rice wine raw materials and products.

	Total sugar	PH	Total acid	CaO	Alcohol	Non-sugar solids	Total score
Rice moisture	−0.426	0.493	0.233	−0.143	−0.424	−0.195	−0.425
Protein	−0.374	0.335	0.16	−0.027	−0.377	−0.332	−0.431
Fat	−0.46	0.543	0.343	−0.554	−0.494	−0.012	−0.444
Crude starch	−0.012	−0.398	0.196	0.16	−0.115	−0.225	0.255
Amylose	−0.052	0	−0.021	−0.061	0.162	0.188	−0.026
Lowest viscosity	0.5	−0.354	−0.436	0.221	0.588	0.417	0.306
Pad value	0.184	−0.354	0.11	−0.289	0.266	−0.189	0.248
Setback	0	−0.021	−0.04	−0.003	0.186	0.133	−0.063

data. A total of 6 yellow rice wine sample data were deleted. Secondly, correlation analysis was carried out between glutinous rice materials and product indexes.

In this paper, Pearson correlation coefficient is mainly used to measure the correlation degree between the indexes of yellow rice wine raw materials and the indexes of products. The values in Table 3 are closer to −1, which indicates a stronger negative correlation, closer to 0, which indicates no correlation, and closer to 1, which indicates a stronger positive correlation. The correlation coefficient can be calculated by the following formula.

$$\rho_{X,Y} = \frac{\text{cov}(X,Y)}{\sigma_X \sigma_Y} \tag{19}$$

X is the raw material index, Y is the product index. $\text{cov}(X,Y)$ is the covariance between rice wine raw materials and products, σ_X and σ_Y are the standard deviations of rice wine raw materials and products respectively.

Step 2: Conduct standardized processing based on the data obtained in Step 1 to obtain standardized data samples. The calculation formula is as follows:

$$x_{ij} = \frac{x_{ij} - \bar{x}_i}{\sigma_{xi}}, y_{ij} = \frac{y_{ij} - \bar{y}_i}{\sigma_{yi}} \quad i = 1, 2, \cdots, m \quad j = 1, 2, \cdots, n \qquad (20)$$

Where x_{ij} is the raw material sample data set, $\bar{x}_i = \frac{\sum_{j=1}^{n} x_{ij}}{n}$ is the raw material sample mean, and $\sigma_{xi} = \sqrt{\sum_{j=1}^{n} (x_{ij} - \bar{x}_i)/n}$ is the raw material sample standard deviation. Similarly, y_{ij}, $\bar{y}_i = \frac{\sum_{j=1}^{n} y_{ij}}{n}$ and $\sigma_{yi} = \sqrt{\sum_{j=1}^{n} (y_{ij} - \bar{y}_i)/n}$ are respectively the data set, mean value and standard deviation of yellow rice wine products sample.

Step 3: Perform multicollinearity analysis on the data samples obtained after standardization, the results are shown in Table 4 for the multicollinearity diagnosis of yellow rice wine:

Table 4. Multicollinearity diagnosis of rice wine.

Model	Tolerance	VIF
Rice moisture	0.466	2.148
Protein	0.372	2.687
Fat	0.899	1.113
Crude starch	0.575	1.74
Amylose	0.083	11.991
Lowest viscosity	0.243	4.116
Pad value	0.613	1.632
Setback	0.074	13.553

The two indexes of amylose and VIF of reappreciation are all greater than 10, which proves the existence of multicollinearity among the data samples.

Step 4: According to the above analysis, multiple stepwise regression, principal component regression and ridge regression can be used to eliminate the multicollinearity among data. Therefore, this paper will carry out multiple stepwise regression, principal component regression, ridge regression, etc. on the data of yellow rice wine respectively, and select the optimal regression method to predict yellow rice wine products. And obtained the above three regression Model R^2 line diagram, as shown in Fig. 3 below.

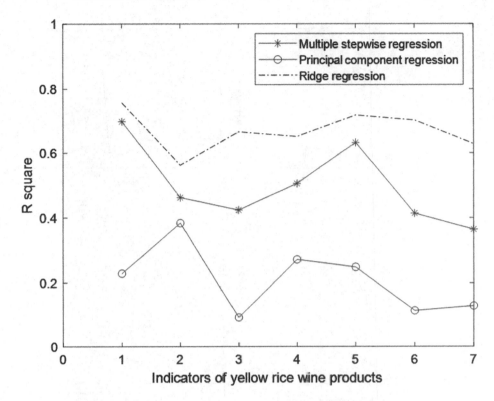

Fig. 3. Broken line chart of three regression R-square models of yellow rice wine.

The R square in the figure above reflects the interpretation rate of the regression prediction model to the sample data. Its value varies from 0 to 1, generally above 0.5, indicating that the regression model obtained by training has a good regression effect. According to Fig. 3, it can be concluded that R square, which is used to predict rice wine products with ridge regression, generally has a higher prediction accuracy than the other two regression models. Therefore, ridge regression is used to predict rice wine products in this paper.

Step 5: After the optimal regression model is selected, the software SPSS24.0 is used to solve it, and the results are as follows.

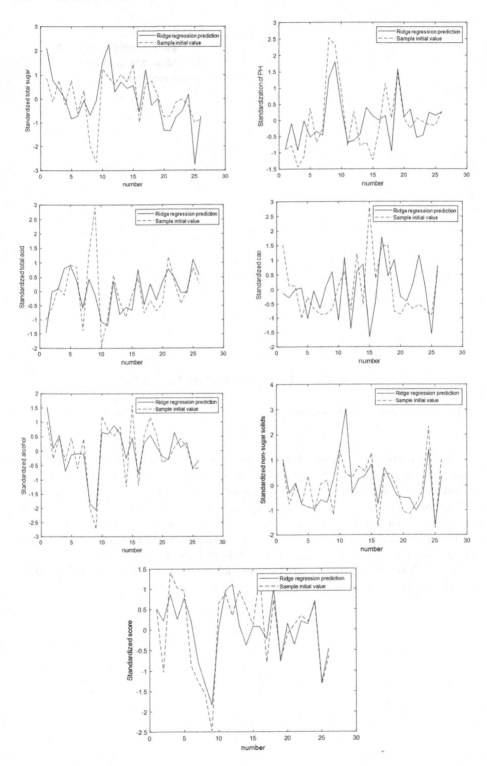

Fig. 4. Broken line chart of predicted value and actual value of yellow rice wine product.

Table 5. Sample set of rice flour ingredients.

Number	Indicators of rice flour raw material										
	Moisture	Starch content	Amylose content	Gel consistency	Protein content	Fat	Fatty acid value	Water soluble	Swelling force	The final viscosity	Gelatinization temperature
1	13.01	72.8	11.3	70	7.74	0.61	50.82	3.7	7.7	2619	81.9
2	14.35	71.7	12.2	72	7.05	0.77	35.89	3.15	8.24	3401.5	85.05
3	12	70.53	12.3	46.5	8.55	1.31	198.71	3.72	8.53	2793.5	78.28
					......						
15	11.95	69.43	24.6	24	8.03	1.33	72.82	4.21	7.37	3963	91.88
16	12.58	73.61	19.8	61	8.39	1.06	53.14	3.32	8.33	3365	81.93
17	11.3	72.67	24.8	48	7.88	0.96	65.33	4.24	8.34	2858	82.23

$$
\begin{cases}
y_1 = -0.2204x_1 - 0.2442x_2 - 0.3362x_3 - 0.3079x_4 - 0.4211x_5 \\
\quad +0.6846x_6 - 0.7884x_7 - 0.3631x_8 - 0.1565x_9 \\
y_2 = 0.2303x_1 + 0.0145x_2 + 0.4197x_3 - 0.1968x_4 - 0.2905x_5 \\
\quad -0.3245x_6 - 0.2201x_7 + 0.5558x_8 + 0.0943x_9 \\
y_3 = -0.1231x_1 - 0.0535x_2 - 0.0081x_3 + 0.0629x_4 + 0.3072x_5 \\
\quad -0.8498x_6 + 0.3777x_7 + 0.2971x_8 + 0.0591x_9 \\
y_4 = 0.9609x_1 - 0.3057x_2 - 0.4703x_3 - 0.0768x_4 + 0.1474x_5 \\
\quad +0.3493x_6 - 0.4372x_7 - 0.5059x_8 + 0.4787x_9 \\
y_5 = -0.3259x_1 + 0.0511x_2 - 0.3282x_3 - 0.2788x_4 - 0.0804x_5 \\
\quad +0.7673x_6 + 0.0826x_7 - 0.3485x_8 - 0.3650x_9 \\
y_6 = -0.1519x_1 - 0.8013x_2 - 0.0342x_3 - 0.3886x_4 + 0.6892x_5 \\
\quad +0.3302x_6 - 0.7705x_7 - 1.2108x_8 + 0.5124x_9 \\
y_7 = -0.4408x_1 - 0.4905x_2 - 0.4237x_3 - 0.2926x_4 + 0.9116x_5 \\
\quad +0.0350x_6 + 0.1094x_7 - 1.3631x_8 - 0.0223x_9
\end{cases} \tag{21}
$$

Figure 4 shows the line diagram of the ridge regression model for the predicted values and the standardized values of the original data of 7 yellow rice wine products.

According to Fig. 4, the predicted value obtained by ridge regression was close to the actual value, which further verified that ridge regression was suitable for the prediction of yellow rice wine products, and laid a good foundation for the solution of the index standard of special raw materials for yellow rice wine below.

Standard Forecasting Model of Rice Flour Specialized Raw Material Index. The second set of 17 sample sets of rice noodles were analyzed with the following data, using SPSS 24.0 software. Table 5 is the indicator sample set of the actual measured initial rice flour raw materials, and Table 6 is the indicator sample set of rice flour products.

Step 1: Process step 1 the same as step 1 of yellow rice wine. Firstly, the data of the initial rice flour raw materials and the index sample set of rice flour products measured above were cleaned up, and the data of article 4 and

Table 6. Sample set of rice flour products.

Number	Indicators of rice flour products					
	Taste the total score	Cooking loss	Rehydration time	Taste	Moisture	Natural breakage rate
1	32.8	8.87	22.75	5.4	12.3	17.54
2	30.8	9.58	24.15	5.1	11.9	17.3
3	41	4.2	26.3	6.3	12.5	24.22
			......			
15	39.9	3.07	28.5	6.1	12.9	9.93
16	33.9	5.29	30.75	5.7	13.1	16.21
17	38.8	6.81	31.25	6.4	11.8	11.69

Table 7. Multicollinearity diagnosis of rice flour.

Model	The eigenvalue	Conditional indicator
Moisture	3.525	1.000
Starch content	2.233	1.256
Amylose content	1.589	1.490
Gel consistency	1.187	1.724
Protein contente	1.000	1.878
Fat content	0.771	2.138
Fatty acid value	0.599	2.426
Water soluble	0.448	2.806
Swelling force	0.318	3.329
The final viscosity	0.216	4.042
Gelatinization temperature	0.089	6.294
Total score of taste	0.026	11.716

article 17 of the rice flour samples were deleted in total. Secondly, the data were standardized to eliminate dimensionality. Finally, the correlation analysis was carried out on the processed rice flour raw materials and product data.

Step 2: Multicollinearity analysis was performed on the data samples obtained after standardization, and the results were shown in Table 7 for the multicollinearity diagnosis of rice flour:

Step 3: Like rice wine, compare the three regression prediction methods and select the best regression method for rice noodle prediction. Line diagrams of three regression R square models of rice flour are obtained, as shown in Fig. 5 below: VIF is greater than 10, proving the existence of multicollinearity among data samples.

It can be seen from the figure above that although R square of ridge regression is better than multivariate stepwise regression in predicting the rehydration time, it is obviously not as good as multivariate stepwise regression in other indicators, and the significance of multivariate stepwise regression is also better than that of ridge regression. Therefore, rice noodles will use multiple stepwise regression for prediction. Matlab software was used to solve the problem, and the results were as follows:

$$\begin{cases} y_1 = -0.575531x_1 - 0.657025x_4 - 0.342976x_6 \\ \quad +0.306272x_7 - 0.381385x_8 \\ y_2 = 0.522997x_1 - 0.312214x_2 + 0.417285x_4 + 0.298353x_6 \\ \quad -0.855269x_7 + 0.876483x_8 - 0.666966x_{11} \\ y_3 = 0.838026x_3 \\ y_4 = -1.06618x_1 - 0.426554x_2 - 0.64822x_5 - 0.436612x_6 \\ \quad +0.742512x_8 + 0.840577x_9 + 0.669782x_{10} - 0.458376x_{11} \\ y_5 = 0.611828x_2 - 0.587119x_4 + 0.806832x_5 \\ \quad -0.51783x_6 + 0.744066x_{11} \\ y_6 = -0.422137x_2 - 0.327122x_5 + 0.3476x_6 + 0.174812x_7 \\ \quad -0.328412x_8 - 0.567842x_{11} \end{cases} \quad (22)$$

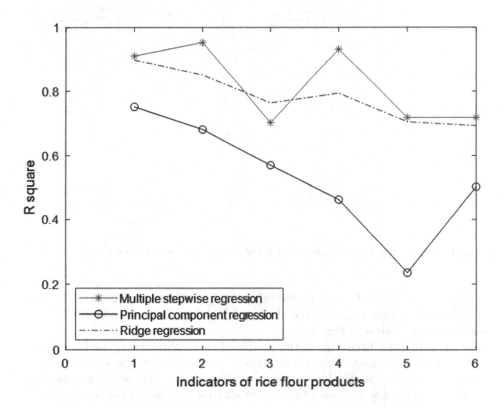

Fig. 5. Broken line chart of three regression R-square models of rice flour.

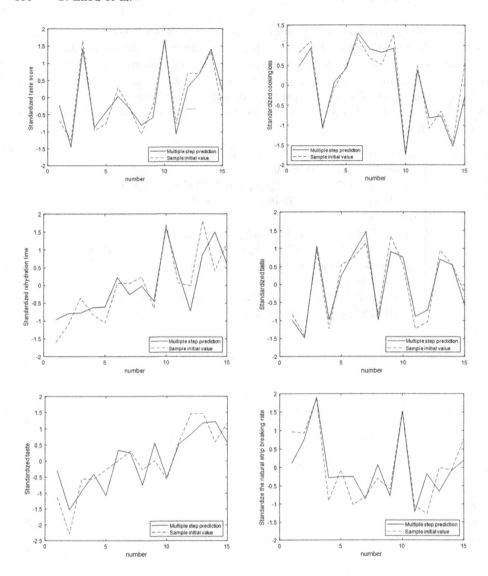

Fig. 6. Broken line chart of predicted value and actual value of rice flour product.

The line diagram of the predicted value of the multivariate stepwise regression model and the standardized value of the original data for six rice flour products was drawn, as shown in Fig. 6.

As can be seen from Fig. 6, the predicted value obtained by multiple stepwise regression is close to the actual value, which further verifies that multiple stepwise regression is suitable for the prediction of rice flour products, and lays a foundation for the solution of the index standard of special raw materials for rice flour below.

Table 8. Sample set of glutinous rice raw materials.

Number	Indicators of glutinous rice raw material							
	Peak viscosity	Breakdown viscosity	Moisture	Amylose content	Protein content	Setback	Gelatinization temperature	Viscosity
1	1571.333	445.333	12.278	1.989	7.14	226	73.917	763.795
2	2518.333	670.667	11.515	2.519	8.062	271.66	82.433	802.125
3	2785.333	1077.667	11.773	2.837	6.515	392.333	78.183	553.18
			......					
20	1101.667	555.333	15.121	2.932	7.408	170.667	72.283	676.469
21	959.667	290	14.994	0.904	7.557	176.667	77.65	372.124
22	1197.667	589.667	14.518	2.957	7.943	180.667	72.3	1163.802

Table 9. Sample set of glutinous rice products.

Number	Indicators of glutinous rice products						
	Adhesiveness	Elasticity	Hardness	Cohesion	Sticky	Chewiness	Resilience
1	−4996.697	0.675	1431.627	0.547	763.795	517.522	0.313
2	−2497.218	0.837	1180.033	0.697	802.125	666.852	0.144
3	−1163.346	0.447	952.677	0.58	553.18	240.516	0.198
			......				
20	−4957.446	0.356	1509.755	0.446	676.469	240.952	0.239
21	−3111.187	0.404	822.904	0.441	372.124	144.88	0.159
22	−3059.268	0.412	1687.199	0.688	1163.802	482.547	0.201

Table 10. Multicollinearity diagnosis of glutinous rice products.

Model	The eigenvalue	Conditional indicator
Peak viscosity	3.801	1.000
Breakdown viscosity	1.840	1.437
Moisture	1.581	1.550
Amylose content	1.002	1.948
Protein contente	0.407	3.058
Setback	0.188	4.501
Gelatinization temperature	0.134	5.329
Viscosity	0.044	9.338
Elasticity	0.004	31.480

Standard Prediction Model of Specialized Raw Materials for Glutinous Rice Products. The third set of 22 samples of glutinous rice products were collected, and the following data were analyzed according to their data characteristics. The software used was SPSS 24.0. Table 8 is the sample set of the actual measured initial glutinous rice raw materials, and Table 9 is the sample set of the indicators of glutinous rice products.

Step 1: Process step 1 the same as step 1 of yellow rice wine. First of all the above measured initial rice raw materials and rice noodles products by data cleaning sample set, a total of deletes data rice flour samples 3, 5, 10 and so on three samples, the second to standardize data processing, eliminate dimension, finally, the rice vermicelli raw material and products after processing the data correlation analysis, concluded that index of raw material viscosity will directly affect the viscous products indicators.

Step 2: Multicollinearity analysis was performed on the data samples obtained after standardization, and the results were shown in Table 10 for multicollinearity diagnosis of rice flour:

VIF is greater than 10, proving the existence of multicollinearity among data samples.

Step 3: Like rice wine, compare the following three regression prediction methods, and select the best regression method for the prediction of glutinous rice products. Three regression models of glutinous rice products, r square line diagrams, are obtained, as shown in Fig. 7 below:

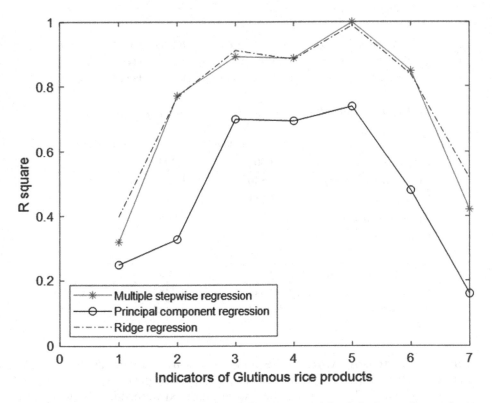

Fig. 7. Broken line chart of three regression R-square models of glutinous rice products.

According to Fig. 7, it can be concluded that the general accuracy of R square used by using ridge regression and multiple stepwise regression for predicting glutinous rice products is similar. However, as far as the first glutinous rice index and the seventh glutinous rice index are relevant, ridge regression is more effective than multiple stepwise regression in predicting glutinous rice products. Therefore, ridge regression is used to predict glutinous rice products. SPSS 24.0 software was used to solve the problem, and the result is Eq. 23.

$$
\begin{cases}
y_1 = -0.0027x_1 + 0.6078x_2 - 0.1712x_3 - 0.1307x_4 - 0.0917x_5 \\
\qquad -0.2567x_6 + 0.0662x_7 - 0.0165x_8 \\
y_2 = -0.0204x_1 + 0.3075x_2 - 0.8217x_3 + 0.1692x_4 + 0.0753x_5 \\
\qquad -0.4793x_6 + 0.2259x_7 - 0.1468x_8 \\
y_3 = -0.1641x_1 - 0.3229x_2 - 0.0737x_3 + 0.1685x_4 - 0.1541x_5 \\
\qquad -0.1904x_6 - 0.1501x_7 + 0.5768x_8 \\
y_4 = 0.3993x_1 + 0.4342x_2 + 0.0013x_3 - 0.0202x_4 + 0.1917x_5 \\
\qquad +0.1334x_6 - 0.0330x_7 + 0.4718x_8 \\
y_5 = 0.0271x_1 - 0.0136x_2 - 0.0108x_3 + 0.0590x_4 - 0.0101x_5 \\
\qquad -0.0393x_6 - 0.0506x_7 + 0.8582x_8 \\
y_6 = 0.0886x_1 + 0.2607x_2 - 0.5613x_3 + 0.1357x_4 + 0.0890x_5 \\
\qquad -0.4989x_6 + 0.1267x_7 + 0.5302x_8 \\
y_7 = -0.2606x_1 - 0.4437x_2 - 0.4005x_3 + 0.2323x_4 - 0.1915x_5 \\
\qquad +0.4057x_6 - 0.3427x_7 - 0.3345x_8
\end{cases} \tag{23}
$$

Figure 8 shows the line graph of the predicted value and the standardized value of the original data drawn by the ridge regression model of seven glutinous rice products. It can be seen from Fig. 8 that the predicted value obtained by ridge regression is close to the actual value, which further verifies that ridge regression is suitable for the prediction of glutinous rice products, and lays a foundation for the solution of the following index standard of special raw materials for glutinous rice products.

4.2 The Standard Optimization Model of Three Kinds of Specialized Raw Materials Is Solved

This section is mainly about the prediction model based on the optimization model in Sect. 2 and combined with the above three products. The index standard of specialized raw materials for rice wine, rice flour and glutinous rice products was solved, and the more suitable raw material ratio of the above three products was obtained.

To Solve the Standard Optimization Model of the Index of Specialized Rice Wine Raw Materials. The solution of the index standard of specialized raw materials for yellow rice wine can be divided into three steps. The specific implementation steps are as follows:

Step 1: Determine the lower and upper bounds of the quality indexes of rice wine raw materials, Use the expression as $x^{low} = [x_1^{low}, x_2^{low}, \cdots, x_8^{low}, x_9^{low}]; x^{up} = [x_1^{up}, x_2^{up}, \cdots, x_8^{up}, x_9^{up}]$.

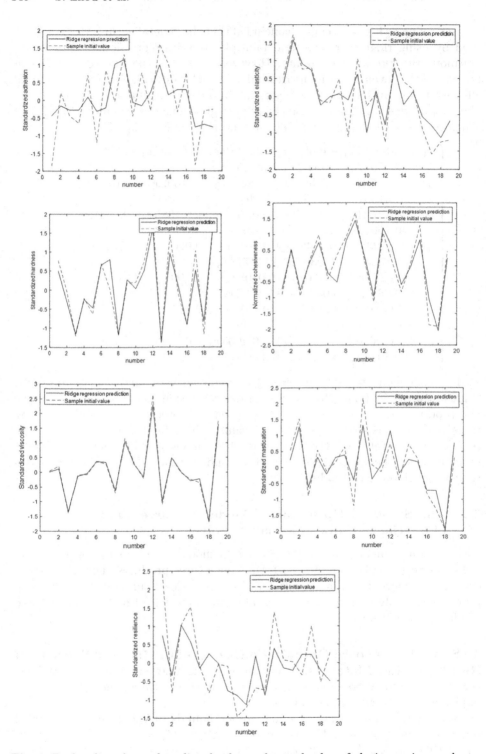

Fig. 8. Broken line chart of predicted value and actual value of glutinous rice product.

Table 11. Multicollinearity diagnosis of glutinous rice products.

α	Rice moisture	Protein	Fat	Crude starch	Amylose	Lowest viscosity	Pad value	Setback	Gelatinization point
l_α	−1.70541	−1.99916	−1.38876	−3.83344	−0.9143	−2.08311	−2.03823	−1.00092	−1.26824
u_α	1.95222	1.78484	1.74782	2.33644	2.04714	1.23952	2.09488	2.14277	2.19887

Table 12. The limit of yellow rice wine products restricts the upper and lower bounds.

k	Total sugar	PH	Total acid	CaO	Alcohol	Non-sugar solids	Total score
L_k	−2.65624	−1.43394	−1.91465	−1.01597	−2.72084	−1.71911	−2.47389
U_k	1.451	2.53	2.90979	2.80728	1.579	2.32323	1.41281

1) Based on the physical and chemical properties of yellow rice wine raw material quality, the first type of constraint was determined: "Restriction of yellow rice wine raw material". Suppose the feasible range of yellow rice wine raw material index is $l = (l_1, l_2, \cdots, l_9)$, $u = (u_1, u_2, \cdots, u_9)$, which represents the lower bound and the upper bound of yellow rice wine raw material index respectively (Table 11).

2) Based on the prediction model and the quality requirements of the target yellow rice wine products, the second constraint was determined: "Restriction constraint of yellow rice wine products". Suppose the feasible range of yellow rice wine product index is $L = (L_1, L_1, \cdots, L_7)$, $U = (U_1, U_2, \cdots, U_7)$, which respectively represents the lower and upper bounds of yellow rice wine quality index (Table 12).

Based on the above two constraints, a standard model for the index of special raw materials for yellow rice wine was established:

$$\min f_2 = \sum_{n=1}^{8} x_n^{low}, \max f_3 = \sum_{n=1}^{8} x_n^{up}$$

$$s.t. \quad \begin{cases} y_m^{low} \le y_m = f(x_1, x_2, ..., x_n) \le y_m^{up} & m = 1, 2, \cdots, 7 \; n = 1, 2, \cdots, 9 \\ x_{ij}^{low} \le x_\alpha^{low}, x_\alpha^{up} \le x_{ij}^{up} & \alpha = 1, 2, ..., 9 \end{cases} \quad (C)$$

where x_n^{low} and x_n^{up} re the maximum and minimum values of the nine yellow rice wine raw materials; y_m^{low} and y_m^{up} are the maximum and minimum values of seven yellow rice wine products, x_α^{low} and x_α^{up} are the required indexes of rice wine raw materials.

3) Based on the requirement of target region maximization, the third type of constraint, diffusion factor constraint, is determined. Since there are many indexes of yellow rice wine raw materials, it is impossible to unify them. Therefore, these indexes can be high-dimensioned, and then "diffusion factor" can be added to obtain the final result by linear weighting method, so that the difference between the final result of the index standard of yellow rice wine raw materials solved can be as large as possible. Set as "diffusion factor", then the third type of constraint is:

$$x_\alpha^{low} + \delta \le x_\alpha^{up} \quad \alpha = 1, 2, \cdots 9 \quad (24)$$

The third type of constraint was added to (C), and the solution was programmed in Lingo to obtain the maximum diffusion factor: $\delta=1.30964$.

4) Set the objective function of rice wine.

step 1: The initial weight of each index β_α is set as 0.0556, that is, the weight of upper and lower bounds of each index in the objective function is the same, and the sum is 1. Set β to 1000 to ensure that it is the first goal. The objective of the linear weighting method is:

$$\min\left[\sum_{\alpha}^{8} 0.0556 * (x_\alpha^{low} - x_\alpha^{up}) - 1000 * \delta\right] \tag{25}$$

Step 2: Establish the optimization model of the quality standard of rice wine raw materials. The multi-objective optimization model of rice wine raw materials is as follows:

$$\min\left[\sum_{\alpha}^{8} 0.0556 * (x_\alpha^{low} - x_\alpha^{up}) - 1000 * \delta\right]$$

According to the above optimization model, three constraint expressions of yellow rice wine are obtained:

$$\begin{cases} -1.70541 \leq x_1^{low}, x_1^{up} \leq 1.95222 \\ -1.99916 \leq x_2^{low}, x_2^{up} \leq 1.78484 \\ -1.38876 \leq x_3^{low}, x_3^{up} \leq 1.74782 \\ -3.83344 \leq x_4^{low}, x_4^{up} \leq 2.33644 \\ -0.9143 \leq x_5^{low}, x_5^{up} \leq 2.04714 \\ -2.08311 \leq x_6^{low}, x_6^{up} \leq 1.23952 \\ -2.03823 \leq x_7^{low}, x_7^{up} \leq 2.09488 \\ -1.00092 \leq x_8^{low}, x_8^{up} \leq 2.14277 \\ -1.26824 \leq x_9^{low}, x_9^{up} \leq 2.19887 \end{cases} \tag{1}$$

$$\begin{cases} -2.65624 \leq -0.2204x_1 - 0.2442x_2 - 0.3362x_3 - 0.3079x_4 - 0.4211x_5 \\ \qquad +0.6846x_6 - 0.7884x_7 - 0.3631x_8 - 0.1565x_9 \leq 1.451 \\ -1.43394 \leq 0.2303x_1 + 0.0145x_2 + 0.4197x_3 - 0.1968x_4 - 0.2905x_5 \\ \qquad -0.3245x_6 - 0.2201x_7 + 0.5558x_8 + 0.0943x_9 \leq 2.53 \\ -1.91465 \leq -0.1231x_1 - 0.0535x_2 - 0.0081x_3 + 0.0629x_4 + 0.3072x_5 \\ \qquad -0.8498x_6 + 0.3777x_7 + 0.2971x_8 + 0.0591x_9 \leq 2.90979 \\ -1.01597 \leq 0.9609x_1 - 0.3057x_2 - 0.4703x_3 - 0.0768x_4 + 0.1474x_5 \\ \qquad +0.3493x_6 - 0.4372x_7 - 0.5059x_8 + 0.4787x_9 \leq 2.80728 \\ -2.72084 \leq -0.3259x_1 + 0.0511x_2 - 0.3282x_3 - 0.2788x_4 - 0.0804x_5 \\ \qquad +0.7673x_6 + 0.0826x_7 - 0.3485x_8 - 0.3650x_9 \leq 1.579 \\ -1.71911 \leq -0.1519x_1 - 0.8013x_2 - 0.0342x_3 - 0.3886x_4 + 0.6892x_5 \\ \qquad +0.3302x_6 - 0.7705x_7 - 1.2108x_8 + 0.5124x_9 \leq 2.32323 \\ -2.47389 \leq -0.4408x_1 - 0.4905x_2 - 0.4237x_3 - 0.2926x_4 + 0.9116x_5 \\ \qquad +0.0350x_6 + 0.1094x_7 - 1.3631x_8 - 0.0223x_9 \leq 1.41281 \end{cases} \tag{2}$$

$$x_\alpha^{low} + \delta < x_\alpha^{up} \tag{3}$$

Step 3: In order to make the specific raw material index standard of yellow rice wine more accurate. This paper mainly from the following two aspects of the special raw materials for yellow rice wine index standards for regulation.

1) The key is to determine the weight of each indicator. In this paper, the weight of each optimization objective solved by information entropy method is:

$$\beta = (\beta_1, \beta_2, \beta_3, \beta_4, \beta_5, \beta_6, \beta_7, \beta_8, \beta_9)$$
$$= (0.1021, 0.0866, 0.1400, 0.0311, 0.1801, 0.1050, 0.0764, 0.1571, 0.1216)$$

2) Adjust the third type of constraint $x_\alpha^{low} + \delta \leq x_\alpha^{up}$, add relaxation factor ρ and floating variables γ.

$$x_\alpha^{low} + \delta_0 * (1 - \rho) + \beta_\alpha * \gamma \leq x_\alpha^{up} \tag{26}$$

where $\alpha = 1, 2, \cdots, 9$,relaxation factor $\rho \in [0, 0.5]$. The secondary modeling is as follows:

$$\max \left[\sum_\alpha^9 \beta_\alpha * (x_\alpha^{low} - x_\alpha^{up}) + 1000 * \gamma \right]$$
$$\begin{cases} & \qquad\qquad\qquad\qquad\qquad\qquad (1) \\ & \qquad\qquad\qquad\qquad\qquad\qquad (2) \\ x_\alpha^{low} + 1.30964 * (1 - \rho) + \beta_\alpha * \gamma \leq x_\alpha^{up} \end{cases}$$

x_α^{low} and x_α^{up} are the minimum and maximum standard values of various quality indicators of rice wine raw materials finally solved. The above optimization model is solved as follows (Table 13):

Table 13. The final optimization criteria of 9 raw material indexes.

	Rice moisture	Protein	Fat	Crude starch	Amylose	Lowest viscosity	Pad value	Setback	Gelatinization point
x_α^{low}	−0.3299	−1.9992	−1.3888	−2.1579	−0.2535	−1.8823	−0.04571	1.2386	1.3632
x_α^{up}	0.4681	−1.2309	−0.5176	−1.4969	0.6950	−1.0786	0.7028	2.1428	2.1989

Step 4: The index standard of special raw materials for yellow rice wine was reversed standardized. According to the standard deviation σ_i and mean $\bar{x}_i$ of the data standardization process, i represents the ith raw material quality index, the solution of the final results x_α^{low} and x_α^{up} is treated with anti-standardization,The optimization range of each raw material index is obtained $\overline{x_i^{low}} = (\overline{x_1^{low}}, \overline{x_2^{low}}, \cdots, \overline{x_8^{low}}, \overline{x_9^{low}})$, $\overline{x_i^{up}} = (\overline{x_1^{up}}, \overline{x_2^{up}}, \cdots, \overline{x_8^{up}}, \overline{x_9^{up}})$. The anti-standardization formula is as follows:

$$\overline{x_i^{low}} = x_\alpha^{low} * \sigma_i + \bar{x}_i \tag{27}$$

$$\overline{x_i^{up}} = x_\alpha^{up} * \sigma_i + \bar{x}_i \tag{28}$$

Table 14 below is the calculation result of each index of special raw materials for yellow rice wine.

Table 14. The final optimization standard of 9 yellow rice wine raw material indexes

	Rice moisture	Protein	Fat	Crude starch	Amylose	Lowest viscosity	Pad value	Setback	Gelatinization point
x_α^{low}	13.213	5.943	0.783	27.812	5.958	595.688	1021.653	1132.56	82.989
x_α^{up}	14.171	6.582	0.979	31.267	13.025	943.280	1291.043	1530.33	87.343

To Solve the Standard Optimization Model of the Index of Specialized Rice Flour Raw Materials. The solution of the index standard of rice flour specialized raw material is the same as the model of the index standard of specialized rice wine raw material. This section will simply introduce the solution of the index standard of rice flour specialized raw material.

Establish the optimization model of rice flour raw material quality standards:

$$\min \left[\sum_\alpha^{11} 0.0455 \left(x_\alpha^{low} - x_\alpha^{up} \right) - 1000 * \delta \right]$$

s.t. $\begin{cases} -1.0528 \le x_1^{low}, x_1^{up} \le 2.64484 \\ -1.86636 \le x_2^{low}, x_2^{up} \le 1.26042 \\ -1.143 \le x_3^{low}, x_3^{up} \le 1.92019 \\ -2.24049 \le x_4^{low}, x_4^{up} \le 1.18577 \\ -1.80542 \le x_5^{low}, x_5^{up} \le 1.62714 \qquad\qquad (1) \\ -1.56976 \le x_6^{low}, x_6^{up} \le 1.79883 \\ -0.99163 \le x_7^{low}, x_7^{up} \le 1.85355 \\ -1.4925 \le x_8^{low}, x_8^{up} \le 1.5339 \\ -1.53534 \le x_9^{low}, x_9^{up} \le 1.3932 \\ -1.0917 \le x_{10}^{low}, x_{10}^{up} \le 2.31423 \\ -1.77034 \le x_{11}^{low}, x_{11}^{up} \le 1.82856 \\ -1.24428 \le -0.575531x_1 - 0.657025x_4 - 0.342976x_6 + 0.306272x_7 \\ \qquad\qquad -0.381385x_8 \le 1.68622 \\ -1.68187 \le 0.522997x_1 - 0.312214x_2 + 0.417285x_4 + 0.298353x_6 - 0.855269x_7 \\ \qquad\qquad +0.876483x_8 - 0.666966x_{11} \le 1.2724 \\ -1.597 \le 0.838026x_3 \le 1.81016 \qquad\qquad (2) \\ -1.42701 \le -1.06618x_1 - 0.426554x_2 - 0.64822x_5 - 0.436612x_6 + 0.742512x_8 \\ \qquad\qquad +0.840577x_9 + 0.669782x_{10} - 0.458376x_{11} \le 1.34773 \\ -2.28382 \le 0.611828x_2 - 0.587119x_4 + 0.806832x_5 \\ \qquad\qquad -0.51783x_6 + 0.744066x_{11} \le 1.45857 \\ -1.27174 \le -0.422137x_2 - 0.327122x_5 + 0.3476x_6 + 0.174812x_7 \\ \qquad\qquad -0.328412x_8 - 0.567842x_{11} \le 1.8755 \\ x_\alpha^{low} + \delta < x_\alpha^{up} \qquad\qquad (3) \end{cases}$

where $\alpha = 1, 2, \cdots, 11$, just like the indexes of rice wine raw materials, the weights of the indexes of rice flour solved by information entropy method are as follows:

$$\beta = (\beta_1, \beta_2, \beta_3, \beta_4, \beta_5, \beta_6, \beta_7, \beta_8, \beta_9, \beta_{10}, \beta_{11})$$
$$= (0.1139, 0.1009, 0.1047, 0.1047, 0.1242, 0.1127, 0.1127, 0.1218, 0.1044, 0, 0)$$

According to the weight of the last two raw material indexes corresponding to the above rice flour products is 0, the influence factor of solving the raw material standard in WIP is very small, therefore, this paper will mainly solve the first nine raw material index standards. And adjust the third type of constraint. The quadratic modeling is as follows:

$$\max \left[\sum_\alpha^{11} \beta_\alpha * (x_\alpha^{low} - x_\alpha^{up}) + 1000 * \gamma \right]$$
$$\begin{cases} \qquad\qquad (1) \\ \qquad\qquad (2) \\ x_\alpha^{low} + 2.84518 * (1 - \rho) + \beta_\alpha * \gamma \leq x_\alpha^{up} \end{cases}$$

Based on quadratic modeling, the final solution result of rice noodles obtained by using LinGO11 is as follows (Table 15):

Table 15. The final optimization results of 8 raw material indexes of glutinous rice product.

	Moisture	Starch content	Amylose	Gel consistency	Protein	Fat	Fatty acid value	Water soluble	Swelling force
x_α^{low}	12.3727	69.5387	11.4759	18.3525	7.9412	1.5219	53.1523	4.1996	7.2884
x_α^{up}	12.3727	69.8456	24.9046	57.5021	8.5207	1.5219	194.6655	4.1996	8.5011

To Solve the Standard Optimization Model of Specialized Raw Materials for Glutinous Rice Products. The solution of the index standard of rice flour specialized raw material is the same as the model of the index standard of specialized rice wine raw material. This section will simply introduce the solution of the index standard of rice flour specialized raw material.

Establish the optimization model of rice flour raw material quality standards:

$$\min \sum_\alpha^8 0.0625 \left(x_\alpha^{low} - x_\alpha^{up} \right) - 1000 * \delta$$

$$\text{s.t.} \begin{cases} -1.50903 \le x_1^{low}, x_1^{up} \le 1.34384 \\ -1.77185 \le x_2^{low}, x_2^{up} \le 1.82776 \\ -1.59307 \le x_3^{low}, x_3^{up} \le 1.86228 \\ -3.00049 \le x_4^{low}, x_4^{up} \le 0.91651 \\ -1.45923 \le x_5^{low}, x_5^{up} \le 1.82919 \qquad (1) \\ -1.35666 \le x_6^{low}, x_6^{up} \le 1.80235 \\ -1.02422 \le x_7^{low}, x_7^{up} \le 3.0974 \\ -1.69437 \le x_8^{low}, x_8^{up} \le 2.64188 \\ -1.858 \le -0.0027x_1+0.6078x_2-0.1712x_3-0.1307x_4-0.0917x_5 \\ \qquad -0.2567x_6+0.0662x_7-0.0165x_8 \le 1.61293 \\ -1.58002 \le -0.0204x_1+0.3075x_2-0.8217x_3+0.1692x_4+0.0753x_5 \\ \qquad -0.4793x_6+0.2259x_7-0.1468x_8 \le 1.71678 \qquad (2) \\ -1.32823 \le -0.1641x_1-0.3229x_2-0.0737x_3+0.1685x_4-0.1541x_5 \\ \qquad -0.1904x_6+0.1501x_7+0.5768x_8 \le 1.92123 \\ -1.91276 \le 0.3993x_1+0.4342x_2+0.0013x_3-0.0202x_4+0.1917x_5 \\ \qquad +0.1334x_6-0.0330x_7+0.4718x_8 \le 1.67692 \\ -1.69437 \le -0.0271x_1-0.0136x_2-0.0108x_3+0.0590x_4-0.0101x_5 \\ \qquad -0.0393x_6-0.0506x_7+0.8582x_8 \le 2.64188 \\ -1.95982 \le 0.0886x_1+0.2607x_2-0.5613x_3+0.1357x_4+0.0890x_5 \\ \qquad -0.4989x_6+0.1267x_7+0.5302x_8 \le 2.17328 \\ -1.46418 \le -0.2606x_1-0.4437x_2-0.4005x_3+0.2323x_4-0.1915x_5 \\ \qquad +0.4057x_6-0.3427x_7-0.3345x_8 \le 2.41271 \\ x_\alpha^{low} + \delta < x_\alpha^{up} \qquad (3) \end{cases}$$

where $\alpha = 1, 2, \cdots, 8$, just like the indexes of rice wine raw materials, the weights of the indexes of rice flour solved by information entropy method are as follows:

$$\begin{aligned} \beta &= (\beta_1, \beta_2, \beta_3, \beta_4, \beta_5, \beta_6, \beta_7, \beta_8) \\ &= (0.1803, 0.1221, 0.1221, 0.0620, 0.1461, 0.1570, 0.1212, 0.0892) \end{aligned}$$

And adjust the third type of constraint. The quadratic modeling is as follows:

$$\max \left[\sum_\alpha^8 \beta_\alpha * (x_\alpha^{low} - x_\alpha^{up}) + 1000 * \gamma \right]$$
$$\begin{cases} (1) \\ (2) \\ x_\alpha^{low} + 2.85287 * (1 - \rho) + \beta_\alpha * \gamma \le x_\alpha^{up} \end{cases}$$

Based on quadratic modeling, the final solution result of rice noodles obtained by using LinGO11 is as follows (Table 16):

Table 16. The final optimization results of 8 raw material indexes of glutinous rice product.

	Peak viscosity	Breakdown viscosity	Moisture	Amylose content	Protein	Setback	Gelatinization point	Viscosity
x_α^{low}	652.114	284.856	10.999	1.916	7.029	228.633	71.236	555.154
x_α^{up}	1622.456	872.118	13.121	2.902	8.055	378.281	78.642	996.097

4.3   The Final Results of the Indexes and Standards of the Three Specialized Raw Materials

Through the above data analysis, the indexes of specialized raw materials for rice wine, rice flour and glutinous rice products are obtained respectively, as shown in the following table (Table 17, 18 and 19):

Table 17. Yellow rice wine raw material index standard.

Indicators of rice wine raw materials	Scope of raw material
Rice moisture (%)	13.213–14.171
Protein (%)	5.943–6.582
Fat	0.783–0.979
Crude starch (%)	27.812–31.267
Amylose (%)	5.958–13.025
Lowest viscosity	595.688–943.28
Attenuation	1021.653–1291.043
Setback	1132.564–1530.331
Gelatinization temperature (°C)	82.989–87.343

Table 18. Index standard of rice flour raw material.

Index of rice flour raw material	Scope of raw material
Moisture (%)	12.3727–12.3727
Starch content (%)	69.5387–69.8456
Amylose (%)	11.4759–24.9046
Gel consistency	18.3525–57.5021
Protein	7.9412–8.5207
Fat	1.5219–1.5219
Fatty acid value	53.1523–194.6655
Water soluble	4.1996–4.1996
Swelling force	7.2884–8.5011

Table 19. Standard for raw materials of glutinous rice products.

Raw material index of glutinous rice products	Scope of raw material
Peak viscosity	652.114–1622.456
Breakdown viscosity	284.856–872.118
Moisture (%)	10.999–13.121
Amylose (%)	1.916–2.902
Protein	7.029–8.055
Setback	228.633–378.281
Gelatinization point (°C)	71.236–78.642
Viscosity	555.154–996.097

The raw material indicators and standards for the three products in the above table can help enterprises to produce the corresponding products and reduce the waste of resources in the process of processing and production.

5   Conclusion

In this paper, the national standard method is adopted and the data obtained from targeted experiments designed according to the index set are analyzed, establish and optimize the model between the raw materials and the three products. By comparing three prediction models of ridge regression, multiple stepwise regression and principal component regression, the optimal prediction model was selected for product prediction. Aiming at the specialized raw material standard model, the raw material index standard range corresponding to three kinds of products was solved. By comparing the calculated standard with the original experimental data through the simulation model, the results are roughly the same, which proves that the calculated standard is reliable and effective, and the standard has certain reference significance for processing enterprises.

Acknowledgement. Subproject of the National Key Research and Development Program of China (Grant No. 2017YFD0401102-02).

References

1. Huang, G., Mao, J., Ji, Z., Fu, J., Zou, H.: Pattern recognition of Chinese rice wine from different rice varieties by DR-FTIR and SIMCA. Food Sci. **34**(14), 285–288 (2013). (in Chinese)
2. Gao, X., Zhang, W., Zhou, G.: Effects of glutinous rice flour on the physiochemical and sensory qualities of ground pork patties. LWT-Food Sci. Technol. **58**(1), 135–141 (2014)
3. Wang, H., Xiao, N., Wang, X., Zhao, X., Zhang, H.: Effect of pregelatinized starch on the characteristics, microstructures, and quality attributes of glutinous rice flour and dumplings. Food Chem. **283**, 248–256 (2019)

4. Li, C., Sun, S., Qi, Q.: Study on the influence of raw material variety on corn processing characteristics. J. Cereals Oils **20**(3), 35–38 (2005). (in Chinese)
5. Wang, J., Shen, Y., Lu, W., Qian, Y.: Situation and development trend of Chinese rice wine research. Brewed China **31**(11), 15–20 (2012). (in Chinese)
6. Xu, E., et al.: Improved bioaccessibility of phenolics and antioxidant activity of glutinous rice and its fermented Chinese rice wine by simultaneous extrusion and enzymatic hydrolysis. J. Funct. Foods **17**, 214–226 (2015)
7. Chen, S., Xu, Y., Qian, M.C.: Comparison of the aromatic profile of traditional and modern types of Huang Jiu (Chinese rice wine) by aroma extract dilution analysis and chemical analysis. Flavour Fragrance J. **33**(3), 263–271 (2018)
8. Gao, X., Tong, L., Zhong, Q., Liu, L., Zhou, X.: Study on quality evaluation index of fresh rice flour. J. Nuclear Agron. **28**(09), 1656–1663 (2014). (in Chinese)
9. Gao, X., Tong, L., Zhong, Q., Liu, L., Zhou, X.: Selection of special raw materials for fresh rice flour processing. Chinese J. Cereals Oils **30**(02), 1–5 (2015). (in Chinese)
10. Li, L., Chen, J., Wang, Y., Chen, L.: The raw material selection of instant fresh rice noodle. Food Ind. **40**(06), 177–182 (2019). (in Chinese)
11. Srikaeo, K., Laothongsan, P., Lerdluksamee, C.: Effects of gums on physical properties, microstructure and starch digestibility of dried-natural fermented rice noodles. Int. J. Biol. Macromol. **109**, 517–523 (2018)
12. Fan, Z.: Inflfluence of ingredients and chemical components on the quality of Chinese steamed bread. Food Chem. **163**, 154–162 (2014)
13. Avula, B., Cohen, P.A., Wang, Y.-H.: Chemical profiling and quantification of monacolins and citrinin in red yeast rice commercial raw materials and dietary supplements using liquid chromatography-accurate QToF mass spectrometry: chemometrics application. J. Books Food Chem. **100**, 243–253 (2014)
14. Yoenyongbuddhagal, S., Noomhorm, A.: Effect of raw material preparation on rice vermicelli quality. Starch/Stärke **54**, 534–539 (2002)
15. Zhang, B., et al.: Suitability evaluation of apple for chips-processing based on BP artificial neural network. Chin. Agric. Sci. **52**(01), 129–142 (2019). (in Chinese)
16. Yang, B., Zhang, X., Zhao, F., Yang, Y., Liu, W., Li, S.: Suitability evaluation of different potato cultivars for processing products. J. Agric. Eng. **31**(20), 301–308 (2015). (in Chinese)
17. Wang, Z.-M., Han, N., Yuan, Z.-M., Wu, Z.-H.: Feature selection for high-dimensional data based on ridge regression and SVM and its application in peptide QSAR modeling. J. Phys. Chem. **29**(03), 498–507 (2013). (in Chinese)
18. Huang, M.: Study on the formula and pretreatment of high quality rice flour. Fujian Light Text. **2**, 38–46 (2019). (in Chinese)
19. Sørensen, K.M., Khakimov, B., Engelsen, S.B.: The use of rapid spectroscopic screening methods to detect adulteration of food raw materials and ingredients. Curr. Opinion Food Sci. **10**, 45–51 (2016)
20. Yang, J., Zhang, Y.: Protein structure and function prediction using I-TASSER. Curr. Protoc. Bioinform. **52**(1), 5–8 (2015)
21. Gracheva, A.Y., et al.: Enhancement of efficiency of storage and processing of food raw materials using radiation technologies. Phys. Atomic Nuclei **79**(14), 1682–1687 (2016)
22. Deng, G.F., Li, K., Ma, J., Liu, F., Dai, J.J., Li, H.B.: Aluminium content of some processed foods, raw materials and food additives in China by inductively coupled plasma-mass spectrometry. Food Addit. Contam. **4**(4), 248–253 (2011)

23. Ropodi, A.I., Panagou, E.Z., Nychas, G.J.: Data mining derived from food analyses using non-invasive/non-destructive analytical techniques; determination of food authenticity, quality safety in tandem with computer science disciplines. Trends Food Sci. Technol. **50**, 11–25 (2016)
24. Wang, X., Cui, H., Shi, J., Zhao, X., Zhao, Y., Wei, Z.: Relationship between bacterial diversity and environmental parameters during composting of different raw materials. Bioresour. Technol. **198**, 395–402 (2015)
25. Ghani, I.M.M., Ahmad, S.: Stepwise multiple regression method to forecast fish landing. Procedia-Soc. Behav. Sci. **8**, 549–554 (2010)
26. Rahimi-Ajdadi, F., Abbaspour-Gilandeh, Y.: Artificial neural network and stepwise multiple range regression methods for prediction of tractor fuel consumption. Measurement **44**(10), 2104–2111 (2011)
27. Xuan, Y., Yue, Q.: Forecast of steel demand and the availability of depreciated steel scrap in China. Resour. Conserv. Recycl. **109**, 1–12 (2016)
28. Yang, X., et al.: Analysis of grey relational degree of amino acid balance between protein feed raw materials and hirudinaria manillensis. J. Yunnan Agric. Univ. (Nat. Sci.) **34**(01), 43–49 (2019)
29. Yao, Y., Gu, X., Shang, F., Qiu, J., Li, J., Li, J.: Investigation and analysis of main antinutritional factors in soybean and extruded soybean. Chin. Agric. Sci. **49**(11), 2174–2182 (2016). (in Chinese)
30. Chen, M., Zheng, W.: A study on optimum mixture ratio of reactive powder concrete. In: Advances in Materials Science and Engineering (2018)
31. Wang, Y., et al.: Influence of the S: Ni ratio in raw materials on the NixSy electrocatalysts. Appl. Surface Sci. **491**, 590–594 (2019)

A Hybrid Harmony Search Algorithm Based on Data Analysis to Solve Multi-objective Grain Transportation Problem

Hang Shu[1], Kang Zhou[1]($\boxtimes$)(iD), Xinyue Hu[1](iD), Zhixin He[1](iD), Jian Zhou[2],
and Guangbin Li[3]

[1] College of Mathematics and Computer Science,
Wuhan Polytechnic University, Wuhan 430023, China
zhoukang65@whpu.edu.cn
[2] College of Food Science and Engineering, Wuhan Polytechnic University,
Wuhan 430023, China
[3] Enterprise-School Joint Innovation Center,
Qianjiang Jujin Rice Industry Co., Ltd., Hubei, China

Abstract. This paper presents a hybrid harmony search algorithm based on data analysis (HSA-DA) to solve multi-objective grain transportation problem. The grain transportation problem can be summarized as the vehicle routing problem with time windows (VRPTW). It is a well-known NP-hard discrete optimization problem with two objectives: to minimize the total distance cost and to minimize the number of vehicles. In the HSA-DA, we use data analysis method to analyze the historical data of each different neighborhood search operators, and feed back the analysis results to the parameters. Consequently, a more suitable parameter settings can be determined adaptively to match different phases of the search process. Moreover, the related factors of exploration and exploitation are used as the indicators of data analysis for balancing their ability. To assess performance, this paper chooses Solomon benchmark instances as testing sets and the simulated results show that HSA-DA outperforms the compared algorithms in some benchmark instances, which verified the feasibility of the algorithm in solving multi-objective VRPTW.

Keywords: Data analysis · Neighborhood search · Harmony search algorithm · Grain transportation · Multi-objective optimization

1 Introduction

With the development of society and the progress of science and technology, a growing number of multi-objective optimization problems [1] need to be solved urgently. Especially when major disasters such as geological disasters, viruses,

© Springer Nature Singapore Pte Ltd. 2021
L. Pan et al. (Eds.): BIC-TA 2020, CCIS 1363, pp. 151–173, 2021.
https://doi.org/10.1007/978-981-16-1354-8_12

climate disasters and so on suddenly come, we often need to solve the transportation problems of relief supplies such as medicine, food, medical equipment by using optimal models for saving resource, cost and time. Therefore, the design of advanced optimization method becomes fundamental and important for the new challenges.

In the optimization field, there are many problems having more than one (often conflicting) objectives that we aim to optimize at the same time. One of these problems, the vehicle routing problem (VRP), was first detailed introduce in 1959 [2]. After decades of development, a series of VRP variants have been proposed, and most of them become a popular research problem in operational research and is also an important application in the areas of transportation and supply chain management [3,4]. Among them, the vehicle routing problem with time windows (VRPTW) is one of an important variants of VRP. The problem involves a depot, geographical scattered customers and some cargo. And, each customer must be serviced once by a vehicle within a specified time window. For the combinatorial optimization problem, many classical heuristic algorithms [5,6] such as genetic algorithm [7], ant colony algorithm [8], particle swarm algorithm [9] and so on have received extensive attention. Furthermore, many scholars improve these classical algorithms from different areas such as algorithm design, scalability and hyper-heuristics [1] for improving the search ability of algorithm.

The harmony search algorithm (HSA), which is a relatively new population-based metaheuristic optimization algorithm, is introduced by Geem et al. [10]. It is inspired by the process where musicians play musical instruments to search for a perfect state of harmony. HSA has been successfully applied to many complex problems such as the combined economic emission dispatch problem [11], the flexible job shop scheduling problem [12], the network reconfiguration problem [13], dynamic optimization and several other optimization problems [14–16]. Because of the wide application of harmony search algorithm in various fields, HSA has attracted the attention of many scholars. Reference [17] introduced in detail the characteristics and various variants of harmony search algorithm. These variants were summarized in two aspects: (1) Variants based on hybridization of HS with other metaheuristic. (2) Variants based on parameters setting. Reference [18] summarized the shortcomings of basic HSA in solving some real life problems. (1) It can be easily trapped and lead to a local optimum solution. (2) Its optimization performance is quite sensitive to the value of a few key control parameters like other metaheuristic algorithms. (3) It has some difficulties in striking a good balance between exploration and exploitation. In order to compensate for those weakness, some researchers combine the unique characteristics of HSA to improve the basic harmony search algorithm. Mahdavi et al. [19] presented an improved harmony search algorithm for solving engineering constraint optimization problems. Ouyang et al. [20] proposed an improved HS algorithm called LHS to improve solution precision and enhance the ability of escaping local optima. Ponz-Tienda et al. [21] presented an innovative improved and adaptive harmony search algorithm to improve the solution of the RLP with multiple resources. Zhang [22] presented a hybrid harmony search algorithm with differential evolution for day-ahead scheduling problem of a microgrid with consideration of power flow constraints. Yassen et al. [25] proposed a hybrid HSA that aims to retain a balance between the exploitation and exploration by providing the appropriate selection of the HSA components as well as the local search configurations. Assad et al. [26] proposed a novel algorithm based on hybridization of Harmony search and Simulated Annealing to remove the limitation of premature convergence.

According to the above discussion, harmony search algorithm possess unique search way, that is, each new solution is generated based on the entire harmony memory. Moreover, the structure of the HS algorithm is relatively easy, which makes it very flexible to combine HSA with other metaheuristic algorithms. However, this relatively simple structure also leads to the problems that it is easy to trap in local optimum and difficulties to strike a good balance between exploration and exploitation when solving multi-objective optimization problems. For improving the search ability of basic HSA in solving multi-objective VRPTW, we present a hybrid harmony search algorithm based on data analysis (HSA-DA). Different from the algorithm mentioned above, in order to realize the effective adaptive adjustment of parameters in the iterative process, HSA-DA uses data analysis method to analyze the historical data of four different neighborhood search operators. Moreover, at different stages of evolution, the sensitive parameters of HSA-DA need to be adjusted adaptive through the feedback results of data analysis. And to balance the ability of exploration and exploitation, data analysis of relevant indicators of exploration and exploitation is inevitable. The main contributions of this paper include the followings:

1) In order to compensate for the weakness of getting trapped in the local optimal solution, several different neighborhood search operators are used to improve the search ability of HSA.
2) In order to realize the effective adaptive adjustment of parameters in the iterative process, the method of data analysis is adopted to analyze the historical data of each neighborhood search operators. And the analysis results are fed back to the parameters to realize the adaptive adjustment of HMCR and PAR.

The remainder of this paper is organized as follows. Section 2 mainly introduces the mathematical model of multi-objective VRPTW. Section 3 describes the proposed HSA-DA and introduces the data analysis method and related analysis indicators in detail. Finally, in the Sect. 4, we analyze the experimental results of HSA-DA and compare with other excellent algorithms.

2   Problem Definition

For multi-objective VRPTW, there are two objectives as follows: the number of vehicles and the total distances cost. The mathematical model can be defined on an undirected graph $G = (V, E)$, where $V = \{v_i | i = 0, 1, ..., N\}$ is the set of vertices, $E = \{e_{ij} | i, j = 0, 1, ..., N\}$ is the set of edges between vertices and

$M = \{1, 2, ..., m\}$ is a set of vehicles. Vertex v_0 denotes the depot such that all vehicles should start from the depot and return to the depot once their tasks are finished. Each customer must be served by only one vehicle in time window $[T_{si}, T_{ei}]$, where T_{si} and T_{ei} are the earliest and latest service time of customer v_i. A vehicle must arrive before the closing time of client v_i. It is noted that any vehicle must wait if its arriving time is less than the earliest service time, and a customer cannot be served by the current vehicle if the vehicle arrives after the end of the customer's time window. Assume the following variables:

d_{ij} the distance between v_i and v_j.
r_i the demand of v_i.
W the capacity of the vehicle.
T_{ik} the time of the k-th vehicle arrives at customer v_i.
t_{ij} travel time from v_i to v_j.

Decision variables:

$$x_{ijk} = \begin{cases} 1 & if \ v_i \ and \ v_j \ are \ visited \ by \ vehicle \ k \\ 0 & otherwise \end{cases}$$

The mathematical model of multi-objective VRPTW is as follows:

$$\min f_1 = \sum_{k \in M} \sum_{j \in N} x_{0jk} \tag{1}$$

$$\min f_2 = \sum_{k \in M} \sum_{i \in N} \sum_{j \in N} d_{ij} x_{ijk} \tag{2}$$

$$\sum_{k \in M} \sum_{j \in N} x_{ijk} = 1, \forall i \in N \tag{3}$$

$$\sum_{i \in N} (r_i \sum_{j \in N} x_{ijk}) \leq W, \forall k \in M \tag{4}$$

$$\sum_{j \in N} x_{0jk} = \sum_{i \in N} x_{i0k} \leq 1, \forall k \in M \tag{5}$$

$$\sum_{i \in N} x_{ihk} = \sum_{j \in N} x_{hjk}, \forall h \in N, \forall k \in M \tag{6}$$

$$T_{ik} + t_{ij} - K(1 - x_{ijk}) \leq T_{jk}, \forall i, j \in N, \forall k \in M, K >> 0 \tag{7}$$

$$\sum_{k \in M} \sum_{i,j \in D} x_{ijk} \leq |D| - 1, \forall D \subseteq N \tag{8}$$

Equations (1) and (2) represent the two objectives, where objective (1) is the number of vehicles; objective (2) is the total distance cost of all the vehicles in a route; Constraints (3–8) ensure that the quantity of goods transported in a route does not exceed the capacity of the vehicle, require that the arrival time at all customers is within their corresponding time window, ensure that each customer vertex is visited by at least one route, and require that the total number of vertices visited is equal to the number of customers.

3 The Hybrid Harmony Search Algorithm Based on Data Analysis

A hybrid harmony search algorithm based on data analysis (HSA-DA) is proposed to solve multi-objective VRPTW. In Sect. 3.1, we introduce the basic elements of HSA-DA, including the parameters, the harmony memory initialization and the basic harmony search algorithm. In Sect. 3.2, the procedure of HSA-DA is described in detail. Section 3.3 introduces the process of four neighborhood search operators. Finally, Sect. 3.4 and Sect. 3.5 respectively introduce the data analysis method and the process of parameter adaptive adjustment. The detailed introduction is as follows.

3.1 Basic Elements of HSA-DA

In this work, we introduce the parameters of HSA-DA, the initialization of harmony memory and the basic harmony search algorithm.

A: The Parameters of HSA-DA

a: Harmony memory size (HMS) -The numbers of solutions in harmony memory.
b: Harmony memory consideration rate (HMCR) -The HMCR value considered in this study is set between zero and one. According to the HMCR, the decision variable of the generated solution will be either chosen from the HM or selected arbitrarily from the available range.
c: Pitch adjustment rate (PAR) -The PAR value is set between zero and one. Here, PAR is divided into three intervals, each representing a different neighborhood search strategy.
d: The number of improvisations (NI) -The number of iterations or the termination criterion of algorithms.
e: The number of samples (NS) – The number of samples for data analysis.

B: Harmony Memory Initialization
The harmony memory (HM) is a matrix of solutions with the size of HMS, where each harmony memory vector represents one solution. In this step, the solutions are randomly constructed. The harmony memory is represented as follows:

$$HM = \begin{bmatrix} x_1^1 & x_2^1 & \cdots & x_n^1 \\ x_1^2 & x_2^2 & \cdots & x_n^2 \\ \vdots & \vdots & \cdots & \vdots \\ x_1^{HMS} & x_2^{HMS} & \cdots & x_n^{HMS} \end{bmatrix}$$

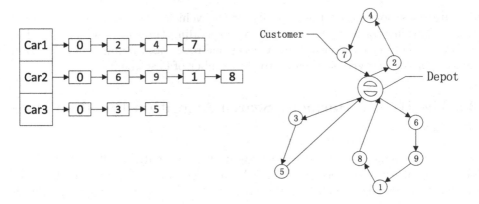

Fig. 1. Solution and the routes

Here, we use the method in reference [23] to express a solution $X = \{x_1^k, x_2^k, ..., x_n^k\}, k \in \{1, 2, ..., HMS\}$. As shown in Fig. 1 (left), for a solution $X_k = \{2, 4, 7, 6, 9, 1, 8, 3, 5\}$ with nine customers, three vehicles are required to serve. And the route of each vehicle is shown in Fig. 1 (right).

C: Basic Harmony Search Algorithm

The structure of basic harmony search algorithm, including improvisation operators, memory consideration, pitch adjustment, and random consideration, is relatively easy. According to the literature [25], the basic steps are as follows:

i: *Initialize parameters HMS, HMCR, PAR and NI.*
ii: *Generate an empty solution X.*
iii: *Produce a random number r between 0 and 1.*
iv: *If r is less than the HMCR, choose and add one customer from HM to X. Otherwise, a new customer is randomly generated and appended to X.*
v: *Any selected customer from the HM is going to be adjusted with regard to the PAR as follows:*
   – *Create a random number r between 0 and 1.*
   – *If the value of r is smaller than PAR, then the current customer will be modified via a neighboring strategy.*
vi: *Repeat steps iii–iv until a new solution is generated.*

The following subsections discuss the improvisation process of HSA-DA, neighborhood search operators and data analysis method in more detail.

3.2 Improvisation Process

In this work, we illustrate the whole procedure of HSA-DA, which is improved on the basic harmony search algorithm framework. This improvement mainly includes the following several aspects: (1) At the beginning of the algorithm, we add a selection mechanism to improve the competitive advantage of excellent solutions in the iterative process. (2) The selected solution is adjusted by a variety of neighborhood search operators to generate a new solution. (3) We use the data analysis method to make the parameters HMCR and PAR adaptively adjusted instead of fixed. The general algorithm to solve a multi-objective VRPTW interactively is summarized in Algorithm 1. First, the tournament selection strategy [24] is adopted to select a solution X from HM, which is the beginning for generating a new solution. Then, according to the parameters PAR and HMCR, the corresponding neighborhood search operators are selected to adjust solution X. Finally, the data generated in the iterative process is analyzed by data analysis method, and the data are fed back to parameters PAR and HMCR to adjust the search strategy adaptively.

3.3   Neighborhood Search Operators

Each selected solution X needs to be adjusted n times (the number of customers) to produce a new solution, and each adjustment needs to select one of the following four neighborhood search operators. Customer x is used to adjust the selected solution, which is either randomly generated or selected from the harmony memory.

Algorithm 1. the process of HSA-DA

Input :
    HM : the harmony memory;
    Initialization parameters: $HMS, HMCR, PAR, NS$ and NI;
Output :
    solutions;
1:**Initialization :**
    Randomly generate an initial harmony memory $HM = \{X^1, X^2, ..., X^{HMS}\}$.
2: **Step 1:**
    Select a solution X from HM.
3: **Step 2:**
    Produce a random number r between 0 and 1.
4: **Step 3:**
    If r less than the $HMCR$, randomly generate a customer and use random
    operator (mentioned in section 3.3(A)) to adjust X. Then calculate each data
    analysis indicator (mentioned in section 3.4) of random operator.
5: **Step 4:**
    Otherwise, the selected customer from the HM is going to be adjusted with
    regard to the PAR as follows:
6:**Step 4.1:**
    Create a random number r between 0 and 1.
7:**Step 4.2:**
    According to number r, choose the corresponding neighborhood search
    operator (mentioned in section 3.3 (B, C, D)) to adjust customer.
8:**Step 4.3:**
    Calculate each data analysis indicator of the selected neighborhood search
    operator.
9:**Step 5:**
    Repeat steps 1-5 until a new solution is generated.
10:**Step 6:**
    If the number of samples reaches NS, adjust parameters $HMCR$ and PAR
    (mentioned in section 3.5).
11:**Step 7:**
    Repeat steps 1-6 until the number of iterations reaches NI.

A: Random Operator

For the randomly generated a customer $x \in R_1$ and the customer $x_i \in R_2$ of the i-th position of X (Both vehicle routing R_1 and R_2 belong to solution X), the adjustment is as follows:

- If $R_1 \neq R_2$, insert customer x into the previous and next position of customer x_i. Delete the duplicate customer x in solution X. Then the values of objective function f_2 of solution X before and after insertion are recorded. Finally, according to this record, x is inserted to the position with the minimum value (see Fig. 2(A)).
- If $R_1 = R_2$, exchange the location of customer x and customer x_i. If the distance of this route is smaller after the exchange, the exchange is completed. Otherwise the exchange is abandoned.

It should be noted that the above operations are completed under the VRPTW constraints.

B: Random Adjustment Operator

Choose a customer x from the HM, then the customer x will be adjusted based on the following equation [19]:

$$x = x \pm r * bw$$
$$bw(gn) = bw_{\min} + \frac{bw_{\max} - bw_{\min}}{NI} \times gn$$

Where, the random number $r \in [0, 1]$ within the probability of PAR. $bw(gn)$ is the bandwidth value for each generation, $bw_{\max}$ is the maximum bandwidth, $bw_{\min}$ is the minimum bandwidth and gn is the generation number. Then the process of random adjustment is the same as the process of random operator (see Fig. 2(B)).

C: Customer Adjustment Operator

For the customer $x \in R_1$ selected from HM and the customer $x_i \in R_2$ of the i-th position of X, the adjustment is as follows: First all customers available for exchange in route R_2 are explored, and then x is exchanged with x_i. Finally, the new route with the smallest distance among all routes after exchanging is obtained. It is noted that the feasible locations are seldom due to the existence of time windows (see Fig. 2(C)).

D: Position Adjustment Operator

For the customer $x \in R_1$ selected from HM and the customer $x_i \in R_2$ of the i-th position of X, the adjustment is as follows: Delete the customer x in solution X. Then customer x needs to be inserted to each feasible position of route R_2, and then these positions are recorded in a set F. If $p = \min\{F(p)\}$, then x is inserted to the p-th position. Moreover, if the number of customers of R_1 is less than that of R_2, the original position of x and x_i will not be considered in the set F, otherwise it needs to be considered (see Fig. 2(D)).

Figure 2 shows the operation of several different neighborhood search operators. Among them, operators A and B have the same operation mode, the difference is that the two operators have different customer point selection. It should be noted that Fig. 2 only describes the adjustment of customer points between different routes, which is also applicable to the adjustment of customer points in the same route.

3.4   The Data Analysis Method

An effective data analysis method is the most important part of parameter adaptively adjustment. In reference [27], the associated control parameter values are gradually self-adapted by learning from their previous experiences in generating promising solutions. The basis of parameter control is to calculate the selection probability of different operators by counting the success and failure times of different operators. However, this statistical method cannot reflect comprehensively the search ability of each neighborhood search operator when solving multi-objective VRPTW. In addition, in different stages of search, we need to analyze the search ability of each neighborhood search operator in real time. Therefore, we use a variety of analysis indicators to reflect the search ability of each operator.

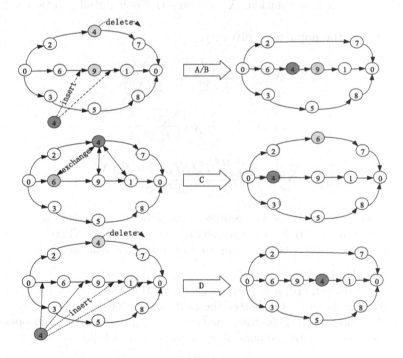

Fig. 2. Neighborhood search operators

A: Data Analysis Indicators

Each new solution will produce a corresponding analysis sample. For the i-th new solution X_i, the vector of its analysis sample can be expressed as $y_i = (w_1^i, w_2^i, w_3^i)$. Each indicator of y_i is represented as follows:

a: w_1 and w_2 mean the improvement degree of each neighborhood operator on objective function f_1 and f_2, respectively.

$$w_{1,t}^i = \sum_{j=1}^{sum^t} \left(\frac{f_1(X_i^{j-1}) - f_1(X_i^j)}{f_1(X_i^0)} \right) \tag{9}$$

$$w_{2,t}^i = \sum_{j=1}^{sum^t} \left(\frac{f_2(X_i^{j-1}) - f_2(X_i^j)}{f_2(X_i^0)} \right) \tag{10}$$

$$\sum_{t=1}^{4} sum^t = n$$

Where, sum^t is the number of times that the t-th ($t \in (1,2,3,4)$) neighborhood operator is selected, X_i^j is the intermediate solution of the adjustment process of the i-th new solution. X_i^0 denotes the i-th initial solution without adjustment.

b: w_3^i means the population diversity.

$$f(X_{i,h}^j) = \frac{f_1(X_{i,h}^j)}{f_1(X_i^0)} + \frac{f_2(X_{i,h}^j)}{f_2(X_i^0)}$$

$$P_h(X_{i,h}^j) = \frac{f(X_{i,h}^j)}{\sum_{h=1}^{HMS} f(X_{i,h}^j)}$$

$$w_{3,t}^i = \sum_{j=1}^{sum^t} \left(-\frac{\sum_{h=1}^{HMS} P_h(X_{i,h}^j) \times \ln P_h(X_{i,h}^j)}{\ln HMS} \right) \tag{11}$$

Population entropy is used to represent the diversity of population [28]. The higher the entropy, the richer the diversity of the population. Where, $X_{i,h}^j$ means that the position of the i-th new solution in the harmony library is h.

B: Statistical Method

According to Eqs. (9), (10) and (11), we can know that the larger the value of the three analysis indicators, the better the performance of the operator in exploration and exploitation. Therefore, for the t-th neighborhood search operator, the result W_t fed back to the parameter is calculated as follows:

$$W_t = \sum_{i=1}^{NS} \left(\frac{w_{1,t}^i + w_{2,t}^i + w_{3,t}^i}{sum^t} \right) \tag{12}$$

3.5   Parameter Adjustment

In the process of parameter adjustment, the trial-and-error scheme is often adopted to search for the most suitable strategy. However, such a trial-and-error searching process requires high computational costs. Moreover, at different stages of evolution, different parameter settings may be required to adjust these neighborhood search operators. Therefore, in order to realize the effective intelligent adjustment of parameters in the iterative process, the data analysis method is adopted to analyze the historical data of four different neighborhood search operators. Then the feedback results are applied to the parameters to realize adaptive adjustment, which can effectively avoid this problem. It is worth noting that in the initial case, the probability of each neighborhood search operator is equal. The parameter adjustment method is as follows:

a: HMCR adjustment strategy:

$$\begin{cases} \frac{W_1}{W_1+\overline{W}} \; random \; operator \\ \\ \frac{\overline{W}}{W_1+\overline{W}} \; other \; operators \end{cases}$$

b: PAR adjustment strategy

$$\begin{cases} \frac{W_2}{\overline{W}} \; random \; adjustment \; operator \\ \\ \frac{W_3}{\overline{W}} customer \; adjustment \; operator \\ \\ \frac{W_4}{\overline{W}} \; position \; adjustment \; operator \end{cases}$$

Where, $\overline{W} = \sum_{t=2}^{4} W_t$. Four neighborhood search operators (random operator, random adjustment operator, customer adjustment operator and position adjustment operator) are introduced in Sect. 3.3.

In the process of adaptive adjustment of parameters HMCR and PAR, if the probability of a neighborhood search operator is zero, we will set a minimum probability parameter θ for automatic adjustment. The adjustment strategy is as follows:

– If the probability of t-th operator W_t is zero, we will set $W_t = \theta$. Then the probability of other three operators will be reduced by $\frac{\theta}{3}$.
– If the probability of more than one operator is zero, we will reset all probabilities to the initial state.

4   Experimental Results and Comparisons

In the experiment, Solomon's VRPTW benchmark [29] is used to evaluate the performance of HSA-DA. The data set is categorized into R1, R2, C1, C1, RC1, and RC2. In the R categories, the distribution of customer location is uniform, and in the C categories, the locations of customers are clustered. The RC categories are a mixture. The R1, C1, and RC1 categories have a shorter scheduling horizon and require more vehicles, whereas the other categories have a longer scheduling horizon and need fewer vehicles. This data set is widely used in the literature on VRPTW. In order to test the performance of the proposed algorithm, the test set of Solomon's benchmarks is adopted for simulation experiments. The plat for simulating the designed experiments: Software: IDEA; Programming language JAVA; Processor: Intel(R) Core (TM)i5-5300CPU 2.3 GHz and Windows10, 64 bits.

A: Benchmark Algorithms
To assess the performance of proposed HSA-DA, we compare the results with eight algorithms. A hybrid multi-objective evolutionary algorithm (HMOEA)[30], multi-objective genetic algorithm (MOGA) [31], multiple ant colony system algorithm hybridized with insertion heuristics (MACS-IH) [32], hybrid shuffled frog leaping algorithm (HSFLA) [33], improved large neighborhood search algorithm (ILNSA) [34], localized genetic algorithm (LGA) [35], a hybrid algorithm of ant colony optimization (ACO) and Tabu search [36] and the motivation of using hybrid ACO (HACO) [8].

B: Parameter Setting
Like the other algorithms, the quality of the solution of HSA-DA can be controlled by the parameters. Therefore, in this work, two different ways are employed to adjust the parameters. (1) The parameter values of HMCR and PAR are given an initial value when starting the evolutionary algorithm and they undergo changes while the evolutionary algorithm is running. (2) Other parameters of HSA-DA are adjusted to the best by the method in reference [8]. After repeatedly testing and adjusting, the harmony memory size, the number of improvisations and the probability parameter θ are set to 50, 1000000 and 0.1, respectively. Moreover, in order to illustrate how those parameters affect the performance of the HSA-DA, the analyses between the approximate optimal solution and the crucial parameters, including HMCR, PAR and NS are carried out on several randomly selected problems C101, R101, RC101, C201, R201 and RC201.

a: parameters HMCR and PAR

Table 1. The approximate optimal objective values obtained by using different HMCR and PAR adjustment strategy

	C101	R101	RC101	C201	R201	RC201
Ave.	(10, 828.94)	(19, 1676.74)	(16, 1708.86)	(3, 591.56)	(5, 1397.85)	(5, 1517.56)
Auto.	(10, 828.94)	(19, 1650.8)	(15, 1636.92)	(3, 591.56)	(4, 1253.23)	(4, 1423.70)

Strategy *Ave.* indicates that the probability of each neighborhood search operator is equal. In this case, parameter values are fixed in the initialization stage and do not change while the evolutionary algorithm is running. Strategy *Auto.* means that the parameters of HMCR and PAR are adjusted adaptively while the evolutionary algorithm is running. As shown in Table 1, for the problems R101, RC101, R201 and RC201, Strategy *Auto.* obviously has a greater advantage. Therefore, HSA-DA adopts strategy *Auto.* to adaptively adjust parameters HMCR and PAR.

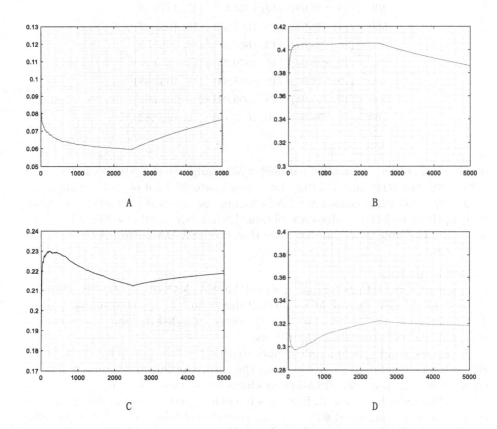

Fig. 3. The probability curve graph of R101. A: random operator; B: random adjustment operator; C: customer adjustment operator; D: position adjustment operator

Figure 3 shows the probability curve graph of each neighborhood search operator when testing example R101. We can see that the probability of each operator selected changes with the running of the algorithm. It indicates that the performance of parameters HMCR and PAR self-adaption is excellent.

b: parameter NS

One of the crucial things in the data analysis method is determining the proper NS. If the NS is too large or too small, the result of data analysis will not be accurate enough. Table 2 represents the approximate optimal objective values obtained by using different NS. For C101, the optimal objective value is always

Table 2. The approximate optimal objective values obtained by using different NS

NS	C101	R101	RC101
100	(10, 828.94)	(19, 1667.27)	(15, 1666.74)
200	(10, 828.94)	**(19, 1650.8)**	**(15, 1636.94)**
300	(10, 828.94)	(20, 1651.05)	**(15, 1636.94)**
400	(10, 828.94)	(19, 1664.62)	(15, 1676.59)
500	(10, 828.94)	(19, 1665.49)	(16, 1669.37)
600	(10, 828.94)	(19, 1667.27)	(16, 1682.88)
700	(10, 828.94)	(19, 1670.25)	(15, 1699.37)
800	(10, 828.94)	(19, 1676.34)	(16, 1682.88)
900	(10, 828.94)	(19, 1666.94)	(16, 1685.09)
1000	(10, 828.94)	(20, 1663.10)	(16, 1687.82)

obtained whenever the value of parameter NS changes in the prespecified interval [100,1000]. For R101 and RC101, the approximate optimal objective values are relatively good when parameter NS is within the interval [200,300], especially their optimal objective values are obtained when NS equals to 200. Therefore, according to Table 2, we can conclude that the HSA-DA performs better when NS is 200.

C: Result Analysis

In this work, HSA-DA is compared with HMOEA, MOGA, MACS-IH, HSFLA, ILNSA, LGA, HACO and ACO-Tabu. Table 3 and 4 give the comparisons of f_1 (smallest number of vehicles) and f_2 (lowest traveled distance) between the HSA-DA and the comparing algorithms.

In Tables 3 and 4, bold numbers indicate that the solutions obtained by HSA-DA are very similar to or better than the results obtained by the comparing algorithms. The proposed HSA-DA produces excellent results with 32 instances in f_1, 4 instances in f_2 and 12 instances in both f_1 and f_2 (out of the Solomon's 56 instances) as compared with the best solutions obtained by other eight algorithms. From Table 3, we can also see that HSA-DA, succeed in finding the best known solutions on C1 instances, performs as well as MACS-IH, HSFLA, LGA, HACO and ACO-Tabu. From Table 4, these nine algorithms perform excellently on C2 instances which have a longer scheduling horizon and need fewer vehicles. Moreover, the smallest number of vehicles obtained by MACS-IH, HSFLA and HSA-DA is relatively better than the results obtained by the other algorithms in general. Thus, we can say that the proposed HSA-DA still appears relatively competitive.

As shown in Table 5, the mean value of f_1 and f_2 is adopted as the estimation index of nine compared algorithms.

In Table 5, bold numbers indicate that better results than other comparing algorithms. In C1, the mean value of f_1 and f_2 obtained by HSA-DA are very similar to the results obtained by other algorithms. Among them, ILNSA and

Table 3. Comparisons between the HSA-DA and other algorithms (C1, R1 and RC1)

Instances	HMOEA		MOGA		MACS-IH		HSFLA		ILNSA		LGA		HACO		ACO-Tabu		HSA-DA	
	f_1	f_2	f_1	f_2	f_1	f_2	f_1	f_2	f_1	f_2	f_1	f_2	f_1	f_2	f_1	f_2	f_1	f_2
C101	10	828.93	10	828.94	10	828.94	10	828.94	10	828.94	10	828.94	10	828.94	10	828.93	**10**	**828.94**
C102	10	828.19	10	828.94	10	828.94	10	828.94	10	828.94	10	828.94	10	828.94	10	828.94	10	828.94
C103	10	828.06	10	828.06	10	828.06	10	828.06	10	839.37	10	828.06	10	828.06	10	828.06	**10**	**828.06**
C104	10	825.54	10	825.65	10	824.78	10	824.78	10	838.98	10	824.78	10	824.78	10	828.2	**10**	**824.78**
C105	10	828.9	10	828.94	10	828.94	10	828.94	10	828.94	10	828.94	10	828.94	10	828.9	**10**	**828.94**
C106	10	828.17	10	828.94	10	828.94	10	828.94	10	842.1	10	828.94	10	828.94	10	828.94	10	828.94
C107	10	829.34	10	828.94	10	828.94	10	828.94	10	828.94	10	828.94	10	828.94	10	828.94	10	828.94
C108	10	832.28	10	828.94	10	828.94	10	828.94	10	832.74	10	828.94	10	828.94	10	830.94	**10**	**828.94**
C109	10	829.22	10	828.94	10	828.94	10	828.94	10	828.94	10	828.94	10	828.94	10	829.22	**10**	**828.94**
R101	18	1613.59	19	1690.28	19	1645.79	19	1650.8	18	1612.29	20	1646.9	19	1669.34	19	1655.03	19	1650.8
R102	18	1454.68	17	1513.74	17	1486.12	17	1486.12	16	1473.31	18	1474.28	17	1443.18	18	1491.18	17	**1443.18**
R103	14	1235.68	14	1237.05	13	1292.68	13	1292.67	12	1279.37	15	1222.68	14	1238.56	14	1243.22	13	1292.68
R104	10	974.24	10	1020.87	9	1007.24	9	1007.31	10	1025.47	11	989.53	10	974.24	10	982.01	10	**974.24**
R105	15	1375.23	14	1415.13	14	1377.11	14	1377.11	14	1377.95	16	1382.78	14	1382.5	16	1380.44	14	1377.11
R106	13	1260.2	13	1254.22	12	1251.98	12	1252.03	12	1276.48	13	1250.11	12	1252.03	13	1265.36	**12**	1252.03
R107	11	1085.75	11	1100.52	10	1104.66	10	1104.66	11	1153.86	12	1083.42	11	1108.8	11	1100.25	11	**1078.82**
R108	10	954.03	10	975.34	9	960.88	9	960.88	10	990.82	10	952.44	10	960.88	9	958.66	10	956.61
R109	12	1157.74	12	1169.85	11	1194.73	11	1194.73	12	1179.73	13	1160.69	12	1222.7	12	1101.99	11	1194.73
R110	12	1104.56	11	1112.21	10	1118.59	10	1118.84	11	1113.1	12	1080.69	11	1114.56	12	1119.53	10	1124.4
R111	12	1057.8	11	1084.76	10	1096.72	10	1096.73	11	1155.39	12	1057.64	10	1096.73	12	1091.11	10	1096.72
R112	10	974.73	10	976.99	9	982.14	9	982.14	10	981.46	10	965	10	976.99	10	974.73	10	971.75
RC101	16	1641.65	15	1636.92	14	1696.94	14	1696.95	15	1671.54	16	1660.55	15	1645.67	14	1650.14	15	**1636.92**
RC102	13	1470.26	14	1488.36	12	1554.75	12	1554.75	13	1447.14	15	1494.92	13	1476.5	13	1514.85	13	1470.26
RC103	11	1267.86	12	1306.42	11	1261.67	11	1261.67	11	1313.79	12	1276.05	11	1262.01	11	1277.11	11	1278.14
RC104	10	1145.49	10	1140.45	10	1135.48	10	1135.48	11	1163.54	10	1151.63	10	1135.48	10	1159.37	10	1135.48
RC105	14	1589.91	14	1616.56	13	1629.44	13	1629.44	13	1502.48	16	1556.21	16	1589.4	15	1617.88	**13**	1633.72
RC106	13	1371.69	12	1454.61	11	1424.73	11	1424.73	12	1406.25	14	1402.25	11	1424.73	13	1387.63	**11**	1427.13
RC107	11	1222.16	12	1254.26	11	1230.48	11	1230.48	11	1278.96	12	1212.83	11	1230.48	11	1280.01	11	1230.48
RC108	11	1133.9	10	1141.34	10	1139.82	10	1139.82	11	1172.83	11	1133.25	10	1142.66	11	1157.44	**10**	1142.66

HACO show comparatively poor performance. In C2, except HACO, HSA-DA is basically on the same level as other algorithms. It indicates that HSA-DA has obvious advantages in computing results in sets C1 and C2. From the result data of R1 and R2, we can see that the results of HSA-DA are better than most of the other eight algorithms. In R1, R2 and RC1, according to the ranking of the results from small to large, we can see that the mean value of the smallest number of vehicles obtained by HSA-DA is in the third order. In RC2, the mean value of the smallest number is in the first order. This shows that HSA-DA has great advantages over other algorithms in the objective of vehicle number. Compared with other algorithms, the performance of HSA-DA in the lowest traveled distance is above the middle level and still has some advantages.

In order to illustrate the mean value ranking of f_1 and f_2 obtained by nine algorithms, we draw two bar charts of the nine algorithms in Table 5 for six test instances (C1, C2, R1, R2, RC1, RC2).

Table 4. Comparisons between the HSA-DA and other algorithms (C2, R2 and RC2)

Instances	HMOEA		MOGA		MACS-IH		HSFLA		ILNSA		LGA		HACO		ACO-Tabu		HSA-DA	
	f_1	f_2	f_1	f_2	f_1	f_2	f_1	f_2	f_1	f_2	f_1	f_2	f_1	f_2	f_1	f_2	f_1	f_2
C201	3	591.58	3	591.56	3	591.56	3	591.56	3	591.56	3	591.56	3	591.56	3	591.58	**3**	**591.56**
C202	3	591.56	3	591.56	3	591.56	3	591.56	3	591.56	3	591.56	3	591.56	3	591.56	**3**	**591.56**
C203	3	593.25	3	596.55	3	591.17	3	591.17	3	591.17	3	591.17	3	591.17	3	593.25	**3**	**591.17**
C204	3	595.55	3	590.6	3	590.6	3	590.6	3	591.17	3	590.6	3	598.72	3	595.55	3	593.93
C205	3	588.16	3	588.88	3	588.88	3	588.88	3	588.88	3	588.88	3	588.16	3	588.88	**3**	**588.84**
C206	3	588.49	3	588.49	3	588.49	3	588.49	3	588.49	3	588.49	3	588.9	3	588.49	**3**	588.88
C207	3	588.88	3	588.29	3	588.29	3	588.29	3	588.29	3	588.29	3	592.46	3	588.88	**3**	**588.29**
C208	3	588.03	3	588.32	3	588.32	3	588.32	3	591.39	3	588.32	3	588.32	3	588.03	3	588.32
R201	5	1206.42	4	1268.44	4	1252.37	4	1252.37	5	1285.9	9	1156.3	4	1252.37	7	1214.22	4	1253.23
R202	4	1091.21	4	1112.59	3	1191.7	3	1191.7	4	1195.1	8	1042.3	4	1091.21	5	1105.2	3	1191.7
R203	4	935.04	3	989.11	3	939.54	3	939.5	3	980.72	6	877.29	4	937.56	4	960.14	3	939.5
R204	3	789.72	3	760.82	2	825.52	2	825.52	3	901.68	4	736.52	3	794.56	4	771.47	3	753.32
R205	3	1049.65	3	1084.34	3	994.42	3	994.42	3	1051.6	6	960.35	3	994.43	4	1050.26	3	994.42
R206	3	940.12	3	919.73	3	906.14	3	906.14	3	941.17	6	894.19	3	906.14	4	954.85	3	912.97
R207	3	852.62	3	825.07	2	890.61	2	890.61	3	843.77	4	800.79	3	825.48	3	870.33	3	814.78
R208	2	790.6	2	773.13	2	726.75	2	726.82	3	744.71	3	706.86	2	726.5	3	777.72	2	726.82
R209	3	974.88	3	971.7	3	909.16	3	909.16	3	938.29	5	860.63	3	855	3	934.21	3	909.16
R210	5	982.31	3	985.38	3	939.34	3	939.37	3	966.5	5	948.82	3	939.37	5	949.02	**3**	**939.37**
R211	4	811.59	3	833.76	2	892.71	2	885.71	3	855.76	5	762.23	4	761.5	4	877.55	2	885.71
RC201	6	1134.91	4	1423.73	4	1406.91	4	1406.91	5	1399.2	10	1281.63	4	1423.7	5	1279.65	4	1423.7
RC202	5	1130.53	4	1183.88	3	1365.65	3	1365.64	4	1382.4	8	1103.47	4	1263.53	5	1157.02	3	1365.64
RC203	4	1026.61	3	1131.78	3	1049.62	3	1049.62	3	1097.6	6	942	4	1048	6	1046.33	3	1060.45
RC204	3	879.82	3	806.44	3	789.41	3	798.46	3	828.55	4	796.12	3	799.52	4	847.33	3	798.46
RC205	5	1295.49	4	1352.39	4	1297.19	4	1297.65	5	1269.4	8	1168.89	4	1410.3	5	1334.55	4	1297.65
RC206	4	1139.55	4	1269.64	3	1146.32	3	1146.32	4	1123	7	1060.52	3	1146.32	5	1112.2	**3**	1153.93
RC207	4	1040.67	3	1140.23	3	1061.14	3	1061.14	3	1090.2	7	970.97	4	1140.67	5	1078.52	3	1060.05
RC208	3	898.49	3	881.2	3	828.14	3	828.14	3	859.13	5	782.7	4	828.71	3	911.15	3	829.69

Table 5. The mean value of f_1 and f_2 obtained by HSA-DA and other algorithms

Algorithms	C1	C2	R1	R2	RC1	RC2
HMOEA	(10, 828.74)	(3, 590.69)	(12.92, **1187.35**)	(3.55, 951.74)	(12.38, **1355.37**)	(4.25, 1068.26)
MOGA	(10, 828.48)	(3, 590.53)	(12.67, 1212.58)	(3.09, 956.73)	(12.38, 1379.87)	(3.50, 1148.66)
MACS-IH	(10, **828.38**)	(3, **589.86**)	(11.92, 1209.89)	(**2.73**, 951.66)	(**11.50**, 1384.16)	(**3.25**, 1119.17)
HSFLA	(10, **828.38**)	(3, **589.86**)	(11.92, 1210.34)	(**2.73**, 951.03)	(**11.50**, 1384.17)	(**3.25**, 1119.29)
ILNSA	(10, 833.10)	(3, 591.31)	(12.25, 1218.28)	(3.27, 964.11)	(12.13, 1369.57)	(3.75,1131.19)
LGA	(10, **828.38**)	(3, 590.39)	(13.50, 1188.85)	(5.55, **886.03**)	(13.25, 1360.96)	(6.88, **1013.29**)
HACO	(10, 838.38)	(3, 644.88)	(12.50, 1203.38)	(3.27, 916.74)	(12.13, 1363.37)	(3.75, 1132.59)
ACO-Tabu	(10, 829.01)	(3, 590.78)	(13, 1105.92)	(4.18, 951.36)	(12.25, 1380.55)	(4.75, 1095.84)
HSA-DA	(10, **828.38**)	(3, 590.32)	(12.25, 1201.09)	(**2.91**, 938.33)	(**11.75**, 1369.35)	(**3.25**, 1123.70)

We can see that the results of the nine algorithms are at the same level in general. This shows that these algorithms have good performance in solving multi-objective VRPTW. Thus, according to Table 5 and Fig. 4, we can say that the proposed HSA-DA still appears relatively competitive, compared with other algorithms.

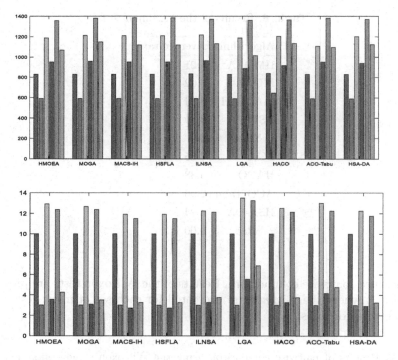

Fig. 4. The bar charts of mean value of f_1 and f_2. (a) Up: Mean value of the lowest traveled distance. (b) Down: Mean value of the smallest number of vehicles.

To further investigate the performance of the nine algorithms, statistical tests are also conducted as experimental tests in the current study. The all results in Tables 6 and 7 were obtained by nonparametric tests in the statistical software SPSS. Given that nonparametric tests do not require explicit conditions to be conducted, the nonparametric Friedman test [38] is employed to determine whether the differences observed between the proposed HSA-DA and those comparing algorithms are statistically significant or not. The T of each instance is considered for the statistical tests.

$$T = \frac{f_1^{algorithms}}{f_1^{best}} + \frac{f_2^{algorithms}}{f_2^{best}}$$

where f_1^{best} and f_2^{best} are calculated on the basis of the best known solution presented in Tables 8 and 9. $f_1^{algorithms}$ and $f_2^{algorithms}$ are calculated on the basis of the solution presented in Tables 3 and 4.

Tables 6 presents average ranks calculated for each algorithm and the *p-value* about acceptance of zero hypothesis for the whole set of instances. Moreover, the *p-value* $(0.00 < 0.05)$ strongly suggests the existence of significant difference among the considered algorithms.

In order to detect differences between particular algorithms, the Wilcoxon signed-ranks nonparametric test [39] is employed to compare two algorithms for

Table 6. Results of the Friedman test

Algorithms	Average rank
HMOEA	6.21
MOGA	6.02
MACS-IH	3.24
HSFLA	3.39
ILNSA	6.3
LGA	7.25
HACO	5.38
ACO-Tabu	2.96
HSA-DA	4.24
p-value	0.00

each instance (pairwise comparison). Results of the Wilcoxon tests are presented in Tables 7, where the *p-values* are presented for each set of instances and for each pair of algorithms.

Table 7. Results of pairwise comparison using the Wilcoxon signed-ranks nonparametric test

HSA-DA *vs*	*p-value*
HMOEA	**0.005**
MOGA	**0.021**
MACS-IH	1.00
HSFLA	1.00
ILNSA	**0.002**
LGA	**0.00**
HACO	1.00
ACO-Tabu	0.491

From Tables 7, pairwise comparison of the HSA-DA with other eight comparing algorithms does not always confirm significant differences between it and other ones. Whereas significant differences are observed for each compared pair between HSA-DA and HOEA, MOGA, ILNSA and LGA for the test instances. It means that HSA-DA outperforms the 4 comparing algorithms while solving the test instances. Although the *p-value* between HSA-DA and MACS-IH, HSFLA, HACO and ACO-Tabu exceed 0.05, we can draw a conclusion that HSA-DA has good performance in solving multi-objective VRPTW by referring to Table 5, 6, 7 and Fig. 4.

Table 8. Comparison of solutions obtained by HSA-DA with the best-known solutions for the test instances of type1 (C1, R1, RC1)

Instances	Best known		HSA-DA		Difference	
	Car	Dis	Car	Dis	Gap (Car)	Gap (Dis)
C101	10	828.94	10	828.94	0	0
C102	10	828.94	10	828.94	0	0
C103	10	828.06	10	828.06	0	0
C104	10	824.78	10	824.78	0	0
C105	10	828.94	10	828.94	0	0
C106	10	828.94	10	828.94	0	0
C107	10	828.94	10	828.94	0	0
C108	10	828.94	10	828.94	0	0
C109	10	828.94	10	828.94	0	0
R101	19	1650.8	19	1650.8	0	0
R102	17	**1434**	17	1443.18	0	0.006
R103	14	**1237.05**	13	1292.68	**−0.071**	0.045
R104	10	974.24	10	974.24	0	0
R105	14	1377.11	14	1377.11	0	0
R106	12	1252.03	12	1252.03	0	0
R107	11	1100.52	11	**1078.82**	0	**−0.020**
R108	10	960.26	10	**956.61**	0	**−0.004**
R109	12	**1169.85**	11	1194.73	**−0.083**	0.021
R110	11	**1112.21**	10	1124.4	**−0.091**	0.011
R111	10	1096.72	10	**1096.72**	0	0
R112	10	976.99	10	**971.75**	0	**−0.005**
RC101	15	1636.92	15	1636.92	0	0
RC102	13	1470.26	13	1470.26	0	0
RC103	11	**1261.67**	11	1278.14	0	0.013
RC104	10	1135.48	10	1135.48	0	0
RC105	16	**1590.25**	13	1633.72	**−0.188**	0.027
RC106	11	1427.13	11	1427.13	0	0
RC107	11	1230.48	11	1230.48	0	0
RC108	10	1142.66	10	1142.66	0	0

D: Comparison of HSA-DA and the Best-known Results

To further evaluate the performance of HSA-DA, Table 8 and Table 9 compare the results obtained by HSA-DA with the best-known solutions [37]. Gap (Car) $= (f_1^{HSA-DA} - f_1^{best})/f_1^{best}$; Gap (Dis) $= (f_2^{HSA-DA} - f_2^{best})/f_2^{best}$.

Table 9. Comparison of solutions obtained by HSA-DA with the best-known solutions for the test instances of type2 (C2, R2, RC2)

Instances	Best known		HSA-DA		Difference	
	Car	Dis	Car	Dis	Gap (Car)	Gap (Dis)
C201	3	591.56	3	591.56	0	0
C202	3	591.56	3	591.56	0	0
C203	3	591.17	3	591.17	0	0
C204	3	**590.6**	3	593.93	0	0.006
C205	3	**588.16**	3	588.84	0	0.001
C206	3	**588.49**	3	588.88	0	0.001
C207	3	588.29	3	588.29	0	0
C208	3	588.32	3	588.32	0	0
R201	5	**1206.42**	4	1253.23	**−0.200**	0.039
R202	4	**1091.21**	3	1191.7	−0.250	0.092
R203	4	**935.04**	3	939.5	**−250**	0.005
R204	3	789.72	3	**753.32**	0	**−0.046**
R205	3	994.42	3	994.42	0	0
R206	3	**833**	3	912.97	0	0.096
R207	3	814.78	3	814.78	0	0
R208	2	726.823	2	726.823	0	0
R209	3	**855**	3	909.86	0	0.064
R210	3	954.12	3	**939.37**	0	**−0.015**
R211	4	**761.1**	2	885.71	**−0.500**	0.164
RC201	6	**1134.91**	4	1423.7	**−0.333**	0.254
RC202	4	**1181.99**	3	1365.64	−0.25	0.155
RC203	4	**1026.61**	3	1060.45	−0.25	0.033
RC204	3	798.46	3	798.46	0	0
RC205	4	1300.25	4	**1297.65**	0	**−0.002**
RC206	**3**	1153.93	3	1153.93	0	0
RC207	4	**1040.67**	3	1060.05	−0.25	0.019
RC208	4	**785.93**	3	829.69	**−0.25**	0.056

From Table 8 and Table 9, we can see that the results obtained by proposed HSA-DA in set C are essentially the same as the best-known solutions. According to test instances C204, C205 and C206, the Gap (Dis) values are 0.006, 0.001 and 0.001. It means that the gap between the solutions obtained by HSA-DA and the best known solutions is small enough. Especially it has the same performance in objective f_1 as the best known. In set R, the overall calculation effect of HSA-DA is not as good as the set C. In the instance R103, R109, R110, R201,

R202, R203 and R211 the performance that HSA-DA solve the smallest number of vehicles is improved while the minimum number is reduced by two vehicles. In the set RC, the mean value of Gap (Car) and Gap (Dis) are -0.095 and 0.035, respectively. It indicates that the accuracy of calculating f_1 is improved, yet the best known outperforms our algorithm in f_2. Thus, According to data in Table 8 and Table 9, we can see that HSA-DA has good performance in solving multi-objective VRPTW.

5 Conclusion

In this paper, we use hybrid harmony search algorithm based on data analysis to solve multi-objective vehicle routing problem with time windows. In order to improve the search ability of harmony search algorithm, we make the following two improvements: (1) A variety of neighborhood search operators are used. (2) We use the data analysis method to adjust the parameters to adjust the evolution direction of each neighborhood search operator. The experimental results show that this improvement effectively improves the search ability of the basic harmony search algorithm.

In the future, this paper can be extended from two aspects. On the one hand, we can use more accurate data analysis model to improve the accuracy of data analysis. On the other hand, the real-world multi-objective VRPTW instances generated in this paper can be seen as benchmarks of many-objective combinatorial problem, which promotes the development of new many-objective algorithms for many-objective combinatorial problems.

Acknowledgement. This work is partially supported by subproject of the National Key Research and Development Program of China (2017YFD0401102-02), Key Project of Philosophy and Social Science Research Project of Hubei Provincial Department of Education in 2019(19D59) and Science and Technology Research Project of Hubei Provincial Department of Education (D20191604).

References

1. Coello, C.A.C., et al.: Evolutionary multiobjective optimization: open research areas and some challenges lying ahead. Complex Intell. Syst. **6**(2), 221–236 (2020)
2. Dantzig, G.B., Ramser, J.H.: The truck dispatching problem. Manag. Sci. **6**(1), 80–91 (1959)
3. Dorling, K., Heinrichs, J., Messier, G.G., Magierowski, S.: Vehicle routing problems for drone delivery. IEEE Trans. Syst. Man Cybern.: Syst. **47**(1), 70–85 (2016)
4. Wang, J., Weng, T., Zhang, Q., et al.: A two-stage multiobjective evolutionary algorithm for multiobjective multidepot vehicle routing problem with time windows. IEEE Trans. Syst. Man Cybern. **49**(7), 2467–2478 (2019)
5. Baldacci, R., Mingozzi, A., Roberti, R.: Recent exact algorithms for solving the vehicle routing problem under capacity and time window constraints. Eur. J. Oper. Res. **218**(1), 1–6 (2012)
6. El-Sherbeny, N.A.: Vehicle routing with time windows: an overview of exact, heuristic and metaheuristic methods. J. King Saud Univ.-Sci. **22**(3), 123–131 (2010)

7. Vidal, T., Crainic, T.G., Gendreau, M., et al.: A hybrid genetic algorithm for multidepot and periodic vehicle routing problems. Oper. Res. **60**(3), 611–624 (2012)
8. Zhang, H., Zhang, Q., Ma, L., et al.: A hybrid ant colony optimization algorithm for a multi-objective vehicle routing problem with flexible time windows. Inf. Sci. **490**, 166–190 (2019)
9. Lagos, C., Guerrero, G., Cabrera, E., et al.: An improved particle swarm optimization algorithm for the VRP with simultaneous pickup and delivery and time windows. IEEE Lat. Am. Trans. **16**(6), 1732–1740 (2018)
10. Geem, Z.W., Kim, J.H., Loganathan, G.V.: A new heuristic optimization algorithm: harmony search. SIMULATION **76**(2), 60–68 (2001)
11. Elattar, E.E.: Modified harmony search algorithm for combined economic emission dispatch of microgrid incorporating renewable sources. Energy **159**(15), 496–507 (2018)
12. Gaham, M., Bouzouia, B., Achour, N., et al.: An effective operations permutation-based discrete harmony search approach for the flexible job shop scheduling problem with makespan criterion. Appl. Intell. **48**(6), 1423–1441 (2017)
13. Rao, R.S., Narasimham, S.V., Raju, M.R., et al.: Optimal network reconfiguration of large-scale distribution system using harmony search algorithm. IEEE Trans. Power Syst. **26**(3), 1080–1088 (2011)
14. Turky, A.M., Abdullah, S., Sabar, N.R.: A hybrid harmony search algorithm for solving dynamic optimisation problems. Procedia Comput. Sci. **29**, 1926–1936 (2014)
15. Turky, A., Abdullah, S.: A multi-population harmony search algorithm with external archive for dynamic optimization problems. Inf. Sci. **272**, 84–95 (2014)
16. Ouyang, H., Gao, L., Li, S., et al.: Improved novel global harmony search with a new relaxation method for reliability optimization problems. Inf. Sci. **305**, 14–55 (2015)
17. Alia, O.M., Mandava, R.: The variants of the harmony search algorithm: an overview. Artif. Intell. Rev. **36**(1), 49–68 (2011)
18. Wu, W., Ouyang, H., Mohamed, A.W., et al.: Enhanced harmony search algorithm with circular region perturbation for global optimization problems. Appl. Intell. **50**(3), 951–975 (2020)
19. Mahdavi, M., Fesanghary, M., Damangir, E.: An improved harmony search algorithm for solving optimization problems. Appl. Math. Comput. **188**(2), 1567–1579 (2007)
20. Yang, H.O., Gao, L., Li, S., et al.: On the iterative convergence of harmony search algorithm and a proposed modification. Appl. Math. Comput. **247**, 1064–1095 (2014)
21. Ponztienda, J.L., Salcedobernal, A., Pellicer, E., et al.: Improved adaptive harmony search algorithm for the resource leveling problem with minimal lags. Autom. Constr. **77**, 82–92 (2017)
22. Zhang, J., Wu, Y., Guo, Y., et al.: A hybrid harmony search algorithm with differential evolution for day-ahead scheduling problem of a microgrid with consideration of power flow constraints. Appl. Energy **183**, 791–804 (2016)
23. Qi, Y., Hou, Z., Li, H., et al.: A decomposition based memetic algorithm for multi-objective vehicle routing problem with time windows. Comput. Oper. Res. **62**, 61–77 (2015)
24. Deb, K., Agrawal, S., Pratap, A., Meyarivan, T.: A fast elitist non-dominated sorting genetic algorithm for multi-objective optimization: NSGA-II. In: Schoenauer, M., et al. (eds.) PPSN 2000. LNCS, vol. 1917, pp. 849–858. Springer, Heidelberg (2000). https://doi.org/10.1007/3-540-45356-3_83

25. Yassen, E.T., Ayob, M., Nazri, M.Z., et al.: Meta-harmony search algorithm for the vehicle routing problem with time windows. Inf. Sci. **325**, 140–158 (2015)
26. Assad, A., Deep, K.: A hybrid harmony search and simulated annealing algorithm for continuous optimization. Inf. Sci. **450**, 246–266 (2018)
27. Qin, A.K., Huang, V.L., Suganthan, P.N., et al.: Differential evolution algorithm with strategy adaptation for global numerical optimization. IEEE Trans. Evol. Comput. **13**(2), 398–417 (2009)
28. Chen, S., Chen, R., Gao, J., et al.: A modified harmony search algorithm for solving the dynamic vehicle routing problem with time windows. Sci. Program. **2017**, 1–13 (2017)
29. Solomon, M.M.: Algorithms for the vehicle routing and scheduling problem. Oper. Res. **35**(2), 254–65 (1987)
30. Tan, K.C., Chew, Y.H., Lee, L.H.: A hybrid multiobjective evolutionary algorithm for solving vehicle routing problem with time windows. Comput. Optim. Appl. **34**(1), 115–151 (2006)
31. Ombuki, B., Ross, B.J., Hanshar, F.: Multi-objective genetic algorithms for vehicle routing problem with time windows. Appl. Intell. **24**(1), 17–30 (2006)
32. Balseiro, S.R., Loiseau, I., Ramonet, J.: An ant colony algorithm hybridized with insertion heuristics for the time dependent vehicle routing problem with time windows. Comput. Oper. Res. **38**(6), 954–966 (2011)
33. Luo, J., Li, X., Chen, M.R., Liu, H.: A novel hybrid shuffled frog leaping algorithm for vehicle routing problem with time windows. Inf. Sci. **316**, 266–292 (2015)
34. Hong, L.: An improved LNS algorithm for real-time vehicle routing problem with time windows. Comput. Oper. Res. **39**(2), 151–163 (2012)
35. Ursani, Z., Essam, D., Cornforth, D., Stocker, R.: Localized genetic algorithm for vehicle routing problem with time windows. Appl. Soft Comput. **11**(8), 5375–5390 (2011)
36. Yu, B., Yang, Z.Z., Yao, B.Z.: A hybrid algorithm for vehicle routing problem with time windows. Expert Syst. Appl. **38**(1), 435–441 (2011)
37. Ghannadpour, S.F., Noori, S., Tavakkolimoghaddam, R., et al.: A multi-objective dynamic vehicle routing problem with fuzzy time windows: model, solution and application. Appl. Soft Comput. **14**, 504–527 (2014)
38. Garcia, S., Molina, D., Lozano, M., et al.: A study on the use of non-parametric tests for analyzing the evolutionary algorithms' behaviour: a case study on the CEC'2005 special session on real parameter optimization. J. Heuristics **15**(6), 617–644 (2009)
39. Rostami, S., Oreilly, D., Shenfield, A., et al.: A novel preference articulation operator for the evolutionary multi-objective optimisation of classifiers in concealed weapons detection. Inf. Sci. **295**, 494–520 (2015)

Chicken Swarm Optimization Algorithm Based on Hybrid Improvement Strategy

Chi Liu[1,2], Jiao Jiao[1,2], Yanfeng Wang[1,2], and Yingcong Wang[1,2(✉)]

[1] School of Electrical and Information Engineering,
Zhengzhou University of Light Industry, Zhengzhou 450002, China
[2] Henan Key Lab of Information-Based Electrical Appliances,
Zhengzhou 450002, China

Abstract. To solve the problem of high dimensional complex optimization, a global Hybrid Improved Chicken Swarm Optimization (HICSO) algorithm is proposed. Firstly, the initial population is constructed by a hybrid chaotic mapping to increase the diversity of the population. Then, according to the searching algorithms characteristics, the nonlinear dynamic inertial strategy equilibrium algorithm is introduced to improve the exploration capability and mining capability. Finally, the reverse learning search strategy of "failed" rooster is proposed to improve the search performance of the algorithm. Through the simulation results on six test functions, this paper verifies the comprehensive optimization performance of HICSO algorithm.

Keywords: Chicken swarm optimization algorithm · Chaotic mapping · Dynamic inertial strategy · Reverse learning

1 Introduction

Swarm intelligence optimization algorithm is a stochastic optimization algorithm based on the simulation of living patterns of organisms in nature. By simulating the physical laws of natural phenomena, foraging and survival habits of various biological populations and various behavioral characteristics, the optimization model was established and the optimization strategy was extracted. After years of development of swarm intelligence algorithms, More common swarm intelligence algorithms include Particle Swarm Optimization (PSO) [1]. Ant Colony Optimization (ACO) [2], and Artificial Bee Colony (ABC) [3], The Artificial Fish Swarm Algorithm (AFSA) [4], and the Bat Algorithm (BA) [5], etc. A series of swarm intelligence algorithms provide an excellent solution to the optimization

Project supported by the National Science Foundation, China (No. 61702463), in part by the Joint Funds of the National Natural Science Foundation of China under Grant U1804262, in part by the Zhongyuan Thousand Talents Program under Grant 204200510003, the Research Program of Henan Province, China (No. 192102210111), and the Doctoral Scientific Research Foundation of Zhengzhou University of Light Industry, China (No. 2017BSJJ004).

L. Pan et al. (Eds.): BIC-TA 2020, CCIS 1363, pp. 174–188, 2021.
https://doi.org/10.1007/978-981-16-1354-8_13

problems in multiple domains and are widely used in scientific computing, mathematical statistics, and other fields. As the field of engineering and technology has evolved, increasingly complex and high dimensional data appears as a norm. New intelligent algorithms and their related improvement strategies are constantly being studied and proposed to solve these problems.

Chicken Swarm Optimization (CSO) is a swarm-intelligence algorithm based on the population characteristics of a natural flock of chickens proposed by Meng et al. [6] in 2014. In nature, the whole flock is divided into N subgroups. Each subgroup is equivalent to a small independent team consisting of a rooster, hens, and a brood of chicks; Different individuals in the same subgroup learn from each other through a hierarchical system and actively learn from elite individuals. The subgroups follow the biological evolutionary elimination rules that simulate the natural world, and the individuals within the species are evaluated and replaced after several generations; different subgroups maintain mutual learning and competition relationship. Chicken swarm algorithm has the advantages of high efficiency, fast convergence rate and strong global search ability. CSO has been successfully applied to SVC model parameter identification [7], multiple classifier coefficient optimization [8], DTI-FA image alignment [9], communication carrier [10] and other fields, which indicates that this algorithm has a good application prospect.

The chicken swarm algorithm has been widely studied and applied once it was proposed. However, like most intelligent algorithms, the chicken swarm algorithm also has its own shortcomings, such as premature convergence [11], easy to fall into local optimum, and slower convergence speed. Many scholars have optimized and improved the chicken swarm algorithm. Shi [12] and others combined the chicken swarm algorithm with the artificial bee colony algorithm to balance the algorithm's global and local search capabilities. Zhang [13]and others proposed a cock forward learning and reverse learning strategy to improve the algorithm's ability to jump out of local extremes. Wu et al. [14] introduced improved factors to enhance the algorithm's optimization ability, and at the same time added deduplication operators to improve the diversity of the population. Gu and others [15] proposed an adaptive dynamic learning strategy to optimize the overall performance of the algorithm.

The above-mentioned improved algorithm improves the optimization ability of the original chicken swarm algorithm to a certain extent, but it still has shortcomings. For example, some improved algorithms only improve part of the chicken swarm, and do not optimize the chicken swarm globally. Some algorithms take too much into consideration the global search ability of the chicken group, but fail to take into account the search accuracy of the algorithm. Aiming at the current problems of the chicken swarm algorithm, this paper proposes a chicken swarm optimization algorithm based on a hybrid improvement strategy, which used hybrid chaotic sequence [16] to initialize the population and increase the initial population diversity of the algorithm. The inertia weight factor that changes with the sine is introduced into the iterative formula of the rooster and the hen, which balances the exploration and mining capabilities of the algorithm. A reverse learning strategy for failed roosters is proposed, which increases the optimization performance of the algorithm while ensuring search efficiency. Through the simulation results on six test functions, this paper verifies the superiority of the Hybrid Improved Chicken Swarm Optimization (HICSO) algorithm over ABC, PSO, CSO and an Improved Chicken Swarm Optimization (ICSO) algorithm in optimizing performance, and verifies the effectiveness of each HICSO's optimization strategy.

2   Basic Chicken Swarm Optimization Algorithm

The swarm algorithm is a bionic swarm intelligence algorithm based on the population characteristics and foraging behavior of a swarm of chickens. In nature, the whole flock is divided into N subgroups, each of which is equivalent to a small, independent flock consisting of a rooster, hens and a brood of chicks; individuals in the same sub-group learn from each other through a hierarchy [17] and actively learn from elite individuals; the different subgroups maintain learning and competitive relationships with each other. The most important feature of this algorithm is the introduction of population division, elite individual and role assignment relationships, and the derivation of followership and learning rules based on these dominant relationships. In a given flock system, different chickens follow different learning patterns, maintaining the status of dominant individuals in the swarm, and ensuring sufficient prospecting capacity. The behavior of the swarm is ideally described by the following rules:

(a) There are several different subgroups in the flock. Each subgroups consists of a dominant rooster, at least one hen, and some chicks.
(b) The flock is divided into groups, and the identity of the chickens (rooster, hen, chicks) is determined by order of the fitness values of each chicken. Chickens with good fitness values served as roosters, chickens with suboptimal fitness values served as hens, and the rest with average fitness values served as chicks, while the mother-chick relationship between hens and chicks was determined randomly.
(c) Under the competitive followership system of the group, the relationship between individuals in the swarm remains unchanged over several generations. However, since we take into account the natural flock growth and mortality criterion, we can set the population state parameter G to indicate that these states of the group are updated every few G's of time.
(d) The more dominant chickens compete for food, the higher the adaptation function evaluation index will be, and the individuals with the highest evaluation value will be randomly assigned to roosters according to the number of randomly generated subgroups. Hens and chicks will be assigned to each subpopulation in turn according to the adaptation value.

The main learning rules for individual groups are as follows:

Rooster: learning from itself and learning from the rest of the subgroup of roosters. The roosters' learning pattern can be called the elite learning pattern, which helps to increase the adaptation advantage, search faster for the optimal solution, and reduce useless searches.

Hens: learn from themselves, from the roosters in their subgroups, and from all the highly adapted hens in the population. The hens are the most active part of the flock, maintaining the learning pattern of their own subclan on the one hand, and searching for the optimal solution globally on the other hand, which helps to jump out of the local optimum.

Chickens: learn from themselves and from the hens in their subgroups. The learning pattern of the chicks maintains the evolutionary pattern of competition within the swarm.

There are three types of chicks in the whole swarm, and the number of individuals is N. The number of roosters, hens, and chicks is RN, HN, and CN, respectively. Roosters are the most adaptable individuals in the population, so they have a larger food search range. The updated formula for rooster locations is as follows:

$$x_{i,j}^{t+1} = x_{i,j}^t \times (1 + randn(0, \sigma^2)) \tag{1}$$

$$\begin{cases} f_i < f_k, & \sigma^2 = 1 \\ f_i \geq f_k, & \sigma^2 = exp[(f_k - f_i)/(|f_i| + \varepsilon)] \end{cases} \tag{2}$$

where $k \neq i$, $x_{i,j}^t$ represents the position of the first iteration of the rooster, $randn(0, \sigma^2)$ denotes a Gaussian distribution with mean 0 and standard deviation σ^2, ε denotes a very small constant, and k is any body of all roosters excluding the i-th individual.

Hens are the most complex groups in the population with the most complex learning pattern, which is crucial to the search performance of the algorithm. The hen's position is updated as follows:

$$x_{i,j}^{t+1} = x_{i,j}^t + c_1 \times rand(x_{r1,j}^t - x_{i,j}^t) + c_2 \times rand(x_{r2,j}^t - x_{i,j}^t) \tag{3}$$

where c1 and c2 represent the learning factor;

$$c1 = exp[(f_i - f_{r1})/(abs(f_i) + \varepsilon)] \tag{4}$$

$$c2 = exp(f_{r2} - f_{i1}) \tag{5}$$

Rand is a random number from 0 to 1; r1 is the rooster in the group of the i-th hen; r2 is an arbitrary individual randomly selected from the roosters and hens in the whole flock, and $r1 \neq r2$.

Chicken is one of the most unfit individuals in the algorithm population. Its foraging pattern follows the hierarchical entourage system. After generation G, the individual in the chicken population will be re-evaluated, and the chicken population will be selected according to the fitness. The position of the chicken is updated as follows:

$$x_{i,j}^{t+1} = x_{i,j}^t + FL \times (x_{m,j}^t - x_{i,j}^t) \tag{6}$$

where: m is the hen (and mother hen) corresponding to the i-th chick; FL is a random number obeying a uniform distribution of $[0.4, 1]$, representing the behavioral pattern of chicks following the hen foraging.

3   Chicken Swarm Optimization Algorithm Based on Hybrid Improvement Strategy

3.1   Chaotic Mapping Initialization Strategy

The performance of group intelligence algorithm to find the best performance is related to the population diversity of the initial population [14]. Generally, the population initialization of group intelligence algorithm uses the rand function to randomly generate the initial population, if the randomly generated initial population is poorly distributed, it will have an impact on the convergence speed and accuracy of the algorithm. The chaotic variables are random and traversable, and the scatterplots generated by the rand function and chaotic logistic sequences were analyzed [18], and the results show that the chaotic sequences are more traversable than the rand function and generate a higher diversity of initial populations. The more widely cited mapping in the current literature is the logistic [19], but studies have shown that it has a high probability of taking values in the intervals [0, 1] and [0.9, 1], and that the speed of the search for excellence is affected by its inhomogeneity of traversal. Tent mapping [20] has better traversal uniformity and faster convergence than the logistic mapping, but tent also suffers from small periodicity and the problem of unstable periodic points. In this paper, a chaotic iterative mapping-hybrid mapping [21] combining logistic mapping and Tent mapping is introduced. The expression is as follows:

$$z_{k+1} = f(z_k) = \begin{cases} b(1 - u_1 z_k^2), & -1 < Z_k \leq 0 \\ 1 - u_2 z_k, & 0 < Z_k < 1 \end{cases} \tag{7}$$

According to the study [22], when the parameters of the above formula are set to $u_1 = 1.8$, $u_2 = 2.0$, b $= 0.85$, and the initial value x_0 is taken as 0.82, this mapping is in a chaotic state. The resulting chaotic sequence was plotted in the laboratory as Fig. 1.

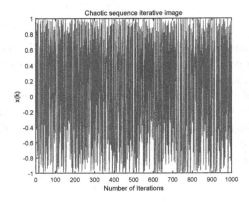

Fig. 1. Chaotic sequence iteration chart.

In Fig. 1, the horizontal axis is the number of iterations k of the chaotic sequence, and the vertical axis is the chaotic state space variable X_k generated after each iteration. The initial populations based on hybrid chaotic sequences are as follows:

$$x_{i,j} = x_{min}^j + Z_{k,j}(x_{max}^j - x_{min}^j) \qquad (8)$$

In this paper, hybrid chaotic mapping is used to initialize the flock, so that the initial swarm particles are more uniformly distributed in the search space, and to improve the swarm algorithm's ability to find the best value.

3.2 Cosine Inertia Weighting Strategy

Inspired by the particle swarm algorithm, this paper introduces the inertial weighting factor [23] into the search strategy of the swarm algorithm, which is a mechanism to coordinate the exploration and exploitation capabilities of the population, and can effectively balance the local and global search capabilities of the flock particles.

Generally, in the early stages of the algorithm run, we want the flock particles to search for feasible solutions in a broader region so that we can quickly determine the approximate range of regional extremes in the entire solution space and avoid the algorithm from falling into premature local optimality. In the later stages of the algorithm iteration, we would like to have the flock particles reduce the search step size and refine the search for neighborhood feasible solutions under the leadership of each flock rooster particle, so as to maintain the dominant position of elite individuals within the flock, avoid missing the global optimum, and solve the problem of low convergence accuracy in the later stages of evolution.

The introduction of inertial weighting coefficients in the swarm algorithm has been proven to be a more effective and can significantly improve the optimization performance of the algorithm. Huang [24] used a random inertial weighting strategy that obeys a Gaussian distribution. This strategy plays a certain optimization role in the result verification, but it cannot control the random change of inertia weight in the early and late iteration of the algorithm. Zheng [25] proposed an adaptive inertial weight that changes with population aggregation. Li et al. [26] proposed a weight update strategy based on linear variation, Han [27] was inspired by the preference for random wandering process in the cuckoo algorithm and introduced a weight update strategy based on decreasing exponential function, all of these improvements improve the performance of the algorithm to some extent.

In this paper, a method to control the inertia weight change according to the cosine function is used, and the advantages of this weight change strategy are: The decreasing rate of this function is relatively slow in the initial stage of the interval, which is convenient for the chicken swarm particles to search for feasible solutions in a relatively large range at the beginning. The decreasing function also maintains a relatively gentle rate of change at the end of the period, which is convenient for the fineness search of swarm particles in the later period. Compared to Gaussian random variation, it can effectively control the algorithm's search mode at different periods of iteration; compared to linear decreasing weights with constant decreasing amplitude. It can make the transition of pre-late search requirements more smoothly; compared to decreasing weights with exponential function, its cosine decreasing curve is more consistent with the search strategy of the chicken particles in the search cycle. This nonlinear decreasing weight strategy allows the algorithm to achieve a balance between global search and local exploration, effectively. The updating formula of the inertia weight w of cosine change is:

$$w_k = (w_{max} - w_{min}/2)\cos(\pi k/k_{max}) + (w_{max} + w_{min}/2) \qquad (9)$$

where, w_{max} and w_{min} are the maximum and minimum values of the inertia weight coefficient, generally 0.95 and 0.4 respectively. k and k_{max} represent the current number of iterations and the maximum number of iterations. w_k represents the inertia weight value corresponding to the k-th iteration. In Fig. 2, w_1 is the nonlinear cosine curve, w_2 is the linear curve, and w_3 is the image with the inertia weight constant value of 0.7.

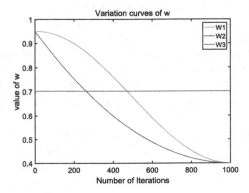

Fig. 2. Inertia weight iteration chart.

Rooster has the highest fitness ranking among the whole flock of chickens. Only the inertia weight, which decreases linearly with the sine change, is added to improve the search performance of the algorithm. The improved rooster position update formula is as follows:

$$x_{i,j}^{t+1} = w * x_{i,j}^t * (1 + randn(0, \sigma^2)) \qquad (10)$$

where, w is the adaptive inertia weight introduced. The formula shows that the rooster is engaged in dynamic inertia self-learning.

The hen plays a connecting role in the whole flock. In order to maintain the stability of the following leading mechanism of the flock, only the inertia weight factor, which decreases nonlinearly with the change of sine, is introduced. The improved hen position updating formula is as follows:

$$x_{i,j}^{t+1} = w * x_{i,j}^t + c_1 \times rand(x_{r1,j}^t - x_{i,j}^t) + c_2 \times rand(x_{r2,j}^t - x_{i,j}^t) \qquad (11)$$

The formula shows that the hen keeps the learning effect on the roosters and other dominant individuals in the group, and at the same time carries on the dynamic inertial self-learning.

Chicken is one of the worst individuals in fitness ranking. In order to maintain the leading role of hen to chicken, the search strategy of chicken does not introduce inertia adaptive weight, but continues to use the original position updating formula.

3.3 Reverse Learning Strategy

In view of the problem that chicken swarm algorithm is prone to fall into local optimal and difficult to jump out when encountering high-dimensional multi-peak functions. Inspired by the fact that failed roosters in the natural world search for food farther away, this paper introduces a search strategy of "failed" roosters reverse learning [28]. The so-called "failed" roosters are the lower performers after an iterative fitness evaluation of the population. The chicken swarm algorithm has a unique hierarchy and leading mechanism, which determines that the rooster is an elite individual, and its position plays a great guiding role in the position update of the hen and chick. Once the rooster falls into the local minimum, the hen and chick in the subgroups of the rooster are also prone to fall into the local optimal under the leading mechanism. Rather than letting this part of "failed" roosters continue the iterative search in the neighborhood with a high probability of being locally optimal, it is better to find the optimal solution in a broader solution space. In this paper, the reverse learning mechanism is used to update the location information of failed roosters.

In probability science, there's usually a half chance that a solution is not as good as its inverse solution. When solving some high-dimensional multi-peak functions, the rooster particle is easily trapped in one or several troughs (when the fitness function takes the minimum value) and difficult to jump out. However, the reverse solution updating strategy can greatly improve the global search ability of the algorithm, and more efficiently find the valleys that may "hide" the global optimal solution, thus creating favorable conditions for the fine search in the later stage of the algorithm. The algorithm introducing the reverse learning strategy is described as follows:

In the algorithm, set the current position of "failed" rooster particle i as x_i and the reverse position as $\hat{x}_i$, and make the failed rooster particle jump to the corresponding reverse solution position through the reverse learning strategy. If the position of the rooster particle i in the j-th dimension is $x_{i,j}$, then its corresponding reverse solution position [25] can be defined as:

$$\hat{x}_{i,j} = x_{min}^j + x_{max}^j - x_{i,j} \qquad (12)$$

where, x_{min}^j and x_{max}^j are the minimum and maximum values of the rooster particle in the j-th dimension respectively.

This represents the failure of the rooster to find food in the opposite region of the solution space. Considering the convergence accuracy, convergence speed and robustness of the algorithm, we set that after the status update of the chicken population every G generation, the rooster particles in the bottom quarter of the fitness ranking in the rooster library are failed roosters. The failed rooster update frequency is consistent with the flock reset frequency.

The search strategy of reverse learning of failed roosters is introduced, which can not only maintain the elite status of roosters with high fitness ranking and maintain the current optimal solution, but also not waste the search potential of the population of roosters with low fitness, but also give consideration to the global exploration ability of the algorithm and search efficiency, which can greatly improve the search performance of the algorithm.

3.4   Framework of HICSO

The detailed process of the global hybrid improved chicken swarm algorithm is as follows:

Step1: set relevant parameters of the algorithm, the maximum iteration number of the algorithm T, spatial dimension D, population size N, rooster, hen, chicken scale factor, update algebra G, etc. The initial population is constructed by chaotic mapping.

Step2: Calculate the fitness value Fitness of N individual chickens, initialize the individual optimal and global optimal, and set the number of iterations $t = 1$.

Step3: If mod $(t, G) = 1$, sort the individuals according to the fitness value of the individuals, establish the hierarchy of the population and assign the subordination relation of the subgroups.

Step4: Consider the bottom quarter of roosters in the rooster library as "failed roosters" and implement the reverse learning strategy. The failed rooster update frequency is consistent with the flock reset frequency.

Step5: Update the position of the flock according to the improved formula, calculate the individual fitness value, and update the individual optimal and global optimal.

Step6: $t = t + 1$. If the iteration stop condition is met, end the iteration and output the optimal value; Otherwise go to Step3 and iterate (Fig. 3).

4   Experiment and Analysis

In order to verify the effectiveness of HICSO, six complex multimodal test functions are selected in this paper for the simulation test. The optimization results were compared with ABC, PSO, CSO and ICSO under fixed optimization iteration parameters. Each algorithm was tested independently for 50 times and

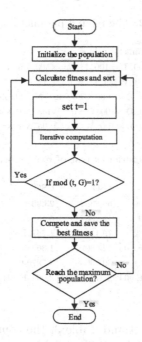

Fig. 3. HICSO algorithm flow chart.

Table 1. Benchmark function

Benchmark function	Foumula	Search interval	d	f_{min}
Levy	$f_1 = \sum_{i=1}^{d-1}(x_i-1)^2[1+sin^2(3\pi x_{i+1})] + sin^2(3\pi x_1) + |x_d-1|[1+sin^2(3\pi x_d)]$	$[-10, 10]$	100	0
Ackley	$f_2 = -20exp(-0.2\sqrt{\frac{1}{30}\sum_{i=1}^{30}x_i^2}) + 20 + e$	$[-32, 32]$	100	0
Alpine	$f_3 = \sum_{i=1}^{d} |x_i sin(x_i) + 0.1x_i|$	$[-10, 10]$	100	0
Griewank	$f_4 = 1 + \sum_{i=1}^{30}\frac{x_i^2}{4000} + \prod_{i=1}^{30} cos(\frac{x_i}{\sqrt{i}})$	$[-600, 600]$	100	0
Rastrigin	$f_5 = \sum_{i=1}^{30}(x_i^2 - 10cos(2\pi x_i) + 10)$	$[-5, 5]$	100	0
Schwefel2.26	$f_6 = 418.9839d - \sum_{i=1}^{d} x_i sin(\sqrt{|x_i|})$	$[-500, 500]$	100	0

then the search performance was evaluated comprehensively. Figure 4 (a) to (f) shows the optimization result curve of the above five algorithms after testing the function. Table 3 records the optimal value found after running the above five algorithms for 50 times respectively.

In addition, in order to verify the effectiveness of each strategy of HICSO, a single strategy control experiment was adopted in this paper. HICSO-1, HICSO-2, and HICSO-3 are respectively named for the improved algorithm that only adopts chaotic initialization strategy, nonlinear inertia weight strategy, and failed rooster reverse learning strategy. Figure 5 (a) to (f) shows the optimization curve of the CSO, the single strategy optimization algorithm and the hybrid strategy optimization algorithm on the six test functions (Tables 1 and 2).

Table 2. The related parameter values.

Algorithms	The related parameter values
ABC	N = 100, NF = 50, D = 100, Mmax = 500, Limit = 0.5N
PSO	N = 100, D = 100, W = 1, C1 = 1.5, C2 = 2
CSO	N = 100, G = 10, D = 100, NR = 0.2N, NH = 0.6N NC = 0.2N, NM = 0.1NH
ICSO	N = 100, G = 10, D = 100, C = 0.4 Wmax = 0.9 Wmin = 0.4
HICSO	N = 100, G = 10, D = 100, Wmax = 0.95 Wmin = 0.4

Table 3. Convergence characteristics test of five algorithms (average of 50 runs).

Benchmark function	ABC	PSO	CSO	ICSO	HICSO
Levy	390.4196	66.8362	23.9080	7.6408	6.3463
Ackley	21.0099	12.2307	4.1312	2.7305E-04	8.8818E-16
Alpine	233.3282	79.1184	1.7672E-01	2.7243E-07	9.0652E-104
Griewank	1.1157E+03	123.8090	1.36380	3.9681E-07	0
Rastrigin	380.1701	897.9036	3.7879E-05	2.0182E-08	0
Schwefel2.26	3.0842E+04	3.3741E+04	3.0643E+04	3.0622E+04	1.7706E+04

It can be seen from Fig. 4 and Table 3, the comprehensive performance of HICSO is superior to other algorithms in the optimization of f1 function and f2 function. Especially in the test of f2 function, HICSO's optimization speed is faster, and according to the data recorded in Table 3, the global optimization accuracy reaches about 16 decimal places, which is much higher than the optimization accuracy of other algorithms. The functions of f3, f4, and f5 are typical nonlinear multimodal functions with extensive search space and a large number of local extreme values. The optimization precision of ABC, PSO, CSO and ICSO in these test functions does not differ much, while HICSO shows good optimization capability in these high-dimensional complex problems and directly finds the global minimum point of f4 and f5 functions. f6 function has a large number of local optimal values near the global optimum, and the function oscillates strongly. HICSO's optimization performance on f6 function is also higher than that of other algorithms. The above results indicate that HICSO has certain advantages in dealing with the optimization of high-dimensional multi-local extremum functions.

In the comparison experiment of a single strategy, we can see that the improved algorithm using the optimization strategy has a certain performance improvement compared with CSO. The HICSO-2's optimization performance using the nonlinear inertia weight strategy has a large improvement range, the HICSO comprehensive optimization performance using the mixed optimization strategy has the best performance. In the optimization test of f6 function, HICSO-1 has a better optimization effect than HICSO-2. This result shows that HICSO-2 also has certain limitations in its optimization ability, which further demonstrates the advantage of the hybrid improvement strategy adopted in this paper when solving multiple complex function problems.

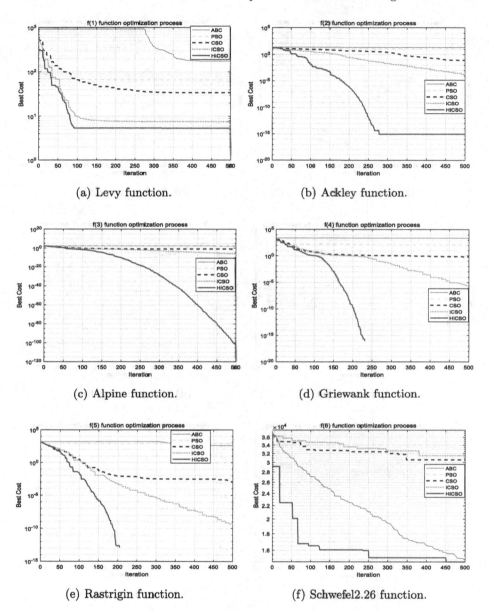

(a) Levy function.

(b) Ackley function.

(c) Alpine function.

(d) Griewank function.

(e) Rastrigin function.

(f) Schwefel2.26 function.

Fig. 4. Test results of five algorithms.

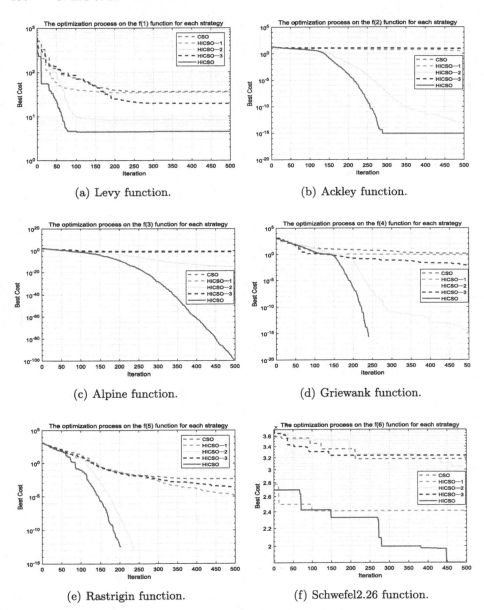

(a) Levy function.

(b) Ackley function.

(c) Alpine function.

(d) Griewank function.

(e) Rastrigin function.

(f) Schwefel2.26 function.

Fig. 5. Test results for effectiveness of each strategy.

5   Conclusion

In this paper, a global Hybrid Improved Chicken Swarm Optimization (HICSO) algorithm is proposed to solve the problem of high dimensional complex optimization due to the defects of the traditional Chicken Swarm Optimization

(CSO) algorithm, such as slow convergence speed and easy to fall into the local optimum. Firstly, the algorithm uses the characteristics of chaotic sequence to initialize the population and improve the diversity of the initial population. Then a nonlinear inertia weight factor is introduced, which makes the algorithm balance the global exploration ability and the mining ability of the optimal solution, Then a reverse learning search strategy of "failed" rooster is proposed to ensure the efficiency and precision of the algorithm. In this paper, 6 test functions were selected for simulation experiment. First, HICSO was compared with ABC, PSO, CSO and ICSO for optimization performance. Then, a controlled experiment was used to compare the optimization effect of each optimization strategy and mixed optimization strategy. The experimental results show that HICSO has good robustness and global convergence performance for complex functions with different characteristics, effectively avoids the premature convergence problem of the original algorithm, and greatly improves the search performance of the algorithm.

References

1. Kennedy, J., Eberhart, R.: Particle swarm optimization. In: Proceedings of ICNN 1995 - International Conference on Neural Networks, vol. 4, pp. 1942–1948 (1995)
2. Dorigo, M., Maniezzo, V., Colorni, A.: Ant system: optimization by a colony of cooperating agents. IEEE Trans. Syst. Man Cybern. Part B Cybern. 26(1), 29–41 (1996)
3. Akbari, R., Ziarati, K.: Multiobjective bee swarm optimization. Int. J. Innovative Comput. Inf. Control IJICIC 8(1b), 715–726 (2012)
4. Li, X.L., Shao, Z.J., Qian, J.X.: An optimizing method based on autonomous animate: fish swarm algorithm. Syst. Eng.-Theory Pract. 22(11), 32–38 (2002)
5. Yang, X.S.: A new metaheuristic bat-inspired algorithm. In: González, J.R., Pelta, D.A., Cruz, C., Terrazas, G., Krasnogor, N. (eds.) Nature Inspired Cooperative Strategies for Optimization (NICSO 2010), pp. 65–74. Springer, Heidelberg (2010). https://doi.org/10.1007/978-3-642-12538-6_6
6. Meng, X., Liu, Y., Gao, X., Zhang, H.: A new bio-inspired algorithm: chicken swarm optimization. In: Tan, Y., Shi, Y., Coello, C.A.C. (eds.) ICSI 2014. LNCS, vol. 8794, pp. 86–94. Springer, Cham (2014). https://doi.org/10.1007/978-3-319-11857-4_10
7. Pourbeik, P., Bostrom, A., Ray, B.: Modeling and application studies for a modemn static VAr system installation. IEEE Trans. Power Deliv. 21(1), 368–377 (2006)
8. Hong, Y., Yu, F.Q.: Improved chicken swarm optimization and its application in coefficients optimization of multi-classifier. Comput. Eng. Appl. 53(9), 158–161 (2017)
9. Zheng, W., Jiang, C., Liu, S., Zhao, J.: Improved chicken swarm optimization algorithm and its application in DTI-FA image registration. Comput. Sci. 45, 285–291 (2018)
10. Yi, Z., Liu, J., Wang, S., et al.: PAPR reduction technology based on CSO algorithm in CO-OFDM system. In: The International Conference on Optical Communications Networks (2017)
11. Liang, J.H., Wang, L.F., Ma, M., Zhang, J.: A fast SAR image segmentation method based on improved chicken swarm optimization algorithm. Multimedia Tools Appl. 77(24), 31787–31805 (2018)

12. Shi, X.D., Gao, Y.L.: Hybrid algorithm based on chicken swarm optimization and artificial bee colony. J. Hefei Univ. Technol. (Nat. Sci.) **41**, 589–594 (2018)
13. Zhang, M.X., Zhang, D.M., Yang, J.Q., et al.: An improved chicken algorithm based on positive learning and reverse learning. Microelectron. Comput. (2018)
14. Wu, D.H., Kong, F., Gao, W.Z., Shen, Y.X., Ji, Z.C.: Improved chicken swarm optimization. In: IEEE International Conference on Cyber Technology in Automation (2015)
15. Gu, Y.C., Lu, H.Y., Xiang, L., et al.: Adaptive dynamic learning chicken swarm optimization algorithm. Comput. Eng. Appl. (2020)
16. Tong, X.J.: Design of an image encryption scheme based on a multiple chaotic map. Commun. Nonlinear Sci. Numer. Simul. **18**(7), 1725–1733 (2017)
17. Wu, Y., Yan, B., Qu, X.J.: Improved chicken swarm optimization method for reentry trajectory optimization. Math. Probl. Eng. **2018**(PT.2), 1–13 (2018)
18. Lee, T.F.: Enhancing the security of password authenticated key agreement protocols based on chaotic maps. Inf. Sci. **290**, 63–71 (2015)
19. Zuppa, L.A.: Chaotic logistic map implementation in the PIC12F629 microcontroller unit. IFAC Proc. **43**(24), 167–170 (2010)
20. Song, J.H., Wang, G.Q., Ma, H.B., Wang, Y.L.: A digital watermark method based on DWT and tent mapping. Int. J. Adv. Comput. Technol. **28**(007), 1262–1265 (2006)
21. Luo, Q.B., Zhang, J.: A new approach to generate chaotic pseudo-random sequence. J. Electron. Inf. Technolo. **28**(7), 1262–1265 (2006)
22. Li, M.T., Zhao, Z.M.: New method to generate chaotic pseudo-random sequence. Appl. Res. Comput. **28**(1), 341–344 (2011)
23. Chen, C., Chellali, R., Xing, Y.: Improved grey wolf optimizer algorithm using dynamic weighting and probabilistic disturbance strategy. J. Comput. Appl. (2017)
24. Xia, H., et al.: Chicken swarm optimization algorithm of hybrid evolutionary searching strategy. Comput. Eng. Appl. (2018)
25. Zheng, J.M., Chellali, R., Chen, C., Xing, Y.: Improved chicken swarm optimization algorithm with adaptive features. Microelectron. Comput. **35**(10), 93–98 (2018)
26. Li, C.H., Lu, A.J., Shao, L.P.: Rooster algorithm based on linear decrement weight update. Intell. Comput. Appl. **2**, 43–47 (2020)
27. Han, F.F., Zhao, Q.H., Du, Z.H.: Enhanced chicken swarm algorithm for global optimization. Enhanced Chicken Swarm Algorithm Glob. Optim. **36**(008), 2317–2319, 2327 (2019)
28. Dyer, A.G., Dorin, A., Reinhardt, V., Garcia, J.E., Rosa, M.G.P.: Bee reverse-learning behavior and intra-colony differences: simulations based on behavioral experiments reveal benefits of diversity. Ecol. Modelling **277**, 119–131 (2014)
29. Kong, F., Wu, D.H.: An improved chicken swarm optimization algorithm. J. Jiangnan Univ.: Nat. Sci. Edition **14**(6), 681–688 (2015)

A Data-Driven Model Analysis Method in Optimizing Raw Materials Standard for Glutinous Rice Products

Zhixin He[1] , Zhou Kang[1]([⊠]) , Jian Zhou[2], Hua Yang[1], Xuechun Shang[1],
and Guangbin Li[3]

[1] College of Mathematics and Computer Science,
Wuhan Polytechnic University, Wuhan 430023, China
zhoukang65@whpu.edu.cn
[2] School of Food Science and Engineering,
Wuhan Polytechnic University, Wuhan 430023, China
[3] Enterprise-School Joint Innovation Center,
Qianjiang Jujin Rice Industry Co., Ltd., Hubei, China

Abstract. The main method to ensure the stable quality of glutinous rice products is to assure that the raw materials of glutinous rice flour meet the specified quality requirements. Therefore, the prediction about the quality standard of raw materials for glutinous rice flour is extremely important. The existing researches rarely take into account such a prediction method for predicting the quality standard of raw materials for glutinous rice flour. In this paper, we apply the quality standard of high-quality glutinous rice products to predict raw materials for glutinous rice flour which meets requirements. In order to solve the raw material standard formulation problem for the glutinous rice product(RMSP-GRP for short), we propose an analysis method based on a three-stage data-driven model which consists of prediction, modeling and regulation. The first stage is to use the quality index of raw materials of glutinous rice flour to predict the quality index of glutinous rice products, in order to perfect the process of transforming the quality requirements of high-quality glutinous rice into the requirements of raw materials of glutinous rice flour. In the second stage, the multi-objective optimization model with priority objective was established to set the upper and lower boundaries of the quality index of raw materials of glutinous rice flour as decision variables and the correction factors were introduced based on the goodness of fit of the prediction function to improve the reliability of the feasible region. The optimization model mentioned above is to search for an optimal hypercube within the feasible region defined by the constraints of raw materials of glutinous rice flour and the constraints of glutinous rice products. In other words, the hypercube can reach the maximum state of the required shape when all vertices of the hypercube are in the feasible region. Based on the quartile data characteristics of the experimental samples and some conclusions in the second stage, we adjust the optimization model to expand the range of quality index of raw materials of glutinous rice flour in the third stage.

Keywords: Special raw materials · Quick-frozen rice dumplings ·
Data-driven · Multi-objective optimization · Quality standard

© Springer Nature Singapore Pte Ltd. 2021
L. Pan et al. (Eds.): BIC-TA 2020, CCIS 1363, pp. 189–220, 2021.
https://doi.org/10.1007/978-981-16-1354-8_14

1   Introduction

As one of the Chinese traditional food crops, glutinous rice can be used to make more than 100 kinds of foods and drinks. Although a lot of foods on the market are made of the general glutinous rice flour, they cannot meet the various characteristics of diversified glutinous rice products [3]. And the formulation of quality standard of the glutinous rice product could help companies to rapidly manage products of different quality. It plays important role in guiding the process adjustment or selection during production.

The production of glutinous rice products is restricted to complicated factors in the cause of diversified manufacturing or environment. Therefore, the formulations of quality standard for raw materials and glutinous rice product are difficult, especially the raw materials. Product quality standard can be obtained by directly testing the target product through quality measurement experiments, but the raw material quality standard is different. It is hard to build a method of converting product quality into raw quality on the condition that the product quality standard and manufacturing are given. Based on the method we proposed, people can accurately obtain raw material quality standard.

The research on the production of glutinous rice products is as follows: explore the correlation of indexes through data analysis; set up comparative experiments of raw material in different conditions such as different kinds of raw material, the products made of raw material on different storage conditions and so on; analyze the impact of glutinous rice flour preparation or manufacturing on quality indexes. The research status of these three directions is analyzed as follows: Some scholars [6–8] implied a data analysis method, for two common glutinous rice products, to study the numerical relationship between the characteristics of glutinous rice flour and the quality of glutinous rice products and drew quantitative conclusions from the correlation analysis of indexes. Some scholars [15, 21, 23] studied the changes in the storage properties of glutinous rice flour and products, elaborated the mechanism of the influence of storage conditions, such as temperature on the quality of glutinous rice products, and explained that the control of production and storage conditions has great significance on improving the product quality. Reference shows that the manufacturing will affect the quality of glutinous rice products in the same initial state (the experimental measurement is similar or identical). References [9, 24, 25] show that the preparation process of glutinous rice flour will affect the characteristics of glutinous rice flour, and then products. In a word, scholars mainly focused on the influence of the quality of glutinous rice products, and studied the quality of glutinous rice products from various aspects. For example, storage conditions, selection of raw materials, control of indexes, and equipment technology. They also formulated some quality standard of the glutinous rice product. However, there are very few researches about a data analysis based method for obtaining the quality index standard of glutinous rice flour from the quality index standard of glutinous rice products.

Wiedermann (1978) proposed an appropriate formula to regulate and control the procedure of butter for achieving the ideal product characteristics and improving the production efficiency. In 2013, Anupam, Lal, Bist, Sharma and Swaroop used a simple weighting method to classify and select paper materials based on the decision units composed of the near chemical, physical, and morphological characteristics of the raw materials [1]. Kim, Lee, Kim and Kim used fuzzy analytic hierarchy process to comprehensively consider all relevant factors for formulating index weights that assesses the criticality of raw material indexes [10]. In a series of articles by Koji Muteki, a data-driven approach was proposed to solve similar optimization problems such as raw material procurement, processed food ingredients, and polymer materials mixed into polymers. In this method, a partial least squares (PLS) method was used to establish a formulation model which combines the characteristics of raw materials with a database of previous process operations. The approach builds an optimization model based on the final product quality to optimize the purchase decision of raw materials. In the end, the raw materials are replaced and the total cost of raw materials is minimized while maintaining the same product performance [14]. Garcia Munoz and Mercado (2013) used mixed integer nonlinear programming and multiple latent variable regression models to study products with better quality from three perspectives: (i) physical properties of input materials; (ii) raw material formulation Ratio; (iii) production route and processing conditions (process development) [4]. Current studies focus on the index development, without studying how to use a certain standard to predict another.

In this paper, we propose a data-driven model analysis method to predict the quality standard of glutinous rice flour when the quality of the raw materials of the goal product is specified. The method is an organic fusion of learning algorithms and multi-objective optimization strategies. Therefore, the glutinous rice flour can produce qualified goal glutinous rice products in a given production process.

During the establishment of the method, we use the learning algorithms to train the model, and the obtained model is used to establish a numerical relationship between the quality of raw materials of glutinous rice flour and the quality of the products. The challenge in the model training is how to use appropriate information extracted from multivariate index data to accurately describe this relationship. Based on the existing conclusions, this paper takes the principal component as explanatory variables and then uses the multiple linear regression model [2] to predict the glutinous rice products. Further, the formulation of raw material quality indexes includes optimizing the multiple indexes and multiple decision variables. We use standard of product quality to predict standard of raw material quality. The essence is to use multiple linear prediction models to convert the constraints of products quality into the quality of the raw materials. Therefore, the core of this paper is to construct a multi-objective linear programming model (Springer Science & Business Media, 2012) to calculate the best quality standard of the raw materials of glutinous rice flour.

The paper is organized as follows. The second part introduces the definition about formulating the raw material standard for glutinous rice products and the basic concepts extracted from the production. The method and process of solving RMSP-GRP are analyzed from the perspective of the manufacturing.

The contribution of this paper lies in the construction of a three-stage data-driven model analysis method. The third part introduces the design idea and detailed modeling steps of the three-stage method. The fourth part details the experimental steps and data conclusions. The fifth part summarizes the conclusions and research prospects of this paper.

2   Problem Description and Methods

This section introduces the definition and basic concepts of the raw material standard formulation problem for the glutinous rice product(RMSP-GRP) in detail and provides the basic method to solve this problem from a macro perspective.

2.1   Raw Material Standard Formulation Problem for the Glutinous Rice Product

The raw material standard formulation problem for the glutinous rice product (RMSP-GRP): under the condition that the quality standard of the glutinous rice product is determined, a method is designed to predict the optimal quality range of glutinous rice flour raw materials, so that as many varieties of glutinous rice flour that meet the standard can produce qualified glutinous rice product.

As the production experience or simple comparative test, we can judge what kind of raw materials of glutinous rice flour input will get what kind of products. This method can improve the production efficiency of glutinous rice products. In this context, a systematic and scientific method is designed to solve raw material standard formulation problem for the glutinous rice product(RMSP-GRP).

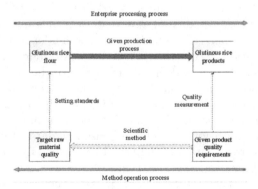

Fig. 1. Relationship between production of glutinous rice products process and method flow

The solution about RMSP-GRP in this article comes from the actual enterprise manufacturing procedure. Many enterprises produce the glutinous rice products according to the Fig. 1.

In summary, solving RMSP-GRP has four constructive meaning for the gluti-nous rice industry:

(1) The quality of glutinous rice products is controlled through the blending of different quality glutinous rice flour raw materials, and the construction of an enterprise raw material blending information system platform is carried out in this way.
(2) Based on the blending system, through the storage characteristics of gluti-nous rice flour and the optimization results of the raw material blending system.
(3) The best plan combined with the market situation for the procurement of raw material of glutinous rice flour is given. The plan is based on the raw material blending system and storage system.
(4) Solving the problem of formulating quality standard of raw material can serve the formulation of raw material standard for different glutinous rice products, such as national standard, line standard, and provincial standard.

The first three meaning are mainly aimed at enterprise, the last one is aimed at industry or related government departments.

2.2   Method for Solving the Raw Material Standard Formulation Problem for the Glutinous Rice Product

The method to solve RMSP-GRP is shown as follows.

In the step 1, we design a set of quality indexes for the raw materials of glutinous rice flour and glutinous rice products, and then, establish an index system for measuring the raw materials of glutinous rice flour and glutinous rice products in the manufacturing procedure.

In the step 2, we choose the most typical one of the many manufacturing procedure of the glutinous rice product.

In the step 3, the sampling and procurement schemes are given according to the variety of the raw materials. And then, all index data about glutinous rice flour raw materials samples are collected into the database.

In the step 4, according to step 2, carry out production experiments on raw material samples, and collect the corresponding indicators of products. Then, based on the data set of raw materials and products, the database is obtained after data preprocessing, which is convenient for subsequent data analysis.

In the step 5, based on a high-quality database, a three-stage data-driven model analysis method is used to calculate the quality standard of glutinous rice flour raw materials.

Figure 2 shows the process for solving RMSP-GRP. The above five step process is complete to solve RMSP-GRP. The key details of each step are described below.

Step 1 Establish an index system of raw materials and products for gluti-nous rice flour and determine the indexes which can evaluate raw materials and products through investigation and theoretical research.

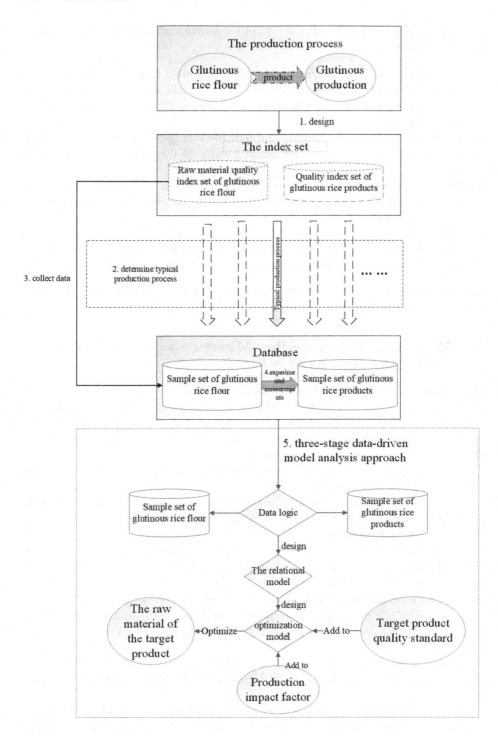

Fig. 2. Problem resolution process

Step 2 Demonstrate the universality and advancement of the technological process by the investigation and theoretical research. The most typical technological process of the glutinous rice product was determined as the technological process used in the production experiment.

Step 3 The sampling and purchasing plan for glutinous rice flour raw materials is:

a. According to the demands of the research, all varieties of food ingredients and market pricing are obtained in the determined area.
b. According to the factors in common, cost performance and quality difference of the raw materials, the weight was set, and the stratified sampling method was used to determine the sampling and procurement plan of the glutinous rice flour raw materials.

Step 4 Obtain glutinous rice products by production experiments. Establish database and data preprocessing.

a. The raw materials of glutinous rice flour are produced through the most typical manufacturing procedure experiment of the product selected in the second step to obtain the corresponding glutinous rice product.
b. Collect the standard index values of glutinous rice products to obtain the index data set of glutinous rice products.
c. The database is established after introducing the index set of food products to the database.
d. Preprocess the data on the database, check whether there is data omission, data duplication, obvious data errors, etc.
e. If the errors in the database are caused by incorrect entries or inconsistent measurement units, manual corrections shall be made. Otherwise, re-experiment the problematic data items, collect the glutinous rice flour raw materials and glutinous rice product index data, and finally get a high-quality database.

Step 5 Calculate the quality standard of the raw materials required for the glutinous rice product by applying the three-stage data-driven model analysis method.

2.3   The Design Idea of Three-Stage Data-Driven Model Analysis Method

After obtaining the sample data sets, a modeling analysis was performed to solve the RMSP-GRP. We designed a three-stage data-driven model analysis method. This method is shown in step 5 of the method flow shown in Fig. 2. According to RMSP-GRP, this paper should solve the problem: for the determined glutinous rice product quality, the range of quality index of raw materials is obtained through analysis. The raw materials obtained in this range are aimed to obtain a goal product. Therefore, the core of data and model analysis in this problem is to construct a model for the quality index of raw materials (optimization model). In order to improve the accuracy of the model for the quality index of raw materials, the data is preprocessed to ensure the accuracy of the prediction model, and then modified the model of the quality index of raw materials. In order to include as many raw materials varieties as possible within the established the range of quality index of raw materials, the structure and parameters of the model for the quality index of raw materials are adjusted, that is, a model of the quality index of raw materials is improved to obtain a regulation model.

As a result, the three-stage data-driven model analysis method have been formed–prediction, modeling, and regulation. The design ideas of the three stages of this method are described below.

Prediction Stage. RMSP-GRP need to use the product standard to predict the raw materials standard. The standard of the product is determined, so we set the index of the product as the response variable, the index of the raw materials as the predictive variable. Then the constraints on product standard are translated into constraints on raw materials standard. There are two problems: use raw materials indexes to predict product indexes and the accuracy of translating prediction results into constraints on raw materials standard.

In order to improve the prediction accuracy, firstly find the logical relationship between the two normalized index sets and perform low-dimensional processing through data analysis, so that the low-dimensional data set meets the training requirements of subsequent relationship models (prediction models) and reduces the training difficulty. Then perform regression prediction. Due to the strong linear correlation between quality indexes, a multiple linear regression model was used as the prediction model.

In order to solve the accuracy problem, a correction factor based on regression prediction accuracy is introduced into the constraints on the raw materials standard for reforming the constraint conditions. For this reason, the optimized raw materials can maximize the guarantee of obtaining products that meet the quality standard, and the credibility of optimization decisions is improved.

Modeling Stage. RMSP-GRP is to find the appropriate range of raw materials indexes. On the one hand, the products produced from raw materials that meet this range must meet the standard. On the other hand, the range contains as many varieties of raw materials as possible, so this problem can be solved by building an optimization model, which is called the optimization model for the quality standard of raw materials.

According to the restriction of the index for the raw materials of glutinous rice flour and glutinous rice product index, the constraint conditions of the optimization model for the quality standard of raw materials are mainly divided into two categories:

The first kind of constraints: "restriction constraint of the raw materials of glutinous rice flour". This constraint limits the solution range according to the basic characteristics of the raw materials of glutinous rice flour. The basic characteristics refer to the theoretically reasonable range of the quality index value.

If one of the glutinous rice flour raw materials indexes, the peak viscosity is in the range of 1000cp-2000cp under normal production conditions, this constraint limits the optimal solution result of the peak viscosity to this range.

The second kind of constraints: "restriction constraint of glutinous rice products". This constraint relies on the relationship model (prediction model) of raw materials and products. It transfers the restrictions on products to the restrictions onraw materials. The accuracy correction of the relationship model also needs to be considered. For the sake of simplicity, the two glutinous rice flour raw materials indexes and the two glutinous rice product indexes are used as examples to study the principle of constructing a glutinous rice products restriction constraint, which can be extended to the case of higher dimensional space.

Assuming that the prediction variables (raw materials indexes) are two, x_1, x_2, and the response variables (product indexes) are two, y_1, y_2. The training prediction model are $y_1 = f_1(x_1, x_2)$, $y_2 = f_2(x_1, x_2)$. $y_1^l ow$ represents the lower bound of the glutinous rice product index standard, $y_1^u p$ represents the upper bound. Establish glutinous rice products restriction constraint as in Eq. 1.

$$\begin{cases} y_1^{low} \leq y_1 = f_1(x_1, x_2) \leq y_1^{up} \\ y_2^{low} \leq y_2 = f_2(x_1, x_2) \leq y_2^{up} \end{cases} \tag{1}$$

The geometric description of the restriction of glutinous rice products restriction constrains is as follows: As shown in Fig. 3, the four oblique straight lines form the boundary of the glutinous rice products restriction constrains. The area enclosed by the four oblique straight lines is the restricted domain of glutinous rice products, that is, a parallelogram area. The raw materials quality index represented by the coordinate point (x_1, x_2) in this area is mapped to the product index through the relationship model f_1 and f_2 without considering the glutinous rice flour raw materials restriction constraint, and in theory, all the mapped product indexes meet the glutinous rice products restriction constraint.

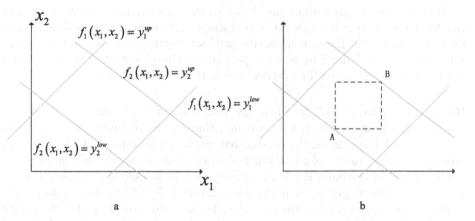

Fig. 3. Glutinous rice products restriction constraint (a) and the target area (b) in the constraints are expressed in a two-dimensional space

As shown in Fig. 3(a), if the constraint domain of glutinous rice product restriction is combined with the first kind of constraint, the quality of the raw material that meets the product requirements will be obtained, that is, the target area of the quality standard we need is selected within this area. Therefore, the target area of the solution is a rectangle in the quality range area of the glutinous rice flour raw materials. The rectangular area containing as many raw materials varieties as possible in the quality area of raw materials that meets the requirements of the quality standard of raw materials. The objective of the optimization model is to make all the vertices of the target area in the area that meets the quality standard of raw materials and make the point farthest from the origin to the farthest and the nearest point to the nearest.

As shown in the two points A and B in the figure, the coordinate values of these two points are exactly the optimization modeling result–the upper and lower bounds of the raw materials quality index. The rectangular area drawn from the two points A and B is the dotted area in Fig. 3(b). Therefore, the objective of the optimization model is to find the coordinates of the two points A and B, so the coordinates of these two points are set as the optimization target. The setting requirements of the optimization objective are described with reference to the rectangle in Fig. 3:

1) The length of each edge indicates the value range of the quality index represented by this edge, so it should be as long as possible. If it is too short, the index range is too small, which makes it more difficult to find the raw materials that meet this range.
2) From 1) knowing the sum of any two perpendicular sides of a rectangle can measure the range of all (two) raw materials quality indexes determined by this rectangular area, so the sum of the length of the sides of the rectangle should also be sought within the feasible region.
3) The ratio of the quality range of each index finally solved should conform to the discrete characteristics of each raw materials quality index.

If the solution space dimension is set to the index number of the glutinous rice flour raw materials index set, the glutinous rice flour raw materials restriction constraint and the glutinous rice product restriction constraint will form a feasible region defined by some hyperplanes. The objective of modeling and optimization is to search for a hypercube in this feasible region.

Regulation Stage. In (2), when applying the linear weighting method, the optimization weight of each side is equal, that is, the rectangle is regarded as a square, and the side length is regarded as the most important optimization objective. At this time, the maximum and equal range of each quality index of the raw materials of glutinous rice flour was obtained by modeling, but it was not the "optimal quality range" in the definition of RMSP-GRP. According to the results of descriptive data analysis, the data distribution characteristics of each quality index in the sample sets are not completely consistent, but present a dumbbell type, normal type, and uniform type distribution. Therefore, it is necessary to regulate the previous optimization principles through weight optimization.

The main means of regulation is to adjust the weight of the objective function. In order to make the regulation results cover as many varieties of raw materials as possible, this paper uses the quartiles of the discrete measure to adjust the weight. After calculating the length of the quartile, the weight is obtained through normalization, and it is substituted into the model in the modeling stage for secondary modeling. The ratio of the length of each side of the rectangle obtained by the secondary modeling is the ratio of the dispersion of the indexes. Then, the sensitivity analysis is performed to explore whether the sum (the sum of the lengths of the sides) of the ranges of the indexes is still possible to improve, and then obtain the most suitable optimization result.

Based on the primary modeling, the secondary modeling performs the following regulation:

1) The maximum side length in the primary modeling results is substituted into the constraint, and the optimal weight of each side length is set as the dispersion of each index of the sample data.
2) Set the reduction step size for the maximum side length in 1), and perform several optimization solutions.

The first step is to optimize parameters based on result of primary modeling and redefine the proportional constraints of each side length. The second step is to set up a comparative experiment for sensitivity analysis, analyze the change of the range and get the optimal solution.

By determining the rectangular area within the parallelogram area, the optimal quality range of the raw materials quality index is obtained. The disadvantage is that the coordinates in the parallelogram area and outside the rectangular area are not within the conclusion of the optimization model. Some feasible solutions have been deleted, which has increased the difficulty of selecting raw materials based on the optimization conclusion.

To sum up, the three stages of "prediction, modeling and regulation" constitute a whole. Each stage is based on data-driven, progressive step by step, and each stage is interrelated and interactive. This paper systematically solves RMSP-GRP through the three-stage data-driven modeling analysis method.

2.4   The Three-Stage Data-Driven Modeling Analysis Method

Suppose that the initial data set obtained by the experiment is preprocessed (denoising, identifying and deleting outliers) as in Eq. 2.

$$\{x_1, x_2, \cdots, x_m, y_1, y_2, \cdots, y_n\} = D^{`} = (D_M \mid D_N)$$

$$= \begin{bmatrix} a_{11} & a_{12} & \cdots & a_{1m} & b_{11} & b_{12} & \cdots & b_{1n} \\ a_{21} & a_{22} & \cdots & a_{2m} & b_{21} & b_{22} & \cdots & b_{2n} \\ \vdots & \vdots & \ddots & \vdots & \vdots & \vdots & \ddots & \vdots \\ a_{t1} & a_{t2} & \cdots & a_{tm} & b_{t1} & b_{t2} & \cdots & b_{tn} \end{bmatrix}$$

where $x_i (i = 1, 2, \cdots, m)$ is the variable of the i-th index of raw materials,$y_j (j = 1, 2, \cdots, n)$ is the varibale of the j-th index of products. $(a_{1i}; a_{2i}; \cdots; a_{ti})^T$ is a sample set of glutinous rice flour raw materials, $(b_{1j}; b_{2j}; \cdots ; b_{tj})^T$ is a sample set of index of glutinous rice products. t is the sample number. The detailed calculation process of each stage of the three-stage data-driven model analysis method is as follows.

First Stage: Prediction. The prediction stage includes three processing parts: standardization, Principal component dimension reduction, and prediction of the quality index of glutinous rice products using the quality index of glutinous rice flour raw materials. The specific implementation steps in the prediction stage are as follows.

Step 1 Normalize the glutinous rice flour raw materials sample set D_M and the glutinous rice product sample set D_N for obtaining the normalized data samples. The calculation formula is:

$$a'_{pi} = \frac{a_{pi} - \bar{a}_i}{\sigma_i} \qquad (i = 1, 2, \cdots, m, p = 1, 2, \cdots, t)$$

$$b'_{pj} = \frac{b_{pj} - \bar{b}_j}{\sigma_j} \qquad (j = 1, 2, \cdots, n, p = 1, 2, \cdots, t)$$

(2)

where $\bar{a}_i = \frac{\sum_{p=1}^{t} a_{pi}}{t}$, $\bar{b}_j = \frac{\sum_{p=1}^{t} b_{pj}}{t}$, standard deviation is:

$$\sigma_i = \sqrt{\sum_{p=1}^{t} \sum_{i=1}^{m} (a_{pi} - \bar{a}_i)^2 / t} \qquad (i = 1, 2, \cdots, m)$$

$$\sigma_j = \sqrt{\sum_{p=1}^{t} \sum_{j=1}^{n} (b_{pj} - \bar{b}_j)^2 / t} \qquad (j = 1, 2, \cdots, n)$$

(3)

The normalized sample set is still recorded as: D_M, D_N.

Step 2 Based on the normalized sample set D_M, perform the principal component dimensionality reduction processing on the quality index of glutinous rice flour raw materials.

(1) Perform the pearson correlation analysis on unnormalized data. If there is a strong correlation between the indexes, then the principal component dimension reduction is performed, and a multiple linear regression model is used to predict the quality of the glutinous rice products in a given production scenario.

(2) Principal component dimension reduction. In the PCA process, m is the dimension of the glutinous rice flour sample set, d is the dimension of the data after dimensionality reduction, and it is also the number of explanatory variables of the second-stage regression model. This paper specifies d by observing the proportion of variance interpretation of the data before and after dimensionality reduction. After PCA, the eigenvectors with smaller eigenvalues are discarded. The discarding rule is: ensure that the cumulative

variance exceeds 95%. The number of reduced dimensions is m-d. The purpose of dimensionality reduction is to reduce the cost of training calculation while making the input training data meet one of the basic assumptions of the multivariate linear model-there is no correlation between explanatory variables. Then get the principal component factor loading matrix as in Eq. 6.

$$\boldsymbol{\vartheta} = \begin{bmatrix} \vartheta_{11} & \vartheta_{12} & \cdots & \vartheta_{1d} \\ \vartheta_{21} & \vartheta_{22} & \cdots & \vartheta_{2d} \\ \vdots & \vdots & \ddots & \vdots \\ \vartheta_{m1} & \vartheta_{m2} & \cdots & \vartheta_{md} \end{bmatrix} \tag{4}$$

The factor load is used to calculate each principal component expression used to map the principal component variable to raw materials quality index variable in step 3. The principal component expression is:

$$z_j = F_j(x_1, x_2, \cdots, x_m) = \sum_{i=1}^{m} \eta_{ij} * x_i \qquad (j = 1, 2, \cdots, d) \tag{5}$$

where $\eta_{ij} = \vartheta_{ij}/\sqrt{\lambda_j}$ is the coefficients of the main component with respect to each raw materials quality index, λ_j is the selected d eigenvalues.

Step 3 Based on the reduced sample data $\boldsymbol{D_d}$, predict the quality indexes of the glutinous rice flour products by applying the quality indexes of glutinous rice flour raw materials.

When training the regression model, $\boldsymbol{D_d}$ and the normalized sample set $\boldsymbol{D_n}$ constitute a training set $(\boldsymbol{D_d}|\boldsymbol{D_n})$. z_{td} means the d-th index of the t-th sample of glutinous rice flour raw material. Because the multivariate linear regression model predicts only one predictive variable, the sample set input for each solution using the least squares method is:

$$(\boldsymbol{D_d}|b_j) = \begin{bmatrix} z_{11} & z_{12} & \cdots & z_{1d} & b_{1j} \\ z_{21} & z_{22} & \cdots & z_{2d} & b_{2j} \\ \vdots & \vdots & \ddots & \vdots & \vdots \\ z_{t1} & z_{t2} & \cdots & z_{td} & b_{tj} \end{bmatrix}$$

The function y_j of predicting raw meterials index is obtained through regression analysis.

$$y_j = G_j(z_1, z_2, \cdots, z_d) = \sum_{i=1}^{d} \phi_{ij} * z_i \qquad (j = 1, 2, \cdots, n) \tag{6}$$

Bring the Eq. (5) into Eq. (6) to get the regression function of the j-th glutinous rice product index which is shown as Eq. (7).

$$y_j = f_j(x_1, x_2, \cdots, x_m) = G_j(F_1(x_1, x_2, \cdots, x_m), \cdots, F_d(x_1, x_2, \cdots, x_m))$$
$$= \sum_{i=1}^{m} \theta_{ij} * x_i \qquad (j = 1, 2, \cdots, n) \tag{7}$$

where θ_{ij} is calculated by Spss. The goodness of fit R_j^2 of the multiple linear regression function $f_j(x_1, x_2, \cdots, x_m)$ ranges from $[0,1]$.

Second Stage: Modeling. The modeling stage is divided into three parts: determination of decision variables, determination of optimization models and calculation of optimization models. The specific implementation steps in the modeling stage are as follows.

Step 1 Determine the lower and upper bounds of the quality index of glutinous rice flour raw materials in products as x^{low}, x^{up}, and $x^{low} = [x_1^{low}, x_2^{low}, \cdots, x_m^{low}]$; $x^{up} = [x_1^{up}, x_2^{up}, \cdots, x_m^{up}]$.

Step 2 Determine the optimization model of raw materials quality standard.

(1) Based on the physical and chemical properties of the quality of glutinous rice flour raw materials, the first kind of constraint was determined: "glutinous rice flour raw materials restriction constraint".It means that the indexes of raw materials of products meet the prescribed range of raw materials.

$$l_i \leq x_i^{low} \leq x_i^{up} \leq u_i \qquad (i = 1, 2, \cdots, m) \tag{8}$$

where l_i and u_i are the prescribed indexes range of raw materials,x_i^{low} or x_i^{up} is the minimum or maximum index of glutinous rice flour raw materials in products.

(2) Based on the regression model and the quality requirements of the target glutinous rice products, second kind of constraint was determined: "glutinous rice products restriction constraint".

1) Determinate the glutinous rice products quality standard.
   The feasible range of the quality index of glutinous rice products are $L = (L_1, L_2, \cdots, L_n)$ and $U = (U_1, U_2, \cdots, U_n)$ which represents the lower and upper bounds, respectively.

2) Determinate the correction factors.
   The goodness of fit obtained during the prediction stage is $R^2 = (R_1^2, R_2^2, \cdots, R_n^2)$. The specific correction method is:
   a. Calculate $\Delta_j = L_j - U_j$, where $j = 1, 2, \cdots, n$, Δ_j is the initial range value.
   b. Calculate the correction factor of the goodness of fit R_j^2 for each regression function:

$$\epsilon_j = 1 - R_j^2 \qquad (j = 1, 2, \cdots, n) \tag{9}$$

   c. Calculate the correction amount of each index according to the correction factor, and reduce and increase the upper and lower standard of the same size.

$$[L_j^{'}, U_j^{'}] = [L_j + 0.5 * \epsilon_j, U_j - 0.5 * \epsilon_j] \qquad (j = 1, 2, \cdots, n) \tag{10}$$

   where 0.5 means that the upper and lower bound correction amount is evenly shared.

3) glutinous rice products restriction constraint.

From step 1) 2), set the glutinous rice products restriction constraint:

$$L_j^{`} \le f_j(x_i) \le U_j^{`} \qquad (i = 1, 2, \ldots, m, j = 1, 2, \ldots, n)$$
$$l_i \le x_i^{low} \le x_i^{up} \le u_i \qquad (i = 1, 2, \cdots, m) \tag{11}$$

It can be seen that the feasible region of the objective function is m-dimensional hypercube. We use X to represent the multi-dimensional hypercube restricted by the objective function in two kinds of constraint spaces.

$$X = \left\{ (x_1, x_2, \cdots, x_m) \,\middle|\, x_i = x_i^{low} \text{ or } x_i^{up}, i = 1, 2, \cdots, m \right\} \tag{12}$$

where $|X| = 2^m$. It means that the hypercube has 2^m vertices. If all vertices of the hybercube mentioned above subject to $L_j^{`} \le f_j(x_k) \le U_j^{`}, x_k \in X$, the Eq. (11) and (12) meet constraints.

(3) Based on the purpose of maximizing the target area, a third kind of constraint is determined: "diffusion factor constraint".

The "diffusion factor" was set in the high-dimensional target space composed of several glutinous rice flour raw materials indexes, and was substituted into the linear weighting method to meet the following requirements:

1) Reasonable range. To ensure that the glutinous rice flour raw materials range is a high confidence range given by taking the prediction error into account.

2) The widest range. To make the final solution cover the feasible range of the "glutinous rice flour raw materials restriction constraint" and "glutinous rice products restriction constraint" as much as possible.

Let x^{low}, x^{up} be the lower and upper bounds of the final solution of each raw materials, and δ be the "diffusion factor", then

$$x_i^{low} + \delta \le x_i^{up} \qquad (i = 1, 2, \cdots m) \tag{13}$$

(4) Set of the objective function.

The range of quality index of glutinous rice flour raw materials solved by the model should cover a wide range on the premise of satisfying the constraint conditions, so, first, it should satisfy the maximum of δ. This is the primary objective:

$$\max f_1 = \delta \tag{14}$$

And the upper and lower bounds of the solution must meet the maximum and minimum, respectively, so the following secondary objectives are:

$$\min f_2 = \sum_{i=1}^{m} x_i^{low}, \max f_3 = \sum_{i=1}^{m} x_i^{up} \tag{15}$$

In summary, the raw materials quality standard optimization model is a multi-objective optimization mathematical model, specifically expressed as:

$$P_1 \ \max f_1 = \delta$$

$$P_2 \ \min f_2 = \sum_{i=1}^{m} x_i^{low}, \max f_3 = \sum_{i=1}^{m} x_i^{up}$$

$$s.t \begin{cases} \grave{L_k} \le f_j(x_k) \le \grave{U_j} & j = 1, 2, \cdots, n; x_k \in X \\ l_i \le x_i^{low} \le x_i^{up} \le u_i & i = 1, 2, \cdots, m \\ x_i^{low} + \delta \le x_i^{up} & i = 1, 2, \cdots, m \end{cases}$$

where P_1 and P_2 are optimization goals with priority, and the priority of P_1 is far greater than P_2, that is, $P_1 \gg P_2$.

Step 3 Establish the optimization model of the raw materials quality standard.

The linear weighting method is used to set weight values with magnitude differences according to the priority of the target and the importance of the target at the same level. This method converts the optimization target into a single target:

$$\max \left\{ \beta'\delta + \sum_{i=1}^{m} \left[\beta_i * \left(x_i^{up} - x_i^{low} \right) \right] \right\} \tag{16}$$

where β_i is the weight of each index, and each of it is equal and $\sum_{i=1}^{m} \beta_i = 1$. β' is the weight of the diffusion factor, and it is generally one or two orders of magnitude larger than β_i when a suitable solution is obtained. LINGO is used to calculate the model for getting the optimal solutions.

In a high-dimensional space constructed from all raw materials index variables, the constraint of raw meterial limits the basic value range of variables in each dimension of the space, forming a hypercube space. And the constraint of products constructs a hyper-dimensional space with irregular shape through the linear functions of L, U and each dimension variable. There are two cases of these two spaces in high-dimensional space: containing or partially overlapping. The purpose of setting the objective function is to find a hypercube in the overlapping area of these two high-dimensional spaces. The hypercube has 2^m vertices, and the coordinates of two points are $\left(x_1^{low}, x_2^{low}, \cdots, x_m^{low} \right)$ and $\left(x_1^{up}, x_2^{up}, \cdots, x_m^{up} \right)$. These two coordinates contain all the vertices information of X. Therefore, we only need to determine them, the index range of raw materials for glutinous rice flour can be obtained.

Third Stage: Regulation. The regulation stage is divided into three parts: the determination of the regulation range, the determination of the regulation model, and the acquisition of quality standard of the special glutinous rice flour raw materials. The specific implementation steps in the regulation stage are as follows. LINGO is used to calculate the model for getting the optimal solutions.

Step 1 Determinate the regulation range.

Using the optimal solution calculated by the model in the second stage, the specific optimization process for the third kind of constraint is:

(1) Calculate the quartiles of the normalize data of raw materials, that is, the quartiles arrange all the values from small to large and divide them into quarters, and are the values at the three division points.

(2) The value at the 25% position (called the lower quartile) and the value at the 75% position (called the upper quartile) are selected to calculate the difference:

$$R = (r_1, r_2, \cdots, r_m) \tag{17}$$

(3) Apply the data normalization to calculate the new decision variables and the constraint weights.

$$\beta_i = r_i / \sum_{j=1}^{m} r_j \qquad (i = 1, 2, \cdots, m) \tag{18}$$

(4) Adjust the third kind constraint $x_\alpha^{low} + \delta \leq x_\alpha^{up}$ according to the diffusion factor δ_0 solved in the second stage, and modify it to

$$x_i^{low} + \delta_0 * (1 - \rho) + \beta_i * \gamma \leq x_i^{up} \qquad (i = 1, 2, \cdots, m) \tag{19}$$

where ρ is a "relaxation factor", which is used to reduce the diffusion factor so that the coordinates of the final solution space (hypercube) have a relaxation space of the size $\delta_0 * \rho$ and each vertex can be adjusted and changed in this space. γ is a "floating variable", which is used to control the final solution of each index to float according to the discrete characteristics of data samples to obtain different results in a range.

Step 2 Determinate the regulation model.

The adjusted multi-objective optimization model is:

$$P_1 \ \max f_4(\gamma) = \gamma$$

$$P_2 \ \min f_5(x^{low}) = \sum_{i=1}^{m} x_i^{low}, \max f_6(x^{up}) = \sum_{i=1}^{m} x_i^{up}$$

$$s.t. \begin{cases} L_k' \leq f_j(x_k) \leq U_j' & j = 1, \cdots, n \ x_k \in X \\ l_i \leq x_i^{low}, x_i^{up} \leq u_i & i = 1, \cdots, m \\ x_i^{low} + \delta_0 * (1 - \rho) + \beta_i * \gamma \leq x_i^{up} & i = 1, \cdots, m \end{cases}$$

Where P_1 is much larger than P_2, and the value range of "relaxation factor" ρ is $[0, 0.5]$, that is, at most half the value of the diffusion factor δ_0 is used as the floating range of the hypercube coordinates, and a step size of 0.05 is set.

β_α is an updated optimization weight. Finally, the solution was performed 11 times and the results were compared to obtain the most reasonable solution range.

Step 3 Calculate the regulation model.

When solving by linear weighting method, the new optimization weights of each decision variable are substituted, and multi-objective is turned into a single objective:

$$\max\left\{\beta'\gamma + \sum_{i=1}^{m}\left[\beta_i * \left(x_i^{up} - x_i^{low}\right)\right]\right\} \tag{20}$$

where β' is higher in order of magnitude than β_α.

Step 4 Obtain the quality standard of the raw materials of the glutinous rice flour

Model conclusion denormalization. According to the standard deviation σ_i and mean value $\bar{x}_i$ of the data normalization process, the solution result x^{low}, x^{up} is de-normalized to obtain the optimized range of each raw materials index $[\overline{x^{low}}, \overline{x^{up}}]$. Where i represents the serial number of raw materials quality index, and

$$\begin{aligned}\overline{x^{low}} &= \left(\overline{x_1^{low}}, \overline{x_2^{low}}, \cdots, \overline{x_m^{low}}\right)\\ \overline{x^{up}} &= \left(\overline{x_1^{up}}, \overline{x_2^{up}}, \cdots, \overline{x_m^{up}}\right)\end{aligned} \tag{21}$$

The data denormalization formula is:

$$\begin{aligned}\overline{x_i^{low}} &= x_i^{low} * \sigma_i + \overline{a_i}\\ \overline{x_i^{up}} &= x_i^{up} * \sigma_i + \overline{a_i} \qquad (i = 1, 2, \cdots, m)\end{aligned} \tag{22}$$

2.5   Experimental Data

The experimental materials include glutinous rice flour sealed under the conditions of vacuum, CO_2 gas sealing, N_2 gas sealing, and natural air packaging at 20 °C, 25 °C, 30 °C, and 35 °C. Quality data of glutinous rice flour raw materials stored for 6 months and quality data of quick-frozen rice dumplings made from raw materials corresponding to the storage conditions. The viscosity change during the gelatinization process of glutinous rice flour was measured by a rapid viscometer. The operation steps were mainly referred to the GB/T 24852-2010 RVA analysis. The quality of the quick- frozen dumplings was tested by texture TPA and sensory evaluation. Table 1 and Table 2 show the initial measured index data sets of the glutinous rice flour and quick-frozen rice dumplings. Where the basic physical and chemical indexes of glutinous rice flour, the gelatinization characteristics RVA, the indexes of the TPA test structure of quick-frozen rice dumplings are continuous random variables, and the sensory scores are discrete random variables.

Table 1. Glutinous rice flour raw materials sample set.

Sample number	Basic physical and chemical indexes			Pasting properties (RVA)				
	Fatty acid value	Acidity	Malondialdehyde	Peak viscosity	Minimum viscosity	Disintegration value	Final viscosity	Pick-up value
1	7.69	0.52	0.455	1914	1134	780	1486	7.69
2	18.64	0.82	0.476	2061	1270	791	1624	18.64
3	21.13	0.85	0.49	2231	1362	869	1743	21.13
4	23.61	0.91	0.515	2319	1407	912	1812	23.61
5	27.34	0.94	0.547	2809	1691	1118	2164	27.34
⋮								
47	34.95	0.8	0.632	3969	2386	1583	3047	661
48	36.25	0.82	0.628	3997	2402	1595	3054	652
49	35.6	0.82	0.619	4126	2501	1625	3203	702

Table 2. Quick frozen dumpling sample set

Sample number	TPA							Sensory score						
	Hardness	elasticity	Cohesion	Chewy	Resilience	Relaxation time	Paste soup rate	Odor	Luster	Completion	Viscosity	Elasticity	hardness degree	taste
1	647.624	0.826	0.664	355.156	0.314	3.37	1.1	5	5	22	17	15	14	5
2	743.417	0.689	0.669	327.54	0.288	3.23	1.089	5	5	22	17	15	14	5
3	716.329	0.736	0.682	359.526	0.344	3.345	1.07	5	5	20	17	15	14	5
4	819.159	0.732	0.673	403.95	0.353	3.625	1.028	5	5	20	16	15	13	5
...														
47	1812.493	1.223	0.728	964.837	0.435	3.878	0.485	3	3	18	15	12	7	3
48	1801.493	1.198	0.731	925.483	0.442	3.891	0.428	3	3	18	15	12	7	3
49	1773.992	1.172	0.723	917.355	0.408	3.788	0.492	3	3	18	14	12	7	3

The initial data was pre-processed, and a total of 7 sample data were eliminated, and normalization was performed and a Box-plot of 8 glutinous rice flour raw materials indexes was drawn as shown in Fig. 4. Box-plot shows that there are different distribution characteristics between the basic physical and chemical indexes, while the pasted characteristics RVA indexes are similar.

2.6 Statistical Analysis

Data were analyzed by SPSS 25 with ANOVA, principal component analysis, and multiple linear regression. All analyses were carried out in triplicate at least. Significance of differences was defined as the 5% level ($p < 0.05$). Lingo 18 was used for multi-objective optimization modeling. MATLAB R2016a is used for anti-standardization.

3 Results

3.1 Results of Each Step of the Prediction Stage

(1) The correlation matrix obtained by Pearson correlation analysis for each glutinous rice flour raw materials index is shown in Table 3. The correlation analysis used unnormalized sample data, and the correlation matrix results show that there is a significant linear single correlation between the pasted characteristics RVA indexes, which just verified the conclusion of the previous research on the raw rice flour index.

Table 3. Correlation matrix (The indexes indicated by each symbol are shown in Table 6.)

	x_1	x_2	x_3	x_4	x_5	x_6	x_7	x_8
x_1	1	0.682	0.584	0.348	0.355	0.334	0.344	0.301
x_2		1	0.061	0.114	0.128	0.099	0.111	0.034
x_3			1	0.298	0.301	0.304	0.304	0.287
x_4				1	0.999	0.996	0.998	0.984
x_5					1	0.992	0.999	0.983
x_6						1	0.993	0.979
x_7							1	0.987
x_8								1

(2) Get the principal component. Principal component analysis was performed on 8 physical and chemical indexes (fatty acid value, acidity, and malondialdehyde) and pasting properties (peak viscosity, minimum viscosity, disintegration value, final viscosity, and pick-up value) of glutinous rice raw

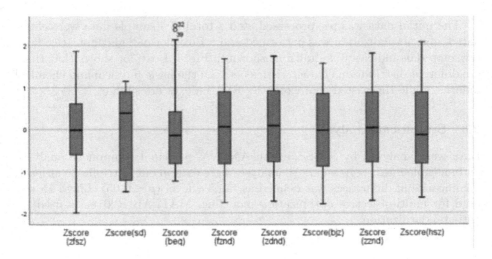

Fig. 4. Box-plot of 8 glutinous rice flour raw materials quality indexes. (The meaning of the symbols is shown in Table 6.)

materials using standardized data. We use $x_1, x_2, \cdots, x_8$ to express these 8 indexes. Based on the variance percentage of the initial eigenvalue in the Table 4 as the basis for selecting the principal components, when the first three principal components were selected, the accumulation reached 98%. Finally, three principal components were selected and the results are shown in Tables 4, Table 5 and Fig. 5.

Table 4. Total variance explanation

Ingredient	Initial eigenvalue			Sum of squared loads		
	Total	Variance percentage	Accumulation (%)	Total	Variance percentage	Accumulation %
1	5.271	65.890	65.890	5.271	65.890	65.890
2	1.669	20.864	86.754	1.669	20.864	86.754
3	.901	11.257	98.012	.901	11.257	98.012
4	.130	1.628	99.640			

Table 6 shows the initial factor load of the principal components. The values in each column represent the degree of influence of each raw materials index on each principal component, that is, the coefficient of the variable when constructing the principal component linear expression. Calculate three principal component expressions based on the component coefficients (factor loads) in Table 5 and eigenvalues in Table 4.

Table 5. Component matrix

Variables[a]	Component		
	1	2	3
x_1	0.475	0.839	0.048
x_2	0.194	0.794	−0.545
x_3	0.412	0.467	0.767
x_4	0.988	−0.139	−0.058
x_5	0.988	−0.127	−0.064
x_6	0.983	−0.150	-0.044
x_7	0.988	−0.140	−0.052
x_8	0.971	−0.201	−0.019

$$z_1 = F_1(x_1, x_2, \cdots, x_8) = 0.2068x_1 + 0.0843x_2 + 0.1794x_3 + 0.4302x_4$$
$$+ 0.4304x_5 + 0.4283x_6 + 0.4303x_7 + 0.4231x_8$$
$$z_2 = F_2(x_1, x_2, \cdots, x_8) = 0.6492x_1 + 0.6143x_2 + 0.3614x_3 - 0.1075x_4$$
$$- 0.0986x_5 - 0.0986x_6 - 0.1161x_7 - 0.1553x_8 \quad (23)$$
$$z_3 = F_3(x_1, x_2, \cdots, x_8) = 0.0508x_1 + 0.5743x_2 + 0.8083x_3 - 0.0612x_4$$
$$- 0.0674x_5 - 0.0465x_6 - 0.0546x_7 - 0.0198x_8$$

(3) Calculate the regression model. Three principal components were used as explanatory variables, and each product index was used as a predictive variable for regression analysis. Table 6 shows the regression results of each product index. We use $y_1, y_2, \cdots, y_7$ to express the 7 indexes (hardness, Elasticity, Cohesion, Chewing property, Resilience, relaxation time, Paste soup rate) of the product. In the table, the R-square reflects the interpretation rate of the regression prediction model on the sample data. The value range is from 0 to 1. If the R square is above 0.5, it means that the regression model obtained by training has a good regression effect.

Table 6. Regression results

	F1	F2	F3	Adjusted R square	R square	Durbin-Watson	F-test	Significance
y_1	0.355	0.143	0.253	0.738	0.757	1.441	39.528	.000
y_2	0.261	0.022	0.581	0.637	0.663	1.331	24.971	.000
y_3	0.300	−0.107	0.361	0.582	0.612	1.179	19.994	.000
y_4	0.342	0.185	0.317	0.747	0.766	1.382	41.377	.000
y_5	0.345	0.043	0.355	0.726	0.746	1.882	37.128	.000
y_6	0.221	0.180	−0.491	0.493	0.530	1.446	14.282	.000
y_7	−0.274	−0.448	0.197	0.746	0.765	0.677	41.217	.000

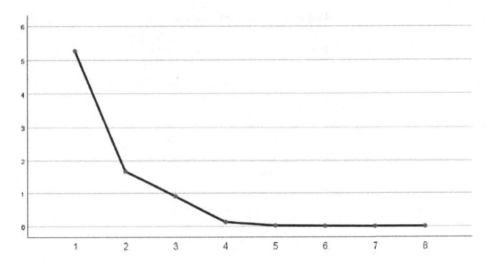

Fig. 5. Gravel figure

(4) Evaluate the regression models. The DW test values in Table 6 indicate that there is no autocorrelation among the explanatory variables of the regression model except for the paste soup rate. F-test results on the model: if the F value of each regression model is greater than $F_i(j-1, n-j)$ by checking the standard table, the null hypothesis is rejected, and the significance sig < 0.05, indicating that the regression model is significant, that is, the combination explanatory variables of principal component have a significant effect on the product indexes, and all regression models in the table are accepted.

Table 7. Regression model coefficients with principal components mapped to raw materials indexes

	x_1	x_2	x_3	x_4	x_5	x_6	x_7	x_8
y_1	0.1791	−0.0275	0.3199	0.1219	0.1216	0.1237	0.1234	0.123
y_2	0.0811	−0.1098	0.2593	0.0944	0.0931	0.0975	0.0961	0.102
y_3	0.0109	−0.2477	0.307	0.1185	0.1153	0.1241	0.121	0.1364
y_4	0.1894	−0.0561	0.3747	0.1108	0.1102	0.1134	0.1127	0.1139
y_5	0.1173	−0.1484	0.3644	0.1221	0.1203	0.1263	0.1244	0.1323
y_6	0.1376	0.4112	−0.2922	0.1058	0.1105	0.0966	0.1023	0.0753
y_7	−0.3375	−0.4114	−0.0518	−0.0818	−0.087	−0.0745	−0.0799	−0.0503

(5) Variable mapping. The regression coefficient matrix after mapping the explanatory variables in the regression model to the eight raw materials

indexes according to the rules (7), (8), and (9) is shown in Table 7. The general form of the regression model for each glutinous rice product index is:

$$y_j = G_j(x_1, x_2, \cdots, x_8) = f_j(F_1(x), F_2(x), F_3(x))$$
$$= \omega_{j1} * x_1 + \omega_{j2} * x_2 + \omega_{j3} * x_3 + \omega_{j4} * x_4 \qquad (24)$$
$$+ \omega_{j5} * x_5 + \omega_{j6} * x_6 + \omega_{j7} * x_7 + \omega_{j8} * x_8$$

where the meaning of the vector F is shown in Table 6. The constituent elements $\omega_{ji}(i = 1, 2, \cdots, 8, j = 1, 2, \cdots, 7)$ of the vector ω represent the values of the j-th row and the i-th column in Table 7. The specific expression of the regression model is:

$$y_1 = 0.1791x_1 - 0.027x_2 + 0.319x_3 + 0.1219x_4$$
$$+ 0.1216x_5 + 0.1237x_6 + 0.1234x_7 + 0.123x_8 \qquad R^2 = 0.757$$
$$y_2 = 0.0811x_1 - 0.1098x_2 + 0.2593x_3 + 0.0944x_4$$
$$+ 0.0931x_5 + 0.0975x_6 + 0.0961x_7 + 0.102x_8 \qquad R^2 = 0.663$$
$$y_3 = 0.0109x_1 - 0.2477x_2 + 0.307x_3 + 0.1185x_4$$
$$+ 0.1153x_5 + 0.1241x_6 + 0.121x_7 + 0.1364x_8 \qquad R^2 = 0.612$$
$$y_4 = 0.1894x_1 - 0.0561x_2 + 0.3747x_3 + 0.1108x_4$$
$$+ 0.1102x_5 + 0.1134x_6 + 0.1127x_7 + 0.1139x_8 \qquad R^2 = 0.766$$
$$y_5 = 0.1173x_1 - 0.1484x_2 + 0.3644x_3 + 0.12218x_4$$
$$+ 0.1203x_5 + 0.1263x_6 + 0.1244x_7 + 0.1323x_8 \qquad R^2 = 0.746$$
$$y_6 = 0.1376x_1 + 0.4112x_2 - 0.2922x_3 + 0.1058x_4$$
$$+ 0.1105x_5 + 0.0966x_6 + 0.1023x_7 + 0.0753x_8 \qquad R^2 = 0.530$$
$$y_7 = -0.3375x_1 - 0.4114x_2 - 0.0518x_3 - 0.0818x_4$$
$$- 0.087x_5 - 0.0745x_6 - 0.0799x_7 - 0.0503x_8 \qquad R^2 = 0.765$$

Draw a line chart as in Fig. 6 that compares predicted values with sample values.

3.2 Results of Each Atep of Modeling Stage

(1) glutinous rice products restriction constraint and glutinous rice flour raw materials restriction constraint. The correction factors were set to adjust the range according to the R square in Table 7. In Table 8, the upper and lower bounds of the glutinous rice products restriction constraint were obtained. And Table 9 shows the glutinous rice flour raw materials restriction constraint.

(2) Set the "diffusion factor" and the objective function. Let the initial index weight $\beta_i = 0.0625$ according to Eq. (9), that is, the weights of the upper and lower bounds of each index in the objective function are equal, and the sum

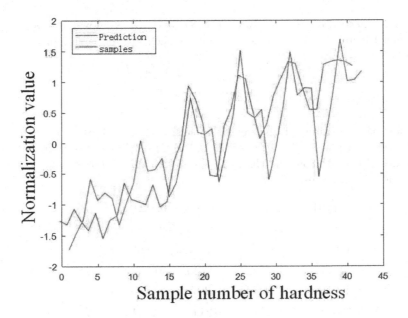

Fig. 6. Predicted values and sample values

Table 8. Upper and lower bounds for glutinous rice products restriction constrains

j	1	2	3	4	5	6	7
L_j	−1.2971	−1.0789	−1.2972	−1.348	−2.4834	−1.8913	−0.6112
U_j	0.2897	−0.1664	0.4154	0.2724	-0.4303	0.0977	2.0289

Table 9. Upper and lower bounds of raw materials restrict constraints

1	1	2	3	4	5	6	7	8
l_i	−1.99848	−1.49456	−1.23453	−1.7573	−1.72689	−1.79174	−1.71258	−1.6366
u_i	1.85863	1.14845	2.46063	1.6787	1.73789	1.56662	1.80019	2.06455

is 1. Let $\beta' \equiv 1000$ to ensure that δ is the primary objective. The objective function solved is:

$$\min \left[\sum_{i=1}^{8} 0.0625 * \left(x_i^{low} - x_i^{up} \right) - 1000 * \delta \right] \quad (25)$$

The inequality constraints (material quality constraint) of 8 variables and the inequality constraints (product restriction constraint) of 7 regression models are recorded as group (I) and group (II) for subsequent calls.

$$(I) \begin{cases} -1.99848 \le x_1^{low}, x_1^{up} \le 1.85863 \\ -1.49456 \le x_2^{low}, x_2^{up} \le 1.14845 \\ -1.23453 \le x_3^{low}, x_3^{up} \le 2.46063 \\ -1.7573 \le x_4^{low}, x_4^{up} \le 1.6787 \\ -1.72689 \le x_5^{low}, x_5^{up} \le 1.73789 \\ -1.79174 \le x_6^{low}, x_6^{up} \le 1.56662 \\ -1.71258 \le x_7^{low}, x_7^{up} \le 1.80019 \\ -1.6366 \le x_8^{low}, x_8^{up} \le 2.06455 \end{cases}$$

$$(II) \begin{cases} -1.2971 < \boldsymbol{X}_{\mathrm{coe1}} * \boldsymbol{X}_1^T < 0.2897 \\ -1.0789 < \boldsymbol{X}_{\mathrm{coe2}} * \boldsymbol{X}_1^T < -0.1664 \\ -1.2972 < \boldsymbol{X}_{\mathrm{coe3}} * \boldsymbol{X}_1^T < 0.4154 \\ -1.348 < \boldsymbol{X}_{\mathrm{coe4}} * \boldsymbol{X}_1^T < 0.2724 \\ -2.4834 < \boldsymbol{X}_{\mathrm{coe5}} * \boldsymbol{X}_1^T < -0.4303 \\ -1.8913 < \boldsymbol{X}_{\mathrm{coe6}} * \boldsymbol{X}_1^T < 0.0977 \\ -0.6112 < \boldsymbol{X}_{\mathrm{coe7}} * \boldsymbol{X}_1^T < 2.0289 \\ \cdots \\ -1.2971 < \boldsymbol{X}_{\mathrm{coe1}} * \boldsymbol{X}_{28}^T < 0.2897 \\ -1.0789 < \boldsymbol{X}_{\mathrm{coe2}} * \boldsymbol{X}_{28}^T < -0.1664 \\ -1.2972 < \boldsymbol{X}_{\mathrm{coe3}} * \boldsymbol{X}_{28}^T < 0.4154 \\ -1.348 < \boldsymbol{X}_{\mathrm{coe4}} * \boldsymbol{X}_{28}^T < 0.2724 \\ -2.4834 < \boldsymbol{X}_{\mathrm{coes}} * \boldsymbol{X}_{28}^T < -0.4303 \\ -1.8913 < \boldsymbol{X}_{\mathrm{coe6}} * \boldsymbol{X}_{28}^T < 0.0977 \\ -0.6112 < \boldsymbol{X}_{\mathrm{coe7}} * \boldsymbol{X}_{28}^T < 2.0289 \end{cases}$$

$$\boldsymbol{X}_{coe} = \begin{bmatrix} 0.1791 & -0.0275 & 0.3199 & 0.1219 & 0.1216 & 0.1237 & 0.1234 & 0.123 \\ 0.0811 & -0.1098 & 0.2593 & 0.0944 & 0.0931 & 0.0975 & 0.0961 & 0.102 \\ 0.0109 & -0.2477 & 0.307 & 0.1185 & 0.1153 & 0.1241 & 0.121 & 0.1364 \\ 0.1894 & -0.0561 & 0.3747 & 0.1108 & 0.1102 & 0.1134 & 0.1127 & 0.1139 \\ 0.1173 & -0.1484 & 0.3644 & 0.1221 & 0.1203 & 0.1263 & 0.1244 & 0.1323 \\ 0.1376 & 0.4112 & -0.2922 & 0.1058 & 0.1105 & 0.0966 & 0.1023 & 0.0753 \\ -0.3375 & -0.4114 & -0.0518 & -0.0818 & -0.087 & -0.0745 & -0.0799 & -0.0503 \end{bmatrix}$$

The coefficient matrix is $\boldsymbol{Xcoe}$. Then the second set of constraints are group (II).

According to Tables (9), (10) and the objective function, the single-objective expression and the initial multi-objective optimization model are:

$$\min \left[\sum_{i=1}^{8} 0.0625 * \left(x_i^{low} - x_i^{up} \right) - 1000 * \delta \right]$$

$$s.t. \begin{cases} (I) \\ (II) \\ x_i^{low} + \delta \le x_i^{up} \quad i = 1, \cdots, 8 \end{cases}$$

(3) The above optimization model was programmed and solved in Lingo, and the maximum diffusion factor and initial solutions were obtained as shown in Table 10.

Table 10. Solution without relaxation factor

$\delta = 0.75138, \beta' = 1000$								
i	1	2	3	4	5	6	7	8
x_i^{low}	−1.5175	3.97E-01	−0.270915	−0.5153837	−1.72689	−1.79174	−1.71258	−1.6366
x_i^{up}	−0.7661	1.14845	4.80E-01	0.2359964	−0.97551	−1.04036	−0.9612	−0.88522
$x_i^{up} - x_i^{low}$	0.75138	0.75138	0.7513801	0.75138	0.75138	0.75138	0.75138	

3.3 Results of Each Step of Regulation Stage

(1) Solving weights. The weights for each optimization objective based on the quartile are:

$$\beta = (\beta_1, \beta_2, \beta_3, \beta_4, \beta_5, \beta_6, \beta_7, \beta_8)$$
$$= (0.139, 0.096, 0.134, 0.124, 0.125, 0.121, 0.127, 0.134)$$

(2) Adjust constraints. According to the conclusion of the modeling stage, the value of the maximum diffusion factor δ_0 was obtained, and then the different relaxation factors ρ was set according to the diffusion factor to establish a comparative experiment and analyze the effect of different relaxation factors on the index solutions of raw materials. Floating variables and relaxation factors were substituted into (13):

$$x_i^{low} + \delta_0 * (1 - \rho) + \beta_i * \gamma \leq x_i^{up} \qquad (26)$$

where $\alpha = 1, \cdots, 8$, the floating variable γ is the primary optimization objective of the optimized model after adjustment, and other constraints are not modified. Relaxation factor $\rho \in [0, 0.5]$. The secondary modeling is:

$$\max \left[\sum_{i=1}^{8} \beta_\alpha * \left(x_i^{low} - x_a^{up} \right) + 1000 * \gamma \right]$$

$$\text{s.t.} \begin{cases} \text{(I)} \\ \text{(II)} \\ x_i^{low} + 0.75138 * (1 - \rho) + \beta_i * \gamma \leq x_i^{10} \quad i = 1, \cdots, 8 \end{cases}$$

(3) Set the step size for comparison experiment. In the comparison experiment, the relaxation factor step size was set to 0.05 for each experiment, and a total of eleven optimization experiments were carried out. The results were obtained in Table 11.

Through the comparative analysis of the eleven conclusions in the Table 11, it can be found that the larger the relaxation factor, the larger the sum of the solution range of each index.

(4) Denormalization. According to the criterion that the sum of the ranges is the largest, the calculated results of each index when ρ=0.5 were selected for denormalization to obtain the final objective solution as shown in Table 12.

Table 11. Results of 11 solves in steps of 0.05

ρ	0.5	0.45	0.4	0.35	0.3	0.25	0.2	0.15	0.1	0.05	0
γ	3.1414	2.8273	2.5131	2.199	1.8848	1.5707	1.2566	0.9424	0.6283	0.3141	0
x_1^{low}	-1.5178	-1.5178	-1.5178	-1.5178	-1.5177	-1.5177	-1.5177	-1.5177	-1.5176	-1.5176	-1.5178
x_2^{low}	0.271	0.2836	0.2962	0.3089	0.3215	0.3341	0.3467	0.3593	0.3719	0.3845	0.271
x_3^{low}	-0.2595	-0.2607	-0.2618	-0.2629	-0.2641	-0.2652	-0.2664	-0.2675	-0.2686	-0.2698	-0.2595
x_4^{low}	-0.5449	-0.5419	-0.539	-0.536	-0.5331	-0.5301	-0.5272	-0.5242	-0.5213	-0.5183	-0.5449
x_5^{low}	-1.7269	-1.7269	-1.7269	-1.7269	-1.7269	-1.7269	-1.7269	-1.7269	-1.7269	-1.7269	-1.7269
x_6^{low}	-1.7917	-1.7917	-1.7917	-1.7917	-1.7917	-1.7917	-1.7917	-1.7917	-1.7917	-1.7917	-1.7917
x_7^{low}	-1.7126	-1.7126	-1.7126	-1.7126	-1.7126	-1.7126	-1.7126	-1.7126	-1.7126	-1.7126	-1.7126
x_8^{low}	-1.6366	-1.6366	-1.6366	-1.6366	-1.6366	-1.6366	-1.6366	-1.6366	-1.6366	-1.6366	-1.6366
x_1^{up}	-0.8455	-0.8376	-0.8297	-0.8217	-0.8138	-0.8059	-0.7979	-0.79	-0.7821	-0.7741	-0.8455
x_2^{up}	1.1485	1.1485	1.1485	1.1485	1.1485	1.1485	1.1485	1.1485	1.1485	1.1485	1.1485
x_3^{up}	0.4038	0.4115	0.4191	0.4268	0.4345	0.4421	0.4498	0.4575	0.4651	0.4728	0.4038
x_4^{up}	0.2461	0.2451	0.2441	0.2431	0.2421	0.2411	0.24	0.239	0.238	0.237	0.2461
x_5^{up}	-0.9417	-0.945	-0.9484	-0.9518	-0.9552	-0.9586	-0.962	-0.9654	-0.9687	-0.9721	-0.9417
x_6^{up}	-0.9979	-1.0022	-1.0064	-1.0107	-1.0149	-1.0191	-1.0234	-1.0276	-1.0319	-1.0361	-0.9979
x_7^{up}	-0.934	-0.9367	-0.9394	-0.9422	-0.9449	-0.9476	-0.9503	-0.953	-0.9558	-0.9585	-0.934
x_8^{up}	-0.8513	-0.8547	-0.8581	-0.8615	-0.8649	-0.8683	-0.8717	-0.8751	-0.8784	-0.8818	-0.8513
$x_1^{up} - x_1^{low}$	0.6723	0.6802	0.6881	0.696	0.7039	0.7118	0.7197	0.7277	0.7356	0.7435	0.7514
$x_2^{up} - x_2^{low}$	0.8774	0.8648	0.8522	0.8396	0.827	0.8144	0.8018	0.7892	0.7766	0.764	0.7514
$x_3^{up} - x_3^{low}$	0.6633	0.6722	0.681	0.6898	0.6986	0.7074	0.7162	0.725	0.7338	0.7426	0.7514
$x_4^{up} - x_4^{low}$	0.791	0.787	0.7831	0.7791	0.7751	0.7712	0.7672	0.7633	0.7593	0.7553	0.7514
$x_5^{up} - x_5^{low}$	0.7852	0.7819	0.7785	0.7751	0.7717	0.7683	0.7649	0.7615	0.7582	0.7548	0.7514
$x_6^{up} - x_6^{low}$	0.7938	0.7896	0.7853	0.7811	0.7768	0.7726	0.7684	0.7641	0.7599	0.7556	0.7514
$x_7^{up} - x_7^{low}$	0.7786	0.7759	0.7731	0.7704	0.7677	0.765	0.7623	0.7595	0.7568	0.7541	0.7514
$x_8^{up} - x_8^{low}$	0.7853	0.7819	0.7785	0.7751	0.7717	0.7683	0.7649	0.7615	0.7582	0.7548	0.7514
Sum of ranges	6.1469	6.1333	6.1198	6.1062	6.0926	6.079	6.0654	6.0518	6.0382	6.0246	6.011

Table 12. The optimized quality standard of glutinous rice flour raw materials

	Fatty acid value	acidity	Malondialdehyde	Peak viscosity	Minimum viscosity	Disintegration value	Final viscosity	Pick-up value
x_*^{low}	22.835	1.495	0.569	2789.64	1269.998	791.009	1623.99	354
x_*^{up}	28.702	1.84	0.642	3265.022	1548.971	988.138	1973.973	427.838

4 Conclusions

In the optimal quality range finally solved by the three-stage model, some indexes such as acidity lie in the upper bound of the first kind constraint. It is speculated that the higher the acidity of glutinous rice flour, the more satisfactory the quality of dumplings. The upper and lower bounds of the final solution range are not in the first kind of constrain, which means that when selecting the glutinous rice flour raw materials of the target product, it is necessary to carefully grasp this quality index to ensure the product quality. The optimal range of the quality index of glutinous rice flour raw materials in Table 12 almost includes all the raw materials with high sensory scores in the sample data. Therefore, the conclusion of this paper is reliable. The three-stage data-driven model can be used to solve the problem of predicting the optimal raw materials of the target products in a certain production environment, not just limited to the glutinous rice industry. In the prediction stage, aiming at higher prediction accuracy, the prediction model can be adjusted according to the characteristics of the samples. In the next two stages, the widest quality range is obtained through two modeling, which reduces the difficulty of selecting raw materials when constraints allow in product process.

Acknowledgement. This work is partially supported by subproject of the National Key Research and Development Program of China (Grant No. 2017YFD0401102-02), Key Project of Philosophy and Social Science Research Project of Hubei Provincial Department of Education in 2019(19D59) and Science and Technology Research Project of Hubei Provincial Department of Education (D20191604).

References

1. Anupam, K., Lal, P.S., Bist, V., Sharma, A.K., Swaroop, V.: Raw materials selection for pulping and papermaking using TOPSIS multiple criteria decision making design. Environ. Progress Sustain. Energy **33**, 1034–1041 (2013). https://doi.org/10.1002/ep.11851
2. Breiman, L., Friedman, J.H.: Predicting multi-variate responses in multiple linear regression. J. Royal Stat. Soc. B (Stat. Methodol.) **59**, 3–54 (1997). https://doi.org/10.1111/1467-9868.00054
3. Dang, Y., Lv, Q., Zhou, J.: Research progress of special rice for glutinous rice products. Cereal Feed Ind. **06**, 23–27 (2018). (in Chinese)
4. Garcia-Munoz, S., Mercado, J.: Optimal selection of raw materials for pharmaceutical drug product design and manufacture using mixed integer nonlinear programming and multivariate latent variable regression models. Ind. Eng. Chem. Res. **52**, 5934–5942 (2013). https://doi.org/10.1021/ie3031828

5. Huang, Y.: Correlation between the characteristics of glutinous rice flour and the quality of rice dumplings. (Master's thesis). Jiangnan University. (2014) http://kns.cnki.net/kns/detail/detail

6. Huang, Z., et al.: Correlation analysis between the characteristics of glutinous rice flour and the quality of quick-frozen rice dumplings. Sci. Technol. Food Ind. **40**, 93–99 (2019). (in Chinese)

7. Hao, Y., Zhao, H., Lin, J.: Prediction of mechanical properties of squeezed aluminum alloy based on machine learning. Spec. Cast. Nonferrous Alloy. **39**, 859–862 (2019). (in Chinese)

8. Huang, R., Wang, J., Liu, Z., Zhang, H., Zhang, Z.: Research on evapotranspiration and its influencing factors based on principal component regression. J. Grassland Sci. **26**, 1454–1457 (2018)

9. Hu, W., Chen, J., Xu, F., Chen, L.: Gelation behavior and rice cake quality of different glutinous rice / japonica rice blend systems. Food Sci. **40**, 85–95 (2019)

10. Kim, J., Lee, J., Kim, B.C., Kim, J.: Raw materials criticality assessment with weighted indicators: an application of fuzzy analytic hierarchy process. Resour. Policy **60**, 225–233 (2019). https://doi.org/10.1016/j.resourpol.2019.01.005

11. Muteki, K., MacGregor, J.F., Ueda, T.: Rapid development of new polymer blends: the optimal selection of materials and blend ratios. Ind. Eng. Chem. Res. **45**, 4653–4660 (2006). https://doi.org/10.1021/ie050953b

12. Muteki, K., MacGregor, J.F.: Multi-block PLS modeling for L-shaped data structures with applications to mixture modeling. Chemom. Intell. Lab. Syst. **85**, 186–194 (2007). https://doi.org/10.1016/j.chemolab.2006.06.018

13. Muteki, K., MacGregor, J.F., Ueda, T.: Mixture designs and models for the simultaneous selection of ingredients and their ratios. Chemom. Intell. Lab. Syst. **86**, 17–25 (2007). https://doi.org/10.1016/j.chemolab.2006.08.003

14. Muteki, K., MacGregor, J.F., Ueda, T.: Estimation of missing data using latent variable methods with auxiliary information. Chemom. Intell. Lab. Syst. **78**, 41–50 (2005). https://doi.org/10.1016/j.chemolab.2004.12.004

15. Pan, Z., Luo, Y., Ai, Z., Yang, L., Fan, W., Huang, Z.: Quality changes and mechanisms of quick frozen rice dumplings under different freezing temperatures. Trans. Chin. Soc. Agric. Eng. **34**, 304–310 (2018). (in Chinese)

16. Tamiz, M.: Multi-Objective Program-Ming and Goal Programming: Theories and Applications. Springer, Heidelberg (1996). https://doi.org/10.1007/978-3-642-87561-8

17. Tao, Q., Xu, Y., Ding, W., Zhuang, K.: Effect of physicochemical indexes of glutinous rice flour on its regeneration characteristics. Food Sci. Technol. **43**, 137–141 (2018). (in Chinese)

18. Wei, C., et al.: Study on the correlation between the basic ingredients of glutinous rice and the quality of coriander. Food Sci. Technol. **43**, 158–163 (2018). (in Chinese)

19. Wang, D.: Robust data-driven modeling approach for real-time final product quality prediction in batch process operation. IEEE Trans. Ind. Inform. **7**, 371–377 (2011). https://doi.org/10.1109/tii.2010.2103401

20. Wiedermann, L.H.: Margarine and margarine oil, formulation and control. J. Am. Oil Chem. Soc. **55**, 823–829 (1978). https://doi.org/10.1007/bf02682655

21. Wang, Y., Jiang, R., Lei, F., Wang, Y.: Research on storage characteristics of glutinous rice flour. China Brewing **33**, 101–105 (2014). (in Chinese)

22. Xie, S., Zhou, H., He, J., Dai, L.: The application of principal component regression in hospital target management. China Health Stat. **29**, 717–718 (2012). (in Chinese)

23. Zhou, X., Ma, P., Hu, Y., & Zhang, Y.: Effects of Frozen Storage Temperature Fluctuation on Cooking Characteristics of Quick Frozen Rice Dumplings. (in Chinese). Cereal and Feed Industry 1, 16–19 (2015)
24. Zhang, Y., Tian, J., Gao, J., Zhou, X.: Effects of glutinous rice flour preparation technology on its starch damage and quality characteristics. J. Henan Univ. Technol. (Nat. Sci. Ed.) 38, 1–31 (2017). (in Chinese)
25. Zhou, X., Wu, F., Zhang, Y., Gao, J., Lu, J.: Effect of semidry milling process on the quality and characteristics of glutinous rice flour. J. Henan Univ. Technol. Nat. Sci. Ed. 39, 1–28 (2018). (in Chinese)
26. Zhuang, K., et al.: Effects of different milling methods of glutinous rice flour on the cooking and taste quality of glutinous rice dumplings. Food Technol. 45, 245–250 (2020). (in Chinese)

Incorporating the Confusion Effect into the Simulated Evolution of Crowded Selfish Herds

Wen-Chi Yang[✉]

Computer Vision Lab, NeuHelium Co., Ltd., Shanghai 200090, China
wenchi.yang@neuhelium.com

Abstract. Regarding collective animal behaviour, a gap has long existed between perspectives from the anti-predator benefit and the evolutionary dynamic. On the one hand, studies on natural swarm intelligence rarely consider how this advantage keeps stable in evolution. On the other hand, evolutionary theories used to neglect the change of absolute fitness at the group level. Nevertheless, social profits are not evenly distributed to individuals. An anti-predator function, therefore, may affect the relative fitness and shape the behavioural evolution in an animal population. To investigate this issue, we adopted the crowded-selfish-herd model with minimum modification to include the confusion effect, a common anti-predator function of prey crowds. Three arguments are proposed from our simulations. First, the negative correlation between the effect strength and the emergent group density shows the confusion effect is restrained by intraspecific competition. Secondly, highly coordinated movements are primary stable states, which geometry is moulded by the degree of the confusion effect. Lastly, a strong confusion effect promotes a branch of stable states where selfish herds exercise as swarms of millipedes. These findings hint that the geometry of collective patterns is possible to identify the existence of confusion effects in nature.

Keywords: Selfish herd · Confusion effect · Intraspecific competition · Complex adaptive system · Artificial life · Evolutionary spatial game

1 Introduction

The emergence of movement coordination in social animals, such as fish, birds, and insects, has long attracted studies of two primary interests. One focus is on the self-organising mechanism that emerges collective behaviour from the interaction among relatively simple individuals, i.e., the *proximate* causation [12]. Based on these studies, swarm intelligence algorithms are developed for solution search, optimisation, and robot designs [1]. The other focus is on the evolutionary dynamics that drive individuals into such stable states, known as the *ultimate* causation [12]. This interest arises in research domains like evolutionary game theory, adaptive dynamic, and mechanism design [15]. The extended applications in computational intelligence include the analysis, prediction, and control of a crowd [18,21].

© Springer Nature Singapore Pte Ltd. 2021
L. Pan et al. (Eds.): BIC-TA 2020, CCIS 1363, pp. 221–234, 2021.
https://doi.org/10.1007/978-981-16-1354-8_15

Regarding researches towards collective animal behaviours, a missing link exists between these two mainstream approaches [13]. From the *proximate* aspect, many empirical works and computational simulations have been proposed to support that collective animal behaviour can effectively increase the overall survival fitness of individuals, as phenomena of natural swarm intelligence [10]. For example, one of the most significant anti-predator functions is the *confusion effect* [11]. It indicates that predators meet more difficulties, or are less frequently, hunting the central individuals of a prey aggregate. This effect has usually been documented from empirical studies on predatory fish [6–8]. Also, the observations have often served as an imprecise explanation about why social animals exhibit collective motion.

In contrast, from the evolutionary viewpoint, selection and adaptation should happen at the individual level (for mating and reproduction rely on individuals) [5,17], or even at the gene level [4]. And the group-level benefit has long been considered indirect or insignificant, for it hardly affects the relative fitness among conspecifics [15,17]. In other words, given excess short-term fitness is available from damaging the group benefit, an optimal collective state cannot remain stable in evolution. Unfortunately, this puzzle might arise in reality from several observations. For example, it has been reported that in a mobile fish aggregate, the leaders at the frontal positions bear more risk than their followers [2]. Hence, collective motion in fish seems to violate the evolutionary principle. Fish individuals should have evolved to repulse from leading the group, and, consequently, the mobility of fish schools should have been minimised [13].

Apart from typical attempts based on evolutionary trade-offs or individual differences [3,9,13], the *crowded selfish herd* scenario proposed in recent years has provided a rather bright and robust interpretation of this conundrum [22]. The related modelling works have demonstrated that collective motion can evolve from purely egoistic prey individuals, by further considering the physical restrictions of individual mobility in a crowded environment [19,20,22]. As a sequel of the famous selfish herd scenario [5], these works demonstrated that in a crowded and dense group, intraspecific competition should lead to a collective departure of outer individuals, for this departure exposes inner neighbours to the dangerous border region, and hence evens the risk distribution. The crowded selfish herd scenario reveals that movement coordination in social animals is explainable from both *proximate* and *ultimate* aspects, with the precondition that individuals make decisions subject to a local receptive field and a limited locomotion ability.

Although the crowded selfish herd scenario has shown its potential to cross the gap between the two research interests, the inferences in the original works would somewhat provoke the debate about group benefit versus individual selection in collective animal behaviours. These works may overemphasise that group-level benefits are unnecessary for the emergence of collective motion, such that anti-predator functions' efficacy was also challenged. Fairly to say, there can be no conflict if movement coordination can evolve from selfish individuals while bringing in additional fitness to group members. Mathematically speaking, given the promise that if anti-predator functions are beneficial, then collective motion emerges (i.e., $p \rightarrow q$), the only contradiction happens when the existence of anti-predator benefits restrains selfish individuals from evolving into collective motion (i.e., $p \wedge \neg q$).

In this work, we utilise computational simulations to investigate the research question about how the confusion effect, as a primary anti-predator function, shapes the behavioural evolution of selfish prey individuals. To obtain more reliable findings, we elaborately integrated the confusion effect into the previous crowded-selfish-herd model framework, with minimum adjustments. The aim is to understand: (1) whether the confusion effect can drive selfish individuals into coordinated movements in evolution, and (2) whether the geometry of emergent patterns varies from different effect intensities.

2   Model Design

2.1   Mathematical Formulation

Since mating and reproduction happen at the individual level, it has long been indicated that intraspecific competition is the primary force that shapes the evolution of a population [17]. Following this viewpoint, the *selfish herd* theory [5] has proposed an adaptive dynamic that the gain of individual survival fitness from hiding into a crowd is sufficient to drive selfish prey into flocking behaviours. However, the movement coordination that emerges from many animal aggregates was left unanswered.

The *crowded selfish herd* scenario [22] has complemented this remaining question by further considering the limitation for an outer individual to enter a crowded and dense group. When squeezing into the crowd centre is infeasible, staying at the boundary and protecting those inner conspecifics can be less adapted than leaving the group collectively and forcing those internal individuals to be at the risky border positions. For example, letting X_C and X_B denote the predation risks at the central and border positions of a compact group ($X_C \ll X_B$ in the *selfish herd* scenario), X_L denotes the predation risk of leaving the group, and N_C and N_B denote the number of prey at the associative positions, then a collective departure of n border individuals must happen when

$$\frac{X_B}{N_B X_B + N_C X_C} > \frac{X_L}{n X_L + N'_B X_B + N'_C X_C} . \tag{1}$$

Notably, N_B and N_C maintain a relation by construction. For example, assuming the crowded group forms a round shape in a two-dimensional space, it must hold that

$$N_B : N_C \approx 2\pi r : \pi r^2 , \tag{2}$$

and equivalently,

$$N_B = \sqrt{4\pi(N_B + N_C)} . \tag{3}$$

Hence, the departure of n border individuals will change the amount of border prey into

$$N'_B = \sqrt{4\pi(N_B + N_C - n)} . \tag{4}$$

When $N_B + N_C > 4\pi$, i.e., a dense group of more than 12 individuals, the amount $N_B' + n$ is always greater than N_B for any positive n. Therefore, once the risk X_L is less, or even slightly greater, than X_B, a continuous departure of border prey should emerge, and the population then exhibits movement coordination.

2.2 Adopted Model Framework

The above mathematical description has proven the validity of the *crowded selfish herd* scenario. To further capture the geometry and morphology of collective patterns in this kind of evolutionary spatial game, simulation has been a popular soft-computing approach [14]. We adopted the original lattice gas model framework and made some minor adjustments to simulate the confusion effect in our experiments. The universal designs are stated here, and we leave the modifications in the next subsection.

The same as the original works [20,22], we prepared a 120 × 120 wrapped-around lattice for 200 prey agents to play at, where each cell accommodates at most one agent. At each time step, every prey agent moves towards one of its four adjacent cells, according to its local perceptions. If another agent has already occupied the target cell, one has to stay at the same place for the crowding effect; otherwise, the move occurs. After sufficiently many time steps (set by 5000 in our experiments), the 5% least fitted agents are eliminated and replaced by the same amount of new agents reproduced from the survivors. We repeat the reproduction cycles, i.e., generations, until a stable state has been observed in the simulated evolution, which was set by 8000 generations in the following experiments.

Our agent design also follows the relevant models [19,20]. The cognition of an agent is a NEAT neural network [16] with ten input neurons and four output neurons. Regarding the input design, we use eight neurons to record the four adjacent cells' occupancy states (a binary signal about whether this cell is occupied) and neighbourhood densities (the ratio of occupied cells to all cells in the receptive field). Besides, the last two input neurons submit a constant value and a random value, respectively. The four output neurons represent the four adjacent cells, and the one with the maximal value triggers a move towards the corresponding cell.

At the reproduction stage, the mating probability is set by the rank selection scheme with a selection intensity 1.02 [20,22]. After a pair of survival agents have been selected as parents, the operator to generate an offspring agent is directly based on the NEAT algorithm [16].

2.3 Adjustments and Metrics

The fitness function to evaluate individual absolute fitness is specifically designed as follows. Given T is the amount of time steps in a generation, i.e., 8000 by our setting, and $n_i(t)$ denotes agent i's neighbourhood density at time t, we define the fitness value by

$$u_i = \frac{1}{T} \sum_{t=1}^{T} n_i(t)^\omega \,, \tag{5}$$

where ω adjusts the strength of the confusion effect, and $\omega = 1$ was the original design [22].

From an ex-post viewpoint, unless a certain gregarious species is endangered, its population size should generally oscillate at the growth barrier regardless of whether anti-predator benefits exist. In other words, at the population level, the confusion effect is to reallocate risk distributions among conspecifics of different traits. When we consider the confusion effect from the perspective about how it affects the relative fitness among individuals at various positions, it becomes reasonable to connect this effect with the value ω. For example, with the increase of ω, the central areas become much safer than other positions, which reflects the observations that predators are confused by abundant prey and have to attack the isolated or outer ones [6–8].

Besides, in previous models, the receptive field of an agent was set by the Moore neighbourhood of range 1 (the 8 surrounding cells) [22], or even the von Neumann neighbourhood of range 1 (the 4 adjacent cells) [19]. Although these settings are sufficient to demonstrate the crowded selfish herd scenario, we found that a larger receptive field brings in more information about the geometry and morphology of prey groups under different risk distributions. In the present work, we set this sensing range as the von Neumann neighbourhood of range 3, that means any two agents within a Manhattan distance of 3 are neighbours, and the area contains 24 cells.

Four metrics are introduced to quantify the simulation outputs. The first is the mean neighbourhood density, which is the expected neighbourhood density per capita per time step [22]. The second is the mean mobility degree, that is the expected frequency an agent changes its cell [22]. The third is the cohesiveness degree, which is the proportion of central prey, defined as those with their neighbourhood densities higher than 0.5 [20]. The last one is the mean group size, given two individuals are in the same group if there is a social connection via their neighbours (and neighbours' neighbours, etc.) [20].

3   Results

3.1   Simulation Overview

We ran 400 independent simulations in the experimental range $0 \le \omega \le 3$ to acquire the features of emergent patterns shaped by the confusion effect in evolution. Before close inspections, we look for a general trend from the correlation values in Table 1 and the distributions in Fig. 1.

According to the statistics, the strength of the confusion effect considerably forms a negative correlation with group density and cohesiveness. Specifically, the group density reaches its maximum at around $\omega = 1$, and the cohesiveness degrees of the final states decrease and converge with the growth of the effect strength. These outputs reveal that even if a stronger confusion effect can

Table 1. Correlations between the confusion effect and the four metrics. The metrics are abbreviated at the header row.

	D	M	C	G.S
Strength (ω)	**−0.38**	**0.14**	**−0.34**	**0.06**
Density	1	**−0.76**	−0.02	−0.03
Mobility	−0.76	1	**0.51**	0.09
Cohesiveness	−0.02	0.51	1	0.06
Group Size	−0.03	0.09	0.06	1

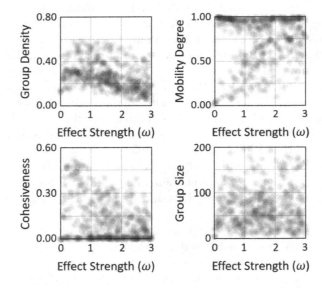

Fig. 1. Distributions of the final states of 400 simulation runs. Branches are observed from the metrics about mobility and cohesiveness.

improve the group-level survival fitness, the bias of advantages towards those prey at dense and central positions causes this social benefit cannot be stable in evolution. Actually, from the viewpoint of individual short-term fitness, the adaptation to stronger confusion effects for those exposed prey is exactly leaving the border positions to avoid being the compensatory target of their predators. However, it is interesting that the average group size, 67.38 prey per group, is generally independent from the strength of the confusion effect.

The correlation value shows the mobility degree of prey gradually increases as the confusion effect enhances. In detail, there are two branches of stable states in our simulations. We apply more dimensions in Fig. 2 and Fig. 3 to better display the clusters of simulated stable states under different degrees of confusion effects. It shows one branch is composed of those states with mobility degrees greater than around 0.75. These states exhibit high individual mobility regardless of the effect strength, but a stronger confusion effect lowers the density and cohesiveness of selfish herds. The other branch, with mobility degrees between 0 and 0.75, displays an elevation of the mobility degree and a dilution of the group density along with the ω value. In the following parts, we investigate the geometry of these two evolutionary branches.

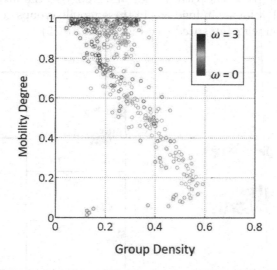

Fig. 2. Correlations between mobility, density and the effect strength. It displays two branches of stable states. One is those states with their mobility close to 1, which branch is attainable regardless of the degree of confusion effects.

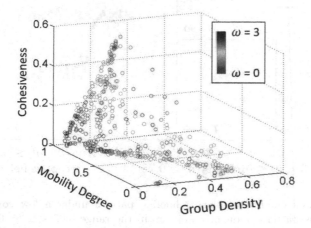

Fig. 3. The scatter plot with maximum information. The measurement about mean group sizes is omitted for being relatively independent of the effect strength and the other metrics. (Color figure online)

3.2 The Emergent Schooling Patterns

We have observed that given any strength of the confusion effect, a fixed ratio of about 60% simulations reach a kind of stable state (quantified as states with their mobility degrees higher than 0.75), where prey agents evolve to assemble highly polarised and fast-moving aggregates (see Fig. 2). We refer to these collective behaviours as *schooling* patterns, for an analogy to the highly coordinated movements in fish schools. Individuals in these mobile groups generally move in the same direction with full speed (see Fig. 4 and Fig. 5).

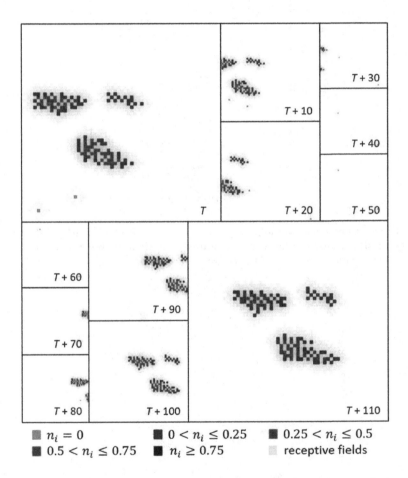

Fig. 4. Snapshots of an exemplary schooling pattern under a low confusion effect ($\omega = 0.2$). This pattern frequently appears in the range $0.05 < \omega < 0.85$. For better visualisation, only a quarter of the arena is displayed.

While the emergence of a schooling pattern brings in scant information about the strength of the confusion effect, the geometry of selfish herds still reveals several indications. We can realize that schooling patterns with little confusion effect (blue dots in Fig. 3) exhibit both higher group densities, i.e., the number of neighbours per individual, and greater cohesiveness, i.e., the proportion of central positions in a group, compared with those undergoing a strong confusion effect (red dots in Fig. 3).

The snapshots in Fig. 4 and Fig. 5 display the typical geometry and locomotion of schooling patterns shaped by low and high confusion effects, respectively. A schooling group exhibits a round shape with a central area when there is little confusion effect, i.e., the predation risk is almost impartial between the boundary and centre of a group. In contrast, when the confusion effect is intensive, prey agents evolve into elongated groups that contain rare central positions. These mobile, elongated, and loosely constructed selfish herds then usually become gigantic aggregation through a series of fusion processes.

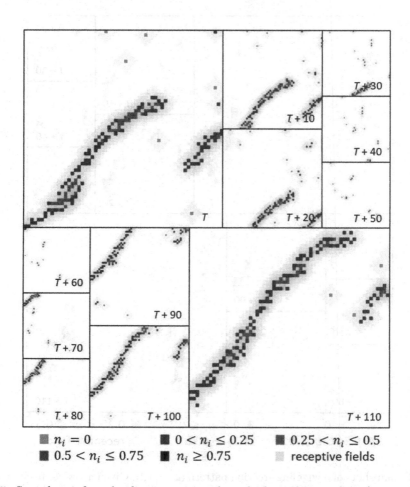

| ■ $n_i = 0$ | ■ $0 < n_i \leq 0.25$ | ■ $0.25 < n_i \leq 0.5$ |
| ■ $0.5 < n_i \leq 0.75$ | ■ $n_i \geq 0.75$ | receptive fields |

Fig. 5. Snapshots of a schooling pattern under a high confusion effect ($\omega = 2.8$). In the range around $2 < \omega < 3$, agents frequently evolve into elongated, loose and mobile herds. Only a quarter of the arena is displayed.

Regarding why the schooling patterns are stable in our simulated evolution, we observed that the full-speed movement of selfish herds mitigates the squeezing attempts of group members such that overcrowding is avoided. Once the group density reaches its equilibrium under a given ω value, the leaders are more adapted to lead their herds than to stop, for a halt causes the current flock much denser and primarily profits the followers. As the followers keep chasing those leaders to maintain their advantageous positions, schooling patterns emerge.

3.3   The Emergent Wiggling Patterns

We mentioned that the comparatively loose structure of schooling patterns provides leading individuals with enough fitness to retain their positions. However,

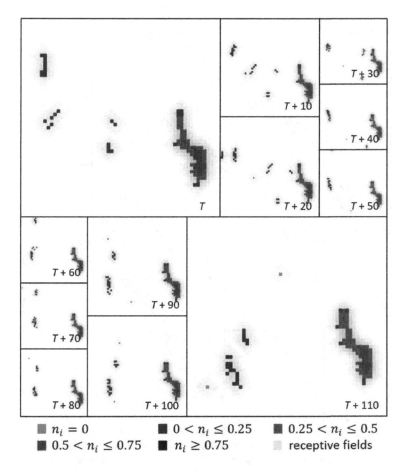

Fig. 6. Snapshots of a wiggling-freezing pattern ($\omega = 0.2$). Given a low confusion effect, selfish herds evolve to wiggle if the group size is small, and freeze when the volume is more significant. Only a one-fourth arena is shown.

this is not the only equilibrium of this evolutionary spatial game. The other 40% simulation runs experience another branch of evolutionary trajectory, and reach an equilibrium of wiggling and freezing patterns.

When movement coordination has not emerged from a stochastic evolutionary process, prey agents evolve into overcrowded groups that touch the physical upper bound of the density level. In this situation, outer agents have to gain their relative fitness by shifting around the dense herd and exposing their inner neighbours. It is the *dodger strategy* documented in the original work [22]. However, although the *dodger strategy* can improve one's fitness rank among group members, this tactic also harms the own absolute fitness such that one's relative fitness in a population may, however, regress. In other words, there is a balance of when to practise the *dodger strategy*.

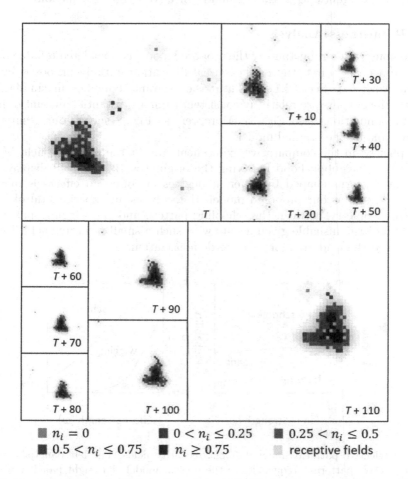

$\blacksquare$ $n_i = 0$ $\blacksquare$ $0 < n_i \leq 0.25$ $\blacksquare$ $0.25 < n_i \leq 0.5$
$\blacksquare$ $0.5 < n_i \leq 0.75$ $\blacksquare$ $n_i \geq 0.75$ $\blacksquare$ receptive fields

Fig. 7. Snapshots of a wiggling pattern ($\omega = 2.8$). Under a strong confusion effect, a type of stable states is the emergence of dense herds that wiggle in a clear direction. This pattern is similar to the collective motion of insect swarms.

The simulation outputs demonstrate that this balance is highly sensitive to the intensity of the confusion effect. Given a low effect strength (see Fig. 6), agents evolve to shift along or depart from the boundary of small groups, that self-organises a collective wiggling behaviour. However, when being on the boundary of a large group, agents evolve to cease the *dodger strategy* for better absolute fitness than individuals of other groups, even though this action profits the inner neighbours.

With the enhancement of the confusion effect, the predation risk biases to the margin of a herd such that harming the survival fitness of inner neighbours becomes increasingly beneficial. Therefore, this branch of stable states composes of more wiggling patterns and less freezing patterns with the growth of the ω value (see Fig. 2). Figure 7 shows an example that under a strong confusion effect, even a gigantic aggregate exhibits collective wiggling behaviour.

3.4 Robustness Analysis

The demonstration robustness of the proposed model is considered reliable based on three aspects. First, the mathematical derivation initially proposed by the present work (see Sect. 2.1) validates the relevant dynamics in simulations. Besides, the outputs are relatively consistent from a substantial amount of independent simulations (see Fig. 3). Moreover, as Fig. 8 shows, our results are reproducible by the original model.

Explicitly, in the comparative experiment, we set the receptive field by the basic Moore neighbourhood following the original work. Figure 8 displays the emergent patterns shaped by different degrees of confusion effects is qualitatively the same as our proposed model. However, as an experimental observation, the geometry between the schooling pattern and the wiggling pattern is visually indistinguishable given agents with such a small receptive field. Hence, we enlarged the field area for a better demonstration.

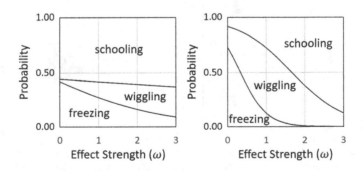

Fig. 8. Collective patterns under different receptive fields. The left panel shows the three collective patterns' frequencies in the present model. The right panel shows the same measurement given the receptive field is the basic Moore neighbourhood, as the traditional setting. The results are approximated by the basic logistic regression.

4 Discussions

In this work, we adopted the framework of crowded-selfish-herd models to launch experiments for disclosing the role of the confusion effect in evolution. According to the simulation outputs, the two proposed research questions have become addressable to a reasonable extent. About whether the confusion effect can enhance the degree of animal movement coordination, our results strongly support this statement from the *ultimate* aspect. Our model demonstrated that even if selection and adaptation are purely at the individual level, the effect strength is positively correlated with the group mobility in evolutionarily stable states.

Regarding the second research question, the impact of the confusion effect on collective animal behaviours is visible. We demonstrated that the confusion effect significantly shapes the geometry and locomotion of selfish herds, such that identifying the degree of a confusion effect by these group-level features seems possible. For example, those highly coordinated and fast-moving animal groups, e.g., the schooling pattern of sardines and the aerial display of starlings, should exhibit elongated shapes if their predators confront a severe confusion effect, and, on the other hand, should exhibit round shapes if the confusion effect is insignificant. Besides, a collective wiggling behaviour, similar to mobile swarms of insects, also reflects a rather strong confusion effect in our model. In contrast, the evolution of a stationary swarm in prey implies the absence of the confusion effect.

This work proposes a novel attempt to integrate anti-predator functions into the evolutionary dynamics, with useful soft-computing approaches. It is clear that the outcome of simulations can be sensitive to the model design. That issue happens in any mathematical model, along with the setting of preconditions. With formulated derivations and robustness analyses, we hope the findings and inferences are generalisable, and we look forward to collaboration with biologists for further empirical validation. In the future works, we aim to simulate more anti-predator functions, e.g., the information transfer effect, from the evolutionary viewpoint. At the same time, we are completing the mathematical derivation of the crowded selfish herd dynamics to draw a rigorous explanation from the findings of agent-based simulations.

References

1. Bonabeau, E., Dorigo, M., Theraulaz, G.: Swarm Intelligence: From Natural to Artificial Systems. Oxford University Press, Oxford (1999)
2. Bumann, D., Rubenstein, D., Krause, J.: Mortality risk of spatial positions in animal groups: the danger of being in the front. Behaviour **134**(13–14), 1063–1076 (1997)
3. Conradt, L.: When it pays to share decisions. Nature **471**(7336), 40–41 (2011)
4. Dawkins, R.: The Selfish Gene. Oxford University Press, Oxford (2016)
5. Hamilton, W.D.: Geometry for the selfish herd. J. Theor. Biol. **31**(2), 295–311 (1971)

6. Herbert-Read, J.E., Rosén, E., Szorkovszky, A., Ioannou, C.C., Rogell, B., Perna, A., Ramnarine, I.W., Kotrschal, A., Kolm, N., Krause, J., et al.: How predation shapes the social interaction rules of shoaling fish. Proc. Royal Soc. B: Biol. Sci. **284**(1861), 20171126 (2017)
7. Hogan, B.G., Hildenbrandt, H., Scott-Samuel, N.E., Cuthill, I.C., Hemelrijk, C.K.: The confusion effect when attacking simulated three-dimensional starling flocks. Royal Soc. Open Sci. **4**(1), 160564 (2017)
8. Ioannou, C., Tosh, C., Neville, L., Krause, J.: The confusion effect-from neural networks to reduced predation risk. Behav. Ecol. **19**(1), 126–130 (2008)
9. Ioannou, C.C., Dall, S.R.: Individuals that are consistent in risk-taking benefit during collective foraging. Sci. Rep. **6**, 33991 (2016)
10. Krause, J., Ruxton, G.D., Ruxton, G.D., Ruxton, I.G., et al.: Living in Groups. Oxford University Press, Oxford (2002)
11. Milinski, M., Heller, R.: Influence of a predator on the optimal foraging behaviour of sticklebacks (gasterosteus aculeatus l.). Nature **275**(5681), 642–644 (1978)
12. Nesse, R.M.: Tinbergen's four questions, organized: a response to bateson and laland. Trends Ecol. Evol. **28**(12), 681–82 (2013)
13. Parrish, J.K., Edelstein-Keshet, L.: Complexity, pattern, and evolutionary trade-offs in animal aggregation. Science **284**(5411), 99–101 (1999)
14. Roca, C.P., Cuesta, J.A., Sánchez, A.: Evolutionary game theory: temporal and spatial effects beyond replicator dynamics. Phys. Life Rev. **6**(4), 208–249 (2009)
15. Smith, J.M.: Evolution and the Theory of Games. Cambridge University Press, Cambridge (1982)
16. Stanley, K.O., Miikkulainen, R.: Evolving neural networks through augmenting topologies. Evol. Comput. **10**(2), 99–127 (2002)
17. Williams, G.C.: Adaptation and natural selection: a critique of some current evolutionary thought, vol. 75. Princeton University Press (2018)
18. Xi, J.Y.S., Chan, W.K.V.: Simulation of knife attack and gun attack on university campus using agent-based model and gis. In: 2019 Winter Simulation Conference (WSC), pp. 263–272. IEEE (2019)
19. Yang, W.C.: When the selfish herd is too crowded to enter. In: 2017 IEEE Symposium Series on Computational Intelligence (SSCI), pp. 2247–2254. IEEE, November 2017. https://doi.org/10.1109/SSCI.2017.8285189
20. Yang, W.C.: When the selfish herd is unsafe in the middle. In: 2018 22nd Asia Pacific Symposium on Intelligent and Evolutionary Systems (IES), pp. 55–62. IES 2018 Program Committee, December 2018
21. Yang, W.C., Lee, Y.H., Yang, K.S.: Modeling the impact of social comparison on student engagement by the equity theory. In: Artificial Life Conference Proceedings, pp. 605–613. MIT Press (2020)
22. Yang, W.C., Schmickl, T.: Collective motion as an ultimate effect in crowded selfish herds. Sci. Rep. **9**(1), 1–11 (2019)

Multiobjective Brainstorm Optimization with Diversity Preservation Mechanism for Nonlinear Equation Systems

Yi Zhao and Zelin Zhu$^{(\boxtimes)}$

Key Laboratory of Image Processing and Intelligent Control of Education Ministry
of China, School of Artificial Intelligence and Automation, Huazhong University
of Science and Technology, Wuhan 430074, China
{zy56865,m201972839}@hust.edu.cn

Abstract. In many fields of engineering and science, it is necessary
to solve nonlinear equation systems (NESs). When using multiobjective
optimization to solve NESs, there are two problems: 1) how to transform an NES into a multiobjective optimization problem and 2) how to
design an algorithm to solve the transformed problems. In this work,
we propose a multilayer bi-objective transformation technique, which
can transform an NES into a bi-objective optimization problem, and it
overcomes the curse of dimensionality and the problem of missing roots
caused by the decrease of solutions discernibility in previous transformation techniques. Then, combining the multilayer bi-objective transformation technique, we design a multiobjective brainstorm optimization with
a diversity preservation mechanism, which can effectively locate multiple roots of NESs in a single run. Compared with several state-of-art
methods on 30 NESs with different features, our approach provides very
competitive performance with the highest root ratio and success ratio.

Keywords: Multiobjective optimization · Nonlinear equation system ·
Brainstorm optimization · Diversity preservation mechanism

1 Introduction

Many problems in the real world can be abstracted as nonlinear equation systems
(NESs) [18,22]. For example, in the electronic circuit design [1], the nonlinear
terms will exist in the equations of circuit analysis when nonlinear elements are
used, which will make the circuit analysis equations become NESs. In the field
of systems control [11], integration, exponential and trigonometric functions are
sometimes needed in the motion control analysis, which turns analysis equations
into time-varying NESs. Besides, solving NESs is widely used in molecular conformations computing [4], power modulation [5], generalized Nash equilibrium
problems [6], and other fields. Without loss of generality, a nonlinear equation

© Springer Nature Singapore Pte Ltd. 2021
L. Pan et al. (Eds.): BIC-TA 2020, CCIS 1363, pp. 235–250, 2021.
https://doi.org/10.1007/978-981-16-1354-8_16

system can be formulated as follows:

$$\begin{cases} e_1(\mathbf{x}) = 0, \\ \quad \vdots \\ e_m(\mathbf{x}) = 0, \end{cases} \tag{1}$$

where m is the number of equations; $\mathbf{x} = (x_1, ..., x_D)^T \in \mathbb{S}$ is a decision vector containing D decision variables; $\mathbb{S} \in \mathbb{R}^D$ denotes the feasible region of search space, and $\mathbb{S}$ is usually defined as $\mathbb{S} = \prod_{j=1}^{D} \left[\underline{x_j}, \overline{x_j} \right]$, where $\underline{x_j}, \overline{x_j}$ are the lower and upper bounds of x_j, respectively. In general, at least one nonlinear equation is in an NES. If $\mathbf{x}^* \in \mathbb{S}$ satisfies $\mathbf{e}(\mathbf{x}^*) = \mathbf{0}$, then $\mathbf{x}^*$ is a root of the NES.

In general, an NES may contain more than one root, and these roots are important equally. Therefore, the main task of solving NESs is to locate multiple roots. However, it is a challenge for numerical computation to locate multiple roots simultaneously [14].

In the field of numerical computation, there are many classical numerical methods for solving NESs, such as Newton's method [24], homotopy method [17, 28], interval-Newton method [3,28], and quasi-Newton method [27]. However, these classical numerical methods have many limitations, such as some of them are sensitive to the initial points and require differentiation. In particular, most of them cannot find multiple roots simultaneously in a single run.

In recent years, many researchers have introduced evolutionary algorithms (EAs) into solving NESs. Benefiting from the fact that EAs work with a population of candidate solutions, EAs have the ability to locate multiple roots simultaneously in a single run. Generally, the EA-based methods can be classified into three categories: i.e., repulsion-based methods, niching-based methods, and multiobjective optimization-based methods.

The repulsion techniques penalize the solutions around the roots that have been found, which enhance the diversity of the population. Hirsch et al. introduced the repulsion method and multi-start strategy into C-GRASP method to solve NESs [13]. Cooperated with the repulsion technique, Gong et al. designed a diversity preservation mechanism and adaptive parameter control to find multiple roots for NESs simultaneously [8]. In [16], a dynamic repulsion technique was proposed to change the radius of repulsion adaptively, in which the radius of the repulsion area decreases with the process of evolution dynamically.

The niching-based methods divide the population into some sub-populations to maintain the diversity of the population. NichePSO [2] combined the niching technique and particle swarm optimization (PSO) to locate multiple roots. In [31], a clustering-based Multistart and Minfinder method was proposed. Pourjafari et al. used a clustering method, then the IWO algorithm was used for each cluster to locate the exact position of the root [23]. He et al. designed a fuzzy neighborhood-based differential evolution with orientation to locate multiple roots simultaneously [12].

In multiobjective optimization [19,20], the main goal is to find a set of Pareto optimal solutions (PS) [21], which is similar to locating multiple roots for NESs. Therefore, many researchers tried to use multiobjective optimization-based methods to solve NESs. In principle, solving NESs by multiobjective optimization can be considered as a two-step procedure. In the first step, it is necessary to design a transformation technique to transform an NES into a multiobjective optimization problem. Then, an optimization algorithm should be designed to solve the transformed problem. Grosan *et al.* proposed a new approach for NESs, named CA, in which an NES with m equations was transformed into an m-objective optimization problem [10]. However, it will suffer from the curse of dimensionality. In [25], an $(m+1)$-objective transformation technique was presented for solving NESs, where m is the number of equations. Similar to CA, its performance will significantly degrade with the increase of m. Song *et al.* transformed the NESs into a bi-objective optimization problem, in which the first dimension of the solution is used to distinguish different objectives [30]. However, since only the first dimension of the solution is used to construct the location function, MONES may lose some roots if the first dimension of multiple roots is the same. Gong *et al.* extended the work presented in [30] and proposed the weighted bi-objective transformation technique (WeB), in which all the dimensions of the solution are considered in the location function [9]. However, due to a weighted linear combination, the discernibility of the transformed solutions are reduced, which will make many roots similar in the objective space, resulting in some of them might be lost.

In this paper, we propose a multilayer bi-objective transformation technique, which overcomes the aforementioned curse of dimensionality and the problem of missing roots caused by the decrease of solutions discernibility. With this transformation technique, a novel multiobjective brainstorm optimization (BSO) algorithm, namely MOBSO, is proposed for solving NESs effectively.

The main contributions of this paper are as follows:

1. A multilayer bi-objective transformation technique is proposed. It can transform an NES into a bi-objective optimization problem, which avoids the curse of dimensionality and the problem of missing roots caused by the decrease of solutions discernibility.
2. A multiobjective BSO algorithm with a diversity preservation mechanism is presented. We combine BSO algorithm with multiobjective optimization and design a diversity preservation mechanism for them, which can penalize clusters with too many individuals and allows multiple clusters to develop in a balanced manner.
3. By combining the multilayer bi-objective transformation technique and multiobjective BSO algorithm, MOBSO is proposed for solving NESs. Results from experiments using 30 test problems verify that MOBSO has better performance than other methods in locating multiple roots of different NESs at a single run.

The rest of the paper is organized as follows. Section 2 describes the proposed method in detail. In Sect. 3, the experimental study and discussions are given. We conclude this paper and outlines the future work in Sect. 4.

2   Proposed Approach

In this section, a multilayer bi-objective transformation technique is proposed to transform an NES into a bi-objective optimization problem. Then, we design a multiobjective brainstorm optimization algorithm with a diversity preservation mechanism, which combined with the multilayer bi-objective transformation technique can effectively locate multiple roots of NESs in a single run.

2.1   Multilayer Bi-objective Transformation Technique

In the existing multiobjective transformation techniques, most of them designed the optimization objectives by the combination of location function and system function. However, their location functions have some limitations. For example, in MONES [30], only the first dimension of the solution is used to construct the location function, it may lose some roots if the first dimension of multiple roots is the same. If an NES has roots $x_1(0.4, 0.5)$, $x_2(0.5, 0.5)$, $x_3(0.5, 0.6)$, $x_4(0.6, 0.6)$, after the transformation of MONES, the distribution of roots in the objective space is shown in Fig. 1. As we can see, MONES cannot distinguish between x_2 and x_3, which may eventually cause one of them to be lost. In the WeB [9], all the dimensions of the solution are considered in the location function. However, due to the weighted linear combination, the discrimination of the transformed solutions is reduced, which will make many roots similar in the objective space, and WeB might lose some of them. For instance, if an NES has roots $x_1(0.3, 0.6)$, $x_2(0.6, 0.3)$ and the weight vector is $w = (0.45, 0.55)$, after transforming by WeB, their location function will be $\alpha_1 = 0.465$ and $\alpha_2 = 0.435$, respectively. The distance between the two roots in the objective space drops from 0.3 (MONES) to 0.03, and the algorithm may not be able to distinguish them, which will cause WeB to lose one of them.

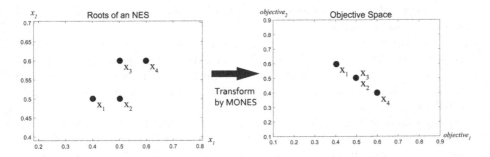

Fig. 1. The transformation process of MONES

In this study, the location function of the multilayer bi-objective transformation is defined as

$$\begin{cases} layer_1 \begin{cases} \min x_1 \\ \min 1 - x_1 \end{cases} \\ \quad\vdots \\ layer_l \begin{cases} \min x_j \\ \min 1 - x_j \end{cases} \\ \quad\vdots \\ layer_{max} \begin{cases} \min x_D \\ \min 1 - x_D \end{cases} \end{cases} \tag{2}$$

where l is the number of layers, and $l = 2, 3, ..., max\_layer$; $max\_layer = \min(D, 5)$ in this study, where D is the dimension of the decision variable; j is defined as $j = \lceil \frac{(l-1)D}{max\_layer-1} \rceil$. The multilayer bi-objective transformation can be obtained by combining the location function with the system function:

$$\begin{cases} layer_1 \begin{cases} \min x_1 + \sum_{i=1}^{m} e_i^2(\mathbf{x}) \\ \min 1 - x_1 + \sum_{i=1}^{m} e_i^2(\mathbf{x}) \end{cases} \\ \quad\vdots \\ layer_l \begin{cases} \min x_j + \sum_{i=1}^{m} e_i^2(\mathbf{x}) \\ \min 1 - x_j + \sum_{i=1}^{m} e_i^2(\mathbf{x}) \end{cases} \\ \quad\vdots \\ layer_{max} \begin{cases} \min x_D + \sum_{i=1}^{m} e_i^2(\mathbf{x}) \\ \min 1 - x_D + \sum_{i=1}^{m} e_i^2(\mathbf{x}). \end{cases} \end{cases} \tag{3}$$

After the transformation, the algorithm is optimized simultaneously on multiple layers. Besides, for every quarter of evolution, the layers would communicate with each other. In the communication, they will exchange information about their population with each other, as depicted in Fig. 2.

For the multilayer bi-objective transformation technique, we can give the following comments. (1) The number of objectives in each layer does not increase as the number of equations increases, thus it can avoid the curse of dimensionality. (2) The information on multiple dimensions of decision variables is used to design the location function, which solves the problem in MONES. (3) Only a single dimension of variables is considered in the location function for each layer, so it does not reduce the discrimination of the solutions.

2.2 Multiobjective BSO Algorithm with Diversity Preservation Mechanism

BSO algorithm is proposed by Shi *et al.* [29], which imitates the human brain-storming process, and it is often used to deal with multi-modal optimization problems. In human society, getting a group of people together to brainstorm is a good way to solve problems. BSO algorithm abstracts group discussions, inter-group communication and individual thinking in the process of brainstorming as

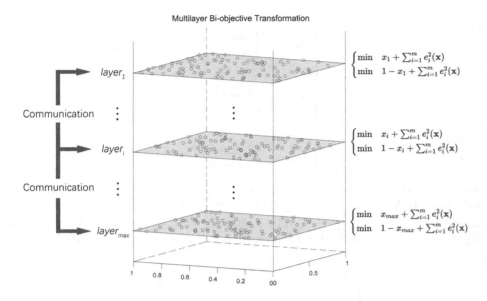

Fig. 2. Multilayer bi-objective transformation technique

the population behaviors in the swarm intelligence algorithm. The process of generating offspring by BSO is depicted in Algorithm 1, where the pre-determined parameters $p_{5a}, p_{6b}, p_{6biii}, p_{6c}$ are the same as the setting of [29], and $rand_1$ to $rand_4$ are random values between 0 and 1.

In the experiments, we found that the number of individuals in each cluster may be different significantly, and clusters with more individuals generally evolve faster than those with fewer individuals. Therefore, clusters with fewer individuals are easily eliminated resulting in missing solutions. To address this problem, we proposed a diversity preservation mechanism with aging characteristics. This mechanism can protect clusters with few individuals and allows all the clusters to maintain a balanced evolution, thereby enhancing the diversity of the population. After the offspring are added into the population, individuals in each cluster will be punished differently according to the number of individuals in their cluster:

$$fitness_i = fitness_i + \frac{nc_i}{popsize} * old$$

$$old = logsig(1.5 - 8.5 * \frac{Gen}{Max\_Gen}) \tag{4}$$

where $fitness_i$ is the fitness values of the individuals in the i-th cluster; nc_i is the number of individuals in the i-th cluster; $popsize$ is the size of the population; old is the aging control parameter, which will dynamically change during the evolution process to adapt to different evolution stages. Since the mechanism will assign penalty values to the individuals in each iteration, the longer the individual stays in the population, the greater the penalty value, and the easier

---

Algorithm 1. BSO

Input: Control parameters: n, p, K
Output: The offspring population
1: Cluster n individuals into K clusters
2: Record the best individual as cluster center in each cluster
3: **if** $rand_1 < p_{5a}$ **then**
4:     Randomly generate an individual to replace a random cluster center
5: **end**
6: **while** n is less than the number of new individual **do**
7:     **if** $rand_2 < p_{6b}$ **then**
8:         Randomly select a cluster
9:         **if** $rand_3 < p_{6biii}$ **then**
10:            Select the cluster center and add random values to it to generate a new individual
11:        **else**
12:            Randomly select an individual from this cluster and add random values to the individual to generate a new individual
13:        **end**
14:    **else**
15:        Randomly select two clusters
16:        **if** $rand_4 < p_{6c}$ **then**
17:            The two cluster centers are combined and then added with random values to generate new individual
18:        **else**
19:            Two individuals from each selected cluster are randomly selected to be combined and added with random values to generate a new individual
20:        **end**
21:    **end**
22: **end**

---

it is to be eliminated. This aging strategy is also in line with the law that new things would replace the old ones in the natural world.

Cooperated with the multilayer bi-objective transformation technique, we propose MOBSO algorithm with the diversity preservation mechanism for solving NESs. After the multilayer populations are initialized, a series of offspring are generated through the BSO algorithm and added to the population. Individuals at each layer are evaluated according to their objective functions by Eq. 3. Then, use the clustering information to punish the individuals correspondingly through Eq. 4. Finally, through fast non-dominated sorting and crowding distance selection, the parent individuals for the next iteration are selected, and if it reaches the specified number of iterations, inter-layer communication will be carried out, otherwise, it will continue to loop until the maximum number of iterations is reached. The pseudo-code of MOBSO is given in Algorithm 2.

Algorithm 2. MOBSO

Input: Control parameters: Max_Gen, n, p, K
Output: The final population
1: Generate an initial population randomly for each layer and evaluate them
2: $Gen = 0$
3: **while** $Gen < Max\_Gen$ **do**
4:     **for** each layer **do**
5:         Generate offspring by Algorithm 1
6:         Evaluate the offspring by Equation 3 and add the them to the population
7:         Apply diversity maintenance to individuals in the population by Equation 4
8:         Fast non-dominated sorting and crowding distance selection
9:     **end**
10:     **if** $Gen\%(floor(Max\_Gen/4) + 1) == 0$ **then**
11:         Pass the cluster center information of this layer to the next layer
12:     **end**
13:     $Gen = Gen + 1$
14: **end**

---

3   Experimental Study and Discussions

This section demonstrates the results of the experimental study and discusses the performance of our approach.

3.1   Test Functions and Performance Criteria

We choose 30 NESs with different features to comprehensively evaluate the performance of different methods [4,7,10,16,32]. Table 1 shows partial information about the 30 NESs.

Based on [15] and [30], two performance metrics, i.e., Root Ratio (RR) and Success Ratio (SR), are used to evaluate the performance of different methods solving NESs.

RR measures the average ratio of all known roots found over multiple runs. The mathematical expression for RR is as follows:

$$RR = \frac{\sum_{i=1}^{N_r} R_i}{R \cdot N_r}$$

where N_r is the number of independent runs; R is the number of known roots of a NES; R_i is the number of roots found in the ith run. In this study, for a solution $\mathbf{x}$, if it satisfies $\sum_{i=1}^{m} e_i^2(\mathbf{x}) < $ 1e-5, then $\mathbf{x}$ can be considered a root of the NES.

SR measures the rate of success runs, which can be expressed as:

$$SR = \frac{N_{sr}}{N_r}$$

where N_{sr} is the number of successful runs. A successful run means that all known roots of an NES are found in a single run.

To make the comparison meaningful, each algorithm is run independently 30 times for each NES. We use multiple-problem Wilcoxon's test and Friedman's test, based on RR and SR value, to test the statistical differences among different algorithms.

3.2   Comparison with Other State-of-Art Methods

This subsection will describe five methods compared with MOBSO and their parameter settings. Then the results of the comparison are shown later. The five state-of-art methods to compare with our approach are namely MONES [30], A-WeB [9], DR-JADE [16], NCDE and NSDE [26].

MONES and A-WeB are multiobjective optimization-based methods. MONES uses the first dimension of the decision variable to design the location function. In A-WeB, all the dimensions of the decision variable are linearly weighted to construct the two objective functions.

DR-JADE is a repulsion-based method. In DR-JADE, a dynamic repulsion technique is used. With the help of this technique, the repulsive radius is controlled dynamically during the evolutionary process.

NCDE and NSDE are two neighborhood-based differential evolution methods. Crowding selection and species are used to form the neighborhood, respectively. They achieve good results in solving multimodal problems.

The parameter settings of five compared methods are shown in Table 2, which are the same as the original.

The comparison results about the average of RR and SR values are shown in Table 3. MOBSO provides the highest average RR value 0.9172 and the highest average SR value 0.8611, followed by DR-JADE, A-WeB, NSDE, NCDE, MONES. The detailed results in terms of RR and SR are respectively reported in Table 4 and Table 6, respectively. Next, we will discuss the experimental results from the following five aspects.

(1) MOBSO performs the best in comparison with the other five methods since it obtains both the highest average RR value and the highest average SR value. In addition, achieves 100% RR and 100% SR on 24 test instances, which means that it succeeds in locating all the roots over all 30 runs. Moreover, the PR and SR values derived from MOBSO are larger than zero for all the test instances except F17.

(2) With the help of the dynamic repulsion technique, DR-JADE has the capability to successfully solve 19 NESs. However, for the instances F06 and F17, two 20-dimension problems, both the RR and SR of DR-JADE are zero. The reason might be that the search ability of DR-JADE decreases when D increases.

(3) NCDE and NSDE show similar performance on most problems, and both of them can achieve 100% successful runs on only five test instances.

(4) In WeB transformation technique, all the dimensions of the solution are considered in the location function, so A-WeB can locate some roots on all the test instances except F21. However, it cannot succeed in every run.

Table 1. Some information of the 30 NES problems, where n is the number of the decision variable; LE is the number of the linear equations; NE is the number of the nonlinear equations; NoR is the number of the roots; Max_FEs is the maximal number of function evaluations.

Prob.	n	LE	NE	NoR	Max_FEs
F01	2	0	2	2	10,000
F02	2	0	2	3	50,000
F03	3	0	3	2	100,000
F04	2	0	2	3	100,000
F05	3	1	2	2	50,000
F06	20	0	20	2	50,000
F07	2	1	1	11	50,000
F08	2	0	2	15	50,000
F09	2	0	2	13	50,000
F10	2	1	1	8	50,000
F11	4	0	4	1	50,000
F12	5	4	1	3	100,000
F13	2	0	2	10	50,000
F14	2	0	2	9	50,000
F15	2	0	2	13	50,000
F16	2	0	2	6	50,000
F17	20	19	1	2	200,000
F18	3	0	3	7	50,000
F19	3	0	3	8	100,000
F20	3	0	3	2	50,000
F21	3	0	3	12	50,000
F22	2	0	2	2	50,000
F23	2	0	2	4	50,000
F24	2	0	2	4	50,000
F25	2	0	2	2	50,000
F26	3	0	3	1	50,000
F27	3	0	3	1	50,000
F28	2	0	2	3	50,000
F29	2	0	2	2	50,000
F30	3	0	3	5	50,000

This is because the weighted linear combination reduces the discernibility of the solutions, which will make many roots similar in the objective space, resulting in some of them might be lost.

Table 2. The parameter settings of the five compared methods.

Algorithm	Parameter
DR-JADE	$NP = 10, c = 0.1, u_{CR} = 0.9, u_F = 0.1$
A-WeB	$NP = 100, H_m = 200$
MONES	$NP = 100, H_m = 200$
NCDE	$NP = 100, F = 0.5, CR = 0.9, m = 5$
NSDE	$NP = 100, F = 0.5, CR = 0.9, m = 5$

(5) The performance of MONES is worse than other methods with the lowest RR and SR. The reason is that, since only the first dimension of the solution is used to construct the location function, MONES may lose some roots if the first dimension of multiple roots is the same.

Table 3. Average RR and SR values of MOBSO and the five compared methods for all test problems.

Algorithm	RR	SR
MOBSO	**0.9172**	**0.8611**
DR-JADE	0.8963	0.7756
A-WeB	0.8626	0.6957
MONES	0.6765	0.5067
NCDE	0.7082	0.5389
NSDE	0.7700	0.5900

Additionally, the results of the Wilcoxon's test and the Friedman's test are reported in Table 7 and Table 5. As shown in Table 7, MOBSO provides higher R+ values than R- value in all the cases for both the RR and SR metrics. Especially, MOBSO significantly outperforms NCDE, A-WeB, NSDE, MONES in that all the p-values are less than 0.05. Besides, we can clearly observe that MOBSO get the best average rankings compared with other methods by the Friedman's test as shown in Table 5. Therefore, from these results, we can conclude that the proposed MOBSO method can be an effective alternative to locate multiple roots of NESs in a single run simultaneously.

Table 4. Experimental Results of MOBSO, DR-JADE, NCDE, A-WEB, NSDE, MONES on 30 test problems in terms of the RR

Prob.	MOBSO	DR-JADE	A-WeB	NCDE	NSDE	MONES
F01	**1.0000**	**1.0000**	0.7250	**1.0000**	**1.0000**	**1.0000**
F02	**1.0000**	**1.0000**	0.8800	**1.0000**	0.9778	0.9778
F03	0.3667	0.8167	0.5450	0.9897	0.9256	**1.0000**
F04	**1.0000**	**1.0000**	0.9900	0.6556	0.9222	0.8111
F05	**1.0000**	**1.0000**	0.8300	**1.0000**	**1.0000**	**1.0000**
F06	0.3500	0.0000	0.6200	0.9833	**1.0000**	0.9833
F07	**1.0000**	0.9970	**1.0000**	0.9848	0.9485	0.9758
F08	**1.0000**	0.9578	0.9573	0.9778	0.9644	0.9422
F09	**1.0000**	**1.0000**	**1.0000**	0.4641	0.5436	0.5923
F10	**1.0000**	0.9583	0.9400	0.8708	0.8833	**1.0000**
F11	**1.0000**	**1.0000**	0.4200	0.0667	0.1333	0.0333
F12	**1.0000**	**1.0000**	0.8933	0.0000	0.0111	0.0000
F13	**1.0000**	0.8767	0.8880	0.9933	0.9533	0.8333
F14	0.9407	**1.0000**	0.9733	0.9185	0.9333	0.1963
F15	**1.0000**	**1.0000**	**1.0000**	0.9821	0.9359	**1.0000**
F16	**1.0000**	**1.0000**	0.9433	0.9944	**1.0000**	**1.0000**
F17	0.0000	0.0000	**0.6200**	0.0000	0.0000	0.0000
F18	**1.0000**	**1.0000**	0.9514	0.9762	0.9952	0.7190
F19	**1.0000**	0.9125	0.8550	**1.0000**	**1.0000**	0.7333
F20	**1.0000**	**1.0000**	**1.0000**	**1.0000**	0.9833	0.5000
F21	0.9250	0.9167	0.0933	0.9750	0.9389	**1.0000**
F22	**1.0000**	**1.0000**	**1.0000**	0.7833	0.9167	0.8333
F23	**1.0000**	**1.0000**	**1.0000**	0.9167	0.9917	0.8583
F24	**1.0000**	**1.0000**	**1.0000**	0.4500	0.9250	**1.0000**
F25	**1.0000**	0.5000	**1.0000**	0.0000	0.0000	**1.0000**
F26	**1.0000**	**1.0000**	**1.0000**	0.0000	0.0000	0.0000
F27	**1.0000**	**1.0000**	0.8800	0.3667	0.8667	0.1667
F28	**1.0000**	**1.0000**	**1.0000**	0.7889	0.9889	**1.0000**
F29	0.9333	**1.0000**	0.9400	0.3000	0.5000	0.0000
F30	**1.0000**	0.9533	0.9320	0.8067	0.8600	0.1400
Avg	**0.9172**	0.8963	0.8626	0.7082	0.7700	0.6765

Table 5. Rankings of the six compared methods by the Friedman's test.

Algorithm	Ranking (RR)	Ranking (SR)
MOBSO	**2.3667**	**2.4000**
DR-JADE	2.7333	2.8000
NCDE	4.2333	4.1333
A-WeB	3.4500	3.4167
MONES	4.2667	4.2167
NSDE	3.9500	4.0333

Table 6. Experimental Results of MOBSO, DR-JADE, NCDE, A-WEB, NSDE, MONES on 30 test problems in terms of the SR

Prob	MOBSO	DR-JADE	A-WeB	NCDE	NSDE	MONES
F01	**1.0000**	**1.0000**	0.5300	**1.0000**	**1.0000**	**1.0000**
F02	**1.0000**	**1.0000**	0.6800	**1.0000**	0.9333	0.9333
F03	0.0667	0.6667	0.2000	0.8667	0.3667	**1.0000**
F04	**1.0000**	**1.0000**	0.9700	0.2667	0.8000	0.4333
F05	**1.0000**	**1.0000**	0.6500	**1.0000**	**1.0000**	**1.0000**
F06	0.0667	0.0000	0.3600	0.9667	**1.0000**	0.9667
F07	**1.0000**	0.9667	**1.0000**	0.8333	0.5667	0.7667
F08	**1.0000**	0.4667	0.5800	0.8000	0.6333	0.4333
F09	**1.0000**	**1.0000**	**1.0000**	0.0000	0.0000	0.0000
F10	**1.0000**	0.6667	0.6000	0.3000	0.2667	**1.0000**
F11	**1.0000**	**1.0000**	0.4200	0.0667	0.1333	0.0333
F12	**1.0000**	**1.0000**	0.6800	0.0000	0.0000	0.0000
F13	**1.0000**	0.0333	0.2800	0.9333	0.8000	0.2333
F14	0.4667	**1.0000**	0.7600	0.4000	0.4667	0.0000
F15	**1.0000**	**1.0000**	**1.0000**	0.7667	0.4333	**1.0000**
F16	**1.0000**	**1.0000**	0.6600	0.9667	**1.0000**	**1.0000**
F17	0.0000	0.0000	**0.2400**	0.0000	0.0000	0.0000
F18	**1.0000**	**1.0000**	0.7000	0.8333	0.9667	0.0333
F19	**1.0000**	0.4333	0.1400	**1.0000**	**1.0000**	0.0333
F20	**1.0000**	**1.0000**	**1.0000**	**1.0000**	0.9667	0.0333
F21	0.3667	0.2667	0.0000	0.7667	0.4667	**1.0000**
F22	**1.0000**	**1.0000**	**1.0000**	0.5667	0.8333	0.6667
F23	**1.0000**	**1.0000**	**1.0000**	0.6667	0.9667	0.4667
F24	**1.0000**	**1.0000**	**1.0000**	0.0333	0.7667	**1.0000**

(continued)

Table 6. (*continued*)

Prob	MOBSO	DR-JADE	A-WeB	NCDE	NSDE	MONES
F25	**1.0000**	0.0000	**1.0000**	0.0000	0.0000	**1.0000**
F26	**1.0000**	**1.0000**	**1.0000**	0.0000	0.0000	0.0000
F27	**1.0000**	**1.0000**	0.8800	0.3667	0.8667	0.1667
F28	**1.0000**	**1.0000**	**1.0000**	0.4333	0.9667	**1.0000**
F29	0.8667	**1.0000**	0.8800	0.0000	0.0000	0.0000
F30	**1.0000**	0.7667	0.6600	0.3333	0.5000	0.0000
Avg	**0.8611**	0.7756	0.6957	0.5389	0.5900	0.5067

Table 7. Results obtained by the multiple-problem Wilcoxon's test for the five compared methods. The highlight values indicate that MOBSO significantly outperforms the method with p-values less than 0.05.

MOBSO VS	RR			SR		
	R+	R-	p-value	R+	R-	p-value
DR-JADE	301.5	163.5	1.53E−01	303.5	161.5	1.41E−01
NCDE	393.0	72.0	**7.95E−04**	393.5	71.5	**6.30E−04**
A-WeB	333.5	131.5	**3.63E−02**	364.5	100.5	**6.16E−03**
NSDE	372.0	63.0	**7.78E−04**	372.0	63.0	**3.80E−04**
MONES	362.0	73.0	**1.62E−03**	360.0	75.0	**1.05E−03**

4 Conclusions

In this paper, we propose a multilayer bi-objective transformation technique to transform an NES into a bi-objective optimization problem. This technique overcomes many problems in the previous transformation technique, such as the curse of dimensionality [10], missing roots caused by the reduction of solution discrimination [9], and the many-to-one mapping from roots of an NES to Pareto front [30]. Subsequently, we present a multiobjective BSO algorithm with a diversity preservation mechanism as the optimization algorithm, which combined with the multilayer bi-objective transformation technique can locate multiple roots of NESs simultaneously in a single run effectively. In the experimental study, we choose 30 NESs as the test instances to evaluate the performance of MOBSO. Moreover, the proposed MOBSO has shown its competitive performance compared to the other state-of-art methods with the highest RR and SR. Furthermore, we use multiple-problem Wilcoxon's test and Friedman's test, based on RR and SR value, to prove that MOBSO is better than the other five methods in statistics. In the future, we will study how to improve the solution accuracy of MOBSO and apply MOBSO to deal with complex real-world NESs.

References

1. Amaya, I., Cruz, J., Correa, R.: Solution of the mathematical model of a nonlinear direct current circuit using particle swarm optimization. Dyna **79**(172), 77–84 (2012)
2. Brits, R., Engelbrecht, A.P., Van den Bergh, F.: A niching particle swarm optimizer. In: Proceedings of the 4th Asia-Pacific Conference on Simulated Evolution and Learning, vol. 2, pp. 692–696. Orchid Country Club, Singapore (2002)
3. Chen, C.Y.: A performance comparison of the zero-finding by extended interval newton method for peano monosplines. Appl. Math. Comput. **219**(12), 6919–6930 (2013)
4. Emiris, I.Z., Mourrain, B.: Computer algebra methods for studying and computing molecular conformations. Algorithmica **25**(2–3), 372–402 (1999)
5. Enjeti, P., Lindsay, J.: Solving nonlinear equations of harmonic elimination PWM in power control. Electron. Lett. **23**(12), 656–657 (1987)
6. Facchinei, F., Kanzow, C.: Generalized Nash equilibrium problems. Ann. Oper. Res. **175**(1), 177–211 (2010)
7. Floudas, C.A.: Recent advances in global optimization for process synthesis, design and control: enclosure of all solutions. Comput. Chem. Eng. **23**, S963–S973 (1999)
8. Gong, W., Wang, Y., Cai, Z., Wang, L.: Finding multiple roots of nonlinear equation systems via a repulsion-based adaptive differential evolution. IEEE Transactions on Systems, Man, and Cybernetics: Systems (2018)
9. Gong, W., Wang, Y., Cai, Z., Yang, S.: A weighted biobjective transformation technique for locating multiple optimal solutions of nonlinear equation systems. IEEE Trans. Evol. Comput. **21**(5), 697–713 (2017)
10. Grosan, C., Abraham, A.: A new approach for solving nonlinear equations systems. IEEE Trans. Syst. Man Cybernet. Part A: Syst. Hum. **38**(3), 698–714 (2008)
11. Guo, D., Nie, Z., Yan, L.: The application of noise-tolerant ZD design formula to robots' kinematic control via time-varying nonlinear equations solving. IEEE Trans. Syst. Man Cybernet. Syst. **48**(12), 2188–2197 (2017)
12. He, W., Gong, W., Wang, L., Yan, X., Hu, C.: Fuzzy neighborhood-based differential evolution with orientation for nonlinear equation systems. Knowl. Based Syst. **182**, 104796 (2019)
13. Henderson, N., Sacco, W.F., Platt, G.M.: Finding more than one root of nonlinear equations via a polarization technique: an application to double retrograde vaporization. Chem. Eng. Res. Des. **88**(5–6), 551–561 (2010)
14. Karr, C.L., Weck, B., Freeman, L.M.: Solutions to systems of nonlinear equations via a genetic algorithm. Eng. Appl. Artif. Intell. **11**(3), 369–375 (1998)
15. Li, X., Engelbrecht, A., Epitropakis, M.G.: Benchmark functions for cec'2013 special session and competition on niching methods for multimodal function optimization. RMIT University, Evolutionary Computation and Machine Learning Group, Australia, Technical report (2013)
16. Liao, Z., Gong, W., Yan, X., Wang, L., Hu, C.: Solving nonlinear equations system with dynamic repulsion-based evolutionary algorithms. IEEE Trans. Syst. Man Cybernet. Syst. (2018)
17. Mehta, D.: Finding all the stationary points of a potential-energy landscape via numerical polynomial-homotopy-continuation method. Phys. Rev. E **84**(2), 025702 (2011)
18. Mehta, D., Grosan, C.: A collection of challenging optimization problems in science, engineering and economics. In: 2015 IEEE Congress on Evolutionary Computation (CEC), pp. 2697–2704. IEEE (2015)

19. Pan, L., He, C., Tian, Y., Wang, H., Zhang, X., Jin, Y.: A classification-based surrogate-assisted evolutionary algorithm for expensive many-objective optimization. IEEE Trans. Evol. Comput. **23**(1), 74–88 (2018)
20. Pan, L., Li, L., Cheng, R., He, C., Tan, K.C.: Manifold learning-inspired mating restriction for evolutionary multiobjective optimization with complicated pareto sets. IEEE Trans. Cybern. (2019)
21. Pan, L., Li, L., He, C., Tan, K.C.: A subregion division-based evolutionary algorithm with effective mating selection for many-objective optimization. IEEE Trans. Cybern. (2019)
22. Pinter, J.: Solving nonlinear equation systems via global partition and search: some experimental results. Computing **43**(4), 309–323 (1990)
23. Pourjafari, E., Mojallali, H.: Solving nonlinear equations systems with a new approach based on invasive weed optimization algorithm and clustering. Swarm Evol. Comput. **4**, 33–43 (2012)
24. Press, W.H., Teukolsky, S.A., Flannery, B.P., Vetterling, W.T.: Numerical recipes in Fortran 77: volume 1, volume 1 of Fortran numerical recipes: the art of scientific computing. Cambridge University Press, Cambridge (1992)
25. Qin, S., Zeng, S., Dong, W., Li, X.: Nonlinear equation systems solved by many-objective hype. In: 2015 IEEE Congress on Evolutionary Computation (CEC), pp. 2691–2696. IEEE (2015)
26. Qu, B.Y., Suganthan, P.N., Liang, J.J.: Differential evolution with neighborhood mutation for multimodal optimization. IEEE Trans. Evol. Comput. **16**(5), 601–614 (2012)
27. Ramos, H., Monteiro, M.T.T.: A new approach based on the newton's method to solve systems of nonlinear equations. J. Comput. Appl. Math. **318**, 3–13 (2017)
28. Schwandt, H.: Parallel interval newton-like Schwarz methods for almost linear parabolic problems. J. Comput. Appl. Math. **199**(2), 437–444 (2007)
29. Shi, Y.: An optimization algorithm based on brainstorming process. In: Emerging Research on Swarm Intelligence and Algorithm Optimization, pp. 1–35. IGI Global (2015)
30. Song, W., Wang, Y., Li, H.X., Cai, Z.: Locating multiple optimal solutions of nonlinear equation systems based on multiobjective optimization. IEEE Trans. Evol. Comput. **19**(3), 414–431 (2014)
31. Tsoulos, I., Stavrakoudis, A.: On locating all roots of systems of nonlinear equations inside bounded domain using global optimization methods. Nonlinear Anal. Real World Appl. **11**(4), 2465–2471 (2010)
32. Wang, C., Luo, R., Wu, K., Han, B.: A new filled function method for an unconstrained nonlinear equation. J. Comput. Appl. Math. **235**(6), 1689–1699 (2011)

Solving Nonlinear Equations Systems with a Two-Phase Root-Finder Based on Niching Differential Evolution

Lianlang Duan and Fei Xu[✉]

Key Laboratory of Image Processing and Intelligent Control of Education Ministry of
China, School of Artificial Intelligence and Automation, Huazhong University of
Science and Technology, Wuhan 430074, China
{m201872614,fxu}@hust.edu.cn

Abstract. Solving nonlinear equation systems (NESs) is a challenging
problems in numerical computation. Two goals should be considered for
solving NESs. One is to locate as many roots as possible and the other
is to improve the solving precision. In this work, in order to achieve
these two goals, a two-phase niching differential evolution (TPNDE) is
proposed. The innovation of TPNDE is mainly reflected in the following
three aspects. First, a probabilistic mutation mechanism is designed to
increase the diversity of the population. Second, a novel reinitialization
procedure is proposed to detect converged individuals and explore more
new regions that may contain global optima. Third, distribution adjustment local search (DALS) is proposed to deal with the isolated solution
and enhance the convergence of the algorithm. To evaluate the performance of TPNDE, we test our TPNDE and 5 state-of-the-art algorithms
on 20 NESs with diverse features. The experimental results show that
the proposed TPNDE algorithm is better than the other methods.

Keywords: Nonlinear equation system · Differential evolution ·
Reinitialization · Distribution adjustment

1 Introduction

A system of nonlinear equations can be formulated as follows:

$$\begin{cases} e_1(\boldsymbol{x}) = 0, \\ e_2(\boldsymbol{x}) = 0, \\ ... \\ e_m(\boldsymbol{x}) = 0, \end{cases} \tag{1}$$

where m is the number of equations; $\boldsymbol{x} = (x_1, x_1, ..., x_D)^T \in \boldsymbol{S}$ is a decision
vector containing D decision variables; $\boldsymbol{S} = \prod_{i=1}^{n} [\underline{x_i}, \overline{x_i}]$ is the decision space, $\underline{x_i}$
and $\overline{x_i}$ are the lower bound and upper bound of x_i, respectively. If a vector $\boldsymbol{x}^*$
subjects to $\forall j \in [1, m], e_j(\boldsymbol{x}^*) = 0$, $\boldsymbol{x}^*$ is called an optimal solution of an NES.

© Springer Nature Singapore Pte Ltd. 2021
L. Pan et al. (Eds.): BIC-TA 2020, CCIS 1363, pp. 251–268, 2021.
https://doi.org/10.1007/978-981-16-1354-8_17

In general, NESs are widely found in the fields of science and engineering [1]. An NES usually contains more than one root and the purpose of solving NESs is to simultaneously locate multiple roots. Therefore, solving NESs is a challenging task in numerical computation [2].

Traditional numerical calculation methods [3–6] (e.g., Newton method, gradient descent method) for solving NESs have a common defect that they cannot locate multiple roots in a single run. Due to this reason, solving NESs by evolutionary algorithms (EAs) has been gaining increasing attention in the past decade. The current popular transformation technique [7] generally transforms an NES into an optimization problem as follows:

$$\min \sum_{i=1}^{m} |e_i(\boldsymbol{x})| \tag{2}$$

or

$$\min \sum_{i=1}^{m} e_i^2(\boldsymbol{x}) \tag{3}$$

The converted problem is a single objective function and the function may contain multiple optima, which is similar to solving multimodal problems. Since there exist more than one optimal solution to be found simultaneously, EAs are not directly suitable for solving the converted problem because they have been originally designed for single-objective optimization which contains only one optimal solution and they performance poorly on preserve the population diversity. The "niching" techniques [8] are proposed to address such an issue.

The "niching" techniques [10,11] are widely used in evolutionary algorithms to maintain population diversity. The working principle of niching is to partition the whole population into several subpopulations and preserve diverse subpopulations converging toward different optimal solutions. Traditional niching methods include: crowding techniques [12], speciation [9,13], fitness sharing [14], clustering [15]. However, the performance of these approaches is often sensitive to parameter settings since the clustering parameters (e.g., crowding size, niching radius) are fixed. The dynamic cluster size niching [16] avoids this problem by adopting a dynamic clustering parameter and it is less sensitive to parameter settings.

Recently, several researches have combined niching techniques and EA for solving multiple optima problem. Ebrahim proposed a two-phase algorithm based on invasive weed optimization [18] and clustering niching techniques for solving NESs [17]. Qu et al. proposed a distance-based locally informed particle swarm (LIPS) algorithm, where LIPS uses several local bests to guide the search of each particle [19]. Yang et al. combined current niching methods with ant colony optimization (ACO) algorithms, where a differential evolution mutation operator is alternatively utilized to construct new solutions [20]. Most recently, Gong et al. proposed a fuzzy neighborhood-based differential evolution with orientation (FNODE) for solving NESs, where the orientation information is integrated into the mutation to produce promising offspring [21]. Among these

EAs, the DE variants have shown promising performance since neighborhood information is well utilized when applying DE within the subpopulation and the neighborhood information can effectively improve the performance of niching. Therefore, in this work, we focus on the DE-based algorithm.

In the DE-based methods [22–25], niching techniques are used to gather the solutions into different clusters to locate different roots of NESs. Sacco designed a hybrid metaheuristic to solve NESs, where the fuzzy clustering means have been used to find more than one root [26]. Wang *et al.* designed a novel dual-strategy differential evolution (DSDE), where the affinity propagation clustering has been used to locating as many peaks as possible from different optimal regions [27]. Biswas *et al.* proposed an improved information-sharing mechanism for inducing efficient niching behavior, where they designed two different reproduction operators for two types of candidate solutions [28]. These researches show that sharing the local information among the species plays an important role in improving the niching behavior.

Many DE variants have been successfully extended to solve NESs, however, there are still some drawbacks of these algorithms as follows.

1. It is difficult to design an appropriate reproduction scheme for different types of subpopulations. For example, for the concentrated subpopulation, we hope a greedy mutation scheme which can help converge to the optimal solution; while for the random subpopulation, an exploratory mutation scheme is required, so as to find more globally optimal regions.
2. Many EA-based algorithms for solving NESs wasted computational resources on converged individuals. It is not necessary to allocate fitness evaluations to the converged individuals.
3. The isolated solutions (the solutions that have no neighbors) often occur in the evolutionary processes and the accuracy of these solutions are poor. However, how to handle the isolated solutions has not been mention in almost all EA-based algorithms.

In this work, to solve these drawbacks, a two-phase niching differential evolution (TPNDE) algorithm is proposed. TPNDE consists of two parts: global search based on probabilistic reproduction mechanism with a reinitialization procedure and distribution adjustment local search. The main contributions of this paper can be summarized as follows.

1. In the global search, we design a probabilistic mutation mechanism for individuals to choose exploiting or exploring mutation strategy. In this way, fitter individuals have a higher probability to choose a greedy mutation scheme while poor individuals are more likely to select the exploratory mutation scheme.
2. We propose a novel reinitialization procedure to detect converged individuals and reinitialize a part of converged individuals to explore new regions.
3. Distribution adjustment local search (DALS) is proposed to deal with the isolated solution and enhance the solution accuracy. DALS can change the distribution of the solution in the population to improve the accuracy of isolated solutions.

The rest of this paper is organized as follows. Section 2 gives a detailed description of the proposed TPNDE algorithm. Experimental setup and results are presented and compared in Sect. 3. Finally, we conclude this paper in Sect. 4.

2   Proposed Algorithm

Based on the above introduction, two major goals need to be considered and achieved: 1) diversity, which helps discover more global optima and 2) convergence, which enables the solutions to be more accurate. To accomplish these two goals, a two-phase differential evolution (TPDE) is proposed, which consists of two phases: global search and local search. Specifically, the global search seeks for approximate locations of solutions, followed by the local search that finds the exact locations of roots.

Algorithm 1. Speciation Clustering

1: Sort the population from better to worse according to fitness value;
2: **for** $i = 1$ **to** N/M **do**
3:     The best individual x is set as the species seed;
4:     The x and its nearest $M - 1$ individuals form a new species;
5:     Remove the M individuals from the population;
6: **end for**

2.1   Global Search

At the global search, differential evolution based on speciation clustering [9] is employed to find the approximate locations of roots. The speciation cluster niching method is shown in Algorithm 1.

We first describe the dynamic cluster sizing, which is utilized in our global search. Traditional neighborhood techniques generate a neighborhood population with a fixed size, in which the subpopulation search is limited. The large subpopulation will lead to converging slowly while the small subpopulation will increase the difficulty in finding the optimal of the edge region. Suppose the population size is NP, and the cluster size M is chosen randomly from a fixed interval. The interval for M is set as $[4, NP/10]$, due to the fact that DE must have at least four individuals. Then the total number of niches is $\lceil NP/M \rceil$. When $NP\%M = 0$, the last niche contains $NP\%M$ individuals, where % stands for the modulo operation.

Probabilistic Reproduction Mechanism. After partitioning the whole population into niches, offspring generation operators are applied in each niching. The mutation strategy employed by DE largely governs the tendency of offspring

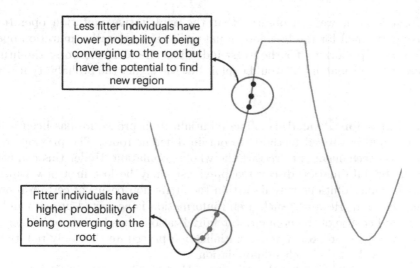

Less fitter individuals have lower probability of being converging to the root but have the potential to find new region

Fitter individuals have higher probability of being converging to the root

Fig. 1. Illustration of probabilistic reproduction mechanism.

that concentrate or scatter around parents. This in turn indicates that different types of problems apply different mutation strategies.

In Fig. 1, black dots denote the less fitter individuals and red dots denote the fitter individuals, respectively. These individuals are chosen from the same species. Fitter individuals have a higher probability of being converging to the global optima. Thus, the fitter the individual is, the greater chance it should exploit. The exploitative mutation strategy DE/best/1 can be used to locally enhance the exploitation and accelerate the convergence speed, which is suitable for fitter individuals. On the contrary, less fitter individuals are away from optima, which should explore further areas and maintain population diversity. The explorative variant DE/current-to-rand/1 can detect other basins of attraction and shows good diversity, which is suitable for less fitter individuals.

We propose a probabilistic model for mutation operator, where the probability of exploiting or exploring for an individual is associated with its fitness. Since the optimization problem which NESs convert into is a minimization problem, the mathematical form of the probability model is as follows:

$$P_i = \frac{f_{max} - f_i}{f_{max} - f_{min} + \delta} \tag{4}$$

where f_{max} and f_{min} are the maximum and minimum fitness values of individuals in the subpopulation, f_i is the fitness value of ith individual in the subpopulation. To accommodate the case where f_{max} is equal to f_{min}, a small positive value δ is introduced and is set as $1E - 8$. P_i is the probability to use DE/best/1 for ith individual in the subpopulation. The dual mutation strategy is as follows:

$$\begin{cases} \text{use DE/best/1, } rand < P_i, \\ \text{use DE/current-to-rand/1, otherwise.} \end{cases} \tag{5}$$

From Eq. (5), we can observe that the exploitative mutation operator is always performed for the best individual while the explorative mutation operator is always performed for the worst individual. Besides, the worse the fitness, the lower the probability it would exploit but the higher the probability it would explore.

Reinitialization Procedure. The reinitialization procedure has been widely used in repulsion-based methods to obtain different roots. The previous reinitialization mechanism is to restart the whole population. Under this condition, some useful information discovered previously may be lost in a new run. For example, some solutions may lie within the attraction basins of certain roots in the current run. However, such useful information is neglected unreasonably in a new run because of the population reinitialization, thus leading to inefficiency. In this work, we propose a new reinitialization procedure that only reinitializes partial individuals for each subpopulation.

The x_{seed_i} is the seed of the ith subpopulation. The situation that $f(x_{seed_i})$ reaches the required accuracy level θ indicates that the solution within the attraction basins of the ith subpopulation is found and there is no need to continue exploring solutions that have already been found. In order to make good use of the limited FEs budget, we only preserve the seed and those solutions that are far from the seed, since those solutions may contain useful information about other roots. Individuals around the seed need to be reinitialized. In this way, the found solution is reserved and more FEs are used to search unexplored regions of the search space. The reinitialization procedure is described as follows:

Algorithm 2. Reinitialization Procedure

1: **for** each species **do**
2:     Calculate fitness f_i of the $seed_i$ of current species using Eq.(3);
3:     **if** $f_i \leq \theta$ **then**
4:         **for** each individual x_{ij} in the current species **do**
5:             Calculate the Euclidean distance between $seed_i$ and x_{ij};
6:             **if** $0 < d < \lambda$ **then**
7:                 Randomly initialize the individual x_{ij};
8:             **end if**
9:         **end for**
10:    **end if**
11: **end for**

Complete Global Search. Based on the above description, the pseudo code of the complete procedure of global search is outlined in Algorithm 3. The major process and superiority of Global Search is shown as follows.

Algorithm 3. Global Search

Input: control parameters: F, CR, $MaxFEs$
Output: the evolved population P

1: Randomly initialize the population;
2: $FEs = 0$
3: **while** $FEs < \frac{MaxFEs}{2}$ **do**
4:     Randomly generate an integer as the cluster size M;
5:     Partition the population into several species using Algorithm 1;
6:     **for** each species **do**
7:         **for** each individual x_i in the current species **do**
8:             Calculate P_i of individual x_i using Eq.(4);
9:             **if** $rand < P_i$ **then**
10:                 Using DE/best/1 strategy for x_i to generate the offspring u_i;
11:             **else**
12:                 Using DE/current-to-rand/1 strategy for x_i to generate u_i;
13:             **end if**
14:             Find the closest solution x_c to u_i in the current species;
15:             **if** $f(u_i) < f(x_c)$ **then**
16:                 $x_c = u_i$;
17:                 $f(x_c) = f(u_i)$;
18:             **end if**
19:         **end for**
20:     **end for**
21:     Perform Reinitialization Procedure using Algorithm 2;
22:     $FEs = FEs + 1$;
23: **end while**

2.2 Distribution Adjustment Local Search (DALS)

After the global search, we acquire the approximate locations of roots, and the next work is to refine the solution accuracy of each optimal region. We note that the distribution of individuals in the evolved population was uneven. Many individuals gathered in the higher precision area, while for the less precise individuals, they have no neighborhood around them. We call these less precise and neighborless individuals "Isolated Solutions". Isolated solutions are difficult to converge due to lacking neighborhood information. Figure 2 shows an example of isolated solutions in the evolved population.

In order to handle isolated solutions, we cluster the individuals according to their distribution. The clustering method is shown as Algorithm 4. The clustering radius R plays a vital role in the clustering process. Here, R is dynamically adjusted as follows:

$$R = \frac{t_{max} - t}{t_{max}} \times (R_{max} - R_{min}) + R_{min} \qquad (6)$$

where R_{max} and R_{min} are respectively the maximal and minimal values of the clustering radius, t and t_{max} are the current and maximum number of generations. From Eq. (6) we can see that R decreases as the number of iterations

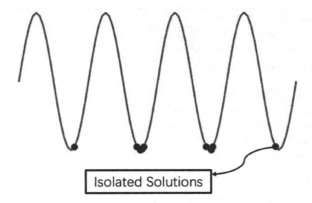

Fig. 2. An example of isolated solutions

Algorithm 4. Clustering

Input: the clustering radius R
Output: species set S_{set}
1: Sort the population from better to worse according to fitness value;
2: **while** the population is not empty **do**
3:     The best individual x is set as the species seed;
4:     Calculate the distance between x and other individuals;
5:     The x and individuals with distance less than or equal to R form a new species;
6:     Append the new species to S_{set} and remove these individuals from the population;
7: **end while**

---

increases. In the early stage, the population may contain local optimal solutions, so we set the large clustering radius to help individuals jump out of the area of local optima. As the search proceeds, the radius gradually reduces so that different roots are distributed in different subpopulations.

After clustering, the whole population is partitioned into many species. The DE operators cannot be directly used in the species that contain isolated solutions since the number of individuals in these species may less than 3. Inspired by the fact that fitter species contain a large number of individuals, we adjust the distribution of solutions by reducing the individuals in fitter species and increasing the individuals in less fitter species. Distribution adjustment is not suitable for each species, so we set two parameters to limit improper species: θ denotes the accuracy level and θ_{local} denotes the minimum accuracy level. Only when the function evaluation value of a fitter species' seed reaches the accuracy level θ and the function evaluation value of a less fitter species' seed reaches minimum the accuracy level θ_{local}, we pair these two species and adjust their distribution. Specific details are shown in Algorithm 5.

Algorithm 5. DALS

Input: control parameters: F, CR, $MaxFEs$, the evolved population P, accuracy level θ, local solution threshold θ_{local}

Output: the final population P

1: FEs=0;
2: **while** $FEs < \frac{MaxFEs}{2}$ **do**
3:      Calculate the clustering radius R using Eq.(6);
4:      Cluster the population using Algorithm 4 and get the species set S_{set};
5:      Calculate the number of species, denoted as N_s;
6:      **for** $i = 1$ to $N_s/2$ **do**
7:          $S_1 = S_{set}(i)$, $S_2 = S_{set}(N_s + 1 - i)$;
8:          $N_1 = size(S_1)$, $N_2 = size(S_2)$; // size: the individual number of species;
9:          $x_1 = best(S_1)$, $x_2 = best(S_2)$; // best: the best individual of species;
10:         **if** $f(S_1(x_1)) \leq \theta$ and $f(S_2(x_2)) \leq \theta_{local}$ **then**
11:             **if** $size(S_1) > size(S_2)$ **then**
12:                 **while** $size(S_1) \geq s/2$ **do**
13:                     Remove the worst individual from S_1;
14:                     Adopt Gaussian distribution to sample a solution x on x_2;
15:                     Append x to S_2;
16:                 **end while**
17:             **end if**
18:         **end if**
19:     **end for**
20:     **for** each species S_i **do**
21:         **if** the number of individuals $N_i > 3$ **then**
22:             Using DE/best/1 for each individual in S_i to generate the offspring;
23:             Perform selection operator in species S_i;
24:         **else**
25:             Adopt Gaussian distribution to sample a offspring for each individual;
26:             Perform selection operator in species S_i;
27:         **end if**
28:     **end for**
29:     $FEs = FEs + 1$;
30: **end while**

2.3 TPNDE

TPNDE consists of the global search and local search. In order to balance the exploration and exploitation, we set the FEs of global search and local search half to half. The main framework of TPNDE is represented in Algorithm 6.

Algorithm 6. TPNDE

Input: the maximum number of FEs $MaxFEs$, population size NP
Output: The optimal solution set S
1: P = GlobalSearch($MaxFEs/2$);
2: /*Using algorithm 3*/
3: S = LocalSearch(P, $MaxFEs/2$);
4: /*Using algorithm 5*/

---

3   Experiments

3.1   Test Functions and Performance Metrics

In this section, we use 20 NES problems chosen from the literature to evaluate the performance of different algorithms. These functions can be classified into three groups. The first group includes the first ten functions F1–F10 which are low-dimensional base functions. The second group consists of the next five functions F11–F15 which are low-dimensional composition functions with a huge number of local optima. The third group consists of the last five functions F16–F20 that are high-dimensional composition function. Table 1 provides the information on these 20 test problems.

Here, all the roots of NESs are known as a priori. If a solution x subjects to $\exists root_k, \|x, root_k\| \leq \lambda$ and $f(x) \leq \theta$ is can be a root of the NES and root $root_k$ is considered to be found. If $n \leq 5$, we set $\lambda = 0.01$ and $\theta = 1E - 6$; otherwise, $\lambda = 0.1$ and $\theta = 1E - 4$.

In order to evaluate the performance of a method solving NESs problems, two judgment metrics of multimodal optimization are introduced here.

Root Ratio (RR). RR denotes the average percentage of the optimal solutions found over multiple runs.

$$RR = \frac{\sum_{i=1}^{N} NOF_i}{NOR \times N} \quad (7)$$

where N is the number of independent runs, NOF_i is the number of roots found in the ith run, and NOR is the number of known roots of a NESs as shown in Table 1.

Success Rate (SR). SR evaluates the percentage of the successful runs.

$$SR = \frac{N_s}{N} \quad (8)$$

where N_s is the number of successful runs. If all known roots have been found in single execute, it can be called successful run.

Table 1. Characteristics of 20 test instances, where n is the number of decision variables; LE is the number of linear equations; NE is the number of nonlinear equations; NOR is the number of known optimal solutions of a NES; $MaxFEs$ is the maximal number of function evaluations.

Prob	n	LE	NE	NOR	$MaxFEs$
F_1	2	0	2	2	10000
F_2	2	0	2	2	50000
F_3	3	0	3	1	50000
F_4	2	0	2	3	50000
F_5	2	0	2	2	50000
F_6	3	0	3	5	50000
F_7	2	0	2	4	50000
F_8	2	0	2	3	100000
F_9	2	0	2	2	50000
F_{10}	2	0	2	6	50000
F_{11}	2	1	1	11	50000
F_{12}	2	0	2	13	50000
F_{13}	2	0	2	13	50000
F_{14}	2	0	2	10	50000
F_{15}	3	0	3	12	50000
F_{16}	20	0	2	2	50000
F_{17}	10	0	10	1	50000
F_{18}	5	4	1	3	100000
F_{19}	8	1	7	16	100000
F_{20}	20	19	1	2	200000

3.2   Effects of TPNDE Components

The main components of TPNDE are: 1) probabilistic reproduction Mechanism; 2) reinitialization Procedure; 3) distribution adjustment local search. In this section, the working principle of each component is discussed. For visualization, test question F13 that contains two decision variables was chosen to illustrate the principle. Three TNPDE variants are corresponding with three components: 1) TPNDE-RM, where the probabilistic reproduction mechanism is replaced by a base DE strategy DE/rand/1; 2) TPNDE-RP, where the reinitialization procedure was removed; 3) TPNDE-DA, in which we eliminated the distribution adjustment local search algorithm. For fair comparison, the same parameters of the algorithms are set as: $F = 0.5$, $CR = 0.9$, $NP = 100$, $MaxFEs = 50000$. The results of TPNDE and its three variants are respectively described in Fig. 3.

In Fig. 3(a), 3(b), and 3(c) show the evolution of TPNDE-RM when $FEs = 10000$, 30000, and 50000. FNODE-RM succeeded in finding all the roots of F13. However, the convergence rate is not fast enough since TPNDE-RM only used a base DE strategy. As can be seen in (b), TPNDE-RM only located 12 roots of F13 and remained one solution that didn't converge when $FEs = 30000$; Fig. 3(d), 3(e), and 3(f) show the evolution of TPNDE-RP when $FEs = 10000$, 30000, and 50000. TPNDE-RP failed to find all the roots at the end of evolution and the final population converged to several roots. TPNDE-RP lost diversity when the reinitialization procedure was removed. Figure 3(g), 3(h), and 3(i) show the evolution of TPNDE-DA when $FEs = 10000$, 30000, and 50000. TPNDE-DA also failed to locate all the roots. In Fig. 3(i), some individuals had already gathered around the near of the roots, however, the values of these individuals didn't reach the accuracy level. It's because of the slow convergence speed of isolated solutions. Figure 3(j), 3(k), and 3(l) show the evolution of TPNDE when $FEs = 10000$, 30000, and 50000. TPNDE found all the roots very quickly. When $FEs = 30000$, TPNDE already located all the roots. The fast convergence and good diversity of TPNDE are benefited from the combined effect of probabilistic reproduction mechanism, reinitialization procedure and distribution adjustment local search.

To more effectively evaluate the effects of the three components of TPNDE, we apply TPNDE and the three variants to solve the 20 NESs. The results were analyzed statistically by the Friedman's test, shown in Table 2. TPNDE ranks first in both RR and SR criteria.

Table 2. Ranking of the four compared methods by the Friedman's test.

Algorithm	Ranking (RR)	Ranking (SR)
TPNDE	**1.975**	**1.975**
TPNDE-RM	2.475	2.475
TPNDE-DA	2.675	2.775
TPNDE-RP	2.875	2.775

3.3 Comparisons with Other Methods

To further evaluate the performance of TPNDE, we compare TPNDE with several state-of-the-art methods on F1–F20, i.e., FNODE [21], RADE [29], DR-JADE [30], MONES [31], A-WeB [32]. To make a fair comparison, the parameters of FNODE, RADE, DR-JADE, MONES and A-WeB are set to be the same as used in their original literature. $MaxFEs$ is given in the last column

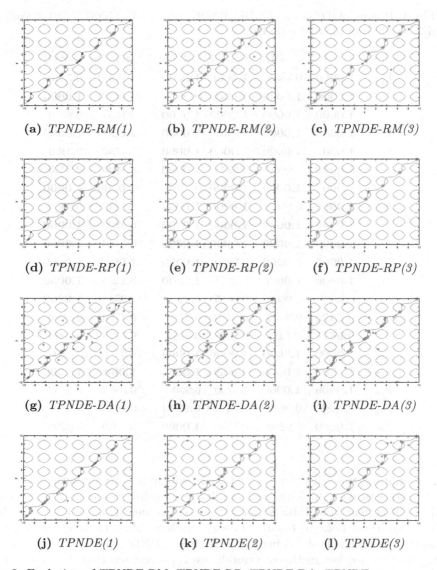

(a) *TPNDE-RM(1)*   **(b)** *TPNDE-RM(2)*   **(c)** *TPNDE-RM(3)*

(d) *TPNDE-RP(1)*   **(e)** *TPNDE-RP(2)*   **(f)** *TPNDE-RP(3)*

(g) *TPNDE-DA(1)*   **(h)** *TPNDE-DA(2)*   **(i)** *TPNDE-DA(3)*

(j) *TPNDE(1)*   **(k)** *TPNDE(2)*   **(l)** *TPNDE(3)*

Fig. 3. Evolution of TPNDE-RM, TPNDE-RP, TPNDE-DA, TPNDE over a typical run on F13. Circles denote the individuals in the population; asterisks denote the found roots.

of Table 1. Table 3 and Table 4 present the comparison results of RR and SR, where all results are averaged over 50 runs. For clarity, the best RR and SR are highlighted in boldface. As can be seen in Table 3 and 4, TPNDE got the best result in most of the test problem.

Table 3. Results of TPNDE, FNODE, RADE, DR-JADE, MONES and A-WeB on F1-F20 in terms of the root ratio RR.

Prob.	TPNDE	FNODE	RADE	DR-JADE	MONES	A-WeB
F_1	**1.0000**	0.7800	**1.0000**	**1.0000**	**1.0000**	0.7250
F_2	**1.0000**	**1.0000**	**1.0000**	0.9667	**1.0000**	**1.0000**
F_3	**1.0000**	**1.0000**	**1.0000**	**1.0000**	0.1667	0.8800
F_4	**1.0000**	**1.0000**	0.9967	**1.0000**	**1.0000**	**1.0000**
F_5	**1.0000**	**1.0000**	**1.0000**	**1.0000**	0.8750	0.9400
F_6	**1.0000**	0.9960	0.9940	**1.0000**	0.8220	0.9320
F_7	**1.0000**	**1.0000**	**1.0000**	0.9867	**1.0000**	**1.0000**
F_8	**1.0000**	0.8667	**1.0000**	**1.0000**	0.8440	0.9900
F_9	**1.0000**	**1.0000**	**1.0000**	**1.0000**	0.9800	**1.0000**
F_{10}	**1.0000**	**1.0000**	**1.0000**	**1.0000**	0.5300	**1.0000**
F_{11}	**1.0000**	**1.0000**	0.9900	**1.0000**	**1.0000**	**1.0000**
F_{12}	**1.0000**	**1.0000**	0.9954	**1.0000**	0.4369	**1.0000**
F_{13}	0.9877	0.9600	0.9015	0.7267	0.9346	**1.0000**
F_{14}	**0.9420**	0.8640	0.6310	0.7740	0.4360	0.8880
F_{15}	**0.9517**	0.7383	0.8908	0.9267	0.5433	0.0933
F_{16}	**1.0000**	**1.0000**	**1.0000**	**1.0000**	0.9450	0.6200
F_{17}	**1.0000**	**1.0000**	**1.0000**	**1.0000**	**1.0000**	**1.0000**
F_{18}	**1.0000**	**1.0000**	0.9700	0.9905	0.8867	0.8933
F_{19}	0.9888	0.9850	0.9444	**0.9974**	0.1663	0.6688
F_{20}	**1.0000**	0.9300	0.7950	**1.0000**	0.3050	0.6200

In addition, the Wilcoxon test and the Friedman test are performed to evaluate the statistical significance of the results, the results are shown in Table 5 and Table 6. It is clear from Table 5 that TPNDE performed significantly better than other algorithms because the $R+$ values were large than $R-$ and the p-values was less than 0.05. From Table 6, we see that TPNDE had the best rankings compared with other methods. Overall, we can conclude that TPNDE generally outperform other five algorithms in comparison and TPNDE is effective in simultaneously locating multiple roots of NESs.

Table 4. Results of TPNDE, FNODE, RADE, DR-JADE, MONES and A-WeB on F1-F20 in terms of the success rate SR.

Prob.	TPNDE	FNODE	RADE	DR-JADE	MONES	A-WeB
F_1	**1.0000**	0.6400	**1.0000**	**1.0000**	**1.0000**	0.5200
F_2	**1.0000**	**1.0000**	**1.0000**	0.9333	**1.0000**	**1.0000**
F_3	**1.0000**	**1.0000**	**1.0000**	**1.0000**	0.1667	0.8800
F_4	**1.0000**	**1.0000**	0.9800	**1.0000**	**1.0000**	**1.0000**
F_5	**1.0000**	**1.0000**	**1.0000**	**1.0000**	0.7800	0.8800
F_6	**1.0000**	0.9800	0.9800	**1.0000**	0.1300	0.6600
F_7	**1.0000**	**1.0000**	**1.0000**	0.9333	**1.0000**	**1.0000**
F_8	**1.0000**	0.7600	**1.0000**	**1.0000**	0.5000	0.9800
F_9	**1.0000**	**1.0000**	**1.0000**	**1.0000**	0.9600	**1.0000**
F_{10}	**1.0000**	**1.0000**	**1.0000**	**1.0000**	0.0000	**1.0000**
F_{11}	**1.0000**	**1.0000**	0.9000	**1.0000**	**1.0000**	**1.0000**
F_{12}	**1.0000**	**1.0000**	0.9400	**1.0000**	**1.0000**	**1.0000**
F_{13}	0.8600	0.5200	0.3100	0.0000	0.6700	**1.0000**
F_{14}	**0.5600**	0.2800	**1.0000**	0.0000	0.0000	0.2800
F_{15}	**0.5200**	0.0200	0.1900	0.2400	0.0000	0.0000
F_{16}	**1.0000**	**1.0000**	**1.0000**	**1.0000**	0.9300	0.3600
F_{17}	**1.0000**	**1.0000**	**1.0000**	**1.0000**	0.0000	0.0000
F_{18}	**1.0000**	**1.0000**	0.9100	0.9333	0.6600	0.6800
F_{19}	0.8400	0.7600	0.4300	**0.9667**	0.0000	0.0000
F_{20}	**1.0000**	0.8600	0.6900	**1.0000**	0.0700	0.2400

Table 5. Results obtained by the multiple-problem Wilcoxon's test for the five compared methods.

TPNDE VS	RR			SR		
	R+	R−	p-value	R+	R−	p-value
FNODE	171.0	39.0	**1.208E−2**	171.0	39.0	**1.208E−2**
RADE	182.5	27.5	**2.519E−3**	182.5	27.5	**2.519E−3**
DR-JADE	103.0	87.0	$\geq$2E−1	100.0	90.0	$\geq$2E−1
MONES	199.5	10.5	**9.346E−5**	199.5	10.5	**9.346E−5**
A-WeB	182.0	28.0	**2.712E−3**	180.0	30.0	**3.654E−3**

Table 6. Ranking of the six compares methods by the Friedman's test.

Algorithm	Ranking (RR)	Ranking (SR)
TPNDE	**2.425**	**2.425**
DR_JADE	2.85	2.85
FNODE	3.15	3.175
RADE	3.65	3.7
A-WeB	4	4.025
MONES	4.9	4.825

4   Conclusion

A two-phase niching differential evolution (TPNDE) was proposed for solving NESs in this paper. Probabilistic reproduction mechanism and reinitialization procedure were designed to enhance the diversity and ensure the global search being able to find the approximate location of roots. Distribution adjustment local search was proposed to refine the solution accuracy. Twenty NES problems were chosen to evaluate the performance of TPNDE and results showed that our algorithm can achieve a promising performance on locating multiple roots of NESs.

Acknowledgements. The National Natural Science Foundation of China (62072201), China Postdoctoral Science Foundation (2020M672359), and the Fundamental Research Funds for the Central Universities (HUST: 2019kfyXMBZ056).

References

1. Mehta, D., Grosan, C.: A collection of challenging optimization problems in science, engineering and economics. In: IEEE Congress Evolutionary and Computing (CEC), pp. 2697–2704 (2015)
2. Karr, C.L., Weck, B., Freeman, L.M.: Solutions to systems of nonlinear equations via a genetic algorithm. Eng. Appl. Artif. Intell. **11**(3), 369–375 (1989)
3. Seiler, M.C., Seiler, F.A.: Numerical recipes in C: the art of scientific computing. Risk Anal. **9**(3), 415–416 (1989)
4. Barzilai, J., Borwein, J.M.: Two-point step size gradient methods. IMA J. Numer. Anal. **8**(1), 141–148 (1988)
5. Ramos, H., M.T.T.: A new approach based on the newtons method to solve systems of nonlinear equations. J. Comput. Appl. Math. **3**(13), 318 (2017)
6. Gritton, K.S., Seader, J.D.: Global homotopy continuation procedures for seeking all roots of a nonlinear equation. Comput. Chem. Eng. **25**(7), 1003–1019 (2001)
7. Brits, R., Engelbrecht, A.P.: Solving systems of unconstrained equations using particle swarm optimization. In: IEEE International Conference on System Man Cybernitics **3**, 6–9 (2002)
8. Shir, O.M.: Niching in evolutionary algorithms. In: Handbook of Natural Computing, pp. pp. 1035–1069, Heidelberg, Germany (2012)

9. Li, X.: Efficient differential evolution using speciation for multimodal function optimization. In: Conference on Genetics Evolution Computing, Washington, DC, USA, pp. 873–880 (2005)
10. Li, J.P., Balazs, M.E., et at.: A species conserving genetic algorithm for multimodal function optimization. Evol. Comput. **10**(3), 207–234 (2002)
11. Gan, J., Warwick, K.: Dynamic niche clustering: a fuzzy variable radius niching technique for multimodal optimisation in GAs. In: IEEE Congress Evolution Computing, Seoul, South Korea, pp. 215–222 (2001)
12. Thomsen, R.: Multimodal optimization using crowding-based differential evolution. In: Proceedings of the 2004 Congress on Evolutionary Computation, vol. 2, no. 2, pp. 1382–1389 (2004)
13. Stoean, C.L., Preuss, M., et at.: Disburdening the species conservation evolutionary algorithm of arguing with radii. In: Conference Genetics Evolutionary Computation, London, U.K, pp. 1420–1427 (2007)
14. Goldberg, D.E., Richardson, J.: Genetic algorithms with sharing for multimodal function optimization. In: 2nd International Conference on Genetic Algorithms, Cambridge, MA, USA, pp. 41–49 (1987)
15. Gao, W., Yen, G.G., Liu, S.: A cluster-based differential evolution with self-adaptive strategy for multimodal optimization. IEEE Trans. Cybern. **44**(8), 1314–1327 (2014)
16. Yangetal, Q.: Multimodal estimation of distribution algorithms. IEEE Trans. Cybern. **47**(3), 636–650 (2017)
17. Pourjafari, E., Mojallali, H.: Solving nonlinear equations systems with a new approach based on invasive weed optimization algorithm and clustering. Swarm Evol. Comput. **4**, 33–43 (2012)
18. Mehrabian, A.R., Lucas, C.: A novel numerical optimization algorithm inspired from weed colonization. Ecol. Inf. **1**(4), 355–366 (2006)
19. Qu, B.Y., Suganthan, P.N., Das, S.: A distance-based locally informed particle swarm model for multimodal optimization. IEEE Trans. Evol. Comput. **17**(3), 387–402 (2013)
20. Yang, Q., et al.: Adaptive multimodal continuous ant colony optimization. IEEE Trans. Evol. Comput. **21**(2), 191–205 (2017)
21. He, W., Gong, W., Wang, L., et al.: Fuzzy neighborhood-based differential evolution with orientation for nonlinear equation systems. Knowl. Based Syst. **182**(15), 104796.1–104796.12 (2019)
22. Pan, L.Q., Li, L.H., He, C., et al.: A subregion division-based evolutionary algorithm with effective mating selection for many-objective optimization. IEEE Trans. Cybern. **50**(8), 3477–3490 (2020)
23. Pan, L.Q., He, C., Tian, Y., et al.: A region division based diversity maintaining approach for many-objective optimization. Integr. Comput. Aided Eng. **24**, 279–296 (2017)
24. He, C., Tian, Y., Jin, Y.C., Pan, L.Q.: A radial space division based evolutionary algorithm for many-objective optimization. Appl. Soft Comput. **61**, 603–621 (2017)
25. Pan, L.Q., He, C., Tian, Y., et al.: A classification-based surrogate-assisted evolutionary algorithm for expensive many-objective optimization. IEEE Trans. Evol. Comput. **23**(1), 74–88 (2019)
26. Sacco, W., Henderson, N.: Finding all solutions of nonlinear systems using a hybrid metaheuristic with fuzzy clustering means. Appl. Soft Comput. **11**(8), 5424–5432 (2011)

27. Wang, Z.J., et al.: Dual-strategy differential evolution with affinity propagation clustering for multimodal optimization problems. IEEE Trans. Evol. Comput. **22**, 894–908 (2017)
28. Biswas, S., Kundu, S., Das, S.: Inducing niching behavior in differential evolution through local information sharing. IEEE Trans. Evol. Comput. **19**(2), 246–263 (2015)
29. Gong, W., Wang, Y., Cai, Z., Wang, L.: Finding multiple roots of nonlinear equation systems via a repulsion-based adaptive differential evolution. IEEE Trans. Syst. Man Cybern. Syst. 1–15 (2018)
30. Liao, Z., Gong, W., Yan, X., Wang, L., Hu, C.: Solving nonlinear equations system with dynamic repulsion-based evolutionary algorithms. IEEE Trans. Syst. Man Cybern. Syst. 1–12 (2018)
31. Song, W., Wang, Y., Li, H., Cai, Z.: Locating multiple optimal solutions of nonlinear equation systems based on multi-objective optimization. IEEE Trans. Evol. Comput. **19**(3), 414–431 (2015)
32. Gong, W., Wang, Y., Cai, Z., Yang, S.: A weighted biobjective transformation technique for locating multiple optimal solutions of nonlinear equation systems. IEEE Trans. Evol. Comput. **21**(5), 697–713 (2017)

Energy-Efficient Data Gathering Scheme Based on Compressive Sensing and Directional Walk Routing in Lossy WSNs

Zhe Han[1] ⓘ, Chuanfeng Li[1](✉), Xia Zhang[2], and Guangyi Liu[2]

[1] Luoyang Institute of Science and Technology, Luoyang 471023, China
hanzheyou@lit.edu.com
[2] National Digital Switching System Engineering and Technological Research Center,
Zhengzhou 450002, China
zhangxiaatzz@sina.com

Abstract. For a multi-hop outdoor wireless sensor network (WSN), data gathering is full of challenges due to the unreliable wireless link and resource-limited nodes. In this paper, a sparse compressive sensing (CS) data gathering scheme based on directional random walk is proposed to resist the impact of packet loss on CS reconstruction accuracy and reduce the energy consumption. Nodes are unevenly deployed in the ring topology network. Data gathering is initiated by nodes located at the outermost ring with a certain probability and transmits forward along the directional walk paths until the CS-based data receiving buffer area is reached. A sparse measurement matrix is designed to collaborate with the CS projections. Additionally, we propose a random path selection scheme for the nodes visited by the projections to guarantee the reliable delivery of transmission and balanced energy consumption. Simulation results show that our proposed scheme can effectively resist the impact of packet loss on the CS reconstruction accuracy and significantly decrease the energy consumption compared to the existing schemes using the dense measurement projections and random walk projections.

Keywords: Wireless sensor network · Compressive sensing · Packet loss ·
Directional walk

1 Introduction

Internet of Things (IOT) technology is regarded as a promising technology that will promote social automation and intelligence in the future. As an important supporting technology of IOT, wireless sensor networks (WSNs) have attracted the interest of many researchers. Distributed wireless nodes in which energy resources are constrained are intensively deployed in the monitoring area in the WSNs. Researches on network energy consumption are accompanied by the development of network. Although traditional technologies such as sleep scheduling [1], information fusion, routing mechanism, distributed source coding and data compression can reduce the overall energy consumption,

© Springer Nature Singapore Pte Ltd. 2021
L. Pan et al. (Eds.): BIC-TA 2020, CCIS 1363, pp. 269–282, 2021.
https://doi.org/10.1007/978-981-16-1354-8_18

they cannot avoid the "energy hole" problem [2], which the network lifetime has not been substantially extended.

As a promising technology, compressive sensing (CS) provides a new way to reduce and balance network energy consumption and extend network lifetime in WSNs by exploiting the data correlation [3–7]. CS has been shown to reduce data transmission with less measurement. For the large-scale WSNs, data gathering based on multi-hop communication is usually utilized. Luo et al. in [8] proposed the compressive data gathering (CDG) algorithm in multi-hop WSNs. CDG exploited the dense measurement matrix to sample the whole network data under the minimum spanning tree routing, which involved entire sensor nodes in which high data correlation exists. Compared with the traditional data gathering, Reference [9] indicated that CS data gathering would increase the energy consumption of leaf nodes and proposed hybird-CS algorithm. By combining CS-based data gathering and non-CS data collection, hybird-CS algorithm further reduced the overall energy consumption of the network. However, hybird-CS requires all sensor nodes to participate in the data collection processing, a random sparse measurement matrix based on minimum spanning tree projection is produced in [10] to optimize the number of participating nodes in CS-based data collection under the premise of ensuring reconstruction accuracy. The algorithm used in [10] required a precise routing control that will impose high communication overhead on sensor nodes, namely the mismatch between sparse projection and data collection route. Further, the problem is applied to other sparse measurement projection processing [11, 12]. It is wise to integrate random walk (RW) and CS-based data collection, without precise routing algorithm [13, 14]. They focused on combining the data gathering route with sparse projection by allowing each node to select randomly its next hop from its neighbors, while the multi-hop transmission process of CS measurement results at the end of RW usually leads to the unbalanced energy distribution and excessive energy consumption when random walk terminates.

As for the practical application scenarios, most CS-based data gathering algorithms are difficult to be applied in multi-hop WSNs since the packet loss will seriously deteriorate the CS reconstruction performance [15]. Reference [16] investigated the impact of the packet loss on CS reconstruction through simulations and theoretical analysis in the multi-hop WSNs and indicated that the CS reconstruction accuracy does not meet the requirements when the packet loss ratio exceeded 5%. However, wireless links in practical WSNs are usually vulnerable and unreliable. There is an average 30% packet loss rate [17], which will constrain the practical application for the CS-based data gathering. Reference [18] proposed SR-BDM algorithm to resist the influence of packet loss by employing the sparsest random measurement matrix in cluster topology networks. However, cluster topology networks are not applied to the large-scale WSNs.

In order to address and promote the implementation of the CS-based data gathering algorithm in multi-hop practical WSNs, there are two challenges: (1) how to resist the impact of packet loss on CS-based data gathering; (2) how to decrease and balance the network energy consumption. In this paper, we propose a directional random walk CS-based data gathering scheme based on the non-uniform ring cluster (CS-DWR) to address the abovementioned challenges. The main contributions of this paper can be summarized as follows:

- The relevance of packet loss in multi-hop practical WSNs is considered and reliable delivery scheme in directional walk path is adopted to resist the impact of packet loss by designing a random path selection scheme for the nodes visited by the CS projections.
- We adopt a directional random walk scheme based on ring topology to integrate the CS-based data gathering with the transmission of CS measurement results. This way can effectively decrease the transmission packets and break the overlong projection path by dividing one traditional random walk path into several paths.
- We present a non-uniform distribution method to balance network energy consumption, which can address the challenge of unbalanced energy consumption caused by the directional random walk scheme based on ring topology. The distribution density of nodes in each ring region is also evaluated in this paper.

2 Preliminaries

2.1 CS Background

Compressive sensing theory consists of sparse representation of signals, measurement matrix and signal reconstruction. The process of data sampling and compression is implemented simultaneously in the CS-based data gathering. CS offers a promising compressive technique to project the original sensor signals from high dimension to low dimension, which can break through the limitation of Shannon's sampling theorem and greatly decrease the total number of transmission. Let $S = [s_1, s_2, \cdots, s_N]^T$ represents the native sensor dataset. S can be defined to be compressive if there is an orthogonal transformation basis $\Psi_{N \times N}$ to make $\alpha = \Psi^T S$ with k nonzero entries, where $k \ll N$. The measurement matrix is denoted by $\Phi = (\phi_{ij})_{M \times N}$, where M represents the measurement times of CS and $M = O(k \log N / k) \ll N$. Then, the measurement of native data can be expressed as:

$$Y = (y_i)_{M \times 1} = \Phi S = \Phi \Psi \alpha = \Theta \alpha \tag{1}$$

where $\Theta = \Phi \Psi$ is a sensing matrix. Sink node can reconstruct the native sensor data from the M measurements by solving the optimization problem of l_1-norm as follows:

$$\hat{S} = \arg\ min \|S\|_{l_1} \quad s.t.\ Y = \Theta S \tag{2}$$

It has been demonstrated that l_1-optimization algorithm can perform an accurate reconstruction if matrix Φ satisfies the restricted isometry property (RIP) [19] as shown below in (3).

$$(1 - \varepsilon)\|S\|_2^2 \le \|\Phi * S\|_2^2 \le (1 + \varepsilon)\|S\|_2^2 \tag{3}$$

To compute the accuracy of CS-based data reconstruction, the normalized mean absolute error (NMAE) can be defined as (4).

$$NMAE = \frac{\left\|\hat{S} - S\right\|_2}{\|S\|_2} \tag{4}$$

2.2 Problem Formulation and Network Model

Most of the existing algorithms are based on the research of how to reduce network energy consumption under the ideal wireless link. Previous researches [15, 16, 18] have verified that CS-based data gathering is highly sensitive to the packet loss through theory and simulation analysis, especially in the multi-hop WSNs, and the traditional guarantee techniques of link reliability cannot satisfy the demand of CS-based data gathering. Once a node fails in the multi-hop network, the CS projection data of all its descendants is unable to be transmitted to the sink, that is, the packet loss is interrelated in the CS-based data gathering.

Consider a multi-hop WSN consisting of N nodes and a sink as shown in Fig. 1. The CS-based measurement process in one multi-hop link is terminated ahead of schedule due to the relevance of packet loss in the unreliable link. Then the CS measurement data acquired by sink node can be drastically reduced, which will result in insufficient CS sampling rate of the whole network. Compared with deterministic routing, random walk routings randomly select the next hop from neighbor nodes and have a natural advantage in dealing with the packet loss. However, the existing CS-based random walk schemes focused on reducing the energy consumption, without considering how to resist the impact of packet loss on the CS-based data gathering. Additionally, omnidirectional random walk made the final nodes of random walk link randomly distributed in the whole network. There usually have overlong multi-hop paths from the final nodes to sink for the transmissions of CS measurement results, which results in the unbalanced energy distribution and additional energy consumption. More importantly, the deterministic routings are required during the transmissions and the packet loss is still a concern. In order to address abovementioned challenges, a directional random walk scheme based on the ring topology is proposed in the lossy WSNs, which can also break the overlong measurement paths to relieve the relevance of packet loss as one random walk path is divided into several paths.

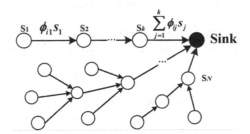

Fig. 1. CS-based data gathering in the multi-hop WSN

In this paper, WSN distribution area is partitioned into k evenly spaced rings, where the ring width is D as shown in Fig. 2. The ring region outward from the center of the circle is denoted by $A_1, A_2, \cdots, A_k$. N sensor nodes are randomly distributed in ring regions. The distribution density of nodes in each ring region is respectively $\rho_1, \rho_2, \cdots, \rho_k$. The center circular area with radius D is defined as the CS-based data receiving buffer area, which sink node is located at the center of receiving buffer area. Assume the communication radius of the sensor nodes is denoted by $r(n)$, where $r(n) \geq D$. [20] indicated that WSNs has strong connectivity with high probability when the radius is scaled as $O\left(\sqrt{logN/N}\right)$. Let the Euclidean distance between node i and node j is $d(i,j) = \sqrt[2]{(x_i - x_j)^2 + (y_i - y_j)^2}$. The WSN can be modelled as an undirected graph $G = (V, E)$, where $V = \{v_i | i = 1, 2, \cdots, N\}$, $E = \{e_{ij} | d(i,j) \leq r\}$. Neighbors of vertex v_i can be defined as $\Gamma v_i = \{v_j \in V | (v_i, v_j) \in E\}$. To simplify and facilitate analysis, we assume each vertex in undirected graph G has the same degree and the nodes in the monitoring area have strong connectivity.

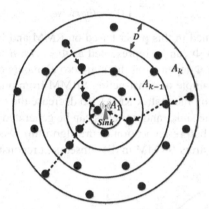

Fig. 2. Network model

3 Proposed Solution

3.1 Constructing Sparse Random Matrix

We assume that l nodes are randomly selected to initiate simultaneous directional RWs at a measurement instant. Note that directional RWs from l initiate nodes to sink result in one random projection of measurement matrix, which can shorten the length of each RW and relieve the impact of the packet loss. In this paper, we construct sparse random measurement matrix (SRMM) by combining the random measurement projection with directional RW routings.

Definition 1: (Random Measurement Matrix, RMM) Construct $M \times N$ measurement matrix $A = (a_{ij})_{M \times N}$. If arbitrary matrix values a_{ij} satisfy Eq. (5), we regard matrix A as RMM. The value of parameter s determines the sparsity of the RMM. When $s = 1$, RMM is the dense measurement matrix.

$$a_{ij} = \sqrt{s} \begin{cases} 1, & with\ prob.\ p = \frac{1}{2s} \\ 0, & with\ prob.\ p = 1 - \frac{1}{s} \\ -1, & with\ prob.\ p = \frac{1}{2s} \end{cases} \qquad (5)$$

Definition 2: (Node State Matrix, NSM) It's well known that each round of CS-based data gathering is divided into M measurements. Let NSM be a binary matrix denoted by $B = (b_{ij})_{M \times N}$, where b_{ij} represents the participation state of node j in the i-th measurement. For nodes participating in the aggregation and transmission processing, the corresponding element of the NSM is 1. Otherwise, the corresponding element is 0. Suppose that the set of nodes in the i-th directional RW measurement paths is called Ω_i, then

$$b_{ij} = \begin{cases} 1, & j \in \Omega_i \\ 0, & otherwise \end{cases} \qquad (6)$$

The SRMM is designed in this paper based on RMM and NSM. Let the SRMM is denoted by $\Phi_{M \times N}$, then Φ can be represented as $\Phi = A \circ B = (a_{ij} \cdot b_{ij})_{M \times N}$, where the non-zero element of Φ depends on the non-zero elements of B in the condition of $s = 1$. Figure 3 is an example of constructing SRMM from one directional walk path, where ϕ_{ij} is determined by the matrix RMM. To decrease the overhead of constructing the RMM and NSM at the sink, random seeds can be generated by each node through a pseudo-random number before invocation of the algorithm. We can adopt node ID and the random seeds to construct SRMM in the subsequent reconstruction.

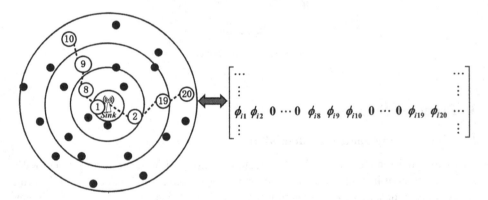

Fig. 3. A construction example of sparse random measurement matrix

4 Proposed CS-DWR Algorithm

Based on the network model mentioned above, we propose CS-DWR algorithm to resist the impact of packet loss and increase the network energy efficiency. The operation of the CS-DWR is detailed below.

Stage 1: N sensor nodes are distributed in the k evenly spaced rings. Suppose that each node can acquire its own ring number through the distribution information. In the initialization phase, neighbor set Γ_{node} can be generated for each node through the node detection mechanism.

Stage 2: At the beginning of data gathering, each node located in ring A_k is randomly selected as source node initiating the directional random walk with a probability p_s. Once node i is selected as source node, it generates an initial packet based on native sensor data and measurement coefficient and selects one neighbor node as the next hop from the set $N_o = \{j \in \Gamma_{node}(i) | j \in A_{k-1}\}$. The detailed procedure of walk path selection is described in Algorithm 1. Note that it is not allowed in our scheme for one measurement projection revisiting to the same node.

$$T(n) = \begin{cases} \frac{1}{n_0 - t(n) \bmod n_0}, & n \in Q \\ 0, & otherwise \end{cases} \tag{7}$$

In (7), n_o is the node number of set N_o and Q is node set that has not been selected as the next hop during the last n_o elections. The sequence number of election is expressed as $t(n)$.

Stage 3: In the following, the nodes visited by the walks repeat the selection process for the next hop node according to algorithm 1 until the projections are transmitted along the walk paths to the CS-based data receiving buffer area. The receiving nodes in the receiving buffer area perform the CS-based data gathering and transmit the projections to sink.

Stage 4: After receiving all projections in the i-th measurement, the sink generates a measurement value. The measurement vector $Y_{M \times 1}$ can be constructed until M measurements are completed. Then, sink reconstructs the native data of the whole network via Eq. (2).

Algorithm 1: Path selection for directional random walk

Input: Set of next hop $N_0(i)$
Output: The next hop node j

1: **If** $N_0(i) \neq \emptyset$
2:   Each node in the set of $N_0(i)$ generates a random number δ from 0 to 1;
3:   Calculate $T(n)$ via Eq. (7);
4:   **While** $\delta < T(n)$
5:     elect node n as the candidate node;
6:     node n sends a communication request to the upper node;
7:     **if** the link between node n and the upper node is invalid;
8:       reselect the next node based on Eq. (7);
9:     **else if** the upper node receives the request and send packet to node n
10:      Output the next hop node n;
11:      remove node n from set $N_0(i)$
12:    **break**
13:    **end if**
14:   **end while**
15: **else if** $N_0(i) = \emptyset$
16: Updata $N_0(i)$.
17: **End if**

---

5 Analysis of the Energy Balance

In our network, the ring area decreases gradually from the outer ring to the inner ring, that is, $A_k > A_{k-1} > \cdots > A_1$. If overall nodes are uniformly distributed, there will be a non-uniform transmission load distribution, which causes the nodes near sink to be overloaded and invalid in advance. In order to balance the transmission load, we propose a non-uniform distribution scheme. The distribution density of nodes satisfies the condition $\rho_1 > \rho_2 > \cdots > \rho_k$ as shown in the Fig. 4, where the color depth represents the distribution density.

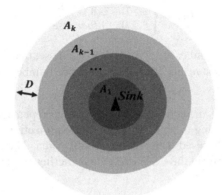

Fig. 4. The distribution density of sensor nodes

Theorem 1: Make sure that the distribution density ratio of nodes in adjacent ring domains satisfies $\rho_{i+1}/\rho_i = 2i - 1/2i + 1$, where $0 \le i \le k$, the transmission load of nodes in the network will be preserved balance.

Proof. Suppose that the radius of distribution area is denoted by $R = D * k$, the transmission load generated by overall source nodes in one measurement projection can be expressed as:

$$load = p_s \rho_k \left[\pi R^2 - \pi \left(R - D \right)^2 \right] \tag{8}$$

In the ring domain A_i, the average transmission load of nodes is

$$\overline{load_t} = \frac{p_s \rho_k [\pi R^2 - \pi (R-D)^2)}{\rho_i \{ \pi (iD)^2 - [\pi (i-1)D]^2 \}} = \frac{p_s \rho_k (2k-1)}{\rho_i (2i-1)} \tag{9}$$

According to the CS-DWR algorithm, the average transmission load of nodes in ring domain A_k can be represented by p_s. In order to ensure the load balance of the whole network, let $\overline{load_t} = p_s$, that is

$$\frac{p_s \rho_k (2k - 1)}{\rho_i (2i - 1)} = p_s \tag{10}$$

Then, we can demonstrate the condition of $\rho_{i+1}/\rho_i = 2i - 1/2i + 1$.

6 Performance Evaluation and Analysis

In order to evaluate the performance of CS-DWR, the real sensor data set collected from the GreenOrbs system [21] is selected to run the simulation. The simulation parameters are set as shown in Table 1. For comparison, CDG [8] and CS-RWR [13] schemes are also implemented. The performance comparison is evaluated from three aspects: the reconstruction accuracy, the number of overall packet transmission and network lifetime. First of all, Fig. 5(a) plots the reconstruction accuracy comparison with 10% packet loss ratio. We can observe that CS-DWR performance outperforms the other algorithms, which CDG algorithm accuracy has a sharp deterioration. The reason is that the relevance of packet loss in the CS-based multi-hop projection is taken into account in CS-DWR scheme, avoiding the premature termination of data projection. Meanwhile, we investigate the performance of our algorithm with the ideal link in Fig. 5(b). From the figure, it can be observed that, the reconstruction accuracy increases with the number of measurements and tends to be consistent in the condition of $M > 30$. When the number of measurements is in the condition of $M \leq 30$, the performance of the scheme using CDG is better than the others due to adopting the dense measurement projection. This indicates that the sparse degree of measurement projection may influence the reconstruction performance in the CS-based data gathering.

Table 1. Default simulation parameters

Parameters		Value
Number of sensor nodes	N	400
Radius of layout area	R	100
Ring width	D	10
Selection probability of sources	$\vec{p_s}$	5%
Maximum communication radius of node	$\vec{r}$	30
Length of packet	L	128(Byte)
Transform basis	$\vec{\Psi}$	DCT
Reconstruction algorithm		OMP

In order to evaluate our proposed scheme CS-DWR in terms of the energy consumption, the number of overall packet transmission is calculated based on the fact that the packet transmission process is the major energy consumption. With a similar reconstruction accuracy, Fig. 6 evaluates the number of overall packet transmission in our algorithm compared with the schemes using CDG and CS-RWR. A noticeable observation in Fig. 6 is that our scheme using CS-DWR requires the least transmissions than the other schemes under the different network sizes. Compared with CS-RWR scheme, our proposed scheme can provide about 20%-40% transmission cost reduction in the different network size. This is because our proposed scheme integrates the random walk

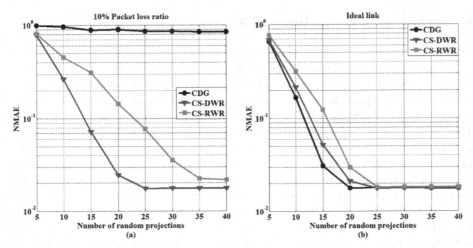

Fig. 5. Performance comparison in terms of reconsrtuction accuracy for different CS-based algorithms

processing with the transmission of CS measurement results by the directional walk based on the ring topology, which can avoid the transmission cost of CS measurement results.

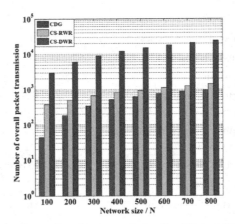

Fig. 6. The number of overall packet transmission for different CS-based algorithms

To further evaluate the network lifetime of our algorithm, the communication energy consumption that has been regarded as the majority energy consumption of sensor nodes is modeled as follows:

$$E_T = \left(\alpha_1 + \alpha_2 \times d^2\right) \times L \tag{11}$$

$$E_R = \alpha_1 \times L \tag{12}$$

E_T represents the energy consumption for the transmitting packet and E_R represents the energy consumption for the receiving packet. d denotes the transmission distance between nodes. L denotes the bit length of the packet. α_1 is the circuit energy consumption coefficient of sensor nodes, and α_2 is the distance attenuation factor.

Figure 7 plots the network lifetime of different schemes, in which the initial energy of sensor node is set to 1 J, $\alpha_1 = 50 \times 10^{-9}$J/b and $\alpha_2 = 10 \times 10^{-12}J/m^2 * $b. As the CDG scheme requires all nodes to participate in the data gathering, the appearance of first dead node is regarded as the critical point of network lifetime. For the random walk scheme, the critical point is loose as the network can still function normally when only one node dies. As shown in Fig. 7, our proposed scheme has great advantages comparing to the schemes using CDG and CS-RWR. The reason is that our scheme allows sensor nodes to alternately participate in data gathering comparing to the CDG scheme and maintain the energy consumption balance comparing to the CS-RWR scheme.

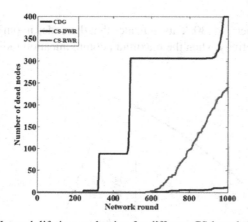

Fig. 7. Network lifetime evaluation for different CS-based algorithms

To further explore the impact of the sparse degree of measurement projection for our CS-DWR scheme, we implemented the simulation by changing the source selection probability p_s. In Fig. 8, with the change of probability p_s, the reconstruction accuracy is evaluated in different network size. The reconstruction performance increases with the probability p_s and tends to be stable when the probability p_s is higher than 0.05. Moreover, large network size will also contribute to the performance improvement. This is because the spatial correlation of sensor data is stronger in large network size, which can help to reduce the necessary sparse degree of measurement projection. It indicates that our proposed algorithm has the advantage of lower data sampling rate and energy consumption in large network size.

We then investigate the impact of maximum communication radius r on our proposed algorithm in Fig. 9. The maximum communication radius of sensor nodes will impact the number of candidate nodes, which is evaluated as shown in Fig. 9(a). It can be observed that the number of candidate nodes increase with the maximum communication radius. When $r = 30$, the average number of candidate nodes is 12. Moreover, Fig. 9(b) plots the impact of r on the NMAE. Increasing r will lead to a NMAE decrease and NMAE

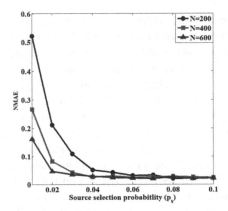

Fig. 8. The probabilities of source selection in terms of reconstruction accuracy

tends to be stable when $r \geq 30$. This indicates that the nodes in our proposed algorithm have a strong connectivity when the maximum communication radius of nodes reaches 30.

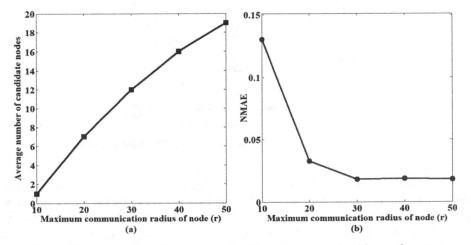

Fig. 9. The impact of maximum communication radius on our algorithm performance

7 Conclusion

In this paper, our goal is to resist the impact of packet loss on CS reconstruction accuracy and reduce the network energy consumption. We propose a sparse directional random walk scheme based on CS. Compared with the traditional CS-based data gathering scheme without considering the packet loss, we considered the relevance of packet loss in multi-hop WSNs and designed a path selection scheme in directional random walk paths by utilizing the natural advantage of random walk to guarantee the reliable delivery of transmission and balanced energy consumption of candidate nodes. In order to further decrease the number of overall transmission packets, we integrated the data gathering with the transmission of CS measurement results by adopting directional random walk scheme. The simulation results have shown that our proposed algorithm outperforms the other algorithms in the practical WSNs and will be a more promising and practical alternative in the data gathering applications.

Acknowledgments. This work was supported by the National Natural Science Foundation of China (grant numbers 61503173); Science and Technology Key Project of Henan Province (grant numbers 162102410051); Luoyang Institute of Science and Technology Advance Research (grant numbers 2019YZ06); Natural Science Foundation of Henan Province (grant numbers 202300410286).

References

1. Subramanian, R., Fekri, F.: Sleep scheduling and lifetime maximization in sensor networks: fundamental limits and optimal solutions. In: International Conference on Information Processing in Sensor Networks. IEEE Press, New York (2006). https://doi.org/10.1145/1127777. 1127813
2. Asharioun, H., Asadollahi, H.: A survey on analytical modeling and mitigation techniques for the energy hole problem in corona-based wireless sensor network. Wirel. Pers. Commun. (2015). https://doi.org/10.1007/s11277-014-2122-3
3. Candes, J., Wakin, B.: An introduction to compressive sampling. IEEE Signal Process. Mag. **25**(2), 21–30 (2008). https://doi.org/10.1109/MSP.2007.914731
4. Aziz, A., Singh, K., Osamy, W., Khedr, A. M.: An efficient compressive sensing routing scheme for internet of things based wireless sensor networks. Wirel. Pers. Commun. **12** (2020). https://doi.org/10.1007/s11277-020-07454-4
5. Luochong, W., Feng, S., Jun, C., Chang, W.: Efficient measurement generation and pervasive sparsity for compressive data gathering. IEEE Trans. Wirel. Commun. **9**(12), 3728–3738 (2010). https://doi.org/10.1109/TWC.2010.092810.100063
6. Srisooksai, T., Keamarungsi, K., Lamsrichan, P.: Practical data compression in wireless sensor networks: a survey. J. Netw. Comput. Appl. **35**(1), 37–59 (2012). https://doi.org/10.1016/j. jnca.2011.03.001
7. Mahmudimanesh, M., Suri, N., Khelil, A.: Balanced spatio-temporal compressive sensing for multi-hop wireless sensor networks. In: IEEE International Conference on Mobile Ad-hoc & Sensor Systems. IEEE Press, New York (2012). https://doi.org/10.1109/mass.2012.6502539
8. Luo, C., Wu, F.: Compressive data gathering for large-scale wireless sensor networks. In: the 15th Annual International Conference on Mobile Computing and Networking, pp. 145–156. ACM Press, New York (2009). US8280671 B2
9. Luo, J., Xiang, L., Rosenberg, C.: Does compressed sensing improve the throughput of wireless sensor networks? In: 2010 IEEE International Conference on Communications. pp. 1–6. IEEE Press, Cape Town (2012). https://doi.org/10.1109/icc.2010.5502565
10. Ebrahimi, D., Assi, C.: Compressive data gathering using random projection for energy efficient wireless sensor networks. Ad Hoc Netw. **16**, 105–119 (2014). https://doi.org/10.1016/j. adhoc.2013.12.004

11. Quer, G., Masiero, R., Munaretto, D., Rossi, M., Widmer, J., Zorzi, M.: On the Interplay between routing and signal representation for compressive sensing in wireless sensor networks. In: Proceedings of the Information Theory and Applications Workshop, pp. 206–215. IEEE Press, New York (2009). https://doi.org/10.1109/ita.2009.5044947
12. Ebrahimi, D., Assi, C.: On the interaction between scheduling and compressive data gathering in wireless sensor networks. IEEE Trans. Wirel. Commun. **15**(4), 2845–2858 (2016). https://doi.org/10.1109/TWC.2015.2512272
13. Nguyen, T., Teague, A.: Compressive sensing based random walk routing in wireless sensor networks. Ad Hoc Netw. **54**, 99–110 (2017). https://doi.org/10.1016/j.adhoc.2016.10.009
14. Haifeng, Z., Feng, Y., Xiaohua, T.: Data gathering with compressive sensing in wireless sensor networks: a random walk based approach. IEEE Trans. Parallel Distrib. Syst. **26**(1), 35–44 (2015). https://doi.org/10.1109/tpds.2014.2308212
15. Xuangou, W., Panlong, Y., Taeho, J.: Compressive sensing meets unreliable link: sparsest random scheduling for compressive data gathering in lossy WSNs. In: the 15th ACM International Symposium on Mobile Ad Hoc Networking and Computing, pp. 13–22. ACM Press, New York (2014). https://doi.org/10.1145/2632951.2632969
16. Zhe, H., Xia, Z., Ou, L.: Data gathering algorithm based on compressive sensing under lossy WSN. J. Softw. **28**(12), 3257–3273 (2017). https://doi.org/10.13328/j.cnki.jos.005246
17. Linghe, K., Mingyuan, X., Xiaoyang, L.: Data loss and reconstruction in sensor networks. In: Proceedings of the IEEE INFOCOM, pp. 1654–1662. IEEE Press, Italy (2013). https://doi.org/10.1109/infcom.2013.6566962
18. Ce, Z., Ou, L., Yanping, Y., Guangyi, L., Tong, X.: Energy-efficient data gathering algorithm relying on compressive sensing in lossy WSNs. Measurement (2019). https://doi.org/10.1016/j.measurement.2019.106875
19. Baraniuk, R.: Compressive sensing. IEEE Signal Process. Mag. **24**, 118–124 (2007). https://doi.org/10.1109/MSP.2007.361585
20. Gupta, P., Kumar, R.: The capacity of wireless networks. IEEE Trans. Inf. Theor. **46**(2), 388–404 (2002). https://doi.org/10.1109/18.825799
21. Lufeng, M., Yuan H., Yunhao, L., Jizhaong, Z.: Canopy closure estimates with greenorbs: sustainable sensing in the forest. In: Proceedings of the 7th ACM Conference on Embedded Networked Sensor Systems, pp. 99–112. ACM Press, New York (2009). https://doi.org/10.1145/1644038.1644049

Neural Network and Machine Learning

Predicting Locus-Specific DNA Methylation Based on Deep Neural Network

Baoshan Ma[1]([⊠]), Jiaxin Dong[1], Shuzheng Zhang[1], Haowen Yan[1], Jianqiao Pan[1],
Chongyang Li[1], Guanghui Liu[2], Zongjiang Gao[3], and Xinyu Zhang[3]([⊠])

[1] College of Information Science and Technology,
Dalian Maritime University, Dalian 116026, China
mabaoshan@dlmu.edu.cn
[2] Dahua Technology Co., Ltd., Hangzhou 310051, China
[3] Maritime Intelligent Transportation Research Group,
Dalian Maritime University, Dalian 116026, China
zhangxy@dlmu.edu.cn

Abstract. The next generation sequencing technologies have enabled DNA methylation levels to be assayed at single-base resolution in the whole genome, but this method is relatively expensive. At present, many traditional machine-learning methods have been actively proposed for predicting DNA methylation status, but the prediction accuracy of various models needs to be enhanced because they cannot fully extract important feature information. Therefore, the prediction method of DNA methylation based on state-of-the-art model is still a challenging topic. In the paper, we developed a deep-learning-based framework to address the issue by integrating a deep neural network (DNN) with random forest (RF). Initially, the DNN extracted potential and highly representative features from neighboring formation, genomic position, DNA sequence properties and cis-regulatory element information with its unsupervised learning process and multi-layer structure. Furthermore, we systematically evaluated and compared prediction performance using each kind of feature of DNA methylation and their combinations. Ultimately, the extracted DNA methylation features were combined with the standardized features to train the RF model and further enhance the prediction accuracy. The results showed the proposed method achieved an accuracy of 92.2% and Area Under Curve of 0.97, and outperformed the existing deep-learning-based methods. In summary, our study could contribute to providing a potential framework for the application of deep learning in DNA methylation prediction.

Keywords: DNA methylation · Deep learning · Feature selection · Random forest · Prediction

1 Introduction

As the most common epigenetic biomarker, DNA methylation is closely related to many biological processes, such as cell differentiation, gene expression, embryonic development and immune regulation. Previous study [1] has shown that suppressor gene of

© Springer Nature Singapore Pte Ltd. 2021
L. Pan et al. (Eds.): BIC-TA 2020, CCIS 1363, pp. 285–297, 2021.
https://doi.org/10.1007/978-981-16-1354-8_19

complex diseases can lose expression by methylation. So the assay of DNA methylation status has emerged as a promising tool for disease sub-classification [2] and tumor diagnosis [3].

Up to now, there were several sequencing methods existed to detect DNA methylation at CpG site resolution, such as whole-genome bisulfite sequencing [4] and methylated DNA immunoprecipitation [5]. These methods have enabled the assay of genome-wide DNA methylation to be more accurate, which contributed the mechanism in epigenetic to be better understood by researchers [6]. But they are prohibitively expensive and experimentally difficult for many studies. Machine learning is a powerful tool to predict DNA methylation [7] and is also a convenient alternative to analyze multi-tissue and multi-cell genome-wide methylation patterns [8, 9]. Recently, researchers' primary interest is to utilize various machine-learning algorithms to extract deep features from DNA methylation datasets, and then a classifier is trained by using these deep features [10]. The trained classifier can predict DNA methylation more accurately. However, DNA methylation dataset has the high dimensionality and non-linearity characteristics, which make the previous feature extraction technology based on traditional machine learning unable to effectively capture potential features.

Recent advances in deep learning have allowed researchers to introduce it into bioinformatics [11–15]. Through unsupervised or semi-supervised training, a multi-layer and interactive neural network can be built to automatically extract unobserved information hidden in biomedical data. The great power of neural network lies in its perfect fitting ability [16] that can approximate any complex function. Up to now, some deep learning models have been developed to predict DNA methylation [11, 13–15, 17, 18]. These deep learning methods used one-hot encoding DNA sequences as input and applied convolutional networks for pattern recognition. In 2017, Zeng et al. [15] introduced the CpGenie, a sequence-based deep learning framework that predicted the effect of genomic sequence variation on DNA methylation at the proximal CpG site. The results showed that CpGenie effectively predicted disease-associated variants and expression quantitative trait loci. Angermueller et al. [11] reported DeepCpG, a computational method based on deep neural networks for predicting DNA methylation status in single cell. This method learned predictive DNA sequence and methylation patterns in a data-driven manner based on a modular architecture. The results showed that DeepCpG produced more accurate predictions of DNA methylation status than previous approaches across all cell types. Fu et al. [13] designed a hybrid sequence-based deep learning model (MHCpG). They integrated both MeDIP-seq data and histone modification data with sequence information and built a convolutional network to explore sequence patterns. Moreover, they extracted more high-level features by a 3-layer feed forword neural network from statistical data. The results suggested that MHCpG could achieve more excellent performance than other methods.

In the study, we proposed a deep-learning-based framework to predict single-CpG-site methylation status by integrating a DNN and a RF model, using features that include neighboring CpG site methylation status, genomic position, local genomic characteristics and co-localization with coding regions and others. In this framework, we could directly learn the feature representation and effectively capture non-linear feature mapping of DNA methylation data. Firstly, we preprocess the raw DNA methylation data features through quality control and standardization. The preprocessed features are defined as standardized features. And then we utilize DNN to extract potential features from the standardized features. The extracted features are defined as abstract features. Furthermore, we apply the abstract features to train the RF model and then predict the DNA methylation. Finally, we combine both abstract features and standardized features to train the RF model. The results show that combining both the abstract features extracted from DNN and the standardized features can obtain the state-of-the-art prediction accuracy.

2 Materials and Methods

In this part, we described the proposed deep learning method in detail. The framework automatically extracts the abstract features from the raw feature data and predicts DNA methylation. The overall framework is shown in Fig. 1.

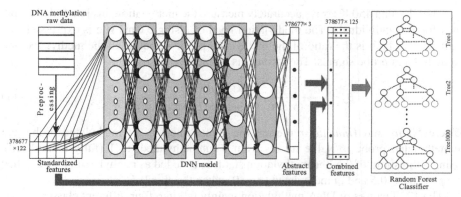

Fig. 1. DNA methylation prediction using a deep neural network and random forest model: DNN as the feature extractor, and random forest as the classifier.

2.1 Overall Framework

The process of DNA methylation prediction is regard as the supervised learning [19]. The first step is to preprocess the raw DNA methylation data; in this step, the raw dataset of DNA methylation is converted into the standardized data that are more conducive for DNN model to extract features. The standardized data are input to the next step, that is, the feature extraction with a DNN. It consists of an input layer, four hidden layers and an output layer. Each hidden layer contains a fully connected layer and an activation function. The features are extracted in the full connected layer and then the extracted features are transformed nonlinearly by the activation function tanh and fed into the next fully connected layer. The features extracting from the deep learning model have strong generalization ability, and can be combined with the raw features to further improve the prediction performance. Previous studies [20] showed that integration of abstract features and raw features could make the model yield better performance. Therefore, we will combine the abstract features with the standardized features to train the RF model for classification of DNA methylation status.

In order to optimize the parameters and verify the generalization ability of the model, 378677 DNA methylation samples were divided into training and testing datasets, in which the training set accounted for 80% of all samples, the testing set accounted for 20% of all samples, then 10% of samples of the training set were randomly selected as validation set.

2.2 Dataset

In this paper, we collected high-throughput DNA methylation microarray data as Zhang et al. [21]. It was measured from 100 unrelated human participants in the TwinsUK cohort (GEO: GSE62992) [22], using HumanMethylation450 array (Illumina 450 K). The 100 volunteers contained 97 female and 3 male participants (age range 27 to 78) [23].

The Illumina 450 K arrays accurately measure the methylation level of 482421 CpG sites for 100 individuals. The methylation level of a single CpG site is expressed as a variable β, which is the ratio of the methylated probe signal to all the methylated and unmethylated probe signals. The formula is defined as:

$$\beta = \frac{\max(Methy, 0)}{\max(Methy, 0) + \max(Unmethy, 0) + \alpha} \tag{1}$$

Where *Methy* and *Unmethy* represent the signal intensity of methylated probe and unmethylated probe. β value ranges from 0 (unmethylated) to 1 (fully methylated). Using a threshold of 0.5, the methylation status is encoded as methylated ($\tau = 1$) when the β value ≥ 0.5 and unmethylated ($\tau = 0$) when the $\beta < 0.5$.

The 122 features of DNA methylation mainly fall into four different classes:

(1) Neighbors: Neighboring CpG site features include genomic distances, binary methylation status of one upstream and one downstream neighboring CpG site.
(2) Genomic position: including promoters, gene body, intergenic region, CGIs, CGI shores and shelves, and so on.
(3) DNA sequence properties: GC content, integrated haplotype scores (iHSs), recombination rate and genomic evolutionary rate profiling (GERP).
(4) Cis-regulatiory elements: CREs, DHS, TFBSs and so on.

We acquired the neighbor features from the Methylation 450 K Array and the position features from the Methylation 450 K Annotation file. For the DNA sequence properties, we acquired recombination rate data from HapMap [24] and GC content data from the raw data that were used to encode the gc5Base track on hg19 from the UCSC Genome Browser. We downloaded iHSs data from the HGDP selection browser iHS data of smoothed Americas [25] and downloaded GERP data from SidowLab GERP++ tracks on hg19. With regard to the CRE features, we acquired DHS data from the DNase-seq data of GM12878 cell line (UCSC accession [wgEncode: EH000534]) and acquired Chromatin immunoprecipitation sequencing data for 79 specific TFBSs from the GM12878 cell line.

We collected ten histone modifications in the peak files from the GM12878 cell line at the ENCODE website and obtained 15 chromatin status from the Broad ChromHMM data from the GM12878 cell line (UCSC accession [wgEncode: EH000033]).

2.3 Preprocessing

The main purpose of data preprocessing is to remove GpG sites with poor quality from DNA methylation dataset. We removed CpG sites with missing values and CpG sites overlapped with SNPs. The CpG sites on X and Y chromosome were further excluded since the genome-wide DNA methylation was only predicted on autosome in this study. After preprocessing DNA methylation data, the total number of CpG site with complete informationis is 378677. The format of DNA methylation data is a 2-D matrix, in which each row contains 378677 CpG sites and each column includes 122 feature values corresponding to each CpG site. Furthermore, each column feature values across the whole CpG sites were standardized to ensure the same scale for training the model. The standardized formula is defined as:

$$x' = \frac{x - \overline{X}}{S} \tag{2}$$

Where the $\overline{X}$ and S refer to the mean and standard deviation of each column feature values, respectively.

2.4 Feature Extraction with DNN

DNN is the extension of artificial neural network and it is an effective method for extracting important and non-linear features by utilizing the multi-layer structure. The two adjacent layers of DNN structure are considered as a restricted boltzmann machine (RBM) [26].

RBM consists of a visible layer and a hidden layer [27], in which the neurons are connected undirectionally. RBM model can represent any probability distribution by using general distribution model on the basis of energy [28]. Its structure is shown in Fig. 2.

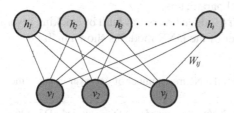

Fig. 2. RBM model structure.

The energy function of RBM is defined as follows:

$$E(v, h) = -\sum_{i=1}^{V}\sum_{j=1}^{H} v_i h_j w_{ij} - \sum_{i=1}^{V} v_i a_i^v - \sum_{j=1}^{H} h_j b_j^h \tag{3}$$

Where v represents the visible unit and v_i represents the ith visible unit status, and h represents the hidden unit, h_j refers to the jth neuron status of hidden layer, w_{ij} refers to the connection weight between ith neuron and jth neuron, and a, b are the visible and hidden biases, respectively. After the parameters are determined, the joint probability distribution of (v, h) is obtained by the energy function, defined as follow,

$$p(v, h) = \frac{e^{-E(v,h)}}{\sum_u \sum_g e^{-E(v,g)}} \tag{4}$$

Where u and g denote the probability status of neuron in all visible layers and all hidden layers, respectively. Marginal probability distribution and conditional probability distribution can be derived from the joint probability distribution, as shown from (5) to (8),

$$p(v) = \frac{\sum_h e^{-E(v,h)}}{\sum_{v,h} e^{-E(v,h)}} \tag{5}$$

$$p(h) = \frac{\sum_v e^{-E(v,h)}}{\sum_{v,h} e^{-E(v,h)}} \tag{6}$$

$$p(v|h) = \frac{e^{-E(v,h)}}{\sum_v e^{-E(v,h)}} \tag{7}$$

$$p(h|v) = \frac{e^{-E(v,h)}}{\sum_h e^{-E(v,h)}} \tag{8}$$

Firstly, we calculated the logarithm of probability $p(v)$ for status v, and then the weight w_{ij} was differentiated to obtain the update formula w_{ij} between visual layer and hidden layer, as shown in (9).

$$\Delta wij = \varepsilon(<v_ih_j>\text{data} - <v_ih_j>\text{model}) \tag{9}$$

Where $<v_ih_j>$data represents the statistical average of real data distribution, $<v_ih_j>$model represents the statistical average of model, and ε represents the learning rate for updating model parameters.

A DNN model with 4 hidden layers was built by stacking several RBMs. The number of neurons in each layer of the DNN model is shown in Table 1.

Table 1. Neuron number of per layer in DNN model.

Network layer	I1	D2	D3	D4	D5	O6
Neuron	122	51	26	10	5	3

In order to bring the advantage of DNN structure into play, the precondition is that we should ensure the network parameters are optimized after determining DNN structure.

The effectiveness and efficiency of the network model are largely determined by the activation function. The activation function tanh is good at feature mapping with a large signal gain in the middle region and an inhibition at both ends. So tanh was applied to the nonlinear transform of sample data in DNN, defined as follow,

$$\tanh = f(z) = \frac{e^z - e^{(-z)}}{e^z + e^{(-z)}} \tag{10}$$

Where z represents a combination of input signals.

After determining the structure and main parameters of the model, we used standardized training dataset to train the network model and updated the weight parameters of network through multiple iterations. Furthermore, the validation dataset was input into the updated model to verify the prediction accuracy. When the prediction accuracy of the validation dataset was no longer improved, that is to say, the whole DNN model was fitted at this time. And then the most representative abstract features of training dataset were output. Similarly, we input the testing dataset into the trained DNN model to generate the most representative abstract features of testing dataset.

2.5 RF Classifier

In the paper, our method can automatically extract the highly representative features by using a DNN model. In most existing studies, the DNN is used to extract features and simultaneously make a final prediction. In this investigation, the RF model was applied to predict DNA methylation status instead of DNN model. RF classifier is an ensemble model that contains a collection of decision trees and produces a single prediction by combining the predictions from all the trees. The output of RF model is determined by the proportion of trees in the fitted forest. So it overcomes the overfitting by utilizing the average of all tree predictions [29]. Since the RF classifier's parameter settings (including the number of trees) are robust, most of the parameters in the RF model were kept as default. The n-tree was set to 1,000 to balance efficiency and accuracy in high-dimensional data. In addition, the cutoff 0.5 was utilized as threshold to classify the methylation status of each CpG site.

The deep learning model has a strong ability to quickly generalize features. Therefore, we proposed to combine the abstract features with the standardized features to enhance the prediction accuracy. Initially, the DNN was applied to extract the abstract features. Then the RF model was applied to predict DNA methylation using the abstract features and the standardized features.

2.6 Evaluation Methods

In the process of designing DNA methylation prediction model, the selection of performance metric is very important for optimizing the model. As the same as most binary classification problems, each CpG site may be judged as one of the following four indices: true positive (TP), false positive (FP), false negative (FN), true negative (TN).

We quantified the above four indices using following classifier performance metrics:

Accuracy (ACC) measures the proportion of correct predictions. The formula is shown in (11).

Sensitivity (SE) represents the proportion of judging the correctness of the positive samples. The formula is shown in (12).

Specificity (SP) refers to the proportion of judging the correctness of the negative sample. The formula is shown in (13).

$$ACC = \frac{TP + TN}{TP + TN + FN + FP} \tag{11}$$

$$SE = \frac{TP}{TP + FN} \tag{12}$$

$$SP = \frac{TN}{TN + FP} \tag{13}$$

Area under curve (AUC) is an area under the receiver operating characteristic (ROC) curve. The ROC curve is drawn with the true positive fraction (SE) versus the false positive fraction (1-SP) by altering the model's positive cut off. The larger AUC represents that model has a better classification performance.

The deep-learning-based framework was implemented by PYTHON 2.7 in a PC with a 3.4 GHZ CPU (Core i7), 8 GB memory.

3   Experimental Results and Discussions

The performance of the deep learning framework proposed in the paper was evaluated by the experiment on high-throughput data. We used the DNN model to extract the abstract features from the standardized features. The abstract features could be directly used to train RF model or combined with the standardized features to train RF model.

In this paper, the standardized training set and testing set were respectively input into the DNN model to obtain the abstract features of training set and testing set which can well reflect the characteristic information of DNA methylation data. Then the RF model was trained by the abstract features of training set, and the prediction accuracy of the method was verified by the abstract features of testing set.We compared the prediction performance using each kind of feature of DNA methylation and their combinations. The compared results were showed in Table 2.

Table 2. Prediction results of different feature sets.

Feature set	ACC(%)	AUC
Gene_pos	78.60	0.8444
Gene_pos + seq_property	79.42	0.8555
Gene_pos + seq_property + TFBS	85.69	0.9156
Gene_pos + seq_property + CRES	88.78	0.9399
Neighbors	90.70	0.9406
Abstract features	91.11	0.9572

Table 2 represents the prediction results obtained by using different feature combinations to train the RF model. As shown in Table 2, the ACC and AUC of abstract features are much higher than other feature combinations. It can be concluded that we can better predict DNA methylation using abstract features. It also suggests that the DNN can automatically learn the feature representations that reflect the more essential data structure properties of DNA methylation through the layer by layer feature extraction.

To improve the prediction accuracy, we further combined both the abstract features and the standardized features to train the RF model, which was compared with the raw features in Zhang's paper [21]. Figure 3 shows the comparison of AUC curves for the two methods. In Fig. 3, the red line represents the AUC curve obtained by integrating the abstract features together with standardized features, and the blue line indicates the AUC curve obtained by using raw features.

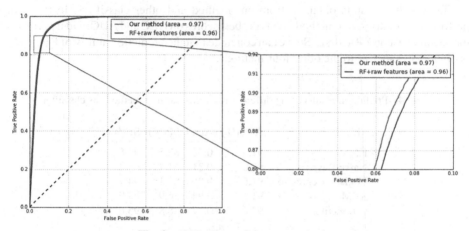

Fig. 3. AUC values of the two methods.

As shown in Fig. 3, our method achieves better prediction performance than the existing RF method in Zhang's paper [21]. The figure suggests that the abstract features combined with the standardized features could help the proposed method capture more comprehensive information, thus improved prediction accuracy of DNA methylation.

Next, we compared our method using abstract features and standardized features with other four traditional machine-learning methods only performing on raw features, including k-Nearest Neighbor (KNN), Naive Bayes, Logistic Regression and SVM. The prediction results were summarized in Table 3.

Table 3 summarizes the prediction results of different models, we observe that our method gains higher ACC, SP and AUC scores over other methods. Among these metrics, SP of our method is obviously higher than other methods. So, it can be concluded that our method can better express the structural characteristics of DNA methylation and suggests a relatively accurate prediction result.

In order to evaluate the prediction capability of the RF classifier more comprehensively, we compared our method with SVM, KNN, Naive Bayes and Logistic Regression

Table 3. Prediction results of different models.

Model	ACC(%)	AUC	SP(%)	SE(%)
KNN	73.2	0.80	72.6	73.7
Naïve Bayes	80.8	0.91	64.4	94.2
Logistic Regression	91.1	0.96	87.3	94.1
SVM	91.3	0.96	86.6	95.1
RF	91.8	0.96	87.9	95.1
Our method	92.2	0.97	88.8	95.0

to predict the DNA methylation based on abstract features and standardized features as input.

Table 4 lists results obtained from our method and other classifiers. In terms of performance metrics, our method yields the best scores on ACC and AUC, and it performs the second best on SP and SE. So we can conclude that the prediction ability of RF model is obviously superior to the other four methods.

Table 4. Prediction results using different machine-learning methods as classifier.

Model	ACC(%)	AUC	SP(%)	SE(%)
KNN	91.5	0.96	87.5	94.8
Naïve Bayes	80.0	0.81	61.7	95.2
Logistic Regression	91.6	0.96	89.1	94.7
SVM	91.3	0.94	86.9	94.9
Our method	92.2	0.97	88.8	95.0

To validate the performance of our method, we also compared our method with the existing deep learning models that include CpGenie [15], DeepCpG [11] and MHCpG [13]. The proposed method and the other three deep learning approaches were performed on our dataset. As shown in Fig. 4, our method achieved the best prediction results compared to CpGenie, MHCpG and DeepCpG. Therefore, our method is better than other existing methods.

Distinct with the existing deep learning methods for predicting DNA methylation at single-CpG-site resolution, our method used the high-throughput microarray data as model input, and incorporated a diverse set of predictive features. Furthermore, we utilized the RF model as a classifier instead of the fully connected layer, which avoided the overfitting problem, thus producing more reliable and accurate results.

This paper proposed a deep-learning-based framework to predict DNA methylation. From the experiment results, our method outperforms the state-of-the-art prediction approaches. Although our study has made some improvements in predicting DNA methylation, there are still some defects. For example, the number of features used for DNA methylation prediction is not very large, which leads to DNN model may only

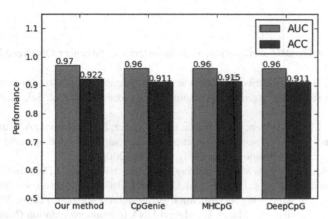

Fig. 4. The prediction results of our method and other existing deep learning methods with our dataset.

learn a limited number of information. Subsequently we will collect more methylation features to enhance the prediction accuracy.

4 Conclusion

DNA methylation is associated with occurrence and development of various diseases, so it is of great significance to diagnose the stage or grade of disease by detecting DNA methylation. In this study, we developed a deep-learning-based framework to predict DNA methylation. Firstly, we compared the prediction results using different feature combinations. We found that the prediction accuracy using the abstract features is better than those using traditional feature combinations. Next, we compared our method using abstract features and standardized features with the existing machine-learning models. The results suggest that combining abstract features with the standardized features can better express the structural characteristics of DNA methylation. Then we applied SVM, KNN, Naive Bayes and Logistic Regression classifier to predict DNA methylation based on abstract features and standardized features. Experimental results show that RF classifier achieves better prediction accuracy than other classifiers. Finally, we compared our method with CpGenie, MHCpG and DeepCpG models. From the result, we found that our method obtained the best performance over other deep learning models. In the future, we will collect more feature information to improve the prediction performance of DNA methylation.

Availability of Data and Materials. The PYTHON source code and data that accompany this paper are available at (https://github.com/lab319/Predicting_methylation_s tatus).

Acknowledgment. This work was supported by the Dalian Science and Technology Innovation Fund (2020JJ27SN066).

References

1. Robertson, K.D.: DNA methylation, methyltransferases, and cancer. Oncogene **20**(24), 3139–3155 (2001)
2. Mehta, A., et al.: Validation of tuba1a as appropriate internal control for normalization of gene expression analysis during mouse lung development. Int. J. Mol. Sci. **16**(3), 4492–4511 (2015)
3. Bianco, T., Chenevix-Trench, G., Walsh, D.C., Cooper, J.E., Dobrovic, A.: Tumour-specific distribution of BRCA1 promoter region methylation supports a pathogenetic role in breast and ovarian cancer. Carcinogenesis **21**(2), 147–151 (2000)
4. Crary-Dooley, F.K., Tam, M.E., Dunaway, K.W., Hertz-Picciotto, I., Schmidt, R.J., LaSalle, J.M.: A comparison of existing global DNA methylation assays to low-coverage whole-genome bisulfite sequencing for epidemiological studies. Epigenetics **12**(3), 206–214 (2017)
5. Jacinto, F.V., Esteban, B., Manel, E.: Methyl-DNA immunoprecipitation (MeDIP): hunting down the DNA methylome. Biotechniques **44**(1), 35–43 (2008)
6. Peat, J.R., Dean, W., Clark, S.J., Krueger, F., Reik, W.: Genome-wide bisulfite sequencing in zygotes identifies demethylation targets and maps the contribution of TET3 oxidation. Cell Rep. **9**(6), 1990–2000 (2014)
7. Jianlin, H., Ming-An, S., Zhong, W., Qianfei, W., Qing, L., Hehuang, X.: Characterization and machine learning prediction of allele-specific DNA methylation. Genomics **106**(6), 331–339 (2015)
8. Baoshan, M., et al.: Predicting DNA methylation level across human tissues. Nucleic Acids Res. **42**(6), 3515–3528 (2014)
9. Ma, B., et al.: Locus-specific DNA methylation prediction in cord blood and placenta. Epigenetics **14**(4), 405–420 (2019)
10. Wong, N.C., Pope, B.J., Candiloro, I.L., Korbie, D., Trau, M., Wong, S.Q., et al.: MethPat: a tool for the analysis and visualisation of complex methylation patterns obtained by massively parallel sequencing. BMC Bioinf. **17**(1), 98 (2016)
11. Angermueller, C., Lee, H.J., Reik, W., Stegle, O.: Erratum to: DeepCpG: accurate prediction of single-cell DNA methylation states using deep learning. Genome Biol. **18**(1), 90–90 (2017)
12. Korfiatis, P., Kline, T.L., Lachance, D.H., Parney, I.F., Buckner, J.C., Erickson, B.J.: Residual deep convolutional neural network predicts MGMT methylation status. J. Digit. Imaging **30**(5), 622–628 (2017)
13. Fu, L., Peng, Q., Chai, L.: Predicting DNA methylation states with hybrid information based deep-learning model. IEEE/ACM Trans. Comput. Biol. Bioinf. **17**, 1721–1728 (2019)
14. Wang, Y., Liu, T., Xu, D., Shi, H., Zhang, C., Mo, Y.-Y., et al.: Predicting DNA methylation state of CpG Dinucleotide using genome topological features and deep networks. Sci. Rep. **6**(1), 19598 (2016)
15. Zeng, H., Gifford, D.K.: Predicting the impact of non-coding variants on DNA methylation. Nucleic Acids Res. **45**(11), e99 (2017)
16. Bengio, Y.: Deep learning of representations for unsupervised and transfer learning, J. Mach. Learn. Res **27**, 17–37 (2012)
17. Ni, P., et al.: DeepSignal: detecting DNA methylation state from Nanopore sequencing reads using deep-learning. Bioinformatics **35**(22), 4586–4595 (2019)
18. Tian, Q., Zou, J., et al.: MRCNN: a deep learning model for regression of genome-wide DNA methylation. BMC Genomics **20**(2), (2019)
19. Model, F., Adorjan, P., Olek, A., Piepenbrock, C.: Feature selection for DNA methylation based cancer classification. Bioinformatics **17**, 157–164 (2001)

20. Prasoon, A., Petersen, K., Igel, C., Lauze, F., Dam, E., Nielsen, M.: Deep feature learning for knee cartilage segmentation using a triplanar convolutional neural network. In: Mori, K., Sakuma, I., Sato, Y., Barillot, C., Navab, N. (eds.) MICCAI 2013. LNCS, vol. 8150, pp. 246–253. Springer, Heidelberg (2013). https://doi.org/10.1007/978-3-642-40763-5_31

21. Zhang, W., Spector, T.D., Deloukas, P., Bell, J.T., Engelhardt, B.E.: Predicting genome-wide DNA methylation using methylation marks, genomic position, and DNA regulatory elements. Genome Biol. **16**(1), 14 (2015)

22. Alireza, M., Hammond, C.J., Valdes, A.M., Spector, T.D.: Cohort profile: TwinsUK and healthy ageing twin study. Int. J. Epidemiol. **42**(1), 76–85 (2013)

23. Bibikova, M., Barnes, B., Chan, T., Ho, V., Klotzle, B., Le, J.M., et al.: High density DNA methylation array with single CpG site resolution. Genomics **98**(4), 288–295 (2011)

24. Belmont, J.W., Boudreau, A., Leal, S.M., et al.: A haplotype map of the human genome. Nature **437**(7063), 1299–1320 (2005)

25. Gross, L.: Clues to our past: mining the human genome for signs of recent selection. PLOS Biol. **4**(3), e94 (2006)

26. Si, Z., Yu, H., Ma, Z.: Learning deep features for DNA methylation data analysis. IEEE Access **4**, 2732–2737 (2016)

27. Lu, N., Li, T., Ren, X., Miao, H.: A deep learning scheme for motor imagery classification based on restricted boltzmann machines. IEEE Trans. Neural Syst. Rehabil. Eng. **25**(6), 566–576 (2016)

28. Manukian, H., Pei, Y.R., Bearden, S.R.B., et al.: Mode-assisted unsupervised learning of restricted Boltzmann machines. Commun. Phys. **3**(105) (2020)

29. Zhu, X., Du, X., Kerich, M., Lohoff, F.W., Momenan, R.: Random forest based classification of alcohol dependence patients and healthy controls using resting state MRI. Neurosci. Lett. **676**, 27–33 (2018)

Pulse Recognition of Cardiovascular Disease Patients Based on One-Dimensional Convolutional Neural Network

Yi Jiao[1], Nan Li[1], Xiaobo Mao[1], Guoliang Yao[1], Yuping Zhao[2], and Luqi Huang[2(✉)]

[1] School of Electrical Engineering, Zhengzhou University, Zhengzhou 450001, China
[2] China Academy of Chinese Medical Sciences, Beijing 100020, China

Abstract. In the clinical diagnosis and treatment of traditional Chinese medicine (TCM), The classification of pulse is an important diagnostic method. The pulse signal of patients with cardiovascular disease is quite different from that of normal people. In pulse classification, traditional methods generally need to manually extract feature information of the time domain and frequency domain, and then perform pulse classification through machine learning methods such as KNN and SVM. However, the manually extracted features may not really represent the true features of the signal. Convolutional neural network (CNN) can automatically extract local features through different convolution kernels, and it can extract the original features of the signal very well. This paper designs a one-dimensional convolution (1D-CNN) residual neural network structure to identify the pulse signal. First, the original data is sliced and normalized, and then the data set is divided into training set and test set, Then take the processed pulse signal directly as input. This allows the computer to perform feature self-learning through the network structure, Finally, it is classified through the fully connected layer. The final classification accuracy rate can reach 97.14%, which is better than traditional machine learning classification methods such as SVM and KNN, It provides new ideas and methods for the classification and objectification of pulse signals.

Keywords: Deep learning · Pulse recognition · 1D-CNN · Residual network structure

1 Introduction

Pulse diagnosis is very important in traditional Chinese medicine. Most researches focus on obtaining objective evidence of Chinese medicine. Pulse diagnosis analysis is an important objective method of traditional Chinese medicine [1]. Early research found that pulse signal can reflect some symptoms of hypertensive

---

Supported by key project at central government level (2060302).

patients. Research found that pulse signal can reflect some symptoms of hypertensive patients. This proves that the pulse condition can be used to predict whether a person suffers from hypertension, which shows that hypertension has a very important relationship with pulse signal. In the theory of traditional Chinese medicine, it is believed that the pulse of most patients with cardiovascular disease is relatively weak [3–5]. It is possible to classify and identify the pulse of patients with cardiovascular disease and the pulse of normal people to achieve the prediction of cardiovascular disease and carry out early intervention treatment.

In the traditional pulse classification methods, most scholars use artificial definition of features, Then use traditional machine learning classification methods such as KNN and SVM to conduct pulse recognition research, However, there is a relatively complex non-linear mapping relationship between the pulse category and the pulse characteristics, and it is difficult to find a suitable characteristic data set for pulse recognition. In recent years, convolutional neural networks have developed rapidly due to their ability to automatically extract features, If there are enough data sets and labels, convolutional neural network (CNN) has a very excellent performance one-dimensional convolutional neural network (1D-CNN) can process time series signals very well, and has good performance in fault detection and other fields. Since 1D-CNN only performs scalar multiplication and addition, 1D-CNN has very good real-time performance and low hardware requirements [6]. This paper proposes a 1D-CNN-based pulse recognition network structure, which is implemented by the deep learning framework Pytorch. The overall research block diagram is shown in Fig. 1.

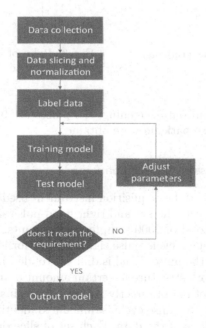

Fig. 1. The overall framework of the system.

2   Pulse Data Collection and Processing

2.1   Pulse Data Collection

In the traditional Chinese medicine theory, the collection and analysis of pulse signal are generally divided into three different positions: Cun, Guan and Chi. The Guan pulse signal is the position with the strongest signal among the three positions, and the influence of the Guan pulse signal by the noise signal is relatively small. And the signal is also the easiest to observe and obtain. Therefore, in order to ensure the stability and reliability of the pulse data, The data collected in this article are all signals at the Guan position, and the collection equipment used is ZM-300, and the collection frequency of the pulse diagnosis instrument 200 Hz. The pulse signal collection objects are the students of Zhengzhou University and the patients with cardiovascular disease in the Affiliated Hospital of Zhengzhou University. The pulse signal of patients suffering from cardiovascular disease is generally weak. In traditional Chinese medicine theory, this kind of pulse signal is generally called Xuan mai. The pulse conditions of college students and those of cardiovascular patients are shown in Fig. 2 and Fig. 3.

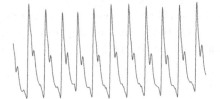   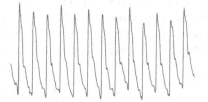

Fig. 2. Pulse of college students.   **Fig. 3.** Pulse of a patients with cardiovascular disease.

After data collection and data screening, the pulses of 60 college students and 54 cardiovascular disease patients were obtained.

2.2   Data Preprocessing and Expansion

The sampling frequency of the acquisition instrument used in this article 200 Hz, and each individual collects the left and right hand pulse signal. Each signal has a length of 10 s and a total of 2000 sampling data points. For pulse signal classification, generally a single cycle pulse signal is used for identification research, However, the period of the pulse signal is difficult to identify and determine. For the deep learning network structure, a certain amount of data set is required, so this article adopts a method of directly slicing the original data, This not only solves the problem that the pulse cycle is difficult to identify, but also maintains the original characteristics of the data, Each set of slice data basically contains three pulse cycle signals [8], and the acquisition time is set to 3.2 s. Because the data samples are too less, the overlapped part can be appropriately increased during the data slicing process. Since the patient's sample data is lower than the university student's sample data, in order to ensure the consistency of the data, the repetition rate of the patient's signal during the sectioning process is slightly higher. This expanded data is more conducive to the training of deep learning networks, The process of data processing is shown in Fig. 4.

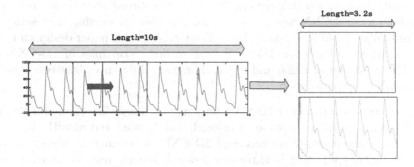

Fig. 4. The process of data slice processing.

After slicing the data, there are a total of 500 sample data. The pulse data of students and cardiovascular disease patients are shown in Table 1.

Table 1. Data type and quantity after slicing operation.

Pulse type	College students	Cardiovascular disease patients
Quantity	250	250

Finally, normalize the sliced data, which is more conducive to the computer training network. And it is necessary to label the processed data, using 0 and 1 to represent normal college students and patients with cardiovascular disease. The pulse data processed in this way can be directly used as the original input of the network structure. The network is trained through the training set and the classification accuracy of the network is verified on the test set.

3 Neural Network Structure of Pulse Classification

3.1 The Difference Between 1D-CNN and 2D-CNN

With the rapid improvement of computer hardware and computing power, deep convolutional neural networks such as "AlexNet" and "GogleNet" appeared, these convolutional neural networks have excellent performance on public data sets. Convolutional neural networks can automatically extract features, while traditional machine learning methods are to manually define features, these manually defined features are sub-optimal, Convolutional neural networks can extract optimized features from the original data to obtain high Accuracy [6]. However, most of the above network structures are for processing two-dimensional signals, and these neural network structures cannot be directly used to process one-dimensional time series signals. To solve this problem, Kiranyaz et al. in 2015 proposed the first compact adaptive 1D-CNN that can directly manipulate patient-specific ECG data. Pranav Rajpurkar [9] developed an algorithm that surpasses cardiologists in detecting widespread arrhythmia using electrocardiogram. 1D-CNN has a great advantage when processing time series signals, and pulse signal is a typical time series signal, so this paper designs a neural network structure based on 1D-CNN. The working principles of 1D-CNN and 2D-CNN are shown in Fig. 5 and Fig. 6. The main differences between 1D-CNN and 2D-CNN are as follows:

- The convolution kernel of 1D-CNN only moves in one direction, and the data of input and output are two-dimensional, mainly used to deal with time series problems; the convolution kernel of 2D-CNN moves in two directions, both input and output data Is three-dimensional, mainly used to process image signals
- 1D-CNN generally uses a lower network depth than the 2D-CNN network structure, and fewer parameters need to be learned during the training process, making it easier to obtain training results
- 1D-CNN usually only uses the computer's CPU to run, while 2D-CNN usually requires a special GPU for accelerated calculations. Compared with 2D-CNN, 1D-CNN has better real-time performance and lower hardware Equipment requirements.

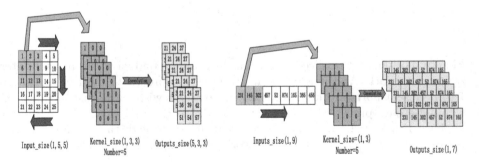

Fig. 5. The working principle of 2D-CNN.   **Fig. 6.** The working principle of 1D-CNN.

3.2   Network Structure

In convolutional neural networks, it is not purely increasing the depth of the network to increase the accuracy of prediction. In the process of training the network, it is necessary to use the backpropagation algorithm to continuously pass the gradient to the front network. When the gradient is passed to the front network, the gradient value will be very small, so that the weight value of the front network cannot be effectively adjusted. In order to avoid the problem of gradient disappearance, a residual network structure is added to the hidden layers. The residual network structure connects the input directly to the output part, so that the learning target can be changed to the difference between the desired output H(x) and the input x [10] The network structure is mainly composed of one-dimensional convolution layer, activation function layer, batch normalization layer, dropout layer, and residual block. The specific network structure diagram is shown in Fig. 7.

Input Layer: It directly converts the sliced signal into a two-dimensional signal as input. The two-dimensional signal represents the number of channels and the length of the signal. The signal dimension of the input layer is 1 * 640 in this article, where 1 represents only one input channel, and 640 represents the length of the signal. The specific structure diagram is shown in Fig. 8.

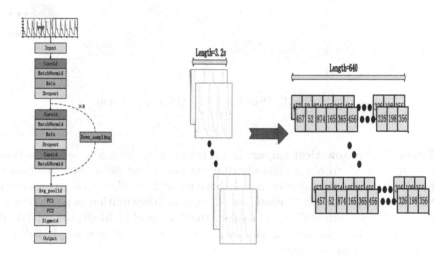

Fig. 7. Block diagram of neural network.

Fig. 8. Structure diagram of the input layer.

Convolutional Layer: The convolutional layer is the most important layer in the neural network. The core part of the convolutional layer is the convolution kernel. Various local features of the original signal can be extracted through convolution kernels. The convolution kernel has two attributes of size And the number, The size and number of the convolution kernel are manually specified, and these weight values of convolution kernels are constantly adjusted during the training process, so that the convolution kernel can learn the optimal weight value. Convolution operation also has the advantages of local connection and weight sharing, The number of parameters is only related to the size and number of the convolution kernel and the number of channels of the input signal. The calculation method of the size of the output signal is shown in formula 1:

$$L = (L_1 - F + 2 * P)/S + 1 \qquad (1)$$

L represents the length of the output signal; L1 represents the length of the input signal; F represents the length of the convolution kernel, P represents the number of zero padding at the end, and S represents the step length of the convolution kernel.

As shown in Fig. 9, the size of the convolution kernel is 1 * 3, where the value [0.1, 0] in the convolution kernel represents the weight value of the convolution kernel. During the training process, the convolution kernel will be adjusted continuously. The weight value will finally get an optimal model.

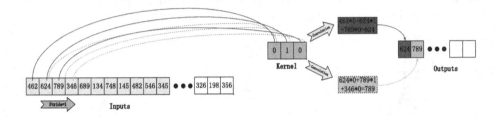

Fig. 9. Principle of 1D-CNN calculation.

Batch Normalization Layer: In deep learning, the main task is to train the neural network to obtain the distribution law of the data. The function of the batch normalization layer is to distribute the data as close to the origin as possible, make the data distribution meet the normal distribution as much as possible, reduce the absolute difference between the data, and highlight the relative difference of the data, so as to accelerate the training of the network, It will perform well in classification tasks.

Activation Function Layer: There is a complex nonlinear mapping relationship between the input and output of the network. If only linear multiplication of the matrix or array is used, then the deep network Will become meaningless, In order to map the nonlinear relationship between input and output, an activation function layer is generally added after the convolutional layer. Commonly used activation functions are sigmoid and Relu.

Pooling Layer: The pooling layer is mainly to maintain the invariance of signal characteristics, improve the robustness of signal characteristics, while reducing the number of parameters and reducing the amount of calculation, which can effectively prevent overfitting, while the pooling layer is generally Including maximum pooling and average pooling, etc. The principle of average pooling is shown in Fig. 10.

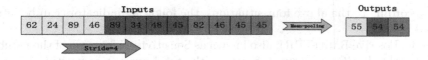

Fig. 10. Principle of average pooling.

Fully Connected Layer: A series of detailed features of the signal will be extracted from the front convolutional layer and pooling layer, and the function of the fully connected layer is to combine these detailed features to determine whether it is a feature of a signal. The number of neurons in the last layer is the number of classified categories.

4   The Results and Analysis of the Experiment

4.1   Prepare the Data Set

The original pulse data was screened, and a total of 114 data samples were obtained, Data labels are marked by experts from China Academy of Chinese Medical Sciences. Divide the sliced data set into two parts: test set and training set. In order to ensure that the trained model has sufficient generalization ability, the sample of training set and the test set are completely independent, and the distribution of the training set and the test set is shown in Table 2.

Table 2. Allocation table of training set and test set.

Label of sample	Training set	Test set
College students	180	70
Cardiovascular disease patients	180	70
Total	360	140

4.2   Analysis of Results

In the classification model, the test set will be divided into two types, positive and negative, which will produce the following four situations respectively [11]:

- True Positive (TP): The true label of the sample is positive, and the model predicts that the label of the sample is positive
- False Negative (FN): The true label of the sample is positive, but the model predicts that the sample label is negative
- False Positive (FP): The true label of the sample is negative, but the model predicts that the sample label is positive
- True Negative (TN): The true label of the sample is negative, and the model predicts that the label w of the sample is negative

According to the above four situations, the following indicators can be introduced:

True Positive Rate (TPR), also known as Sensitivity: The ratio of the number of correctly classified positive samples to the total number of positive samples: as shown in formula (2):

$$TPR = \frac{TP}{TP + FN} \tag{2}$$

True Negative Rate (TNR): the ratio of the number of correctly classified negative samples to the number of negative samples, as shown in formula (3)

$$TNR = \frac{TN}{FP + TN} \tag{3}$$

Accuracy: the proportion of the number of correctly classified samples to the number of all samples [11], as shown in formula (4)

$$accuracy = \frac{TP + TN}{TP + FN + FP + TN} \tag{4}$$

Precision: The proportion of the number of correctly classified positive samples to the number of positive samples in the classifier, as shown in formula (5)

$$precision = \frac{TP}{TP + FP} \tag{5}$$

F1-Score: the harmonic average of precision rate and recall rate, the calculation method is shown in formula (6)

$$F1 = \frac{2 * precision * recall}{precision + recall} \tag{6}$$

The cross entropy function is selected as the loss function in the training process, and the optimization algorithm uses the batch gradient descent algorithm. The cross entropy function is shown in formula (7).

$$loss = -\frac{1}{N} \sum_{n=1}^{N} y_n \log \widehat{y}_n + (1 - y_n) \log(1 - \widehat{y}_n) \tag{7}$$

The indicators and parameters of the classifier are shown in Table 3.

The hardware platform used to train the neural network model is CPU i5-4210H@2.9 GHZ, the memory is 12G running memory, the operating system platform is Windows10, the deep learning framework based on Pytorch. The classification accuracy rate can reach about 97.14%. The loss function and accuracy rate of the training set and test set are shown in Fig. 11. The ROC curve describes the relationship between the True Positive Rate (TPR) and the False Positive Rate (FPR) of the classifier [12]. The ROC curve of the classifier designed in this paper is shown in Fig. 12.

Table 3. Indicators and parameters of the classifier.

The name of each evaluation index	Parameter values of evaluation index
TPR	0.9851
TNR	0.9571
Accuracy	0.9714
Precision	0.9583
F1-score	0.9715

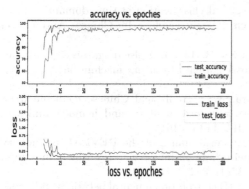

Fig. 11. The change curve of the accuracy rate and the loss function of the training set and the test set.

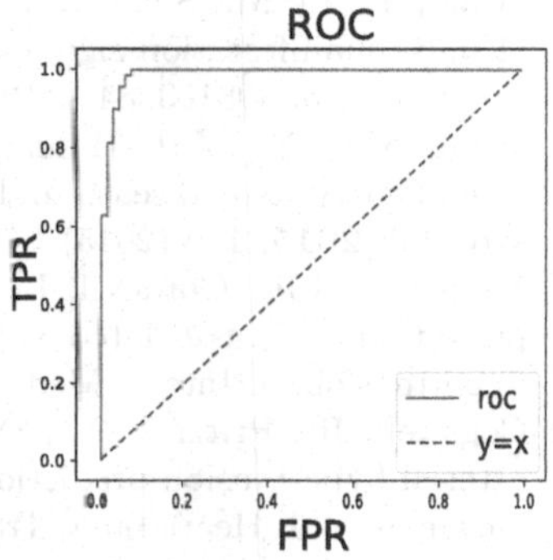

Fig. 12. Curve of ROC.

Compared with the traditional manual definition of features, and finally classification with machine learning methods[7], The accuracy of traditional classification methods such as SVM and KNN is basically around 85% [2]. The one-dimensional convolutional neural network used in this paper can automatically identify features [13] and has a 97.14% accuracy rate. Compared with traditional methods, the neural network in this article has lower computational complexity and higher accuracy.

5   Conclusion

Pulse diagnosis occupies an important position in traditional Chinese medicine. The pulse signal can reflect the physical condition of the human body to a certain extent. In this paper, a 1D-CNN pulse classification is proposed by analyzing the pulse conditions of cardiovascular disease patients and normal people. In the test set, a classification accuracy rate of 97.14% is achieved, which proves that the pulse signal has a certain relationship with cardiovascular disease, and has certain practical value for future clinical diagnosis of Chinese medicine. However, because the data samples in this article are not particularly large, the trained model may not have sufficient generalization ability. Therefore, the next step is to obtain as many data samples as possible to improve the generalization ability of the model.

References

1. Hu, X.J., Zhang, J.T., Xu, B.C., Liu, J., Wang, Y.: Pulse wave cycle features analysis of different blood pressure grades in the elderly. In: Evidence-Based Complementary and Alternative Medicine 2018, pp. 1–12 (2018)
2. Wang, Y., Li, M., Shang, Y.: Analysis and classification of time domain features of pulse manifestation signals between different genders. In: Chinese Automation Congress, pp. 3981–3984 (2019)
3. Wang, N.Y., Yu, Y.H., Huang, D.W., Xu, B., Liu, J.: Pulse diagnosis signals analysis of fatty liver disease and cirrhosis patients by using machine learning. Sci. World J. **2015**, 1–9 (2015)
4. Moura, N.G.R., Cordovil, I., Ferreira, A.S.: Traditional Chinese medicine wrist pulse-taking is associated with pulse waveform analysis and hemodynamics in hypertension. J. Integr. Med. **14**(2), 100–113 (2016)
5. Cogswell, R., Pritzker, M., De, M.T.: Performance of the REVEAL pulmonary arterial hypertension prediction model using non-invasive and routinely measured parameters. J. Heart Lung Transpl. **33**(4), 382–387 (2014)
6. Kiranyaz, S., Avci, O., Abdeljaber, O.: 1D convolutional neural networks and applications: a survey. arXiv preprint arXiv:1905.03554 (2019)
7. Zhang, D., Zuo, W., Wang, P.: Generalized feature extraction for wrist pulse analysis: from 1-D time series to 2-D matrix. In: Computational Pulse Signal Analysis, pp. 169–189. Springer, Singapore (2018). https://doi.org/10.1007/978-981-10-4044-3_9
8. Urtnasan, E., Park, J.-U., Joo, E.-Y., Lee, K.-J.: Automated detection of obstructive sleep apnea events from a single-lead electrocardiogram using a convolutional neural network. J. Med. Syst. **42**(6), 1–8 (2018). https://doi.org/10.1007/s10916-018-0963-0
9. Hannun, A.Y., Rajpurkar, P., Haghpanahi, M., Tison, G.H., Bourn, C.: Cardiologist-level arrhythmia detection and classification in ambulatory electrocardiograms using a deep neural network. Nat. Med. **25**(1), 65 (2019)
10. He, K., Zhang, X., Ren, S., Sun, J.: Deep residual learning for image recognition. In: Proceedings of the IEEE Conference on Computer Vision and Pattern Recognition 2016, pp. 770–778 (2016)
11. Kiranyaz, S., Zabihi, M., Rad, A.B., Ince, T., Hamila, R., Gabbouj, M.: Real-time phonocardiogram anomaly detection by adaptive 1D convolutional neural networks. Neurocomputing (2020)
12. Arji, G., Safdari, R., Rezaeizadeh, H., Abbassian, A., Mokhtaran, M., Ayati, M.H.: A systematic literature review and classification of knowledge discovery in traditional medicine. Comput. Methods Programs Biomed. **168**, 39–57 (2019)
13. Li, F., et al.: Feature extraction and classification of heart sound using 1D convolutional neural networks. EURASIP J. Adv. Signal Process. **2019**(1), 1–11 (2019). https://doi.org/10.1186/s13634-019-0651-3

Machine Learning Meets Big Data: An Overview of Diagnostic and Prognostic Prediction for Cancer

Baoshan Ma[1,2](✉), Bingjie Chai[1], Mingkun Fang[1], Jishuang Qi[1], Xiaoyu Hou[1], Xinyu Zhang[3], Zongjiang Gao[3], Fanyu Meng[1], and Fengju Song[4](✉)

[1] College of Information Science and Technology,
Dalian Maritime University, Dalian 116026, China
mabaoshan@dlmu.edu.cn

[2] Institute of Environmental Systems Biology, College of Environmental Science and Engineering, Dalian Maritime University, Dalian 116026, China

[3] Maritime Intelligent Transportation Research Group,
Dalian Maritime University, Dalian 116026, China

[4] Department of Epidemiology and Biostatistics, Key Laboratory of Cancer Prevention and Therapy, Tianjin, National Clinical Research Center of Cancer, Tianjin Medical University Cancer Institute and Hospital, Tianjin 300000, China
songfengju@tmu.edu.cn

Abstract. The past decades have witnessed the rapid development on biological technology and artificial intelligence (AI). Large amounts of omics data have been produced and accumulated by high-throughput sequencing technology. The accumulation of multi-omics data and the innovation of machine-learning provide a variety of resources for diagnostic and prognostic prediction of cancer, which efficiently enhance clinical decision making, improve prognosis, and accelerate the progress of precision medicine. In this review, first we reviewed the common omics data. Second, we briefly introduced several popular machine learning methods. Thirdly, we systematically summarized the substantial achievements obtained in a number of prediction studies of cancer, including breast cancer (BRCA), kidney renal clear cell carcinoma (KIRC), glioblastoma multiforme (GBM). Lastly, it is promising that the advanced AI technologies such as deep learning will be widely applied to facilitate diagnosis and treatment for cancer patients as massive omics data are efficiently and accurately measured.

Keywords: Machine learning · Multi-omics · Diagnostic prediction · Prognostic prediction · Precision Medicine

1 Introduction

Today, cancer remains one of the major causes of death in the world. The American Cancer Society estimates that 1,806,590 new cancer cases and 606,520 cancer deaths are projected to occur in the United States in 2020 [1]. Furthermore, the overall number of deaths caused by cancer is still rising throughout the world. A main reason is that the

© Springer Nature Singapore Pte Ltd. 2021
L. Pan et al. (Eds.): BIC-TA 2020, CCIS 1363, pp. 309–321, 2021.
https://doi.org/10.1007/978-981-16-1354-8_21

patients were usually diagnosed with cancer at the medium or late stages. Therefore, one of the important solutions is to make accurate diagnostic prediction in advance, which holds the promise of facilitating the treatment decisions for patients and understanding the mechanisms of cancer occurrence and development.

With the recent advancement in sequencing technologies [2, 3] and the advent of "era of precision medicine" [4, 5], it has become more efficient and convenient to obtain massive biological data. Vast amounts of cancer data have been collected and deposited, including genomics and proteomics, which are publicly available to the medical research. The analyses of large-scale molecular data are beneficial for many aspects of oncology research, which can help to classify the possible subtypes, stages and grades of cancer. However, the traditional biostatistical models usually have some drawbacks in cancer predictions based on big data, for instance, the Cox regression model reduces its power in the sense that it does not allow for the identification of interactions between genomic features [6]. In addition, some traditional biostatistical models lack efficiency in dealing with big data. Advanced machine learning methods have been the powerful tools for big data mining and have a growing trend on the applications for cancer prediction [7, 8].

Previously, single type of molecular data was applied for diagnostic and prognostic prediction of cancer. The prediction models often performed low accuracy, approximately 70% [9, 10]. As the progress of sequencing technology, an obvious trend on cancer prediction is to integrate multi-omics data. For example, Yuan and Allen et al. predicted patient survival using diverse molecular data, including somatic copy number alteration (CNA), DNA methylation and mRNA, microRNA and protein expression, from 953 samples of four cancer types (kidney renal clear cell carcinoma (KIRC), glioblastoma multiforme (GBM), ovarian serous cystadenocarcinoma (OV) and lung squamous cell carcinoma (LUSC)), and found that the random survival forest based model incorporating molecular data with clinical variables significantly improves predictions for three cancers (GBM, KIRC, OV) [11]. Isik and Ercan attempted to combine various data sources (RNA-seq, Reverse Phase Protein Array, protein-protein interaction) with machine learning (Support Vector Machine, Random Forest) to predict the survival time of cancer patients, including LUSC, GBM and KIRC [12]. The results showed that the prediction models based on multi-omics data have better accuracy and utility for guiding clinical therapy and improving prognosis. Consequently, the accumulation of multi-omics data and the innovation of machine learning will certainly accelerate the progress of diagnostic and prognostic prediction for cancer.

In this review, we first reviewed the common omics data. Secondly, we briefly introduced several popular machine learning methods. Thirdly, we systematically summarized the substantial achievements obtained in a number of cancer prognostic prediction studies. Lastly, we discussed and analyzed some of the existing challenges and believed that the advanced AI technologies such as deep learning will be widely applied to facilitate diagnosis and treatment for cancer patients.

2   Omics Data

In molecular biology field, omics contains genomics, proteomics, transcriptomics, metabolomics, lipidomics, immunomics, glycomics and so on, that is shown in Fig. 1.

Massive omics data have a growing trend on the applications for cancer prediction, a list of publications relevant to omics data applied in predicting cancers is shown in Table 1 [13–23]. In this section, we will give the general concepts of several main omics.

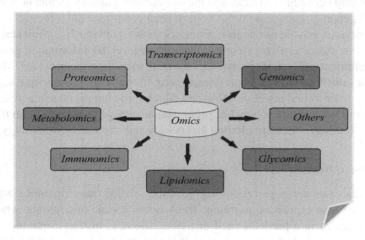

Fig. 1. Omics contents

Table 1. Publications relevant to omics data applied for cancer prediction.

Reference	Cancer type	Omics data name
Fan et al. [13]	Esophagus cancer	RNA-Seq
Hayes et al. [14]	Glioblastoma	microRNA
Chen et al. [15]	Lower grade glioma	Gene expression
Margolin et al. [16]	BRCA[a]	Gene expression, copy number
Seoane et al.[17]	BRCA	Gene expression, CNV
Zhang et al. [18]	GBM[b]	Copy number, gene expression, gene methylation and miRNA expression
Kim et al. [19]	OV[c]	Gene expression, CNV, methylation, miRNA
Ray et al. [20]	OV	Gene expression, methylation, CNV
Ruffalo et al. [21]	BRCA, GBM	Gene expression, mutation, PPI
Jennings et al. [22]	GBM	mRNA, methylation, copy number
Zhao et al. [23]	GBM, BRCA, AML[d], LUSC[e]	Gene expression, DNA methylation, microRNA, copy number

[a] Breast Cancer (BRCA), [b] Glioblastoma Multiforme (GBM), [c] Ovarian Cancer (OV), [d] Acute Myeloid Leukemia (AML),[e] Lung Squamous Cell Carcinoma (LUSC)

2.1 Genomics

In the 1980s, genomics came into being. In more detail, genomics is field of science of researching the composition of the genome of organisms, the structure of each gene, the relationship between each other and the associated regulatory elements. Since 1995, nearly 300 genome-sequencing projects have been completed [24]. From the comparison with previous genetic researches, genomics shows a obviously "wholeness", which describes gene characteristics in terms of the genome level. Bioinformatics, gene expression measurement and genetic analysis are the main tools for genomics [25]. MicroRNA sequencing (miRNA-seq) can be performed using Illumina high-throughput sequencing platform in order to find novel miRNAs and their expression profiles in a given sample [26]. The miRNA-seq technology has prominent advantages compared with traditional RT-PCR technology, Northern blotting technology and microarray technology.

2.2 Transcriptomics

A new subject was developed following genomics, called transcriptomics, sometimes referred to as gene expression profiling. Transcriptomics can measure the whole set of mRNA molecules in a particular cell or tissue. The field of transcriptomics provides information about both the presence and the relative abundance of RNA transcripts, thus indicating the active ingredients in the cell [24]. After the Human Genome Project completed the sequencing work, transcriptomics has been receiving a lot of attention [27]. Scientists found genes that do not encode proteins are not useless, which contain many very important regulatory originals that are associated with regulated genes [28]. RNA sequencing (RNA-seq), one major method for studying the transcriptome, generated from the innovation of sequencing technology [29]. It can identify the full catalog of transcripts, precisely define the structure of genes, and accurately measure gene expression levels. It offers numerous advantages over microarrays.

2.3 Proteomics

Proteomics refers to entire set of proteins translated from the gene, it is the complementary to genomics because it focuses on the gene products. Comparing with genomics, proteomics is more complex. Proteomics aims to gain a comprehensive understanding of all kinds of proteins and their relationship with the surrounding environment, which involves in specific physiological or pathological state. For a living organism in different parts of its body and different stages of the life cycle, there may be many differences in protein expression. For this reason, the amount of expression, post-translational modification and subcellular distribution of proteins and so on, can be reflected in proteomics [24]. The techniques such as two-dimensional gel electrophoresis analysis and protein chip analysis can be used in obtaining and analyzing proteomics data [30].

3 Machine Learning Techniques

Vast amounts of data to be analyzed and interpreted are growing rapidly with the continuous accomplishment of various genome projects. Machine learning is a branch of

AI, which has been gradually regarded as a powerful tool to analyze biological data by using a variety of statistical, probabilistic and optimized techniques. Machine learning techniques can discover and identify the relationships among complex data sets. In addition, these techniques have shown their effective performance in predicting cancer, which provide important technical support for cancer prediction [31, 32]. There are many machine learning methods for cancer prediction. A list of publications relevant to above aspect is shown in Table 2, where machine learning methods, cancer types and prediction accuracy in the publications are recorded [33–39].

In this section, we mainly introduce the following machine learning algorithms for classification, dimension reduction and data integration on cancer prediction.

3.1 Classification

Naive Bayes (NB) models have been widely used for clustering and classification due to their simplicity, efficiency and accuracy [40]. In the general procedure of applying NB for classification purpose, the classes of unlabeled samples can be inferred using the learned network.

Decision Tree (DT) is a hierarchical data structure, which implements the divide-and-conquer strategy. DT is simple to interpret and quick to learn [41]. It can be used for both classification and decision analysis. The class of a new sample can be conjectured when traversing the tree for the classification.

Support Vector Machine (SVM) is a set of related supervised learning methods, which is usually used for classification and regression analysis [42]. The algorithm basically finds the optimum separating hyper-plane, which maximizes the margin between the samples of two classes given by the training data [43]. The SVM is less affected by outliers in the samples and can be used for the reliable classification of new samples. Its prediction accuracy is generally high and over-fitting problems is less [44].

Artificial Neural Network (ANN) is computer-based algorithm, which is modeled on the structure and behavior of neurons in the human brain. The algorithm can be trained to handle a variety of classification or pattern recognition problems [35]. As a classification method, ANN achieved high performance for the cancer survival prediction [45].

Extreme gradient boosting (XGBoost) algorithm is proposed by Chen et al. in 2016 [46]. XGBoost is a regression tree that has the same decision rules as decision tree. It supports both regression and classification. Recently, this algorithm has been widely applied to medicine, image and signal processing, data mining and other fields [47, 48]. As a type of gradient boosting machine, XGBoost is mainly improved in two aspects: speeding up the tree construction and proposing a new distributed algorithm for tree searching [49].

3.2 Dimension Reduction

LASSO is a regression analysis method that enhances the prediction accuracy and interpretability of the statistical model by variable selection and regularization. As a sparse linear discriminative model, LASSO [50] plays a crucial role in the classification, regression and feature selection of multi-class data.

Minimum Redundancy Maximum Relevance (mRMR) feature selection method sorts variables according to their mutual information [51]. The method is shown to achieve high accuracy by eliminating irrelevant and redundant features [52]. The mRMR method was applied in [53] to filter noisy and redundant genes in high dimensional microarray data in order to find a candidate gene set.

3.3 Data Integration

Similarity Network Fusion(SNF) approach uses networks of samples as a basis for integration [54]. The SNF can get useful information even from a small number of samples and it is robust to noise and data heterogeneity. The approach constructs networks of samples for each available data type and then efficiently fuses these into one network that represents the full spectrum of underlying data. The final fused network is used for classification.

Table 2. Publications relevant to machine learning methods applied for cancer prediction.

Reference	Machine learning method	Cancer type	Accuracy
Bhalla [33]	SVM[a]	ccRCC[b]	72.64%
Ahmad et al. [34]	SVM	BRCA	95%
Chen et al. [35]	ANN[c]	Lung cancer	83%
Jagga et al. [36]	RF[d]	KIRC[e]	0.8 (AUC)
Deng et al. [37]	NLLP[f]	KIRC	0.852
Ogunleye et al. [38]	XGBoost[g]	CKD[h]	100%
Ding et al. [39]	XGBoost	Pan-cancer	0.95 (AUC)

[a] Support Vector Machine (SVM), [b] Clear Cell Renal Cell Carcinoma (ccRCC), [c] Artificial Neural Network (ANN), [d] Random Forest (RF), [e] Kidney Renal Clear Cell Carcinoma (KIRC), [f] Network-based LASSO Label Prediction (NLLP), [g] Extreme Gradient Boosting (XGBoost), [h] Chronic Kidney Disease (CKD)

Multiple Kernel Learning (MKL) [55] is an intermediate integration technique that can integrate different data types to one model. The MKL calculates different kernel (or similarity) matrices separately and integrates these matrices to generate a final kernel matrix to be used.

4   Diagnostic and Prognostic Prediction for Cancer

4.1   Prognosis Prediction of Breast Cancer

Breast cancer (BRCA) is one of the most common cancers worldwide, which is diagnosed in approximately 30% in all cancer cases. The efforts related to BRCA prediction have been made, as that can facilitate the subsequent clinical therapy of patients and reduce BRCA mortality efficiently [56–58].

Dokyoon Kim et al. proposed a new integrative framework to predict cancer patient prognosis [59]. The framework aimed to achieve both integration of different omics data types and discovery of the interactions between meta-dimensional genomic features, so that predictive power of survival models can be improved. This study analyzed breast cancer data with 476 patients from TCGA. Four different genomic data types were used to represent different dimensions (CNA as genome dimension, methylation as epigenome dimension, gene expression as transcriptome dimension, and protein data as proteome dimension). 'Analysis Tool for Heritable and Environmental Network Associations' (ATHENA) and grammatical evolution neural network (GENN) were applied in this study [60]. ATHENA can establish the meta-dimensional models by analyzing meta-dimensional genomic data simultaneously [61–63]. The final GENN model was a kind of optimized neural network, which was employed in order to build interaction models between genomic features associated with survival outcomes. These four single-dimensional genome data and age were integrated to generate a meta-dimensional genome and an independent validation dataset was used to test the resulting multi-dimensional model. Compared with traditional Cox regression approach and binary classification approach, the proposed framework can identify interactions between meta-dimensional omics data associated with survival, which is associated with heterogeneous disease such as breast cancer prognosis. In addition, the advantage of the proposed model is that the sex, age, or stage are included in this study, as potential confounders. However, it should be noted that this study only used age as a clinical covariate because there were many missing values in other clinical variables. Future work will be a follow-up study to take other clinical variables (such as cancer stage, grade, etc.) in to account.

4.2   Prediction of Kidney Renal Clear Cell Carcinoma's Stage

Kidney cancer is one of ten most common cancers. Kidney renal clear cell carcinoma (KIRC) is the most common type of kidney cancer by far. The treatment and prognosis depend, to a large extent, on the cancer's stage. Thus, predicting the stage of cancer is regarded as one of the most important issues in the field of cancer therapy.

To deal with the diversity and big volume of cancer omics data, some methods have been proposed to integrate these data to predict cancer. A machine learning approach, iCluster [64], uses a joint latent variable model for integrative clustering. However, iCluster is sensitive and fussy on data preprocessing step. Wang B et al. proposed the SNF method to integrate mRNA expression, DNA methylation and miRNA of cohort cancer patients for tumor subtyping and survival prediction, achieved effective results [54]. SNF was also applied on the following study. Su-Ping Deng et al. integrated two types of data in order to construct a fused network for identifying the stages of KIRC better [37]. The authors created the networks for gene expression network and DNA methylation respectively and fused both networks into a similarity network by SNF [54] approach. And then they tested the potential of network-based approach in identifying the stages of KIRC from above three networks. Network-based semi-supervised learning (NSSL) method was used for predicting the label of a new sample. The authors used a network-based LASSO lable prediction method to predict the lables of unlabled samples. In order to verify the validity of the model, the authors used resample (1000 times) to evaluate. The NLLP method had the best performance as compared to the four methods of k nearest neighbors (k = 7), Maximum link weight (MLW) [65] and Large link weight and small difference of degree centrality (WDC) [66]. The limitation of this study is that the amount of data samples is too small, only 66. In order to compensate for this insufficiency, researchers randomly sampled value of each stage of both gene expression data and DNA methylation data and generated a simulated sample. The simulated KIRC dataset and the true KIRC dataset downloaded from TCGA were then integrated into a mixed KIRC dataset. NLLP method was applied to the mixed dataset, the results further confirmed that the proposed approach achieved accurate performance. Moreover, authors claimed that the proposed model can generalize to other cancers for the early diagnosis and therapy.

4.3 Prediction of Glioblastoma Multiforme

Among numerous cancers, glioblastoma multiforme (GBM) is a type of gliomas that has higher mortality. Moreover, this disease is highly aggressive. Approximately 175,000 people suffer from GBM each year worldwide, with only 50,000 survivals [67, 68]. Therefore, it is essential to accurately predict GBM. Owing to the complexity of the tumor initiation and progression, it is not sufficient to predict GBM through a single biomolecular data. Researchers have attempted to combine multiple types of data [69, 70], however, the results are not very reliable. And it is hard to apply these attempts on clinical therapy.

In 2017, Shu-Guang Ge et al. proposed a novel data-integration method for cancer subtypes identification, namely Scluster [71]. When dealing with large volumes of high-dimensional data integration, this approach could address the issue of clustering cancer samples in subspaces. A total number of 215 patients were considered in this study, which including mRNA expression (12,042 genes), DNA methylation (1,491 genes) and miRNA expression (534 genes). A set of coefficient matrixes were calculated by an optimal PCA method and the indicator matrices were calculated separately by an adaptive sparse reduced-rank regression (S-rrr) method [72]. To integrate these low-dimensional subspaces simultaneously, the authors combined different subspaces and then integrated these subspaces into a patient-by-patient similarity matrix [73]. Finally, cancer subtypes were identified by using the spectral clustering method. According to the results, based on gene expression data and DNA methylation data, Scluster can effectively extract biology feature and identify cancer subtypes. Compared with other advanced integrative methods, including SNF [54] and iCluster [64], the proposed framework is an unsupervised method to find the principal low-dimension subspace and develops a strongly concordant structure without data preprocessing step. Moreover, researchers further analyzed the subtypes of GBM and explored the reaction of survival for treatment with a drug (temozolomide) in different GBM subtypes patients. This study demonstrates the effectiveness of Scluster to predict survival and identify cancer subtypes, which presents the foundation for the future studies of different clusters.

5   Challenges For Clinical Application

The application of machine learning in combination with omics data for cancer prediction still exists some challenges. There are some confusions caused by inconsistent nomenclatures of patients data across different databases. Moreover, many missing values for some clinical variables are found in the patients data sources, which influence, to a certain extent, on the construction of machine learning model and the prediction results. Most of omics data contain noise, so in some experiments, data preprocessing is essential. For example, as a clustering method, iCluster has higher demand on preprocessing [64].

In addition, omics data (such as DNA methylation and mRNA) are high-dimensional data. The issue of analyzing high-dimensional dataset has recently been regarded as one of the main challenges, owing to these datasets are characterized by a major imbalance of the sample volume and the gene volume. Due to the complexity and heterogeneity of cancer, it is also a difficulty to determine the interaction between the different dimension of omics data and take the potential affect associated with cancer prediction into account [71]. We believe that with the maturation of related technologies, these problems will be more tractable and that is just around the corner.

6 Future Directions

Along with the development of high-throughput sequencing technology and the reduction of sequencing cost, the field of bioinformatics has entered into the era of big data, which is characterized by massive high-throughput omics data. Vast amounts of omics data, including genomics and transcriptomics, are continuously accumulated and provide the foundation for the cancer prediction studies.

As a new domain of machine learning, DL is the extension and expansion of ANN. The application of this algorithm has improved speech recognition, image processing and drug discovery to a large extent [74–76]. It is speculated that DL is considered as having huge potential in cancer prediction. For example, Kumardeep Chaudhary et al. proposed a research to stratify patients into different categories, where in a DL approach was employed to discover the association between the multi-omics features and the differential survival of hepatocellular carcinoma (HCC) patients [77]. A total number of 360 patient samples data, including RNA-seq, miRNA-seq and methylation data from TCGA, were used to train the DL model. The proposed model achieved good performance in terms of patients survival and model fitness, $P = 7.13e^{-6}$, C-index $= 0.68$. In brief, we believe that there is room for further development on the application of DL in clinical prediction of cancer, and we also look forward to its remarkable effect not only on cancer diagnosis and prognosis, but also on the therapy.

7 Conclusion

Huge volume of omics data have been produced and accumulated by high-throughput sequencing technology, which provide the big data foundation for bioinformatics. The wide application of machine learning combined with diverse omics data is driving the progress of diagnostic and prognostic prediction for cancer. Improving the accuracy of cancer prediction methods will be one of the most important topics in bioinformatics. In this review, we outline the application of machine learning technology and highlight the advanced progress of these methods based on omics data in cancer prediction. Despite existing several challenges, these approaches have gradually been improved and will achieve significant progress in the field of cancer diagnosis and therapy.

Funding. This work was supported by the National Natural Science Foundation of China (61471078), Dalian Science and Technology Innovation Fund (2020JJ27SN066) and the Fundamental Research Funds for the Central Universities (3132014306,3132015213, 3132017075).

References

1. Siegel, R.L., Miller, K.D., Jemal, A.: Cancer statistics. CA: A Cancer J. Clin. **70**(1), 7–30 (2020)
2. Barretina, J., et al.: The cancer cell line encyclopedia enables predictive modelling of anticancer drug sensitivity. Nature **483**(7391), 603–607 (2012)
3. Heather, J.M., Chain, B.: The sequence of sequencers: the history of sequencing DNA. Genomics **107**(1), 1–8 (2016)
4. Shin, C., Han, C., Pae, C.-U., Patkar, A.A.: Precision medicine for psychopharmacology: a general introduction. Expert Rev. Neurother. **16**(7), 831–839 (2016)
5. Buguliskis, J.S.: Pharmacogenomics serves as the critical driver for precision medicine. Clinical OMICs **2**(6), 12–14, 16 (2015)
6. Gui, J., Moore, J.H., Kelsey, K.T., Marsit, C.J., Karagas, M.R., Andrew, A.S.: A novel survival multifactor dimensionality reduction method for detecting gene–gene interactions with application to bladder cancer prognosis. Hum. Genet. **129**(1), 101–110 (2011)
7. Ma, B., Geng, Y., Meng, F., Yan, G., Song, F.: Identification of a sixteen-gene prognostic biomarker for lung adenocarcinoma using a machine learning method. Journal of Cancer **11**(5), 1288 (2020)
8. Rahimi, A., Gönen, M.: Discriminating early- and late-stage cancers using multiple kernel learning on gene sets. Bioinformatics **34**(13), i412–i421 (2018)
9. Daéid, N.N., Waddell, R.J.: The analytical and chemometric procedures used to profile illicit drug seizures. Talanta **67**(2), 280–285 (2005)
10. Listgarten, J., et al.: Predictive models for breast cancer susceptibility from multiple single nucleotide polymorphisms. Clin. Cancer Res. **10**(8), 2725–2737 (2004)
11. Yuan, Y., et al.: Assessing the clinical utility of cancer genomic and proteomic data across tumor types. Nat. Biotechnol. **32**(7), 644–652 (2014)
12. Isik, Z., Ercan, M.E.: Integration of RNA-Seq and RPPA data for survival time prediction in cancer patients. Comput. Biol. Med. **89**, 397–404 (2017)
13. Fan, Q., Liu, B.: Identification of a RNA-Seq based 8-long non-coding RNA signature predicting survival in esophageal cancer. Med. Sci. Monit. Int. Med. J. Exp. Clin. Res. **22**, 5163–5172 (2016)
14. Hayes, J., et al.: Prediction of clinical outcome in glioblastoma using a biologically relevant nine-microRNA signature. Mol. Oncol. **9**(3), 704–714 (2015)
15. Chen, B., Liang, T., Yang, P., Wang, H., Liu, Y., Yang, F., You, G.: Classifying lower grade glioma cases according to whole genome gene expression. Oncotarget **7**(45), 74031–74042 (2016)
16. Margolin, A.A., et al.: Systematic analysis of challenge-driven improvements in molecular prognostic models for breast cancer. Sci. Transl. Med. **5**(181), 181re181–181re181 (2013)
17. Seoane, J.A., Day, I.N., Gaunt, T.R., Campbell, C.: A pathway-based data integration framework for prediction of disease progression. Bioinformatics **30**(6), 838–845 (2014)

18. Zhang, Y., Li, A., Peng, C., Wang, M.: Improve glioblastoma multiforme prognosis prediction by using feature selection and multiple kernel learning. IEEE/ACM Trans. Comput. Biol. Bioinf. **13**(5), 825–835 (2016)
19. Kim, D., Li, R., Lucas, A., Verma, S.S., Dudek, S.M., Ritchie, M.D.: Using knowledge-driven genomic interactions for multi-omics data analysis: metadimensional models for predicting clinical outcomes in ovarian carcinoma. J. Am. Med. Inform. Assoc. **24**(3), 577–587 (2017)
20. Ray, P., Zheng, L., Lucas, J., Carin, L.: Bayesian joint analysis of heterogeneous genomics data. Bioinformatics **30**(10), 1370–1376 (2014)
21. Ruffalo, M., Koyutürk, M., Sharan, R.: Network-based integration of disparate omic data to identify "silent players" in cancer. PLoS Comput. Biol. **11**(12), (2015)
22. Jennings, E.M., Morris, J.S., Carroll, R.J., Manyam, G.C., Baladandayuthapani, V.: Bayesian methods for expression-based integration of various types of genomics data. EURASIP J. Bioinf. Syst. Biol. **2013**(1), 13 (2013)
23. Zhao, Q., Shi, X., Xie, Y., Huang, J., Shia, B., Ma, S.: Combining multidimensional genomic measurements for predicting cancer prognosis: observations from TCGA. Brief. Bioinform. **16**(2), 291–303 (2015)
24. Joyce, A.R., Palsson, B.Ø.: The model organism as a system: integrating 'omics' data sets. Nat. Rev. Mol. Cell Biol. **7**(3), 198–210 (2006)
25. Mikkelsen, T., et al.: Initial sequence of the chimpanzee genome and comparison with the human genome. Nature **437**(7055), 69–87 (2005)
26. Rounge, T.B., Lauritzen, M., Langseth, H., Enerly, E., Lyle, R., Gislefoss, R.E.: MicroRNA biomarker discovery and high-throughput DNA sequencing are possible using long-term archived serum samples. Cancer Epidemiol. Biomark. Prev. : A Publ. Am. Assoc. Cancer Res. Cosponsored Am. Soc. Prev. Oncol. **24**(9), 1381–1387 (2015)
27. McGettigan, P.A.: Transcriptomics in the RNA-seq era. Curr. Opin. Chem. Biol. **17**(1), 4–11 (2013)
28. Zhang, W., Li, F., Nie, L.: Integrating multiple 'omics' analysis for microbial biology: application and methodologies. Microbiology **156**(2), 287–301 (2010)
29. Wang, Z., Gerstein, M., Snyder, M.: RNA-Seq: a revolutionary tool for transcriptomics. Nat. Rev. Genet. **10**(1), 57–63 (2009)
30. Pandey, A., Mann, M.: Proteomics to study genes and genomes. Nature **405**(6788), 837–846 (2000)
31. Mitchell, T.M.: The discipline of machine learning. Carnegie Mellon University, School of Computer Science, Machine Learning, USA (2006)
32. Biship, C.M.: Pattern recognition and machine learning (information science and statistics). Springer, New York (2007)
33. Bhalla, S., et al.: Gene expression-based biomarkers for discriminating early and late stage of clear cell renal cancer. Sci. Rep. **7**(1), 1–13 (2017)
34. Ahmad, L.G., Eshlaghy, A., Poorebrahimi, A., Ebrahimi, M., Razavi, A.: Using three machine learning techniques for predicting breast cancer recurrence. J. Health Med. Inf. **4**(2), 1–3 (2013)
35. Chen, Y.-C., Ke, W.-C., Chiu, H.-W.: Risk classification of cancer survival using ANN with gene expression data from multiple laboratories. Comput. Biol. Med. **48**, 1–7 (2014)
36. Jagga, Z., Gupta, D.: Classification models for clear cell renal carcinoma stage progression, based on tumor RNAseq expression trained supervised machine learning algorithms. BMC Proc. **8**(6), S2 (2014)
37. Deng, S.-P., Cao, S., Huang, D.-S., Wang, Y.-P.: Identifying stages of kidney renal cell carcinoma by combining gene expression and DNA methylation data. IEEE/ACM Trans. Comput. Biol. Bioinf. **14**(5), 1147–1153 (2016)
38. Ogunleye, A.A., Qing-Guo, W.: XGBoost model for chronic kidney disease diagnosis. IEEE/ACM Trans. Comput. Biol. Bioinf. (2019)

39. Ding, W., Chen, G., Shi, T.: Integrative analysis identifies potential DNA methylation biomarkers for pan-cancer diagnosis and prognosis. Epigenetics **14**(1), 67–80 (2019)
40. Zhang, H.: The optimality of Naive Bayes. In: International Flairs Conference, Florida, USA (2004)
41. Mitchell, T.M.: Machine Learning. China Machine Press, McGraw-Hill Education (Asia) (2003)
42. Aruna, S., Rajagopalan, S., Nandakishore, L.: Application of GIST SVM in cancer detection. arXiv preprint (2012)
43. Statnikov, A., Wang, L., Aliferis, C.F.: A comprehensive comparison of random forests and support vector machines for microarray-based cancer classification. BMC Bioinf. **9**(1), 319 (2008)
44. Noble, W.S.: What is a support vector machine? Nat. Biotechnol. **24**(12), 1565–1567 (2006)
45. Ayer, T., Alagoz, O., Chhatwal, J., Shavlik, J.W., Kahn Jr., C.E., Burnside, E.S.: Breast cancer risk estimation with artificial neural networks revisited: discrimination and calibration. Cancer **116**(14), 3310–3321 (2010)
46. Chen, T., Guestrin, C.: Xgboost: a scalable tree boosting system. In: Proceedings of the 22nd ACM SIGKDD International Conference on Knowledge Discovery and Data Mining, pp. 785–794. (2016)
47. Ma, B., Meng, F., Yan, G., Yan, H., Chai, B., Song, F.: Diagnostic classification of cancers using extreme gradient boosting algorithm and multi-omics data. Comput. Biol. Med. **121**, (2020)
48. Long, J.-M., Yan, Z.-F., Shen, Y.-L., Liu, W.-J., Wei, Q.-Y.: Detection of epilepsy using MFCC-based feature and XGBoost. In: 2018 11th International Congress on Image and Signal Processing, BioMedical Engineering and Informatics (CISP-BMEI), pp. 1–4. IEEE, New York (2018)
49. Torlay, L., Perrone-Bertolotti, M., Thomas, E., Baciu, M.: Machine learning–XGBoost analysis of language networks to classify patients with epilepsy. Brain Inform **4**(3), 159–169 (2017)
50. Tibshirani, R.: Regression shrinkage and selection via the lasso. J. R. Stat. Soc. Ser. b-Methodol. **58**(1), 267–288 (1996)
51. Peng, H., Long, F., Ding, C.: Feature selection based on mutual information criteria of max-dependency, max-relevance, and min-redundancy. IEEE Trans. Pattern Anal. Mach. Intell. **27**(8), 1226–1238 (2005)
52. Ding, C., Peng, H.: Minimum redundancy feature selection from microarray gene expression data. J. Bioinf. Comput. Biol. **3**(2), 185–205 (2005)
53. El Akadi, A., Amine, A., El Ouardighi, A., Aboutajdine, D.: A new gene selection approach based on minimum redundancy-maximum relevance (MRMR) and genetic algorithm (GA). In: 2009 IEEE/ACS International Conference on Computer Systems and Applications, pp. 69–75. IEEE, New York (2009)
54. Wang, B., et al.: Similarity network fusion for aggregating data types on a genomic scale. Nat. Methods **11**(3), 333–337 (2014)
55. Gönen, M., Alpaydın, E.: Multiple kernel learning algorithms. J. Mach. Learn. Res. **12**, 2211–2268 (2011)
56. Bochare, A.: Integrating Domain Knowledge in Supervised Machine Learning to Assess the Risk of Breast Cancer Using Genomic Data. University of Maryland, Baltimore County (2012)
57. Jerez, J.M., et al.: Missing data imputation using statistical and machine learning methods in a real breast cancer problem. Artif. Intell. Med. **50**(2), 105–115 (2010)
58. Sumbaly, R., Vishnusri, N., Jeyalatha, S.: Diagnosis of breast cancer using decision tree data mining technique. Int. J. Comput. Appl. **98**(10), 16–24 (2014)

59. Kim, D., Li, R., Dudek, S.M., Ritchie, M.D.: Predicting censored survival data based on the interactions between meta-dimensional omics data in breast cancer. J. Biomed. Inform. **56**, 220–228 (2015)

60. Motsinger-Reif, A.A., Dudek, S.M., Hahn, L.W., Ritchie, M.D.: Comparison of approaches for machine-learning optimization of neural networks for detecting gene-gene interactions in genetic epidemiology. Genet. Epidemiol.: Official Publ. Int. Genet. Epidemiol. Soc. **32**(4), 325–340 (2008)

61. Holzinger, E.R., Dudek, S.M., Frase, A.T., Pendergrass, S.A., Ritchie, M.D.: ATHENA: the analysis tool for heritable and environmental network associations. Bioinformatics **30**(5), 698–705 (2014)

62. Kim, D., Li, R., Dudek, S.M., Ritchie, M.D.: ATHENA: identifying interactions between different levels of genomic data associated with cancer clinical outcomes using grammatical evolution neural network. BioData Min. **6**(1), 23 (2013)

63. Turner, S.D., Dudek, S.M., Ritchie, M.D.: ATHENA: a knowledge-based hybrid backpropagation-grammatical evolution neural network algorithm for discovering epistasis among quantitative trait Loci. BioData Min. **3**(1), 5 (2010)

64. Shen, R., Olshen, A.B., Ladanyi, M.J.B.: Integrative clustering of multiple genomic data types using a joint latent variable model with application to breast and lung cancer subtype analysis. Bioinformatics **25**(22), 2906–2912 (2009)

65. Denoeux, T.: A k-nearest neighbor classification rule based on Dempster-Shafer theory. IEEE Trans. Syst. Man Cybern. **25**(5), 804–813 (1995)

66. Opsahl, T., Agneessens, F., Skvoretz, J.: Node centrality in weighted networks: generalizing degree and shortest paths. Soc. Netw. **32**(3), 245–251 (2010)

67. Jemal, A., Siegel, R., Ward, E., Hao, Y., Xu, J., Thun, M.J.: Cancer statistics. CA: A Cancer J. Clin. **59**(4), 225–249 (2009)

68. Sun, Y., et al.: A glioma classification scheme based on coexpression modules of EGFR and PDGFRA. Proc. Natl. Acad. Sci. **111**(9), 3538–3543 (2014)

69. Colman, H., Zhang, L., Sulman, E.P., McDonald, J.M., Shooshtari, N.L., Rivera, A., Popoff, S., Nutt, C.L., Louis, D.N., Cairncross, J.G.: A multigene predictor of outcome in glioblastoma. Neuro-oncology **12**(1), 49–57 (2010)

70. Liang, Y., et al.: Gene expression profiling reveals molecularly and clinically distinct subtypes of glioblastoma multiforme. Proc. Natl. Acad. Sci. **102**(16), 5814–5819 (2005)

71. Ge, S.-G., Xia, J., Sha, W., Zheng, C.-H.: Cancer subtype discovery based on integrative model of multigenomic data. IEEE/ACM Trans. Comput. Biol. Bioinf. **14**(5), 1115–1121 (2016)

72. Ma, Z., Sun, T.: Adaptive sparse reduced-rank regression. Statistics (2014)

73. Wei, Y.-C., Cheng, C.-K.: Towards efficient hierarchical designs by ratio cut partitioning. In: 1989 IEEE International Conference on Computer-Aided Design. Digest of Technical Papers, pp. 298–301. IEEE, New York(1989)

74. Tompson, J.J., Jain, A., LeCun, Y., Bregler, C.: Joint training of a convolutional network and a graphical model for human pose estimation. In: Advances in Neural Information Processing Systems, pp. 1799–1807. (2014)

75. Hinton, G., et al.: Deep neural networks for acoustic modeling in speech recognition: the shared views of four research groups. IEEE Sig. Process. Mag. **29**(6), 82–97 (2012)

76. Ma, J., Sheridan, R.P., Liaw, A., Dahl, G.E., Svetnik, V.: Deep neural nets as a method for quantitative structure–activity relationships. J. Chem. Inf. Model. **55**(2), 263–274 (2015)

77. Chaudhary, K., Poirion, O.B., Lu, L., Garmire, L.X.: Deep learning–based multi-omics integration robustly predicts survival in liver cancer. Clin. Cancer Res. **24**(6), 1248–1259 (2018)

The Predictive Model of Esophageal Squamous Cell Carcinoma Differentiation

Yuli Yang[1,2], Haoping Ji[1,2], Junwei Sun[1,2], and Yanfeng Wang[1,2](✉)

[1] Henan Key Lab of Information-Based Electrical Appliances,
Zhengzhou University of Light Industry, Zhengzhou 450002, China
yanfengwang@yeah.net
[2] School of Electrical and Information Engineering,
Zhengzhou University of Light Industry, Zhengzhou 450002, China

Abstract. The diagnosis of the degree of differentiation of tumor cells can help physicians to make timely detection and take appropriate treatment for the patient's condition. The original datasets are clustered into two independent types by the Kohonen clustering algorithm. One type is used as the development sets to find correlation indicators and establish predictive models, while the other type is used as the validation sets to test the correlation indicators and model. Thirteen indicators significantly associated with the degree of differentiation of esophageal squamous cell carcinoma are found by Kohonen algorithm in the development sets. Ten different machine learning classification algorithms are used to predict the differentiation of esophageal squamous cell carcinoma. The artificial bee colony-support vector machine (ABC-SVM) has better prediction accuracy than the other nine algorithms and has a shorter training time. The average accuracy of the 10-fold cross-validation reached 81.5% by ABC-SVM algorithm. In the development sets, a model with the great merit for the degree of differentiation is found based on logistic regression algorithm. The AUC value of the model is 0.672 and 0.753 in the development sets and validation sets, respectively. $p-values$ are less than 0.05. The results are shown that the model has a high predictive value for the differentiation of esophageal squamous cell carcinoma.

This work was supported in part by the National Key Research and Development Program of China for International S and T Cooperation Projects under Grant 2017YFE0103900, in part by the Joint Funds of the National Natural Science Foundation of China under Grant U1804262, in part by the State Key Program of National Natural Science of China under Grant 61632002, in part by the Foundation of Young Key Teachers from University of Henan Province under Grant 2018GGJS092, in part by the Youth Talent Lifting Project of Henan Province under Grant 2018HYTP016, in part by the Henan Province University Science and Technology Innovation Talent Support Plan under Grant 20HASTIT027, in part by the Zhongyuan Thousand Talents Program under Grant 204200510003, and in part by the Open Fund of State Key Laboratory of Esophageal Cancer Prevention and Treatment under Grant K2020-0010 and Grant K2020-0011.

L. Pan et al. (Eds.): BIC-TA 2020, CCIS 1363, pp. 322–335, 2021.
https://doi.org/10.1007/978-981-16-1354-8_22

Keywords: ESCC · Kohonen clustering algorithm · Classification algorithm · ABC-SVM · ROC · Differentiation prediction model

1   Introduction

Esophageal squamous cell carcinoma is one of the most common malignant tumors in China, which has a high mortality rate [1,2]. The degree of tumor cell differentiation of esophageal squamous cell carcinoma is an important reference information in cancer diagnosis and treatment. High differentiation means that the tumor cells are more similar to normal cells, the tumor is less malignant and less likely to metastasize. It is less sensitive to radiotherapy and chemotherapy. And it has better prognosis. The difference between low-differentiated cells and normal cells is very big, and the malignancy of tumor is relatively high. It is easy to metastasize in the clinical process, and it is more sensitive to radiotherapy and chemotherapy, so the prognosis is poor. As long as early detection and timely treatment can be done, the metastatic speed of tumor can be slowed down through integrated treatment of traditional Chinese and western medicine, and achieve better clinical efficacy [3–5].

Cancer cells have the characteristic of differentiating into normal cells. In medicine, this feature is used by doctors to determine the degree of differentiation of tumor cells. After the patient's biopsy pathology, the malignancy and differentiation of the tumor are confirmed, by observing the characteristic state of tumor cells under a microscope. The traditional method of determining the degree of differentiation is complicated and needs to rely on human experience to make decisions. In this paper, we aim to develop a new model to predict the degree of differentiation of esophageal cancer patients based on blood and tumor size parameters. The prediction model can better predict the degree of esophageal cancer tumor differentiation, which can assist professional physicians in making decisions and improve the clinical treatment effect.

The original dataset is clustered into two separate categories of data by Kohonen algorithm. The first dataset is used to develop the prediction model for the degree of esophageal squamous cell carcinoma differentiation. The second dataset is used to validate the prediction model. First, in the development sets, the Kohonen clustering algorithm is used to cluster multiple indicators significantly associated with esophageal squamous cell carcinoma. The results showed that out of the 21 indicators, 13 are clustered and significantly correlated with the degree of differentiation. Based on these 13 indicators, the degree of esophageal squamous cell carcinoma differentiation is well predicted by the ABC-SVM algorithm, with the average accuracy of 81.5% for 10-fold cross validation. Then, the logistic regression is used to find a model that have greater predictive value for the degree of esophageal cancer differentiation. The AUC value of the model in the development sets is 0.672, whose the P value is less than 0.05. The AUC value of the model in the validation sets is 0.753, whose the P value is less than 0.05. The results are shown that the model has some predictive value for the differentiation of esophageal squamous cell carcinoma. Thirteen relevant indicators have a high correlation with the degree of tumor differentiation of esophageal cancer patients. And the ABC-SVM algorithm is used to predict the degree of tumor differentiation of esophageal squamous cell carcinoma which achieve good results.

The main focus of this article is to investigate the indicators significantly associated with the degree of esophageal squamous cell carcinoma differentiation and to develop the model to predict the tumor differentiation of esophageal squamous cell carcinoma. By using Khonen clustering algorithm, ABC-SVM algorithm, logistic regression, and ROC curve method, the model for predicting the degree of esophageal squamous cell carcinoma differentiation is proposed. The main contributions of this article can be summarized as:

(i) Thirteen indicators associated with the degree of esophageal squamous cell carcinoma differentiation are found and are validated in the external validation sets.
(ii) Differentiation of esophageal squamous cell carcinoma is well predicted by ABC-SVM based on the 13 relevant indicators.
(iii) A model with a high predictive value for esophageal squamous cell carcinoma differentiation is found and is validated in the external validation sets.

2 Data Set Analysis

2.1 Data Introduction

The original dataset for this study contains 211 samples, each with 21 indicators. The 21 indicators include: WBC count, lymphocyte count, monocyte count, neutrophil count, eosinophil count, basophil count, red blood cell count, hemoglobin concentration, platelets count, total protein, albumin, globulin, PT, INR, APTT, TT, FIB, tumor site, tumor length, tumor width, tumor thickness. The gender, age, tumor site information and the population proportions of the original data sets are shown in Table 1. The mean, median, range, and variance information of the 20 indicators in the original sample sets are shown in Table 2.

2.2 Clustering of Data Sets

In this paper, in order to ensure that the predictive model has some predictive power and application. The method of Khonen clustering is used to cluster all the samples from the original dataset into two different categories of dataset. One type is used as the development sets to develop a prediction model for the degree of esophageal cancer differentiation. Another category is used as the validation sets to validate the developed prediction model.

Kohonen self-organizing neural network is an unsupervised learning neural network with self-organizing functions, which has the ability to map high dimensional inputs to low dimensions. A two-layer network is composed of an input layer and a competition layer, and the neurons between the two layers implement a two-way connection. The network has no hidden layer.

Table 1. The population proportions of the original data sets.

Project	Category	Number of population	Percentage of population
Genders	Male	135	64%
	Female	76	36%
Ages	≥58[a]	68	32%
	<58	143	68%
Tumor site	Upper chest	26	12%
	Middle chest	139	66%
	Lower chest	46	22%

[a] Critical threshold for age in the sample sets. Age is used as a variable, and the degree of tumor differentiation is used as a categorical variable. The ROC curve is drawn. After calculating the Youden index, the critical threshold of age for the degree of differentiation is determined to be 58. $P<0.05$. The value of AUC is greater than 0.5. The Youden index is calculated by using (1),

$$Youden\ Index = Sensitivity - (1 - Specificity) \quad (1)$$

Khonen self-organizing neural network is adaptive and belongs to an unsupervised network, without distinguishing between the training sets and the test sets [6]. The "near excitation near suppression" function in the brain's nervous system is achieved through competition between neurons [7–9]. As shown in Fig. 1, a self-organizing neural network of 36–21 structure is established. Algorithm 1 presents the main procedures of the Khonen self-organizing neural network algorithm.

As shown in Table 3 the original dataset is partitioned into two separate datasets by the Kohonen clustering algorithm. These are two different classes of datasets, one as development sets and one as validation sets. The development sets data contains 114 samples, with 53 low differentiation samples and 61 medium differentiation samples, each containing 21 indicators. The validation sets contains 97 samples, with 40 samples for low differentiation and 57 samples for medium differentiation, each sample containing 21 indicators.

Table 2. The original data information.

Variable	Mean	Median(Range)	Variance
Tumor length	3.873459716	4(1.5~10.5)	2.548625592
Tumor width	2.538862559	2.5(1~7)	0.941911081
Tumor thickness	1.140758294	1(0.8~5)	0.31937847
WBC count	6.484549763	6(2.5~15.3)	4.841624915
Lymphocyte count	1.869336493	1.8(0.4~11.7)	0.849811939
Monocyte count	0.422985782	0.4(0~1.4)	0.1666239
Neutrophil count	3.8907109	3.4(0.5~10.6)	3.913749492
Eosinophil count	0.133649289	0.1(0~0.6)	0.022338524
Basophil count	0.04985782	0(0~1)	0.007075694
Red blood cell count	5.131516588	4.56(2.93~5.75)	83.44124436
Hemoglobin concentration	139.2938389	140(95~100)	250.5799142
Platelets count	235.6729858	226(100~418)	5328.859219
Total protein	71.32701422	71(46~92)	57.49731438
Albumin	42.54976303	43(26~79)	29.04870232
Globulin	28.87203791	28(17~45)	31.91211916
PT	10.15876777	10.1(7~16.6)	2.333767998
INR	0.775829384	0.77(0.45~1.64)	0.027433952
APTT	37.11374408	36.1(19.7~56.7)	59.97528639
TT	15.45118483	15.6(8.3~21.3)	4.021748589
FIB	349.3134218	344.029(245.68~710.56)	4881.231632

where the unit of tumor length, tumor width, tumor thickness is CM. The unit of WBC count, lymphocyte count, monocyte count, neutrophil count, eosinophil count, basophil count, red blood cell count, hemoglobin concentration, platelets count, total protein, albumin, globulin is g/L. The unit of PT, APTT, TT is second(s). The unit of FIB is mg/L. INR represents the international normalized ratio, which can be expressed by formula 1. *ISI* is the international sensitivity index for measuring reagents.

$$INR = \left(\frac{Patient's\ PT}{PT\ of\ normal\ control\ group} \right)^{ISI} \quad (2)$$

Algorithm 1. Framework of the Khonen self-organizing neural network algorithm for our study.

Input: clustering indicators M, clustering samples N. ($M = M_1, M_2, M_3, ... M_m, N = 221, m = 21$)

Output: Relevant indicator T. ($T = T_1, T_2, ..., T_n, n < N$)

1: Data normalization

$$y = \frac{(y_{max} - y_{min})(x - x_{min})}{(x_{max} - x_{min})} + y_{min} \tag{3}$$

2: Network initialization Randomly set the vector of the initial connection weight value between the mapping layer and the input layer, $k \in [1, 36]$. The initial value η of the learning rate is 0.7, $\eta \in (0, 1)$. The initial neighborhood is set to N_{k0}.

3: Input of initial vector X:

$$X = (x_1, x_2, x_3, \cdots, x_m)^T, m \in [1, 221] \tag{4}$$

4: Calculate the distance between the weight vector of the mapping layer and the initial vector

$$X_i^l = \left(X_1^l, X_2^l, \cdots, X_i^l\right) \tag{5}$$

where i is the i-th node of the mapping layer, $i = 1, 2, ..., 21$, l is the training data, $l = 1, 2, ..., 221$. E is calculated by (6),

$$E = \min_k \|X - W_k\| = \min_k \left[\frac{1}{2} \sum_{i=1}^{21} (x_i - w_{ki})^2\right] \tag{6}$$

where k is the k-th node of the output layer, $k = 1, 2, ..., 36$, w_{ki} is the connection weight value of the i-th neuron of the input layer and the k-th input neuron of the mapping layer.

5: Weight learning

$$\begin{cases} w_k^{t+1} = w_k^t + \Delta w_k \\ \Delta w_k = \eta \delta_{vk} \|X - W_v\| \end{cases} \tag{7}$$

where t is the number of learning cycles, and W_v is the weight of the connection between the neurons surrounding the winning neurons and the initial vector. η is a constant of $[0, 1]$, which gradually decreases to 0 by (8),

$$\eta(t) = 0.2(1 - t/1000) \tag{8}$$

δ_{vk} represents the value of the proximity relationship between the neuron k and the adjacent center v, as in (9),

$$\delta_{vk} = e^{-(D_{vk}/R)^2} \tag{9}$$

where D_{vk} represents the distance of the output neuron k from the center of the network topology to the adjacent center v. R is the radius of the winning neighborhood N_{kt} of neuron k.

6: Winning neurons are labeled.

7: End

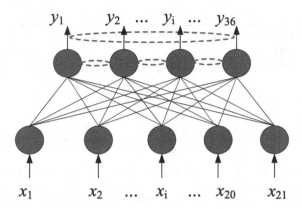

Fig. 1. Khonen neural network of 36-21 structure. There are 21 neurons in the input layer and 36 neurons in the mapping layer. X represents the initial vector, i stands for the i-th node of the input layer, k is regarded as the k-th node of the output layer, ω is considered as the connection weight value, and η is the learning rate.

Table 3. Numbers of samples in the development sets and validation sets.

Project	Development sets		Validation sets		Number of samples
	Male	Female	Male	Female	
Poorly differentiated	37	16	28	14	95
Moderate differentiation	36	25	34	21	116
Total number of samples	114		97		211

3   Correlation Analysis of Indicators

3.1   Clustering of Correlation Indicators

To ensure the rapidity and validity of the predictive model, 21 indicators need to be screened. The Kohonen clustering algorithm is used to screen the indicators that are significantly associated with the differentiation of esophageal squamous cell carcinoma.

In the Algorithm 1, N is set to 21 and M is set to 221. i is 21 and l is 221. In the development set, 21 indicators are clustered by Kohonen clustering algorithm, and finally 13 indicator features that are significantly associated with the degree of esophageal cancer differentiation are found.

The 13 indicators that are significantly correlated with the degree of differentiation are WBC count, lymphocyte count, monocyte count, neutrophil count, eosinophil count, basophil count, red blood cell count, PT, INR, tumor site, tumor length, tumor width, tumor thickness in Table 4.

The Kohonen algorithm has certain limitations and shortcomings. First, the Kohonen algorithm needs to select an appropriate learning rate, and the size of the learning rate determines whether the performance of the Kohonen algorithm

Table 4. Information of 13 indicators that are significantly related to the degree of differentiation in the development sets.

Tumor site	Tumor length	Tumor width	Tumor thickness	WBC count	Lymphocyte count	Monocyte count	Neutrophil count	Eosinophil count	Basophil count	Erythrocyte count	PT	INR	Degree of differentiation
Lower chest	2.5	3	0.5	7.4	2	0.7	4.3	0.4	0	4.09	10	0.75	Poorly differentiated
Middle chest	3.5	3	0.5	10.4	3.9	0.7	5.6	0.1	0.1	5.02	9.6	0.71	Poorly differentiated
Lower chest	4	1	0.6	6	3.4	0.4	2.2	0	0	4.13	7.1	0.46	Poorly differentiated
......													
Middle chest	4	3	1	7.1	3.5	0.3	3	0.3	0	4.31	11.8	0.95	Moderate differentiation
Upper chest	8	5	1	6.6	1.2	0.6	4.8	0	0	4.24	7	0.45	Moderate differentiation
Middle chest	2	2	1.5	7.7	2.1	0.4	5	0.2	0	4.07	8.8	0.63	Moderate differentiation

tends to be stable. Second, sometimes the initial weight vector of a neuron is too far from the input vector, which will cause it to not winning the competition, and thus never learn and become useless neurons.

3.2 Correlation Indicators Validation and Esophageal Cancer Differentiation Prediction

In recent years, machine learning technology has developed rapidly and has outstanding performance in many fields. Common classification algorithms include Support Vector Machine (SVM) [10,11], Classification And Regression Tree (CART), K-Nearest Neighbor (KNN), Ensemble, Extreme Learning Machine (ELM), etc. Different algorithms have their own unique advantages. Various classification prediction problems are successfully solved by these algorithms.

In this study, ten different classification algorithms are used to predict the differentiation of esophageal squamous cell carcinoma. In the development sets, 17 indicators significantly associated with the degree of esophageal cancer differentiation are used as input characteristics and the degree of differentiation as an output. The prediction results of ten classification algorithms are shown in Table 5.

As shown in Table 5, ABC-SVM has a higher average accuracy than the other nine algorithms for 10-fold cross-validation and is more efficient in training. In the development sets, the average accuracy of the 10-fold cross-validation of ABC-SVM predicting the degree of differentiation based on 13 indicators is 81.5%. The average accuracy rate based on 21 indicators is only 75.0%. In the validation sets, the average accuracy of the 10-fold cross-validation of ABC-SVM predicting the degree of differentiation based on 13 indicators is 80.0%. The average accuracy rate based on 21 indicators is only 76.0%. Thus, these 13 indicators screened by the clustering algorithm have a higher correlation with the degree of tumor differentiation of esophageal squamous cell carcinoma. The 13 indicators screened by the clustering algorithm not only improved the prediction accuracy of the differentiation degree, but also reduced the training time of the classification algorithm and improved the training efficiency of the classification algorithm.

For ABC algorithm, the ABC algorithm is used to optimize the main parameters of SVM, including penalty factor c and kernel function parameter g. The artificial bee colony algorithm is an optimized method to simulate the behavior of bees, which can solve multivariate function optimization problems [12,13]. It does not require specific information about the problem and has a faster convergence rate [14–16]. The initial bee colony size is regarded as 20. The number of updates is limited to 100. If the honey source is not updated more than 100 times, the honey source is abandoned. The maximum number of iterations is set 10 times. The number of parameters optimized is 2, the range of parameters is selected from 0.01 to 100, and the algorithm is repeated twice to check the robustness of the ABC-SVM.

4 Development and Validation of the Predictive Model for Esophageal Cancer Differentiation Degrees

The data from the development sets are analyzed by using the multiple logistic regression approach [17]. A multiple logistic regression model is a linear regression model with multiple independent variables. It is used to reveal the linear relationship between the dependent variable and multiple variables. Its mathematical model can be formulated as

$$Y = \beta_0 + \beta_1 x_1 + \beta_2 x_2 + ... + \beta_p x_p \tag{10}$$

Thirteen indicators significantly associated with the degree of esophageal squamous cell carcinoma differentiation are used as inputs and the degree of differentiation as the outputs. The resulting model can be expressed as

$$
\begin{aligned}
Model =\ & 6.59 * X_1 + 3.85 * X_2 + 4.69 * X_3 + 10.005 * X_4 + 11.74 * X_5 \\
& + 47.24 * X_6 + 5.51 * X_7 + 107.13 * X_9 + 5.571 * X_{11} \\
& - 9.66 * X_{12} - 13.01 * X_{13}
\end{aligned}
\tag{11}
$$

where X_1 represents the tumor site and X_2 represents the tumor length. X_3 is the tumor width and the X_4 is the tumor thickness. X_5 represents the WBC count and the X_6 represents the lymphocyte count. X_7 is the monocyte count and X_9 is the eosinophil count. X_{11} represents the red blood cell count and X_{12} represents the PT. X_{13} represents the INR.

The receiver operating characteristic (ROC) curve is also known as the sensitivity curve [18,19]. It can judge the predictive ability of a model [20,21]. The ROC curve of the model in the development sets is shown in Fig. 2 (a). The value of area under curve (AUC) is 0.672, larger than 0.5. $P = 0.0007$. The ROC results for the model in the development sets are shown in Table 6. Therefore, in the validation set, the model has a high predictive value for tumor differentiation of esophageal squamous cell carcinoma.

In this paper, in order to test the validity of the model, the model obtained in the development sets is used for testing and evaluation in the validation sets. The ROC curve of the model in the validation sets is shown in Fig. 2 (b). The ROC analysis of the model in the validation sets is shown in Table 6. The value of area under curve (AUC) is 0.753, larger than 0.5. $P < 0.0001$. In the external validation set, the model has a high predictive value for tumor differentiation in esophageal squamous cell carcinoma. Therefore, the model found in this study has some generalizability and potential application value.

Table 5. The prediction results of the degree of differentiation of ten classification algorithms are based on 21 indicators and 13 indicators.

Data set	Number of samples	Classification algorithm	Number of indicators	Training time	Average accuracy of 10-fold crossover
Development sets	114	SVM	21	0.4339	57.9
			13	0.3941	53
		QDA	21	0.5149	57.9
			13	0.3726	57.4
		CART	21	2.7506	54.4
			13	0.3985	59.1
		LDA	21	1.1738	59.6
			13	0.3570	57.4
		KNN	21	0.4219	57.9
			13	0.3879	53.9
		Ensemble	21	3.1797	61.4
			13	3.3533	61.7
		ELM	21	0.0691	58
			13	0.0121	47
		PSO-SVM	21	134.23	58
			13	109.11	59
		GA-SVM	21	8.4211	51
			13	6.7524	50.01
		ABC-SVM	**21**	**0.9919**	**76.3**
			13	**0.6273**	**81.5**
Validation sets	97	SVM	21	0.3991	58.8
			13	0.3852	54.8
		QDA	21	0.3802	52.6
			13	0.3642	52.3
		CART	21	0.3444	48.5
			13	0.3609	48.7
		LDA	21	0.3929	49.5
			13	0.3568	61.9
		KNN	21	0.4039	60.8
			13	0.3976	53
		Ensemble	21	3.2612	61.9
			13	3.3079	57.4
		ELM	21	0.0541	53
			13	0.0113	53
		PSO-SVM	21	258.12	60
			13	139.68	58.89
		GA-SVM	21	6.4214	58
			13	4.9353	63
		ABC-SVM	**21**	**0.62332**	**76**
			13	**0.5006**	**78**

where SVM is Support Vector Machine and QDA is Quadratic Discriminant Analysis. The CART represents Classification And Regression Tree and the LDA represents Linear Discriminant Analysis. KNN is K-Nearest Neighbor and Ensemble is Ensemble Bagged Tree. The ELM represents Extreme Learning Machine and the PSO-SVM represents Particle Swarm Optimization-Support Vector Machine. GA-SVM is Genetic Algorithm-Support Vector Machine and ABC-SVM is Artificial Bee Colony-Support Vector Machine.

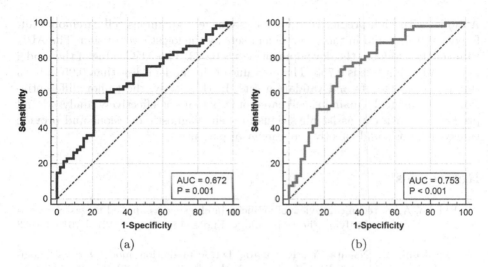

Fig. 2. ROC curves for the model. (a) ROC curves for the model in the development sets. (b) ROC curves for the model in the validation sets. The ordinate is "Sensitivity" and the abscissa is "1-Specificity", the curve is clearly located at the upper left of the diagonal and has a good significance.

Table 6. ROC results of the model in the development sets and validation sets.

Project	Development sets	Validation sets
Area under the ROC curve (AUC)	**0.672**	**0.753**
Standard Error	0.0505	0.0505
95% Confidence interval	0.578 to 0.757	0.655 to 0.835
Z statistic	3.406	4.999
Significance level P (Area = 0.5)	**0.0007**	**<0.0001**
Youden index J	0.3498	0.4404
Associated criterion	>−17.25294	≤−12.37098
Sensitivity	79.25	73.58
Specificity	55.74	70.45

5 Conclusions

In this paper, the Kohonen clustering algorithm, ABC-SVM, logistic regression, and ROC are used to analyze and predict the tumor differentiation of esophageal squamous cell carcinoma. Thirteen indicators significantly associated with esophageal squamous cell carcinoma are found in the development sets by the Kohonen clustering algorithm. Ten classification algorithms are used to predict the tumor differentiation of esophageal squamous cell carcinoma based on 13 significantly correlated indicators. The results showed that ABC-SVM have a good prediction performance, with a 10-fold cross-validation accuracy of 81.5%.

A model with high predictive value for esophageal squamous cell carcinoma differentiation is found in the development sets by the logistic regression. The AUC value of the model in the development sets is 0.672. The AUC value of the model in the validation sets is 0.753. The $p-$ value of the model is less than 0.05 in both the development sets and validation sets. In this study, the tumor differentiation of esophageal squamous cell carcinoma patients is effectively analyzed and predicted, which can assist physicians in their diagnostic decisions and provide timely diagnosis and effective treatment of patients.

References

1. Ebigbo, A.: A technical review of artificial intelligence as applied to gastrointestinal endoscopy: clarifying the terminology. Endos. Int. Open **7**(12), E1616–E1623 (2019)
2. Murakami, Y., Nagata, Y., Kawahara, D.: A prediction model for pathological findings after neoadjuvant chemoradiotherapy for resectable locally advanced esophageal cancer based on PET images using radiomics and machine-learning. J. Clin. Oncol. **38**, 456–456 (2020)
3. Menya, D., Kigen, N., Oduor, M.: Traditional and commercial alcohols and esophageal cancer risk in Kenya. Int. J. Cancer **144**(3), 459–469 (2019)
4. Gillies, C., Farrukh, A., Abrams, R.: Risk of esophageal cancer in achalasia cardia. A Meta-analysis. **3**(3), 196–200 (2019)
5. Haisley, K.R., et al.: Specific tumor characteristics predict upstaging in early-stage esophageal cancer. Ann. Surg. Oncol. **26**(2), 514–522 (2018). https://doi.org/10.1245/s10434-018-6804-z
6. Sun, J., Han, G., Zeng, Z., Wang, Y.: Memristor-based neural network circuit of full-function Pavlov associative memory with time delay and variable learning rate. IEEE Trans. Cybern. **50**(7), 2935–2945 (2020)
7. Sun, J., Yang, Y., Wang, Y., Wang, L., Song, X., Zhao, X.: Survival risk prediction of esophageal cancer based on self-organizing maps clustering and support vector machine ensembles. IEEE Access **8**, 131449–131460 (2020)
8. Sun, J., Zhao, X., Fang, J., Wang, Y.: Autonomous memristor chaotic systems of infinite chaotic attractors and circuitry realization. Nonlinear Dyn. **94**(4), 2879–2887 (2018). https://doi.org/10.1007/s11071-018-4531-4
9. Wang, Y., Li, Z., Sun, J.: Three-variable chaotic oscillatory system based on DNA strand displacement and its coupling combination synchronization. IEEE Trans. Nanobioscience **19**(3), 434–445 (2020)
10. Hou, K., et al.: Research on practical power system stability analysis algorithm based on modified SVM. Protect. Control Modern Power Syst. **3**(1), 1–7 (2018). https://doi.org/10.1186/s41601-018-0086-0
11. El-Saadawi, M., Hatata, A.: A novel protection scheme for synchronous generator stator windings based on SVM. Protect. Control Modern Power Syst. **2**(1), 1–12 (2017). https://doi.org/10.1186/s41601-017-0057-x
12. Mahmoodabadi, M.: Epidemic model analyzed via particle swarm optimization based homotopy perturbation method. Inf. Med. Unlocked **18**, 100293 (2020)
13. Alshamlan, H.M., Badr, G.H., Alohali, Y.A.: ABC-SVM: artificial bee colony and SVM method for microarray gene selection and multi class cancer classification. Int. J. Mach. Learn. Comput. **6**(3), 184 (2016)

14. Grover, P., Chawla, S.: Text feature space optimization using artificial bee colony. In: Das, K.N., Bansal, J.C., Deep, K., Nagar, A.K., Pathipooranam, P., Naidu, R.C. (eds.) Soft Computing for Problem Solving. AISC, vol. 1057, pp. 691–703. Springer, Singapore (2020). https://doi.org/10.1007/978-981-15-0184-5_59

15. Andrushia, A.D., Patricia, A.T.: Artificial bee colony optimization (ABC) for grape leaves disease detection. Evol. Syst. **11**(1), 105–117 (2019). https://doi.org/10.1007/s12530-019-09289-2

16. Watada, J., Roy, A., Wang, B., Tan, S.C., Xu, B.: An artificial bee colony based double layered neural network approach for solving quadratic bi-level programming problems. IEEE Access **8**, 21549–21564 (2020)

17. Christodoulou, E., Ma, J., Collins, G.S., Steyerberg, E.W., Verbakel, J.Y., Van Calster, B.: A systematic review shows no performance benefit of machine learning over logistic regression for clinical prediction models. J. Clin. Epidemiol. **110**, 12–22 (2019)

18. Wen, P., Chen, S., Wang, J., Che, W.: Receiver operating characteristics (ROC) analysis for decreased disease risk and elevated treatment response to pegylated-interferon in chronic hepatitis b patients. Futur. Gener. Comput. Syst. **98**, 372–376 (2019)

19. Tada, T., et al.: Impact of albumin-bilirubin grade on survival in patients with hepatocellular carcinoma who received sorafenib: an analysis using time-dependent receiver operating characteristic. J. Gastroenterol. Hepatol. **34**(6), 1066–1073 (2019)

20. Evcimen, Y., Onur, I.U., Cengiz, H., Yigit, F.U.: Optical coherence tomography findings in pre-eclampsia: a preliminary receiver operating characteristic analysis on choroidal thickness for disease severity. Curr. Eye Res. **44**(8), 916–920 (2019)

21. Jang, E.J., Nandram, B., Ko, Y., Kim, D.H.: Small area estimation of receiver operating characteristic curves for ordinal data under stochastic ordering. Stat. Med. 1–15 (2020)

Analysis of Pregnancy Pulse Discrimination Based on Wrist Pulse by 1D CNN

Nan Li[1], Yi Jiao[1], Xiaobo Mao[1], Yuping Zhao[2], Guoliang Yao[1], and Luqi Huang[1,2(✉)]

[1] College of Electrical Engineering, Zhengzhou University, Zhengzhou 450001, China
[2] China Academy of Chinese Medical Sciences, Beijing 100700, China

Abstract. Wrist pulse contains important information of human health, so the diagnosis and analysis based on pulse signal is of great significance. In this study, a one-dimensional convolutional neural network (1D CNN) model is proposed to distinguish from pregnancy pulse normal pulse. The performance of the proposed 1D CNN was validated with a collected data set consists of 160 subjects. The 1D CNN proposed with clique blocks style architecture and transition blocks is employed. Furthermore, the three clique blocks go through the pooling layer, and extend the one-dimensional data into vectors through the full connection layer, respectively. By using stacked blocks and transition blocks, the proposed CNN leading a promising classification performance. The F-score, accuracy, precision and recall were used to evaluate the effectiveness of this method in pregnancy pulse detection. The experimental results showed that the proposed 1DCNN has a very high averaged accuracy of 97.08%, which indicated that the method can better used for pulse classification.

Keywords: Traditional Chinese medicine · 1D CNN · Pregnancy pulse · F-score

1 Introduction

Traditional Chinese medicine (TCM) is a complete medical system that has widely application in disease diagnosis, treatment and prevention for over 30 centuries [1]. As one of the most important complementary and alternative medicines, TCM has been accepted and used increasingly in the world. In Oriental as well as Western medicine, pulse is considered as a fundamental signal of life, carrying essential information about a persons physical condition and health status [2]. In TCM texts, various pulse qualities have been described [3–5]. The Chinese medical doctors usually use the three fingers of index, middle and ring fingers simultaneously or individually to determine various characteristic features of the pulse [6,7]. It is generally believed that every pulse can reflect people's different physical conditions, which is widely used in aid of diagnosing cardiovascular disease etc. [8–12].

L. Pan et al. (Eds.): BIC-TA 2020, CCIS 1363, pp. 336–346, 2021.
https://doi.org/10.1007/978-981-16-1354-8_23

An important application of pulse diagnosis is the discrimination of pregnancy. A series of physiological changes will take place in women's body, which can be manifested in pulse condition after pregnancy. The pulse condition of pregnancy can objectively reflect a series of changes of the mother's body during pregnancy, which is helpful to judge and understand the health status of the mother. Since the pulse examination has no stimulation, no damage and no radiation, which is better than gynecological examination and is easy to be accepted by pregnant women. Therefore, the in-depth study of pregnancy pulse has clinical application value. A well trained doctor can take the radial pulse to evaluate whether a woman has conceived, to determine the weeks of gestation, and to predict the outcome of pregnancy. Descriptions of the pregnant womens pulse are abundant, as the Huangdi Internal Classic described, but opinions differ on this article [13]. For example, some physicians explain that the slippery pulse is taken on Cun at the first stage of pregnancy, but some describe that the slippery pulse is detected on the cubit during pregnancy. Most doctors believe that Chi pulse is unique compared with inch pulse to pregnant women, and pulse will change with the progress of pregnancy. In addition, there are differences among pulse conditions for pregnant women of different ages. Nevertheless, pulse assessment is a skill that requires long-term experience and is subject to subjective influence. Consequently, an objective and automatic computer assist tool for pregnancy pulse signals analysis is strongly required.

In recent years, more and more attention has been paid to the diagnostic model of combining TCM with artificial intelligence (AI). AI technology can simulate the process of clinical diagnosis thinking and reasoning judgment, automatically analyze and calculate clinical data, and provide a effective way for disease prevention, management, diagnosis and treatment. As the core of AI, deep learning provides an effective way to solve the complex autonomous learning and data analysis problems, such as self coding neural network [14], support vector machine (SVM) [15] and convolutional neural network (CNN) [16], etc. A typical CNN structure is consist of input layer, convolution layer, pooling layer, fully connected layer and softmax layer etc. Owing to the strong feature representation power of deep learning technologies, deep convolutional neural network, as one of the typical deep learning architecture, has achieved tremendous success recently in variety of practical fields. However, CNN is often used to process two-dimensional signals, and the pulse collected is a one-dimensional model. Thus, the 1D pulse signal is usually mapped to a 2D space (for example, a 1D speech signal can be converted into 2D feature maps [17], static feature maps [18], or frequency-time feature [19]) when processing a 1D signal with CNN, which brings inconvenience to signal processing.

In order to meet the characteristics of one-dimensional signal, 1D CNN has become one of the hot spots in the current research. Compared with the 2D CNN, the 1D CNN has the following advantages. Firstly, the 1D temporal signal is directly collected from data acquisition system, so it is more natural to use the 1D input. Secondly, the 2D CNN requires additional 1D-to-2D conversion process (e.g. time-frequency representation method) that may lose some useful information related to faults due to irreversible conversion. Finally, the 2D input signal usually has a higher dimension than the 1D input, which makes the CNN calculation more complex and time-consuming [20,21]. Nowadady, 1D CNN is widely used in image and engineering problems and has achieved good results. Xu et al. study on efficiently real-time behavior recognition algorithm using acceleration sensor. They propose a human behavior recognition method based on improved One-Dimensional Convolutional Neural Networks (1D CNNs) and the method can reach the average accuracy of 98.7% in the recognition of 11 human activities [22]. Wang et al. proposed a novel attention mechanism and multi-attention 1D CNN to diagnose wheelset bearing faults. The 1D CNN used can adaptively recalibrate features of each layer and can enhance the feature learning of fault impulses [23]. Fu et al. study the features in the pulse waves of women during pregnancy. They choose continuous cycles waves with different period length and then do the LSQ regression by 12 harmonics fitting to build mathematical model, then do classification and identification of pregnant women [24]. Chowdhury et al. proposed 1D triplet convolutional neural network to combine the two features (Mel frequency cepstral coefficients and linear predictive coding) in a novel manner, thereby enhancing the performance of speaker recognition in challenging scenarios [25]. Hussain et al. present a new dynamic self-organized network immune algorithm that classifies term and records, over sampling and cross validation techniques are evaluated [26]. These literature show that 1D CNN could be used for TCM clinical diagnosis study with intelligent thought.

In this work, a novel 1D CNN structure is proposed in this paper for effective pregnancy pulse classification. Firstly, each layer of the 1DCNN network adopts the block stack structure, including the block and the transition block. Moreover, a bidirectional connection structure is constructed by using the updated layer to update the previous layer alternately, which the system can obtain effective features. Secondly, the three clique blocks go through the pooling layer, and extend the one-dimensional data into vectors through the full connection layer, respectively. Finally, by combining the feature map blocks of different groups, the fusion of multi-scale features is realized. On this basis, the pulse of pregnant women was identified and the expected effect was achieved. The experiment verifies the feasibility and effectiveness of the proposed method.

The rest of paper is organized as follows. In Sect. 2, some related work will be present. In Sect. 3, the 1D CNN system was proposed and introduced. In Sect. 4 the experimental result and discussion were given. Finally, the conclusions and perspectives of future work are presented in the last section.

2   Related Work

In this part, pulse data acquisition, sample expansion, and train and test data were performed.

2.1   Data Acquisition

A total of 80 health volunteers from Zhengzhou University and 80 pregnant women from the Fifth Affiliated Hospital of Zhengzhou University have been recruited in this study, with a mean age of 24.2 ± 5.5. All volunteers agreed with the exposed terms by signing a written informed consent. In addition, each participant has a questionnaire to ensure the accuracy of the experiment. Data were collected by ZM-300 Intelligent Pulse Meter of Traditional Chinese Medicine, which the sampling frequency 200 Hz. The volunteers were asked to sit still or rest for at least 5 min before the acquisition. During the collecting process, participants were required to sit or stay supine, relax, not talk and breathe normally. Then, the TCM pulse bracelet was placed over the Chi position in the left hand to capture the pulse signals under six pressures for 10 s, respectively. Subjects were excluded from analysis if they lacked complete data for control or outcome variables or had significant disease. Each person collects six groups of data under six different pulse pressures, each group of data consists of 2000 data points. The waveform under the optimal pressure was selected as the experimental object. So the pulse dataset contains a total of 160 pulse signals that are unevenly distributed into normal people and pregnant women. As shown in Fig. 1 and Fig. 2, pulse wave cycle data were obtained in all subjects.

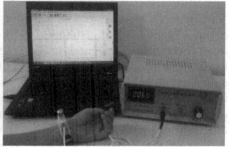

Fig. 1. ZM-300 intelligent pulse meter.   **Fig. 2.** Pulse acquisition.

2.2   Sample Expansion

In order to make better use of the structure of 1D CNN, the data collected is amplified. Since the acquisition frequency 200 Hz and acquisition time of each group data is 10 s, we use 2 s as a segmentation cycle to expand the data and take them as the research object. Therefore, 160 pulse signals were segmented and amplified. Finally, 800 effective waveforms sets were obtained after expanding the data.

2.3   Train and Test Data

1DCNNs require numerous samples to train for improved generalization. However, the data set used in our experiment is relatively small. In order to obtain as much effective information as possible from the limited data, the 10-fold cross

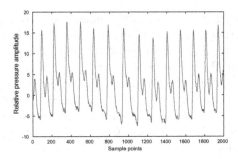 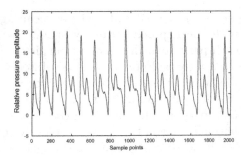

Fig. 3. Original pulse wave.   **Fig. 4.** Filtered pulse wave.

validation was used to process the data and obtained the training set and test sets. The training set contained 560 samples, and the test set contained 240 samples (Figs. 3 and 4).

3 1D CNN Design for the Proposed System

The 1D CNN is analogous to a regular neural network but it has generally raw data as input instead of handcrafted features. Such input data is processed to learn the appropriate representation of the input by several trainable convolution layers. The proposed models consist of batch normalization, residual learning, and down-sampling in the initial layers of the CNN. The structure of the 1D CNNs was simplified as a basic structure of convolution layer, a pooling layer, and a full network layer. The convolution layer had feature maps, and the transfer function was sigmoid. The pooling layer used max-pooling, and the stride was 3. The softmax classifier was used in full network layer to output the posterior probability of each class.

3.1 1D CNN Topology

As described in Fig. 5, the proposed 1D CNN takes pulse set as inputs and outputs predicted results of the corresponding classier. The proposed model is mainly constituted by three clique blocks and two transition blocks. Each transition block connects the subsequent blocks and gradually reduces the mapping features. The feature map of each block is not only input into the next block, but also the original data was compressed in channel dimension. The features connected and compressed by different blocks are sent into pooling to obtain the multi-scale representation. Finally, the compression features of different scales are combined together and the full connect layer is implemented by softmax to achieve the classification results.

3.2 Network Model of 1D CNN

The 1D CNN model has a multi-layer structure, which is mainly divided into the following five parts: input layer, convolution layer (Conv), pooling layer (Pool),

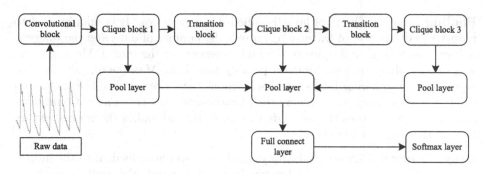

Fig. 5. Flow chart

fully connected layer (FC), and softmax layer. The 1D CNN model structure constructed in this paper is shown in Fig. 6.

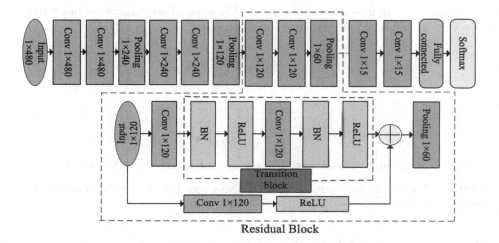

Fig. 6. Network structure of the proposed 1D CNNs

Input Layer: The input layer of 1D CNN can handle one-dimensional data. In this paper, the original data is processed and input in 1×480 form. The hidden layer is composed of convolutional layers, pooling layers, and fully connected layers.

Convolutional Layer: The convolutional layer extracts feature from input data. The pool layer receives the eigenvalues from the convolutional layer and carries out feature selection and information filtering. With the increase of the number of convolution layers, low-level features can be merged into high-level features, and the objects can be classified according to the features. For a typical one-dimensional convolution mechanism, information flows to the next layer through convolution operation and then processed by activation function.

Pooling Layers: The pool layer is called down sampling. It is mainly used to reduce the dimension of features, compress the number of data and parameters, reduce over fitting, and improve the fault tolerance of the model. Mean-pooling and max-pooling are two common pooling functions. Max-pooling divides the input feature mapping into several subregions, while preserving the maximum value of each sub region, reducing the phenomenon that the convolutional layer parameter error causes the estimated mean shift, and makes the image texture information better expressed.

Fully Connected Layers: The fully connected layer is equivalent to the hidden layer in the feed forward neural network, which expands the multidimensional data into vectors and transfers them to the next layer by using the excitation function. The fully connected layer is obtained by adding the weight coefficient to the nodes of the previous layer for many times and adding bias.

Softmax: Softmax is the classifier of this architecture, it makes the prediction using the inputted features. Softmax is a generalization of logistic regression to the problem of multi-class classification. The class label y takes on more than two values. Softmax function can be defined to be

$$w_{ij}z_i = \sum_{j=1}^{N} h_j w_{ij} \tag{1}$$

$$softmax(z)_i = p_i = \frac{e^{z_i}}{\sum\limits_{j=1}^{N} e^{z_i}} \tag{2}$$

where e^{z_i} is the input of softmax, h_i is the activation and w_{ij} is the weight value.

Output Layer: The output layer of 1DCNNs uses the softmax function or the logistic function to output the classification results.

4   Experimental Result and Discussion

In our experiments, the number of iterations is set to 100, and the batch size varies according to the size of the input feature. The models with the best validation accuracy were saved. All experiments were conducted on a desktop computer equipped with Intel Core i7-9700 CPU (72 core, 16.0 GHz) having 16 GB RAM and Nvidia GeForce GTX 1050 GPU. The operating system was Ubuntu version 16.04.

Experiments based on 1D CNNs for pregnancy pulse recognition have effectively improved the recognition accuracy. The curve of accuracy rate and loss rate of the 1D CNN proposed were shown in the Fig. 7 and Fig. 8, respectively. It can be seen from the Fig. 7 that the average accuracy of the identification of pregnancy pulse is 97.08%. ROC curve was shown in Fig. 9. In addition, the $F-score$ was used to indicate the tests accuracy in the statistical analysis of binary classification, The $F-score$ is the harmonic mean of the precision and recall, where an $F - score$ reaches its optimal value at 1 and worst at 0. The $F - score$, precision and recall to quantify the performance of the method in this study, shown in Table 1.

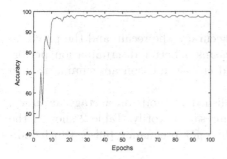

Fig. 7. Test accuracy rate of 1DCNN.

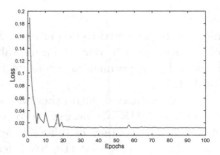

Fig. 8. Test loss rate of 1DCNN.

(1) Accuracy: The ratio of the number of correctly classified samples to the total number of samples.
(2) Precision: The ratio of the number of activities of a certain type to that of all activities of that type. It is an index for predicting results.
(3) Recall: A certain type of activity is correctly predicted as the ratio of the number of such activities to the original total number of such activities. It is an indicator for the original sample instance.

The $F - score$, accyracy, precision and recall can be calculated using the following equation.

$$F - score = 2 \times \frac{\frac{TP}{TP+FP} \times \frac{TP}{TP+FN}}{\frac{TP}{TP+FP} + \frac{TP}{TP+FN}} \tag{3}$$

$$Accyracy = \frac{TP}{TP + TN + FP + FN} \tag{4}$$

$$Precision = \frac{TP}{TP + FP} \tag{5}$$

$$Recall = \frac{TP}{TP + FN} \tag{6}$$

where, TP is the number of activities correctly predicted to be positive, TN is the number of activities correctly predicted to be negative, FP is the number of activities incorrectly predicted to be positive, and FN is the number of activities

Table 1. Displacement spans for different acquisition position.

Criteria	F-score	Accuracy	Precision	Recall
Values	0.9709	0.9708	0.9669	0.9750

incorrectly predicted to be negative. The accuracy, the recall, and the precision range from zero to one. A larger value means a better discrimination performance. The experimental results of 10-fold cross-validation are summarized in Table 1.

When compared with other well-established methods on average accuracy, the designed 1DCNN network also performs satisfactorily. Table 2 showed the classification accuracy of different algorithms for pregnancy pulse, which indicated that the proposed 1DCNN is feasible.

Table 2. Displacement spans for different acquisition position.

Research work	Accuracy
Fu [24]	0.86
Hussain [26]	0.90
The proposed 1DCNN	0.97

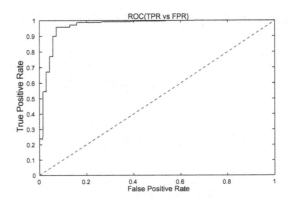

Fig. 9. ROC curve of the proposed 1DCNN

5   Conclusion and Recommendations for the Future

Traditional Chinese medicine believes that human wrist pulse wave contains a lot of important information, which can reflect pathologic changes of the human body condition. In this paper, a 1D CNN model is proposed to distinguish normal pulse from pregnancy pulse. The three clique blocks go through the pooling layer, respectively and extend the one-dimensional data into vectors through the full connection layer. The experimental results show that the accuracy rate of this method is about 97.08% in classifying the pregnancy pulse. In summary, the 1D CNN proposed in this study can effectively improve the classification accuracy of pregnancy pulse.

In the future, the noises factors will be taken into consider to build a model with more robustness for the practical clinical conditions. We will extract more pulse features and use feature dimension reduction to eliminate feature interference caused by feature increase. In addition, the extracted pulse characteristics were used to identify pregnancy pulse from normal pulse, and further verify the new pulse diagnosis method.

Acknowledgments. The work is supported by the key project at central government level (Grant No. 2060302).

References

1. Wu, H.K., Ko, Y.S., Lin, Y.S., et al.: The correlation between pulse diagnosis and constitution identification in traditional Chinese medicine. Complement. Ther. Med. **30**, 107–112 (2017)
2. Velik, R.: An objective review of the technological developments for radial pulse diagnosis in traditional Chinese medicine. Eur. J. Integr. Med. **7**(4), 321–331 (2015)
3. Xiao, J.H., Lei, Z., Jia, T.X., et al.: Pulse wave cycle features analysis of different blood pressure grades in the elderly. Evid. Complement. Alternat. Med. 1–12 (2018). ID 1976041
4. Bilton, K., Zaslawski, C.: Reliability of manual pulse diagnosis methods in traditional East Asian medicine: a systematic narrative literature review. J. Alternat. Complement. Med. **22**(8), 599–609 (2016)
5. Hajar, R.: The pulse in ancient medicine part 1. Heart Views Offic. J. Gulf Heart Assoc. **19**(1), 36 (2018)
6. Qiao, L.J., Qi, Z., Tu, L.P., et al.: The association of radial artery pulse wave variables with the pulse wave velocity and echocardiographic parameters in hypertension. Evid. Complement. Alternat. Med. 1–12 (2018). ID 5291759
7. Huang, Y., Chang, Y., Cheng, S., et al.: Applying pulse spectrum analysis to facilitate the diagnosis of coronary artery disease. Evid. Complement. Alternat. Med. 1–10 (2019). ID 2709486
8. De, M.N., Cordovil, I., De, S.F.A.: Traditional Chinese medicine wrist pulse-taking is associated with pulse waveform analysis and hemodynamics in hypertension. J. Integr. Med. **14**(2), 100–113 (2016)
9. Zhang, Z., Zhang, Y., Yao, L., Song, H., Kos, A.: A sensor-based wrist pulse signal processing and lung cancer recognition. J. Biomed. Inf. **79**, 107–116 (2018)

10. Vallee, A., Petruescu, L., Kretz, S., et al.: Added value of aortic pulse wave velocity index in a predictive diagnosis decision tree of coronary heart disease. Am. J. Hypertens. **32**(4), 375–383 (2019)
11. Alemi, H., Khaloo, P., Mansournia, M.A., et al.: Pulse pressure and diabetes treatments. Medicine **97**(6), e9791 (2018)
12. Wang, N., Yu, Y., Huang, D., et al.: Pulse diagnosis signals analysis of fatty liver disease and cirrhosis patients by using machine learning. Sci. World J. **2015**, 1–9 (2015)
13. Fan, X.D., Wang, R., Chen, W.Y.: Pregnancy outcome of iron-deficiency anemia in third trimester. J. Int. Obstet. Gynecol. **41**(3), 274–276 (2014)
14. Cai, J., Dai, X., Hong, L., et al.: An air quality prediction model based on a noise reduction self-coding deep network. Math. Prob. Eng. **2020**(3), 1–12 (2020)
15. Wang, H., Tan, B., Fang, X., et al.: Precise classification offorest types uses hyperion image based on C5.0 decision tree algorithm. J. Zhejiang AF Univ. **35**(4), 724–734 (2018)
16. Hu, Q., Wang, P., Shen, C., et al.: Pushing the limits of deep CNNs For pedestrian detection. IEEE Trans. Circ. Syst. Video Technol. **28**(6), 1358–1368 (2017)
17. Zhao, J., Mao, X., Chen, L., et al.: Speech emotion recognition using deep 1D–2D CNN LSTM networks. Bio. Signal Proc. Control **47**, 312–323 (2019)
18. Alaa, T., Gaber, Hassanien, T., Ella A.: One-dimensional vs. two-dimensional based features: plant identification approach. J. Appl. Logic **24**, 15–31 (2016)
19. Barrack, D., Goulding, J., Hopcraft, K., et al.: AMP: a new time-frequency feature extraction method for intermittent time-series data. Comput. Sci. **65**, 1–11 (2015)
20. Li, F., Liu, M., Zhao, Y., et al.: Feature extraction and classification of heart sound using 1D convolutional neural networks. J. Adv. Sig. Proc. **2019**(1), 59–70 (2019)
21. Xiao, B., Xu, Y., Bi, X., et al.: Heart sounds classification using a novel 1-D convolutional neural network with extremely low parameter consumption. Neurocomputing **392**, 153–159 (2019)
22. Xu, Z., Zhao, J., Yu. Y, Zeng, H.J.: Improved 1D-CNNs for behavior recognition using wearable sensor network. Comput. Commun. **151**(1), 1153–1156 (2020)
23. Wang, H., Liu, Z., Peng, D., Qin, Y.: Understanding and learning discriminant features based on multiattention 1Dcnn For wheelset bearing fault diagnosis. IEEE Trans. Indust. Infor. **16**(9), 5735–5745 (2020)
24. Wang, N., Yu, Y., Huang, D., et al.: Research of features in the pulse waves of women during pregnancy. In: Bio Informatics Bio Medicine, pp. 730–732 (2010)
25. Chowdhury, A., Ross, A.: Fusing MFCC and LPC features using 1D triplet CNN for speaker recognition in severely degraded audio signals. IEEE Trans. Inf. Forensics Secur. **15**, 1616–1629 (2020)
26. Hussain, A.J., Fergus, P., Al-Askar, D., Al-Jumeily, D.: Dynamic neural network architecture inspired by the immune algorithm to predict preterm deliveries in pregnant women. Neurocomputing **151**, 963–974 (2015)

Perceptron Circuit Design of Second Order Damped System Based on Memristor

Xiao Xiao[1,2], Juntao Han[1,2], Xiangwei Chen[1,2], and Junwei Sun[1,2(✉)]

[1] Henan Key Lab of Information-Based Electrical Appliances,
Zhengzhou University of Light Industry, Zhengzhou 450002, China
junweisun@yeah.net
[2] School of Electrical and Information Engineering,
Zhengzhou University of Light Industry, Zhengzhou 450002, China

Abstract. The development of traditional CMOS-based logic circuits in terms of speed and energy consumption is approaching the limit. Memristor is a kind of bio-inspired hardware with a special structure, which has the advantages of simple structure, low power consumption and easy integration. It has good application prospects in high performance memory and neural network. The invention of memristor provides a new way to develop a more efficient circuit design. In this paper, the second order damping system based on memristor is used to realize the function of human body perceptron. By taking advantage of the variable resistance of memristors, the function of real-time perception can be realized. The second order underdamped state itself is used to realize the sensory adaptation ability of perceptrons. Through theoretical analysis and Pspice simulation, the feasibility of the second order damped system perceptron based on memristor is verified. The human body sensor based on memristor provides a reference for more future intelligent robots. It also provides support for the development and application of bio-inspired hardware.

Keywords: Memristor · Perceptron · Second order damped system · Circuit design

---

This work was supported in part by the National Key Research and Development Program of China for International S and T Cooperation Projects under Grant 2017YFE0103900, in part by the Joint Funds of the National Natural Science Foundation of China under Grant U1804262, in part by the State Key Program of National Natural Science of China under Grant 61632002, in part by the Foundation of Young Key Teachers from University of Henan Province under Grant 2018GGJS092, in part by the Youth Talent Lifting Project of Henan Province under Grant 2018HYTP016, in part by the Henan Province University Science and Technology Innovation Talent Support Plan under Grant 20HASTIT027, in part by the Zhongyuan Thousand Talents Program under Grant 204200510003.

L. Pan et al. (Eds.): BIC-TA 2020, CCIS 1363, pp. 347–358, 2021.
https://doi.org/10.1007/978-981-16-1354-8_24

1 Introduction

With the development of robots, researchers have conducted a lot of researches on the processing of robot sensory activities. Humanoid intelligent devices are constantly being developed, especially those with artificial sensory processing or emotional intelligence algorithms are developing rapidly [1–5]. Linguistically, the word "perception" is defined by the Oxford Dictionary as the ability to see and hear, or to become aware of something through the senses [6]. However, in the relevant theories of psychology, perception is an important basic skill for human survival. Because humans can describe the process of learning information about their environment [7,8]. Human perception can be seen as a complex recognition system [9]. Neurological research has shown that the brain is the core organ of the human sensory system, and that it consists of a complex network of neurons. All kinds of sensory organs of people transmit to the nerve center through neurons so that the brain gets all kinds of information.

In recent years, the perception of robot is a hot topic in the field of human-computer interaction. A model for emotional modulation of the robot periper-sonal space was proposed by [10]. By observing human activities, a semantic perception method to extract low-level information from sensor data and infer high-level information was given by [11]. The localization of perceptual attention is realized by visual and visual emotion recognition [12]. However, all of these methods ignore real-time perception. In real life, human perception is often a continuous process. A perceptron that can continuously perceive makes a machine more humanoid.

Everyone has sensory organs, but the sensory ability of each person is different, some people have strong sensory abilities, others have weak sensory abilities. The same sound is heard by some and not by others. The same size object is visible to some and invisible to others, and that is the difference in sensory ability. Different senses have different acuity. Based on the size of weber's score, we can judge the acuteness of certain senses [13]. The smaller the Weber score, the sharper the sensation. The Wechsler scores of different senses are shown in Table 1. In this study, different memristor-based perceptrons are designed according to different waveforms.

The memristor is a variable and non-volatile resistance. It has nanoscale dimensions and behaves much like synapses in the brains of intelligent creatures. Since it was discovered, it attracted the attention of many researchers. A continuously variable resistor value of a memristor has been used to store analog audio data [14]. When a memristor is used in a circuit, the circuit is very simple and energy consumption is very low.

In this paper, based on the research and design of the human body perception circuit, a kind of human body sensor based on the second order damped system of memristor is proposed to realize the real-time perception ability of robot. Currently the sensory processors in humanoid intelligent devices are mostly built on traditional complementary metal oxide semiconductor (CMOS) devices which combine with other components such as capacitor, operational amplifier and so on [15,16]. However, the capacitor, operational amplifier and other components may increase the area and power of the circuit, which is not conducive to circuit integration. The memristor used in this paper has simple structure and rich switching characteristics, and is an ideal choice for simulating human perception processor.

Table 1. Webster's fraction of different senses.

Feeling	Weber fraction
The sense of visual	1/60
The sense of kinesthetic	1/50
The sense of pain	1/30
The sense of auditory	1/10
The sense of touch	1/7
The sense of smell	1/4
The sense of taste	1/3

In Sect. 2, a threshold memristor model is introduced. Then, in Sect. 3, the circuit of second order damping system based on the memristor is designed. In Sect. 4, the simulation results of second order underdamped system circuit are described in detail. Finally, some conclusions are drawn in Sect. 5.

2   Memristor Model

Memristor originated from the theoretical conjecture proposed by Chua, a Chinese professor at the University of California, Berkeley [17]. There are six mathematical relationships between charge, voltage, current, and magnetic flux, only one between charge and magnetic flux $d\phi/dq$ is unknown. From the perspective of symmetry, in addition to resistance, capacitance and inductance, there should also be a fourth passive electronic component that can associate charge with magnetic flux. The relation between charge and magnetic flux has the same dimension as resistance, whose value is determined by the amount of charge flowing through it. Therefore, such device is called memristor. However, memristor is only a theoretical model, which has not received enough attention. Hewlett-Packard Labs created the memory resistor in an experiment with microcircuits until 2008 [18]. Memristors could play an important role in the next generation of high-performance computers, according to Nature Electronics [19].

Memristor has the property of resistances and is first used in logical operations [20–26]. Secondly, using memristor to construct chaotic circuit can generate complex chaotic phenomena and realize secure communication based on memristor chaos [27–29]. Based on the characteristic of variable resistance and non-volatile resistance of memristor, non-volatile resistance memory can be constructed [30–33].

Since the first memristor was made in the laboratory, a variety of memristors have been made [34–38]. But these memristors are only used in the laboratory. The researchers used computer-aided design to make unconditional contact with the memristor object. Various memory resistor simulation models have been developed for the development of memory resistor circuits [20,21,39–41]. In the paper, the threshold memristor model used to mimic the AIST-based memristor is selected, which matches the I-V characteristics of both repetitive sweeping and sinusoidal inputs [44]. The model is described as

$$M = R_{ON}\frac{w(t)}{D} + R_{OFF}(1 - \frac{w(t)}{D}).(R_{OFF} \gg R_{ON}) \tag{1}$$

where $M(t)$ is the memristance, $w(t)$ is the width of the high doped region, D is the full thickness of memristor material. R_{ON} and R_{OFF} denote the resistance when the memristor is completely high doped or low doped, respectively. The derivative of the state variable $w(t)$ is

$$\frac{dw(t)}{dt} = \begin{cases} \mu_v \frac{R_{ON}}{D} \frac{i_{off}}{i(t)-i_0} f(w(t)), & v(t) > V_{T+} > 0 \\ 0, & V_{T-} \leqslant v(t) \leqslant V_{T+} \\ \mu_v \frac{R_{ON}}{D} \frac{i(t)}{i_{on}} f(w(t)), & v(t) < V_{T-} < 0 \end{cases} \tag{2}$$

where μ_v stands for the average ion mobility, i_0, i_{on} and i_{off}, are constants, i_0 is a very small constant, so that the memristance will decrease when the memristor is applied by a small positive voltage. In this paper, any positive voltage applied to memristor can make $i(t)$ greater than i_0. V_{T+} and V_{T-} are positive and negative threshold voltages, respectively, ensuring that the memristance changes only when the voltage is greater than V_{T+} or less than V_{T-}. $f(w(t))$ is given as a window function

$$f(w(t)) = 1 - (\frac{w(t)}{D} - sgn(-i))^{2p} \tag{3}$$

where p is a positive integer. Applying a positive voltage to a memristor causes an increase in $w(t)$ and a decrease in memristor. The greater the positive voltage is, the slower $w(t)$ increases, and the slower the memristance decreases. The opposite case will occur when the memristor is applied by a negative voltage. The memristor parameters used in the subsequent circuit design are shown in Table 2.

Table 2. The parameters of threshold voltage memristor model.

Parameters	R_{on}	R_{off}	R_{init}	$V_{TH+}(v)$	$V_{TH-}(v)$
Value	1k	800k	8k	0.19	−0.37
Parameters	$D(nm)$	$\mu_v(m^2 s^{-1}\Omega^{-1})$	$i_{off}(A)$	$i_0(A)$	P
Value	3	1.6e−15	1.0e−5	1.0e−3	10

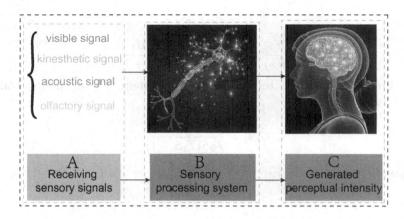

Fig. 1. Schematic diagram of perception processor.

3   Circuit Design

Schematic diagram of perception processor is shown in Fig. 1. It mainly consists of part A: Receiving sensory signals module, part B: Sensory processing module and part C: Generated perceptual intensity module. When it receives a stimulus, it produces a stimulus signal, the sensory signal, and sends it to the body's sensory processor. Perceptual signals are generated by the body's perceptrons, which generate the intensity of perception. And then it goes to the nerve center of the brain. Perceptual signals are generated by the body's perceptors to generate perceived intensity, which is then transmitted to the brain's nerve centers. In this paper, we design a body perceptron using a second-order damping system. It contains a proportional part, an integral part, and an inertia part. The transfer function of the proportional part is

$$c(t) = K_1 r(t) \tag{4}$$

$$\frac{C(s)}{R(s)} = K_1 = \frac{R_2}{R_1} \tag{5}$$

The transfer function of the integral part is

$$T_0 \frac{dc(t)}{dt} = r(t) \tag{6}$$

$$T_0 = R_3 C_1 \tag{7}$$

$$\frac{C(s)}{R(s)} = \frac{1}{T_0 s} = \frac{1}{R_3 C_1 s} \tag{8}$$

The transfer function of the inertia part is

$$T_1 \frac{dc(t)}{dt} + c(t) = K_2 r(t) \tag{9}$$

$$T_1 = R_4C_2 \tag{10}$$

$$\frac{C(s)}{R(s)} = \frac{K_2}{T_1s + 1} = \frac{R_4/M_1}{R_4Cs + 1} \tag{11}$$

These three parts combine to form the entire system. The open-loop transfer function of the system is

$$G(s) = \frac{K_2}{T_0S(T_1S + 1)} \tag{12}$$

The open-loop gain K is

$$K = \frac{K_2}{T_0} \tag{13}$$

The closed loop transfer function of the system is

$$\Phi(s) = \frac{C(s)}{R(s)} = \frac{K_2}{T_0T_1s^2 + T_0s + K_2} = \frac{K_2/T_0T_1}{s^2 + s/T_1 + K_1/T_0T_1} \tag{14}$$

The following parameters can be obtained

$$\frac{K_2}{T_0T_1} = \omega_n^2, \omega_n = \sqrt{\frac{1}{R_3M_1C_1C_2}} \tag{15}$$

$$\frac{1}{T_1} = 2\xi\omega_n, \xi = \sqrt{\frac{R_3M_1C_1}{4R_4^2C_2}} \tag{16}$$

In a second-order damping system, the remaining parameters are

$$M_p = e^{\frac{-\xi\pi}{\sqrt{1-\xi^2}}} = e^{-\sqrt{\frac{\pi^2 R_3M_1C_1}{4R_4^2C_2 - R_3M_1C_1}}} \tag{17}$$

$$t_p = \frac{\pi}{\omega_n\sqrt{1-\xi^2}} = \sqrt{\frac{4\pi^2 R_3R_4^2M_1C_1C_2^2}{4R_4^2C_2 - R_3M_1C_1}} \tag{18}$$

$$t_s = \frac{4}{\xi\omega_n} = 8R_4^2C_2 \tag{19}$$

$$C(t_p) = 1 + e^{\frac{-\xi\pi}{\sqrt{1-\xi^2}}} = 1 + e^{-\sqrt{\frac{\pi^2 R_3M_1C_1}{4R_4^2C_2 - R_3M_1C_1}}} \tag{20}$$

The circuit design of the second-order damping system skin sensor based on memristor is shown in Fig. 2. In the second-order damping system, a is the proportional link, b is the integral link, and c is the inertial link. The memristor based human perceptor consists of four single-memristor body perception circuits that receive and process visual, kinesthetic, auditory, and olfactory signals, respectively, and convert the electrical signals into perceptual intensity while transmitting them to the nerve center. As shown in Fig. 3, this work proposes a circuit with four perceptors acting simultaneously based on the perceptors.

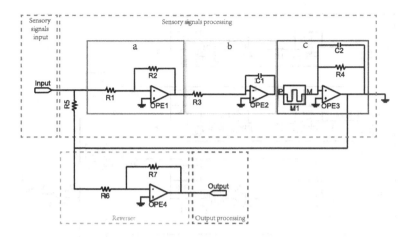

Fig. 2. Schematic diagram of human perceptron circuit for second order damped system based on memristor.

4   Simulation Results

Pspice is used to perform time domain analysis on the designed circuit. After the sensory organs are stimulated by the outside world, the constant stimulation signals change the sensitivity of the sensory organs. The intensity of perception goes through a short period of fluctuation and then enters a relatively stable phase of output. Medium-term perceptual intensity is characterized by small scale fluctuations. For example, if people put their hands in cold water for a long period of time, it may feel icy at first, but over time they may get used to it. It's called sensory adaptation. Therefore, a kind of sensing processor based on second order damping is proposed in this work, which can represent this process well. The performance indexes of the second-order system in the underdamped state are shown in Table 3. It takes $R_1 = R_2 = R_5 = 20$ KΩ, $R_3 = 100$ KΩ, $R_4 = 200$ KΩ, $R_6 = R_7 = 10$ KΩ.

The simulation results of the sensor circuit of the second-order underdamped system based on the memristor are shown in Fig. 4. In Fig. 4(a), the perceptron

Table 3. Performance index of the second-order system in the underdamped state.

Underdamping	Parameter								
	$M_1(\text{K}\Omega)$	K	ω_n	ξ	$C(t_p)$	$C(\infty)$	$M_p(\%)$	$t_p(s)$	$t_s(s)$
$0 < \xi < 1$	8	25	25	0.1	1.73	1	0.73	0.13	1.6
	72	2.778	8.333	0.3	1.37	1	0.37	0.40	1.6
	200	1	5	0.5	1.16	1	0.16	0.73	1.6
	512	0.391	3.125	0.8	1.02	1	0.02	1.67	1.6
	800	0.25	2.5	1	1	NO	NO	NO	1.6

5   Conclusion

In the paper, a second-order damped human body sensor based on memristor has been designed. Perceptron includes the input module, the generating perceptron intensity module and the output module. The function of perceptron real-time perception can be realized by the characteristics of memristor. Theoretical analysis and simulation results show that the designed circuit can realize the functions of real-time perception and sensory adaptation, and finally realize the function of perceptron. In future research, the perceptron circuit of the second order damped system based on memristor will be used to realize more complex functions, so as to realize more humanoid functions of the robot. In addition, the design of memristor circuit will provide a reference for the further development of bionic hardware.

References

1. Jin, X., Su, T., Kong, J., Bai, Y., Miao, B., Dou, C.: State-of-the-art mobile intelligence. Enabling robots to move like humans by estimating mobility with artificial intelligence. Appl. Sci. **8**(3), 1–39 (2018). Article no. 379
2. Cui, C., Bian, G., Hou, Z., Zhao, J., Zhou, H.: A multimodal framework based on integration of cortical and muscular activities for decoding human intentions about lower limb motions. IEEE Trans. Biomed. Circuits Syst. **11**(4), 889–899 (2017)
3. Rasouli, M., Chen, Y., Basu, A., Kukreja, S.L., Thakor, N.V.: An extreme learning machine-based neuromorphic tactile sensing system for texture recognition. IEEE Trans. Biomed. Circuits Syst. **99**(12), 313–325 (2018)
4. Navaraj, W.T., Nunez, C.G., Shakthivel, D., Vinciguerra, V., Labeau, F., Gregory, D.H., Dahiya, R.: Nanowire FET based neural element for robotic tactile sensing skin. Front. NeuroSci. **11**, 501 (2017)
5. Kawasaki, H., Mouri, T.: Humanoid robot hand and its applied research. J. Robot. Mechatron. **31**(1), 16–26 (2019)
6. Pflug, G.: Book review: the oxford dictionary of statistical terms. Biom. J. **46**(2), 284 (2004)
7. Sebrechts, M.M.: The Psychology of Human-Computer Interaction (Book). Erlbaum Associates Inc., New Jersey (1983). American Entist
8. Bills, A.G.: Sensation and perception in the history of experimental psychology. Psychol. Bull. **40**(3), 222–225 (1943)
9. APAFreeman, R.B.: The senses considered as perceptual systems. Q. Rev. Biol. **1**, 8–9 (1969)
10. Belkaid, M., Cuperlier, N., Gaussier, P.: Emotional modulation of peripersonal space as a way to represent reachable and comfort areas. In: Intelligent Robots and Systems, pp. 353–359 (2015)
11. Ramirezamaro, K., Beetz, M., Cheng, G.: Understanding the intention of human activities through semantic perception: observation, understanding and execution on a humanoid robot. Adv. Robot. **29**(5), 345–362 (2015)
12. Chao, L., Tao, J., Yang, M., Li, Y., Wen, Z.: Audio Visual Emotion Recognition with Temporal Alignment and Perception Attention (2016). arXiv: Computer Vision and Pattern Recognition

13. Goldstein, B.E., Brockmole, J.: Sensation and Perception. Cengage Learning, Boston (2016)
14. Duan, S.K., Hu, X.F., Wang, L.D., Li, C.D.: Analog memristive memory with applications in audio signal processing. Sci. China Inform. Sci. **57**(4), 1–15 (2013). https://doi.org/10.1007/s11432-013-4864-z
15. Kaboli, M., Cheng, G.: Robust tactile descriptors for discriminating objects from textural properties via artificial robotic skin. IEEE Trans. Robot. **34**(4), 985–1003 (2018)
16. Gupta, S., Yogeswaran, N., Giacomozzi, F., Lorenzelli, L., Dahiya, R.: Flexible AlN coupled MOSFET device for touch sensing. In: IEEE SENSORS (2018)
17. Chua, L.O.: Memristor-the missing circuit element. IEEE Trans. Circuit Theory **18**(5), 507–519 (1971)
18. Strukov, D.B., Snider, G.S., Stewart, D.R., Williams, R.S.: The missing memristor found. Nature **453**(7191), 80–83 (2008)
19. Li, C., Hu, M., Li, Y., Jiang, H., Xia, Q.: Analogue signal and image processing with large memristor crossbars. Nat. Electron. **1**(1), 52–59 (2018)
20. Lehtonen, E., Laiho, M.: Stateful implication logic with memristors. In: IEEE/ACM International Symposium on Nanoscale Architectures, pp. 33–36 (2009)
21. Xia, Q., et al.: Memristor-CMOS hybrid integrated circuits for reconfigurable logic. Nano Lett. **9**(10), 3640–3645 (2009)
22. Borghetti, J., Snider, G.S., Kuekes, P.J., Yang, J.J., Stewart, D.R., Williams, R.S.: 'Memristive' switches enable 'stateful' logic operations via material implication. Nature **464**(7290), 873–876 (2010)
23. Kvatinsky, S., Wald, N., Satat, G., Kolodny, A., Friedman, E.G.: MRL-memristor ratioed logic. In: International Workshop on Cellular Nanoscale Networks and Their Applications, IEEE (2012)
24. Guckert, L., Swartzlander, E.E.: MAD gates-memristor logic design using driver circuitry. IEEE Trans. Circuits Syst. II Express Briefs **64**(2), 171–175 (2017)
25. Kim, K., Williams, R.S.: A family of stateful memristor gates for complete cascading logic. IEEE Trans.Circuits Syst. **66**(11), 4348–4355 (2019)
26. Papandroulidakis, G., Serb, A., Khiat, A., Merrett, G.V., Prodromakis, T.: Practical implementation of memristor-based threshold logic gates. IEEE Trans. Circuits Syst. **66**(8), 3041–3051 (2019)
27. Muthuswamy, B.: Implementing memristor based chaotic circuits. Int. J. Bifurc. Chaos Syst. **20**(05), 1335–1350 (2010)
28. Sun, J., Zhao, X., Fang, J., Wang, Y.: Autonomous memristor chaotic systems of infinite chaotic attractors and circuitry realization. Nonlinear Dyn. **94**(4), 2879–2887 (2018). https://doi.org/10.1007/s11071-018-4531-4
29. Sun, J., Han, G., Wang, Y., Zhang, H., Wu, L.: Hybrid memristor chaotic system. J. Nanoelectron. Optoelectron. **13**(6), 812–818 (2018)
30. Xu, C., Dong, X., Jouppi, N. P., Xie, Y.: Design implications of memristor-based RRAM cross-point structures. In: 2011 Design, Automation and Test in Europe, pp. 1–6 (2011)
31. Ebong, I., Mazumder, P.: Self-controlled writing and erasing in a memristor cross-bar memory. IEEE Trans. Nanotechnol. **10**(6), 1454–1463 (2011)
32. Shaarawy, N., et al.: Design and analysis of 2T2M hybrid CMOS-Memristor based RRAM. Microelectron. J. **73**, 75–85 (2018)
33. Dubey, S.K., Reddy, A., Patel, R., Abz, M., Srinivasulu, A., Islam, A.: Architecture of resistive RAM with write driver. Solid State Electron. Lett. **2**, 10–22 (2020)

34. Yan, X., Zhao, J., Liu, S., Zhou, Z., Liu, Q., Chen, J.S., Liu, X.: Memristor with Ag-cluster-doped TiO2 films as artificial synapse for neuroinspired computing. Adv. Funct. Mater. **28**(1), 1705320 (2018)

35. Yoon, J.H., et al.: A low-current and analog Memristor with Ru as mobile species. Adv. Mater. **32**(9), 1904599 (2020)

36. Zhou, L., et al.: Tunable synaptic behavior realized in C3N composite based memristor. Nano Energy **58**, 293–303 (2019)

37. Kvatinsky, S., Friedman, E.G., Kolodny, A., Weiser, U.C.: TEAM: threshold adaptive memristor model. IEEE Trans. Circuits Syst. **60**(1), 211–221 (2013)

38. Biolek, D., Biolkova, V., Biolek, Z.: SPICE model of memristor with nonlinear dopant drift. Radioengineering **18**(2), 210–214 (2009)

39. Xu, F., Zhang, J.Q., Huang, S.F., Zhang, J.S., Xie, S.Q., Wang, M.S.: A new nonlinear dopant kinetic model of memristor and its application. Indian Journal of Physics **93**(6), 765–772 (2018). https://doi.org/10.1007/s12648-018-1330-1

40. Rziga, F.O., Mbarek, K., Ghedira, S., Besbes, K.: An efficient Verilog-A memristor model implementation: simulation and application. J. Comput. Electron. **18**(3), 1055–1064 (2019). https://doi.org/10.1007/s10825-019-01357-9

41. Nigus, M., Priyadarshini, R., Mehra, R.M.: Stochastic and novel generic scalable window function-based deterministic memristor SPICE model comparison and implementation for synaptic circuit design. SN Appl. Sci. **2**(1), 1–20 (2019). https://doi.org/10.1007/s42452-019-1888-z

42. Zhang, Y., Wang, X., Li, Y., Friedman, E.G.: Memristive model for synaptic circuits. IEEE Trans. Circuits Syst. II-Express Briefs **64**(7), 767–771 (2017)

Pulse Analysis and Identification of Obese People Based on VGG-16 Net

Guoliang Yao, Yi Jiao, Nan Li, and Xiaobo Mao$^{(\boxtimes)}$

School of Electrical Engineering, Zhengzhou University, Zhengzhou 450001, China

Abstract. The objectification of Traditional Chinese Medicine(TCM) pulse diagnosis has become one of the important development directions of pulse diagnosis analysis. In this paper, Z-M300 intelligent pulse diagnosis instrument was used to collect pulse images of college students with different body weights, and then expert screening, data preprocessing and data marking were carried out to obtain standard data sets. Then, the improved VGG-16 convolutional neural network(VGG-16Net) is used to realize the feature self-extraction of pulse image and establish the pulse image classification model. The experimental results show that the classification accuracy of the method for the pulse image of obese people and normal people reaches 90.28%, which greatly improves the accuracy compared with the traditional method of pulse image classification. This study proves the validity of the one-dimensional convolutional neural network for pulse image classification, which is of great significance for the objectification of pulse diagnosis.

Keywords: Pulse classification · Deep learning · CNN.

1 Introduction

Pulse diagnosis has important research value and clinical significance. During pulse diagnosis, physicians obtain pulse signals by pressing the radial artery pulse at the wrist with their fingers, but the accuracy is affected by the clinical experience of physicians, and there is a lack of objective diagnostic criteria. In this paper, convolutional neural network is applied to the classification of pulse signals, which provides an effective and objective method for medical research, contributes to the standardization of pulse identification, and promotes and advances the inheritance of Traditional Chinese Medicine.

It is of great significance for the modernization of Traditional Chinese Medicine to realize the classification of pulse by feature extraction of pulse. Lin et al. calculated continuous blood pressure values by pulse wave propagation velocity to obtain more accurate continuous blood pressure measurements [1]. Wang et al. proposed the theory of Kernel Extreme Learning Machine(KELM) and applied it to the classification of pulse, and adopted Morlet wavelet function as the kernel function of limit learning machine to realize the accurate classification of pulse, it solves the problem of the lack of quantitative criteria and the low

Supported by key project at central government level (2060302).

© Springer Nature Singapore Pte Ltd. 2021
L. Pan et al. (Eds.): BIC-TA 2020, CCIS 1363, pp. 359–368, 2021.
https://doi.org/10.1007/978-981-16-1354-8_25

recognition rate of traditional pulse classification methods in artificial pulse diagnosis [2]. Thakker B et al. proposed a Dynamic Time Warping (DTW) method to detect abnormal pulse signals. They divided the pulse signals into a single periodic set and identified the abnormal pulse signals based on the similarity of the period of a single cycle [3]. Li et al. use D-S evidence theory is established based on feature fusion in BPW driver fatigue detection model, successful for fatigue driving pulse wave with the normal pulse, the research based on biological information fusion of driving fatigue check models and methods in the driver fatigue detection and monitoring has a good application prospect [4]. Li Fufeng et al. analyzed and extracted the pulse signal using Hilbert-Huang transform (HHT) and time domain method respectively, and gave the time domain parameters and time domain parameters of the pulse signal Hilbert-Huang transform, and obtained the corresponding relationship between the pulse shape of patients with coronary heart disease and the Hilbert transform component [5].

Among the numerous studies on the classification of pulse signals, there are mainly BP Neural Network, linear discriminant analysis, Bayesian classifier, Support Vector Machine (SVM), and Convolutional Neural Network (CNN), which all require the extraction of pulse characteristics manually. However, there is a complex nonlinear relationship between pulse type and pulse characteristics, so it is very difficult to find the feature set that can distinguish different pulse patterns with these methods. In recent years, convolutional neural network has been widely applied in image recognition direction. Through simulating the transmission of neuron information, convolutional neural network can realize the automatic extraction of features. In many studies, these features have been proved to have better characterization effect and better classification effect than manual extraction of features.

Obesity is a chronic metabolic disease caused by the interaction of multiple factors such as genetic factors and environmental factors [6]. In recent years, obesity rates have been rising rapidly around the world. Effective detection of obese people is the basis for analyzing the causes of obesity and then treating them. Therefore, objective identification criteria for obese people have become an urgent problem to be solved [7]. The author proposed to use one-dimensional convolutional neural network to analyze and identify pulse signals of obese people, hoping to provide objective criteria for the determination of obesity.

2   Research Methods

The proposed pulse classification method is shown in Fig. 1, including the following steps.

2.1   Data Collection

Pulse data of obese and healthy individuals used in this paper were collected by researchers from the School of Electrical Engineering, Zhengzhou University.

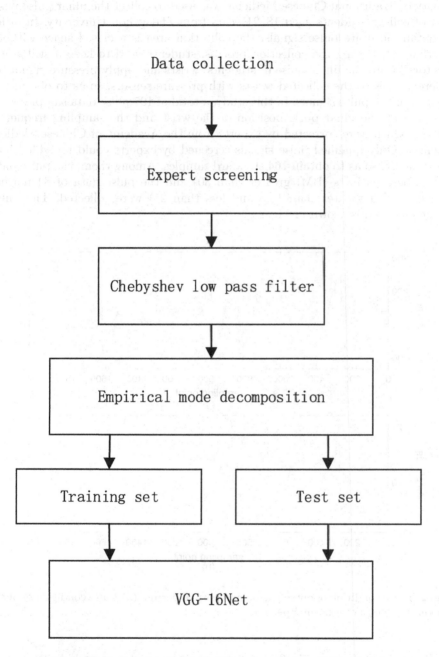

Fig. 1. Block diagram of pulse identification method is presented.

Zm-300 intelligent TCM pulse detection instrument developed by Shanghai University of Traditional Chinese Medicine was used to collect the ulnar pulse position of college students aged 18–21 years from Zhengzhou University. In order to obtain accurate pulse signals, the collection area is a closed space without interference. During the collection process, students need to keep a still state. Doctors locate the ulnar pulse of students' wrists and apply pressure signals of different sizes to the collected wrists with pressure sensors, so as to obtain the most accurate pulse signals. In this study, a total of 197 pulse data samples were collected at the ulnar pulse position of the wrist and the sampling frequency 200 Hz, which were corrected by experts from the Academy of Chinese Medical Sciences. Only qualified pulse signals screened by experts could be added into the data set, so as to obtain 164 standard samples. Among them, the pulse data of 84 obese patients (BMI greater than 30) and the pulse data of 84 normal patients (BMI greater than 18.5 and less than 25) were collected. The pulse image collected is shown in Fig. 2.

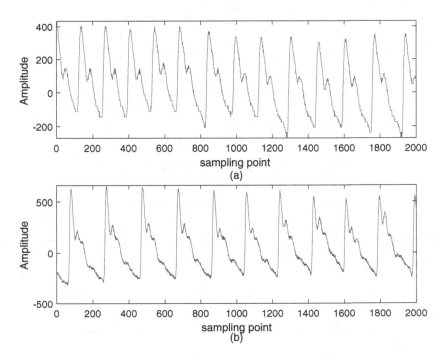

Fig. 2. Pulse condition of obese person and normal person. (a) Pulse condition of obese person. (b) Pulse of a normal person.

It can be seen from Fig. 2 that pulse wave has a strong periodicity. Before using convolutional neural network to classify the data set, complete pulse wave in the data set should be extracted first, and 288 consecutive sampling points should be randomly selected from each data set to obtain complete pulse image.

2.2   Data Denoising

High random interference of power line and baseline drift interference may be brought in the process of collecting pulse signals. There are different denoising methods according to the characteristics of different interfered signals. The frequency range of pulse signals is mainly distributed in 0–20 Hz, so chebyshev low-pass filter is selected for high-frequency signals in this paper to eliminate power line interference and high-frequency random interference above 20 Hz. Then, Empirical Mode Decomposition(EMD) [8] was used to filter baseline drift noise. First, pulse signals were decomposed into 9 IMF components, as shown in Fig. 3.

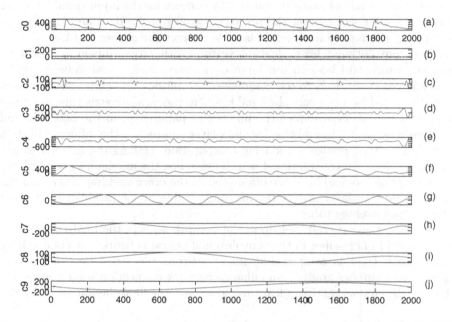

Fig. 3. Empirical modal decomposition results. (a) The original signal. (b)–(j) EMD components.

In the Fig. 3, C0 is the original pulse, C1–C9 is the IMF component, and the original pulse signal is decomposed by EMD into multiple components C1–C9. With the increase of decomposition times, the frequency of components decreases, C1–C4 is the high frequency part, and C5–C9 is the low frequency part. Observation of IMF classification shows that the frequency of signal C5–C9 component is less 1 Hz, while the pulse sampling frequency 200 Hz. Therefore, the reconstructed C5–C9 signal is the disturbance signal, and the de-noised signal can be obtained by subtracting the disturbance signal from the original signal.

2.3   Basic Structure of Convolutional Neural Network

As one of the most important algorithms in deep learning, convolutional neural network is often used for the classification and recognition of speech and images. One dimensional convolutional neural network also shows excellent performance in the processing of sequence data. The principle of the convolutional neural network is similar to that of the artificial neural network, which consists of three important parts: The convolution layer, the pooling layer and the full connection layer.

The convolutional layer contains multiple convolution filters, which have the characteristics of weight sharing and local connection. The convolution filter is the convolution kernel and is an important part of the convolutional layer. The convolution kernel extracts features by convolving the input data. The first convolution filter will extract the primary features of the data and then act as the input of the next convolutional layer to extract the deeper features.

After convolutional layer, feature vectors with larger dimensions will be obtained, which will lead to too large data space, and neural network training of such data will lead to too complex computation. Therefore, pooling layer is usually added between convolutional layers in the network structure to reduce the spatial size of data, reduce the number of parameters in the network, and avoid resource waste. In addition, pooling layer can reduce the influence of data overfitting on the premise of reducing computation, making the network structure more robust. In convolutional neural networks, the maximum pooling layer and the average pooling layer are often used as the downsampling layer, and the maximum pooling layer selects the maximum value in the neighborhood space as the output average value.

All connection generally set up in the network layer of the final location, its have the effect of classifier in the convolutional neural network, the connectivity layer in each layer is composed of many neurons tile structure, its function is nonlinear mapping ability, can enhance network connection layer connection across all the characteristics of learning, to achieve the final classification results.

2.4   VGG-16 Net

VGG-16 net is a kind of convolutional neural network, which is a deep convolutional neural network structure jointly developed by Computer Vision Group of Oxford University and Google Deepmind researcher. This network has simple structure and good classification effect, and can often achieve classification effect at the level of neural networks such as Googlenet Alexnet [9].

VGG-16 net successfully constructed a 16-layer deep convolutional neural network by repeatedly stacking 3 * 3 convolution kernel and 2 * 2 pooling layer. VGG-16 net has 13 convolutional layers and 3 full connection layers, and the maximum pooling layer is added in the 2, 4, 7, 10 and 13 convolutional layers. Based on the structure of VGG-16 network and the characteristics of pulse signal, the VGG-16 network is reformed in this paper to achieve better classification effect of one-dimensional signals. The structure of the original VGG-16 is shown in Table 1.

Table 1. Detailed parameter configuration of the model.

Sequence	Type of operation
0	Data input
1	Conv3-64
2	Conv3-64
3	Maxpool
4	Conv3-128
5	Conv3-128
6	Maxpool
7	Conv3-256
8	Conv3-256
9	Conv3-256
10	Maxpool
11	Conv3-512
12	Conv3-512
13	Conv3-512
14	Maxpool
15	Conv3-512
16	Conv3-512
17	Conv3-512
18	Maxpool
19	FC-4096
20	FC-4096
21	FC-1000
22	Softmax

3 Experimental Results and Analysis

In the experiment, the pulse of healthy people was considered a positive sample, and that of obese people was considered a negative sample. Sensitivity (SE), Specificity (SP) and Accuracy (ACC) were used to evaluate the classification effect of the model. SE represents the probability of correct prediction in positive sample, SP represents the probability of correct prediction in negative sample, ACC represents the overall prediction accuracy of positive sample and negative sample, which is defined as follows:

$$SE = \frac{TP}{TP + FN} \tag{1}$$

$$SP = \frac{TN}{TN + FP} \tag{2}$$

$$ACC = \frac{TN + TP}{TN + TP + FN + FP} \tag{3}$$

where TP represents the number of positive samples correctly classified, TN represents the number of negative samples correctly classified, FP represents the number of positive samples incorrectly classified, and FN represents the number of negative samples incorrectly classified. In this paper, an improved VGG-16 network was built through Tensorflow, and the parameters of the network were set as follows: iteration times 150, initial learning rate 0.001, dropout parameter 0.5, and hierarchical sampling was used to divide the data set into training set and test set, with the training set accounting for 80% of the data set and the test set accounting for 20% of the data set.

The experimental results are shown in Fig. 4, the abscissa represents the number of training, the vertical axis represents ACC and the loss function. As shown in Fig. 4, when the number of training times is greater than 50, the accuracy rate has risen to a better effect. In addition, there is a positive correlation between the training accuracy and the loss function. When the loss function mutates, ACC will also go down. The curve shows a wave phenomenon in the process of training, this may be due to too few samples in the data set.

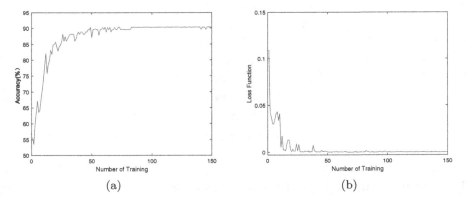

(a)   (b)

Fig. 4. (a) The relationship between accuracy and training times. (b) Relationship between loss function and training times.

In order to verify the effectiveness of the neural network in this paper, the two groups of data were used as the input training model of the improved VGG-16 Net. After ten blank tests, the average ACC was 90.28%, SE and SP were 91.67% and 88.89% respectively. To demonstrate the effectiveness of this experiment, ACC in the experimental results was compared with three traditional pulse classification methods, as shown in Table 2.

Literature [10] combined with time-frequency domain analysis extracted 70 features of pulse conditions, and then fed into support vector machines to classify pulse wave signals from sleep-disordered people and normal people. Literature

Table 2. Pulse classification results.

Method	Accuracy rate(%)
VGG-16Net	90.28
SVM [10]	85.20
Cluster method [11]	81.30
BP neural network [12]	85.00

[12] studied the influence of the classification of impulse signals and the selection of characteristic factors on the classification of impulse signals, and used BP neural network to achieve a high classification accuracy.

As can be seen from the table2, the improved VGG-16 convolutional neural network model in this paper has the best classification effect for pulse images. Compared with SVM, clustering method and BP neural network, the accuracy rate is improved by 5.08%, 8.98% and 5.28%, respectively. Therefore, compared with other methods, the method proposed in this paper has better classification performance.

4   Conclusion

Pulse diagnosis is a simple and effective diagnostic method, but its diagnosis process is often affected by subjective factors. Therefore, the objectification of pulse analysis has attracted the attention of researchers. In this paper, the improved VGG-16 net is used to classify the manifestation of pulses, which can effectively recognize the features of pulse signals and classify pulse signals. In the experiment, standard data sets were obtained through standardized data acquisition, screening and preprocessing, etc., then a convolutional neural network was established to conduct self-learning and training on the data sets to obtain a classification model, and finally pulse signals were classified and recognized.

The experimental results show that the improved VGG-16 net proposed in this paper has an excellent effect on pulse classification, with an average accuracy of 90.28%, which is higher than the current traditional pulse classification method, proving the validity of the one-dimensional convolutional neural network for pulse classification. The next step is to optimize the structure of the convolutional neural network and obtain more similar data sets to achieve better classification effect.

References

1. Xu, L., Gao, K.P.: Calculation method of continuous blood pressure based on PPG signal quality assessment. In: Proceedings of the 27th China Control and Decision-making Conference on IEEE Singapore Industrial Electronics Branch, Northeastern University 2015, vol. 2, pp. 3147–3152. China (2016)

2. Wang, J., Li, Z.: Wavelet core limit learning machine method for pulse classification and recognition. Comput. Eng. Design. **40**(05), 1472–1476 (2019)
3. Thakker, B.: Pulse analysis. World Acad. Sci. Eng. Technol. **55**, 173–176 (2009)
4. Li, X., Zhang, H., Wu, C.Z., Zhang, Q., Sun, Y.F.: Driving fatigue detection method based on pulse wave signal fusion. Chin. J. Highw. **33**(06), 168–181 (2020)
5. Li, F.F., Sun, R.: Pulse signal analysis of patients with coronary heart diseases using Hilbert-Huang transformation and time-domain method. Integr. Med. **21**(5), 355–360 (2015)
6. Jiang, J.Z., Yi, Y.L., Liu, Z.C.: Pathogenesis of obesity. Chin. J. Tradit. Chin. Med. **27**, 1918–1920 (2009)
7. Ju, X.L., Pei, D.M.: Epidemic characteristics and related factors of overweight and obesity in healthy physical examination population. China Prim. Med. **27**(13), 1628–1633 (2020)
8. Yin, L., Chen, F.M., Zhang, Q., Chen, X.: Adaptive ECG denoising method using set empirical mode decomposition and improved threshold function. J. Xi'an Jiaotong Univ. **54**(01), 101–107 (2020)
9. Zhang, H.F., Luo, Z.: Research on bird video image retrieval based on convolutional neural network. Sci. Res. Inform. Technol. Appl. **8**(05), 50–57 (2017)
10. Ramiro, C., Gaston, S.: Sleep-wake stages classification using heart rate signals from pulse oximetry. Heliyon **5**(10), 1–12 (2019)
11. Yang, S.: Pulse Signal Feature Extraction and Pulse Graph Clustering Method. Harbin Institute of Technology, China (2018)
12. Wang, S.H., Jiang, J.L., Lu, X.B.: Study on the classification of pulse signal based on the BP neural network. J. Biosci. Med. **8**(05), 104–112 (2020)

Motion Analysis for Dragon Boat Athlete Using Deep Neural Networks

Chuanzhi Xu[1], Zeyong Wu[2], Bifeng Wu[2], and Yihua Tan[2(✉)]

[1] School of Physical Education, Huazhong University of Science and Technology,
Wuhan 430074, Hubei, People's Republic of China
[2] School of Artificial Intelligence and Automation, Huazhong University of Science
and Technology, Wuhan 430074, Hubei, People's Republic of China
yhtan@hust.edu.cn

Abstract. In the training of sports, video-based motion analysis is important to automatically capture the action of trainees and provide training suggestions. Focusing on the dragon boating which mainly involves periodic rowing actions, this paper proposes a motion analysis method by comparing the action patterns of the athletes in the video and the expert athletes. First, taking a dragon boating video as input, the key points of human body of the dragon boat athlete in every frame are extracted with the deep convolutional neural network HRNET. Second, the extracted key points of athlete's body are constructed as a sequence to represent the motion of human body, and a mathematical analysis method is designed to obtain the related action parameters. Third, the parameters are compared with the standard actions of expert athletes to give the advice for action correction. Experimental results demonstrate that the proposed method can provide reliable suggestions for dragon boat athletes, which is robust to individual differences and non-uniform resolutions caused by different videos.

Keywords: Motion analysis · Deep convolutional neural network · Dragon boat · Key points of athlete's body

1 Introduction

Although current researches of athletes' training have covered different kinds of sports, the related technologies still heavily rely on manual analyses provided by professional workers. Considering the low efficiency and high cost, current manual analyses can hardly be applied in large-scale athletes' training which normally involves different levels. One direction to solve this problem is applying artificial intelligence technologies in the analyses of athlete's actions, which are designed to automatically capture the action of trainees and provide suggestions. Because videos can effectively record the actions of athletes, video-based motion analysis methods are the trend in the research of automatic action analyses.

Generally speaking, video-based motion analysis normally contains two steps. First, taking the video containing the training athletes as input, the key points of human body in

© Springer Nature Singapore Pte Ltd. 2021
L. Pan et al. (Eds.): BIC-TA 2020, CCIS 1363, pp. 369–380, 2021.
https://doi.org/10.1007/978-981-16-1354-8_26

every frame are extracted, which are constructed as a sequence to represent the motion of athletes. Second, the analyses are performed on the sequence of the key points to give advice for the action corrections. However, both the two steps still have unsolved problems.

In the first step, existing methods can hardly achieve both high accuracy and efficiency when the extracting key points of human body in the scene with complex background. Two categories of the key points extraction methods are widely used in video-based motion analyses. The first category is to obtain the global features and consider the pose estimation problems as classification or regression problems [1, 2]. However, the accuracy of such methods is ordinary and this method can only solve the scenes with clean background. The second category is based on the graph structure [3], which expresses the characteristics of individual partial areas. The position of a single area is usually obtained by deformable part-based model, and the relationship between the key points of human body is optimized by considering the pairwise relationship. However, this type of method has an obvious disadvantage, that is, it is difficult to determine the topological model it depends on.

In the second step, existing methods normally analyze every action separately, then integrate them to obtain the final results. This kind of approach can hardly be adapted to the case that the variance of the key points of human body is high. The viewpoint changes lead to the key points which are extracted in a short time are normally unstable, so separately analyzing every action can hardly induce a reliable result.

Focusing on the dragon boating which mainly involves periodic rowing actions, this paper proposes a motion analysis method which can mitigate above two problems. In the first step, we use deep convolutional neural network HRNET [4] to improve the performance of the key points extraction. In the second step, we calculate the statistics for multiple periodic actions to improve the reliability of action analysis. This analysis process can extract various information about an athlete's actions, which is the base to give suggestions for the athlete. Overall, the proposed method has the advantages of high accuracy and efficiency in analyzing athletes' movements, which can reduce the time and cost in the training of dragon boating.

2 Related Work

Nowadays, motion analysis methods based on video analysis technology are mainly divided into two steps. The first step is to extract the human motion information in the video, which is mainly based on the method of extracting the key points of the human body; the second step is to analyze the extracted human action information, which are mainly based on the set rules or the action similarity.

2.1 Extraction of the Key Points of Human Body

In the field of motion analysis, the methods for the extracting key points of the human body are mainly divided into two categories. The first type of methods are to extract the key points of the human body frame by frame [5], and the second type of methods are to use the pose estimation algorithm to extract the key points of the human body.

The specific effect is shown in Fig. 1. Since the latter has greater advantages over the first method in terms of timeliness, accuracy and anti-interference, this paper only discusses the methods of the extracting key points of human body based on the pose estimation algorithm. Current pose estimation methods based on deep convolutional neural networks are mainly divided into top-down and bottom-up methods:

Fig. 1. Key points of human body extraction result

(1) The top-down methods use a detector to distinguish human bodies, within which extraction algorithm of the key points is performed. According to the style of the feature acquisition, there are regression [6–8] and detection [9–12] algorithms. As a typical regression algorithm, Diogo C. Luvizon [8] used specific functions to directly obtain the key points of human body from feature maps, establishing a completely differentiable framework. As for detection algorithm, the estimated heat map output by neural network is exploited to identify the points with the highest heat values as the key points, which is more robust. There are several typical algorithms, such as RMPE which is local multi-person pose estimation [10], Mask-RCNN [11], CPN that is cascaded pyramid network [12].

(2) On the other hand, the bottom-up method performs the key points detection within the whole image, then the key points are connected in terms of the relationships of connection and spatial position among them. The advantage of this method is that the detection time has no relation to the number of persons in an image. The disadvantage is that the dense key points are difficult to be distinguished whether they belong to one person or the another. Some representative algorithms include OpenPose proposed by Zhe Cao [13] and DeepCut proposed by Leonid Pishchulin [14].

2.2 Motion Analysis

When the action information of the persons in the video is obtained, the motion information can be analyzed. Motion analysis mainly solves two problems. One is the recognition of the type of action. Jiang et al. proposed a deep neural network model based on ResNeXt to recognize human actions in video [15]. The other one is to determine how correct the action is when comparing with the standard motion. There are rule-based and action analysis algorithms.

According to the rule-based action analysis methods, Li et al. used a cascaded convolutional neural network to extract facial feature points, and calculates various angle parameters of head movement through the extracted feature points, then the corresponding angle value is compared with the set threshold to determine if it is an abnormal behavior [16]. Zhu et al. applied OpenPose to extract the key points of the human body, so as to obtain the position of the foot joint points, and obtain the distance from the specified safe position to determine whether the person is in safe position [17].

On the other hand, based on action similarity, Li et al. collected the badminton player's swing action in the video by the badminton robot's vision system, and compared it with the standard swing motion to analyze and evaluate the motion in the video [18]. Ji used the OpenPose algorithm to extract golf swing action parameters in the video, and then compared them with the professional golf swing action parameters to analyze and evaluate the standard degree of golf swing action in the video [19].

3   Method

The proposed method includes two steps: (1) convolutional neural network is applied to extract the key points of athlete's body corresponding to the joints, such as elbow, wrist, shoulder, etc., (2) the key points are connected to analyze the motion information of athlete which could be further fed back to the coach for the dragon boat training.

3.1   Extraction of Key Points Using HRNET

Since the accurate extraction of the key points of athlete's body is very crucial for the following motion analysis, we apply high-resolution network (HRNET [4]) to conduct the task. The main reason is that the model structure of HRNET output high resolution feature representation such that the locations of points are more accurate than those recovered from low resolution feature. The overall model structure is shown in Fig. 2. From the structure, we can imply that multi-resolution paths extract rich features as well as accurate locations of points.

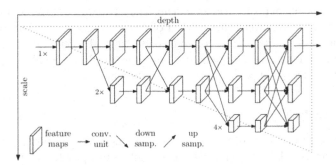

Fig. 2. Model structure of HRNET [4]

In the implementation of HRNET, we follow the design rules of ResNet so that the number of channels of each resolution is refined, and the depth information is embedded to all steps. Finally, a small net and a large net are set up with different parameters:

HRNET-W32 and HRNET-W48, where 32 and 48 represent the width of the high-resolution subnets in the last three steps. The widths of the three parallel subnets in the small network are: 64, 128, and 256, and the widths of the three parallel subnets in the large network are: 96, 192, and 384.

With the trained model, the key points of dragon boat athlete can be extracted from video. An extraction example is shown in Fig. 3. It can be seen that the key points of the human body in Fig. 3 have been clearly marked as blue dots corresponding to the joint location.

Fig. 3. Key points extracted from dragon boat athlete (blue dots). (Color figure online)

3.2 Extraction of Athlete Motion Information

For the rowing action in dragon boat, we mainly pay attention to the movement of the wrist, elbow, shoulder and hip joints. Therefore, we define the following angles to describe the rowing action:

(1) Paddle angle: it refers to the acute angle between the paddle and the horizontal plane when the paddle is inserted into or taken out of water. Paddle angle can be calculated by connecting the two wrist joints;
(2) Shoulder joint angle: it refers to the angle between the upper arm and the trunk;
(3) Elbow joint angle: it refers to the angle between the forearm and the upper arm;
(4) Hip joint angle: it refers to the angle between the trunk and the thigh.

These angles extracted from video are combined to characterize the details of row action, which can be used to judge the motion level of dragon boating athletes.

Basically, rowing action is a periodical motion in which the coordinates of the key point corresponding to a joint form a periodical wave. According to the observation that the location extent of a joint is limited, we can set the time interval between two neighboring maximum locations of the same key point as a cycle. In the following section, we give the specific procedure of finding the cycle of a motion, which is shown as Fig. 4.

Because each key point extracted from HRNET corresponds to a specific joint, we group all the specific key points in time series as an analysis unit. Among the key points in the series, the average number of frames between adjacent points with the maximum

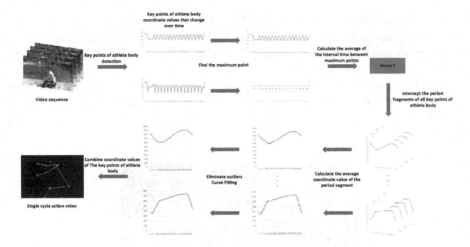

Fig. 4. Scheme flow of the motion information extraction

coordinates is calculated as the average period T of the periodic repetitive actions. By summing and averaging the coordinates of the corresponding points of all the periods, the average curve of the athlete's joint points in a cycle can be obtained. Finally, the corresponding joint angle could be obtained from the cycle information of each key point.

The specific details are as follows:

First, it is necessary to find the maximum points through the periodic law of the coordinates of the key points, and the conditions of the maximum points satisfy Eq. (1):

$$(f_{k,i}, y^k_{f_{k,i}}) = \max\{y^k_{f_{k,i-r}}, y^k_{f_{k,i-r+1}}, \ldots y^k_{f_{k,i+r}})$$ (1)

where $f_{k,i}$ represents the number of frames corresponding to the maximum value of ith coordinate of the key point k in the video sequence, y^k_f represents the coordinate value of the key point k in f^{th} frame, and r represents the search range of the number of frames (It is set to 30 in the experiment, that is, the search range is -30–30, which needs to be less than the estimated motion period).

After all the maximum points are counted, the average period of each repeated motion in the dragon boating can be obtained by taking the difference between two adjacent maximum points and taking the average, as shown in Eq. (2).

$$T = \frac{1}{K(N-1)} \sum_{k=1}^{K} \sum_{i=1}^{N-1} (f_{k,i+1} - f_{k,i})$$ (2)

where T represents the period, K represents the number of the key points, N represents the number of maximum points, and $f_{k,i}$ represents the number of frames corresponding to the key point k at i^{th} coordinate maximum in the video sequence.

The Cycle Average Action can be obtained by adding the corresponding points in each cycle segment and taking the average, as shown in Eq. (3)

$$CAA_j^k = \frac{1}{N} \sum_{i=0}^{N-1} y_{f_0 + T \cdot i + j}^k \tag{3}$$

where CAA_j^k represents the coordinate value of the key point k in j^{th} frame in a single cycle after averaging, y_f^k represents the coordinate value of the key point k in f^{th} frame, and f_0 represents the initial number of frames in the first cycle (Set to 207 in experiment).

After obtaining the required average coordinate value of each key point, the four kinds of angle information required by the paper can be obtained through some angle transformations.

3.3 Motion Transformation Evaluation

After obtaining the required four joint angles, we can evaluate the motion of dragon boat athlete by comparing it with the angle information of the standard action. The angles difference guides the final suggestion, as shown in Eq. (4):

$$\partial_i = \beta_i - \mu_i \tag{4}$$

where β is the angle information in the standard action, μ is the angle information of athlete, ∂ represents the angle difference and i represents the serial number of a certain angle ($i = 1$–4) respectively represent paddle, shoulder, elbow and the hip angles). When $\partial > 5°$ indicates that a certain angle of the athlete is too large during exercise, attention should be paid to reduce the angle appropriately. When $\partial < -5°$ indicates that a certain angle of the athlete is too small during exercise, and the range of this part of the movement needs to be increased, when $-5° < \partial < 5°$ means that a certain angle of the athlete's movement is quite standard.

4 Experiment

4.1 Experimental Results

This paper analyzes the specific actions of the characters through the input of the dragon boat rowing video sequence. First, by key point detection, the coordinates of the key points of athlete's body in each frame are obtained, and the periodic curve of the key points changing with time can be drawn as Fig. 5.

Since the rowing cycle of the dragon boat action is stable, the period fragments of all related joints can be obtained and further fit with polynomial curve after part of the abnormal values are removed, which are shown in Fig. 6.

By the obtained average coordinate values of the key points of human body, a video of the key points of human body motion in a single cycle is obtained, and the representative rowing motion is grouped as shown in Fig. 7.

The average angle change curves of the four angles are also finally drawn as shown in Fig. 8:

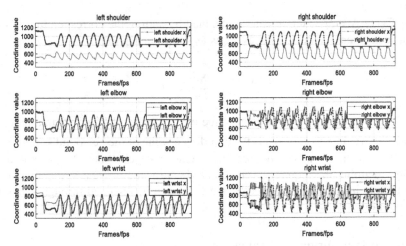

Fig. 5. Coordinate change curve of the key points of athlete

With the above analysis results, an example of suggestions can be drawn as follows:

(1) The change range of the shoulder angle when the dragon boat athlete is in the beginning of paddle is $100°$–$120°$, and the normal range of shoulder joint angle change should be $120°$–$130°$. We can see that $\partial_2 = 10°$–$20° > 5°$ It means that the athlete's shoulders are not extended enough when rowing, resulting in the athlete's failure to obtain a reasonable insertion point;

(2) The dragon boat athlete's elbow angle is $178°$ before entering the water. The normal range should be $165 \pm 5°$. We can see that $\partial_3 = 13° > 5°$. It means that the elbow joint angle is too large and the arm is too stretched away and too stiff. Therefore, the elbow joint angle should be slightly reduced;

(3) The hip angle is $51°$ when the athlete inserts the Paddle. The normal range should be $30°$. We can see that $\partial_4 = 21° > 5°$. It means that the body is too stretched and the lift is too large. It should be controlled at about $30°$ to obtain a reasonable insertion point.

4.2 Comparison Experiment

The method used in this paper has significant advantages in accuracy and efficiency. Compared with the traditional method of analyzing human movements, this method can also obtain better and more accurate human motion information. We compared the results of the method proposed in [5]. For simplicity, only one cycle is measured during the experiment. The changes of the hip angle are compared, and the specific experimental results are shown in Fig. 9:

It can be seen from Fig. 9 that the hip angle change curve obtained by the analysis method in [5] and that of our proposed method are very similar, but our proposed method have two advantages of the method in [5]:

(1) Time complexity is low. The method in [5] needs to analyze the input video frame by frame slowly, and the time cost is too high. However, the method proposed in this

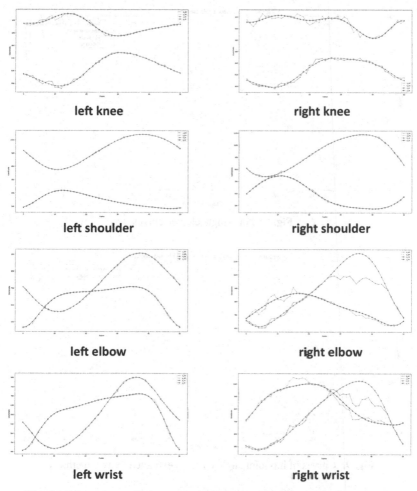

Fig. 6. Comparison of joint curves before and after fitting of each key point

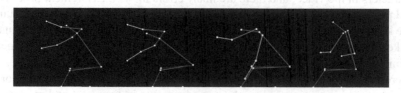

Fig. 7. Rowing sequence represented by the key points of athlete

paper relies purely on algorithm analysis, which can automatically and quickly obtain the required various angles. Generally speaking, using the method in [5] to process a video sequence of an athlete's periodic actions will take nearly 40 min. However, using the method proposed in this paper will only take nearly 10 s.

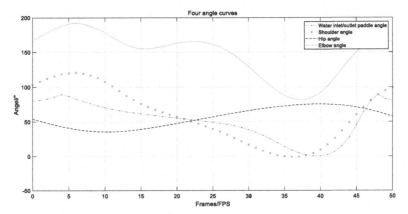

Fig. 8. Four-angle change curves

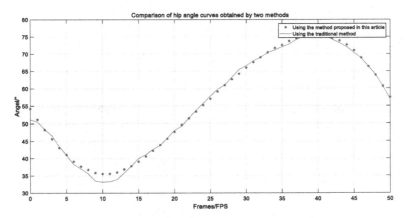

Fig. 9. Curves of hip joint angle changes extracted by two methods

(2) Accuracy is better. The method in [5] needs to manually detect the key angles of the characters in the video, and there are many errors in the measurement process. The method proposed in this paper first uses the posture estimation algorithm to obtain the reliable key points of human body, and then performs some coordinate transformations on the key points coordinates to obtain the required angle. There is no need to measure in the middle, and the accuracy of the experimental results is high.

Therefore, in general, the method of analyzing the rowing movement of dragon boat athletes proposed in this paper has obvious advantages in time cost and measurement accuracy compared with the traditional method of analyzing sports movements.

5   Conclusion

This paper mainly discusses the extraction of the key points of athlete's body and the analysis of dragon boat rowing movements. After obtaining the reliable key points of athlete's body, the average period of each repetitive movement is extracted, which is further used to analyze the motion parameters represented as four joint angles. Finally, the joint parameters are compared with standard action to give some improvement suggestions. The experiments of the action analysis method proposed in this paper demonstrate that it can qualitatively evaluate the action of dragon boat athlete.

In future, there are two directions can be further explored:

First, the optimal design of the key points of human body detection network is very important. To reduce the complexity of training and testing, it is necessary to design lightweight neural networks.

Second, this study only studies motion parameters of paddle, elbow, shoulder and hip angles, so that more complicated motion description framework needs to be studied to further analyze the movement rhythm and the speed of each joint from multiple angles.

References

1. Rogez, G., Rihan, J., Ramalingam, S., et al.: Randomized trees for human pose detection. In: IEEE Conference on Computer Vision & Pattern Recognition, pp. 1–8 (2008)
2. Urtasun, R., Darrell, T.: Sparse probabilistic regression for activity-independent human pose inference. In: IEEE Conference on Computer Vision & Pattern Recognition, pp. 149–156 (2008)
3. Hu, G.: Research of Human Pose Estimation Based on Pictorial Structure Models. Wuhan University of Technology (2014)
4. Sun, K., Xiao, B., Liu, D., et al.: Deep high-resolution representation learning for human pose estimation. IEEE Conference on Computer Vision & Pattern Recognition, pp. 5686–5696 (2019)
5. Qiong-zhu, G., Feng, C.: Sports biomechanical analysis of landing stability of maneuvers in women's Wushu. J. Wuhan Inst. Phys. Educ. **44**(6), 48–52 (2010)
6. Sun, X., Xiao, B., Wei, F., et al.: Integral Human Pose Regression. In: Ferrari, V., Hebert, M., Sminchisescu, C., Weiss, Y. (eds.) Computer Vision – ECCV 2018. Lecture Notes in Computer Science, vol. 11210, pp. 536–553. Springer, Cham (2018)
7. Newell, A., Yang, K., Deng, J.: Stacked hourglass networks for human pose estimation. In: Leibe, B., Matas, J., Sebe, N., Welling, M. (eds.) Computer Vision – ECCV 2016. Lecture Notes in Computer Science, vol. 9912, pp. 483–499. Springer, Cham (2016). https://doi.org/10.1007/978-3-319-46484-8_29
8. Luvizon, D.C., Tabia, H., Picard, D.: Human pose regression by combining indirect part detection and contextual information. Comput. Graph. **85**, 15–22 (2017)
9. Li, S., Liu, Z.Q., Chan, A.B.: Heterogeneous multi-task learning for human pose estimation with deep convolutional neural network. Int. J. Comput. Vis. **113**(1), 19–36 (2015)
10. Fang, H.S., Xie, S., Tai, Y.W., et al.: RMPE: regional multi-person pose estimation. In: IEEE International Conference on Computer Vision, pp. 2353–2362 (2017)
11. He, K., Georgia, G., Piotr, D., et al.: Mask R-CNN. In: IEEE International Conference on Computer Vision, pp. 2980–2988 (2017)
12. Chen, Y., Wang, Z., Peng, Y., et al.: Cascaded pyramid network for multi-person pose estimation. In: IEEE Conference on Computer Vision and Pattern Recognition, pp. 7103–7112 (2017)
13. Cao, Z., Simon, T., Wei, S.E., et al.: Realtime multi-person 2D pose estimation using part affinity fields. In: IEEE Conference on Computer Vision and Pattern Recognition, pp. 1302–1310 (2017)

14. Pishchulin, L., Insafutdinov, E. Tang, S., et al.: DeepCut: joint subset partition and labeling for multi person pose estimation. In: IEEE Conference on Computer Vision and Pattern Recognition, pp. 4929–4937 (2016)
15. Sheng-nan, J., En-qing, C., Ming-yao, Z., et al.: Human action recognition based on ResNeXt. J. Graph. **41**(2), 277–282 (2020)
16. Li, Y.: Abnormal Behavior Detection Based on Head Movement Analyze in Examination Room. Changchun University of Science and Technology (2018)
17. Zhu Jian-bao, X., Zhi-long, SY.-w., et al.: Detection of dangerous behaviors in power stations based on OpenPose multi-person attitude recognition. Autom. Instrum. **35**(2), 47–51 (2020)
18. Li, K.: Capture, Recognition and Analysis of Badminton Players Swing. University of Electronic Science and Technology of China (2020)
19. Ji, Y.: The Research on Golf Swing Action Comparison Based on Video Human Body Pose Estimation. Nanjing University of Posts and Telecommunications (2019)

Memristor-Based Neural Network Circuit of Associative Memory with Multimodal Synergy

Juntao Han[1,2], Xiao Xiao[1,2], Xiangwei Chen[1,2], and Junwei Sun[1,2(✉)]

[1] Henan Key Lab of Information-Based Electrical Appliances,
Zhengzhou University of Light Industry, Zhengzhou 450002, China
junweisun@yeah.net
[2] School of Electrical and Information Engineering,
Zhengzhou University of Light Industry, Zhengzhou 450002, China

Abstract. Information processing tasks in the brain are performed primarily by a network of multiple neurons and synapses that connect them. Most associative memory neural networks based on memristor only discuss the relationship between individual neurons and synapses. In this paper, an associative memory involving multiple neurons and multiple synapses is discussed. A memristive neural network circuit that can realize multimodal associative memory is designed and verified by the simulation results. The designed circuit consists of a neuron module, a synapse module and a synergistic neuron module. The functions such as learning, forgetting, second learning, and synergistic memory are implemented by the circuit.

Keywords: Associative memory · Memristor · Multimodal · Neural network · Synergistic memory

1 Introduction

With the development of biological technology and electronic technology, the demand for efficient and intelligent information processing systems similar to the brain is growing [1–8]. Artificial neural network is a computational model that imitates the structure and function of biological neural network. The model

This work was supported in part by the National Key Research and Development Program of China for International S and T Cooperation Projects under Grant 2017YFE0103900, in part by the Joint Funds of the National Natural Science Foundation of China under Grant U1804262, in part by the State Key Program of National Natural Science of China under Grant 61632002, in part by the Foundation of Young Key Teachers from University of Henan Province under Grant 2018GGJS092, in part by the Youth Talent Lifting Project of Henan Province under Grant 2018HYTP016, in part by the Henan Province University Science and Technology Innovation Talent Support Plan under Grant 20HASTIT027, in part by the Zhongyuan Thousand Talents Program under Grant 204200510003.

ⓒ Springer Nature Singapore Pte Ltd. 2021
L. Pan et al. (Eds.): BIC-TA 2020, CCIS 1363, pp. 381–395, 2021.
https://doi.org/10.1007/978-981-16-1354-8_27

consists of neurons and synapses. Artificial neural network has been widely used in artificial intelligence, information processing, automatic control, computer science, pattern recognition and other fields. Based on the rapid development of the contemporary fields of neurobiology, mathematics, physics and computer science, researchers have moved from building simple mathematical models to study neuronal models and neural network models that more closely matches physiological characteristics [9–13].

The current construction of artificial neural networks is mainly based on CMOS integrated transistors. The performance of neural network is improved by reducing the size of transistor. Neuron hardware implementation requires multiple transistors, which greatly increases the power consumption and design complexity of artificial neural network [14,15]. Scholars predict that CMOS will reach its physical limits within a decade or two. The emphasis in the design of artificial neural networks needs smaller and more capable devices. Scholars are committed to finding new devices to complement CMOS, or eventually replace it altogether, to achieve the performance gains of artificial neural networks. In 1971, Leon Chua predicted the existence of the fourth basic electronic element based on the principle of symmetry, which is memristor [16]. The theory of memristor has never gained valuable advances because no one have been able to come up with a physical model or an example of memristor. Until 2008, Hewlett-Packard built a model with memristor properties that confirmed the existence of memristors [17]. The researchers have conducted numerous experiments to study the application of memristor after the memristor model was proposed.

Memristor is a resistor with memory property. As a novel fundamental component with both storage and computational functions at the nanoscale, the memristor exhibits biological properties similar to neuronal synapses. Its energy efficiency and integration density are very high. The emergence of memristor is expected to make a breakthrough in neural network [18–21]. A bridge memory-resistive synapse was proposed in [22]. The electronic synapse contains four memory resistances and is capable of zero, positive, and negative synaptic weights. A novel memory-blocking synaptic and neuronal model was proposed in [23], which enables positive and negative synaptic weights. Neurons and synapses are the most basic and important structures in biological neural networks. Information processing tasks in the brain are performed primarily by a network of multiple neurons and synapses. The larger and more complex information to be processed, the more neurons and synapses are involved. In terms of memory storage, the number of synapses is much larger than neurons. It means that when a neuron corresponds to multiple synapses, its ability to store and process information is greater [24–27]. Human memory is divided into long-term memory and short-term memory [28]. Neurons will form long-term memory when the brain is stimulated for a long time. It means that neurons remember faster when receiving the same external stimulus again. An associative memory through microcontrollers and memristors is implemented, but the use of microcontrollers significantly increases the complexity and power consumption of the circuit [21]. Different associative memory circuits based on memristor were implemented in

[29–31], but their research was limited to single mode. A multimodal associative memory circuit was proposed in [32], but the synergy among the modals was not considered. In this paper, a multimodal synergistic association memory circuit based on memristor is proposed. One neuron in the circuit corresponds to two synapses, which can process more complex information. Also the circuit can perform multimodal synesthetic learning by connecting each neuron module. In addition, the circuit implements associative memory functions such as learning, forgetting and second learning. Pspice is utilized to simulate and verify its validity of the designed circuit.

The paper is organized as follows: Sect. 2 describes a mathematical model of a memristor with threshold. The design of the circuit is shown in Sect. 3. In Sect. 4, the simulation results and analysis of the circuit are introduced in PSPICE. Section 5 concludes this paper and discusses further works.

2   Memristor Model with Threshold

As an innovative electronic component, memristor has attracted the attention of many scholars. Various memristor models have been developed and simulated in the laboratory [33–38]. A voltage controlled threshold memristor model is proposed in [33]. According to the experimental data, the model is more suitable for the design of synaptic circuits compared with other memristor models. The model can determine the behavior of memory synapses in a neural network based on changes in memristance. In this paper, the threshold memristor model used to mimic the AIST-based memristor is selected, which matches the $I - V$ characteristics of both repetitive sweeping and sinusoidal inputs [33]. The model is described by the following

$$M(t) = R_{ON}\frac{w(t)}{D} + R_{OFF}(1 - \frac{w(t)}{D}) \qquad (1)$$

where $M(t)$ is the memristance, $w(t)$ is the width of the high doped region, D is the full thickness of memristive material. R_{ON} and R_{OFF} denote the resistance when the memristor is completely high doped or low doped, respectively. The derivative of the state variable $w(t)$ is

$$\frac{dw(t)}{dt} = \begin{cases} \mu_v \frac{R_{ON}}{D} \frac{i_{off}}{i(t)-i_0} f(w(t)), & v(t) > V_{T+} > 0 \\ 0, & V_{T-} \leqslant v(t) \leqslant V_{T+} \\ \mu_v \frac{R_{ON}}{D} \frac{i(t)}{i_{on}} f(w(t)), & v(t) < V_{T-} < 0 \end{cases} \qquad (2)$$

where μ_v stands for the average ion mobility, i_0, i_{on} and i_{off}, are constants, i_0 is a very small constant, so that the memristance will decrease when the memristor is applied by a small positive voltage. In this paper, any positive voltage applied to memristor can make $i(t)$ greater than i_0. V_{T+} and V_{T-} are positive and negative threshold voltages, respectively, ensuring that the memristance changes only when the voltage is greater than V_{T+} or less than V_{T-}. $f(w(t))$ is given as a window function

$$f(w(t)) = 1 - (\frac{w(t)}{D} - sgn(-i))^{2p} \qquad (3)$$

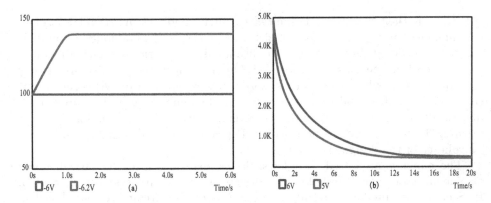

Fig. 1. PSPICE simulation results of memristance change. (a) Memristance change of memristor model in neuron module. (b) Memristance change of memristor synapse model in synapse module. The memristance of memristor model in synergetic neuron is similar to memristor model in neuron module.

where p is a positive integer. When a voltage is applied to the memristor, the memristance of the memristor will change. Applying a positive voltage to the memristor will cause the increase of $w(t)$ and the decrease of the memristance. The greater the positive voltage is, the slower $w(t)$ increases, and the slower the memristance decreases. The opposite case will occur when the memristor is applied by a negative voltage. These parameters of the memristors are shown in Table 1. Figure 1 shows the curves of the memristance when memristors are applied by different voltages. As can be seen in Fig. 1, the memristance of M_1 does not change when the applied voltage does not exceed the negative threshold value. If the applied voltage exceeds the negative threshold value of M_1, then

Table 1. Parameters settings of memristor in three modules

Parameters	$Setting_1$	$Setting_2$	$Setting_3$
$R_{ON}(\Omega)$	100	100	1K
$R_{OFF}(\Omega)$	140	5K	5k
$R_{init}(\Omega)$	100	4.9K	1K
V_{T+} (V)	2	3	5
V_{T-} (V)	−6.05	−0.05	−5
D (nm)	3	3	3
$\mu_v(\mathrm{m^2 s^{-1} \Omega^{-1}})$	1.6e–18	1.6e–18	1.6e–18
i_{on} (A)	1	1	1
i_{off} (A)	1e–5	1e–5	1e–5
i_0 (A)	1e–3	1e–3	1e–3
p	10	10	10

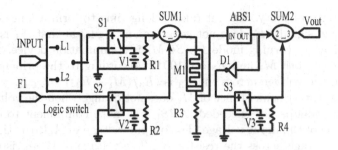

Fig. 2. The circuit schematic of neuron module. S_1, S_2, and S_3 are the voltage-controlled switches, where the closed voltage is 0.5 V. $V_1 = -12$ V, $V_2 = -0.2$ V, $V_3 = -2$ V, $R_1 = R_2 = R_4 = 1$ KΩ, $R_3 = 100$ Ω. D_1 is a NOT gate. F_1 is feedback signal.

the memristance of M_1 rises from 100 Ω to 140 Ω. As can be seen in Fig. 1, the memristance drops of the memristor is non-linear and the memristance of the memristor drops faster at an applied voltage of 5 V than 6 V.

3   Circuits Design

Memristor has non-linear and non-volatile characteristics. Memristor may be more suitable for implementing artificial neural networks than other nanoscale devices. In this paper, memristor is used in a neuron module, a synapse module and a synergetic neuron module. The synapse module is used for the simulation of biological synapses and the measurement of synaptic weights. The neuron module is used to regulate the rate of learning, forgetting and second learning. The synergistic neuron module can realize synergistic work by processing the information of multiple neurons. The memristors for the above modules have different characteristics.

3.1   Neuron Module

There are numerous neurons in a brain that have the ability to receive and process information. The number of synapses is much larger than neurons in the biological brain. It means that neurons can control multiple synapses. The connection between neurons and synapses can greatly increase the efficiency of the brain. As shown in Fig. 2, the logic gate mimics the selection of synapses by neurons in response to external stimulus. When exposed to different external stimulus, the neuron calls different synapses. In this circuit, one neuron corresponds to two synapses. And a high level and a low level correspond to different learning signals. When the input of a neuron is a high level, S_1 is closed. It means that the neuron starts to call up a synapse for learning mode L_1. When the input of a neuron is a low level, the neuron starts to call up another synapse for learning mode L_2. F_1 is a feedback signal to the neuron after the synapse forms long-term memory. Since it takes a long time to form a long-term memory of learning signals, F_1 does not generate any signal at first. V_1 is the input voltage source for learning mode L_1. SUM_1 is a summation device. The initial memristance of both M_1 and R_3 are $100\,\Omega$. According to the principle of voltage division, the voltage across the R_3 is $(R_3/(M_1 + R_3)) * V_{SUM_1} = -6\,\mathrm{V}$. As shown in Fig. 1, the memristance of M_1 does not change when the voltage across its threshold value is not exceeded. ABS_1 is a math component to obtain the absolute value of the input voltage. The output voltage of ABS_1 is the absolute value of the voltage across the resistor R_3. The voltage of V_{ABS_1} is $6\,\mathrm{V}$. If the learning signal remains after synapse formation of long-term memory, S_1 and S_2 are closed. The voltages of $-12\,\mathrm{V}$ and $-0.2\,\mathrm{V}$ are sent to M_1 and R_1 through SUM_1. The voltage at both ends of M_1 decreases from $-6\,\mathrm{V}$ to $-6.1\,\mathrm{V}$. $-6.1\,\mathrm{V}$ is lower than the threshold voltage of M_1, and the memristance of M_1 will increase. The change of memristance of M_1 will affect the voltage at both ends of R_1. The parameters R_{OFF} and R_{ON} of M_1 are set to $140\,\Omega$ and $100\,\Omega$, respectively. As shown in Fig. 1, if the voltage through M_1 is less than or equal to $-6.1\,\mathrm{V}$, the memristance of M_1 will rise from $100\,\Omega$ to $140\,\Omega$ in a short period of time. The change of memristance of M_1 will affect the voltage at both ends of R_3. If the memristance of M_1 is larger, the absolute value of voltage at both ends of R_3 is smaller. The voltage at both ends of R_3 becomes $(R_3/(M_1+R_3))*V_{SUM_1} \approx -5\,\mathrm{V}$ after the memristance of M_1 rises to $140\,\Omega$. The voltage of V_{ABS_1} also changes and finally stabilizes at $5\,\mathrm{V}$. If the neuron begins to learn again, V_{ABS_1} becomes $5\,\mathrm{V}$. It means that they will learn faster than the first time when they receive the same learning signal again after neurons form long-term memory. It can be seen from the rate at which the memristance of the memristor M_2 decreases. When the signal of learning mode L_1 is cut off, S_1 is opened and the voltage of V_{ABS_1} is $0\,\mathrm{V}$. Then D_1 produces a high level, S_3 is closed. The synapses begin to forget the previously learned information, and $-2\,\mathrm{V}$ voltage begins as the new voltage.

3.2   Synapse Module

The nervous system is made up of a large number of neurons. The parts of the neurons that come into contact with each other and transmit information to each other are called synapses. In the nervous system, synapse is a structure that allows electrical or chemical signals to pass from one neuron to another. M_2 is the core of synapse module. The strength of connections between neighboring neurons is determined by synaptic weights. Synaptic weight W is defined as $W = R_5/M_2$. The lower the memristance of M_2 in the synapse module is, the stronger the synaptic weight between neurons. The circuit design determines the degree of learning and forgetting of neurons based on the increase and decrease of the synaptic weights. $Vout$ is used as learning and forgetting voltage of synapse module. When $Vout$ is positive, synapse begins to enter the state of learning. On the contrary, it will enter the state of forgetting. The generation of synaptic weights was simulated by M_2 and OP_1. The combination of ABM_1, OP_2 and OP_3 enables the measurement and determination of synaptic weights. In the absence of a learning signal, D_1 outputs a high level. It will cause the voltage at

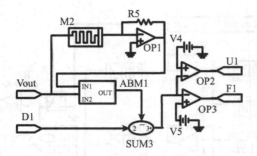

Fig. 3. The circuit schematic of synapse module. $R_2 = 1\,\mathrm{K}\Omega$. $V_4 = 1.4\,\mathrm{V}$, $V_5 = 1.2\,\mathrm{V}$. OP_1, OP_2, and OP_3 are operational amplifiers. ABM_1 is a math component, where $Vout = -V_{IN_2}/V_{IN_1}$. U_1 is the signal that L_1 learning mode is completed. F_1 is feedback signal.

the negative terminal of OP_2 and OP_3 to always be greater than the voltage at the positive terminal. The design simulates that the pre-neuron at the neuron only produces a signal to the post-neuron when the neuron is an activated state and its synaptic weight drops to a threshold. When the neuron has a learning signal, D_1 produces a low level, and $Vout$ produces $6\,\mathrm{V}$. The output voltage of OP_1 is $V_{OP1} = -(R_5/M_2) * Vout$. The synaptic weight information is processed by OP_1 and sent to ABM_1. Output of ABM_1 is $V_{ABM_1} = -V_{IN2}/V_{IN1} = -V_{OP1}/Vout = M_1/1000$. The pre-neuron can not transfer information to the post-neuron because of the low synaptic weight between them. The voltage is summed by SUM_1 and sent to OP_2 and OP_3. The inverting input port of OP_2 and OP_3 receive a signal which indicates the synaptic strength. If $V_{SUM_1} < 1.4\,\mathrm{V}$, then OP_2 outputs $1\,\mathrm{V}$. The degree of connection between the two neurons is strong when V_{SUM_3} is lower than the positive pole of OP_2. It forms short-term memory, not long-term memory. After human has completely forgotten something, it takes the same amount of time as the first contact to recall the event. If V_{SUM_3} is lower than the positive voltage of OP_3, the feedback signal F_1 will produces a high level. It means that neuron forms a long-term memory. After the neuron forms a long-term memory, $Vout$ will change from $6\,\mathrm{V}$ to $5\,\mathrm{V}$. Even human has completely forgotten something after a long-term memory is formed, it takes less time to recall it again than first learning (Fig. 3).

3.3   Synergistic Neuron Module

The processing of information in the brain requires multiple neurons to work together. Unlike the previous neuron modules, the synergistic neuron modules need to process information passed by multiple neurons. The synergistic neuron module is divided into two parts. The green part processes information from the pre-neurons. And the blue part integrates information processed in the green part. $U_1 - U_6$ are the output voltages from the six synapses of the three pre-neurons. U_1 and U_2 represent the voltages of the two synapses of the pre-neuron. If the voltage value of U_1 is $1\,\mathrm{V}$, it means that the pre-neuron has completed

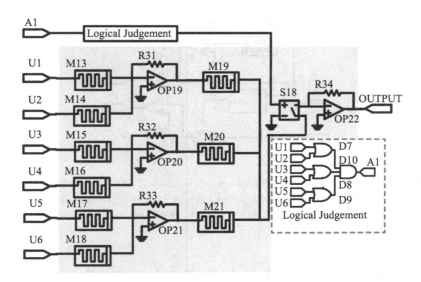

Fig. 4. The circuit schematic of synergistic neuron. $U_1 - U_6$ are signals for the completion of the $L_1 - L_6$ learning mode, respectively. S_3 is the voltage-controlled switch. $R_{31} = R_{32} = R_{33} = R_{34} = 1\,\mathrm{K\Omega}$. R_{init} of M_{13}, M_{15} and M_{17} are $1\,\mathrm{K\Omega}$, $500\,\Omega$ and $250\,\Omega$, respectively. R_{init} of M_{14}, M_{16} and M_{18} are $1\,\mathrm{K\Omega}$. R_{init} of M_{19}, M_{20} and M_{21} are $1\,\mathrm{K\Omega}$. D_7, D_8, and D_9 are OR gates. D_{10} is a AND gate. $OUTPUT$ is the final voltage. (Color figure online)

learning mode L_1. The voltage value of U_2 indicates whether the pre-neuron has completed mode L_2. A pre-neuron can only perform one mode of learning at the same time in this circuit. It is to prevent the information from getting scrambled. M_3, M_4 and OP_4 form a synaptic weight generating module of the post-neuron. The synaptic weights W_1, W_2, W_3, W_4, W_5, and W_6 are defined as $W_1 = R_{31}/M_{13} = 1$, $W_2 = R_{31}/M_{14} \approx 0$, $W_3 = R_{32}/M_{15} = 2$, $W_4 = R_{32}/M_{16} \approx 0$, $W_5 = R_{33}/M_{17} = 4$, and $W_6 = R_{33}/M_{18} \approx 0$, respectively. In order to process the information faster, the synaptic weights of the synergistic neuron module are fixed. When the voltage of U_1 is $1\,\mathrm{V}$, the voltage of OP_4 is $V_{OP_{19}} = -(W_1 * U_1) - (W_2 * U_2) = 1\,\mathrm{V}$. When the voltage value of U_2 is $1\,\mathrm{V}$, the voltage of OP_{19} is very small. Differences in synaptic weights imply that synergistic neurons can process many kinds of information. The information of the pre-neuron is processed by the synaptic weight module then enters the blue part of the weight summation module. M_{19}, M_{20}, M_{21} and OP_{22} form the synaptic weight summation module. S_1 is closed when all three pre-neurons have produce voltages. The synaptic weight row vectors and column vectors of synergistic neurons are $[W_1, W_2, W_3, W_4, W_5, W_6]$ and $[U_1, U_2, U_3, U_4, U_5, U_6]^{\mathrm{T}}$, respectively. The output voltage of OP_{22} is $[W_1, W_2, W_3, W_4, W_5, W_6]*[U_1, U_2, U_3, U_4, U_5, U_6]^{\mathrm{T}}$. The positive and negative threshold voltages of the memristors $M_{13} - M_{21}$ are $5\,\mathrm{V}$ and $-5\,\mathrm{V}$, respectively. It is to prevent the memristance of the memristors changing in information processing (Fig. 4).

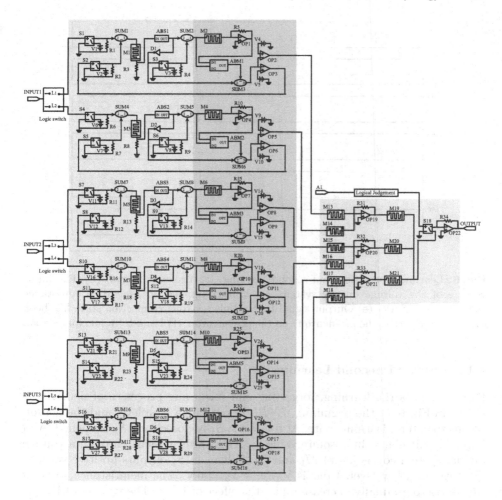

Fig. 5. Complete circuit

3.4   Complete Circuit

The brain requires multiple neurons to perceive external stimulus. And the processing of data after perception requires synergistic neurons. As shown in Fig. 5, three pre-neurons are responsible for judging and processing the external learning signal. According to the processing results of the pre-neurons, the corresponding voltage is produced to the corresponding synapse. The result of each synapse is integrated by the synergistic neurons to produce the final learning information.

4   Simulation

Pspice is used to perform time domain analysis on the designed circuit. (high level is 1 V, low level is 0 V).

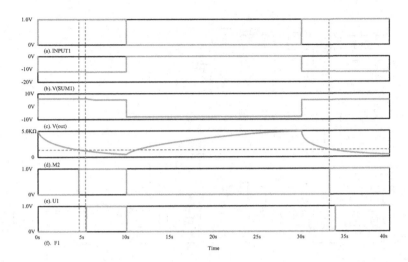

Fig. 6. Learning forgetting and second learning. (a) Learning signal. (b) The input voltage of the voltage divider system. (c) Voltage applied on M_2. (d) Memristance change curve of M_2. (e) Output signal that means a strong connection state has been established between the pre-neuron and the post-neuron. (f) Long-term memory signal.

4.1 First and Second Learning

Figure 6 shows the learning, forgetting and relearning processes of neuron. As shown in Fig. 6, at the beginning, $INPUT_1$ outputs a high level and the neuron begins to enter a learning state. At 0 s −4.6 s, S_1 is closed, and S_2 is opened. And V_{SUM_1} is calculated in absolute value by ABS_1 after passing through a voltage divider system consisting of M_1 and R_3. When ABS_1 outputs positive voltage, D_3 outputs a low level. $Vout$ is $V_{ABS_1} + V_3 = 6$ V. The memristance value of M_2 starts to gradually decrease under the effect of $Vout$. The voltage of V_{SUM_3} decreases as the memristance of M_2 decreases. At 4.6 s, the memristance of M_2 drops to 1.4 KΩ, and the input voltage of the positive terminal of OP_2 begins to be greater than V_{SUM_1}. Then U_1 starts to change the voltage from 0 V to 1 V. It means learning is completed. At 5.4 s, the memristance of M_2 drops to 1.2 KΩ, and OP_3 outputs a feedback signal F_1. With the appearance of feedback signal F_1, S_2 is closed. The voltage of SUM_1 is $V_{SUM_1} = V_1 + V_2 = -12.2$ V. The voltage at both ends of M_1 changes from −6 V to −6.1 V. At 6.4 s, the memristance of M_1 rises to 140 Ω. The voltage of $Vout$ is $Vout = V_{ABS_1} + V_3 \approx 5$ V. At 10 s, $INPUT_1$ outputs a low level. S_1, S_4 are opened, and S_2 is closed. Then $Vout$ produces the forgotten voltage. In order to make the simulation results more intuitive, the forgetting voltage of −2 V is changed to −8 V. At 29 s, the memristance of M_2 returns to its initial value. At 30 s, the $INPUT_1$ produces a high level again and the neuron enters a second learning state. The voltage of $Vout$ is 5 V. At 33.2 s, OP_2 starts to produce voltage of 1 V.

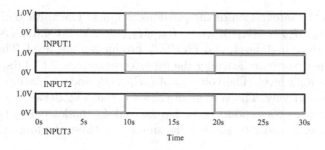

Fig. 7. Synergistic memory. $INPUT_1 - INPUT_3$ are the input signals of the three pre-neurons.

4.2 Synergistic Memory

The synergistic memory process of the three neurons is shown in Figs. 7, 8 and 9. At the beginning, $INPUT_1$ and $INPUT_3$ produce low level, and $INPUT_2$ produces a high level. The three pre-neurons in the system perform L_2, L_3 and L_6 modes. The weights of the learning synapses in the three learning modes gradually decreased from 0 to 4.6 s. Before 4.6 s, the weights of the learning synapses were above the threshold, and $U_1 - U_6$ produce 0 V. At 4.6 s, the weights of the learning synapses were below the threshold. The voltage of U_2, U_3 and U_6 are increased to 1 V. A_1 produces a high level, the synergistic neurons began to work. The synergistic neurons invoke different weighting modules to process the data based on the input signals from different synapses. The voltage of $V_{OP_{11}}$ and $V_{OP_{21}}$ are $V_{OP_{11}} = V_{OP_{21}} = -(R_{31}/M_{14}) * U_2 = -(R_{33}/M_{18}) * U_6 = -0.1\,\text{V} \sim 0$. The voltage of V_{OP_5} is $V_{OP_{20}} = -(R_{32}/M_{15}) * U_3 = -2\,\text{V}$. The output voltage of

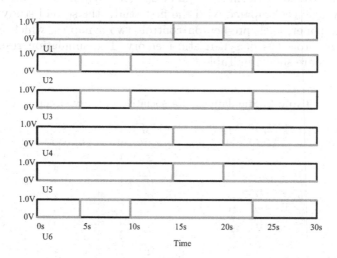

Fig. 8. Synergistic memory. $U_1 - U_6$ are the output voltages from the six synapses of the three pre-neurons.

OUTPUT is the integration of the previous weights. The voltage of OUTPUT is $V = -(R_{34}/M_{19} - (R_{34}/M_{20}) - (R_{34}/M_{21}) = 2\,\text{V}$. At 4.6 s, $INPUT_1$ and $INPUT_3$ produce high level, and $INPUT_2$ produces a low level. The three pre-neurons in the system are learning the other three modes. At 14.6 s, U_1, U_2 and U_5 produce a high level. The voltages of OP_4, OP_5 and OP_6 are $-1\,\text{V}$, $-0.1\,\text{V}$ and $-4\,\text{V}$, respectively. The voltage of OUTPUT is 5 V. Between 10 s and 20 s, the three synapses corresponding to L_2, L_3 and L_6 modes began to enter into forgetting state. In order to shorten the simulation time, the forgetting speed is accelerated.

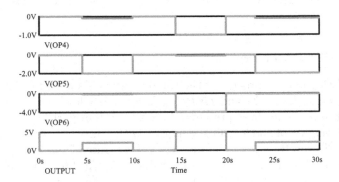

Fig. 9. Synergistic memory. $V_{OP_{19}} - V_{OP_{22}}$ are synaptic weight curves of post-neuron. OUTPUT is the final voltage.

At 20 s, the input signal of the initial moment is reentered. The three pre-neurons in the system perform L_2, L_3 and L_6 modes again. At 23.2S, OUTPUT produces 1 V again. Compared with the first study, the second study takes less time. In this paper, each pre-neuron controls two synapses, which can realize eight different processes of synergistic memory. The simulation results of the eight processes are shown in Table 2.

Table 2. Simulations of associative memory circuit

$INPUT_1$ (V)	$INPUT_2$ (V)	$INPUT_3$ (V)	M_2 (Ω)	M_{22} (Ω)	M_{32} (Ω)	M_{42} (Ω)	M_{52} (Ω)	M_{62} (Ω)	V_{OP_4} (V)	V_{OP_5} (V)	V_{OP_6} (V)	OUTPUT (V)
0	0	0	/	↓	/	↓	/	↓	0	0	0	0
1	0	0	↓	/	/	↓	/	↓	−1	0	0	1
0	1	0	/	↓	↓	/	/	↓	0	−2	0	2
1	1	0	↓	/	↓	/	/	↓	−1	−2	0	3
0	0	1	/	↓	/	↓	↓	/	0	0	−4	4
1	0	1	↓	/	/	↓	↓	/	−1	0	−4	5
0	1	1	/	↓	↓	/	↓	/	0	−2	−4	6
1	1	1	↓	/	↓	/	↓	/	−1	−2	−4	7

5   Conclusion

In this paper, the traditional mode of associative memory is extended to achieve multimodal synergy. Different neurons can work in concert with each other to transform simple information into more complex information. In addition, a neuronal circuit module conforming to the properties of biological neurons is proposed. The circuit can simulate biological memory and second memory. However, there may be a gap between the proposed circuit and the actual neural processing method. In the future, we will focus on the simplification of the circuit structure and the optimization of circuit performance.

References

1. Zhang, X., Han, Q., Wang, J.: Admissible delay upper bounds for global asymptotic stability of neural networks with time-varying delays. IEEE Trans. Neural Netw. **29**(11), 5319–5329 (2018)
2. Zhang, F., Zeng, Z.: Multiple lagrange stability under perturbation for recurrent neural networks with time-varying delays. IEEE Trans. Syst. Man Cybern. 1–13 (2018). https://doi.org/10.1109/tsmc.2018.2793343
3. Silver, D., et al.: Mastering the game of go without human knowledge. Nature **550**(7676), 354–359 (2017)
4. Rasouli, M., Chen, Y., Basu, A., Thakor, N.V.: An extreme learning machine-based neuromorphic tactile sensing system for texture recognition. IEEE Trans. Biomed. Circuits Syst. **12**(2), 313–325 (2018)
5. Silver, D., et al.: Mastering the game of go with deep neural networks and tree search. Nature **529**(7587), 484–489 (2016)
6. Basheer, I.A., Hajmeer, M.: Artificial neural networks: fundamentals, computing, design, and application. J. Microbiol. Methods **43**(1), 3–31 (2000)
7. Hassoun, M.H., Intrator, N., Mckay, S., Christian, W.: Fundamentals of artificial neural networks. Comput. Phys. **10**(2), 137 (1996)
8. Rosenfeld, A., Tsotsos, J.K.: Incremental learning through deep adaptation. IEEE Trans. Pattern Anal. Mach. Intell. **42**(3), 651–663 (2020)
9. Hasan, R., Taha, T.M., Yakopcic, C.: On-chip training of memristor crossbar based multi-layer neural networks. Microelectron. J. **66**, 31–40 (2017)
10. Hu, M., et al.: Memristor-based analog computation and neural network classification with a dot product engine. Adv. Mater. **30**(9), 1705914 (2018)
11. Cruzalbrecht, J., Derosier, T., Srinivasa, N.: A scalable neural chip with synaptic electronics using cmos integrated memristors. Nanotechnology **24**(38), 384011 (2013)
12. Indiveri, G., Linaresbarranco, B., Legenstein, R., Deligeorgis, G., Prodromakis, T.: Integration of nanoscale memristor synapses in neuromorphic computing architectures. Nanotechnology **24**(38),384010 (2013)
13. Berdan, R., Prodromakis, T., Salaoru, I., Khiat, A., Toumazou, C.: Memristive devices as parameter setting elements in programmable gain amplifiers. Appl. Phys. Lett. **101**(24), 243502 (2012)
14. Snider, G.S.: Self-organized computation with unreliable, memristive nanodevices. Nanotechnology **18**(36), 365202 (2007)
15. Junsangsri, P., Lombardi, F.: Design of a hybrid memory cell using memristance and ambipolarity. IEEE Trans. Nanotechnol. **12**(1), 71–80 (2013)

16. Chua, L.: Memristor-the missing circuit element. IEEE Trans. Circuit Theory **18**(5), 507–519 (1971)
17. Strukov, D.B., Snider, G.S., Stewart, D.R., Williams, R.S.: The missing memristor found. nature **453**(7191), 80 (2008)
18. Jo, S.H., Chang, T., Ebong, I., Bhadviya, B., Mazumder, P., Lu, W.: Nanoscale memristor device as synapse in neuromorphic systems. Nano Lett. **10**(4), 1297–1301 (2010)
19. Cantley, K.D., Subramaniam, A., Stiegler, H.J., Chapman, R.A., Vogel, E.M.: Hebbian learning in spiking neural networks with nanocrystalline silicon tfts and memristive synapses. IEEE Trans. Nanotechnol. **10**(5), 1066–1073 (2011)
20. Kim, H., Sah, M.P., Yang, C., Roska, T., Chua, L.O.: Neural synaptic weighting with a pulse-based memristor circuit. IEEE Trans. Circuits Syst. **59**(1), 148–158 (2012)
21. Pershin, Y.V., Ventra, M.D.: Experimental demonstration of associative memory with memristive neural networks. Neural Netw. **23**(7), 881–886 (2010)
22. Adhikari, S.P., Kim, H., Budhathoki, R.K., Yang, C., Chua, L.O.: A circuit-based learning architecture for multilayer neural networks with memristor bridge synapses. IEEE Trans. Circuits Syst. I-regular Pap. **62**(1), 215–223 (2015)
23. Hong, Q., Zhao, L., Wang, X.: Novel circuit designs of memristor synapse and neuron. Neurocomputing **330**, 11–16 (2019)
24. Burkitt, N.: A review of the integrate-and-fire neuron model: I. homogeneous synaptic input. Biol. Cybern. **95**(1), 1–19 (2006)
25. Urbanska, M., Blazejczyk, M., Jaworski, J.: Molecular basis of dendritic arborization. Acta Neurobiol. Exp. **68**(2), 264–288 (2008)
26. Redmond, L., Oh, S., Hicks, C., Weinmaster, G., Ghosh, A.: Nuclear notch1 signaling and the regulation of dendritic development. Nat. Neurosci. **3**(1), 30–40 (2000)
27. Sousa, A.M.M., Meyer, K.A., Santpere, G., Gulden, F.O., Sestan, N.: Evolution of the human nervous system function, structure, and development. Cell **170**(2), 226–247 (2017)
28. Lynch, M.A.: Long-term potentiation and memory. Physiol. Rev. **84**(1), 87–136 (2004)
29. Prezioso, M., Merrikhbayat, F., Hoskins, B.D., Adam, G.C., Likharev, K.K., Strukov, D.B.: Training and operation of an integrated neuromorphic network based on metal-oxide memristors. Nature **521**(7550), 61–64 (2015)
30. Zhang, Y., Li, Y., Wang, X., Friedman, E.G.: Synaptic characteristics of ag/aginsbte/ta-based memristor for pattern recognition applications. IEEE Trans. Electron Devices **64**(4), 1806–1811 (2017)
31. Wang, Z., Wang, X.: A novel memristor-based circuit implementation of full-function pavlov associative memory accorded with biological feature. IEEE Trans. Circuits Syst. I-regular Pap. **65**(7), 2210–2220 (2018)
32. An, H., An, Q., Y.Yi.: Realizing behavior level associative memory learning through three-dimensional memristor-based neuromorphic circuits. IEEE Trans. Emerg. Top. Comput. Intell. (2019). https://doi.org/10.1109/tetci.2019.2921787
33. Zhang, Y., Wang, X., Li, Y., Friedman, E.G.: Memristive model for synaptic circuits. IEEE Trans. Circuits Syst. Ii-express Briefs **64**(7), 767–771 (2017)
34. Singh, Jeetendra, Raj, Balwinder: An accurate and generic window function for nonlinear memristor models. J. Comput. Electron. **18**(2), 640–647 (2019). https://doi.org/10.1007/s10825-019-01306-6
35. Biolek, D., Biolkova, V., Biolek, Z.: Spice model of memristor with nonlinear dopant drift. Radioengineering **18**(2), 210–214 (2009)

36. Li, Y., Zhong, Y., Xu, L., Zhang, J., Xu, X., Sun, H., Miao, X.: Ultrafast synaptic events in a chalcogenide memristor. Sci. Rep. **3**(1), 1619–1619 (2013)
37. Zha, J., Huang, H., Huang, T., Cao, J., Alsaedi, A.: A general memristor model and its applications in programmable analog circuits. Neurocomputing **267**, 134–140 (2017)
38. Kvatinsky, S., Friedman, E.G., Kolodny, A., Weiser, U.C.: TEAM: ThrEshold adaptive memristor model. IEEE Trans. Circuits Syst. I-regular Pap. **60**(1), 211–221 (2013)

Lung Segmentation via Deep Learning Network and Fully-Connected Conditional Random Fields

Yuqin Li, Bo Wang, Weili Shi, Yu Miao, Huamin Yang, and Zhengang Jiang[✉]

Changchun University of Science and Technology, Changchun, China
jiangzhengang@cust.edu.cn

Abstract. Computer-Aided Diagnosis (CAD) benefits to early diagnosis and accurate treatment of lung diseases. As a preprocessing of CAD-based chest radiograph analysis, reliable lung segmentation is a prerequisite step which affects the precision of lesion recognition and classification. The techniques of deep learning have been widely applied for learning task-adaptive features in image segmentation. However, most existing lung fields segmentation methods based on deep learning are unable to ensure appearance and spatial consistency of the lung fields due to the varied boundaries and poor contrasts. In this study, we propose a novel method for lung fields segmentation by integrating U-Net network and a fully connected conditional random field (CRF). In the first step, we train the U-Net network designed in this paper to provide a preliminary probability to each pixel in images. Secondly, a fully connected CRF algorithm is used in this paper to optimize the coarse segmentation according to the intensity and position information of each pixel in images. Comparison with some previous methods on JSRT dataset, the proposed method in this paper shows higher Dice-Coefficient and Jaccard index.

Keywords: Lung fields segmentation · U-Net · Fully connected CRF

1 Introduction

The system of Computer-Aided diagnosis (CAD) is an efficient tool and a prerequisite for automatic medical diagnosis. With the development of medical image processing technology, the performance of CAD is increasing. Nowadays, doctors use the CAD systems to provide more persuasive judgments. Chest X-Ray is a common diagnostic imaging technology, which has been widely applied for lung diseases. Detecting lung fields in chest X-Ray images is important in CAD for lung diseases detection and diagnosis. An automatic and accurate lung fields segmentation method can save doctors' efforts for manual identification. In addition, reliable and automatic lung fields segmentation is an important step for analyzing chest X-Ray images, which ensures that lung diseases detection is not confounded by regions outside lung.

However, an accurate segmentation of lung fields in X-Ray image remains a challenge for several reasons. Lung fields in X-Ray images contain some superimposed structures as Fig. 1 (e.g., clavicles, ribs), which lead to blurred lung boundaries [1]. Besides, there

L. Pan et al. (Eds.): BIC-TA 2020, CCIS 1363, pp. 396–405, 2021.
https://doi.org/10.1007/978-981-16-1354-8_28

are large variations about lung anatomical shapes on account of the heart dimensions or other pathologies among different patients in X-Ray images, which will disturb the boundaries of lung fields. To meet this challenge, many researchers have proposed a lot of methods for lung fields segmentation. The traditional algorithms of lung fields segmentation can be roughly divided into some categories: rule-based methods, pixel-based methods, registration-based methods, shape model-based methods.

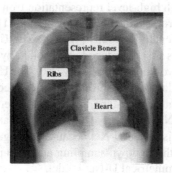

Fig. 1. Some superimposed structures of lung fields in Chest X-Ray images

Rule-based methods consist of a sequence of rules and steps [2–5]. Due to the heterogeneity of lung fields shapes, the rule-based methods always tend to failure. Pixel-based methods regard the segmentation tasks as a classification and use a classifier to label each pixel as ROI or background [6, 7]. However, these methods always cause wrong classification around boundaries. Registration-based methods try to employ a segmented lung database as anatomical atlas to match the objective images [8, 9]. However, these methods depend on the results of nonrigid registration, which are inefficient. Finally, the shape model-based methods [10–13] tend to produce average shapes, which rely on the initial model heavily and also ineffective with abnormal cases.

In recent years, deep learning (e.g., convolutional neural networks) methods have been widely used in image analysis, which is composed of multiple processing layers to achieve high performance by learning the representation of data [14–16]. It has been proven effective for semantic image segmentation. The convolutional neural network-based methods can extract image features automatically and process the images efficiently with its excellent ability of feature extraction and expression. However, these methods need a large number of labeled data to extract the ROIs effectively in the training step. It is also a failure due to the varied shapes and the quality of imaging.

Nowadays, the popular hybrid methods which fuse some advanced techniques have displayed efficient performance [6, 17]. In this paper, a hybrid method for lung fields segmentation is proposed by integrating U-Net network and a fully connected conditional random field (CRF). A fully connected CRF takes the original image and the corresponding predicted probability map as its input. The fully connected CRF uses a highly efficient inference algorithm which defines the pairwise edge potentials by a liner combination of Gaussian kernels in feature space. By using the fully connected CRF as a post processing, the surrounding pixels is considered while assigning the label to some particular pixels.

2 Method

2.1 Deep Learning Networks

Biomedical images contain some objects of interest (e.g., organs or lesions), but the edge of the interesting object is variable. To cope with the object's segmentation with detailed patterns, the skip-architecture that combined appearance representation from shallow encoding layers with high-level representation from deep decoding layers was proposed by Long [18] to produce detailed segmentation. This theory has been proved to produce promising segmentation results [18, 19]. The U-Net network employs the skip-architecture, which was first introduced and applied by Ronneberger [20]. In fact, U-Net is a kind of Fully Convolution Neural Networks. The U-Net network combines the features from shallow and deep layers through multipath confusion effectively, which solves the spatial loss of feature maps and improves the performance of semantic segmentation. The model of U-Net can achieve higher performance for image segmentation on a smaller training set. It is called U-Net because its elegant U type formed by symmetrical structure forms with the down-sampling and the up-sampling in the network. Figure 2 shows a simple symmetrical U-Net model.

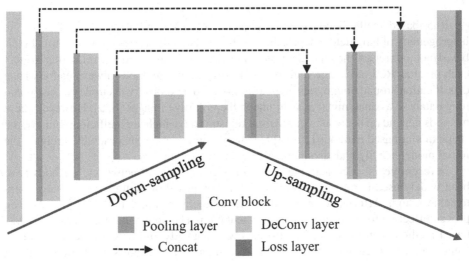

Fig. 2. The architecture of a simple U-Net.

The U-Net network in this paper consists of an encoding (down-sampling) structure and a decoding (up-sampling) structure as shown in Fig. 3. This U-Net network consists of 22 convolutional layers, 4 max-pooling layers, 4 up-sample layers and 4 catenation connections. The green cuboids correspond to multi-channel feature maps, and the transparent cuboids represent copied feature maps. Different operations are indicated by arrows with different colors. The numbers at the top of the cuboid denote the number of channels. The batch size in this model is 8. In this architecture, the last convolutional layer uses the sigmoid activation function, and the remains use ReLu activation function.

To obtain specific information of each region in the images, a receptive field with size of 3 * 3, stride as 1 are involved in this model.

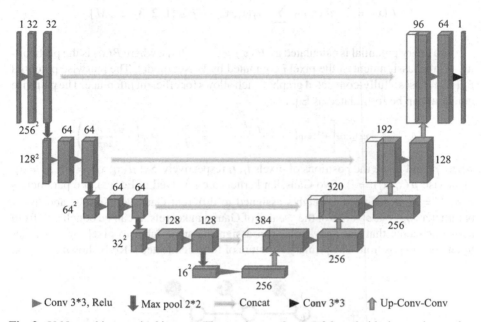

Fig. 3. U-Net architecture in this paper. The numbers at the top of the cuboids denote the number of channels. Different operations are indicated by arrows with different colors

2.2 Fully Connected CRF

In this paper, we use the fully connected conditional random field (CRF) proposed by Krähenbühl [21] to refine the coarse segmentation. The model of CRF evolved from the Markov Random Field (MRF). The model of CRF is an undirected graph in which each node satisfies the properties of Markov [22]. The basic CRF is composed of unary potentials and pairwise potentials, in which the unary potentials are obtained from individual pixels and the pairwise potentials are adjacent pixels. Supposing that an image I is composed of a set of pixels $I = \{I_1, I_2, \ldots, I_M\}$, where M is the number of pixels in image I. The energy function of basic CRF is formulated as Eq. (1):

$$E(x) = \sum_i \theta(x_i) + \sum_{i,j \in N_i} \beta(x_i, x_j), \ i \in \{1, 2, 3, \ldots, M\}, j \in N_i \tag{1}$$

where x is the label assignment for each pixel, x_i represents the label assigned to pixel i, $\theta(x_i)$ is the unary term, and $\beta(x_i, x_j)$ is the pairwise term. N_i denotes the neighborhood of pixel I_i. By minimizing the energy function, a set of x_i can be found to segment the object. In this paper, a fully connected CRF is used to get a global optimized result and improve the segmentation performance. Different from the traditional CRF models, the fully connected CRF computes the pairwise potentials on all pairs of pixels in image I. The energy function of fully connected CRF is written as Eq. (2):

$$E(x) = \sum_i \theta_i(x_i) + \sum_{i<j} \beta_{ij}(x_i, x_j), \ i,j \in \{1, 2, 3, \ldots, M\} \tag{2}$$

The unary potential is calculated as: $\theta_i(x_i) = -logP(x_i)$, where $P(x_i)$ is the probability of label assignment of the pixel i computed by U-Net model. The pairwise potential $\beta_{ij}(x_i, x_j)$ uses a fully-connected graph, which allows for efficient inference. The pairwise potential can be formulated as Eq. (3):

$$\beta_{ij}(x_i, x_j) = \mu(x_i, x_j)\left[w^{(1)} \exp\left(-\frac{\|p_i - p_j\|^2}{2\sigma_\alpha^2} - \frac{\|I_i - I_j\|^2}{2\sigma_\tau^2}\right) + w^{(2)} \exp\left(-\frac{\|p_i - p_j\|^2}{2\sigma_\xi^2}\right)\right] \tag{3}$$

where p_i and p_j are the positions of pixels I_i, I_j respectively. Set $\mu(x_i, x_j) = 1$ if $x_i \neq x_j$, otherwise $\mu(x_i, x_j) = 0$. Two Gaussian kernels are involved in Eq. (3), the parameters $w^{(k)}$, $k = 1, 2$ denote the weights assigned to different Gaussian kernels, and hyper parameters $\sigma_\alpha, \sigma_\tau, \sigma_\xi$ control the "scale" of Gaussian kernels. It can be concluded from above concepts that the first kernel can assign the same label to pixels with similar intensity and position. The primary structure of fully connected CRF is shown as Fig. 4.

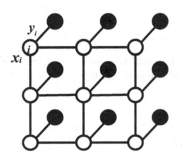

Fig. 4. Fully connected CRF principle structure

3 Experiment

3.1 Dataset

In the experiment, a public available dataset of Japanese Society of Radiological Technology (JSRT) [23] is used to evaluate the proposed method. The JSRT dataset consists of 247 PA chest radiographs from 13 institutions in Japan and one American institution. The images were scanned from films to the size of 2048 * 2048 pixels, with a spatial resolution of 0.175 mm and 12-bit gray levels. The manual segmentation of lung fields in Chest X-Ray images in the JSRT dataset is available at the website: http://www.isi. uu.nl/Research/Databases/SCR/. The JSRT dataset is divided into two folds: fold 1 (124 images) and fold 2 (123 images). In this paper, a two-fold cross-validation method is used to evaluate the segmentation performance. Some examples from the JSRT dataset are illustrated as Fig. 5.

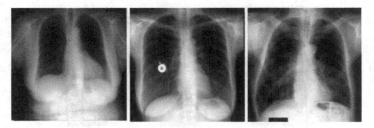

Fig. 5. Some Chest X-Ray images in JSRT dataset

3.2 Indicators

In this paper, we use two widely popular indicators to evaluate the proposed method quantitatively and compare it with other methods for lung fields segmentation. One is the Jaccard index (Ω) and the other is the Dice similarity coefficient (DSC) [24]. The metrics are defined and computed as follows.

1) The Jaccard index is the agreement between the ground truth and the estimated mask over all pixels in image. It is formulated as Eq. (4):

$$\Omega = \frac{|S \cap GT|}{|S \cup GT|} = \frac{|TP|}{|FP| + |TP| + |FN|} \tag{4}$$

where GT is the ground truth and S is the estimated segmentation mask, TP(true positives) represents correctly classified pixels, FP (false positives) denotes the pixels which are classified as object but are background actually, and FN (false negatives) represents pixels which are classified as background but are the object part in fact.

2) The Dice similarity coefficient is the overlap ratio between the ground truth (GT) and the estimated segmentation mask S. It is formulated as Eq. (5):

$$DSC = \frac{|S \cap GT|}{|S| + |GT|} = \frac{2|TP|}{2|TP| + |FN| + |FP|} \tag{5}$$

3.3 Experiment Results

In this paper, a two-fold cross-validation method was used to evaluate the segmentation performance in the experiment of U-Net. We adjusted the size of images without compressing the pixel value to 512 * 512. The resolution of the manual segmentation corresponding to the original dataset was 1024 * 1024. The epoch in U-Net network was set at 200. Figure 6 shows some visualization results about the intermediate layers of U-Net network. Training with the 1024 * 1024 resolution is also feasible but it requires multiple GPUs. By using U-Net network, we obtained a probability for each pixel. As a post processing method, the CRF used a highly efficient inference algorithm which defines the pairwise edge potentials by a liner combination of Gaussian kernels in feature space. Besides, the single U-Net was implemented as a comparison in this experiment. The qualitative results of the proposed method segmentation are presented in Fig. 7. And the comparison results with other methods are summarized as Table 1. From the results, it suggests that the proposed segmentation method can be used to achieve reliable lung fields segmentation.

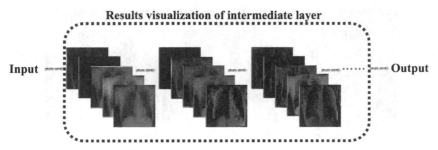

Fig. 6. Some visualization results about the intermediate layers of U-Net network

a. Initial images   b. Ground-Truth   c. Proposed method

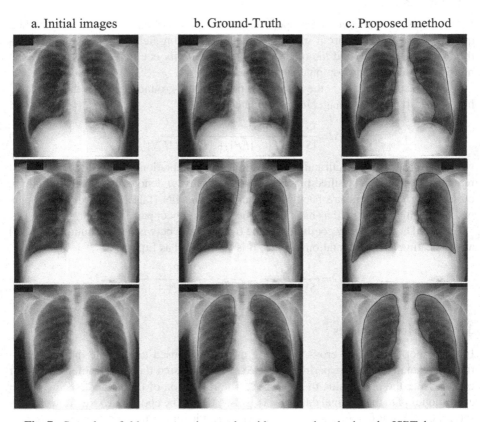

Fig. 7. Some lung fields segmentation results with proposed method on the JSRT dataset.

Table 1. Performance of lung field segmentation in terms of Jaccard index (Ω) and DSC.

Method	Ω (%)	DSC (%)
SIFT-Flow [8]	95.4 ± 1.5	96.7 ± 0.8
Hybrid method [25]	94.6 ± 1.9	97.2 ± 1.0
InvertedNet [14]	94.6 ± 1.9	97.2
Single U-Net	94.9 ± 2.1	97.1 ± 1.7
The proposed method	**95.1 ± 2.1**	**97.3 ± 1.6**

4 Conclusion

In this paper, we proposed a novel method for lung fields segmentation by integrating U-Net network and a fully connected conditional random field (CRF). This integrated model was designed to solve the problem of difficulty in ensuring the consistency of appearance and spatial. Firstly, a two-fold cross-validation method was used to evaluate the segmentation performance in the experiment of U-Net, which provided a preliminary probability to each pixel. Then, this paper used a fully connected CRF to post-process the preliminary coarse segmentation. By considering the pixel's intensity and position information in the images, the proposed method showed higher performance on the JSRT dataset.

Acknowledgments. This work is supported by the Projects of the Science & Technology Development Program of Jilin Province, China: (20190302112GX, 20190201196JC, 20180201037SF), the Project of Development and Reform Commission of Jilin Province: (2018C039-1), the China Guanghua Science and Technology Fund of the First Hospital of Jilin University (NO.JJDYYGH2019003) and The National Key Research and Development Program of China: (2017YFC0108303).

References

1. Yang, W., et al.: Lung field segmentation in chest radiographs from boundary maps by a structured edge detector. IEEE J. Biomed. Health Inf. **22**(3), 842–851 (2017)
2. Brown, M.S., Wilson, L.S., Doust, B.D., Gill, R.W., Sun, C.: Knowledge-based method for segmentation and analysis of lung boundaries in chest X-ray images. Comput. Med. Imaging Graph. **22**(6), 463–477 (1998)
3. Duryea, J., Boone, J.M.: A fully automated algorithm for the segmentation of lung fields on digital chest radiographic images. Med. Phys. **22**(2), 183–191 (1995)
4. Ginneken, B.V., Romeny, B.M.: Automatic segmentation of lung fields in chest radiographs. Med. Phys. **27**(10), 2445–2455 (2000)
5. Gao, Q., Wang, S., Zhao, D., Liu, J.: Accurate lung segmentation for X-ray CT images. In: Third International Conference on Natural Computation (ICNC 2007), pp. 275–279. IEEE, Haikou, China (2007)
6. Ginneken, B.V., Stegmann, M.B., Loog, M.: Segmentation of anatomical structures in chest radiographs using supervised methods: a comparative study on a public database. Med. Image Anal. **10**(1), 19–40 (2006)

7. McNitt-Gray, M.F., Huang, H.K., Sayre, J.W.: Feature selection in the pattern classification problem of digital chest radiograph segmentation. IEEE Trans. Med. Imaging **14**(3), 537–547 (1995)

8. Candemir, S., et al.: Lung segmentation in chest radiographs using anatomical atlases with nonrigid registration. IEEE Trans. Med. Imaging **33**(2), 577–590 (2014)

9. Candemir, S., Antani, S.: A review on lung boundary detection in chest X-rays. Int. J. Comput. Assist. Radiol. Surg. **14**, 563–576 (2019)

10. Dawoud, A.: Lung segmentation in chest radiographs by fusing shape information in iterative thresholding. IET Comput. Vision **5**(3), 185–190 (2011)

11. Soliman, A., et al.: Accurate lungs segmentation on CT chest images by adaptive appearance-guided shape modeling. IEEE Trans. Med. Imaging **36**(1), 263–276 (2017)

12. Shi, Y., Qi, F., Xue, Z., Chen, L., Ito, K., Matsuo, H., Shen, D.: Segmenting lung fields in serial chest radiographs using both population-based and patient-specific shape statistics. IEEE Trans. Med. Imaging **27**(4), 481–494 (2008)

13. Sun, S., Bauer, C., Beichel, R.: Automated 3-D segmentation of lungs with lung cancer in CT data using a novel robust active shape model approach. IEEE Trans. Med. Imaging **31**(2), 449–460 (2012)

14. Novikov, A.A., Lenis, D., Major, D., Hladůvka, J., Wimmer, M., Bühler, K.: Fully convolutional architectures for multiclass segmentation in chest radiographs. IEEE Trans. Med. Imaging **37**(8), 1865–1876 (2018)

15. Harrison, A.P., Xu, Z., George, K., Lu, L., Summers, R.M., Mollura, D.J.: Progressive and multi-path holistically nested neural networks for pathological lung segmentation from CT images. In: Descoteaux, M., Maier-Hein, L., Franz, A., Jannin, P., Collins, D., Duchesne, S. (eds.) Medical Image Computing and Computer Assisted Intervention − MICCAI 2017. Lecture Notes in Computer Science, vol. 10435, pp. 621–629. Springer, Cham (2017). https://doi.org/10.1007/978-3-319-66179-7_71

16. Negahdar, M., Beymer, D., Syeda-Mahmood, T.: Automated volumetric lung segmentation of thoracic CT images using fully convolutional neural network. In: Medical Imaging 2018: Computer-Aided Diagnosis. SPIE Medical Imaging, Houston, Texas, United State (2018)

17. Coppini, G., Miniati, M., Monti, S., Paterni, M., Favilla, R., Ferdeghini, E.M.: A computer-aided diagnosis approach for emphysema recognition in chest radiography. Med. Eng. Phys. **35**(1), 63–73 (2013)

18. Long, J., Shelhamer, E., Darrell, T.: Fully convolutional networks for semantic segmentation. In: Proceedings of the IEEE Conference on Computer Vision and Pattern Recognition (CVPR), pp. 3431–3440. IEEE, Boston, MA, USA (2015)

19. Drozdzal, M., Vorontsov, E., Chartrand, G., Kadoury, S., Pal, C.: The importance of skip connections in biomedical image segmentation. In: Carneiro, G., et al. (eds.) Deep Learning and Data Labeling for Medical Applications (DLMIA 2016). Lecture Notes in Computer Science, vol. 10008, pp. 179–187. Springer, Cham Deep Learning and Data Labeling for Medical Applications (DIMIA) (2016). https://doi.org/10.1007/978-3-319-46976-8_19

20. Ronneberger, O., Fischer, P., Brox, T.: U-Net: convolutional networks for biomedical image segmentation. In: Navab, N., Hornegger, J., Wells, W., Frangi, A. (eds.) Medical Image Computing and Computer-Assisted Intervention – MICCAI 2015. Lecture Notes in Computer Science, vol. 9351, pp. 234–241. Springer, Cham (2015). https://doi.org/10.1007/978-3-319-24574-4_28

21. Krähenbühl, P., Koltun, V.: Efficient inference in fully connected CRFs with gaussian edge potentials. In: Advances in Neural Information Processing Systems (NIPS), pp. 109–117. MIT Press, Granada, Spain (2011)

22. Feng, N., Geng, X., Qin, L.: Study on MRI medical image segmentation technology based on CNN-CRF model. IEEE Access **8**, 60505–60514 (2020)

23. Shiraishi, J., et al.: Development of a digital image database for chest radiographs with and without a lung nodule: receiver operating characteristic analysis of radiologists' detection of pulmonary nodules. Am. J. Roentgenol. **174**(1), 71–74 (2000)
24. Dice, L.R.: Measures of the amount of ecologic association between species. Ecology **26**(3), 297–302 (1945)
25. Shao, Y., Gao, Y., Guo, Y., Shi, Y., Yang, X., Shen, D.: Hierarchical lung field segmentation with joint shape and appearance sparse learning. IEEE Trans. Med. Imaging **33**(9), 1761–1780 (2014)

HSDet: A Representative Sampling Based Object Detector in Cervical Cancer Cell Images

Xiaoli Yan and Zhongsi Zhang[✉]

Key Laboratory of Image Processing and Intelligent Control of Education
Ministry of China, School of Artificial Intelligence and Automation,
Huazhong University of Science and Technology, Wuhan 430074, China
{xiaoliyan,zzs}@hust.edu.cn

Abstract. Automated detection of cervical cancer cells has the potential to reduce error and increase productivity in cervical cancer screening. However, the existing object detection methods to detect the cervical cancer cells make inadequate use of negative samples and fail to balance the number of hard samples and easy samples. In this work, we propose a image-level sampling method, called pair sampling, which can extract the representative negative samples and generate the sample pair image. Then, based on the sample pair image, we propose the hybrid sampling, a proposal-level sampling method, to balance the number of hard samples and easy samples. Combining the proposed sampling methods, we design a representative sampling based cervical cell detector, which can detect the cervical cancer cells effectively. In order to comprehensively evaluate our method, we use a dataset which is consisted of 16000 annotated cervical cell images with size of 1024×1024. The experimental result shows that our method achieves 57.1% mean Average Precision (mAP), and it is higher than cascade R-CNN and Faster R-CNN by 4.7% and 5.8%, respectively.

Keywords: Pair sampling · Hybrid sampling · Object detection · Cervical cancer screening

1 Introduction

Cervical cancer is the most highly aggressive cancer and a major health problem in females, and a leading cause of cancer-related deaths worldwide. Cervical cytology is the most common and effective screening method for cervical cancer and precancerous cervical lesions [5]. The method is to conduct a cytological analysis of the collected cells that have been smeared on a glass slide and stained under the microscope, then finally give a diagnosis report according to the descriptive diagnosis method of the Bethesda system (TBS) [8]. However, manual examination for detecting abnormal cells in a cervical cytology slide is tedious and time-consuming for an expert pathologist. Therefore, there is a need for an automated and computer-assisted technique for cervical screening.

© Springer Nature Singapore Pte Ltd. 2021
L. Pan et al. (Eds.): BIC-TA 2020, CCIS 1363, pp. 406–418, 2021.
https://doi.org/10.1007/978-981-16-1354-8_29

Over the past 30 years, extensive research has attempted to develop automated assisted screening methods. The mainstream method is to divide the detection of cervical cell images into three stages: divide the cells in the images, extract the features of the cells, and finally identify the cancer cells through a classifier [1,3,19]. Due to the objective reasons such as the production technique and the microscope image environment, the collected cell images inevitably have some noise such as uneven illumination, background shadow, and inconsistent staining depth, and there are a large number of overlapping cells in the cells. As segmentation affects the accuracy of classification, precise segmentation under complex conditions is of great importance. Many deep learning based methods have been proposed for gland/nuclei instance segmentation tasks [4,9,14]. IRNet is the first end-to-end deep learning method for overlapping cell segmentation in Pap smear image [20], its segmentation accuracy of the nucleus and cytoplasm is far superior to the traditional method. Compared with the level-set based method [13], the IRNet [20] effectively improves cytoplasm Average Jaccard Index (AJI) from 19.74% to 71.85% and nuclei AJI from 31.67% to 54.96%.

However, the ground truth for deep learning based instance segmentation requires to mark the contours of the cells. The pathologist's marking workload is too much, which is not conducive to clinical application. Therefore, some methods based on deep learning based object detection have recently appeared, only need to mark two points of the cell's bounding box, so that the work of labeling is 1/tens of the segmentation. Liang et al. combined the general object detection method and the small sample learning method to achieve good detection results in the case of insufficient picture samples of cervical cancer cells [10]. Xiang et al. cascaded an additional task-specific classifier to improve the classification performance of hard examples which are four highly similar categories [18].

In this work, we propose a cell detector based on cascade R-CNN, which has chosen HRNet as a feature extraction network for that it can maintain high-resolution representations through the whole process, which is especially suitable for small cell feature extraction. We also proposed a pair sampling strategy in our detector called HSDet, to sample from both images with objects and images without objects, which could decrease the false detections. Moreover, we propose a hybrid sampling strategy in HSDet, to choose representative examples, which could extract representative difficult samples when foreground and background are difficult to distinguish. Extensive experiments demonstrate the effectiveness of our method, our HSDet achieves 57.1% mean Average Precision 50 (mAP50), and it is higher than cascade R-CNN and Faster R-CNN by 4.7% and 5.8%, respectively.

Our contributions are summarized as follows. 1) The general object detection algorithm uses random sampling in the image-level sampling. But most of the cervical cell images are negative images, and directly put these negative images into training will degrade the performance of the detection network. So we proposed a pair sampling strategy to fully exploit the samples in the negative images. 2) In the region proposal level sampling, the most advanced algorithms used for object detection are OHEM [16] and Focal Loss [12]. However, experiments have proved that these two methods do not work on the cervical cell datasets. In order to mine more representative samples for training, we propose a Hybrid Sampling strategy.

2   Related Work

2.1   CerVical Cell Segmentation and Classification

With the continuous development of pattern recognition technology and image processing technology, the mainstream method for image recognition of cervical cancer cells is to firstly segment each cell in the image, then extract the features of the cells, and finally identify the cancer cells through a classifier.

Traditional cytological criteria for the classification of cervical cell abnormalities are based on the changes in the nucleus to cytoplasm ratio, nucleus size, irregularity of nucleus shape, and membrane. Therefore, a great deal of work has been focused on the segmentation of cells or cell components using traditional image segmentation methods as well as segmentation methods based on convolutional neural networks [3,17]. Based on accurate segmentation of the cervical cell images, the patches that contain a single cell can be clipped from the regions around the cervical nucleus, then the cervical cells in the patches can be extracted features to identify abnormal cells. First, manually designed features were used for feature extraction, and then sent to the classifier [3]. Later, the convolutional neural network was used to extract feature and classification [10]. Due to the problems of adhesion and overlap in cervical cell images, the segmentation of cells or cell components is still an open problem, and the accuracy of segmentation will affect the accuracy of classification. Many deep learning based methods have been proposed for gland/nuclei instance segmentation tasks [4,9,14]. IRNet is the first end-to-end deep learning method for overlapping cell segmentation in Pap smear image [20], its segmentation accuracy of the nucleus and cytoplasm is far superior to the traditional method. Compared with the level-set based method [13], the IRNet [20] effectively improves cytoplasm Average Jaccard Index (AJI) from 19.74% to 71.85% and nuclei AJI from 31.67% to 54.96%.

2.2   Cervical Cell Object Detection

Although deep learning based instance segmentation has greatly improved the accuracy of cervical image recognition, the ground truth for deep learning based instance segmentation requires to mark the contours of the cells. The pathologist's marking workload is too much, which is not conducive to clinical application. Therefore, some methods based on deep learning based object detection have recently appeared, only need to mark two points of the cell's bounding box, so that the work of labeling is 1/tens of the segmentation. Liang et al. combined the general object detection method and the small sample learning method to achieve good detection results in the case of insufficient picture samples of cervical cancer cells [10]. Xiang et al. cascaded an additional task-specific classifier to improve the classification performance of hard examples which are four highly similar categories [18].

Current state-of-the-art object detectors with deep learning can be mainly divided into two major categories: two-stage detectors and one-stage detectors. Two-stage detectors first generate region proposals which may potentially be objects and then make predictions for these proposals. Faster R-CNN [15] is a representative two-stage detector, which was able to make predictions at 5 FPS on GPU and achieved state-of-the-art results on many public benchmark datasets, such as Pascal VOC 2007, 2012 and MSCOCO. Currently, there are a huge number of detector variants based on Faster R-CNN for different usage [2,11]. Cascade R-CNN [2] extend Faster R-CNN to a multi-stage detector through the classic yet powerful cascade architecture. Mask R-CNN [6] extends Faster R-CNN to the field of instance segmentation. Based on Mask R-CNN, Huang et al. proposed a mask-quality aware framework, named Mask Scoring R-CNN, which learned the quality of the predicted masks and calibrated the misalignment between mask quality and mask confidence score [7]. In the region proposal level sampling, the most advanced algorithms used for object detection are OHEM [16] and Focal Loss [12]. OHEM is a simple and intuitive algorithm that eliminates several heuristics and hyperparameters in common use and it yields consistent and significant boosts in detection performance on benchmarks like PASCAL VOC 2007 and 2012. Focal Loss [12] focuses training on a sparse set of hard examples and prevents the vast number of easy negatives from overwhelming the detector during training.

3   Proposed Method

3.1   Detection Network

As there are a large number of small cells in the patch, we choose HRNet as the feature extraction network based on the state-of-art two-stage detector, cascade R-CNN, as shown in Fig. 1.

HRNet can maintain the features of high resolution through a parallel connection of high-resolution and low-resolution networks, and has a better effect on the recognition of small objects. It conducts repeated multi-scale fusions such that each of the high-to-low resolution representations receives information from other parallel representations over and over, leading to rich high-resolution representations.

3.2   Pair Sampling

The region of interest (RoI) typically has millions of pixels. Since the size of cells is too small for the RoI, the cell features will disappear if we directly sent the RoI as an input image into the object detection networks. In this work, we use a redundant cropping method to cut the whole slide image (WSI) into small pieces, which is shown in Fig. 2. First, we obtain the RoI from WSI, and then use a

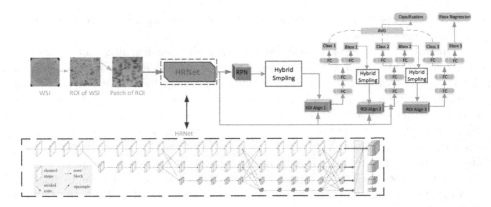

Fig. 1. The structure of HSDet. Its input are patches automatically cropped from WSI. It is made up of backbone network HRNet and the cascade head. The orange circle represents the head, classification and bounding box regression are tackled independently. The red circle show the proposed sampling method when choosing the regional proposal. (Color figure online)

1024×1024 slide window, in a stride of 512, from left to right and top to bottom, to crop the patches. For these patches, if an abnormal cell is contained in them and the retained area of cells in the patch is more than a preset threshold, it is a positive patch and the coordinates of the cell relative to the patch are recorded and the patch is put into the training set. The other patches are negative patches. As for cropping the test set, since there is no ground truth, all patches are sent into the test set, then detected using our HSDet, and the patches with detection results will be spliced back to the original image in accordance with the cropping sequence.

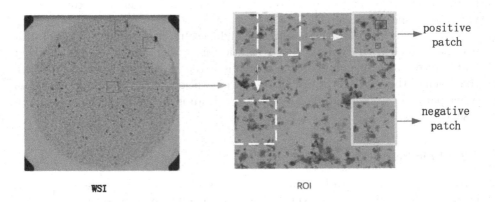

Fig. 2. Our redundant croping method for WSI.

However, most of the patches cut from RoI do not contain abnormal cells. In order to fully use these negative patches, we try to put these negative patches directly into the training set, but the performance degrades. In order to further explore whether negative patches are useful, we first train a model with only positive patches and test the model on negative patches. We find that the model produces a large number of false positives on negative patches, which indicates that we could mine negative samples from negative patches to decrease false detections. To mitigate false positives, we propose an image-level sampling method called pair sampling. As shown in Fig. 3, the details are discussed below.

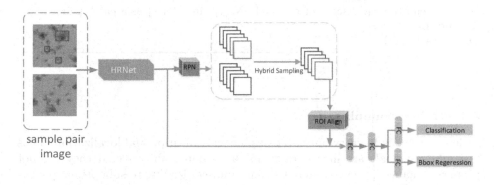

Fig. 3. Sample pair images and the detection network. Each sample pair contains a positive image and a negative image. In the right detection network, a green box indicates a positive region proposal coming from a positive image, and a red box indicates a negative region proposal coming from a positive image or a negative one. (Color figure online)

Our pair sampling method uses image-level sampling to mitigate sample imbalance in a batch. After cutting the WSIs, the number of negative patches is much greater than the number of positive patches. For efficiency, we first train a model with only positive patches, and then test on all negative patches, keeping negative samples with false positive confidence greater than a preset threshold. Then we randomly select negative patches with the same number of positive patches from the retained negative patches, which ensures that the positive and negative samples in a batch are balanced. When performing training sampling, we first sample a positive patch and then a negative patch, which forms a patch pair. When sampling a batch, the patch pair is the basic sampling unit. The positive samples in a patch pair are sampled from the positive patch, and the negative samples in a patch are sampled from the positive patch and negative patch. The process of pair sampling is described in Algorithm 1.

Algorithm 1. Pair Sampling

Input: the negative patches set $\{N\}$, the positive patches set $\{P\}$, the preset threshold α, the number of positive patches num, the sample pair set $\{Pair\}$ (Initialize to empty set).

Output: the patch pair set get by Pair Sampling.

1: Train a model M with positive patches $\{P\}$
2: Test M on negative patches N
3: Keep the negative patches with false detection confidence greater than α
4: Sample num patches from $\{N\}$ randomly, get $\{N_{sub}\}$
5: Randomly shuffle the elements in $\{P\}$ and $\{N_{sub}\}$
6: **for** $i = 1, 2, \cdots, num$ **do**
7:     append the ith element of $\{P\}$ and $\{N_{sub}\}$ into $\{Pair\}$ as a patch pair
8: **end for**
9: return $\{Pair\}$

3.3 Hybrid Sampling

A detector needs to carry out two tasks, i.e. classification and localization. Thus two different goals are incorporated in the training objective. If they are not properly balanced, one goal may be compromised, leading to suboptimal performance overall. The case is the same for the involved samples during the training process. If they are not properly balanced, the small gradients produced by the easy samples may be drowned into the large gradients produced by the hard ones, thus limiting further refinement.

In order to solve the problem of sample imbalance, OHEM [16] chooses difficult samples to participate in training. However, in the scene of cervical cancer cell slices, there will be lots of noise due to staining, which causes OHEM to focus too much on noises and ignore the easy samples. Focal Loss [12] alleviates the problem of sample imbalance by increasing the proportion of difficult sample loss. But it works when there are a large number of easy samples. When coming to the scene of cervical cancer cell slices, where foreground and background are difficult to distinguish, Focal Loss does not work. To mitigate the problem of sample imbalance, we propose a hybrid sampling method that can take into account the difficult samples and easy samples.

For better description of the algorithm, some notations are given first. For a training sample, $(x_{a1}, y_{a1}, x_{a2}, y_{a2})$ represents the coordinates of ground truth box A, $(x_{b1}, y_{b1}, x_{b2}, y_{b2})$ denotes the coordinates of the matched default box B. First, we calculate the IoU of box A and B:

$$IoU_{AB} = \frac{A \cap B}{A \cup B} \tag{1}$$

B is a positive sample only if IoU_{AB} is larger than a preset threshold. If B is a positive sample, then we calculate the smallest enclosing convex object C for A and B:

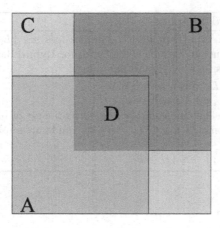

Fig. 4. A, B are two arbitrary shapes, C is the smallest enclosing convex of A and B, D is the [IoU] of A and B.

$$x_{c1} = \min(x_{a1}, x_{b1}) \tag{2}$$

$$y_{c1} = \min(y_{a1}, y_{b1}) \tag{3}$$

$$x_{c2} = \max(x_{a2}, x_{b2}) \tag{4}$$

$$y_{c2} = \max(y_{a2}, y_{b2}) \tag{5}$$

where $(x_{c1}, y_{c1}, x_{c2}, y_{c2})$ are the coordinates of C. For the regression part, we choose GIoU loss function. It is reasonable to use GIoU as loss function for boxes regression. It considers not only overlapping areas but also non-overlapping areas, which better reflects the overlap of the boxes. The GIoU of two arbitrary shapes A and B is defined as:

$$GIoU_{AB} = IoU_{AB} - \frac{C - U}{C} \tag{6}$$

where $U = A + B - IoU_{AB}$, IoU_{AB} and C are calculated by Eq. 1–Eq. 5. Figure 4 is a schematic diagram of GIoU. Then, we use G_i to denote the GIoU of the i-th predicted box and the ground truth, E_i to represent the cross entropy of the i-th predicted box. Then loss of the i-th predicted box is defined as:

$$L_i = G_i + E_i \tag{7}$$

After getting the sample loss, we can select some difficult samples according to the loss size. Then we select some easy samples based on random sampling. The process of hybird sampling is described in Algorithm 2.

Algorithm 2. Hybird Sampling

Input: the number of total samples N, samples loss set $\{L_i : 0 < i < N + 1\}$, the number of samples we use to train k, scale factor for Hybird Sampling α.
Output: the samples set get by Hybird Sampling.
1: Construct the loss L_i shown as in Eq. 7
2: Sort the loss set $\{L_i : 0 < i < N + 1\}$
3: Get the first $\alpha * k$ elements from the loss set as the set of hard samples: $\{H\}$
4: Get $(1 - \alpha) * k$ elements from $\{L_i - H\}$ by random sampling as the set of easy samples: $\{E\}$
5: return training sample set $\{H + E\}$

---

4   Experiments

4.1   Dataset and Evaluation

The dataset for cervical cancer cell recognition consists of 1000 whole slide images at 20x magnification whose length and width are over 10,000 pixels. The numbers of the training set, validation set, and test set are 600, 200, and 200. Among the training set and validation set, there were 500 positive WSIs and 300 negative WSIs in the training set and the test set. Positive WSIs will provide multiple candidate regions of interest, whose length and width are ranging from 4000 to 5000. The location of abnormal squamous epithelial cells is labeled in the ROI area, while the negative WSIs do not contain abnormal squamous epithelial cells and are not labeled. The abnormal squamous epithelial cells discussed in the preliminary round mainly include four types: High Intraepithelial Lesion (HSIL), atypical squamous cells cannot be clearly defined (ASC-US), atypical squamous cells tend to be high in epithelial cells (ASC-H), low-grade intraepithelial lesions (LSIL).

In this work, we use 10 metric for all experiments, the main performance measure used in this benchmark is shown by mean Average Precision (mAP), which is calculated with $IoU = 0.5$.

4.2   Experimental Settings

Experiments are implemented based on the deep learning framework PyTorch and executed on a workstation with two Intel 32 Core i7 CPUs with 64 GB RAM and two NVIDIA GTX-1080 GPUs with 20 GB memory. The operating system is Ubuntu 16.04.

Before training, a 1024×1024 slide window with the stride of 512 was used to crop the RoI of WSIs into patches, while before testing, a 1024×1024 slide window with the stride of 256 was used. Our dataset contains a training set of 14400 patches and a testing set of 1600 patches. The dataset was rotated by 90°, 180°, and 270°, and was flipped horizontally and vertically, for data augmentation. During training and testing, input images were all in multi-scale, including the size of 1024×1024, 1224×1224, and 1536×1536. The network was trained by the stochastic gradient descent method, the batch size was set as 6, and the learning rate was set as 0.01. The learning rate was reduced to 0.001 after 4 epochs were iterated, and the training was terminated when 10 epochs were iterated.

4.3 Experimental Results

This section we show the results of the experiments and discuss the perfomancce of our method in three parts.

(1) We conduct the experiments about pair sampling, the results are shown in Table 1. We use Faster R-CNN as the baseline with backbone ResNet-101. Then we found that mAP is increasing when we use HRNet-32 as backbone instead. HRNet keeps the characteristic of high discrimination and has a better effect on the recognition of small targets, so HRNet is especially suitable for the feature extraction of cervical cancer cell images. As high-quality proposals can produce higher-quality bounding boxes, so connect multiple R-CNNs and set different thresholds can produce a higher-quality detector. The cascade structure mitigates the mismatch of a single regression, and the three regressions help to reinforce the classification mismatch, so the AP50 is also significantly improved. From Table 1, we can also get that, the performance degrades when we take the negative patches directly into the training set. To solve this problem, we propose pair sampling, which defines the patch pair and could take advantage of negative patches.

(2) For the experiments about hybrid sampling, the results are shown in Table 2. We verify the effectiveness of our method on Faster R-CNN and cascade R-CNN. In order to extract difficult samples, we first try OHEM. However, from Table 2, we can get that the performance drops when we use OHEM. We believe that OHEM only chooses the most difficult samples, and can not represent the entire sample distribution. Then we use Focal Loss, but the effect is still not ideal. We think the reason is that there are not a lot of simple samples in the cervical cancer data. Finally, our proposed method, Hybrid Sampling, can select more representative samples, and the experimental results also show the effectiveness of our method.

(3) We conduct the experiments to verify the orthogonality of our methods, the results are shown in Table 3. Based on cascade R-CNN, we proposed a pair sampling method to take advantage of the negative patches, which significantly reduces false detections. It can be seen that its AP50 has been greatly improved compared with cascade R-CNN. Then, a Hybrid Sampling method is proposed to sample representative examples, which mitigates the problem of sample imbalance when foreground and background are difficult to distinguish. When our two methods were used in combination, they produce a significant performance improvement.

Table 1. Experiments results on cervical cancer dataset, PP means positive patches, NP means negative patches

Method	Backbone	Training set	mAP0.5
Faster R-CNN	ResNet	PP	50.2
Faster R-CNN	HRNet	PP	51.3
Faster R-CNN	HRNet	PP+NP	**50.5**
Faster R-CNN + pair sampling	HRNet	PP+NP	**53.5**
Cascade R-CNN	HRNet	PP	52.4
Cascade R-CNN	HRNet	PP+NP	**51.6**
Cascade R-CNN + pair sampling	HRNet	PP+NP	**54.2**

Table 2. Experiments results on cervical cancer dataset, PP means positive patches, NP means negative patches

Method	Backbone	Training set	mAP0.5
Faster R-CNN	ResNet	PP	50.2
Faster R-CNN	HRNet	PP	51.3
Faster R-CNN+hybird sampling	HRNet	PP	**53.2**
Cascade R-CNN	HRNet	PP	52.4
Cascade R-CNN+OHEM	HRNet	PP	**50.5**
Cascade R-CNN+focal loss	HRNet	PP	**51.4**
Cascade R-CNN+hybird sampling	HRNet	PP	**54.4**

Table 3. Experiments results on cervical cancer dataset, PP means positive patches, NP means negative patches

Method	Backbone	Training set	mAP0.5
Faster R-CNN	ResNet	PP	50.2
Faster R-CNN	HRNet	PP	51.3
Cascade R-CNN	HRNet	PP	52.4
Cascade R-CNN + pair sampling	HRNet	PP+NP	**55.2**
Cascade R-CNN + hybird sampling	HRNet	PP	**54.4**
HSDet	HRNet	PP+NP	**57.1**

5   Conclusions

In this work, we proposed a cervical cytology screening model called HSDet. First, the method of pair sampling is proposed to label the normal cells which are similar to the abnormal cells, to decrease the false detections. Then we propose the hybrid sampling method, to choose representative examples, which could mitigate the problem of sample imbalance while foreground and background are difficult to distinguish to the scene of cervical cancer cell slices. Our HSDet achieve an mAP 57.1%, and it is higher than cascade R-CNN and Faster R-CNN by 4.7% and 5.8%, respectively. Our method is deployed to detect the WSI, and the dataset used only requires cytologists to label the abnormal cells locations, so it is of significant practical application value in cervical cancer screening field.

References

1. Birdsong, G.G.: Automated screening of cervical cytology specimens. Hum. Pathol. **27**(5), 468–481 (1996)
2. Cai, Z., Vasconcelos, N.: Cascade R-CNN: delving into high quality object detection. In: Proceedings of the IEEE Conference on Computer Vision and Pattern Recognition, pp. 6154–6162 (2018)
3. Chankong, T., Theeraumpon, N., Auephanwiriyakul, S.: Automatic cervical cell segmentation and classification in pap smears. Comput. Methods Programs Biomed. **113**(2), 539–556 (2014)
4. Chen, H., Qi, X., Yu, L., Dou, Q., Qin, J., Heng, P.A.: Dcan: Deep contour-aware networks for object instance segmentation from histology images. Med. Image Anal. **36**, 135–146 (2017)
5. Davey, E., et al.: Effect of study design and quality on unsatisfactory rates, cytology classifications, and accuracy in liquid-based versus conventional cervical cytology: a systematic review. Lancet **367**(9505), 122–132 (2006)
6. He, K., Gkioxari, G., Dollár, P., Girshick, R.: Mask R-CNN. In: Proceedings of the IEEE International Conference on Computer Vision, pp. 2961–2969 (2017)
7. Huang, Z., Huang, L., Gong, Y., Huang, C., Wang, X.: Mask scoring R-CNN. In: Proceedings of the IEEE Conference on Computer Vision and Pattern Recognition, pp. 6409–6418 (2019)
8. Hyne, S.: The bethesda system for reporting cervical cytology: Definitions, criteria, and explanatory notes: 2nd edition. Pathology **37**(4), 328–329 (2005)
9. Kumar, N., Verma, R., Sharma, S., Bhargava, S., Vahadane, A., Sethi, A.: A dataset and a technique for generalized nuclear segmentation for computational pathology. IEEE Trans. Med. Imaging **36**(7), 1550–1560 (2017)
10. Liang, Y., Tang, Z., Yan, M., Chen, J., Xiang, Y.: Comparison detector: Convolutional neural networks for cervical cell detection. arXiv: Computer Vision and Pattern Recognition (2018)
11. Lin, T.Y., Dollár, P., Girshick, R., He, K., Hariharan, B., Belongie, S.: Feature pyramid networks for object detection. In: Proceedings of the IEEE Conference on Computer Vision and Pattern Recognition, pp. 2117–2125 (2017)
12. Lin, T.Y., Goyal, P., Girshick, R., He, K., Dollár, P.: Focal loss for dense object detection. In: Proceedings of the IEEE International Conference on Computer Vision, pp. 2980–2988 (2017)
13. Lu, Z., Carneiro, G., Bradley, A.P.: An improved joint optimization of multiple level set functions for the segmentation of overlapping cervical cells. IEEE Trans. Image Process. **24**(4), 1261–1272 (2015)
14. Raza, S.E.A., Cheung, L., Shaban, M., Graham, S., Epstein, D., Pelengaris, S., Khan, M., Rajpoot, N.M.: Micro-net: A unified model for segmentation of various objects in microscopy images. Med. Image Anal. **52**, 160–173 (2019)
15. Ren, S., He, K., Girshick, R., Sun, J.: Faster R-CNN: Towards real-time object detection with region proposal networks. IEEE Trans. Pattern Anal. Mach. Intell. **39**(6), 1137–1149 (2016)

16. Shrivastava, A., Gupta, A., Girshick, R.: Training region-based object detectors with online hard example mining. In: Proceedings of the IEEE Conference on Computer Vision and Pattern Recognition, pp. 761–769 (2016)
17. Song, Y., Zhang, L., Chen, S., Ni, D., Lei, B., Wang, T.: Accurate segmentation of cervical cytoplasm and nuclei based on multiscale convolutional network and graph partitioning. IEEE Trans. Biomed. Eng. **62**(10), 2421–2433 (2015)
18. Xiang, Y., Sun, W., Pan, C., Yan, M., Yin, Z., Liang, Y.: A novel automation-assisted cervical cancer reading method based on convolutional neural network. Biocybern. Biomed. Engi. **40**(2), 611–623 (2020)
19. Zhang, L., et al.: Automation-assisted cervical cancer screening in manual liquid-based cytology with hematoxylin and eosin staining. Cytometry A **85**(3), 214–230 (2014)
20. Zhou, Y., Chen, H., Xu, J., Dou, Q., Heng, P.A.: Irnet: instance relation network for overlapping cervical cell segmentation. In: International Conference on Medical Image Computing and Computer-Assisted Intervention, pp. 640–648. Springer (2019)

Identification of Prognostic Signature in Esophageal Cancer Based on Network Analysis

Jianfei Ma[1] and Yabing Huang[2(✉)]

[1] Key Laboratory of Image Information Processing and Intelligent Control,
School of Artificial Intelligence and Automation,
Huazhong University of Science and Technology,
Luoyu Road 1037, Wuhan 430074, China
[2] Department of Pathology, Renmin Hospital of Wuhan University,
Wuhan 430060, China

Abstract. Esophageal cancer is the 6th most common cancer in the world with a five-year survival among 15% to 25% patients. It's of great significance to identify prognostic signature for precise prediction of patient survival. In this work, we use a network-based approach to identify the disease genes of esophageal cancer. We construct the co-expression networks of normal and cancer samples by interpreting the gene expression profile and further divide the networks into inactivated subnetwork and enhanced subnetwork. Functional enrichment analysis shows that phosphoprotein and acetylation are both enriched in the inactivated genes and enhanced genes. Furthermore, 5 kinesin family members, KIF11, KIF23, KIF18A, KIF18B, and KIF2A, are all found to be significantly enhanced, suggesting that kinesin is crucial in promoting the formation of esophageal cancer. The 11 genes both inactivated and enhanced in the process of tumor development are found to be prognosis-associated and perform well in evaluating the survival of esophageal cancer patients. This study provides us fundamental recognition about the functional dysregulation in esophageal cancer and help to identify the biomarker for the further development of therapeutic targets.

Keywords: Esophageal cancer · Prognosis · Coexpression · Network

1   Introduction

Esophageal cancer is the 8th leading cause of cancer related death and the 6th most common cancer in the world. The morbidity and mortality are distributed distinctly between different regions. China is one of the most prevalent region with esophageal cancer in the world, leading to 150 thousands deaths every year. Unlike other cancers, such as lung cancer and breast cancer, that have been studied extensively, the state of molecular and functional characterization of esophageal cancer has not yet been changed and is still unclear in the recent

© Springer Nature Singapore Pte Ltd. 2021
L. Pan et al. (Eds.): BIC-TA 2020, CCIS 1363, pp. 419–431, 2021.
https://doi.org/10.1007/978-981-16-1354-8_30

years. Within all the esophageal cancer, esophageal squamous cell cancer is the major type in most cases with its histopathological form [1]. The genomic and molecular characterization has been studied in some papers [2,3], but the fundamental mechanism underlying the esophageal squamous cell cancer remains elusive and there is no effective approach for the diagnosis and treatment of the esophageal squamous cell cancer, resulting in the outcome of a five-year survival among 15% to 25% patients [4].

Traditional tumor staging system has been widely used in the clinical assessment of patient survival of esophageal cancer. But it doesn't achieve good performance due to the molecular heterogeneity of esophageal cancer. In recent years, extensive studies concentrated on the identification of prognostic signature of esophageal cancer [7]. Infiltrating immune cells are found to be associated with the survival of esophageal cancer [6,8]. Furthermore, specific DNA methylation markers are reported to be associated with the diagnosis and prognosis [5]. However, they don't achieve satisfactory performance in the clinical assessment of prognosis of esophageal cancer due to the expensive and technically difficult usage of these signatures. Besides, most of these analysis are based on the traditional statistical analysis and a network-based method to identify the prognostic signature of esophageal cancer is lacking (Fig. 1).

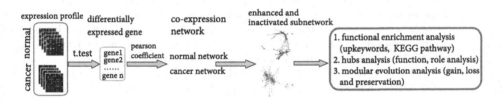

Fig. 1. Schematic workflow for the identification of inactivated and enhanced genes and modules based on co-expression analysis.

In this study, we aim to identify a prognostic signature using network-based approach. We identify the differential co-expression networks between normal and tumor samples which are further classified as inactivated network and enhanced network. Functional enrichment analysis of these two networks identifies the inactivated and enhanced modules in the process from normal to cancer and we identify several key genes which are both inactivated and enhanced in cancer. The hub genes in the dysregulated modules are also observed to be enriched in the KEGG cancer pathways. Finally, we found that most of these hubs are prognosis associated and the signature constructed by these hubs performs well in distinguishing patients with poor survival.

2 Statistical Analysis and Identification of Disease Genes

2.1 Construction of Co-expression Network

Co-expression network is constructed based on the gene expression profile (GSE2 3400, NCBI) [22]. To identify the different part between normal and tumor samples, we choose the top 5000 differentially expressed genes as candidates for co-expression network construction. We use t test to identify the differentially expressed genes between normal and tumor samples and rank them by P value. The top 5000 genes are chosen for network construction and then we use Pearson correlation coefficient to test the linear relationship between any two genes. Positive value indicates the positive relationship and negative value indicates the negative relationship between two genes. The absolute value indicates the strength of the relationship between two genes. We set 0.8 as threshold for link identification.

2.2 Identification of Inactivated and Enhanced Network

We set 0.7 as threshold for identification of inactivated and enhanced network by $|P_n|$-$|P_t|$, in which P_n indicates the correlation coefficient in normal samples and P_t indicates the correlation coefficient in tumors. There is a link in normal network and no link in tumor network if the difference is greater than 0.7. There is a link in tumor network and no link in normal network if the difference is less than -0.7. The networks constructed based on this rule are inactivated network and enhanced network (Table 1).

Table 1. Functional enrichment analysis of these inactivated genes.

Category	Term	Count	PValue
UP_KEYWORDS	Phosphoprotein	611	9.26e−42
UP_KEYWORDS	Acetylation	314	1.11e−31
GOTERM_CC_DIRECT	Nucleoplasm	284	1.54e−29
GOTERM_MF_DIRECT	Protein binding	627	2.29e−22
UP_KEYWORDS	Nucleus	384	5.85e−20
UP_KEYWORDS	Cytoplasm	337	9.48e−14
UP_KEYWORDS	Alternative splicing	627	1.07e−12
UP_KEYWORDS	Ubl conjugation	149	2.59e−12
GOTERM_CC_DIRECT	Cytoplasm	378	4.01e−12
UP_KEYWORDS	Cell cycle	75	1.05e−11

2.3 Identification of Evolution: Gain, Loss, and Preservation

We construct the global co-expression networks of normal and tumor samples with the top 5000 differentially expressed genes. The interactions existing in both

Table 2. Functional enrichment analysis of these enhanced genes.

Category	Term	Count	PValue
UP_KEYWORDS	Phosphoprotein	265	3.62e−31
UP_KEYWORDS	Cell cycle	64	1.33e−27
GOTERM_CC_DIRECT	Nucleoplasm	140	1.70e−25
UP_KEYWORDS	Cell division	47	6.59e−24
UP_KEYWORDS	Mitosis	38	4.84e−22
GOTERM_MF_DIRECT	Protein binding	273	1.07e−20
UP_KEYWORDS	Nucleus	181	1.83e−20
UP_KEYWORDS	Acetylation	137	7.41e−20
GOTERM_BP_DIRECT	Cell division	40	4.48e−17
GOTERM_BP_DIRECT	DNA replication	27	4.94e−16

normal and tumor networks are called preservation, the interactions existing only in normal network are called loss and the interactions existing only in tumor network are called gain. For the evolution analysis of modules, we identify gain, loss and preservation by comparing the two modules in normal and tumor networks consisted of the same genes. We calculate the number of interactions lost in the normal samples, acquired in the tumors and preserved from normal to tumor samples. We divide the total number of nodes in the module to calculate the average gain, loss, and preservation (Table 2).

2.4 Module Identification and Functional Enrichment Analysis

Module identification is performed by maximizing the network's modularity [23] using simulated annealing [24]. The detailed algorithm is presented in [25]. Functional annotation is conducted using the bioinformatics tool (DAVID bioinformatics resource) [26]. Functional clusters are also identified in this online tool. The inactivated genes and enhanced genes are submitted to this tool separately for the identification of functional annotation. Hubs are identified based on their significant inactivation and enhancement. The genes, with at least 10 interactions inactivated, are classified as inactivated hubs. The genes, with at least 10 interactions enhanced, are classified as enhanced hubs. The genes which are both inactivated hubs and enhanced hubs are classified as key genes.

2.5 Enrichment Analysis of These Hub Genes in KEGG Pathway

The cancer-related genes are downloaded from KEGG pathway which are the members involved in cancer pathway. We calculate the number of overlapped genes between hub genes and cancer-related genes S_D. We calculate the number of overlapped genes between cancer-related genes and random set selected from the entire gene set as a control R_D. The value of control group is averaged across

1000 random sampling. The enrichment score is determined by this formula:
$z\ score\ =\ \frac{S_D - mean\ of\ R_D}{SD\ of\ R_D}$.

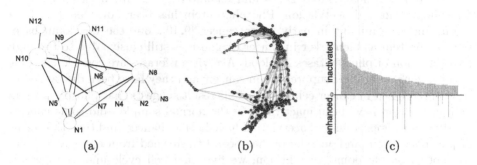

$$(a) \qquad\qquad (b) \qquad\qquad (c)$$

Fig. 2. Functional cartography of inactivated network. (a, b) Inactivated network in the normal samples. It has been divided into 12 modules (N1–N12), the size of the module is proportional to the number of nodes in the module and the width of the line is proportional to the number of links. The nodes with different color are classified as the members within different modules. The network is produced using program Cytoscape. (c) Significantly inactivated hubs (with degree more than 10) in the inactivated network.

3   Prognostic Value and Functional Characterization of Disease Associated Genes

3.1   Construction of Normal and Esophageal Cancer Co-expression Network

The gene co-expression network is constructed based on the gene expression profile. To identify the difference between normal and tumor samples, we choose top 5000 differentially expressed genes as candidates for construction of normal and esophageal cancer co-expression network. By comparing these two networks, we find that some interactions exist in both normal and cancer network, some interactions exist only in normal network and others belong to cancer network. The subnetwork existing in both normal and tumor network is called preservation. The subnetwork existing only in normal network is called inactivated network and the subnetwork existing only in tumor network is called enhanced network. We find that the inactivated network contains 1148 genes and 3221 interactions and the enhanced network contains 1041 interactions and 492 genes.

3.2   Functional Annotation of Dysregulated Genes in Esophageal Cancer

In this study, the unchanged subnetwork is called preservation and thus cancer irrelevant and the remained changed parts which are further classified as loss and gain are cancer associated. Note that we just care about what has been changed between normal and tumor samples and aim to identify the inactivated and enhanced subnetworks and further the dysregulated modules and genes.

We find that inactivated genes and enhanced genes are both enriched in phosphoprotein and acetylation. Phosphoprotein has been considered to be a significant determinant in early stage cancer [9,10], but the development of phosphoprotein as biomarker in cancer diagnosis is still elusive due to the high concentration of phosphatases in blood. Acetyltransferases are considered to be oncoproteins and tumor suppressors in cancers and they have been discovered to be overexpressed in cancer cell [11,12]. This result suggests that phosphoprotein and acetylation have been inactivated in the normal samples and some cancer-specific phosphoprotein and acetylation have been enhanced and thus the status of phosphoprotein and acetylation has been transformed from one stable point to another stable point. In addition, we find that cell cycle and mutagenesis site are both enriched with inactivated and enhanced genes, suggesting that the pathway in cell cycle has been damaged and the abnormal cell cycle pathway related to cancer has been constructed (Fig. 3).

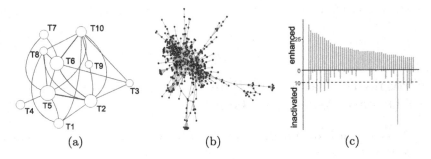

Fig. 3. Functional cartography of enhanced network. (a, b) Enhanced network in the tumors. It has been divided into 10 modules (T1–T10), the size of the module is proportional to the number of nodes in the module and the width of the line is proportional to the number of links. The nodes with different color are classified as the members within different modules. (c) Significantly enhanced hubs (with degree more than 10) in the enhanced network in which 54 nodes are classified as significantly enhanced genes with their significant gain of interaction in the co-expression network under the process of tumorigenesis.

The dysregulated modules are also included in our analysis. We performed enrichment analysis of inactivated and enhanced clusters to determine the functional annotation of these dysregulated genes. We find that inactivated genes are mainly concentrated into 2 clusters. The first cluster, with an enrichment score 7.13, is related with cellular division. The second cluster, with an enrichment score 6.51, contains DNA damage and DNA repair. It shows that these two clusters associated with cell division and DNA repair have been mainly damaged. Enrichment analysis of these enhanced genes shows that they are clustered mainly into 5 clusters. Interestingly, we find that cell division related cluster and DNA repair related cluster are also enriched in the inactivated genes. It suggests that these two clusters play significant roles in both normal and tumor samples. In addition to these two clusters, three more clusters are found to be enhanced. One is related with DNA replication, the other one is related with Centromere, Kinetochore, and Chromosome and the final one is associated with ATP binding and Nucleotide binding.

3.3 Functional Cartography of Inactivated Network

Community structure in biological network is considered to be functional [13,14]. The nodes which are involved in the same module tend to have the same and similar function and participate in the same pathway. The nodes in the same module are connected with each other tightly and the nodes in different modules are connected with each other sparsely. To identify the structure and modular function of the inactivated network, we divide the inactivated network into 12 modules (N1–N12). We find that phosphoprotein is enriched in 6 modules (N1, N5, N6, N8, N9, N10), suggesting that phosphoprotein is widespread in the normal tissues and play a significant role in the development of tumorigenesis. In addition to phosphoprotein, we find that acetylation is also widespread in the inactivated modules (N1, N5, N6, N8). It suggests that the signature of phosphoprotein and acetylation is distinct between the normal and cancer samples and the distinct signature may give us some clues for cancer diagnosis and used as potential drug target in the therapeutic treatment. Furthermore, sequence variant is observed to be enriched in N7. We can see from the modular graph that N7 is connected tightly with N8 and N10, suggesting that modules N8 and N10 are significantly affected by sequence variant (Table 3).

Scale-free distribution is a common feature of most biological networks in which most of the nodes in the network have a small degree and only a small number of hubs have a large amount of interactions. It suggests that most of the genes participate in the regulation of cellular activity and have supplemental function but a few genes play a determinant role in the regulation of critical pathways. This distribution provides the network beneficial attributes of network robustness for random node failure and a short distance between any two nodes. Due to the important role in the network, the hubs in biological network tend to be essential, evolutionarily conserved across different species and key determinant in disease. Based on these reasons, we try to identify the inactivated hubs in the normal network. We rank the inactivated nodes by their degree and then set 10 as threshold for hubs identification (the nodes with at least 10 interactions are classified as inactivated hubs). We find that 192 genes are identified as inactivated hubs with their significant loss of function in the process of tumorigenesis.

Table 3. Functional enrichment analysis of these modules.

Module	Term	PValue	Module	Term	PValue
N1	Acetylation	7.19e−09	T1	Cell cycle	6.64e−13
N1	Phosphoprotein	3.21e−06	T1	Cell division	1.80e−11
N5	Phosphoprotein	4.38e−15	T2	Cell cycle	1.26e−10
N5	Acetylation	1.42e−10	T2	Mitosis	5.63e−10
N6	Acetylation	1.98e−09	T4	Signal	8.52e−12
N6	Phosphoprotein	4.56e−09	T4	signal peptide	7.63e−12
N7	Sequence variant	2.14e−05	T5	Acetylation	0.000014
N7	Polymorphism	3.31e−05	T5	Phosphoprotein	0.000154
N8	Nucleoplasm	6.77e−11	T6	Phosphoprotein	2.40e−14
N8	Phosphoprotein	2.73e−10	T6	Nucleus	1.21e−10
N11	Nucleoplasm	1.97e−11	T6	Cell cycle	3.12e−08
N11	Nucleus	8.80e−07	T6	Cell division	3.73e−08
N10	Cell cycle	2.68e−11	T10	Cell cycle	5.03e−08
N10	Mitosis	6.45e−11	T10	Cell division	7.06e−08
N9	Nucleus	1.83e−20	T10	Nucleus	3.06e−06
N9	Acetylation	7.41e−20	T10	Mitosis	1.44e−05

3.4   Functional Cartography of Enhanced Network in Cancer

Loss of function and gain of function coexsit in the process of tumorigenesis. Comparing between the inactivated and enhanced networks, We find that the inactivated network is larger than enhanced network with its large number of nodes and links, most attributable to the natural property of mutation in which most of the inactivation may be passenger alteration, suggesting that the evolution from normal to cancer is just a process of degeneration. Thus it seems that the enhanced network play a more significant role than the inactivated part and we should concentrate on the enhanced part.

The enhanced network is divided into 10 modules (T1–T10). We find that cell division, cell cycle, and mitosis are enriched in 4 modules (T1, T2, T6, and T10), suggesting that these pathways have been significantly enhanced in tumors. These 4 modules are connected with each other tightly, suggesting that they play different roles in the regulation of cell division and participate in the regulation of similar function. In addition, we also observe that phosphoprotein is widespread in the enhanced modules, suggesting that phosphoprotein has a high level of expression and it is a potential key biomarker for cancer diagnosis by identifying cancer-specific phosphoprotein. Comparing with the inactivated pathways, we find that enhanced pathways concentrate mainly on the level of cell cycle, cell division, and mitosis.

Enhanced hubs are also identified in this study. Similar with the above approach in the inactivated network, we classify these nodes with at least 10 interactions as enhanced hubs. Fifty-four genes are classified as significantly enhanced hubs in which 10 genes are inactivated hubs. Comparing with the observation that inactivated hubs are hardly enhanced, we can conclude that the inactivated genes may not be enhanced and the enhanced genes will also be inactivated, leading to a result that some key modules and pathways have been both inactivated and enhanced in tumorigenesis.

3.5 Evolution Analysis of Esophageal Cancer

Evolution is a long-time process and be with us all the time without beginning and ending. Mutations exist in all species and happen in our DNA randomly. Good mutations help us to adapt to the change of environment and bad mutations will lead to the extinction of species. As we have illustrated above, the process from normal to cancer can be regarded as evolution in which inactivation and enhancement coexist. With the mutations happening in our DNA, genetic interactions have been changed a lot and therefore lead to the inactivation of original pathways and construction of some abnormal pathways. Note that we just care about the changed part in the evolution which is further classified as loss and gain (Fig. 4).

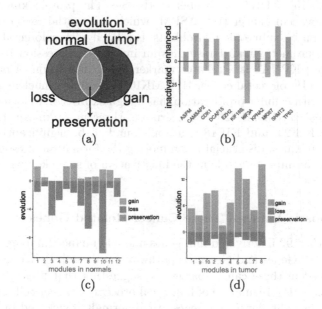

Fig. 4. Modular and genetic evolution in the process of tumorigenesis. (a) Cancer is a result of evolution in which specific inactivation and enhancement are combined. Unchanged part in this evolution is called preservation, changed parts are further classified as inactivation and enhancement. (b) Eleven genes are classified as key genes with their significant loss and gain in the evolution. (c) Evolution analysis of 12 inactivated modules in the normal network. (d) Evolution analysis of 10 enhanced modules in the tumor network.

Loss, gain, and preservation are defined by comparing the two networks of normal and tumors consisted of the same gene set. Evolution analysis of 12 inactivated modules shows that loss is mainly enriched in these modules and 3 modules (N1, N5, and N6) are enriched with both loss and gain. Functional analysis shows that these three modules are enriched in phosphoprotein and acetylation, suggesting that the status of phosphoprotein and acetylation is transformed from one high level to another high level. We can observe from the graph that N10 has a significant enrichment score with loss, suggesting that cell cycle, cell division, and mitosis in module N10 have been damaged seriously. Evolution analysis of 10 enhanced modules shows that these modules are enriched with gain and some of them are also enriched with loss, suggesting that cancer-related enhanced modules have been transformed from one stable status to another stable status in which the original pathway has been damaged and the new abnormal pathway has been constructed.

Eleven genes are classified as key genes (which are both significantly inactivated and enhanced). They are ASPM, CAMSAP2, CDK1, DCAF15, EZH2, KIF18B, KIF2A, KPNA2, MK167, SHMT2, and TP63, in which KIF18B and KIF2A belong to the kinesin family member; TP63, belonging to the p53 family member, is a tumor protein; SHMT2, encoding the mitochondrial form of a pyridoxal phosphate-dependent enzyme, is a valuable prognostic biomarker in breast cancer [15]; CDK1, a member of the Ser/Thr protein kinase family, is related with ovarian cancer [16]; ASPM, which is essential for normal mitotic spindle function in embryonic neuroblasts, is related with colorectal cancer [17]; EZH2, a histone methyltransferase, has an increased expression in Merkel cell carcinoma [18]; KPNA2 is a reliable marker for identification of patients with high-risk stage II colorectal cancer [19]; MKI67, encoding a nuclear protein that is associated with cellular proliferation, has a high expression in locally advanced nasopharyngeal carcinoma [20]. Furthermore, three more kinesin family members, KIF11, KIF23, and KIF18A, are all found to be significantly enhanced, suggesting that kinesin is crucial in promoting the formation of esophageal cancer and plays an important role in the inactivation of some key pathways in the normal samples.

3.6   Prognostic Value of These Cancer-Related Genes

We validate the 192 inactivated hub genes and 54 enhanced hub genes in Kyoto Encyclopedia of Genes and Genomes pathway database [21]. We find that they are all enriched in these cancer pathways, suggesting that these genes play an important role in the regulation of biological process in cancer cell. Furthermore, we find that these 11 significant genes are abnormally expressed in The Cancer Genome Atlas database. These genes are combined together by proportional hazards model to give a risk score for each sample. After the computation of the risk score of each sample, we divide the samples into two groups based on the median (these samples with risk score less than the median are classified as low risk group and other samples are classified as high risk group). Survival analysis of these esophageal carcinoma samples shows that these two groups have distinct survival curve and they are separated with each other. Low risk group has a good prognosis and high risk score has a poor prognosis. The expression profile of these 11 genes is distinct between these two groups (Fig. 5).

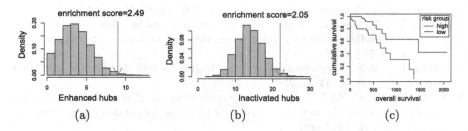

(a)   (b)   (c)

Fig. 5. Validation of the 11-gene signature in TCGA cohort. (a, b) Enrichment analysis of 192 inactivated hub genes and 54 enhanced hub genes in KEGG cancer pathway. Red arrow is the number of overlapped genes between inactivated hubs (enhanced hubs) and the genes in cancer pathway. The grey area is the distribution of the overlapped genes between cancer pathway and random set selected from the total gene set randomly across 1000 times. (c) Validation of the 11-gene signature in TCGA cohort. Patients are divided into two groups based on the median of risk score.

4   Conclusion

In this study, we proposed differential network analysis in esophageal cancer by interpreting the gene expression profile. Disease associated genes of esophageal cancer have been identified in this study which can further be classified as inactivated and enhanced genes. The approach used in this study can also be applied in other disease for discovery of inactivated and enhanced genes. Furthermore, combination of these inactivated and enhanced genes leads to a overlap in 11 genes in which 5 genes belong to the kinesin family, suggesting the significant role of these genes in driving the development of esophageal cancer. Further analysis demonstrates the prognostic value of these genes in identification of high risk patients. In conclusion, this study has proved that network-based analysis is feasible in identification of prognostic signature of esophageal cancer and the potential value of these genes in driving the development of esophageal cancer and therapeutic target is of great significance for the further investigation.

References

1. Xu, Y., Yu, X., Chen, Q., et al.: Neoadjuvant versus adjuvant treatment: which one is better for resectable esophageal squamous cell carcinoma? World J. Surg. Oncol. **10**(1), 1–8 (2012)
2. Song, Y., Li, L., Qu, Y., et al.: Identification of genomic alterations in oesophageal squamous cell cancer. Nature **509**(7498), 91 (2014)

3. Lin, D., Hao, J., Nagata, Y., et al.: Genomic and molecular characterization of esophageal squamous cell carcinoma. Nat. Genet. **46**(5), 467 (2014)

4. Pennathur, A., Gibson, M.K., Jobe, B.A., et al.: Oesophageal carcinoma. Lancet **381**(9864), 400–412 (2013)

5. Li, D., Zhang, L., Liu, Y., et al.: Specific DNA methylation markers in the diagnosis and prognosis of esophageal cancer. Aging **11**(23), 11640–11658 (2019)

6. Li, Y., Lu, Z., Che, Y., et al.: Immune signature profiling identified predictive and prognostic factors for esophageal squamous cell carcinoma. OncoImmunology **6**(11), e1356147 (2017)

7. Huang, F., Yu, S.: Esophageal cancer: risk factors, genetic association, and treatment. Asian J. Surg. **41**(3), 210–215 (2018)

8. Yi, L., Huang, P., Zou, X., et al.: Integrative stemness characteristics associated with prognosis and the immune microenvironment in esophageal cancer. Pharmacol. Res. **161**, 105144 (2020)

9. Iliuk, A.B., Arrington, J.V., Tao, W.A.: Analytical challenges translating mass spectrometry-based phosphoproteomics from discovery to clinical applications. Electrophoresis **35**(24), 3430–3440 (2014)

10. Chen, I., Xue, L., Hsu, C., et al.: Phosphoproteins in extracellular vesicles as candidate markers for breast cancer. Proc. Natl. Acad. Sci. **114**, 201618088 (2017)

11. Yu, M., Gong, J., Ma, M., et al.: Immunohistochemical analysis of human arrest-defective-1 expressed in cancers in vivo. Oncol. Rep. **21**(4), 909–915 (2009)

12. Kalvik, T., Arnesen, T.: Protein n-terminal acetyltransferases in cancer. Oncogene **32**(3), 269 (2013)

13. Girvan, M., Newman, M.E.: Community structure in social and biological networks. Proc. Natl. Acad. Sci. **99**(12), 7821–7826 (2002)

14. Hartwell, L.H., Hopfield, J.J., Leibler, S., et al.: From molecular to modular cell biology. Nature **402**(6761), C47–C52 (1999)

15. Zhang, L., Chen, Z., Xue, D., et al.: Prognostic and therapeutic value of mitochondrial serine hydroxyl-methyltransferase 2 as a breast cancer biomarker. Oncol. Rep. **36**(5), 2489–2500 (2016)

16. Yang, W., Cho, H., Shin, H., et al.: Accumulation of cytoplasmic CDK1 is associated with cancer growth and survival rate in epithelial ovarian cancer. Oncotarget **7**(31), 49481 (2016)

17. Choi, E.J., Kim, M.S., Yoo, N.J., et al.: Frameshift mutation of ASPM gene in colorectal cancers with regional heterogeneity. Pathol. Oncol. Res. **22**(4), 877–879 (2016)

18. Harms, K.L., Chubb, H., Zhao, L., et al.: Increased expression of EZH2 in Merkel cell carcinoma is associated with disease progression and poorer prognosis. Hum. Pathol. **67**, 78–84 (2017)

19. Jeong, D., Kim, H., Ban, S., et al.: Karyopherin α-2 is a reliable marker for identification of patients with high-risk stage II colorectal cancer. J. Cancer Res. Clin. Oncol. **143**(12), 2493–2503 (2017)

20. Zhao, Y., Shen, L., Huang, X., et al.: High expression of Ki-67 acts a poor prognosis indicator in locally advanced nasopharyngeal carcinoma. Biochem. Biophys. Res. Commun. **494**(1–2), 390–396 (2017)

21. Ogata, H., Goto, S., Sato, K., et al.: KEGG: kyoto encyclopedia of genes and genomes. Nucleic Acids Res. **27**(1), 29–34 (2000)

22. Su, H., Hu, N., Yang, H.H., et al.: Global gene expression profiling and validation in esophageal squamous cell carcinoma (ESCC) and its association with clinical phenotypes. Clin. Cancer Res. **17**(9), 2955–66 (2011)

23. Newman, M.E., Girvan, M.: Finding and evaluating community structure in networks. Phys. Rev. E **69**(2), 026113 (2004)
24. Kirkpatrick, S., Gelatt, C.D., Vecchi, M.P.: Optimization by simulated annealing. Science **220**(4598), 671–680 (1983)
25. Guimera, R., Amaral, L.A.N.: Functional cartography of complex metabolic networks. Nature **433**(7028), 895 (2005)
26. Huang, D.W., Sherman, B.T., Lempicki, R.A.: Systematic and integrative analysis of large gene lists using DAVID bioinformatics resources. Nat. Protoc. **4**(1), 44 (2008)

Prediction of Drug-Disease Associations Based on Long Short-Term Memory Network and Gaussian Interaction Profile Kernel

Han-Jing Jiang[1], Yan-Bin Wang[2], and Yabing Huang[3(✉)]

[1] Key Laboratory of Image Information Processing and Intelligent Control of Education Ministry of China, Institute of Artificial Intelligence, School of Artificial Intelligence and Automation, Huazhong University of Science and Technology, Wuhan 430074, China
`jianghanjing@mail.hust.edu.cn`
[2] College of Computer Science and Technology, Zhejiang University, Hangzhou 315000, China
`11921107@zju.edu.cn`
[3] Department of Pathology, Renmin Hospital of Wuhan University, Wuhan 430060, China

Abstract. Drug-disease association depicts the accessibility landscape of the association at the molecular level, thereby revealing the intermolecular reaction in the process of drug reposition. However, the scarcity of drug-disease association data often complicates the drug reposition. In this work, we present a method for predicting drug-disease association, which is called drug-disease association prediction via Gaussian interaction profile kernel and long short-term memory network (G-LSTM). G-LSTM combines a recurrent network framework with a Gaussian interaction profile kernel to learn underlying features that accurately characterize drug-disease-association data. We have verified G-LSTM models on the two benchmark datasets Fdataset and Cdataset, respectively. The experimental results show that the predictive performance was significantly improved, with AUC of 0.9527 and 0.9705, respectively.

Keywords: Long short-term memory · AdaBoost classifier · Drug-Disease association

1 Background

Researchers have confirmed that drug reposition is an effective way to save resources for drug development. As reported, a novel drug typically takes 10–17 years from development to market, costing an average of $ 2–3 billion. Therefore, an approach that can reduce the cost of drug development and shorten the drug development cycle is urgently needed. About 30 percent of all new drugs approved by the U.S. Food and Drug Administration (FDA) are drug

© Springer Nature Singapore Pte Ltd. 2021
L. Pan et al. (Eds.): BIC-TA 2020, CCIS 1363, pp. 432–444, 2021.
https://doi.org/10.1007/978-981-16-1354-8_31

reposition-based products each year. Therefore, a key task in the post-genome era is to discover as many new drug-disease association pairs as possible [11].

The advantage of drug repositioning is that existing drugs have passed the clinical trials and can be quickly introduced to market. On this basis, a lot of time and economic costs can be saved [23]. For example, sildenafil was actually used to treat cardiovascular disease before it was widely recognized as a treatment for erectile dysfunction. The artemisinin was originally used for the treatment of malaria, and now it has been found to have the potential to treat rectal cancer. Although it will take 4–5 years to fully confirm the application value of artemisinin for rectal cancer, the speed has doubled compared to the drug development process [25].

In recent years, under the development of multiple data sources such as targets, drug pathways, mold, and drug substructure information, several computational methods for predicting drug-disease association have been proposed. For example, some methods predict drug-disease association using miRNA-disease association [26]. Another popular method to predict drug-disease association is to use drug target information [4]. The Ion channels of drugs are also thought to be a source of information for predicting drug-disease associations [5]. But these methods cannot be implemented without pre-existing information.

Compared with existing information sources, the substructure of the drug and the semantics of the disease are the most effective information [6]. Previous studies have confirmed that drug molecular fingerprints play a pivotal role in predicting drug-disease associations [10]. Therefore, methods for extracting drug molecular characteristics and disease semantic information have attracted much attention [7]. In these methods, feature representation methods are usually used to represent each drug fingerprint and disease as a vector. Then the drug-disease pair vector is fed into the machine learning algorithm to train the predictor. Therefore, the feature representation of the drug-disease pair is the core part of predicting the drug-disease association model [20].

Over the last few years, several drug-disease pair feature extraction methods have been reported with the development of the drug-disease prediction methods [8]. For example, Liang et al. used the LRSSL model to extract the features of drug molecular fingerprints, extracted important drug features from multiple drug feature profiles under the constraints of L1-norm [12]. Zhang et al. proposed to use 0–1 matrix to represent features, which can only represent the presence or absence of substructures, targets or drug interactions [24]. The calculation of drug reposition can also consider the application of deep learning to extract features.

In this work, we propose a computational model based on long short-term memory (LSTM) to predict unknown drug-disease association. The Gaussian interaction profile kernel and long short-term memory (G-LSTM) model includes three steps: (i) The feature representation of drug-disease pairs. We use drug-disease association to calculate the Gaussian interaction profile kernel of drug and disease respectively. We then use drug fingerprints to calculate drug structural similarity, and to calculate disease semantic similarity in disease MeSH terms. [13]. (ii) Feature fusion. We then calculated drug similarity and disease similarity and fused to obtain the final feature representation. (iii) Prediction task. We validated the effectiveness of G-LSTM in extracting latent features that characterize the distributions of input drug-disease association datasets, and used Adaboost classifier execute prediction task [19]. We implement this method on two important drug-disease associated datasets including Fdataset and Cdataset. The results show that this method can provide excellent performance for the latest disease-drug association prediction algorithms.

2   Materials and Methods

In this section, we propose a novel deep learning model based on G-LSTM to predict drug-disease association. Specifically, we use the Gaussian interaction profile kernel to obtain drug features and disease features, then integrate them with semantic similarity of disease and structural similarity of drug respectively. Finally, input the composed feature vector into LSTM to judge the association between the drug and the disease. The flow of our proposed model is shown in Fig. 1.

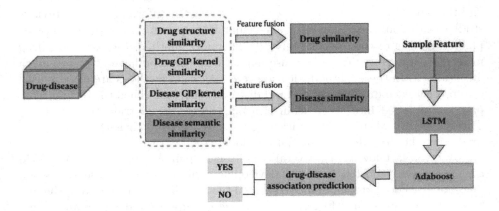

Fig. 1. Flowchart of G-LSTM model to predict potential drug-disease associations.

2.1   Dataset

In this work, we obtain the drug-disease association data from two public dataset, as show in Table 1. The first dataset is gold standard dataset which collected by Gottlieb et al. which is called Fdataset [1]. The Fdataset includes 593 drugs from DrugBank [22], 313 diseases from Online Mendelian Inheritance in Man (OMIM), and 1933 validated drug-disease associations [2]. This drug-disease data set is considered as the gold standard for evaluating the performance of the proposed method. The other dataset was Cdataset collected by Luo et al., consisting of 663 drugs, 409 diseases, and 2532 associations between them [14].

In this study, we use the known drug-disease associations provided in the Cdataset and Fdataset as the positive sample set. In order to construct balanced datasets, we randomly select the same number of associations as the negative sample set from other unknown drug-disease associations. Although unproven drug-disease pairs with associations can be used as negative samples, they can be ignored from a probability point of view. In the end, the positive samples and negative samples in the dataset we constructed accounted for half. We construct the drug-disease adjacency matrix M based on dataset, and its rows correspond to drugs and columns correspond to diseases.

Table 1. General statistics on Fdataset and Cdataset

Datasets	Drugs	Diseases	Interactions
Cdataset	663	409	2532
Fdataset	593	313	1933

2.2 Gaussian Interaction Profile Kernel Similarity for Disease

The Gaussian interaction profile kernel similarity of disease is based on the assumption that similar diseases are usually associated with drugs with similar functions. The Gaussian interaction profile kernel can map two-dimensional data to a high-dimensional space, which can better cluster similar samples, achieve linear separability, and describe similarity. We define the binary vector $W(h(i))$ to represent the association between disease $h(i)$ and each drug in the dataset. Thus, the Gaussian interaction profile kernel similarity for diseases $GD(h(i), h(j))$ of disease $h(i)$ and disease $h(j)$ can be calculated using the following formula:

$$GD(h(i), h(j)) = exp(-\theta_h[||W(h(i)) - W(h(j))||^2)$$ (1)

The calculation formula of parameter θ_h is as follows:

$$\theta_h = \frac{1}{m}\sum\nolimits_{i=1}^{m} ||W(h(i))||^2$$ (2)

where m is the number of rows of the adjacency matrix M.

2.3 Gaussian Interaction Profile Kernel Similarity for Drug

For the Gaussian interaction profile kernel of drug similarity, we use the binary vector $W(l(i))$ to represent the interaction profile of the drugs, where $l(i)$ corresponds to the column vector of the adjacency matrix M. The Gaussian interaction profile kernel of drug similarity $GR(l(i), l(j))$ can be calculated by the following formula:

$$GR(l(i), l(j)) = \exp\left(-\theta_l|W(l(i)) - W(l(j))||^2\right)$$ (3)

$$\theta_l = \frac{1}{n} \sum_{i=1}^{n} \|W(l(i))\|^2 \tag{4}$$

where θ_l is the width parameter, n is the number of columns of the matrix M.

2.4 Drug Structure Similarity

We download the drug's SMILE (simplified molecular input line input specification) from DrugBank [21]. The CHEMICAL Development Kit calculates the similarity of the Tanimoto score Sim_r using the molecular fingerprints of the two drugs [16]. The logical function $L(x) = 1/\left(1 + e^{lx+h}\right)$ is used to adjust the similarity [18], where x represents the value of Sim_p, and l and h are parameters for adjusting Sim_p. Logical functions can convert small similarity values to values close to zero.

Through the above steps, the drug similarity Sim_p is converted to the new similarity Sim_r. It is assumed that the two drugs are more similar when the indications are shared. Given that shared information can further improve drug similarity Sim_r, we establish a weighted drug sharing network based on known drug-disease associations, where nodes represent drugs and weights represent the number of shared diseases between drugs. In this work, graphic clustering method, ClusterONE, is used to identify potential drug clusters. The cohesion of cluster V was defined by ClusterONE [15]:

$$f(v) = \frac{E_{in}(V)}{(E(V) + E_{bound}(V) + P(V))} \tag{5}$$

where $E_{in}(V)$ represents the total weight of each edge in vertex group V, $E_{bound}(V)$ represents the total weight of connecting this group to the rest of the edges in the graph, and $P(V)$ is the penalty term. We hypothesize that drugs belonging to the same cluster had a stronger correlation. Assuming that the cohesion of two drugs in the same cluster is Q, the similarity between drugs can be defined as $(1 + QC) * Sim_r$. When a similarity is greater than or equal to 1, it is replaced with 0.99.

2.5 Disease Semantic Similarity

The disease similarity Sim_i was measured by calculating the similarity between the grid terms appearing in the medical description of the disease in the OMIM database [17]. The disease similarity Sim_h is adjusted by building the disease sharing correlation network through the ClusterONE, as the adjustment of the similarity of the drug shown in Subsect. 2.4.

2.6 Multi-source Data Fusion

We fusion the feature of the calculated disease similarity and drug similarity to obtain the final feature descriptor. The fused features contain multiple information, which can dig deeper potential associations. For diseases, we merge disease semantic similarity and disease Gaussian interaction profile kernel similarity. If there is Gaussian interaction profile kernel similarity between disease $h(i)$ and (j), the disease Gaussian interaction profile kernel similarity model is used to construct the descriptor $DI(h(i), h(j)$; otherwise, disease semantic similarity is used, which is formulated as follows.

$$DI(h(i), h(j)) = \begin{cases} GD(h(i), h(j)), & \text{if } h(i) \text{ and } h(j) has \\ & \text{Guassian similarity,} \\ Sim_h, & \text{otherwise.} \end{cases} \quad (6)$$

Similar to disease similarity, the formula for drug similarity is as follows:

$$DR(l(i), l(j)) = \begin{cases} GR(l(i), l(j)), & \text{if } l(i) \text{ and } l(j) has \\ & \text{Guassian similarity,} \\ Sim_r, & \text{otherwise.} \end{cases} \quad (7)$$

2.7   G-LSTM Model

In this subsection, we introduce G-LSTM model used to predict drug-disease association, which combines the Gaussian interaction profile kernel similarity and the LSTM. In what follows, we first recall LSTM [3], then introduce G-LSTM model.

Comparing with the traditional RNN model, LSTM is an improved RNN structure that can utilize the information of long dependance [3].within a standard RNN model, the repeating model, such as tanh layer, tend to has a simple structure. Cell state is the most significant factor in the LSTM in which the edge representing the cell state moves horizontally across graph of Fig. 2. Cell state consists of a Sigmoid neural network layer and a point multiplication operation. LSTM has three gates to protect and control the state of cells. The Sigmoid layer of the "forget gate" decides what information to discard from the cell state. It looks at $h_{(t-1)}$ (previous output) and x_t (current input), and outputs a number between 0 and 1 for each digit in the cell state $C_{(t-1)}$ (previous state). The next tanh layer creates a candidate vector C_t that will be added to the state of the cell. In the next step, combine the two vectors to create the update value. This results in new candidate values, measured by how much we decide to update each status value. The status value $C_{(t-1)}$ update to C_t, C_t will be on a status value multiplied by the f_t, express forward to forget, then get the value of the combined with $i_t * \breve{c}_t$. Finally, the sigmoid layer decides which parts of the cell state to output.

G-LSTM is an integrated algorithm that combines the Gaussian interaction profile kernel similarity and traditional LSTM model to evaluate the distribution of drug-disease association data. Then, the fused features are calculated by similarity features and they are taken as the LSTM input.

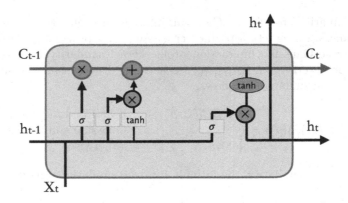

Fig. 2. The key to the LSTM is the cell state, and the line representing the cell state runs horizontally across the top of Fig. 2.

3   Results

We use the final feature descriptor as the input of the Adaptive Boosting (Adaboost) classifier. Adaboost is a classic ensemble learning algorithm that combines multiple weak classifiers into a strong classifier. The adaptation of Adaboost lies in the fact that the weight of the sample that was misclassified by the previous weak classifier (the weight corresponding to the sample) will be strengthened, and the sample with the updated weight will be used to train the next weak classifier again. In each round of training, we use the population (sample population) to train a new weak classifier to generate a new sample weight and the speech power of the weak classifier, and iterate until the predetermined error rate is reached or the specified maximum number of iterations is reached. Therefore, we use Adaboost to obtain the final drug-disease association prediction results.

3.1   Evaluation Criteria

To evaluate the performance of G-LSTM, we use four types of evaluation criteria to evaluate the performance of the proposed model, i.e., Precision (Prec.), F1-score, Recall, and Accuracy (Acc.).

$$Prec. = \frac{TP}{(TP + FP)}, \tag{8}$$

$$Recall. = \frac{TP}{(TP + FN)} \tag{9}$$

$$F1\text{-}score = \frac{2PR}{(P + R)} \tag{10}$$

$$Acc. = \frac{(TP + TN)}{(TP + TN + FP + FN)} \tag{11}$$

where TP, FP, and FN represent the number of positive samples correctly predicted in the model, the number of correctly predicted negative samples, the number of falsely predicted positive samples and the number of false predicted negative samples, respectively.

3.2 Evaluate Prediction Performance

The statistical results of the prediction performance of the G-LSTM model on the two data sets are listed in Table 2 and Table 3. We use the 10-fold cross validation method to verify two datasets, and our model gives satisfactory results. 92.32% accuracy, 90.59% precision, 94.46% recall and 92.48% F1-score were obtained on the Fdataset. Their standard deviations are 1.09%, 1.35%, 1.57%, and 1.09%, respectively. On the Cdataset, the accuracy is as high as 90.56%, the precision is 87.81%, the recall is 86.57%, and the F1-score is 88.04%. Their standard deviations are 1.13%, 1.62%, 1.19%, and 1.04%, respectively.

Table 2. Experimental results of 10-fold cross validation yielded by G-LSTM on Fdataset.

Test set	Acc. (%)	Pre. (%)	Recall. (%)	F1-score. (%)
1	93.02	89.90	96.89	93.27
2	91.73	88.89	95.34	92.00
3	91.47	88.83	94.82	91.73
4	93.28	92.00	94.85	93.40
5	94.32	93.43	95.36	94.39
6	92.25	91.00	93.81	92.39
7	91.97	90.10	94.30	92.15
8	93.26	91.54	95.34	93.40
9	91.45	90.00	93.26	91.60
10	90.41	90.21	90.67	90.44
Average	92.32 ± 1.09	90.59 ± 1.35	94.46 ± 1.57	92.48 ± 1.09

In addition, we draw the ROC curve generated by the model on the Fdataset and the Cdataset, and calculated their AUC respectively. As shown in Fig. 3, after 10-fold cross validation, the ROC curve of the model can reach the upper left of the figure. The average values of AUCs are 95.46%, and 95.27%. The standard deviations were 0.68%, and 0.84%.

3.3   Comparison Among Different Classifier

In order to evaluate the impact of Adaboost on the overall performance of the G-LSTM model, we compare it with the support vector machine classifier (SVM). More specifically, we keep the other parts of the model unchanged and only replace the last part of the classifier [9]. The support vector machine model was implemented using 10-fold cross validation on the Fdataset and Cdataset. Table 3 lists the experimental results of the 10-fold cross-validation of the SVM model. Figure 4 shows the ROC curve verified by the SVM model on two data sets. Table 4 and Table 5 intuitively show that the G-LSTM model is better than the SVM model in the four indexes of accuracy, precision, recall, and F1-score in the two data sets. Figure 4 shows the ROC curve obtained by SVM after

Table 3. Experimental results of 10-fold cross-validation yielded by G-LSTM on Cdataset.

Test set	Acc. (%)	Pre. (%)	Recall. (%)	F1-score. (%)
1	89.15	84.91	95.28	89.80
2	91.91	88.73	96.06	92.25
3	89.74	87.08	93.28	90.08
4	91.91	88.97	95.65	92.19
5	88.93	86.35	92.49	89.31
6	89.53	86.76	93.28	89.90
7	90.71	88.72	93.28	90.94
8	91.70	90.42	93.28	91.83
9	90.32	86.69	95.26	90.77
10	91.70	89.51	94.47	91.92
Average	90.56 ± 1.13	87.81 ± 1.62	94.23 ± 1.19	90.90 ± 1.04

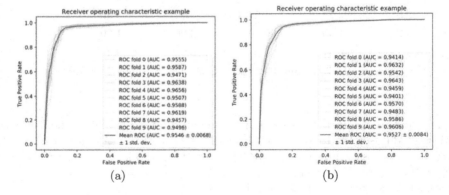

Fig. 3. 3(a) and 3(b) show the ROC curves yielded by G-LSTM using 10-fold cross validation on the Fdataset and Cdataset, respectively.

Table 4. Experimental results of 10-fold cross-validation yielded by SVM on Fdataset.

Test set	Acc. (%)	Pre. (%)	Recall. (%)	F1-score. (%)
1	93.02	92.35	93.78	93.06
2	92.76	90.24	95.85	92.96
3	91.73	88.15	96.37	92.08
4	90.96	88.41	94.33	91.27
5	93.28	90.38	96.91	93.53
6	88.63	85.05	93.81	89.22
7	94.04	91.67	96.89	94.21
8	90.93	89.11	93.26	91.14
9	92.75	89.47	96.89	93.03
10	92.23	90.15	94.82	92.42
Average	92.03 ± 1.47	89.50 ± 1.94	95.29 ± 1.38	92.29 ± 1.37
G-LSTM	92.32 ± 1.09	90.59 ± 1.35	94.46 ± 1.57	92.48 ± 1.09

Table 5. Experimental results of 10-fold cross-validation yielded by SVM on Cdataset.

Test set	Acc. (%)	Pre. (%)	Recall. (%)	F1-score. (%)
1	88.17	82.99	96.06	89.05
2	89.54	85.02	96.06	90.20
3	88.95	84.81	94.86	89.55
4	88.76	83.79	96.05	89.50
5	87.55	83.45	93.68	88.27
6	89.13	84.86	95.26	89.76
7	89.72	84.78	96.84	90.41
8	88.34	83.68	95.26	89.09
9	89.92	85.56	96.05	90.50
10	89.92	85.56	96.05	90.50
Average	89.00 ± 0.76	84.45 ± 0.86	95.62 ± 0.84	89.68 ± 0.70
G-LSTM	90.56 ± 1.13	87.81 ± 1.62	94.23 ± 1.19	90.90 ± 1.04

10-fold cross validation on two data sets. According to these results, the intuitive comparison shows that the G-LSTM model is significantly better than SVM in the performance of the two datasets.

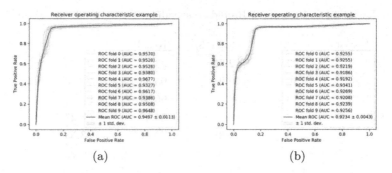

Fig. 4. (a) and (b) show the ROC curves yielded by SVM using 10-fold cross validation on the Fdataset and Cdataset, respectively.

3.4 Comparison with Previous Studies

To further evaluate the prediction performance of G-LSTM, we compared its performance against five other state-of-the-art methods based on Fdataset and Cdataset. Table 6 lists six models of DrugNet, MBiRW, HGBI, DRRS, KBMF and G-LSTM for 10-fold cross validation of AUC values on Fdatasets and Cdataset. Directly observing Table 6, we can find that G-LSTM is significantly better than other high-cited methods. The results show that the G-LSTM model combined with Adaboost classifier can excavate the deep characteristics of drug-disease pair.

Table 6. Comparison of results of different models on Fdataset and Cdataset.

Model	Fdataset	Cdataset
DrugNet	0.778	0.804
MBiRW	0.917	0.933
HGBI	0.829	0.858
DRRS	0.930	0.947
KBMF	0.915	0.928
G-LSTM	0.955	0.953

4   Conclusion

In this work, we propose a deep learning-based approach to infer potential drug-disease associations. This approach create new frame to fuse the structural features of drugs, semantic features of diseases, and Gaussian interaction profile kernel features of pair of drugs and diseases by long-short term memory network. The prediction was conducted by training a adaboost classifier with our hybrid features. To assess our method, we compare it with several methods. It is conclude that the proposed method is superior to other methods. We also can see the proposed method has a good application effect in the case of small data sets. All experimental results provide a strong evidence for the effectiveness of this method in predicting drug-disease association.

Acknowledgements. This work was supported by National Natural Science Foundation of China (61902342).

References

1. Gottlieb, A., Stein, G.Y., Ruppin, E., Sharan, R.: Predict: a method for inferring novel drug indications with application to personalized medicine. Mol. Syst. Biol. **7**(1), 496 (2011)
2. Hamosh, A., Scott, A.F., Amberger, J.S., Bocchini, C.A., McKusick, V.A.: Online mendelian inheritance in man (OMIM), a knowledgebase of human genes and genetic disorders. Nucleic Acids Res. **33**(suppl_1), D514–D517 (2005)
3. Hochreiter, S., Schmidhuber, J.: Long short-term memory. Neural Comput. **9**(8), 1735–1780 (1997)
4. Huang, Y.A., Chan, K.C., You, Z.H.: Constructing prediction models from expression profiles for large scale lncRNA-miRNA interaction profiling. Bioinformatics **34**(5), 812–819 (2018)
5. Huang, Y.A., Hu, P., Chan, K.C., You, Z.H.: Graph convolution for predicting associations between miRNA and drug resistance. Bioinformatics **36**(3), 851–858 (2020)
6. Huang, Y.A., You, Z.H., Chen, X.: A systematic prediction of drug-target interactions using molecular fingerprints and protein sequences. Curr. Protein Pept. Sci. **19**(5), 468–478 (2018)
7. Ji, B.Y., You, Z.H., Jiang, H.J., Guo, Z.H., Zheng, K.: Prediction of drug-target interactions from multi-molecular network based on line network representation method. J. Transl. Med. **18**(1), 1–11 (2020)
8. Jiang, H.J., Huang, Y.A., You, Z.H.: Predicting drug-disease associations via using gaussian interaction profile and kernel-based autoencoder. Biomed. Res. Int. **2019**, 1–11 (2019)
9. Jiang, H.J., Huang, Y.A., You, Z.H.: SAEROF: an ensemble approach for large-scale drug-disease association prediction by incorporating rotation forest and sparse autoencoder deep neural network. Sci. Rep. **10**(1), 1–11 (2020)
10. Jiang, H.J., You, Z.H., Huang, Y.A.: Predicting drug- disease associations via sigmoid kernel-based convolutional neural networks. J. Transl. Med. **17**(1), 382 (2019)
11. Jiang, H.-J., You, Z.-H., Zheng, K., Chen, Z.-H.: Predicting of drug-disease associations via sparse auto-encoder-based rotation forest. In: Huang, D.-S., Huang, Z.-K., Hussain, A. (eds.) ICIC 2019. LNCS (LNAI), vol. 11645, pp. 369–380. Springer, Cham (2019). https://doi.org/10.1007/978-3-030-26766-7_34
12. Liang, X., et al.: LRSSL: predict and interpret drug-disease associations based on data integration using sparse subspace learning. Bioinformatics **33**(8), 1187–1196 (2017)
13. Lipscomb, C.E.: Medical subject headings (MeSH). Bull. Med. Libr. Assoc. **88**(3), 265 (2000)

14. Luo, H., et al.: Drug repositioning based on comprehensive similarity measures and Bi-Random walk algorithm. Bioinformatics **32**(17), 2664–2671 (2016)
15. Nepusz, T., Yu, H., Paccanaro, A.: Detecting overlapping protein complexes in protein-protein interaction networks. Nat. Methods **9**(5), 471 (2012)
16. Steinbeck, C., Hoppe, C., Kuhn, S., Floris, M., Guha, R., Willighagen, E.L.: Recent developments of the chemistry development kit (CDK)-an open-source java library for chemo-and bioinformatics. Curr. Pharm. Des. **12**(17), 2111–2120 (2006)
17. Van Driel, M.A., Bruggeman, J., Vriend, G., Brunner, H.G., Leunissen, J.A.: A text-mining analysis of the human phenome. Eur. J. Hum. Genet. **14**(5), 535–542 (2006)
18. Vanunu, O., Magger, O., Ruppin, E., Shlomi, T., Sharan, R.: Associating genes and protein complexes with disease via network propagation. PLoS Comput. Biol. **6**(1), e1000641 (2010)
19. Wang, Y.B., You, Z.H., Yang, S., Yi, H.C., Chen, Z.H., Zheng, K.: A deep learning-based method for drug-target interaction prediction based on long short-term memory neural network. BMC Med. Inform. Decis. Mak. **20**(2), 1–9 (2020)
20. Wang, Y., You, Z., Li, L., Chen, Z.: A survey of current trends in computational predictions of protein-protein interactions. Front. Comput. Sci. **14**(4), 144901 (2020)
21. Weininger, D.: SMILES, a chemical language and information system. 1. Introduction to methodology and encoding rules. J. Chem. Inf. Comput. Sci. **28**(1), 31–36 (1988)
22. Wishart, D.S., et al.: DrugBank: a knowledgebase for drugs, drug actions and drug targets. Nucleic Acids Res. **36**(suppl_1), D901–D906 (2008)
23. Wu, C., Gudivada, R.C., Aronow, B.J., Jegga, A.G.: Computational drug repositioning through heterogeneous network clustering. BMC Syst. Biol. **7**(S5), S6 (2013)
24. Zhang, W., et al.: Predicting drug-disease associations by using similarity constrained matrix factorization. BMC Bioinform. **19**(1), 1–12 (2018)
25. Zheng, K., You, Z.H., Li, J.Q., Wang, L., Guo, Z.H., Huang, Y.A.: iCDA-CGR: identification of circRNA-disease associations based on chaos game representation. PLoS Comput. Biol. **16**(5), e1007872 (2020)
26. Zheng, K., You, Z.H., Wang, L., Zhou, Y., Li, L.P., Li, Z.W.: DBMDA: a unified embedding for sequence-based miRNA similarity measure with applications to predict and validate miRNA-disease associations. Mol. Ther.-Nucleic Acids **19**, 602–611 (2020)

DNA Computing and Membrane Computing

Label-Free Fluorescence Detection of Carbohydrate Antigen 15-3 via DNA AND Logic Gate Based on Graphene Oxide

Wenxiao Hu[1] , Luhui Wang[1], Yue Wang[2], Mengyao Qian[2], and Yafei Dong[1,2](✉)

[1] College of Life Science, Shaanxi Normal University, Xi'an 710119, China
dongyf@snnu.edu.cn
[2] School of Computer Sciences, Shaanxi Normal University, Xi'an 710119, China

Abstract. In this work, we have developed a DNA AND logic gate based on graphene oxide (GO) absorbing single DNA and G-quadruplex interacting with N-methyl mesoporphyrin IX(NMM) for detecting breast cancer biomarker carbohydrate antigen 15-3 (CA15-3). With CA15-3 and NMM as the two inputs, the fluorescence intensity of the NMM is the output signal. A hairpin DNA probe is designed, consisting of CA15-3 aptamer and partly anti-CA15-3 aptamer sequences as a long stem and G-rich sequences as a quadruplex-forming oligomer. In the presence of CA15-3 or NMM alone, there is no significant fluorescence enhancing, and the output of the signal is "0". While in the presence of CA15-3 protein and NMM, the fluorescence signal was dramatically increasing and the output of the signal is "1". This biosensor platform also exhibited good reproducibility, selectivity and showed high sensitivity for CA15-3 protein in a range of 10U/mL-500U/mL with the detection limit of 10U/mL. In addition, the fluorescence DNA AND logic gate can successfully be applied to the determination of CA15-3 in spiked human serum. In summary, the proposed fluorescent DNA AND logic gate could construct a simple, fast, label-free and highly specific sensing methods for CA15-3.

Keywords: DNA logic gate · CA15-3 · Graphene oxide · Label-free detection · Fluorescence biosensor

1 Introduction

Molecular logic system is a device to realize logical processing of molecular information based on the interaction between molecular modules in physical, chemical and biological processes [1]. Through the combination of molecular logic system and all kinds of analysis and detection technology, it can construct a digital, multi-group differentiation, intelligent biochemical sensing device, which has a wide application prospect in nanotechnology, biomedicine, biochemical analysis, environmental analysis and other fields. For instance, Huo et al. [2] successfully constructed a series of colorimetric and fluorescent logic gate (AND, NAND, OR, NOR, INHIBIT and IMPLICATION) based on the interaction of TMPipPrOPP and G-Quadruplex to realize pH-sensing. Lu et al. [3]

© Springer Nature Singapore Pte Ltd. 2021
L. Pan et al. (Eds.): BIC-TA 2020, CCIS 1363, pp. 447–456, 2021.
https://doi.org/10.1007/978-981-16-1354-8_32

used the recovery of fluorescence intensity and no fluorescence recovery as the output signal to detect arginine and Cu^{2+}. Moreover, Deng et al. [4] finished a pathogenic bacterial gene-induced logically reversible logic gate, which is good for implement advanced computational processing. Molecular logic gate attracted extensive attention in terms of biosensors [5], intelligent diagnosis [4] and molecular computing [6] in recent years. Although obtained many progressive results, it is challenging to construct easy-to-design, versatile and robust logic circuits integrated on a molecular scale.

However, molecular logic gate always used fluorescent dyes to realize fluorescence signal, [7, 8] this method is relatively expensive, low yield and singly labeled impurities and fluorescent labeling may have a certain effect on the affinity between the target and the aptamer. As a result, non-fluorescent labeled fluorescent aptamer biosensor technology has been developed. G-quadruplex is a kind of DNA or RNA secondary structure, which contains guanine-rich bases. Every four guanine-rich bases are connected by Hoogsteen hydrogen bond and fold into a helix formation, which is first discovered in 1962 [9]. The G-quadruplex is stabilized through K^+, Na^+ and Mg^{2+}, etc. [10, 11]. Furthermore, hemin, N-methylmesoporphyrin IX (NMM) or Thioflavine T can be inserted into the structure of G-quadruplex to construct colorimetric and fluorescent biosensors [12–16], which can lower the fluorescence back signal. Two-dimensional graphene oxide nanosheets have been widely used in fluorescent aptasensor because of their good properties [17–21]. GO can absorb single strand DNA via π-π stacking between nucleobases and GO, rather than double-stranded DNA, triple-strand DNA or aptamer–target complexes [22, 23]. Owing to simple and specific interactions between targets and aptamers, good water dispersibility and biocompatibility of GO [24], many GO-based fluorescent aptasensor have been constructed for a variety of targets detection [25–30].

Here we constructed a DNA AND logic gate based on graphene oxide (GO) absorbing single DNA and G-quadruplex interacting with NMM for detecting breast cancer biomarker carbohydrate antigen 15-3 (CA15-3). CA15-3 can specifically interact with aptamer and open the hairpin structures, leading the G-rich sequence fell off from GO and G-quadruplex stabilized through K^+. And then, NMM can be bind to G-quadruplex, which caused a great fluorescence enhancement. In contrast, the hairpin structures cannot be opened without CA15-3 added into experiment, which are strongly absorbed on GO resulting no fluorescent signal. Therefore, a DNA AND logic gate can be constructed using CA15-3 and NMM as the two inputs, and the fluorescence signal as the output. Furthermore, this fluorescent DNA AND logic gate was used for the assay of CA15-3 in a biological sample and satisfactory experimental results were obtained.

2 Materials and Methods

2.1 Reagents and Materials

The carbohydrate antigen 15-3 (CA15-3) were purchased from Shanghai Linc-Bio Science Co. Ltd. Graphene oxide was purchased from XFNANO Co. Ltd. (Nanjing, China, http://www.xfnano.com). The healthy human serum and streptavidin (SA) were obtained from solarbio (Beijing, China, http://www.solarbio.com). The lysozyme, thrombin and bovine serum albumin (BSA) were purchased from Sigma (St. Louis, MO, USA). The hpDNA (5'GAAGTGAATATGACAGATCACAACTAA

TGGGTAGGGCGGGTGGGAGTTGTGATCTGTCA-3') were synthesized by Sangon Biological Engineering Technology Co. Ltd. (Shanghai, China, http://www.sangon.com) and purified using high performance liquid chromatography. The underline indicates the CA15-3 aptamer, and the bold denotes the stem region of the G-rich sequences. N-methylmesoporphyrin IX (NMM) was purchased from J&K Scientific Ltd. (Beijing, China). All of the reagents were diluted to the required concentration with working buffer (10 mM PBS, pH = 7.2) before use.

2.2 Assay Procedures

Firstly, 250 nM hpDNA and 5 mg mL^{-1} GO was first mixed and kept at 37 °C for 30 min, followed by adding 100U mL^{-1} of CA15-3. 30 min later, the reaction solution was added with 20 mM K$^+$, 1 μM NMM and incubated at 37 °C for 25 min, then the solution was diluted to 100μL. Finally, the fluorescence of the mixture was carried out on an EnSpire ELIASA from PerkinElmer. In control experiments, the measurement process was all the same with the above except the addition of CA15-3. Unless otherwise noted, each fluorescence measurement was repeated three times, and the standard deviation was plotted as the error bar.

3 Results

3.1 Principle of Design

In the present study, the principle of AND logic gate was constructed (Fig. 1). In the absence of NMM and CA15-3 input, the result shows no prominent fluorescence band at 610 nm output 0. Operation by NMM as (Input 1) to this mixture solution, the output remained '0' and with the sole addition of another input CA15-3 (input 2), the output remained '0' again. In the simultaneous presence of both the chemical inputs (1 and 2), the output becomes '1'. Thus, the strategy of detecting CA15-3 for AND molecular logic gate is turned out. The implementation of this fluorescence AND logic platform is mainly due to the hairpin DNA probe consisting of CA15-3 aptamer and partly anti- CA15-3 aptamer sequences as a long stem and a G-rich sequences as a quadruplex-forming oligomer. In the absence of CA15-3, the GO can strongly adsorb single-stranded nucleic acids, thus, the hpDNA is adsorbed onto the surface of GO via π–π stacking between DNA bases and GO, resulting in low fluorescence signal. Upon adding the CA15-3, the aptamer sequences could be specific recognized by CA15-3 to form aptamer/CA15-3 complexes, leading to explode G-rich sequence. Then, when the K$^+$ and NMM are added, G-rich sequence can fold into a quadruplex by K$^+$, and then G-quadruplex interacts with NMM, which is a specific G-quadruplex binder, leading to a dramatic increase in fluorescence of NMM. The quantities of CA15-3 can be achieved by fluorescence increment.

3.2 Feasibility Analysis of the Developed Method for CA15-3 Detection

To further verify the feasibility of our strategy, Fig. 2 shows the fluorescence emission spectra under different conditions. When mixture solution containing GO, hp DNA and

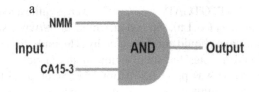

b

Truth Table

Input		Output
NMM	CA15-3	FL Intensity
0	0	0
1	0	0
0	1	0
1	1	1

c

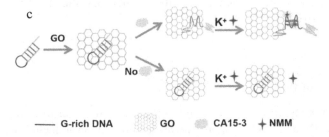

——— G-rich DNA   GO   CA15-3   + NMM

Fig. 1. Schematic description of the Label-free fluorescence detection of CA 15-3 via DNA AND logic gate based on graphene oxide and G-quadruplex. (a) Schematic diagram of the "AND" logic gate; (b) fluorescence truth table; (c) Schematic diagram of label-free fluorescence detection of CA 15-3.

K^+, there also was low fluorescence (black line), showing that hpDNA can strongly be absorbed on GO sheets. The fluorescence signal produced by mixture solution containing hpDNA, GO, K^+ and NMM (red line) is relatively weak in the absence of CA15-3, because CA15-3 cannot specifically bind to aptamer and open the hairpin DNA. And then, when mixture solution containing hpDNA, GO, K^+ and CA15-3, there was low fluorescence (blue line), since no NMM interacting with G-quadruplex. However, upon adding NMM and CA15-3, significant enhancement of the fluorescence intensity was observed (green line), as a result of the specific binding of aptamer to CA15-3, leading to the aptamer/CA15-3 complex formation, and keep the hpDNA away from GO. The G-rich sequence can fold into a quadruplex by K^+, and then G-quadruplex interacts with NMM. Taking the above results together, the feasibility of the proposed aptasensor for CA15-3 detection by our design was confirmed.

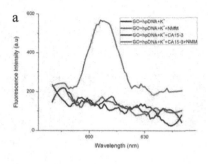

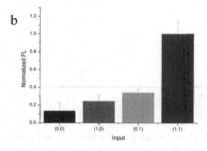

Fig. 2. Fluorescence signals of the "AND" logic gate; (b) histograms of the "AND" logic gate in 10 nM PBS buffer (pH 7.2) (Colour figure online).

3.3 Optimization of Reaction Conditions

To achieve optimal sensing performance, several reaction conditions such as the concentration of hpDNA, the concentration of GO, the CA15-3 incubated time and incubated temperature were optimized. While the F and F0 were the fluorescence intensities in the presence and absence of CA15-3, respectively. The fluorescence intensity and the value of F/F0 are selected to evaluate the effects of the reaction conditions on the sensing performance of the method. As shown in Fig. 3(a), Maximum F/F0 value is observed when the concentration of hpDNA was 250 nM, however, F/F0 value decreases obviously along with the further increasing of hpDNA concentration. Thus, the hpDNA concentration of 250 nM was confirmed as the optimized concentration.

At the same time, the concentration of GO is another important factor affecting fluorescence intensity. As depicted in Fig. 3(b), with the increase in the concentration of GO, the fluorescence intensity initially increased and then gradually decrease, and maximum F/F0 values is observed when the concentration of GO is 5 mg mL^{-1}. Thus, 5 mg mL^{-1} GO are used in the subsequent experiments.

In addition, the CA15-3 incubation time and incubation temperature are another important reaction condition affecting fluorescence intensity for this sensor. Figure 3(c) shows that the incubation temperature could obviously affect the sensitivity; the F/F0 value reached a maximum when the incubate temperature was 37 °C and then decreased gradually. Therefore, 37 °C was confirmed as the optimized incubate temperature. The fluorescence intensity and the value of F/F0 change is related to the CA15-3 incubation

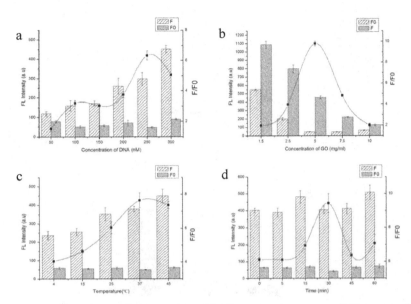

Fig. 3. (a) The effect of DNA Concentration on the fluorescence response of this system; (b) The effect of GO Concentration on the fluorescence response of this system; (c) The effect of CA15-3 incubation temperature on the fluorescence response of this system; (d) The effect of CA15-3 incubation time on the fluorescence response of this system.

time. As shown in Fig. 3(d), maximum F/F0 value is observed when time is 30 min. Thus, 30 min of CA15-3 incubated time was selected for the rest of the experiments.

3.4 Sensitivity and Specificity

Under the optimal reaction conditions, the sensitivity of the sensor for detection of CA15-3 is investigated. Figure 4(a) shows the fluorescence emission spectra of the biosensor incubated in different concentrations of CA15-3. We found that the fluorescence dramatically enhanced with the increasing concentration of CA15-3 from 0 to 3000 U mL^{-1}. It illustrates a highly concentration dependence of the sensor for detection of CA15-3. At the same time, Fig. 4(b) shows a good linear correlation between the fluorescence intensity and the concentration of CA15-3 in the range from 10 UmL^{-1} to 500 UmL^{-1}. The calibration plot of the linear equation is given as y = 4.635x + 243.73 (R2 = 0.9848), where x is concentration of CA15-3 and y is the fluorescence intensity. Furthermore, the LOD calculated using S/N ratio of three was 10 UmL^{-1}. In addition, for the specificity study, adding different control proteins was investigated, including thrombin (0.1 µg mL^{-1}), lysozyme (0.1 µg mL^{-1}), streptavidin (0.1 µg mL^{-1}), BSA (0.1 µg mL^{-1}). As shown in Fig. 5, in the presence of other control proteins (0.1 µg mL^{-1}), the significant increase of fluorescence signal is observed in the presence of the CA15-3 (0.1 µg mL^{-1}), indicating that this proposed strategy exhibited good specificity for CA15-3 detection.

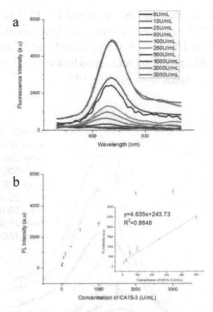

Fig. 4. (a) Fluorescence spectra of NMM towards different concentrations (0, 10, 50, 100, 250, 500, 1000, 2000 and 3000 U mL^{-1}) of CA15-3 in PBS buffer; (b) The relationship between the fluorescence intensity of NMM and different concentrations of CA15-3 in PBS buffer. The concentrations of hpDNA, GO, K$^+$ and NMM were 250 nM, 5 mg mL^{-1}, 20 mM and 1·μM, respectively.

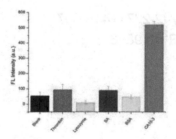

Fig. 5. Fluorescence intensity (at the emission wavelength of 610 nm) of the sensor in the presence of blank, thrombin (10 μgmL^{-1}), lysozyme (10 μgmL^{-1}), streptavidin (10 μgmL^{-1}), BSA (10 μgmL^{-1}) and CA15-3 (10 μgmL^{-1}), respectively. Error bars: SD, n = 3.

3.5 CA15-3 Assay in Real Samples

To further verify the potential applicability of this present strategy in biological sample, the detection of CA15-3 in biological sample by spiking CA15-3 to human serum diluted to 0.1% with buffer solution with the different concentration of CA15-3 were performed. As shown in Fig. 6, a significant increase in biological sample was observed, compared with no spiking biological sample. These results clearly demonstrate that this sensor can be a potential analytical method to detect CA15-3 in real samples sensitively. The recoveries for the various concentrations of spiked CA15-3 in human serum were in the range of 86.97–106.13%, with the relative standard deviations (RSDs) of 8.76%, 5.05%, 2.14% and 5.50% at 100, 250, 500 and 1000 U mL^{-1} of CA15-3, respectively. This indicated an acceptable precision and reproducibility of the present approach for detecting CA15-3 in real samples (n = 3) (Table 1).

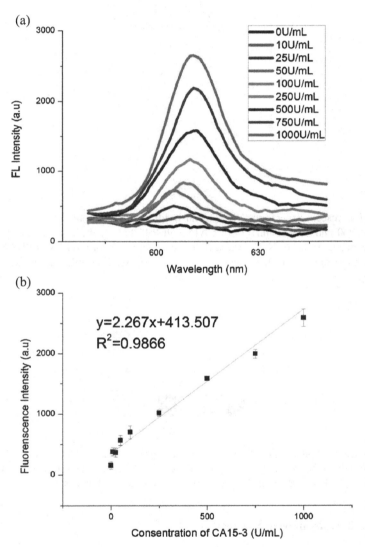

Fig. 6. (a) Fluorescence intensity of solution after different CA15-3 in diluted human serum; (b) linear relationship between fluorescence intensity value and CA15-3 concentration in diluted human serum.

Table 1. Recovery of CA15-3 spiked in human serum samples

Serum sample	Added (U mL^{-1})	Founded (U mL^{-1})	Recovery (%)	RSD (%)
1	100	86.97	86.97	8.76
2	250	265.33	106.13	5.05
3	500	517.35	103.47	2.14
4	1000	960.52	96.05	5.50

4 Discussion

This study successfully developed a DNA AND logic gate based on graphene oxide (GO) absorbing single DNA and G-quadruplex interacting with N-methyl mesoporphyrin IX(NMM) for detecting breast cancer biomarker carbohydrate antigen 15-3 (CA15-3). This system responded to CA15-3 linearly in the concentration ranging from 10 to 500U mL^{-1}, and the LOD of 10 U mL^{-1}, which was lower than the level of CA15-3 in healthy people blood. Under laboratory conditions, the method has the advantages of high sensitivity, good specificity, fewer steps and low cost. Furthermore, the system also applied to diluted healthy human serum and trustworthy for detection and measurement of CA15-3 is confirmed. But this method has some shortcomings, for instance, this method needs further experiments to lower the detection limit of CA15-3. It is expected that this system has great potential application of CA15-3 clinical diagnostics in vitro.

References

1. de Silva, A.P., McClenaghan, N.D.: Molecular-scale logic gates. Chem. (Weinheim an der Bergstrasse, Germany) **10**, 574–586 (2004)
2. Huo, Y.-F., Zhu, L.-N., Li, X.-Y., Han, G.-M., Kong, D.-M.: Water soluble cationic porphyrin showing pH-dependent optical responses to G-quadruplexes: applications in pH- sensing and DNA logic gate. Sens. Actuator B-Chem. **237**, 179–189 (2016)
3. Wenjing, L., Yifang, G., Yuan, J., Shaomin, S., Chenzhong, L., Chuan, D.: Carbon nano-dots as a fluorescent and colorimetric dual-readout probe for the detection of arginine and Cu2+ and its logic gate operation. Nanoscale **9**(32), 11545–11552 (2017)
4. Jiankang, D., et al.: A target-induced logically reversible logic gate for intelligent and rapid detection of pathogenic bacterial genes. Chem. Commun. **54**(25), 1–10 (2018). Cambridge, England
5. Yingying, Z., Luhui, W., Yafei, D.: A Label-free and Universal Platform for the Construction of Various Logic Circuits Based on Graphene Oxide and G-Quadruplex Structure. Anal. Sci. **35**(2), 181–187 (2019)
6. de Silva, A.P., Uchiyama, S.: Molecular logic and computing. Nat. Nanotechnol. **2**(2), 399–410 (2007)
7. Li, W., et al.: Graphene-based aptamer logic gates and their application to multiplex detection. ACS Nano. **6**, 6659–6666 (2012)
8. Jing, Y., et al.: Fluorescent nanoparticle beacon for logic gate operation regulated by strand displacement. ACS Appl. Mater. Interfaces **5**, 5393–5396 (2013)
9. Gellert, M., Lipsett, M.N., Davies, D.R.: Helix formation by guanylic acid. Proc. Nat. Acad. Sci. India A. **48**, 2013–2018 (1962)
10. Jiande, G., Leszczynski, J.: Origin of Na$^+$/K$^+$ selectivity of the guanine tetraplexes in water: the theoretical rationale. J. Phys. Chem. A **106**, 529–532 (2002)

11. Balaratnam, S., Basu, S.: Divalent cation-aided identification of physico-chemical properties of metal ions that stabilize RNA G-quadruplexes. Biopolymers **103**, 376–386 (2015)
12. Li, R., Liu, Q., Jin, Y., Li, B.: G-triplex/hemin DNAzyme: an ideal signal generator for isothermal exponential amplification reaction-based biosensing platform. Anal. Chim. Acta **1079**, 139–145 (2019)
13. Zhang, Y., Wang, L., Wang, Y., Dong, Y.: Label-free optical biosensor for target detection based on simulation-assisted catalyzed hairpin assembly. Comput. Biol. Chem. **78**, 448–454 (2019)
14. Wei, Y., Wang, L., Zhang, Y., Dong, Y.: An enzyme- and label-free fluorescence aptasensor for detection of thrombin based on graphene oxide and G-quadruplex. Sensors **19**, 3–11 (2019)
15. Khusbu, F.Y., Zhou, X., Chen, H., Ma, C., Wang, K.: Thioflavin T as a fluorescence probe for biosensing applications. Trac-Trends Anal. Chem. **109**, 1–18 (2018)
16. Li, Y., Wang, Y., Zhang, B., He, Y., Wang, J., Wang, S.: A rapid fluorometric method for determination of aflatoxin B1 in plant-derived food by using a thioflavin T-based aptasensor. Microchim. Acta **186**, 1–7 (2019)
17. Rao, C.N.R., Sood, A.K., Subrahmanyam, K.S., Govindaraj, A.: Graphene: the new two-dimensional nanomaterial. Angew. Chem.-Int. Edit. **48**, 7752–7777 (2009)
18. Zhou, Q., et al.: Ultra- sensitive enzyme-free fluorescent detection of VEGF (165) based on target-triggered hybridization chain reaction amplification. RSC Adv. **8**, 25955–25960 (2018)
19. Ning, Y., Hu, J., Wei, K., He, G., Wu, T., Lu, F.: Fluorometric determination of mercury (II) via a graphene oxide-based assay using exonuclease III-assisted signal amplification and thymidine-Hg (II)-thymidine interaction. Microchim. Acta. **186**, 3–8 (2019)
20. Huang, Z., Luo, Z., Chen, J., Xu, Y., Duan, Y.: A facile, label-free, and universal biosensor platform based on target-induced graphene oxide constrained DNA dissociation coupling with improved strand displacement. ACS Sens. **3**, 2423–2431 (2018)
21. Zhou, J., Meng, L., Ye, W., Wang, Q., Geng, S., Sun, C.: A sensitive detection assay based on signal amplification technology for Alzheimer's disease's early biomarker in exosome. Anal. Chim. Acta **1022**, 124–130 (2018)
22. Lu, C.-H., Yang, H.-H., Zhu, C.-L., Chen, X., Chen, G.-N.: A graphene platform for sensing biomolecules. Angew. Chem.-Int. Edit. **48**, 4785–4787 (2009)
23. Park, J.S., Goo, N.-I., Kim, D.-E.: Mechanism of DNA adsorption and desorption on graphene oxide. Langmuir **30**, 12587–12595 (2014)
24. Lee, J., Kim, J., Kim, S., Min, D.-H.: Biosensors based on graphene oxide and its biomedical application. Adv. Drug Deliv. Rev. **105**, 275–287 (2016)
25. Wang, Y., Wei, Z., Luo, X., Wan, Q., Qiu, R., Wang, S.: An ultrasensitive homogeneous aptasensor for carcinoembryonic antigen based on up conversion fluorescence resonance energy transfer. Talanta **195**, 33–39 (2019)
26. Li, X., Ding, X., Fan, J.: Nicking endonuclease-assisted signal amplification of a split molecular aptamer beacon for biomolecule detection using graphene oxide as a sensing platform. Analyst **140**, 7918–7925 (2015)
27. He, Y., Lin, Y., Tang, H., Pang, D.: A graphene oxide-based fluorescent aptasensor for the turn-on detection of epithelial tumor marker mucin 1. Nanoscale **4**, 2054–2059 (2012)
28. Wang, H., Chen, H., Huang, Z., Li, T., Deng, A., Kong, J.: DNase I enzyme-aided fluorescence signal amplification based on graphene oxide-DNA aptamer interactions for colorectal cancer exosome detection. Talanta **184**, 219–226 (2018)
29. Dolati, S., Ramezani, M., Nabavinia, M.S., Soheili, V., Abnous, K., Taghdisi, S.M.: Selection of specific aptamer against enrofloxacin and fabrication of graphene oxide based label-free fluorescent assay. Anal. Biochem. **549**, 124–129 (2018)
30. Xu, J., et al.: A fluorescent aptasensor based on single oligonucleotide-mediated isothermal quadratic amplification and graphene oxide fluorescence quenching for ultrasensitive protein detection. Analyst **143**, 3918–3925 (2018)

A Novel Autonomous Molecular Mechanism Based on Spatially Localized DNA Computation

Yue Wang[1], Mengyao Qian[1], Wenxiao Hu[2], Luhui Wang[2], and Yafei Dong[1,2(✉)]

[1] School of Computer Science, Shaanxi Normal University, Xi'an 710119, Shaanxi, China
dongyf@snnu.edu.cn
[2] College of Life Science, Shaanxi Normal University, Xi'an 710119, Shaanxi, China

Abstract. Contemporary DNA synthesis technology matures, and the development provides intriguing possibilities for dynamic manipulation of DNA self-assembly, which plays a pivotal role in the behavior of designing versatile nanodevices and generating controllable networks. Similarly, in synthetic molecular circuits, the spatially localized architecture furnishes a different strategy, allowing for immobilized DNA molecules in close vicinity to each other. Herein, the formal modeling language was utilized to mark the address with a specific sequence of location tags, thus a set of routes were precisely arranged at the nanoscale. Beyond building a collection of separate modules, computer simulations were used to explore further complex assemblies of the building blocks. By orchestrating a series of DNA strand displacement operations locally, autonomous movement and addressing operations were realized, completing the group transport and partition storage of dissimilar molecules. The nanodevice gives the DNA molecule its mechanical properties and follows an embedded "molecular program". The simulation results of the Visual DSD tool provided qualitative and quantitative proof for the operation of the system.

Keywords: DNA nanotechnology · Molecular programming · DNA computing · Computer-assisted design

1 Introduction

Modular DNA molecules serve as programmable middleware between input and output due to Weston-Crick base-pairing rules and predictable dynamics, revealing the mystery of molecular programming field. A common molecular computing architecture can be constructed simply by programming nucleotide sequences in DNA. In the face of increasingly complex molecular systems, molecular programming, as an evolutionary algorithm at the molecular level, can systematically analyze and design reaction networks with autonomous functions [1]. Excellent achievements have been made from the points of view of both information processing components [2–4] and dynamic nanometer-scale devices [5, 6].

DNA strand replacement can be rationally engineered to handle nontrivial information processing networks because its unique features including predictability and

L. Pan et al. (Eds.): BIC-TA 2020, CCIS 1363, pp. 457–470, 2021.
https://doi.org/10.1007/978-981-16-1354-8_33

programmability [7]. DNA strand replacement, as a dynamic and multifunctional technology in nanoscale engineering [8], is an effective way of multilevel hierarchically. Toehold-mediated strand displacement reactions (TMSD) is a controlled mechanism that yurke and colleagues have demonstrated for the first time in their availability in information processing [9]. This theoretical machinery shows the feasibility to implement a simple and robust reaction system for a wide range of applications such as digital computation [10, 11], logical reasoning [12], neural networks [13] and image processing [14].

Yet evidently, synthetic DNA system based on sequence specificity only, can design, but it has been a thrilling challenge to extend large-scale parallel systems. Leaks from unwanted binding in a well-mixed solution pose a risk to the performance of DNA circuits [15]. Besides, when considered DNA strands as freely floating reactants, the rate of interaction of the diffusible components is relatively low. The spatial localization of molecular components is conducive to the parallel processing of information and has particular benefits for DNA computing [16]. Moreover, recent evidence indicates that space organization provides a potentially powerful engineering principle for overcoming speed and modular limitations in engineering molecular circuits [17, 18]. Through planning the nanometer motion, DNA origami [19] are potentially useful to package information together to deliver it with good encapsulation. The existing work harnesses this unique feature for creating a high-quality nanoscale platform, to the best of our knowledge [20–25].

This emerging research field has made considerable progress, however, it is still wide open for research. Indeed, further exploration in the aspects of algorithms design and model construction are a necessity. The convergence of multiple interdisciplinary ideas often brings fresh innovative strategies. It is necessary for us to introduce intelligence into molecular robots using computational models [26]. Computer-aided design can not only speculate scientific and reasonable calculation models but also simulate and verify complex systems in advance [27]. The modeling language implemented with Visual DSD software tool allows devices to be programmed using a common syntax and analyzed in varying degrees depending on the algorithm complexity [28, 29]. Lakin and colleagues extended Microsoft Visual DSD with new syntax constructs [30], it was a useful expansion that provided topological and geometric constraints on DNA reaction systems.

In this article, modular units with different divisions of labor were grouped up to optimize the overall layout following bottom-up principles. We reported a synthetic molecular machinery made from DNA that automates the close integration of transmission unit and addressing unit. For our architecture, as shown in Fig. 1, the conveyor was loaded with two or more types of molecules moving forward in trajectory encoded with position coordinates, eventually delivering the molecules to the receiver precisely through specific recognition upon arrival. We encoded the localized DNA-based system with spatial constraints into a formal language. As such, they could be automatically verified by compiling Microsoft DSD code. Both theoretical analysis and computer simulation results manifested that this model was effective.

The remainder of this paper is arranged as follows: Sect. 2 briefly introduces basic concepts of DNA strand displacement and the way of logic programming. In Sect. 3 we

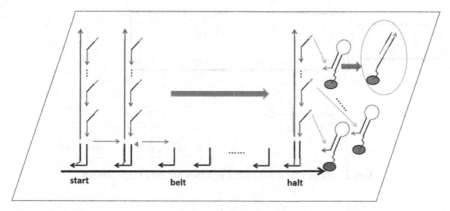

Fig. 1. Schematic of the design showing conveyor locomotion and partition placement.

describe the molecular representation and reaction network of the proposed model in quite a bit of detail. The Computer simulations obtained to evaluates its performance in Sect. 4. We conclude this manuscript in Sect. 5 with a brief discussion about potential implications and researching the value of our model.

2   Background and Methods

In many DNA devices, thermodynamic deviations among the hybridization of DNA strands change the state of the machine, and differences in energy prompt synthetic nanomachines to a thermodynamically stable direction. The extra base pairs in DNA hybridization created enthalpy, combined with increased entropy from the release chain [31], driving the strand displacement system to form a more energetically preferred product. Here's a brief overview about how we coded and implemented it with Visual DSD modeling language, especially the difference between free diffusion and spatial constraints.

2.1   DNA Strand Displacement Reaction

DNA Strand Displacement provides an ideal framework for programmable design. The invading strand docks competitively into the longer backbone strand, and the process of branch migration is gradually combined it with more base pairs to replace the shorter output strand. Figure 2 illustrates the basic process. For clarity, we graphically represented and displayed the corresponding text syntax.

Different nucleic acid strands enclosed in angle brackets consist of a multiset of domains, separated by the whitespace partition, where each domain represents a unique sequence. The direction is rendered 5' to 3' from left to right and arrow in the diagram points to 3' end. Multiple chains split with parallel operators in square brackets make up a specie. Each species may compose of one or more strands, and if a species contains more than one nucleic acid strand, they are divided by the parallel composition operator. The domain is a finite non-empty basic nucleotide sequence, which abstracts the physical

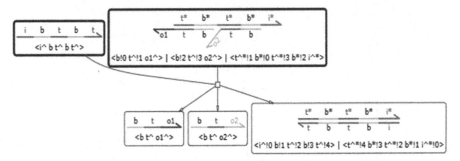

Fig. 2. Basic reaction process of DNA Strand Displacement.

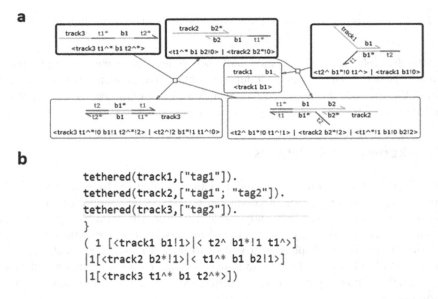

Fig. 3. (a) Localized reaction process of DNA Strand Displacement. (b) The code for the position coordinates and the initial species.

implementation of non-interference. Free or binding domains rest with whether or not the following is a "!" and the binding identifier. For instance, two domains i and $i*$ are bound using the Watson crick (C-G, T-A) by the notation $i!0$ and $i*!0$. A colorful toehold is marked with a caret "^". The toehold of the input strand $i^$ first hybridized with its complementary domain i^* to complete the reversible binding, and then branch migration with the following gray long domain, successively replacing two output strands and producing stable double strand at the same time.

2.2 Localized DNA Computation

In a localized DNA system, the species annotated with a finite number of tags are pinned to the substrate, separating them spatially from each other. The interactions are confined between two strands in close proximity, whereas reactions between species that do not share a common tag are considered impossible.

In the reaction in Fig. 3(a), all three initial reactants are annotated using one or more position tags, as shown in the code block in Fig. 3(b). By virtue of sharing a common tag, the two components are tied together, which represents that they are close enough to interact. Although the two DNA species containing domains *track1* and *track2* respectively have complementary binding domains, react impossibly because they are not adjacent to each other. So we could see that the strand $< t2\hat{} b1* t1\hat{} >$, after the middle node containing domain *track2* handover, could be hybridized with $< track3\ t1\hat{}*$ b1 $t2\hat{}* >$.

3 Principle and Algorithm

With the help from excellent addressing capabilities, geometric constraints were conducive to efficient completion of tasks. The molecular encoding strategy enabled the system to respond to local stimuli and control the transmission of signals. The fixed elements were composed of physical points and mobile lines on which the functional modules of transport and addressing were constructed.

The physical location of the individual components is an important part of the task. We first set up the layout of the physical location fixed to the surface. As can be seen from the code in Fig. 4(a), in addition to three separate physical sites to deposit different objects, a linear track was arranged in this space. Their location relationship is shown in Fig. 4(b), where the connection represented two points adjacent to each other.

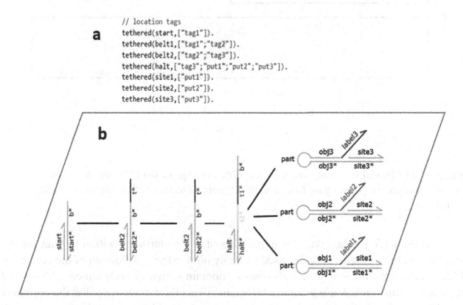

Fig. 4. (a) The code for the position coordinates. (b) The position relation of each component.

Delivery Unit. The system relies on transport operations so as to overcome the spatial distance of molecules, which is accurately transmit multiple nano-objects to the predefined position along a programmed path. Aside from playing the part of a walking element for mechanical movement, the delivery device also acted as a carrier for molecules carrying different objects. This task transmitted molecules forward according to the external input control instructions. By dynamically coupling to a stator fixed to the surface, the conveyor continuously marches in a controlled direction, ending transmission after reaching a specific destination for this type.

We combined dispersed individual molecules to become an automated group transport. The single-stranded DNA in Fig. 5(a) represents different objects. The strand in Fig. 5(b) is called a conveyor, where the domain *part* is used to carry different objects. To perform a movement on a belt, a single-stranded DNA conveyor was designed with four domains *t*, *b*, *t1* and *t2*. There is a *link* domain in the middle that connects two parts and is also used to limit its movement without a trigger signal. The state in Fig. 5(c) is to load different objects on the conveyor. The *t* and *d* domains function independently of the *part* domain, and thus, the conveyor should be able to perform step motion in a programmable way whether or not it is carrying a molecule.

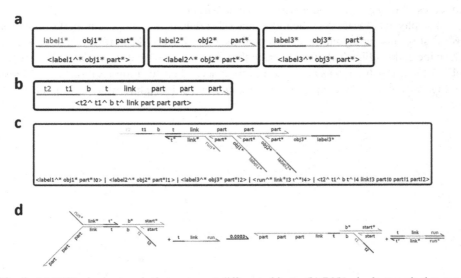

Fig. 5. (a) DNA single strands that represent different objects. (b) DNA single strands that represent conveyor. (c) Conveyors loaded with different objects. (d) The reaction of starting the conveyor.

In order to force the conveyor initially fixed at the starting position to wait for the instruction, the inhibitor strand is used to stably bind to the *link* domain of the conveyor. Meanwhile, the inhibitor strand also has *t** domain which is complementary to *t* and trigger domain *run**. Among them, *t** domain covers the *t* domain so that the conveyor cannot move forward, and *run** domain serves as a toehold to receive the trigger signal. The function of the initiation strand < run link t > is to sense and drive. The conveyor is activated one-time due to a free-spreading initiation strand triggers it. A freely diffused substance is considered near any other substance, in which case its reaction with any other strand is possible. Hence, when the system adds a sufficient amount of the initiation strand, strand displacement reactions occur in the trigger domain run^* exposed by the inhibitor strand and the toehold of the initiation strand $run^$ domain. The inhibitor strand is competitively removed from the double-stranded portion and further produced a double-strand waste [t^* link* run^*], thus making the $t^$ domain free and starting the conveyor (Fig. 5d).

A chain of DNA strands representing belts are arranged and anchored in a straight line. Once the conveyor is activated, it begins to transport the molecules remotely from the start point to the halt point along with belts. The idea of the forward process comes from the "burnt-bridges" [32, 33] mechanism. Powered by enzyme-assisted DNA hybridization, DNA machines are capable of traversing a track of single-stranded. The conveyor takes a step from the present location on the track to its neighboring location. Nicking enzymes can disrupt the belts, which not only provides power to the motor but also imposes directionality. This process drives the conveyor in a constant direction, carrying different objects to its destination. The conveyor strand is partly hybridized with the belt, as two domains d and $t^$, respectively. We defined the context rules to encode the behavior of the nicking reaction with the following code:

nickase (P, Q, [B]) :- recognition([A;B]),

P = C [A!i B!j] [B'!j A'!i],

Q = C [A!i > |<B!j][B'!j A'!i].

recognition ([t^*; b*]).

reaction([P], "nickase", Q):- nickase (P, Q, _).

If the double-stranded region has two bound sites A!i and B!j that contain specific identification sequences without interruption, a nick is introduced at a precise position between the two sites, represented by the nicking pattern A!i > | < B!j. The nick occurs only when domains A and B are the identification site for a nicking enzyme, which is represented by predicate recognition ([A; B]). Here, t^* and $b*$ domains are defined as the identification site according to recognition ([t^*; b*]). Compiling the DSD code obtains the reaction shown in Fig. 6, from which it can be seen that the nickase can cut off the belt and release the t^*, when it identifies the distinct double-stranded region [t^* b*]. The damaged passage provides a "memory point" of direction, which also exposes the $t^$ toehold of conveyor so that it can be bound into the next adjacent position, forming a coherent transport system. The stator at the end of the track is slightly different, replacing t with two toehold domains $t1$ and $t2$, which capture the conveyor when arrive at termination. Furthermore, there is one point worth mentioning that the conveyor along the track when the catalytic hydrolysis of the stator, the front track has been cut off, deserted $t*$ domain ensues. This reaction results in fewer complementary base pairs between the tracks and the conveyors, so the back reaction is basically negligible.

Addressing Unit. It is of great value in computer science, engineering, technology and even life systems to store different molecules in appointing locales. We have assembled a device with multiple receivers that are responsible for placing each type of object in place. Using specificity of DNA sequences, we were able to complete the connection switch

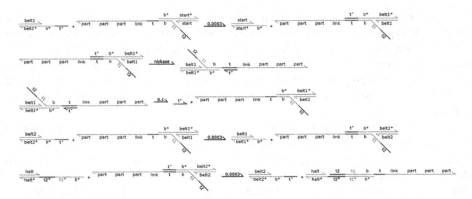

Fig. 6. The reaction process of the conveyor along the track.

through surface automatic addressing. In order to avoid the object sent to the incorrect place, a suitable sequence is contrived for information confirmation in the process of object handover. The conveyor does not have the function of automatic unloading, thus three hairpin structures were designed as receivers to identify the matching objects. Hairpin DNA receivers expose the toehold to specifically recognize objects, and subsequent strand displacement allows molecules to be hand-in-hand between different locations. This unloading process is based on a transition that the conjugate of a carrier and object with partial DNA hybridization converts into a fully hybrid conjugate between receiver and object. The main reaction (see Fig. 7) demonstrates how this process approach proceeds, in a unified manner, the exposed toehold firstly binds with the matched object when the receiver is close to the molecule. If the replacement domain of the hairpin is complementary with the corresponding molecular structure domain, the hairpin will be opened and the object will be irreversibly detached from the conveyor.

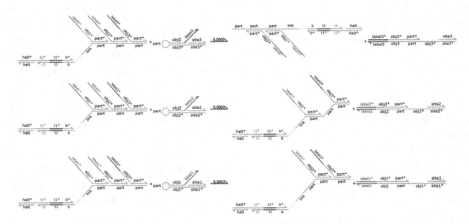

Fig. 7. The reaction process of molecule delivery through specific recognition.

4   Simulation Results and Discussion

Visual DSD tool was used to simulate the qualitative and quantitative behavior of the system. The function describing the DNA reaction was written in a programming language first, and then the collection of DNA species is encoded. Finally the compiler automatically output all possible paths and final results of the reaction.

Figure 8 shows the resulting compiled reaction network of the DNA species collection. We assume that the belt is fixed at four junction anchorage *start*, *belt1*, *belt2*, and *halt*. Simultaneously, the conveyor is initially connected to the first stator *start* while binding different objects and inhibitor strand. For illustration, we exhibited a simplified version with the reason that the overall system contains excessive species and cannot be clearly visualized. Initially, the components coexist stably and do not react with each other until the trigger signal is added. The initiation strand binds to the inhibitor strand on domain *run^* and then displaces domains *link* and *t^*, promoting the removal of the inhibitor strand and producing a stable duplex. As the branch migration continues to the end of the *b* domain, the previously bound *b* domain of the conveyor will disassociate, causing the transport to complete the first step span. The nicking enzyme catalyzes cleavage of the belt strand at a precisely determined position and cuts the domain *t^** to dissociate it so long as the specific recognition site appeared, exposing a short toehold *t^* of the conveyor. The free *t^* domain can be bound to the complementary *t^** domain of a neighboring belt strand, and the *d* domain can be further bound to the *d** to be unassociated with the previous position, resulting in the conveyor moving one step to the next location. Following these continuously repeated steps, the conveyor switches dynamically between different positions via a toehold mediated branch migration reaction and keeps a unidirectional motion. After the conveyor reaches the final position, each type of molecule was delivered to a specified destination until all the molecules were classified into distinct piles. The process can be done autonomously without external control through a natural transition from an unstable high-energy state to a stable low-energy state, which also benefits from localization limitations, greatly simplifying the complexity of the design.

It is feasible to parse the Markov Chain (CTMC) of DSD code generation for continuous-time by computing all possible interleavings of the reactions and the collection of species. The analysis of the CTMC determines the final state of the system after it is allowed to run for a long time. As can be seen from Fig. 9, the initial state was a specified discrete species population, and when the final state was reached the conveyor stayed at the final halt anchor point, indicating that it has made a successful step along a precisely defined track. All the molecules reached the specified location ultimately. These facts provided qualitative evidence that the system can function as expected.

Deterministic simulation was applied as the primary method for analyzing the behavior of systems with the purpose of proving the quantitative characteristics. Running the program can produce the simulation results in the form of tables. For more clarity, a time series was depicted mainly for the trajectory of molecular movement as the simulation progresses (see Fig. 10). In this graph, "start-object1&2&3-lock" represents the state that is fixed at the start position, hence the population of this state gradually towards zero due to the combination of the initiation strand and the inhibition

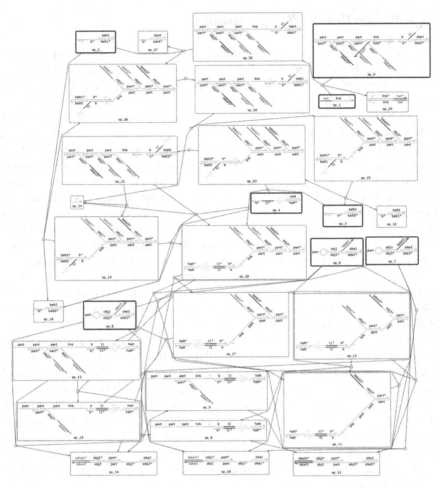

Fig. 8. The reaction Network.

strand. "start-object1-object1-2-3-unlock", "belt1-object1-2-3", "belt2-object1-object1-2-3" and "belt3-object1-2-3" refer to the status of the conveyors in four positions. They produced an ordinal response with a short bout of rising followed by a sustaining fall and reached to zero finally, indicating that the conveyor is carrying different objects along the track successively. The number of "halt-" close to 100 nM over time proving that the conveyor is finally stuck at the halt point. The three final states were "site1-object1", "site2-object2" and "site3-object3", which meant the fact that three different kinds of objects arriving at the specified place was gradually approaching 100, as expected. The system has a certain degree of intelligence due to the reaction can be carried out spontaneously.

For the sake of estimating the approximate mean and variance of CRN, we used a linear noise approximation (LNA) simulator, which shows the final output concentration of the crucial species in Fig. 11. From the results in the figure, the conveyor and the three

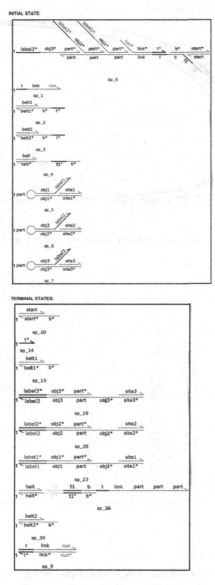

Fig. 9. The initial and final states of a continuous-time Markov chain.

objects end up at the specified position, while the process of travel produces a large <
t^* > .

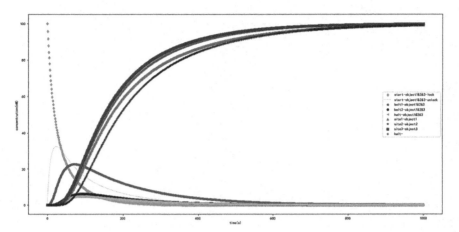

Fig. 10. Time courses for different species in visual DSD.

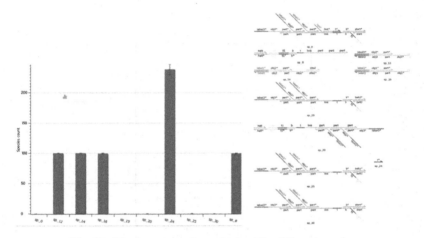

Fig. 11. Final concentrations obtained for different species.

5 Discussion

In conclusion, we proposed a novel DNA-based molecular model that embodied the fundamental principles for developing nanotechnology DNA systems. Molecular programming provides a new perspective for the implementation of local control in complex and scalable networks. In the area of nanoscale space constructed by local DNA, various operations were carried out on the molecule, designing routes to control motion trajectories and move molecules to a specified position. The system was highly organized and integrated with delivery and addressing modules. After the conveyor responded to the initiation command, the different types of nanomaterials were transported remotely in a controlled direction and stopped when they reached the designated location. Addressing operations, furthermore, place materials in specific locations through specific identification of precise partitioning. Analyses and simulations on computers provide deterministic simulation for the proposed design strategy. Judging from the results implemented in Visual DSD, our model has achieved the desired effect and has theoretically verified the feasibility of the model. In the field of reconfigurable nano computing, the development of intelligent molecular systems, according to the required functions is a long-term goal of exploration, which has been achieved step by step with the incessant development of technology. Theoretically, the localization scheme has implemented the molecular trans-fer and addressing strategies, while there is much to explore further. Each module can be developed as a seed of an integrated system, designed as reusable components that per-form independent functions. Exploring potential ways to design and implement smarter nanometer-sized synthesis systems has been the subject of much interest. The ability of programmable computing models enables predictive decision-making. Our approach is expected to provide design inspiration for future integrated molecular systems.

Acknowledgment. This research was supported by National Natural Science Foundation of China (no. 61572302), Natural Science Basic Research Plan in Shaanxi Province of China (no. 2020JM-298). The authors are very grateful to the anonymous reviewers for their valuable comments and suggestions for improving the quality of the paper.

Data Availability. The data used to support the findings of this study are available from the corresponding author upon request.

Conflicts of Interest. The authors declare that they have no competing interests.

References

1. Soloveichik, D., Seelig, G., Winfree, E.: DNA as a universal substrate for chemical knetics. Proc. Natl. Acad. Sci. **134**, 5393–5398 (2009)
2. Song, X., Reif, J.: Nucleic acid databases and molecular–scale computing. ACS Nano **13**(6), 6256–6268 (2019)
3. Schaus, T.E., Woo, S., Xuan, F., Chen, X., Yin, P.: A DNA nanoscope via auto-cycling proximity recording. Nat. Commun. **8**, 1–9 (2017). Article no. 696
4. Gerasimova, Y.V., Kolpashchikov, D.M.: Towards a DNA nanoprocessor: reusable tile–inte-grated DNA circuits. Angew. Chem. Int. Ed. **55**(35), 10244–10247 (2016)
5. Chao, J.: Solving mazes with single–molecule DNA navigators. Nat. Mater. **18**(3), 273–279 (2019)
6. Thubagere, J., Li, W., Johnson, R.F.: A cargo–sorting DNA robot. Science **357**(6356), 1–11 (2017)
7. Lakin, M.R., Stefanovic, D.: Supervised learning in adaptive DNA strand displacement networks. ACS Synth. Biol. **5**(8), 885–897 (2016)
8. Zhang, D.Y., Seelig, G.: Dynamic DNA nanotechnology using strand–displacement reactions. Nat. Chem. **3**(2), 103–113 (2011)
9. Yurke, B., Turberfifield, A.J., Mills, A.P., Simmel, F.C., Neumann, J.L.: A DNA–fuelled molecular machine made of DNA. Nature **406**(6796), 605–608 (2000)
10. Thubagere, A.J., Thachuk, C., Berleant, J., et al.: Compiler–aided systematic construction of large–scale DNA strand displacement circuits using unpurified components. Nat. Commun. **8**(1), 103–113 (2017)

11. Wang, F., Lv, H., Li, Q., et al.: Implementing digital computing with DNA–based switching circuits. Nat. Commun. **11**(1), 1–8 (2020)
12. Ordóñez-Guillén, N.E., Martínez-Pérez, I.M.: Catalytic DNA strand displacement cascades applied to logic programming. IEEE Acces **7**, 100428–100441 (2019)
13. Qian, L., Winfree, E., Bruck, J.: Neural network computation with DNA strand displacement cascades. Nature **475**(7356), 368–372 (2011)
14. Dai, M., Jungmann, R., Yin, P.: Optical imaging of individual biomolecules in densely packed clusters. Nat. Nanotechnol. **11**(9), 798–807 (2016)
15. Song, T.Q.: Improving the Performance of DNA strand displacement circuits by shadow cancellation. ACS Nano **12**(11), 11689–11697 (2018)
16. Dunn, K.E., Trefzer, M.A., Johnson, S., et al.: Investigating the dynamics of surface–immobilized DNA nanomachines. Sci. Rep. **6**(1), 631–633 (2016)
17. Chatterjee, G., Dalchau, N., Muscat, R.A., et al.: A spatially localized architecture for fast and modular DNA computing. Nat. Nanotechnol. **12**(9), 920–927 (2017)
18. Boemo, M.A., Lucas, A.E., Turberfield, A.J., et al.: The formal language and design principles of autonomous DNA walker circuits. ACS Synth. Biol. **5**(8), 878–884 (2016)
19. Rothemund, P.W.K.: Folding DNA to create nanoscale shapes and patterns. Nature **440**(7082), 297–302 (2006)
20. Li, S.P., Jiang, Q., Liu, S.L.: A DNA nanorobot functions as a cancer therapeutic in response to a molecular trigger in vivo. Nat. Biotechnol. **36**(3), 258–264 (2018)
21. Grossi, G., Jepsen, M.D.E., Kjems, J., et al.: Control of enzyme reactions by a reconfigurable DNA nanovault. Nat Commun **8**(1), 65–87 (2017)
22. Kroener, F., Heerwig, A., Kaiser, W., et al.: Electrical actuation of a DNA origami Nanolever on an electrode. J. Am. Chem. Soc. **139**(46), 16510–16513 (2017)
23. Zhou, L.F., Marras, A.E., Huang, C.M., et al.: Paper origami-inspired design and actuation of DNA nanomachines with complex motions. Small **14**(47), (2018)
24. Wang, F., Zhang, X.L., Liu, X.G., et al.: Programming motions of dna origami nanomachines. Small **15**(26), (2019)
25. Kopperger, E., List, J., Madhira, S., et al.: A self–assembled nanoscale robotic arm controlled by electric fields. Science **359**(6373), 296–300 (2018)
26. Hagiya, M., Konagaya, A., Kobayashi, S., et al.: Molecular robots with sensors and intelligence. Acc. Chem. Res. **47**(6), 1681–1690 (2014)
27. Aubert, N., Mosca, C., Fujii, T., et al.: Computer–assisted design for scaling up systems based on DNA reaction networks. J. R. Soc. Interface **11**(93), 1–12 (2014)
28. Lakin, M.R., Youssef, S., Cardelli, L., et al.: Abstractions for DNA circuit design. J. R. Soc. Interface **9**(68), 470–486 (2012)
29. Petersen, R.L., Lakin, M.R., Phillips, A.: A strand graph semantics for DNA–based computation. Theor. Comput. Sci. **632**, 43–73 (2016)
30. Lakin, M.R., Phillips, A.: Automated analysis of tethered DNA nanostructures using constraint solving. Nat. Comput. **17**(4), 709–722 (2017)
31. Zhang, D.Y., Turberfield, A.J., Yurke, B., et al.: Engineering entropy-driven reactions and networks catalyzed by DNA. Science **318**(5853), 1121–1125 (2007)
32. Bath, J., Green, S.J., Turberfield, A.J.: A free-running DNA motor powered by a nicking enzyme. Angew. Chem. **44**(48), 4358–4361 (2005)
33. Wickham, S.F.J., Bath, J., Katsuda, Y., et al.: A DNA–based molecular motor that can navigate a network of tracks. Nat. Nanotechnol. **7**(3), 169–173 (2012)

An Improved Spectral Clustering Based on Tissue-like P System

Xiu Yin and Xiyu Liu[✉]

Business School, Shandong Normal University, Jinan, China
xyliu@sdnu.edu.cn

Abstract. Generally, spectral clustering (SC) includes two steps. First, the similarity matrix is obtained from the original data, then perform k-means clustering based on the similarity matrix. For k-means algorithm, the choice of initial clustering center limits its clustering performance. To solve this problem, this paper proposes an improved spectral clustering algorithm based on tissue-like P system, called ISCTP. It replaces k-means algorithm in spectral clustering with k-means++ to improve the arbitrariness of initial point selection. k-means algorithm needs to artificially determine the initial clustering center, different clustering centers may lead to completely different results. While k-means++ can effectively refine this disadvantage, the basic idea of k-means++ is that the distance of different clustering centers should be as far as possible. In addition, we combine k-means++ with the tissue-like P system that has unique extremely parallel nature and can greatly improves the efficiency of the algorithm. The experimental results of UCI and artificial datasets prove the effectiveness of our proposed method.

Keywords: Spectral clustering · Tissue-like P system · Membrane computing

1 Introduction

Membrane computing belongs to natural computing. During its development, many computing frameworks and biomolecular computing models have been produced. Membrane computing were initiated by PG [2] at the end of 1998. Since then it has received widespread attention from people at home and abroad. Membrane systems (also known as P systems) [1] are distributed parallel computing models that inspired by living cells. P system roughly includes three types: cell-like P systems, tissue-like P systems, and neural-like P systems. And we think that each P system corresponds to a membrane structure. We place a set of objects in the compartments of the membrane structure, then these objects evolve in a synchronous, uncertain, and extremely parallel manner through the rules we define (These rules are related to the membranes) [3, 4]. Because of these characteristics of the P system, people combine it with other algorithms. For example, Liu et al. combine an improved spectral clustering with the cell-like P system to reduce the entire algorithm complexity and improve efficiency, and this method is called SCBK-CP [5].

© Springer Nature Singapore Pte Ltd. 2021
L. Pan et al. (Eds.): BIC-TA 2020, CCIS 1363, pp. 471–480, 2021.
https://doi.org/10.1007/978-981-16-1354-8_34

As we all know, clustering is the process of dividing data points into different groups (or clusters). Through the measure of similarity, some data points are divided into one cluster. The data points are more similar in the same cluster than the data points in different clusters [6], but at first we can't know that it will be divided into several clusters, because clustering has the characteristics of unsupervised learning. Clustering has a variety of applications in many different fields such as object recognition [7, 8], cyber-physical systems [9, 10], or bioinformatics [11].

In recent years, spectral clustering is more and more popular because of its excellent clustering performance and easy to implement [12, 13]. Spectral clustering is a clustering method based on graph theory. In 2000, Shi and Malik [14] proposed Normalized Cuts that established canonical cut objective function for 2-way partition. Then Hagen and Kahng [15] proposed the Ratio Cut. Therefore, the clustering problem is transformed into a graph partitioning problem. According to graph theory, we construct the undirected weighted graph $G = (V, E)$, where $V = \{s_i | 1 \leq s_i \leq n\}$ represents the set of nodes (the set of data point), $E = \{w_{ij} | 1 \leq i, j \leq n, i \neq j\}$ stands for weighted edge and it represents the similarity of two nodes. The main idea of partitioning is to maximize the similarity of the data points inside the subgraphs and minimize the similarity between the subgraphs. Therefore, the spectral clustering algorithm has the advantages of being able to cluster on a sample space of arbitrary shape and converge to a global optimal solution. Ng, Jordan, and Weiss [16] proposed a relatively well-known spectral clustering algorithm, known as the NJW algorithm. NJW algorithm first constructs the similarity matrix according to the dataset, and then obtains the Laplacian matrix. Next, the data is transformed into a new dimension through calculation. [17] Finally, clustering is performed by k-means algorithm. K-means algorithm is a traditional clustering algorithm, it keeps the sum of the variances within each cluster as small as possible, however it is largely limited by the initial choice of clustering centers. Once improperly selected, it will fall into a local optimal deadlock [18]. But k-means++ algorithm can improve the choice of clustering center. This is the motivation for writing this paper.

In this paper, we have improved the NJW algorithm, and use k-means++ instead of k-means as well as construct a tissue-like P system as the framework of the k-means++ algorithm to improve the efficiency of the algorithm, which is called ISCTP. The main contributions of this paper are as follows: (1) k-means++ improves k-means' arbitrariness in choosing initial clustering centers. (2) the tissue-like P system framework we constructed is a distributed parallel computing model, which effectively improves the efficiency of the algorithm.

2   Related Work

2.1   The Tissue-like P System with Membrane

The cell-like P system studies the computer science inside a single cell. However, the tissue-like P Systems study the mutual cooperation and communication between multiple cells, cells and environment. These cells are freely placed in the same environment to complete the entire computer system.

Then, we define a tissue-like P system as $\prod$,

$$\Pi = \left(O, B, H, w_1, \ldots, w_m, E, ch, \left(S_{(i,j)}\right)_{(i,j)\in ch}, \left(R_{(i,j)}\right)_{(i,j)\in ch}, i_0\right)$$

where

(1) O is the finite alphabet of objects;
(2) B represents the states of the alphabet;
(3) H is a collection of membrane markers;
(4) $w_1, \cdots, w_m$ are finite multisets of objects in O which are initially present inside the cells (labeled 1, ..., m);
(5) $E \subseteq O$ is the set of symbol objects present in an arbitrary number of copies in the environment;
(6) $ch \subseteq \{(i,j)|i,j \in \{0, 1, \ldots, m\}, i \neq j\}$ is the set of channels between cells, and cells and environment;
(7) $S_{(i,j)}$ is the initial state of the channel (i,j);
(8) $R_{(i,j)}$ is a finite set of symport/antiport rules of the form $\left(s, x/y, s'\right)$ with $s, s' \in B, x, y \in O^*$;
(9) $i_0 \in \{1, \cdots, m\}$ is the output cell (Fig. 1).

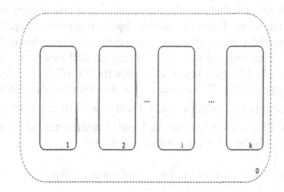

Fig. 1. The membrane structure of a tissue-like P system

2.2 Spectral Clustering Algorithm-NJW

Usually, NJW algorithm usually contains two separate steps [16, 19]. Firstly, all sample points form a dataset $S = \{s_1, s_2, \cdots, s_n\} \in R^{n \times m}$ with k clusters. The similarity matrix of S is obtained through the Gaussian kernel function

$$W = \exp\left(-\frac{\|s_i - s_j\|^2}{2\sigma^2}\right) \tag{1}$$

and then construct the degree matrix D(i, i), which is a diagonal matrix and sum of the i-th row elements of the W. The Laplacian matrix is defined as

$$L = I - D^{-\frac{1}{2}} W D^{-\frac{1}{2}} \tag{2}$$

Calculate the eigenvectors of L and take the first Z largest eigenvectors to form a matrix $V = \{v_1, v_2, \ldots, v_k\} \in R^{n \times K}$, renormalize each row of V to form matrix Y

$$Y = \frac{V_{ij}}{\left(\sum_j V_{ij}^2\right)^{\frac{1}{2}}} \tag{3}$$

Second, think of each row of Y as a point, and then use k-means algorithm [5] for clustering. If the i-th row of the matrix Y belongs to the k-th cluster, the original point s_i belongs to the k-th cluster. This is the general process of spectral clustering.

3 An Improved Spectral Clustering Based on Tissue-like P System

3.1 The Initial Configuration of the Tissue-like P System

After we normalize the first Z feature vectors of Laplacian matrix, we get a new data set Y. We can put Y as the initial object x_1 in any cell. Communication is very important for every P systems, the tissue P system moves objects from one compartment to another by establishing channels in neighboring compartments. The channel between cells i and j is modeled as an ordered pair (i, j). Moreover cell i can communicate with the environment(denoted by 0), the channels between them is $(0, i)$ or $(i, 0)$, which is linked to the symport/antiport rules. This movement of the object is also controlled by a series of finite rules, the form of a rule is $\left(s, x/y, s'\right)$ with $s, s' \in B, x, y \in O^*$, s and s' is a state, this state changes after each rule is applied and it determines which rules are applied subsequently. The specific rules are defined as follows:

- $[a \rightarrow b]_h$ where $h \in H, a \in O$, and $b \in O$ (Object evolution rulers: a evolves into b in a membrane).
- $a[]_h \rightarrow [b]_h$, where $h \in H$, and $a, b \in O$. (The communication rules of send-in: object a may be modified to b during the process of entering membrane h).
- $[a]_h \rightarrow []_h b$, where $h \in H, a, b \in O$, (The communication rules of send-out: the object a in the membrane may be modified to b during entering the environment.).
- $[a]_h \rightarrow [b]_{h_1} [c]_{h_2}$, where $h, h_1, h_2 \in H$ and $a, b \in O$. (Elementary membrane decomposition rules: a membrane may break down into two membranes with different labels, and objects may become other objects in the process.) [20] (Fig. 2).

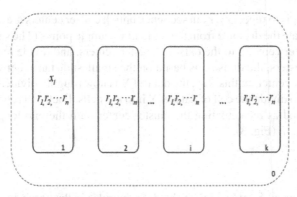

Fig. 2. The initial configuration of the tissue-like P system

3.2 Define the Rules of K-means++ Algorithm in Tissue-like P System

We identify four strategies to apply rules in tissue-like P system: maximally parallel with sequential behavior on channels (denoted by maxsc), maximally parallel, asynchronous, and sequential modes. In this paper, we apply the maxsc strategy that claims at most one rule is applied for each channel in each step. Therefore, the rules of each channel are sequential, but it involves a maximal number of the objects.

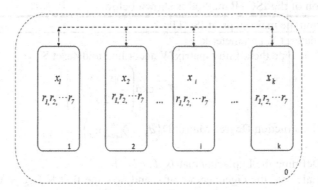

Fig. 3. The calculation process of the tissue-like P system

We specify that whenever an object enters a cell, rule r_1 will be activated, and then rule $r_2, r_3, r_4, \cdots, r_n$ will be performed in sequence. Rule r_1 is defined as randomly selecting a sample point as the first cluster center c_1. Then r_2 is activated to calculate the distance from the remaining sample points to cluster center c_1 and the distance is expressed by $D(x)$. Rule r_3 is defined as calculating the probability P that n-1 sample points are selected as the next cluster center. And we specify that the sample point with the highest probability will be selected as the next cluster center c_2.

$$P = \frac{D(x)^2}{\sum_{x \in X} D(x)^2} \qquad (4)$$

Definition r_4 is to repeat r_2, r_3 in sequence until k cluster centers are selected. Rule r_5 is used to calculate the distance from the remaining sample points (The sample points not selected as cluster centers) to the existing cluster centers, and divide remaining sample points into k clusters, the division is based on the smallest distance between the sample point and cluster center. In this way, the dataset Y is now roughly divided into k clusters. Rule r_6 is used to divide the cell of dataset Y into k-1 cells. Each cell represents a cluster. Rule r_7 is defined as recalculating the cluster center until they no longer change, and then iterating r_5, r_6 (Fig. 3).

3.3 Halting

We divide the dataset Y into k clusters by defining rules in the tissue-like P system. And we put each cluster of data point in a cell. The system halts until the cluster centers no longer changes.

3.4 Description the Main Steps of ISCTP

The k-means++ algorithm improves k-means' choice of initial cluster centers. The tissue-like P system greatly improves the efficiency of the k-means++ algorithm due to its extremely parallel characteristics. For example, it can be performed simultaneously when calculating the distance between each data point and the existing cluster center. The description of the ISCTP method is shown below.

Description the main steps of ISCTP

Inputs: dataset Y, parameter k

Step1: Calculate the affinity matrix W according to dataset S

$$W = \exp\left(-\frac{\left\|s_i - s_j\right\|^2}{2\sigma^2}\right)$$

Step2: Construction Degree Matrix D $\left(d_{ii} = \sum_{j=1}^{n} w_{ij}\right)$

Step3: Defining the Laplacian matrix $L = D^{-\frac{1}{2}} W D^{-\frac{1}{2}}$

Step4: Calculate the eigenvectors of L and take the first K largest eigenvectors to form a matrix $V \in R^{n \times k}$

Step5: Normalize each row of V and think of each row of V as a point, then use k-means++ algorithm for clustering.

Step6: K-means++ algorithm is combined with tissue-like P system, and the dataset Y is divided into k categories by formulating rules. Every category is placed in a cell.

Step8: Use the extremely parallel feature of tissue-like P system to repeatedly calculate the cluster centers until they no longer change. And the sample points are reclassified every time the cluster center is repeatedly calculated.

Output: clusters

---

4 Algorithm Evaluation

4.1 Dataset

This paper uses four UCI datasets and three artificial datasets to evaluate the ISCTP method proposed in this paper. Table 1 shows the specific information of the datasets. Each dataset includes four parts: object, attribute, cluster number, and source.

Table 1. Datasets information

Data sets	Objects	Attributes	Clusters	Source
Glass	241	9	6	UCI
Zoo	150	4	3	UCI
Wine	178	13	3	UCI
Iris	150	4	2	UCI
Threecircles	3603	2	3	Artificial
Spiral	944	2	2	Artificial
Twomoons	1502	2	2	Artificial

4.2 The Method of Assessment

In this paper, we use Purity Index (PUR) as the evaluation criteria. The calculation formula of PUR is as follows:

$$Purity(V, U) = \frac{1}{N} \sum_k \max_j |v_k \cap u_j| \tag{5}$$

where N represents the total number of samples, $V = \{v_1, v_2, \cdots, v_k\}$ represents the division of clusters, $U = \{u_1, u_2, \cdots, u_j\}$ denotes the true classification. Purity $\in [0, 1]$, and the closer its value is to 1, the better the clustering effect.

4.3 Experimental Results

In this paper, we have performed experiments on four UCI datasets and three artificial datasets using four methods. As we all know, spectral clustering algorithm requires input parameter σ to calculate the Gaussian kernel function. σ defines the width of the neighborhood, which affects the similarity among sample points. In other words, it is a reference distance, if the distance among sample points is smaller than it, it is evaluated as similar, otherwise it is not similar. Different datasets have different requirements for σ, and the same dataset produces different clustering effects under different parameter σ. This paper conducts 100 experiments on each dataset and selects the optimal value and worst value of various datasets under various methods.

It can be seen from Table 2 that the accuracy of our proposed ISCTP method is higher than other three comparison algorithms for the datasets Glass and Zoo. For the Wine data set, the optimal value of the ISCTP method is higher than other comparison methods, but the worst value does not improve. For the Iris dataset, the SCBK-CP method has the highest optimal value, and the four methods have the same worst value.

Table 2. Experimental results (the best case/the worst case)

DataSets	K-means	SC	SCBK-CP	ISCTP
Glass	0.6335/0.4159	0.6776/0.4766	0.6776/0.4159	**0.6822/0.4953**
Zoo	0.8614/0.6931	0.8713/0.7228	0.8614/0.7228	**0.8911/0.7327**
Wine	0.7022/**0.6573**	0.7079/0.6067	0.6921/0.6067	**0.7191**/0.6067
Iris	0.8933/0.6667	0.8933/0.6667	**0.9272**/0.6667	0.9067/0.6667

For the artificial dataset, we use the following picture to show the clustering results. The clustering results of the Threecircles dataset are shown in the following Fig. 4.

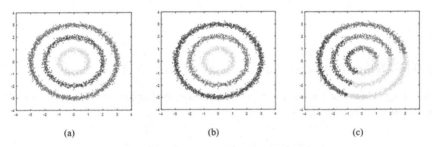

(a)   (b)   (c)

Fig. 4. **a** result of ISCTP, **b** result of spectral clustering, **c** result of k-means

The clustering results of the Spiral dataset are shown in the following Fig. 5.

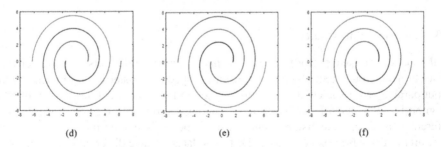

(d)   (e)   (f)

Fig. 5. **d** result of ISCTP, **e** result of spectral clustering, **f** result of k-means

The clustering results of the Twomoons dataset are shown in the following Fig. 6.

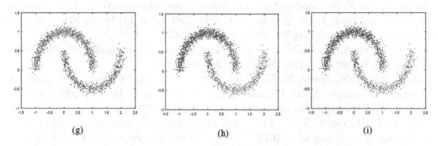

(g)   (h)   (i)

Fig. 6. g result of ISCTP, h result of spectral clustering, i result of k-means

By observing the pictures, we can clearly observe that the clustering effect of ISCTP and spectral clustering algorithms on artificial datasets is significantly higher than k-means. To be honest, there are still some problems in this paper, such as the lack of novelty for improvement and insufficient experiments. These are the directions of our efforts.

5 Conclusion

In this paper, we proposed an improved spectral clustering algorithm based on tissue-like P system, called ISCTP. Although the experimental results are a little unsatisfactory, the k-means++ algorithm dose improve the choice of initial clustering centers and the tissue-like P system we constructed can greatly improve operating efficiency. But this paper does have some problems, such as the improvement points lack novelty, the experimental results is not very convincing, etc. In the future, we will conduct deeper research on spectral clustering, such as improving the Gaussian kernel function, automatically determining the number of clusters, etc.

Acknowledgement. This research project is supported by National Natural Science Foundation of China (61876101, 61802234, 61806114), Social Science Fund Project of Shandong Province, China (16BGLJ06, 11CGLJ22), Natural Science Fund Project of Shandong Province, China (ZR2019QF007), Postdoctoral Project, China (2017M612339, 2018M642695), Humanities and Social Sciences Youth Fund of the Ministry of Education, China (19YJCZH244), Postdoctoral Special Funding Project, China (2019T120607).

References

1. Pan, L., Pérez-Jiménez, M.: Computational complexity of tissue-like P systems. J. Complex. **26**(3), 296–315 (2010)
2. Păun, G.: Computing with membranes. J. Comput. Syst. Sci. **61**(1), 108–143 (2000)
3. Frisco, P.: Computing with Cells: Advances in Membrane Computing. Oxford University Press, Oxford (2009)

4. Daniel, D.-P., Pérez-Jiménez, M.J., Romero-Jiménez, Á.: Efficient simulation of tissue-like P systems by transition cell-like P system. Nat. Comput. **8**(4), 797–806 (2009)
5. Zhang, Z., Liu, X.: An improved spectral clustering algorithm based on cell-like P system. In: Milošević, D., Tang, Y., Zu, Q. (eds.) HCC 2019. LNCS, vol. 11956, pp. 626–636. Springer, Cham (2019). https://doi.org/10.1007/978-3-030-37429-7_64
6. Zhu, X., Zhang, S., He, W., Hu, R., Lei, C., Zhu, P.: One-step multi-view spectral clustering. IEEE Trans. Knowl. Data Eng. **31**(10), 2022–2034 (2019)
7. Gao, B., Liu, T.-Y., Zheng, X., Cheng, Q.-S., Ma, W.-Y., Qin, T.: Web image clustering by consistent utilization of visual features and surrounding texts. In: Proceedings of the 13th Annual ACM International Conference on Multimedia (2005)
8. Yang, Y., Xu, D., Yan, S., Nie, F., Yan, S., Zhuang, Y.: Image clustering using local discriminant models and global integration. IEEE Trans. Image Process. **19**(10), 2761–2773 (2010)
9. Tsekouras, G.J., Hatziargyriou, N.D., Dialynas, E.N.: Two-stage pattern recognition of load curves for classification of electricity customers. IEEE Trans. Power Syst. **22**(3), 1120–1128 (2007)
10. Cao, J., Li, H.: Energy-efficient structuralized clustering for sensor-based cyber physical systems. In: Ubiquitous, Autonomic and Trusted Computing, pp. 234–239 (2009)
11. Yeung, K.Y., Ruzzo, W.L.: Principal component analysis for clustering gene expression data. Bioinformatics **17**(9), 763–774 (2001)
12. Von Luxburg, U., Planck, M.: A tutorial on spectral clustering. Stat. Comput. **17**(4), 395–416 (2007)
13. Verma, D., Meila, M.: A comparison of spectral clustering algorithms. University of Washington Technical report UWCSE030501, pp. 1–18 (2003)
14. Shi, J., Malik, J.: Normalized cuts and image segmentation. IEEE Trans. Pattern Anal. Mach. Intell. **22**(8), 888–905 (2000)
15. Hagen, L., Kahng, A.: New spectral methods for ratio cut partitioning and clustering. IEEE Trans. Comput. Aided Des. Integr. Circuits Syst. **11**(9), 1074–1085 (1992)
16. Ng, A., Jordan, M., Weiss, Y.: On spectral clustering: Analysis and an algorithm. Adv. Neural. Inf. Process. Syst. **2**, 849–856 (2002)
17. Afzalan, M., Jazizadeh, F.: An automated spectral clustering for multi-scale data. Neurocomputing **347**, 94–108 (2019)
18. Tzortzis, G., Likas, A.: The minmax k-means clustering algorithm. Pattern Recogn. **47**(7), 2505–2516 (2014)
19. Peng, B., Zhang, L., Zhang, D.: A survey of graph theoretical approaches to image segmentation. Pattern Recogn. **46**(3), 1020–1038 (2013)
20. Jiang, Z., Liu, X., Sun, M.: A density peak clustering algorithm based on the K-nearest Shannon entropy and tissue-like P system. Math. Probl. Eng. **2019**, 1–13 (2019)

Design of Blood Group Pairing Logic Circuit Based on DNA Strand Displacement

Chun Huang[1,2], Yanfeng Wang[2], and Qinglei Zhou[1]($\boxtimes$)

[1] School of Information Engineering, Zhengzhou University,
Zhengzhou 450001, China
huangchunzzuli@yeah.net, ieqlzhou@zzu.edu.cn
[2] College of Electrical and Information Engineering, Zhengzhou University
of Light Industry, Zhengzhou 450002, China

Abstract. DNA strand displacement provides an effective approach to construct complex nano logic circuits. In this work, a blood group pairing logic circuit with DNA materials is designed to complete the function of blood group pairing. First, threshold gate, amplifier gate, fan-out gate and report gate are constructed on the basis of the reaction mechanism of DNA strand displacement, and then the basic computing modules of logic AND and OR are formed. In order to make any digital logic circuit translate into a dual-rail digital circuit with dual-rail strategy conveniently, the universal math model of a dual-rail digital circuit is proposed. Next, with fluorescence labeling technology, the dual-rail digital circuit of blood group pairing is converted into the DNA biochemical logic circuit consisting of fan-out gates, report gates, logic AND and OR gates. The simulation results are obtained by Visual DSD, which shows that the proposed DNA-circuit is stable, effective, and highly sensitive for blood type signals. The method of constructing blood group pairing nano logic circuit proposed in this paper also greatly reduces the difficulty of experimental operation compared with the DNA assembly technology for the same logic function, which can be applied to nano medicine diagnosis and large scale nano logical circuits in the future.

Keywords: DNA strand displacement · Blood group pairing circuit · Dual-rail logic · Math model · Visual DSD

This work was supported in part by the National Key Research and Development Program of China (2016YFB0800100), in part by the National Key Research and Development Program of China for International S and T Cooperation Projects (2017YFE0103900), in part by the Joint Funds of the National Natural Science Foundation of China (U1804262), in part by the Science and Technology Project of Henan Province (202102310202), in part by the Youth Talent Lifting Project of Henan Province (2018HYTP016), and in part by Zhongyuan Thousand Talents Program (204200510003).

© Springer Nature Singapore Pte Ltd. 2021
L. Pan et al. (Eds.): BIC-TA 2020, CCIS 1363, pp. 481–501, 2021.
https://doi.org/10.1007/978-981-16-1354-8_35

1   Introduction

Nowadays nanotechnology and biotechnology have developed into the most concerned frontier areas, and more and more scientists are devoting themselves to it. DNA is not only the carrier of life genetic information, but also the natural nano-biomaterials and components [1]. Because DNA has good biocompatibility, and excellent programmability that can make DNA as a leading material to construct complex nano structures on the basis of Watson-Crick base pairing principle, it has widely applied in the field of nanomedicine, for example, DNA drug delivery, targeted therapy for cancer and so on [2–4]. How to match blood groups quickly and accurately is very important for patients with excessive blood. Here, we propose a novel model based on DNA strand displacement to construct an intelligent DNA molecular system to quickly detect the result of blood type paring for patients.

DNA strand displacement technology is a kind of reliable dynamic nanotechnology, which has widely applied in the field of bio-molecular computation and nano devices manufacturing because of its spontaneity, sensitivity and accuracy [5–8]. Acting as a computing tool, it has solved many problems, such as the directed Hamiltonian path problem [9], the maximal clique problem [10], and some arithmetic calculation problems [11]. In addition, as an excellent nano component, it is also used to make nano robot, or construct a series of nano circuits as basic units to realize biological computer, or design nano sensor to detect thrombin [12–15]. Moreover, DNA strand displacement technology has some other advantages of high-density storage of information, high performance parallel computing and programming. Therefore, it is an inevitable trend to select DNA strand displacement technology for making nano medicine devices [16,17]. Blood type test is an essential operation, and almost all medical care needs it. In order to solve more complex molecule medicine problems, the device of matching blood group may play an important role in the future. The blood groups paring circuit with DNA materials is worth researching, which can combine with other DNA components to complete more complex nano medical problems.

In this work, the novel molecular detector mode of blood type is constructed based on the principle of blood group pairing, which consists of 2 layers logic circuits. The detector has four input signals, which represent four types of blood groups A, B, O, AB, respectively. Meanwhile, it has an output signal to test whether the blood group pairing is successful. If the logic value of output is "1", which indicates that the blood group pairing is successful, then the transfusion therapy can be performed; otherwise, it will not be able to work.

Compared with the existing work [18–20], there are some advantages, which can make our research more attractive and interesting. First, the DNA logic circuit in this paper belongs to a large size nano device, and it is difficult to realize with DNA assembly technology that is more effective in small scale nano structure. Second, dynamic DNA strand replacement technology is adopted, which can reduce the difficulty and complexity of the experiment operation, all biochemical reaction can occur naturally without any enzyme at normal temperature. Third, 114 basic DNA single strands are designed with a kind of toehold strategy in this work, which helps to form a more complex structure with other nano devices. What's more, the dual-rail circuit math models are constructed, which can effectively avoid the generation of uncertain output signals aiming at the situation of logic "NOT" gate without input DNA strand. In summary, the four advantages make our research more interesting and attractive than the previous work.

In this paper, the remaining content is given as follows: the mechanism about the DNA strand displacement is shown in Sect. 2. The Sect. 3 introduces the process of building blood group pairing digital logic circuit and transforming it into the seesaw circuit. The results of simulation are presented in Sect. 4. Finally, the conclusion of blood group pairing circuit on the basis of DNA strand displacement with dual-rail strategy is given in Sect. 5.

2   The Dynamic Behavior of DNA Strand Displacement

DNA strand displacement technology is a kind of dynamic nanotechnology developed from DNA self-assembly technique, which can guide multiple DNA strands to assemble spontaneously based on $Watson - Crick$ complementarity principle [21,22]. There are two kinds of stands involved in DNA strand displacement reaction, one is the single strand called invading strand or input signal, and the other is the partial double strand involved a target stand. The partial double strand has an exposed domain usually called toehold, by which the free single strand (called input signal strand) can first bind to the double strand compound according to the base complementary pairing principle, and then another single strand (called target strand) will be released from the original double-strand after branch migration occurred between the single strand and the partial double strand. During the whole process of DNA strands displacement reaction, another similar reaction (called reversible reaction) will happen if a new toehold domain is generated from the new partial double strand [5]. Finally, the two types of reaction will achieve dynamic balance. If there is no new toehold domain produced, no reversible reaction will occur. In the DNA biochemical reaction networks, the irreversible DNA strand displacement reaction offers the driving force of DNA system to perform the system function from one side to the other. Here, an example is given as shown in Fig. 1, which demonstrates the process of the DNA strand displacement reaction, where each letter represents a different domain composed of non-empty and finite base sequences. Different domains do not interfere with each other, only complementary domains can be bound to each other. In Fig. 1(a), $T1$, R and T are paired with $T1^*$, R^* and T^*, respectively, where T and $T1$ are toehold domains. It demonstrates the reversible reaction mechanism of DNA strand displacement. In the dark black box are the reactants, and in the light box are the generators. The toehold domain T in the single DNA strand $<R\ T>$ firstly binds to the complementary domain T^* exposed on the DNA double strand $<S>[T1\ R]T^*$, and then the process of DNA strand migration is carried out. After the toehold domain binding between T and $T*$, the domain R on the strand $<R\ T^\wedge>$ will gradually replace the domain R on the strand $<S>[T1\ R]T^*$, and bind with the domain R^* on the strand $<S>[T1^\wedge\ R]T^{*\wedge}$. Finally, the strand $<S\ T1^\wedge\ R>$ is released from the double strand $<S>[T1^\wedge\ R]T^{*\wedge}$, and at the same time a new double strand $T1^*[R\ T^\wedge]$ is generated, which has an exposed toehold, so the single strand $<S\ T1^\wedge\ R>$ will implement the reaction of strand displacement with the new double strand $T1^*[R\ T^\wedge]$. From Fig. 1(a), we can see that the arrows are bidirectional, which shows the reaction is reversible. If we define the single strand $<R\ T^\wedge>$ as an input signal, then the single strand $<S\ T1^\wedge R>$ is an output signal, according on the simple reaction mechanism, more complex logic circuit models can be constructed. Obviously, Fig. 1(b) shows the process of irreversible reaction, where $T2$ is the toehold domain, and $R1$ is the branch migration domain, and the new generated double strand $<R1\ T2>$ has no exposed domains. DNA strand displacement reaction can be implemented at a natural temperature without any enzymes or transcription machinery, and its reaction speed can be controlled by changing the length of toehold domain. In a summary, DNA strand displacement technology has some remarkable advantages that are spontaneity, sensitivity, accuracy and expansibility with other nano-devices. Therefore, it is gradually becoming one of the important choices to construct nano-devices.

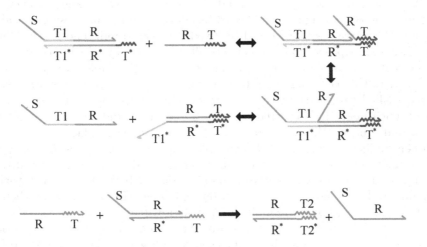

Fig. 1. The reaction mechanism of DNA strand displacement. (a) The reversible reaction of the DNA strand displacement. T and $T1$ are toehold domains, R is a branch migration domain. (b) The irreversible reaction of the DNA strand displacement. $T2$ is the toehold domain, $R1$ is the branch migration domain. These figures are drawn and simulated by soft Visual DSD.

3   Digital Circuit Design of Blood Group Pairing Detector

3.1   Single-Rail Digital Circuit

In the electron digital circuits, there are three basic logical gates, which are logic AND, OR and NOT. The value of output for logic OR gate is logic "0" if all inputs are logic "0", otherwise it is logic "1". The value of output for logic AND gate is logic "1" if all inputs are logic "1", otherwise it is logic "0". The output of logic NOT gate is always the opposite of the input. If the input is logic "1", it is logic "0". Conversely, it is logic "1" if the input is logic "0". The blood group pairing circuit is a digital combinational logic circuit, which is built by some basic logical gates. First, the truth table of blood type pairing between the blood donor and the recipient is constructed, which is shown in Table 1 (a–d). Here, A blood type is represented by the binary number "00", B blood type is represented by the binary number "01", AB blood type is represented by the binary number "11", and O blood type is represented by the binary number "10". The rules of blood transfusion are as follows: A type blood can only be given to the patients with blood type A or AB, B type blood can only be supplied for the patients with blood type B or AB, O type blood can be applied to the patients with any blood type. In general, the same blood type should be considered firstly during the pairing process. Based on the above description and discussion, the logic function expression is shown in Formula (1).

$$Y = F(A, B, C, D) = AB + C\bar{D} + B\bar{C}D + \bar{A}\bar{B}\bar{D} \tag{1}$$

According to Formula (1), one simplified single-rail digital logic circuit for the blood group pairing is built (in Fig. 2), which consists of four NOT gates, three AND gates and one OR gates. The circuit has four inputs indicated with variables A, B, C, D, respectively, the first two of them represent the blood type of recipient, and the last two represent the donor blood type. The output result is represented by the variable Y. If Y is logic "1", it shows that the blood pairing is successful; otherwise, it is failure.

3.2   Math Model of Dual-Rail Logic Circuit

The values of signals are determined by the concentration of a DNA strand in the blood group pairing based on DNA strand displacement, so NOT gate has a hidden trouble probably causing the error output during the process of biochemical reaction. If one input signal is logic "0", it means there is no any DNA species. When the logic "0" signal passes through NOT gate to perform calculation, the gate should output the result of logic "1", and then there is a strange phenomenon occurred that a new single DNA species is generated without any materials, so the following computations in this logic circuit cannot be done normally. To avoid the occurrence of this phenomenon, an idea based on dual-rail logic circuit is proposed, which can improve the work efficiency of blood type paring circuit.

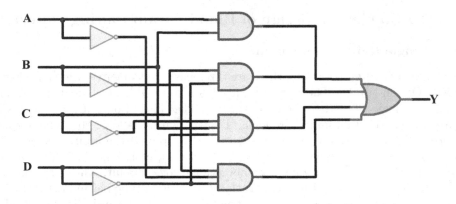

Fig. 2. Single-rail digital logic circuit of the blood group pairing based on DNA strand displacement. A, B, C, and D are input signals, where the combination of A and B represents the recipient's blood type, the combination of C and D represents the donor's blood type. Y is an output signal.

In this paper, a general math model for any dual-rail logic circuit is constructed, which can be applied to design any complex dual-rail logic circuits. The specific process is as follows: suppose that the single-rail logic circuit has m inputs and n outputs, A_i and Y_j represent the i_{th} input and the j_{th} output, respectively. The functional expression of the single-rail logic circuit is as follows:

$$Y_j = F_j(A_1, A_2, ..., A_m) = G_j(A_1, A_2, ..., A_m, \bar{A}_1, ..., \bar{A}_m) \tag{2}$$

In a dual-rail logic circuit, each initial input signal is transformed into two input signals expressed as logic "ON" or "OFF". Here, the logic "ON" is defined as logic "1" and the logic "OFF" is defined as logic "0". For example, the input signal Ai is divided into two signals A_i^0 and A_i^1, where A_i^0 and A_i^1 are represented by two different DNA single strands, respectively. If the input signal A cannot be participated in the reaction, then A_i^0 and A_i^1 will be set to logic "ON" and logic "OFF", respectively. In exactly the same way, Y_j is replaced by $Y_j^P 1$ and Y_j^0, the relation between Y_j^1 and Y_j^0 is: $Y_j^1 = (Y_j^0)$. So the functional expression of the dual-rail logic circuit corresponding to the single-rail logic function expression 3 is as follows:

$$Y_j^1 = F_j(A_1^1, A_2^1, ..., A_m^1) = G_j(A_1^1, A_2^1, ..., A_m^1, A_1^0, ..., A_m^0) \tag{3}$$

$$Y_j^0 = \overline{F_j(A_1^1, A_2^1, ..., A_m^1)} = \overline{G_j(A_1^1, A_2^1, ..., A_m^1, A_1^0, ..., A_m^0}) \tag{4}$$

According to the dual strategy mentioned above, Formula (1) can be converted to Formula (5) and Formula (6):

$$Y^1 = F(A, B, C, D) = A^1 B^1 + C^1 D^0 + B^1 C^0 D^1 + A^0 B^0 D^0 \tag{5}$$

$$Y^0 = \overline{F(A, B, C, D)} = (A^0 + B^0)(C^0 + D^1)(B^0 + C^1 + D^0)(A^1 + B^1 + D^1) \tag{6}$$

Table 1.

(a) Recipient with blood type A				
Input				Output
Recipient		Donor		Y
A	B	C	D	
0	0	0	0	1
0	0	0	1	0
0	0	1	0	1
0	0	1	1	0

(b) Recipient with blood type B				
Input				Output
Recipient		Donor		Y
A	B	C	D	
0	1	0	0	0
0	1	0	1	1
0	1	1	0	1
0	1	1	1	0

(c) Recipient with blood type O				
Input				Output
Recipient		Donor		Y
A	B	C	D	
1	0	0	0	0
1	0	0	1	0
1	0	1	0	1
1	0	1	1	0

(d) Recipient with blood type AB				
Input				Output
Recipient		Donor		Y
A	B	C	D	
1	1	0	0	1
1	1	0	1	1
1	1	1	0	1
1	1	1	1	1

Therefore, the dual-rail logic circuit of the blood type pairing circuit can be built based on Formula (5) and Formula (6), as shown in Fig. 3.

When the inputs signals $A = 0$, $B = 1$, $C = 1$, $D = 0$, it means the recipient with B blood type is going to match the donor with AB blood type. Based on the mentioned above, we can get $A^0 = 1$, $B^1 = 1$, $C^1 = 1$, $D^0 = 1$, $A^1 = 0$, $B^0 = 0$, $C^0 = 0$, $D^1 = 0$. From left to right in Fig. 3, the OR gate W_1 is operated by $A^0 = 1$, $B^0 = 0$, and the output result is $P_1 = [(A^0 = 1) \vee (B^0 = 0)] = 1$; The AND gate W2 is operated by A1 $= 0$, B1 $= 1$, and the out-put result is represented by $P_2 = [(A^1 = 0) \wedge (B^1 = 1)] = 0$; The OR gate W_3 is operated by $C^0 = 0$, $D^1 = 0$, and the output result is $P_3 = [(C^0 = 0) \vee (D^1 = 0)] = 0$; The AND gate W4 is operated by $C^1 = 1$, $D^0 = 1$, the output of which is represented by $P_4 = [(C^1 = 1) \wedge (D^0 = 1)] = 1$; The OR gate W_5 is operated by $B^0 = 0$, $D^0 = 1$, $C^1 = 1$, and the output result is $P_5 = [(B^0 = 0) \vee (D^0 = 1) \vee (C^1 = 1)] = 1$; The sixth AND gate W6 is operated by $C^0 = 0$, $D^1 = 0$, $B^1 = 1$, the output of which is represented by $P^6 = [(C^0 = 0) \wedge (D^1 = 0)(B^1 = 1)] = 0$; The seventh OR gate W_7 is operated by $B^1 = 1$, $A^1 = 0$, $D^1 = 0$, and the output result is $P_7 = [(B^1 = 1) \vee (A^1 = 0) \vee (D^1 = 0)] = 1$; The eighth AND gate W_8 is operated by $B^0 = 0$, $A^0 = 1$, $D^0 = 1$, the output of which is represented by $P_8 = [(B^0 = 0) \wedge (A^0 = 1) \wedge (D^0 = 1)] = 0$. Then, the upstream outputs P_1, P_3, P_5 and P_7 are operated with the AND operation through the AND gate Q_2, and the output result is represented by R_1, that is $R_1 = [(P_1 = 1) \wedge (P_3 = 0) \wedge (P_5 = 1) \wedge (P_7 = 1)] = 0$, so the final output result is $Y_0 = 1$; The upstream outputs P_2, P_4, P_6 and P_8 are computed by the next stage OR gate Q_1, and the output result is indicated by R_2, that is, $R_2 = [(P_2 = 0) \vee (P_4 = 1) \vee (P_6 = 0) \vee (P_8 = 0)] = 1$, the final output result is $Y^1 = 1$, which shows that the blood type can be paired between the donor and the recipient.

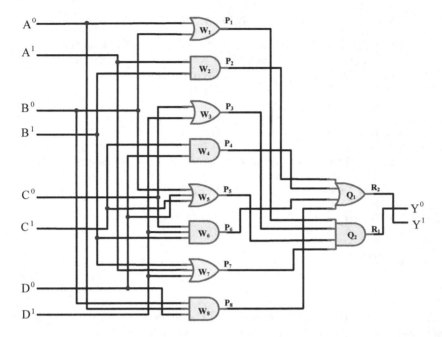

Fig. 3. Dual-rail logic circuit of the blood group pairing based on DNA strand displacement.

4   Design of Basic Calculation Modules for DNA Logic Circuit

In this context, the concentration of a DNA strand is used to represent the logic values of a biochemical logic circuit, and "1" unit concentration" is 10,000 nM in this paper. If the concentration of a DNA strand is more than 0.9 unit concentration, the logic value of this strand is defined as logic 1; if the concentration of a DNA strand is less than 0.1 unit concentration, the logic value of this strand is defined as logic 0.1 during the reaction process of DNA strand displacements, all chemistry reactions can be happened spontaneously at room temperature, and the concentration of DNA strands changes constantly and then affects the reaction speed and the final results. With the DNA strand displacement reactions proceeding, the concentration of the initial DNA strands participating reaction will reduce or increase. Usually, the computation process in a logic circuit is dynamic cascaded, where the output signal of up-stream gate acts as the input signal of downstream. In order to ensure the right output result of every logic gate in the logic circuit, all the DNA strands participating reactions should have proper concentration corresponding the logic values. The DNA threshold gate is designed to reduce the concentration of a DNA signal strand into a target value, and the design of DNA amplification gate is to realize to amplify the concentration of a DNA signal strand to a set value. In addition, Fan-out gate, report-er gate, and the module of AND gate and OR gate are designed too, which are the basis of constructing the blood group pairing logic circuit.

4.1 DNA Threshold Gate

In Fig. 4, the DNA double strand $uR^{*\wedge}T^{*\wedge}[vL^\wedge v\ vR^\wedge]$ is a threshold gate, the single strand $<uL^\wedge u\ uR^\wedge T^\wedge vL^\wedge v\ vR^\wedge>$ represents an input signal strand. The colorful domains except the gray domains in Fig. 4 represent toehold domains. When the threshold strand and the input strand are mixed in solution, the toehold "T" in the input strand binds spontaneously to the toehold "T^*" in the threshold strand because of the complementary property between the two toeholds. As the branch migrating to the right gradually, the strand $<vL^\wedge v\ vR^\wedge>$ is displaced finally and generates two new products: the double strand $<uL^\wedge u>[uR^\wedge T^\wedge vL^\wedge v\ vR^\wedge]$ and the single strand $<vL^\wedge v\ vR^\wedge>$. The reaction is shown in Fig. 4, which is irreversible because new products have no exposed toeholds complemented with each other. So with threshold gate reaction performing, the input strand is consumed constantly, if the amount of threshold strand is enough, the input strand will be consumed entirely. Figure 4 (c) is the simulation of the threshold gate. The concentration of threshold strand can be set according to the requirements of DNA systems

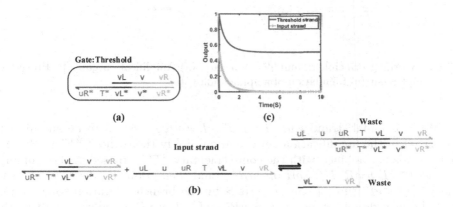

Fig. 4. Reaction between a threshold gate and an input DNA strand. (a) Threshold gate (b) Process of DNA implement (c) Simulation of threshold gate.

4.2 DNA Amplification Gate

A DNA amplification gate includes two parts: an amplifier strand and a fuel strand. As shown in Fig. 5 (a) when a DNA signal strand needs to amplify to a set value, we should adjust the concentration of the amplifier stand and the fuel strand. If the target value of the signal strand's concentration is set to m (m represents a concentration value), then the concentration of the amplifier strand needs to adjust to m, too. The concentration of the fuel stand is greater than twice the concentration of the amplifier strand. Usually, the concentration of the fuel stand is twice than of the amplifier strand, which is enough for DNA system. So the concentration of the fuel strand needs to adjust to $m * 2$. Figure 5 (b) demonstrates how the amplification gate works with a DNA signal strand.

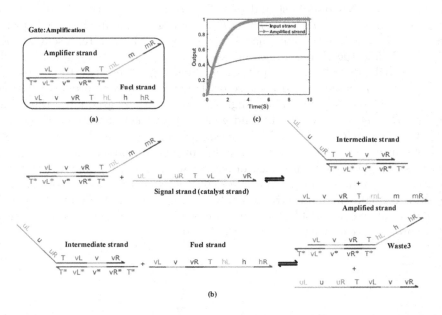

Fig. 5. Working principle of amplification gate. (a) Amplification gate (b) Process of DNA implement (c) Simulation of amplification gate.

When a signal strand $<uL^\circ u \ uR^\circ T^\circ \ vL^\circ v \ vR^\circ>$ needed to be amplified is in-putted in the amplification gate solution, firstly the toehold "T" in the signal strands is combined with the complementary "T^*" exposed in the amplifier strand $T^*[vL^\circ v \ vR^\circ T^\circ] <mL^\circ m \ mR^\circ>$, and then gradually displaces the single strand $<vL^\circ v \ vR^\circ T^\circ mL^\circ m \ mR^\circ>$ by the branch migration to the right, and the new double stand $<uL^\circ u \ uR^\circ> [T^\circ vL^\circ v \ vR]T^*$ is generated at the same time. As can be seen from Fig. 5 (b), this reaction is reversible. Next, the newly generated double strand $<uL^\circ u \ uR^\circ> [T^\circ vL^\circ v \ vR]T^*$ reacts with the fuel strand $<vL^\circ v \ vR^\circ T^\circ hL^\circ h \ hR^\circ>$. The toehold "T" in the fuel strand is bound to the complementary "T^*" exposed in the double strand $<uL^\circ u \ uR^\circ> [T^\circ vL^\circ v \ vR]T^*$, and the branch migration is moving to the left gradually, the single strand $<uL^\circ u \ uR^\circ T^\circ vL^\circ v \ vR^\circ>$ is displaced again, the process of this reaction is shown in Fig. 5 (b) As can be seen from Fig. 5 (b), this reaction is reversible too.

From the reaction process of amplification gate, we can find that the signal strand $<uL^\circ u \ uR^\circ T^\circ vL^\circ v \ vR^\circ>$ is consumed in the first reaction, but it is generated in the second reaction again. So, the signal strand only plays a catalytic role, whose concentration is not changed finally, in other words, the signal strand is equivalent to not participating in the reaction. The double strand $<uL\hat{\ } u\ uR\hat{\ }>$ $[T\hat{\ }vL\hat{\ }v\ vR]T^*$ is generated in the first section, but it is consumed in the second reaction, so the double strand is just an intermediate product. The single strand $<vL\hat{\ }v\ vR\hat{\ }\ T\hat{\ }\ mL\hat{\ }\ m\ mR\hat{\ }>$ is an amplified signal strand, its concentration is same as the amplifier strand's. There-fore, the concentration of the single strand $<vL\hat{\ }v\ vR\hat{\ }T\hat{\ }mL\hat{\ }m\ mR\hat{\ }>$ is m. Figure 5 (c) is the simulation of the amplification gate. In a summary, the amplification gate designed in this paper realized the conversion from low concentration strand to high concentration strand.

4.3   DNA Fan-Out Gate

In the DNA system, every logic gate constructed by some DNA strands is independent, which does not interfere with each other. The signal transmission between gates is accomplished by DNA strands. Sometimes a DNA strand needs to be converted into several different DNA strands representing the same logic value because the concentration of the DNA strand has been reduced in the upstream reaction, while it must take part in the downstream reaction as the same high concentration. Fan-out gates designed in this paper are used to realize this function. Here, a one-input-two-output fan-out gate is constructed, as shown in Fig. 6 (a), which consists of fan-out strand1 $T^*[vL\hat{\ }\ v\ vR\hat{\ }\ T]$ $<m1L\hat{\ }\ m1\ m1R\hat{\ }>$, fan-out strand2 $T^*[vL\hat{\ }\ v\ vR\hat{\ }\ T\hat{\ }]$ $<m2L\hat{\ }\ m2\ m2R\hat{\ }>$ and fuel strand $<vL\hat{\ }\ v\ vR\hat{\ }T\hat{\ }\ hL\hat{\ }\ h\ hR\hat{\ }>$.

When an input signal strand $<uL\hat{\ }\ u\ uR\hat{\ }\ T\hat{\ }\ vL\hat{\ }\ v\ vR\hat{\ }>$ interacts with the fan-out gate, there will be three reactions in the whole computing process, which is shown in Fig. 6 (b) In the first reaction, the toehold "T" in the signal strand is combined with the complementary "T^*" exposed in the fan-out strand1, and then gradually displaces the single strand $<vL\hat{\ }v\ vR\hat{\ }T\hat{\ }m1L\hat{\ }m1\ m1R\hat{\ }>$ by the branch migration to the right, and the new double stand $<uL\hat{\ }u\ uR\hat{\ }>\ [T\hat{\ }vL\hat{\ }v\ vR\hat{\ }]T^*$ is generated at the same time. As can be seen from the Fig. 6 (b), the first reaction is reversible. Just like the first reaction, the input signal reacts with the fan-out strands, and finally the new single stand $<vL\hat{\ }\ v\ vR\hat{\ }\ T\hat{\ }\ m2L\hat{\ }\ m2\ m2R\hat{\ }>$ is generated. Besides of this, the same double strand $<uL\hat{\ }u\ uR\hat{\ }>\ [T\hat{\ }vL\hat{\ }v\ vR]T^*$ is produced in both the first reaction and the second reaction, and it is consumed by the fuel strand $<vL\hat{\ }\ v\ vR\hat{\ }\ T\hat{\ }\ hL\hat{\ }\ h\ hR\hat{\ }>$ in the third reaction, and the initial input signal strand $<uL\hat{\ }\ u\ uR\hat{\ }\ T\hat{\ }\ vL\hat{\ }\ v\ vR\hat{\ }>$ is displaced again. In fact, the input signal needed to be converted into two same logical signals is just a catalytic agent, which has no participation in the whole reaction essentially. If the concentration of the fan-out strand1 and strand2 is set to 1 unit, and the fuel strand's concentration is 4 units, the fan-out gate will output two new single strand $<vL\hat{\ }v\ vR\hat{\ }T\hat{\ }m1L\hat{\ }m1\ m1R\hat{\ }>$ and $<vL\hat{\ }v\ vR\hat{\ }T\hat{\ }m2L\hat{\ }m2\ m2R\hat{\ }>$, whose concentration is same, and the value is 1 unit. If we want to construct a one-input-three-output fan-out gate, we only need to add the fan-out strand3 $<T^*[vL\hat{\ }\ v\ vR\hat{\ }\ T\hat{\ }]<m3L\hat{\ }\ m3\ m3R\hat{\ }>$ to the fan-out gate, and ensure that the concentration of the fuel strand is six times of the fan-out stand1. Figure 6 (c)

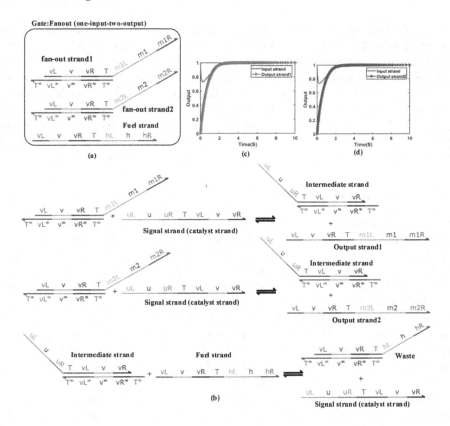

Fig. 6. Working principle of one-input-two-output Fan-out gate. (a) One-input-two-output fan gate (b) Process of DNA implement (c) Simulation of output stand1 (d) Simulation of output stand2.

and Fig. 6 (d) is the simulation. According to the principle of constructing fan-out gate, we can construct any fan-out gate that can convert one signal strand into n strands, which have the same concentration. In particular, the function of fan-out gate is only efficient to the high concentration representing logic "1". If the concentration of the input signal strand represents logic "0", the input signal should be filtered, so a threshold gate should be added to consume the input signal, just like amplification gate.

4.4   DNA Reporter Gate

DNA reporter gate is used to check the final results of DNA system. The structure and function of reporter gates is similar to the threshold gates. The reporter gate includes quenching agent and fluorescent nano gold probe, which has various colors to represent different DNA stands and cannot react with other logic gates. In Fig. 9 (a), the output strand $<nL^\hat{}\ n\ nR^\hat{}\ T^\hat{}\ vL^\hat{}\ v\ vR^\hat{}>$ need to be checked. When the output strand inputs the reporter strand, its toehold "T" is combined with the complementary "T^*" exposed in the reporter strand, and then gradually displaces the flour strand $<vL\hat{}\ v\ vR\hat{}\ Flout>$ by the branch migration to the right, and the new double strand $<nL\hat{}\ n\ nR\hat{}>\ [T\hat{}\ vL\hat{}\ v\ vR]$ is generated at the same time. Because there is no complementary domains between the new double chain and flour chain, the reaction of reporter gate irreversible. With the reaction going on, the output strand is gradually consumed, and the flour strand is getting more and more. Finally, the flour strand can be checked out. Figure 7 (c) is the simulation.

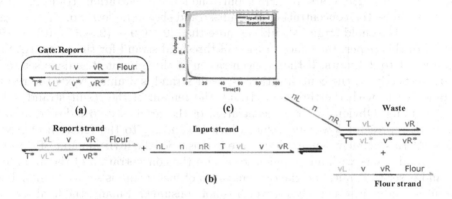

Fig. 7. Working principle of reporter gate. (a) Report gate (b) Process of DNA implement (c) Simulation of report gate.

4.5 The Basic Computing Module Logic AND and OR

The logic circuit of DNA molecule is the basic unit of biological computer, which is mainly composed of DNA logic AND gates and logic OR gates. Here, the logic AND and OR computing modules are designed as shown in Fig. 8 (a), which include AND (OR) gate strand, threshold strand, amplifier strand and fuel strand. The calculation module is not only logic AND gate, but also logic OR gate. We can adjust the concentration of the threshold gate to realize the logic function of different gates simply. As can be seen from Fig. 3, the dual-rail logic circuit of the blood group pairing based on DNA strand displacement needs three kinds of logic gates: two-input-AND (OR) gate, three-input-AND (OR) gate, four-input-AND (OR) gate. The amount of the inputs for logic AND (OR) gate is decided by the concentration of AND (OR) gate strand. If the amount of inputs is n, the concentration of AND (OR) gate strand will be n units. Figure 8 (b) demonstrates how a three-input-AND (OR) gate works. There are three input strands in this AND (OR) gates, and they have the same right part $<T\hat{}\ sL\hat{}\ s\ sR\hat{}>$, which are input strand1 $<m1L\hat{}\ m1\ m1R\hat{}\ T\hat{}\ sL\hat{}\ s\ sR\hat{}>$, input strand2 $<m2L\hat{}\ m2\ m2R\hat{}\ T\hat{}\ sL\hat{}\ s\ sR\hat{}>$, input strand3 $<m3L\hat{}\ m3\ m3R\hat{}\ T\hat{}\ sL\hat{}\ s\ sR\hat{}>$, respectively. When these signal strands are input AND (OR) gate, they react with AND (OR) gate strand, respectively, and the same result strand $<sL^\smallfrown s\ sR^\smallfrown T^\smallfrown eL^\smallfrown e\ eR^\smallfrown>$ is output, as shown in Fig. 8 (b). If the concentration of every input strand is set to 1 unit, the concentration of AND (OR) gate strand should be set to 3 units. Consequently, the concentration of result strand is the sum of three input strands' concentration. The function of threshold strand in AND (OR) gate is to consume the result strand and change its concentration. If the gate performs AND logic functions, how to define the concentration of threshold strand is critical. As we all know, when the concentration of all input strands is high, the concentration of result strand should be high. Therefore, the concentration of threshold should be less than $(3 * 0.9 = 2.7)$ units. If there is only one low concentration strand in three input strands, the concentration of result strand should be low. So, the concentration of threshold strand should be more than $[2 * 0.9 + (2 - 1) * 0.1 = 1.9]$ units. In this paper, the concentration of threshold strand for three-input-AND gate is set to 2.3 units. If then concentration of three input strands is set to 1 unit, respectively, the concentration of result strand is 3 units. Next, the result strand reacts with the threshold strand, the remain of the result strand is $(3 - 2.3)$ units. Obviously, the concentration of the result strand is less than 0.9 units, it represents low logic value, which is contrary to the function of AND gate. At this moment, an amplifier gate is must. So, the little amount of threshold strand reacts with an amplifier gate, and the concentration of the amplifier strand is set to 1 unit, and the concentration of fuel strand is set to 2 units. The result strand is just a catalyzer, which is not consumed. Finally, the final strand $<eL^\smallfrown e\ eR^\smallfrown T^\smallfrown aL^\smallfrown a\ aR^\smallfrown>$ can be output by the AND gate, whose concentration is 1 unit. In summary, three high concentration input strands can make AND gate output high concentration final stand, which complies with the logic function of AND gate. If at least one of three input strands is defined as 0.1 unit concentration and the concentration of threshold strand is still 2.3 units, there is at most 2.1 units concentration result strand $<sL^\smallfrown s\ sR^\smallfrown T^\smallfrown eL^\smallfrown e\ eR^\smallfrown>$ is produced. Obviously, the result strand can be consumed by threshold strand. Therefore, the AND gate outputs logic "0". In conclusion, the three-input-AND gate is composed of these four kinds of strands, which are 3 units concentration AND strand, 2.3 units concentration threshold strand, 1 unit concentration amplifier strand, and 2 units concentration fuel stand. Figure 8(c) is the simulation of three inputs AND computing module.

OR gate has the same structure as the AND gate. If the concentration of thresh-old strand is defined as $[w]_{th}$ units, then

$$0.1 * 3 < [w]_{th} < 0.9 * 1 + (3 - 1) * 0 \tag{7}$$

Here, $[w]_{th}$ is set to 0.7 units. If three input strands are low concentration, then the result strand $<sL^\smallfrown s\ sR^\smallfrown T^\smallfrown eL^\smallfrown e\ eR^\smallfrown>$ has at most 0.3 units after the first three reaction in Fig. 8 (b), which can be consumed completely. If at least one of three input strands is high concentration, then the concentration of the result strand is at least 0.9 units. Next, the result strand reacts with the threshold strand, and remains $(0.9 - 0.7 = 0.2)$ units. The little amount result strand reacts with amplifier gate, and the 1unit concentration final strand

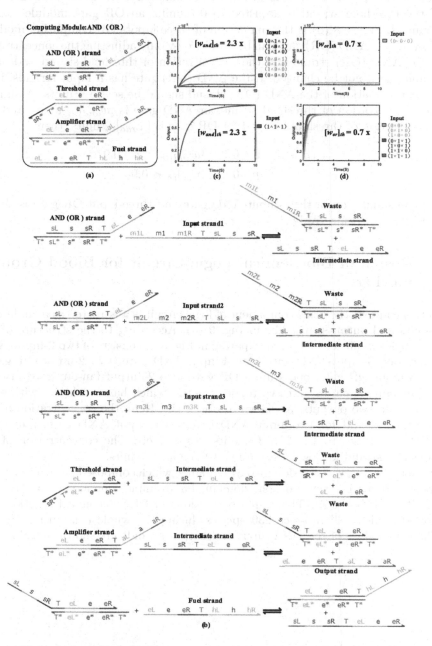

Fig. 8. Three inputs AND (OR) computing module. (a) Computing module of logic three-input AND and OR (b) Process of DNA implement (c) Simulation of three-input logic AND gate (d) Simulation of three-input logic OR gate.

$<eL\hat{}\ e\ eR\hat{}\ T\hat{}\ aL\hat{}\ a\ aR\hat{}>$ is produced. In summary, when the concentration of the threshold strand is adjusted to 0.7 units, an OR gate module can be obtained. Figure 8 (d) is the simulation of three inputs OR computing module. Overall, one AND (OR) gate can be obtained by only adjusting the concentration of the AND (OR) strand and the concentration of threshold strand and other strands need not be changed. If the AND (OR) gate has n input strands, then the concentration of the AND (OR) strand should be set to n units. Assuming the concentration of threshold strand for AND gate is $[w_{and}]_{th}$ units, and the concentration of thresh-old strand for OR gate is $[w_{and}]_{th}$ units, then

$$(n-1)*1+0.1 < [w_{and}]_{th} < n*0.9 \tag{8}$$
$$n*0.1 < [w_{or}]_{th} < 0.9 \tag{9}$$

The simulation of three-input-AND gate and three-input-OR gate is shown in Fig. 8 (b), respectively.

5   Design of Biochemical Logic Circuit for Blood Group Pairing

In this context, the basic component of logic circuit is abstracted as a circle with in-puts and outputs, just like in Fig. 9 (a). According to the structure of the dual logic circuit for blood group paring in Fig. 3, it consists of two 2-input-AND gates, one 3-input-AND gate, one 4-input-AND gate, two 2-input-OR gates, one 3-input-OR gate, one 4-input-OR gate, two 2-output-fan-out gates, two 3-output-fan-out gates, and two reporter gates, which has two layers with eight inputs and two outputs, as shown in Fig. 9 (b). Here, the concentration of the threshold strand for two-input AND gate, three-input AND gate, four-input AND gate is set to 1.2, 2.3, 3.3 units, respectively. The concentration of the threshold strand for logic OR gate is defined as 0.7 units.

In this work, we have designed 87 domains, which composed 86 species. There are 4 6 bases in every toehold domain, for example, domain $T\hat{} = [GCTA]$, $S10R\hat{} = [TAGCCA]$. There are 96 reactions in CRN (chemical reaction networks), which will produce 230 species during the whole computing process. The logic values of the DNA input and output strands are shown in Table 2.

Table 2. Logic values of the input and output strands

Input/outout	DNA strands	Logic value
A0	<S4L^ S4 S4R^ T^ S5L^ S5 S5R>	0
A1	<S6L^ S6 S6R^ T^ S7L^ S7 S7R>	1
B0	<S8L^ S8 S8R^ T^ S9L^ S9 S9R>	0
B1	<S10L^ S10 S10R^ T^ S11L^ S11 S11R>	1
C0	<S12L^ S12 S12R^ T^ S13L^ S13 S13R>	0
C1	<S14L^ S14 S14R^ T^ S15L^ S15 S15R>	1
D0	<S16L^ S16 S16R^ T^ S17L^ S17 S17R>	0
D1	<S18L^ S18 S18R^ T^ S19L^ S19 S19R>	1
Y0	<S56L^ S56 S56R^ Fluor56>	0
Y1	<S58L^ S58 S58R^ Fluor58>	1

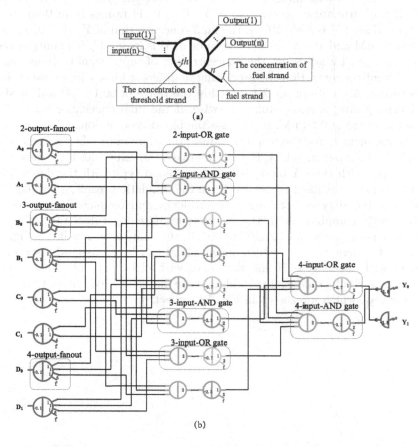

Fig. 9. The biochemical circuit of the blood group pairing based on DNA strand displacement. (a) Abstraction of a component. (b) DNA molecule circuit.

6   Simulation with Visual DSD

For the biochemical logic circuit based on the DNA strand displacement, the soft of Visual DSD is professional for DNA stands design, which can offer some functions of programming, compiling, simulation and analysis. Here, the reaction process of the blood group pairing logic circuit based on DNA strand displacement is investigated by visual DSD. The simulations of the blood group pairing logic circuit based on DNA strand displacement can be shown correctly in Fig. 10 (a–p).

In this logic circuit, there are four input signals, which are A, B, C and D, respectively. When the values of inputs signals A^0, A^1, B^0, B^1, C^0, C^1, D^0 and D^1 are determined, the different output results of Y are gained in the blood group pairing logic circuit. The simulation results corresponding to all combinations of input signals are obtained from 0000 to 1111 in Fig. 10 (a–p). The response time is set to 0000 s, the total input concentration is set to 100 nM. The outputs are represented by two different color curves, where the green is Y^1 and the red is Y^0. If the ultimate concentration of Y^i (i = 0, 1) ranges from 0 to 10 nM, then the value of Y is logic "0". If the final concentration of Y^i (i = 0, 1) varies between 90 nM and 100 nM, then the value of Y is logic "1". The output result can be changed by adjusting the concentration of input signals, input signals with different concentration corresponding to different binary input value. If the final concentration of output $Y1$ is within the range of 90 to 100 nM, it shows blood type paring is successful; otherwise, if the final concentration of Y^1 is within the range of 0 20 nM, it suggests the blood type of donor does not agree with the recipient's, and the blood transfusion therapy cannot be carried out. For example, if the input signals A, B, C, D are taken the value "0001", it means that the recipient with type A blood is matching blood type with the donor whose blood type is B, just like Fig. 10 (b). From the simulation result, Y1 is logic "0", it indicates blood type matching between donor and recipient is unsuccessful, which is fully compliant with the blood type matching rules. With the same method, when input signals $ABCD = 0110$, the simulation result (in Fig. 10g) is achieved, where $Y^1 = 1$, which shows blood can be transfused between the recipient with blood type B and the donor with blood type O. Then, a group of simulation results conforming to blood type matching rules are obtained with the same way, which are shown in Fig. 10 respectively.

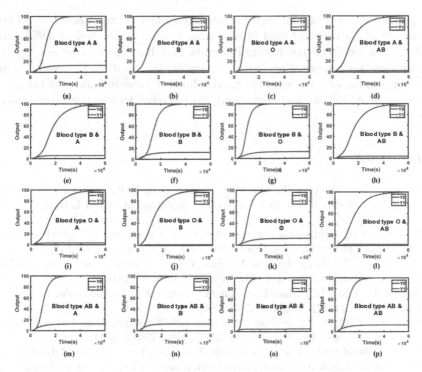

Fig. 10. Sixteen kinds of simulations results of the blood group pairing logic circuit based on DNA strand displacement corresponding to inputs from 0000 to 1111. (a) $ABCD = 0000, Y = 1$ (b) $ABCD = 0001, Y = 0$ (c) $ABCD = 0010, Y = 1$ (d) $ABCD = 0011, Y = 0$ (e) $ABCD = 0100, Y = 0$ (f) $ABCD = 0101, Y = 1$ (g) $ABCD = 0110, Y = 1$ (h) $ABCD = 0111, Y = 0$ (i) $ABCD = 1000, Y = 0$ (j) $ABCD = 1001, Y = 0$ (k) $ABCD = 1010, Y = 1$ (l) $ABCD = 1011, Y = 0$ (m) $ABCD = 1100, Y = 1$ (n) $ABCD = 1101, Y = 1$ (o) $ABCD = 1110, Y = 1$ (p) $ABCD = 1111, Y = 1$. (Color figure online)

7 Conclusion

In this paper, the modules of threshold gate, amplification gate, fan-out gate, reporter gate, AND (OR) gate were designed based on the reaction mechanism of the DNA strand displacement firstly, and then revealed their working principles that are universal and the most basic modules for constructing any DNA logic circuit. Secondly, the math model of any dual logic circuit is proposed. Next, the dual logical circuit model of the blood group pairing has been designed. Thirdly, 114 basic DNA single strands for the blood group pairing are designed. Finally, the reaction process of the DNA biochemical circuit for blood group pairing has been simulated and the results of the logical operations can be displayed correctly through the specialized Visual DSD software. According to the results of the simulation, the displacement of DNA strands is an effective method for logic computation. The Model of blood group pairing logic circuit proposed in this paper has some significance for intelligent medical treatment. In addition, the investigation for the blood type pairing logic circuit based on DNA strand displacement designed by dual-rail circuits may have a great prospect for the development and application in the biological information processing, molecular computing, and so on. Due to the limited experimental conditions, the experiments of DNA strand compound displacement will be the future research directions.

References

1. Li, W., Yang, Y., Yan, H., Liu, Y.: Three-input majority logic gate and multiple input logic circuit based on DNA strand displacement. Nano Lett. **13**(6), 2980–2988 (2013)
2. Cao, M., et al.: Multivalent aptamer-modified DNA origami as drug delivery system for targeted cancer therapy. Chem. Res. Chin. Univ. **36**, 1–7 (2019)
3. Hu, Q., Li, H., Wang, L., Gu, H., Fan, C.: DNA nanotechnology-enabled drug delivery systems. Chem. Rev. **119**(10), 6459–6506 (2018)
4. Konry, T., Walt, D.R.: Intelligent medical diagnostics via molecular logic. J. Am. Chem. Soc. **131**(37), 13232–13233 (2009)
5. Qian, L., Winfree, E.: Scaling up digital circuit computation with DNA strand displacement cascades. Science **332**(6034), 1196–1201 (2011)
6. Qian, L., Winfree, E.: Parallel and scalable computation and spatial dynamics with DNA-based chemical reaction networks on a surface. In: Murata, S., Kobayashi, S. (eds.) DNA 2014. LNCS, vol. 8727, pp. 114–131. Springer, Cham (2014). https://doi.org/10.1007/978-3-319-11295-4_8
7. Song, T., Garg, S., Mokhtar, R., Bui, H., Reif, J.: Analog computation by DNA strand displacement circuits. ACS Synth. Biol. **5**(8), 898–912 (2016)
8. Wang, Y.F., Wang, P.R., Huang, C., Sun, J.W.: Five-input cube-root logical operation based on DNA strand displacement. J. Nanoelectron. Optoelectron. **13**(6), 831–838 (2018)
9. Adleman, L.M.: Molecular computation of solutions to combinatorial problems. Science **266**(5187), 1021–1024 (1994)
10. Ouyang, Q., Kaplan, P.D., Liu, S., Libchaber, A.: DNA solution of the maximal clique problem. Science **278**(5337), 446–449 (1997)
11. Xu, J., et al.: An unenumerative DNA computing model for vertex coloring problem. IEEE Trans. Nanobiosci. **10**(2), 94–98 (2011)
12. Collins, F.: The Language of Life: DNA and the Revolution in Personalised Medicine. Profile Books, London (2010)
13. Ding, B., Seeman, N.C.: Operation of a DNA robot arm inserted into a 2D DNA crystalline substrate. Science **314**(5805), 1583–1585 (2006)
14. Thubagere, A.J., et al.: A cargo-sorting DNA robot. Science **357**(6356), 1112 (2017)
15. Wang, X., Zhou, J., Yun, W., Xiao, S., Chang, Z., He, P.: Detection of thrombin using electrogenerated chemiluminescence based on Ru (bpy) 32+-doped silica nanoparticle aptasensor via target protein-induced strand displacement. Anal. Chimica Acta **598**(2), 242–248 (2007)
16. Yurke, B., Turberfield, A.J., Mills, A.P., Simmel, F.C., Neumann, J.L.: A DNA-fuelled molecular machine made of DNA. Nature **406**(6796), 605–608 (2000)

17. Zhang, P., Jiang, J., Yuan, R., Zhuo, Y., Chai, Y.: Highly ordered and field-free 3d DNA nanostructure: the next generation of DNA nanomachine for rapid single-step sensing. J. Am. Chem. Soc. **140**(30), 9361–9364 (2018)
18. Shi, X., et al.: Programmable DNA tile self-assembly using a hierarchical sub-tile strategy. Nanotechnology **25**(7), 075602 (2014)
19. Wang, Y., Sun, J., Zhang, X., Cui, G.: Full adder and full subtractor operations by DNA self-assembly. Adv. Sci. Lett. **4**(2), 383–390 (2011)
20. Zhao, S., Liu, Y., Wang, B., Zhou, C., Zhang, Q.: DNA logic circuits based on FokI enzyme regulation. N. J. Chem. **44**(5), 1931–1941 (2020)
21. Hong, F., et al.: Layered-crossover tiles with precisely tunable angles for 2D and 3D DNA crystal engineering. J. Am. Chem. Soc. **140**(44), 14670–14676 (2018)
22. Li, J.X., Wang, Y.F., Sun, J.W.: Odd judgment circuit of four inputs based on DNA strand displacement. J. Nanoelectron. Optoelectron. **15**(3), 415–424 (2020)

Three-Variable Chaotic Oscillatory System Based on DNA Chemical Reaction Networks

Haoping Ji[1,2], Yuli Yang[1,2], Xiangwei Chen[1,2], and Yanfeng Wang[1,2(✉)]

[1] Henan Key Lab of Information-Based Electrical Appliances,
Zhengzhou University of Light Industry, Zhenzhou 450002, China
yanfengwang@yeah.net
[2] School of Electrical and Information Engineering,
Zhengzhou University of Light Industry, Zhenzhou 450002, China

Abstract. DNA strand displacement reactions as a new type of nanotechnology have great potential in the constructions of circuits. The classical step signal is realized by DNA chemical reaction networks (CRNs) in the previous work. Up to now, few works have been done to realize chaotic system through DNA CRNs. In this paper, a three-variable chaotic oscillatory system is proposed by DNA CRNs. The chaotic system CRNs is made up of multiplication modules, combination modules and degradation modules, then chemical reaction equations are compiled into a three-variable chaotic oscillatory system by the law of mass action. The simulations are given to show our DNA CRNs can generate chaotic oscillatory signals.

Keywords: DNA strand displacement · Chaotic system · Chemical reaction network

1 Introduction

CRNs are an effective modeling method to describe the relationship of reactant, intermedium and product, and through the law of mass action, ordinary differential equations (ODEs) could be constructed by them [1–4]. CRNs can not only analyze the existing system but also construct the designed system conveniently

This work was supported in part by the National Key Research and Development Program of China for International S and T Cooperation Projects under Grant 2017YFE0103900, in part by the Joint Funds of the National Natural Science Foundation of China under Grant U1804262, in part by the State Key Program of National Natural Science of China under Grant 61632002, in part by the Foundation of Young Key Teachers from University of Henan Province under Grant 2018GGJS092, in part by the Youth Talent Lifting Project of Henan Province under Grant 2018HYTP016, in part by the Henan Province University Science and Technology Innovation Talent Support Plan under Grant 20HASTIT027, in part by the Zhongyuan Thousand Talents Program under Grant 204200510003.

© Springer Nature Singapore Pte Ltd. 2021
L. Pan et al. (Eds.): BIC-TA 2020, CCIS 1363, pp. 502–512, 2021.
https://doi.org/10.1007/978-981-16-1354-8_36

[5,6]. DNA strand displacement reactions are considered to be an ideal carrier for the construction of CRNs [7,8]. This reaction is a DNA molecules spontaneous reaction that a single-chain is driven by intermolecular forces, reacting with a partially complementary double-chain to replace one of the double chain at room temperature [9–11]. Through the property of cascade, complex CRNs can be formed by simple DNA modules which are made up of DNA strand displacement reactions and a circuit system can be built with chemical equations [12,13]. With these advantages, the research of DNA strand displacement reactions has attracted the attention of many experts and has been applied to DNA logic gates, sensors, molecular detection and other aspects [14–17].

Chaos is a common phenomenon of nonlinear dynamical systems and chaotic motion is complex and unpredictable [18,19]. Small disturbances in control parameters will cause huge changes in the chaotic system [20,21]. The movement of the chaotic system is different from the real random movement, and the trajectory of the chaotic system is reproducible [22]. The irregularity and repeatability of chaos has attracted many scholars to participate in this research field. Their purpose is to understand the general laws behind random movement. Chaos theory has been applied to image encryption [23], information transmission [24], weather prediction [25], cryptography [26–30] and so on. Until now, few works has been done for three-variable chaotic systems by DNA strand displacement reactions.

In this work, multiplication modules, combination modules and degradation modules are designed by DNA strand displacement reactions, and these modules can be integrated to realise three-variable chaotic system. Our modules are proved to be correct through the comparison of Visual DSD and Matlab. Compared with previous work, our work use the software of Visual DSD to design DNA modules and realize the construction of a three-variable chaotic system, providing reference for the study of chaos theory at the DNA molecular level.

2   Construction of Modules

There is an inseparable connection between DNA CRNs and ideal CRNs. Ideal CRNs concentrations and DNA CRNs concentrations of main reactants X, Y, Z are represented by $[X_1(t)]$, $[Y_1(t)]$, $[Z_1(t)]$ and $[X(t)]$, $[Y(t)]$, $[Z(t)]$, respectively. The initial concentrations of substance X are represented by $[X(t_0)]$ and $[X_1(t_0)]$ ($[X(t_0)] = [X_1(t_0)]$), respectively. The initial concentrations of substance Y are represented by $[Y(t_0)]$ and $[Y_1(t_0)]$ ($[Y(t_0)] = [Y_1(t_0)]$), respectively. The initial concentrations of substance Z are represented by $[Z(t_0)]$ and $[Z_1(t_0)]$ ($[Z(t_0)] = [Z_1(t_0)]$), respectively.

The DNA CRNs of multiplication reaction (4) consist of the reactant X, auxiliaries A_0, B_0 and A_5. The initial concentration of the reactant X is set to $[X(t_0)]$. Similarly, auxiliaries A_0, B_0 and A_5 are set to C_m ($[X(t_0)] \ll C_m$). Due to DNA reaction (1), $d[X(t)]/dt = -q_i C_m [X(t)]$ is given. $d[X(t)]/dt = 2q_m C_m [sp2(t)]$, $d[X(t)]/dt = q_m C_m [sp2(t)]$ are obtained from DNA reactions (2) and (3), respectively. In DNA strand displacement reaction (1), the reactant

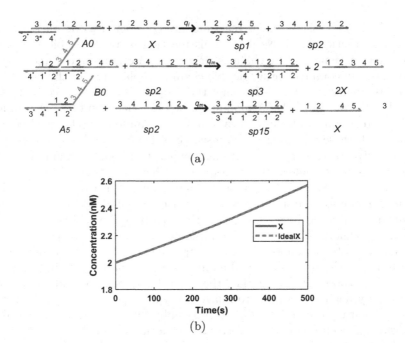

(a)

(b)

Fig. 1. Multiplication reaction (4). (a) DNA chemical reaction networks, (b) Concentration evolutions. The initial concentration of reactant X is 2 nM. In addition, auxiliaries A_0, B_0 and A_5 are 10000 nM. Reaction rates q_i and q_m are $10^{-6}/\text{nM/s}$ and $10^{-3}/\text{nM/s}$, respectively.

X binds to the auxiliary A_0 to form $sp1$ and $sp2$, then intermediate $sp2$ binds to auxiliary B_0 to form $sp3$ and $2X$ in reaction (2). X and $sp15$ are formed by reactant A_5 and intermediate $sp2$ in reaction (3). By comparing the ideal chemical reaction with DNA strand displacement reactions, $q_i = k_1/C_m$ is given due to $q_i \ll q_m$. It is apparent from Fig. 1 that the dynamic behaviors of DNA CRNs and ideal CRNs are consistent.

The DNA CRNs representations are

$$A_0 + X \xrightarrow{q_i} sp1 + sp2 \tag{1}$$

$$B_0 + sp2 \xrightarrow{q_m} sp3 + 2X \tag{2}$$

$$A_5 + sp2 \xrightarrow{q_m} sp15 + X \tag{3}$$

The ideal CRNs representation is

$$2X \xrightarrow{k_1} 3X \tag{4}$$

The DNA CRNs of multiplication reaction (7) consist of the reactant X, auxiliaries A_0 and B_0. The initial concentration of the reactant X is set to $[X(t_0)]$. Similarly, auxiliaries A_0 and B_0 are set to C_m ($[X(t_0)] \ll C_m$). Due to DNA

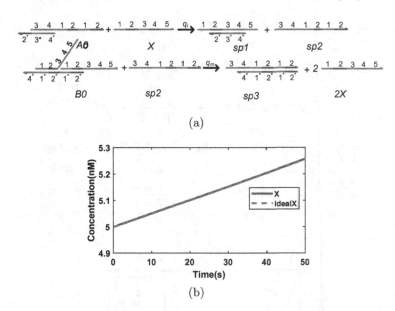

(a)

(b)

Fig. 2. Multiplication reaction (7). (a) DNA chemical reaction networks, (b) Concentration evolutions. The initial concentration of reactant X is 5 nM. In addition, auxiliaries A_0, B_0 are 10000 nM. Reaction rates q_i and q_m are 10^{-6}/nM/s and 10^{-3}/nM/s, respectively.

reaction (5), $d[X(t)]/dt = -q_i C_m [X(t)]$ is given and $d[X(t)]/dt = 2q_m C_m [sp2(t)]$ is obtained from DNA reaction (6). In DNA strand displacement reaction (5), reactant X binds to auxiliary A_0 to form $sp1$ and $sp2$, then intermediate $sp2$ binds to auxiliary B_0 to form X and $sp3$ in reaction (6). By comparing the ideal chemical reaction with DNA strand displacement reactions, $q_i = k_2/C_m$ is given due to $q_i \ll q_m$. It is apparent from Fig. 2 that the dynamic behaviors of DNA CRNs and ideal CRNs are consistent.

The DNA CRNs representations are

$$A_0 + X \xrightarrow{q_i} sp1 + sp2 \tag{5}$$
$$B_0 + sp2 \xrightarrow{q_m} sp3 + 2X \tag{6}$$

The ideal CRNs representation is

$$X \xrightarrow{k_2} 2X \tag{7}$$

The DNA CRNs of combination reaction (13) consist of reactants X, Z, auxiliaries A_{31}, A_{32}, B_3, A_4 and B_4. The initial concentrations of reactants X and Z are set to $[X(t_0)]$ and $[Z(t_0)]$. Similarly, auxiliaries A_{31}, A_{32}, B_3, A_4 and B_4 are set to C_m ($[X(t_0)] \ll C_m$, $[Z(t_0)] \ll C_m$). Due to DNA reaction (8), $d[X(t)]/dt\text{-} = -q_i C_m [X(t)]$ is given. $d[X(t)]/dt = -q_i C_m [X(t)]$ and $d[Z(t)]/dt = q_m C_m [sp10(t)]$ are obtained from DNA reactions (9) and (10), respectively. In

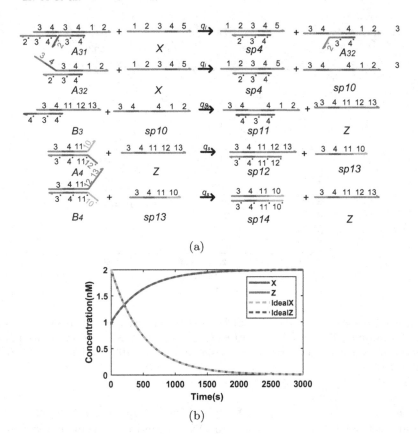

(a)

(b)

Fig. 3. Combination reaction (13). (a) DNA chemical reaction networks, (b) Concentration evolutions. The initial concentrations of reactants X and Z are 2 nM and 1 nM, respectively. In addition, auxiliaries A_{31}, A_{32}, B_3, A_4 and B_4 are 10000 nM. Reaction rates q_i, q_m and q_s are 10^{-6}/nM/s, 10^{-3}/nM/s and 7/nM/s, respectively.

addition, $d[Z(t)]\text{-}/dt = -q_s C_m [Z(t)]$ and $d[Z(t)]/dt = q_s C_m [sp13(t)]$ are obtained from DNA reactions (11) and (12), respectively. In DNA strand displacement reaction (8), reactant X binds to auxiliary A_{31} to form $sp4$ and A_{32}, then intermediate A_{32} binds to reactant X to form $sp4$ and $sp10$ in reaction (9). Z and $sp11$ are formed by intermediate $sp10$ and auxiliary B_3 in reaction (10). In reaction (11), reactant Z binds to auxiliary A_4 to form $sp12$ and $sp13$, then intermediate $sp13$ binds to auxiliary B_4 to form $sp14$ and Z in reaction (12). By comparing the ideal chemical reaction with DNA strand displacement reactions, $q_i = k_3/C_m$ is given due to $q_i \ll q_m$. It is apparent from Fig. 3 that the dynamic behaviors of DNA CRNs and ideal CRNs are consistent.

The DNA CRNs representations are

$$A_{31} + X \xrightarrow{q_i} sp4 + A_{32} \tag{8}$$

$$A_{32} + X \xrightarrow{q_i} sp4 + sp10 \tag{9}$$

$$B_3 + sp10 \xrightarrow{q_m} sp11 + Z \tag{10}$$

$$A_4 + Z \xrightarrow{q_s} sp12 + sp13 \tag{11}$$

$$B_4 + sp13 \xrightarrow{q_s} sp14 + Z \tag{12}$$

The ideal CRNs representation is

$$2X + Z \xrightarrow{k_3} 2Z \tag{13}$$

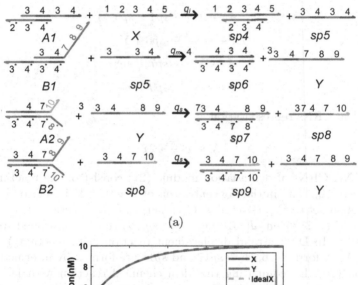

(a)

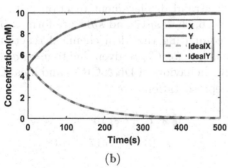

(b)

Fig. 4. Combination reaction (18). (a) DNA chemical reaction networks, (b) Concentration evolutions. The initial concentrations of reactants X and Y are 5 nM. In addition, the auxiliaries A_1, B_1, A_2 and B_2 are 10000 nM. Reaction rates q_i, q_m and q_s are 10^{-6}/nM/s, 10^{-3}/nM/s and 7/nM/s, respectively.

The DNA CRNs of combination module (18) consist of reactants X, Y, auxiliaries A_1, B_1, A_2 and B_2. The initial concentrations of reactants X and Y are set to $[X(t_0)]$ and $[Y(t_0)]$. Similarly, auxiliaries A_1, B_1, A_2 and B_2 are set to C_m, ($[X(t_0)] \ll C_m$, $[Y(t_0)] \ll C_m$). Due to DNA reaction (14), $d[X(t)]/dt = -q_i C_m [X(t)]$ is given. $d[Y(t)]/dt = q_m C_m [sp5(t)]$, $d[Y(t)]/dt = -q_s C_m [Y(t)]$ and $d[Y(t)]/dt = -q_s C_m [sp8(t)]$ are obtained from DNA reactions (15), (16) and (17), respectively. In DNA strand displacement reaction (14), reactant X binds to auxiliary A_1 to form $sp4$ and $sp5$, then intermediate $sp5$ binds to auxiliary B_1 to form Y and $sp6$ in reaction (15). In reaction (16), reactant Y binds to auxiliary A_2 to form $sp7$ and $sp8$, then intermediate $sp8$ binds to auxiliary B_2 to form $sp9$ and Y in reaction (17). By comparing the ideal chemical reaction with DNA strand displacement reactions, $q_i = k_4/C_m$ is given due to $q_i \ll q_m$. It is apparent from Fig. 4 that the dynamic behaviors of DNA CRNs and ideal CRNs are consistent.

The DNA CRNs representations are

$$A_1 + X \xrightarrow{q_i} sp4 + sp5 \tag{14}$$

$$B_1 + sp5 \xrightarrow{q_m} sp6 + Y \tag{15}$$

$$A_2 + Y \xrightarrow{q_s} sp7 + sp8 \tag{16}$$

$$B_2 + sp8 \xrightarrow{q_s} sp9 + Y \tag{17}$$

The ideal CRNs representation is

$$X + Y \xrightarrow{k_4} 2Y \tag{18}$$

The DNA CRNs of degradation module (21) consist of the reactant Y and the auxiliary A_6. The initial concentration of reactant Y is set to $[Y(t_0)]$ and auxiliary A_6 is set to C_m, ($[Y(t_0)] \ll C_m$). Due to DNA reaction (19), $d[Y(t)]/dt = -q_i C_m [Y(t)]$ is given. $d[sp16(t)]/dt = -q_m [sp16(t)]$ is obtained from DNA reaction (20). In DNA strand displacement reaction (19), reactant Y binds to auxiliary A_6 to form $sp16$, then $sp17$ and $sp18$ are formed by intermediate $sp16$ in reaction (20). By comparing the ideal chemical reaction with DNA strand displacement reactions, $q_i = k_5/C_m$ is given due to $q_i \ll q_m$. It is apparent from Fig. 5 that the dynamic behaviors of DNA CRNs and ideal CRNs are consistent.

The DNA CRNs representations are

$$A_6 + Y \xrightarrow{q_i} sp16 \tag{19}$$

$$sp16 \xrightarrow{q_m} sp17 + sp18 \tag{20}$$

The ideal CRNs representation is

$$Y \xrightarrow{k_5} \phi \tag{21}$$

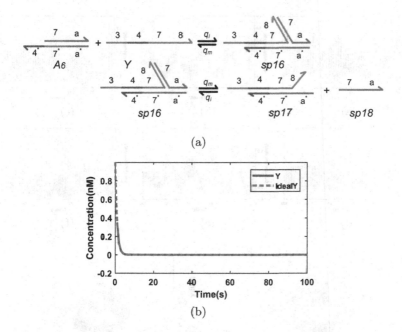

(a)

(b)

Fig. 5. Degradation reaction (21). (a) DNA chemical reaction networks, (b) Concentration evolutions. The initial concentrations of reactant Y is 1 nM and the auxiliary A_6 is 10000 nM. Reaction rates q_i and q_m are 10^{-6}/nM/s and 10^{-3}/nM/s, respectively.

3   Simulation Results

To analyse the performance of our DNA CRNs, the three-variable chaotic system is simulated by Visual DSD and Matlab, respectively. The CRNs are

$$\begin{cases} 2X_1 \xrightarrow{2.1} 3X_1; X_1 \xrightarrow{0.7} 2X_1; Z_1 + 2X_1 \xrightarrow{2.9} 2Z_1 \\ Y_1 + X_1 \xrightarrow{1.1} 2Y_1; Y_1 \xrightarrow{1} \phi; 2Z_1 \xrightarrow{0.5} \phi; Z_1 \xrightarrow{2.7} \phi \end{cases} \tag{22}$$

According to the CRNs (22), the ODEs are

$$\begin{cases} \dot{X}_1 = 2.1X_1^2 + 0.7X_1 - 2.9X_1^2 Z_1 - 1.1X_1 Y_1 \\ \dot{Y}_1 = 1.1X_1 Y_1 - Y_1 \\ \dot{Z}_1 = 2.9X_1^2 Z_1 - 0.5Z_1^2 - 2.7Z_1 \end{cases} \tag{23}$$

The concentration evolutions and chaotic attractors in Matlab and in Visual DSD are given in Fig. 6. It is apparent that they both generate three-variable chaotic oscillatory signals.

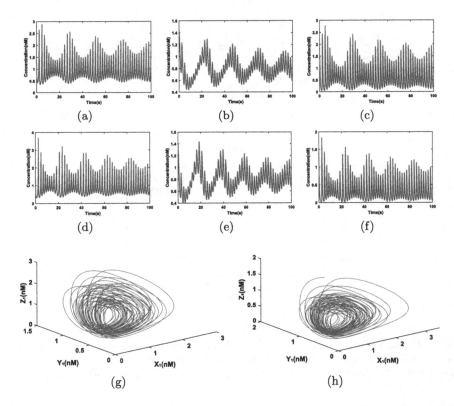

Fig. 6. Simulations of three-variable chaotic system. (a) Time domain waveforms of X_1 in Matlab, (b) Time domain waveforms of Y_1 in Matlab, (c) Time domain waveforms of Z_1 in Matlab, (d) Time domain waveforms of X_1 in Visual DSD, (e) Time domain waveforms of Y_1 in Visual DSD, (f) Time domain waveforms of Z_1 in Visual DSD, (g) Chaotic attractor of $X_1Y_1Z_1$ in Matlab, (h) Chaotic attractor of $X_1Y_1Z_1$ in Visual DSD.

4   Conclutions

In this work, we propose a method for designing a three-variable chaotic oscilla-tory system based on multiplication modules, combination modules and degra-dation modules. These modules are designed by DNA strand displacement reac-tions. In the simulation experiments of Matlab and Visual DSD, our design is proved to be reliable, which can provide reference for the study of chaos theory at the DNA molecular level. Our future work is achieving the PI control of a three-variable chaotic oscillatory system.

References

1. Gunawardena, J.: Chemical reaction network theory for in-silico biologists. Notes available for download at http://vcp.med.harvard.edu/papers/crnt.pdf (2003)
2. Lotka, A.J.: Undamped oscillations derived from the law of mass action. J. Am. Chem. Soc. **42**(8), 1595–1599 (1920)
3. Soliman, S., Heiner, M.: A unique transformation from ordinary differential equations to reaction networks. PloS One **5**(12), 208 (2010)
4. Feinberg, M.: Chemical reaction network structure and the stability of complex isothermal reactors. The deficiency zero and deficiency one theorems. Chem. Eng. Sci. **42**(10), 2229–2268 (1987)
5. Angeli, D.: A tutorial on chemical reaction network dynamics. Euro. J. Control **15**(3–4), 398–406 (2009)
6. Arceo, C.P.P., Jose, E.C., Marin-Sanguino, A., Mendoza, E.R.: Chemical reaction network approaches to biochemical systems theory. Math. Biosci. **269**, 135–152 (2015)
7. Lakin, M.R., Youssef, S., Polo, F., Emmott, S., Phillips, A.: Visual DSD: a design and analysis tool for DNA strand displacement systems. Bioinformatics **27**(22), 3211–3213 (2011)
8. Xing, Y., Yang, Z., Liu, D.: A responsive hidden toehold to enable controllable DNA strand displacement reactions. Angewandte Chemie Int. Edition **50**(50), 11934–11936 (2011)
9. Li, F., Zhang, H., Wang, Z., Li, X., Li, X.F., Le, X.C.: Dynamic DNA assemblies mediated by binding-induced DNA strand displacement. J. Am. Chem. Soc. **135**(7), 2443–2446 (2013)
10. Soloveichik, D., Seelig, G., Winfree, E.: DNA as a universal substrate for chemical kinetics. Proc. National Acad. Sci. **107**(12), 5393–5398 (2010)
11. Zhang, J.X., et al.: Predicting DNA hybridization kinetics from sequence. Nat. Chem. **10**(1), 91–98 (2018)
12. Wang, F., et al.: Implementing digital computing with DNA-based switching circuits. Nat. Commun. **11**(1), 1–8 (2020)
13. Zhang, D.Y., Seelig, G.: Dynamic DNA nanotechnology using strand-displacement reactions. Nat. Chem. **3**(2), 103–113 (2011)
14. Li, W., Yang, Y., Yan, H., Liu, Y.: Three-input majority logic gate and multiple input logic circuit based on DNA strand displacement. Nano Lett. **13**(6), 2980–2988 (2013)
15. Thubagere, A.J., et al.: Compiler-aided systematic construction of large-scale DNA strand displacement circuits using unpurified components. Nat. Commun. **8**(1), 1–12 (2017)
16. Wang, Y., Tian, G., Hou, H., Ye, M., Cui, G.: Simple logic computation based on the DNA strand displacement. J. Comput. Theor. Nanosci. **11**(9), 1975–1982 (2014)
17. Sun, J., Li, X., Cui, G., Wang, Y.: One-bit half adder-half subtractor logical operation based on the DNA strand displacement. J. Nanoelectron. Optoelectron. **12**(4), 375–380 (2017)
18. Li, C., Sprott, J.C., Xing, H.: Constructing chaotic systems with conditional symmetry. Nonlinear Dyn. **87**(2), 1351–1358 (2016). https://doi.org/10.1007/s11071-016-3118-1
19. Pecora, L.M., Carroll, T.L.: Synchronization in chaotic systems. Phys. Rev. Lett. **64**(8), 821 (1990)

20. Aihara, K., Takabe, T., Toyoda, M.: Chaotic neural networks. Phys. Lett. A **144**(6–7), 333–340 (1990)
21. Carroll, T.L., Pecora, L.M.: Synchronizing chaotic circuits. In: Nonlinear Dynamics in Circuits, pp. 215–248. World Scientific (1995)
22. Thompson, J.M.T., Stewart, H.B.: Nonlinear Dynamics and Chaos. Wiley (2002)
23. Guan, Z.H., Huang, F., Guan, W.: Chaos-based image encryption algorithm. Phys. Lett. A **346**(1–3), 153–157 (2005)
24. Schweighofer, N., Doya, K., Fukai, H., Chiron, J.V., Furukawa, T., Kawato, M.: Chaos may enhance information transmission in the inferior olive. Proc. Nat. Acad. Sci. **101**(13), 4655–4660 (2004)
25. Buizza, R.: Chaos and weather prediction january 2000. In: European Centre for Medium-Range Weather Meteorological Training Course Lecture Series ECMWF (2002)
26. Kanter, I., Kopelowitz, E., Kinzel, W.: Public channel cryptography: chaos synchronization and hilbert tenth problem. Phys. Rev. Lett. **101**(8), 101 (2008)
27. Sun, J., Han, G., Zeng, Z., Wang, Y.: Memristor-based neural network circuit of full-function pavlov associative memory with time delay and variable learning rate. IEEE Trans. Cybern. (2019)
28. Sun, J., Wu, Y., Cui, G., Wang, Y.: Finite-time real combination synchronization of three complex-variable chaotic systems with unknown parameters via sliding mode control. Nonlinear Dyn. **88**(3), 1677–1690 (2017). https://doi.org/10.1007/s11071-017-3338-z
29. Sun, J., Yang, Y., Wang, Y., Wang, L., Song, X., Zhao, X.: Survival risk prediction of esophageal cancer based on self-organizing maps clustering and support vector machine ensembles. IEEE Access **8**, 131449–131460 (2020)
30. Sun, J., Zhao, X., Fang, J., Wang, Y.: Autonomous memristor chaotic systems of infinite chaotic attractors and circuitry realization. Nonlinear Dyn. **94**(4), 2879–2887 (2018). https://doi.org/10.1007/s11071-018-4531-4

Reversible Spiking Neural P Systems with Anti-spikes

Suxia Jiang[✉], Yijun Liu, Tao Liang, Bowen Xu, Liying Jiang,
and Yanfeng Wang

School of Electrical and Information Engineering,
Zhengzhou University of Light Industry, Zhengzhou 450002, Henan, China

Abstract. In order to improve the energy efficiency of computers, reversible computing models are proposed. Spiking neural (SN) P systems are a class of bio-inspired computing models, as a matter of course, the reversible spiking neural P systems are constructed, the reversibility and the computational power of SN P systems are investigated. In this paper, we consider reversibility of spiking neural P systems with anti-spikes (ASNP systems, for short) and propose reversible spiking neural P systems with anti-spikes (RASN P systems, for short). Specifically, we prove that RASN P systems with spiking rules of categories $(a, \bar{a})$ and (a, a) without forgetting rules are universal as number generating devices. Change the rule form $(a, \bar{a})$ and (a, a) to $(a, \bar{a})$ and $(\bar{a}, a)$, such systems are proved to be universal. The reversibility of the system is also proved.

Keywords: Bio-inspired computing · Membrane computing · Spiking neural P system · Reversible computing model

1 Introduction

Natural computation is a research field abstracted from observing various biological phenomena in nature. Membrane computing (a new branch of natural computing), a new distributed biological computing model inspired by the structure and function of biological cells, has been proposed (initiated in [1,2]). The computing models is studied in the field of membrane computing are collectively referred to as membrane systems (in short, P systems).

Due to the advantages of distributed parallel computing, the research on membrane computing is also a new force suddenly rises. More and more biological phenomena are discovered and introduced into the membrane system. Inspired by the way neurons in the human brain connect, encode and process information within neurons, and communicate with each other, the spiking neuron P system was proposed in [3] and has become an important research field of membrane computing, such system also are a class of distributed and parallel computing devices. The spiking neuron P system is composed of several neurons (represented by ellipse), which transmit information through the synapse

© Springer Nature Singapore Pte Ltd. 2021
L. Pan et al. (Eds.): BIC-TA 2020, CCIS 1363, pp. 513–533, 2021.
https://doi.org/10.1007/978-981-16-1354-8_37

(represented by directed arcs) according to the number of spikes (represented by singleton a), forgetting rules and spiking rules. SN P systems can be used as computing devices mainly in three ways: generating sets of numbers [3,4], generating strings [5,6], and computing functions [7,8]. SNP systems can be used to (theoretically) solve computationally hard problems in a feasible time (see, e.g., [9,10]). Many variants of SNP systems associated with specific biological features have also been proposed, such as homogenous SNP systems [11], SN P systems with weights [12], time-free SNP systems [13] and SNP systems with astrocytes [14]. Recently, SNP systems have also made progress in application [15–17] Research on the spiking nervous system is continuing and evolving.

Landauer theory in [18] proposed by Landauer in 1961, Landauer believed that unwanted information in computation was a waste that needed produce work to remove, the Landauer theory states that the loss of n bytes of information in the computing process of computing device will generate $nkT \ln 2$ thermodynamic entropy. The traditional computing devices adopts the von Neumann architecture, however, the heat generated by the loss of information is the bottleneck of the development of traditional computers. In order to avoid the loss of computing energy, constructing a reversible computing model is one of the effective methods to improve the computing efficiency of traditional computers. The reversible computing model can trace from the current state of the system to the previous state, thus, it can be realized that there is no loss of information in the calculation process, reducing the energy loss caused by information erasure. Up to now, many models of reversible computation have been constructed, including reversible Turing machine [19], reversible computing universal Turing machine [20], reversible computer embedded in the Thue system [21], Fredkin reversible logic gate [22], computation universal reversible register [23], and so on. Recently, reversible ideas have been introduced into the SN P system [24]. The idea of reversible computation is also introduced into SNP systems in [25].

In this work, we improved the model in [25], a Spiking Neural P Systems with anti-spikes without the delay feature and forgetting rules will be structure. We need to prove the following results: (1) ASNP system with rules of with rules of classifications $(a, \bar{a})$ and (a, a) is reversible and universal as number generating devices; (2) ASNP system with rules of classifications $(a, \bar{a})$ and $(\bar{a}, a)$ is reversible and universal as number generating devices.

2   Preliminaries

It is necessary to some familiarity with basic elements of language theory to better understand, this part of the knowledge can refer to [26], and possess a measure of the theoretical basis of membrane computation, refer to [1]. We here only introduce the necessary prerequisites.

An alphabet V, V^* denotes the set of all finite strings of symbols from V. The empty string is denoted by λ, and the set of all nonempty strings over V is denoted by V^+. When $V = a$ is a singleton, we write simply a^* and a^+ instead of a^* and a^+.

A regular expression over an alphabet V is defined as follows: (1) λ and each $a \in V$ is a regular expression. (2) if E_1 and E_2 are regular expressions over V, then $(E_1)(E_2)$, $(E_1) \cup (E_2)$, and $(E_1)^+$ are regular expressions over V, (3) nothing else is a regular expression over V. With each regular expression E we associate a language $L(E)$, defined in the following way: (1) $L(\lambda) = \{\lambda\}$ and $L(a) = \{a\}$, for all $a \in V$, (2) $L((E_1) \cup (E_2)) = L(E_1) \cup L(E_2)$, $L((E_1)(E_2)) = L(E_1)L(E_2)$, and $L((E_1)^+) = L((E_2)^+)$, for all regular expressions E_1, E_2 over V. Unnecessary parentheses can be omitted when writing a regular expression, and $(E)^+ \cup \{\lambda\}$ can also be written as E^*. By NRE we denote the families of Turing computable sets of numbers. (NRE is the family of length sets of recursively enumerable languages those recognized by Turing machines.

In the universality proofs, the notion of a reversible register machine is used. The detailed description of the reversible register can refer [25]. The reversible register is represented by a register machine $M = \{m, H, l_0, l_H, I\}$. Where m represents the number of registers, H is a finite set of instruction labels in a reversible register, l_0 is the start label, l_H is the halt label, I is a finite set of instructions, each label from H labels the unique instruction from I are of the following four forms:

- l_i: $(CHE(r), l_j, l_k)$(check the number in register, if the number is zero go to instruction l_j, otherwise executed to instruction l_k).
- l_i: $(ADD(r), l_j, l_k)$(ADD instructions: add the number stored in register r by one and execute non-deterministically one of the instructions with labels, l_j, l_k).
- l_i: $(SUB(r), l_j, l_k)$(SUB instructions: subtract 1 from the number stored in register r and execute non-deterministically one of the instructions with labels, l_j, l_k).
- l_h:$HALT$ (stop the compute procedure of register machine).

In a reversible register, for any instruction l_i, if there are more than one instructions which satisfies that l_i is the next instruction to be executed, then there must be only two such instructions. The two instructions operate on the same register. One of the two instructions proceeds to instruction l_i when the value in the register is zero, and the other one proceeds to instruction l_i when the value of the register is positive (greater than zero). The formal description of the reversibility of a register machine is as follows.

For any two different instructions $(l_{i1} : OP(r_1), l_{j1}, l_{k1})$ and $(l_{i2} : OP(r_2), l_{j2}, l_{k2})$ it holds that $l_{j1} \neq l_{j2}$, or if $l_{j1} = l_{j2}$ or $l_{k1} = l_{k2}$, then $OP = CHE$ and $r_1 = r_2$. The configuration of reversible registers is transferred between one-to-one correspondence, that is, in the computation process, any configuration can only uniquely reach the next configuration (The configuration of a register machine at any step is defined by the current instruction and the contents of all registers.)

In the reversible spiking neuron system (In short, RSN P system), at some moment, the number of spikes in each neuron and the open-close status of each neuron contribute to the configuration of the system. A system can transit from one configuration to another by using firing and forgetting rules. Start with the initial configuration, a series of configuration transfer is defined as the computation of system. In the reversible spiking neuron system, the configuration of the system has only one previous configuration at any time, in this way, the system can use the configuration at any time to deduce the previous configuration to avoid information loss. If a configuration can proceed from the initial configuration by a sequence of transitions, then it is called a reachable configuration. The set of all reachable configurations of system Π is denoted by $C(\Pi)$, So the reversible spiking neuron system is defined as: An SN P system Π is called reversible, if for any $c \in (\Pi)$, it has a unique previous configuration. It is necessary for the global transition among configurations of a reversible register machine to be injective [27]. (The configuration of a register machine at any step is defined by the current instructions and the contents of all registers.)

3   Reversible Spiking Neural P Systems with Anti-spikes

The previous section introduced the reader to the basics of regular languages and automata. In this section, we construct a reversible ASNP system of degree $m \geq 1$ in the following form:

$$\Pi = (O, \sigma_1, \sigma_2, \sigma_3, \cdots, \sigma_m, syn, out),$$

- $O = \{a, \bar{a}\}$ is a singleton alphabet, a is called a spike, $\bar{a}$ is called a anti-spike;
- $\sigma_1, \sigma_2, \sigma_3, \cdots, \sigma_m$ are neurons, of the form $\sigma_i = (n_i)$ with $1 \leq i \leq m$, where $n_i \geq 0$ is the number of initial spikes in the neuron σ_i;
- syn is the set of synapses; each element in syn is a pair of the form $((i, j), R_{(i,j)})$, where (i, j) indicates that there is a synapse connecting neurons σ_i and σ_j, with $i, j \in \{1, 2, \cdots, m\}, i \neq j$, and $R_{i,j}$ is a finite set of rules of the following two forms:
  a. $E/b^c \rightarrow b'$, where E is a regular expression over a or $\bar{a}$, while $b, b' \in O$, and $c \geq 1$ (spiking rules);
  b. $b^s \rightarrow \lambda$, Where $b \in 0$ and $s \geq 1$, with the restriction that $b^s \notin L(E)$ for any rule $E/b^c \rightarrow b'$ of type(1) from $R_{i,j}$ (forgetting rules).
- $in, out \in \{1, 2, \cdots, m\}$ indicates the input and output neurons, respectively.

The spiking rules $E/b^c \rightarrow b'$ are used in the following. If the neuron σ_i contains k spikes/anti-spikes, and $b^k \in L(E), k \geq c$, then the rule $E/b^c \rightarrow b'$ can be applied, which means consuming (removing) c spikes/anti-spikes (thus only $k - c$ spikes remain in neuron σ_i), the neuron is fired, and it produces b' spike/anti-spikes immediately (because there's no delay) sent to all neurons σ_i such that $(i, j) \in syn$ if a rule $E/b^c \rightarrow b'$ has $E = b^c$, then it is called pure and written in the simplifed form $b^c \rightarrow b'$.

A forgetting rule $b^s \rightarrow \lambda \in R_{(i,j)}$ is used when the neuron contains exactly s spikes/anti-spikes, and by using the forgetting rule, all s spikes/anti-spikes are removed from the neuron.

The following, we introduce the characteristic properties of the RASN P system: When a spike a and an anti-spike $\bar{a}$ remain in the same neuron, they cannot coexist, instantaneously annihilate each other (both of them will disappear at the same time). Suppose a neuron receives a^r spikes and $(\bar{a})^s$ anti-spikes at same time, the neuron immediately uses the annihilation rule until the applied condition is no longer satisfied, there may be $r - s$ remains in the neuron. It's worth noting that the annihilation rule is instantaneous, It doesn't take any time.

There is a hypothetical global clock in the system, which marks the time for all neurons and synapses. In each unit of time, If neurons can use one of its rules, then this rule must be used. If more rules can be used at the same time, then the use of rules should satisfy the non-deterministic principle (randomly chose one of them to execute). Thus, the rules are used in a sequential manner on each neurons, but each neuron works in parallel. It is restricted that all rules which are applied at any moment should consume the same number of spikes from the given neuron, this way of applying rules is called equal spikes consumption strategy [28].

In the introduction, we recommend concept of system configuration (the number of spikes in each neuron and the open-close status of each neuron). Because of the existence of anti-spikes, the RASN P systems are different from general systems. Because the system does not consider the delay, We can omit the open-close status of each neuron. RASN P system of configuration is donated by $(c_1, c_2, c_3, c_4, c_5, \cdots)$ with $c_i \in Z$ is set of integer, where positive numbers represent the number of spikes, and negative numbers represent the number of anti-spikes. A series of transitions starting from the initial configuration are called computations. A computation halts If there are no rules in the system to use. With any computation, ending up with a spike train, the sequence of symbols 0 and 1 indicating the time interval when the output sends the spike into the environment: 1 indicates a spiking step, 0 indicates a step when no spike exits the system.

The result of computation is the same as the general SNP system. In this work, we consider the time interval between the first two consecutive steps t_1 and t_2 the output neuron spikes, the $t_2 - t_1$ is said to be computed by system Π. The set of all numbers generated in this way is denoted by $N_2(\Pi)$ (the subscript 2 indicates that the computation result is encoded by the time distance between the first two spikes of any computation).

RASN P system can also work in accepting mode. The number n is introduced into the system as a string $10^{n-1}1$. In this way, the number n is equivalent to being received by the system if the computation halts. The set of numbers accepted by system Π is denoted by $N_{acc}(\Pi)$.

We donated by $N_{acc/2}RASNP(cat_p, rule_k, Inh)$, the subscript of N represents the working mode of the system: generating or accepting mode; The subscript p and k represents there are at most two rules and two categories of spiking rules in each neurons; Inh represents inhibitory rules. If only pure form of spiking rules are applied, the indication $rule_k$ is substituted by $prule_k$, and if inhibitory synapses are not used, the indication Inh will be removed from the notation.

4 RASN P Systems with Rules of Classifications $(a, \bar{a})$ and (a, a)

In this section. We prove the RASN P systems with rules of classifications $(a, \bar{a})$ and (a, a) without forgetting rules are universal.

The knowledge of reversible registers is covered in Sect. 2. When register machine M work in the generating mode, and it generates a set of $N(M)$ of numbers in the following way. The initial configuration of register is empty, start with the instruction with label l_0 and proceeds to execute instruction as indicated by the label. If the register machine reaches the halt instruction, then the computation will stop, the value of register 1 at that time is said to be generated by M. The set of number are said Turing computable, hence they characterize NRE.

A register can also be used in the accepting mode, but in this section we only consider the case as an generating mode.

Theorem 1. $N_2RASNP(cate_2, prule_2) = NRE$

Proof. We need to prove that the system without the delay feature and forgetting rules is reversible and universal as number generating devices, the inclusion $N_2RASNP(cate_2, prule_2) \supseteq NRE$ is straightforward, according to $Turing -$ $Church$ thesis, it is adequate to prove the converse inclusion. For the purpose, we use the characterization of NRE by means of reversible register machine applied in generative mode. Let us introduce the reversible register machine $M = \{m, H, l_0, l_h, I\}$. We need to set up a special SNP system Π to simulate the reversible register machine M.

The system is composed of four types of modules: CHE module, ADD module, SUB module, FIN module, the first three modules used to simulate the CHE, ADD, and SUB instructions of M, respectively; the FIN module is used to generate computation result. CHE module, ADD module, SUB module, and FIN module as shown in Fig. 1, Fig. 2, Fig. 3 and Fig. 4 respectively. Each neurons has at most two pure spiking rules of categories of $(a, \bar{a})$ and (a, a), and we dose not use the forgetting rules.

As a rule, neuron σ_r represent each register r of M. The number stored in register r is encoded by the number of spikes present in neuron σ_r. Specifically, if register r holds the number $n \geq 0$, then neuron σ_r contains $n + 2$ spikes. During a computation, if a neuron σ_{l_i} receives one spike, it starts to simulate an instruction $l_i : (OP(r), l_j, l_k)$: proceed from neuron σ_{l_i} firing, it changes or checks the number of spikes in neuron σ_r as instructed by OP, then it transmits one spike into neuron σ_{l_j} or neuron σ_{l_k}, which can be fire in this way. When neuron σ_{l_h} is firing, a computation in M is completely simulated in Π; the FIN module starts to output the computation result (the interval of the first two spikes transmit into the environment by the output neuron corresponds to the number stored in register 1 of M)

- Mode CHE simulating the CHE instruction $l_i : (CHE(r), l_j, l_k)$.

The CHECK instruction is to check the register and execute different instructions based on the results in the register. Let us see the module form Fig. 1. The neuron σ_r retains two spikes in its initial configuration, the number of spikes in the neuron σ_r is greater than 2. At step t, the neuron σ_l receives one spike and begins to simulate the check instruction. The neurons $\sigma_{l_i^{(1)}}$ and $\sigma_{l_i^{(2)}}$ receive one spike at next time, the rule $a \to a$ in the neuron $\sigma_{l_i^{(1)}}$ is fired and send one spike to the neuron $\sigma_{l_i^{(3)}}$, the rule $a \to \bar{a}$ in the neuron $\sigma_{l_i^{(2)}}$ is fired and send one anti-spike to the neuron σ_r. There are two cases as following:

Case I: If the neuron σ_r contain 2 spikes, then the register is empty, the neuron σ_r contain one spike(one spike from neuron σ_r and one anti-spike from neuron $\sigma_{l_i^{(2)}}$ annihilate each other), then the rule $a \to a$ in neurons $\sigma_{l_i^{(3)}}$ and σ_r is fired and send one spike to the neurons $\sigma_{l_i^{(4)}}$, $\sigma_{l_i^{(5)}}$, $\sigma_{l_i^{(6)}}$. At next step, neuron $\sigma_{l_i^{(7)}}$ receives one spike from neuron $\sigma_{l_i^{(4)}}$ and one anti-spike from neuron $\sigma_{l_i^{(6)}}$ and annihilate, hence there is no spike in neuron $\sigma_{l_i^{(7)}}$, in the meantime, neurons $\sigma_{l_i^{(3)}}$ and $\sigma_{l_i^{(3)}}$ sends a spike to neuron $\sigma_{l_i^{(4)}}$ respectively (the CHECK instruction does not change the number of registers). In the next step, neuron $\sigma_{l_i^{(8)}}$ receives one spike from neuron $\sigma_{l_i^{(5)}}$, the rule $a \to a$ is fired and send one spike to neuron σ_j to simulate the instruction l_j.

Case II: If the number of spikes inside the neuron σ_r are great than 2, this means that the register is non-empty. At the step $t+2$, the rule $a \to a$ in the neuron σ_r cannot be activated after receives one anti-spike from neuron $\sigma_{l_i^{(2)}}$, the spike in the neuron σ_r will be reduced by one. The rule $a \to a$ in neuron $\sigma_{l_i^{(3)}}$ is fired and send one spike to $\sigma_{l_i^{(4)}}$, at the next time, neuron $\sigma_{l_i^{(4)}}$ sends one spike to neurons σ_r and $\sigma_{l_i^{(7)}}$. The neuron $\sigma_{l_i^{(7)}}$ sends one spike to the neuron σ_{l_k} to simulate the instruction l_k and returns one spike to the neuron σ_r.

Therefore, the **CHE module** checks if the register is empty by sending one anti-spike to the register. The system fires the neuron σ_{l_j} if the number in register r is 0, otherwise it fires neuron σ_{l_k}.

– Mode ADD simulating the ADD instruction $l_i : (ADD(r), l_j, l_k)$.

Let us assume that at step t, a ADD instruction $l_i : (CHE(r), l_j, l_k)$ has to be simulated. With one spike inside, the rule $a \to a$ in neuron σ_i is empowered, and it fires at t step with sending one spike into neurons $\sigma_{l_i^{(2)}}$, $\sigma_{l_i^{(1)}}$ and σ_r(increment the number of registers r by one). Beacuse of choosing non-deterministically the rule inside neuron $\sigma_{l_i^{(1)}}$, there are following two cases in neuron $\sigma_{l_i^{(1)}}$.

Case I: If the rule $a \to a$ is fired in the neuron $\sigma_{l_i^{(1)}}$ at the step $t+1$, then neuron $\sigma_{l_i^{(3)}}$ received one spike from neuron $\sigma_{l_i^{(1)}}$ and neuron $\sigma_{l_i^{(4)}}$ received one spike from $\sigma_{l_i^{(2)}}$, thus, at step $t+2$, the rule $a \to a$ inside neuron $\sigma_{l_i^{(3)}}$ and the rule $a \to a$ inside neuron $\sigma_{l_i^{(4)}}$ are applied, then one spike is sent to neuron $\sigma_{l_i^{(5)}}$, but the neuron $\sigma_{l_i^{(7)}}$ received two spikes (from neurons $\sigma_{l_i^{(3)}}$ and $\sigma_{l_i^{(4)}}$) that render the rule $a \to a$ unusable, After receiving the spike, neuron $\sigma_{l_i^{(5)}}$ sends one spikes

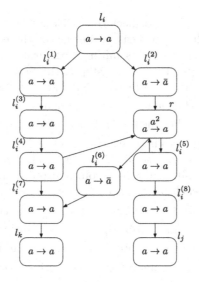

Fig. 1. CHE Module(simulating $l_i : (CHE(r), l_j, l_k)$)

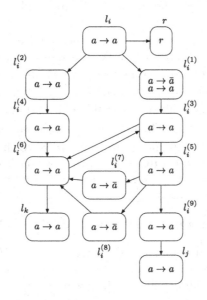

Fig. 2. ADD Module(simulating $l_i : (ADD(r), l_j, l_k)$)

to neuron $\sigma_{l_i^{(7)}}$ and neurons $\sigma_{l_i^{(8)}}$ (two of the anti-spikes sent by neurons $\sigma_{l_i^{(7)}}$ and $\sigma_{l_i^{(8)}}$ annihilate two spikes in neuron $\sigma_{l_i^{(6)}}$), at the same time, $\sigma_{l_i^{(5)}}$ sends one spike to neuron $\sigma_{l_i^{(9)}}$. Then, neuron $\sigma_{l_i^{(9)}}$ sends one spike to neuron σ_{l_j} at $t + 4$. Hence, neuron σ_{l_j} can fire at step $t + 5$ and system starts to simulate instruction l_j of M.

Case II: If the rule $a \to \bar{a}$ is fired in neuron $\sigma_{l_i^{(1)}}$ at the step $t + 1$, then the neuron $\sigma_{l_i^{(3)}}$ receives one anti-spike from neuron $\sigma_{l_i^{(1)}}$, then the rule $a \to a$ is not fired in the neuron $\sigma_{l_i^{(3)}}$, and one spike is sent to neuron $\sigma_{l_i^{(6)}}$. At next step, the neuron $\sigma_{l_i^{(3)}}$ receive one spike from neuron $\sigma_{l_i^{(3)}}$ to counteract the anti-spike inside the neuron $\sigma_{l_i^{(3)}}$, and at the same time, the neuron σ_{l_k} receives one spike and being to simulate instruction l_k of M.

– Mode SUB simulating a SUB instruction $l_i : (SUB(r), l_j, l_k)$.

Because of the **SUB module** uses the same way to make non-deterministic choices with the **ADD module**, the **ADD module** can be reused to simulate the SUB instruction, but we need to add a auxiliary neuron $\sigma_{l_i^{(0)}}$ to subtract 1 from the neuron σ_r. At step t, the rule $a \to a$ inside neuron σ_{l_i} is fired, one spike is sent to the auxiliary neuron $\sigma_{l_i^{(0)}}$, and in next time, one anti-spike is sent to neuron σ_r to counteract one spike (we must make sure that there are spike in the neuron σ_r, hence we need to execute the CHECK instruction before performing the SUB instruction).

– Mode FIN output the result of computation.

When the neuron σ_{l_h} in system receives one spike at some step, which means that the system reaches the halt instruction and start to output the computation result, and neuron σ_1 has $n+2$ spikes (the number of register 1 of M is $n \geq 0$) at that moment. With one spike inside neuron σ_{l_h}, the rule $a \to a$ fired and send one spike to neurons $\sigma_{l_h^{(1)}}$, $\sigma_{l_h^{(2)}}$ and $\sigma_{l_h^{(3)}}$. At step $t + 1$, rule $a \to \bar{a}$ is applied, sending the first anti-spike to neuron σ_1 and this anti-spike immediately annihilates one spike in neuron σ_1 by the annihilating rule $a\bar{a} \to \lambda$, at the same time, the neuron $\sigma_{l_h^{(1)}}$ receives one spike from the neuron $\sigma_{l_h^{(2)}}$, so that the neuron $\sigma_{l_h^{(1)}}$ will continue to send one anti-spike to the neuron σ_1.

At step $t + 2$, the neuron σ_{out} receives the first spike from the neuron $\sigma_{l_i^{(5)}}$, and rule $a \to a$ is applied at the next step, at the same time, the number of spikes inside the neuron σ_r is n. The first spike is sent to the environment by the output neuron at step $t + 3$.

At the step $t + 2$, the rule $a \to a$ in the neurons $\sigma_{l_i^{(2)}}$ and $\sigma_{l_i^{(4)}}$ are applied. Hence, from the step $t + 2$ on, neurons $\sigma_{l_i^{(2)}}$ and $\sigma_{l_i^{(4)}}$ emit one spike to each other at each step, neuron $\sigma_{l_h^{(2)}}$ and neuron $\sigma_{l_i^{(4)}}$ complement each other, at the same time, the rule $a \to \bar{a}$ in the neuron $\sigma_{l_i^{(1)}}$ is applied, continuously sending an anti-spike to neuron σ_1, which annihilates one spike in neuron σ_1 instantly. Starting at step $t + 2$, the spike inside neuron σ_1 decreases by 1 at each step, at step $t+n+1$, neuron σ_1 store one spike ultimately and become fired, at the next time, neurons $\sigma_{l_i^{(2)}}$ and $\sigma_{l_i^{(4)}}$ receive one spike from neuron σ_1, these neuron will stop complementing each other. At the same time, the rule $a \to a$ is also used and one spike is sent to neuron σ_{out}. At step $t+n+3$, neuron σ_{out} contains one spike and emit the second spike to the environment. The interval between these

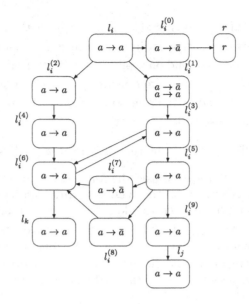

Fig. 3. SUB Module (simulating $l_i : (SUB(r), l_j, l_k)$)

two spike sent out to the environment by the system is $(t + n + 3) - (t + 3) = n$, which is exactly the number stored in register 1 when the computation of M halts.

In a word, it is obvious that the reversible register machine M is correctly simulated by system. Hence we did not use any forgetting rules or delay rules, all rules are of the two categories $(a, \bar{a})$ and (a, a). Therefore, $N_2 RASNP(cate_2, prule_2) = NRE$. Where the categories of spiking rules are $(a, \bar{a})$ and (a, a).

5 RASN P Systems with Rules of Classifications $(a, \bar{a})$ and $(\bar{a}, a)$

In this section, we prove the RASN P systems with rules of classifications $(a, \bar{a})$ and $(\bar{a}, a)$ without forgetting rules are universal. We only use the rules $a \to \bar{a}$ and $\bar{a} \to a$, these two kinds of rules work in the flip-flop way in the sense of changing between spikes an anti-spikes. In the following, we prove that RASN P system that consist of these two kinds of rules can achieve the Turing universality.

Theorem 2. $N_2 RASNP(cate_2, prule_2) = NRE$, where the categories of spiking rules are $(a, \bar{a})$ and $(\bar{a}, a)$.

Proof. Similar to the proof of Theorem 4.1, we construct a particular RASN P system with rules of classifications $(a, \bar{a})$ and $(\bar{a}, a)$ to simulate a reversible register machine $M = \{m, H, l_0, l_h, I\}$. The system Π is composed of CHE

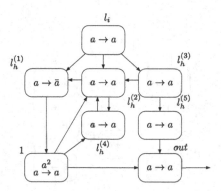

Fig. 4. FIN Module (simulating $l_h : HALT$

modules, SUB modules, ADD modules and FIN modules as shown in Fig. 5, Fig. 6, Fig. 7 and Fig. 8, respectively.

For each register r of M, a neuron σ_r is associated and each label l_i of an instruction in M is also associated with a neuron σ_{l_i}. The number of spikes in neuron σ_r corresponds to the number stored in register r. Especially, a number $n \geq 0$ stored in register 1 is encoded by $n + 2$ spikes, while for register $r \geq 2$, the number of spikes is equal to the value of register r. We think of register 1 as the output register, and the number stored in register 1 is never decremented during any computation. All neurons are empty in the initial configurations, with the exception of neuron σ_1 associated with register 1 and neuron $\sigma_{l_h^{(1)}}$ in the module FIN, which contains two spikes, respectively. During a computation, when neuron σ_{l_i} receives one spike, system Π start to simulate an instruction $l_i : (OP(r), l_j, l_k)$ of M: starting with application of rules inside neuron σ_{l_i}, operating neuron σ_r as demand by OP, then introducing one spike into neuron σ_{l_j} or σ_{l_k}. When neuron σ_{l_h} is useable at certain moment, it means that a computation in M is completely simulate in Π. The neuron σ_{out} will fire twice at step t_1 and t_2, and the time lag $t_2 - t_1$ corresponds to the number stored in register 1 of M.

– Mode CHE simulating the CHE instruction $l_i : (CHE(r), l_j, l_k)$.

At step t, neuron σ_{l_i} receives one spike to simulate a CHE instruction $l_i : (CHE(r), l_j, l_k)$, the rule $a \rightarrow \bar{a}$ is applied, one anti-spike is sent to neurons $\sigma_{l_i^{(1)}}$ and σ_r. We can check whether the number in the register is empty by sending an anti-spike to the neuron σ_r, thus, there are following two case:

Case I: If the neuron σ_r has n spikes (corresponding to that the number stored in register r is n). Then, after one spike is annihilated by the anti-spike from neuron σ_{l_i}, there are no anti-spike in neuron σ_r, the rule $\bar{a} \rightarrow a$ inside the neuron σ_r is not enabled, the number of spikes in neuron σ_r is decreased by one. Similarly, neurons $\sigma_{l_i^{(6)}}$ and $\sigma_{l_i^{(7)}}$ is not fired. Thus the neuron $\sigma_{l_i^{(1)}}$ send one spike to neuron σ_{l_j} through converting between spikes and anti-spikes of the neurons

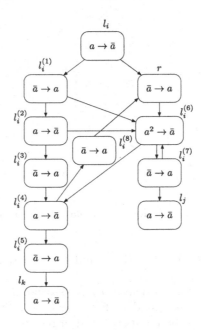

Fig. 5. CHE Module (simulating $l_i : (CHE(r), l_j, l_k)$

$\sigma_{l_i^{(2)}}$, $\sigma_{l_i^{(3)}}$ and $\sigma_{l_i^{(4)}}$, $\sigma_{l_i^{(5)}}$. At step $t + 2$, spike from neuron $\sigma_{l_i^{(2)}}$ and anti-spike from neuron $\sigma_{l_i^{(1)}}$ annihilated. At step $t + 4$, one anti-spike is sent to neuron $\sigma_{l_i^{(8)}}$ to supplementing the spike consumed in the neuron σ_r. Thus, the system starts to simulate instruction l_k of M.

Case II: If the neuron σ_r has no spike at the step t (corresponding to that the number stored in register r is 0), then, the rule $\bar{a} \to a$ inside neuron σ_r is applied at step $t + 1$. At step $t + 2$, neuron $\sigma_{l_i^{(6)}}$ accumulates two spikes (one from neuron $\sigma_{l_i^{(1)}}$ and one from neuron σ_r), then rule $a^2 \to \bar{a}$ is used, sending one anti-spike to neuron $\sigma_{l_i^{(4)}}$ to prevent the system simulate instruction l_j, neuron $\sigma_{l_i^{(7)}}$ also receives a anti-spike from neuron $\sigma_{l_i^{(6)}}$. At the next moment, neuron $\sigma_{l_i^{(7)}}$ sends one anti-spike to annihilate the spike from neuron $\sigma_{l_i^{(2)}}$, At step $t + 3$, neuron $\sigma_{l_i^{(7)}}$ sends one spike to σ_{l_j}, thus, the system starts to simulate instruction l_j of M.

The simulation of CHE instruction check the number of register by sending one anti-spike to neuron σ_r, Therefore, the CHECK module checks if the register is empty by sending one anti-spike to the register. The system fires the neuron σ_{l_j} if the number in register r is 0, otherwise it fires neuron σ_{l_k}.

– Mode ADD simulating the ADD instruction $l_i : (ADD(r), l_j, l_k)$.

When neuron σ_{l_i} receives one spike at t step, a ADD instruction has to be simulated. With one spike inside neuron σ_{l_i}, the rule $a \to \bar{a}$ is applied, neuron

$\sigma_{l_i^{(1)}}$ receives one anti-spike and send one spike to neuron σ_r (increasing the value of register by one). At the moment, neuron $\sigma_{l_i^{(2)}}$ also receives one anti-spike, at step $t+2$, the neurons $\sigma_{l_i^{(5)}}$ receives two anti-spikes and trigger rule to implement nondeterministic selection of instructions. Hence, there are two case in neuron $\sigma_{l_i^{(5)}}$. At step $t+3$, neuron $\sigma_{l_i^{(6)}}$ accept one anti-spike from neuron $\sigma_{l_i^{(4)}}$, hence the rule inside neuron $\sigma_{l_i^{(4)}}$ can not be applied, the anti-spike will remain in the neuron $\sigma_{l_i^{(6)}}$ until one spike enter. Hence, whether neuron $\sigma_{l_i^{(5)}}$ sends one spike or two spike determines whether the system is simulating instruction l_j or l_k (results are non-deterministic). There are two cases as follows.

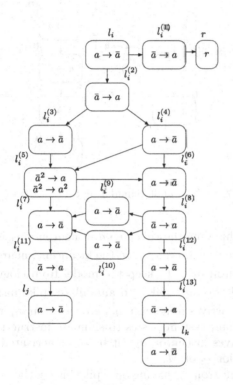

Fig. 6. ADD Module (simulating $l_i : (ADD(r), l_j, l_k)$)

Case I: If the rule $\bar{a}^2 \rightarrow a$ is fired in the neuron $\sigma_{l_i^{(5)}}$ at the step $t+3$, neuron $\sigma_{l_i^{(6)}}$ only accept one spike, which annihilate the anti-spike in neuron $\sigma_{l_i^{(6)}}$, hence, the rule inside neuron $\sigma_{l_i^{(6)}}$ is not be applied. One spike is sent to neuron $\sigma_{l_i^{(7)}}$. The neuron $\sigma_{l_i^{(11)}}$ converts anti-spike from neuron $\sigma_{l_i^{(7)}}$ into one spike and sends it to neuron σ_{l_j} to simulate instruction l_j of M by neuron.

Case II: If the rule $\bar{a}^2 \rightarrow a^2$ is fired in the neuron $\sigma_{l_i^{(5)}}$ at the step $t+3$, neuron $\sigma_{l_i^{(6)}}$ accept two spike, one spike remains after annihilating one anti-spike

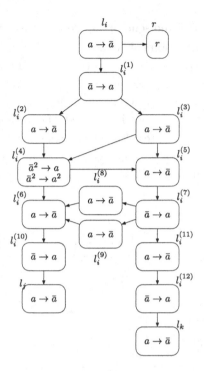

Fig. 7. SUB Module (simulating $l_i : (SUB(r), l_j, l_k))$

in neuron $\sigma_{l_i^{(6)}}$. In this way, the rule $a \rightarrow \bar{a}$ in neuron $\sigma_{l_i^{(6)}}$ is used at step $t + 3$, sending an anti-spike to neuron $\sigma_{l_i^{(8)}}$. In the meantime, neuron $\sigma_{l_i^{(7)}}$ also receives two spikes from neuron $\sigma_{l_i^{(5)}}$, to keep the model from clogging up, the neuron $\sigma_{l_i^{(9)}}$ and $\sigma_{l_i^{(10)}}$ send two anti-spikes to annihilate spike inside neuron $\sigma_{l_i^{(7)}}$. At step $t + 7$, one spike arrives in neuron σ_{l_k}, after neuron σ_{l_k} receives one spike, it becomes activated, and system passes to simulate instruction l_k of M. At step $t + 7$, one spike arrives in neuron σ_{l_k}, it becomes activated, and system passes to simulate instruction l_k of M.

Therefore, from neuron σ_{l_i} having one spike inside, the system adds one spike to neuron σ_r, and one of the two neurons σ_{l_i} and σ_{l_k} receive one spike, which correctly simulate the ADD instruction $l_i : (ADD(r), l_j, l_k)$.

– Mode SUB simulating a SUB instruction $l_i : (SUB(r), l_j, l_k)$.

Same as in the previous section, the SUB module uses the same way to make non-deterministic choices with the ADD module, the ADD module also can be reused to simulate the SUB instruction.

At step t, neuron σ_{l_i} receives one spike and becomes activated, sending one anti-spike to neuron σ_r to subtract the number of spike in neuron σ_r by one (we must make sure that there are spike in the neuron σ_r, hence we need to execute the CHECK instruction before performing the SUB instruction).

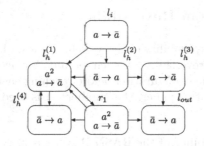

Fig. 8. FIN Module (simulating $l_h : HALT$)

– Mode FIN output the result of computation.

Assume now that the computation in M halts, the halt instruction l_h is reached and the result of computation is placed in register 1, which is never decremented during the computation is placed in register 1. Suppose at step t, neuron σ_1 receives one spike and the number of spikes in neuron σ_1 is $n + 2(n > 0)$, for the number n stored in register 1 of M. With one spike in neuron σ_h, rules $a \to \bar{a}$ are used, sending one anti-spike to neurons $\sigma_{l_h^{(1)}}$ and $\sigma_{l_h^{(2)}}$, respectively. By receiving the one anti-spike, one of the two initial spikes in neuron $\sigma_{l_h^{(1)}}$ is annihilated. At step $t+1$, neuron $\sigma_{l_h^{(1)}}$ ends with one spike inside and rule $a \to \bar{a}$ is used, sending an anti-spike to neuron $\sigma_{l_h^{(4)}}$. Simultaneously, rule $a \to \bar{a}$ is applied, and one anti-spike is sent to neuron σ_1, and this is the first anti-spike arriving σ_1 in neuron σ_1, which immediately annihilates one spike in neuron σ_1 by the annihilating rule $a\bar{a} \to \lambda$, corresponding to that the number of spikes in neuron σ_1 is decreased by one. With one anti-spike in neuron $\sigma_{l_h^{(2)}}$, rules $\bar{a} \to a$ is applied sending one spike to neurons $\sigma_{l_h^{(3)}}$, respectively. At step $t+2$, an anti-spike arrives in neuron σ_{out} from neuron $\sigma_{l_h^{(3)}}$ and rule $a \to \bar{a}$ on the synapse pointing to the environment is applied. The first spike is sent to the environment by the output neuron at step $t+3$.

From step $t+2$ on, at each step, rule $a \to \bar{a}$ is used sending one anti-spike to neuron $\sigma_{l_h^{(4)}}$, and rule $a \to \bar{a}$ is applied emiting one spike to neuron σ, so neurons $\sigma_{l_h^{(1)}}$ and $\sigma_{l_h^{(4)}}$ keep activated. In this way, at each step, rule $a \to \bar{a}$ is also applied, and one anti-spike is continuously sent to neuron $\sigma_{l_h^{(4)}}$, and this anti-spike annihilating a spike in neuron σ_1. At step $t+n+1$, neuron σ_1 ends with one spike inside and rules $a \to \bar{a}$.

From the above description of the modules and their work, it is clear that the reversible register machine M is correctly simulated by system Π. Therefore, it is obtained $N(\Pi) = N(M)$. In the following, we prove that system Π is reversible during the simulation of the computation of M.

6   Proof of System Reversibility

In order to prove the reversibility of the system, First we have to prove that each model of the system is reversible. For each module, We need to demonstrate that the system has a unique configuration before reaching each configuration during the transformation. In this paper, the number -1 is used to represent the anti-spikes in neurons.

– Proof of the reversibility of the RASN P systems of classifications $(a, \bar{a})$ and (a, a)

For the transitions of the **CHE module**, if the number in register r is $n > 0$, the transitions of the module is

$$< \sigma_i, \sigma_r, \sigma_{l_i^{(1)}}, \sigma_{l_i^{(2)}}, \sigma_{l_i^{(3)}}, \sigma_{l_i^{(4)}}, \sigma_{l_i^{(5)}}, \sigma_{l_i^{(6)}}, \sigma_{l_i^{(7)}}, \sigma_{l_i^{(8)}}, \sigma_j, \sigma_k >$$
$$\Rightarrow < 1, n + 2, 0, 0, 0, 0, 0, 0, 0, 0, 0, 0 >$$
$$\Rightarrow < 0, n + 2, 1, 1, 0, 0, 0, 0, 0, 0, 0, 0 >$$
$$\Rightarrow < 0, n + 1, 0, 0, 1, 0, 0, 0, 0, 0, 0, 0 >$$
$$\Rightarrow < 0, n + 1, 0, 0, 0, 1, 0, 0, 0, 0, 0, 0 >$$
$$\Rightarrow < 0, n + 2, 0, 0, 0, 0, 0, 0, 1, 0, 0, 0 >$$
$$\Rightarrow < 0, n + 2, 0, 0, 0, 0, 0, 0, 0, 0, 1, 0 >$$

If the number in register r is $n = 0$, the transitions of the module is

$$< \sigma_i, \sigma_r, \sigma_{l_i^{(1)}}, \sigma_{l_i^{(2)}}, \sigma_{l_i^{(3)}}, \sigma_{l_i^{(4)}}, \sigma_{l_i^{(5)}}, \sigma_{l_i^{(6)}}, \sigma_{l_i^{(7)}}, \sigma_{l_i^{(8)}}, \sigma_j, \sigma_k >$$
$$\Rightarrow < 1, 2, 0, 0, 0, 0, 0, 0, 0, 0, 0, 0 >$$
$$\Rightarrow < 0, 2, 1, 1, 0, 0, 0, 0, 0, 0, 0, 0 >$$
$$\Rightarrow < 0, 1, 0, 0, 1, 0, 0, 0, 0, 0, 0, 0 >$$
$$\Rightarrow < 0, 0, 0, 0, 0, 1, 1, 1, 0, 0, 0, 0 >$$
$$\Rightarrow < 0, 2, 0, 0, 0, 0, 0, 0, 0, 1, 0, 0 >$$
$$\Rightarrow < 0, 2, 0, 0, 0, 0, 0, 0, 0, 0, 0, 1 >$$

For the transitions of the **ADD module**, if the number in register r is n, there are two cases. If the rule $a \to \bar{a}; 0$ is fired in the neuron $\sigma_{l_i^{(1)}}$ at the step $t + 1$, then the transitions of the module is

$$< \sigma_i, \sigma_r, \sigma_{l_i^{(1)}}, \sigma_{l_i^{(2)}}, \sigma_{l_i^{(3)}}, \sigma_{l_i^{(4)}}, \sigma_{l_i^{(5)}}, \sigma_{l_i^{(6)}}, \sigma_{l_i^{(7)}}, \sigma_{l_i^{(8)}}, \sigma_{l_i^{(9)}}, \sigma_j, \sigma_k >$$
$$\Rightarrow < 1, n + 2, 0, 0, 0, 0, 0, 0, 0, 0, 0, 0, 0 >$$
$$\Rightarrow < 0, n + 3, 1, 1, 0, 0, 0, 0, 0, 0, 0, 0, 0 >$$
$$\Rightarrow < 0, n + 3, 0, 0, -1, 1, 0, 0, 0, 0, 0, 0, 0 >$$
$$\Rightarrow < 0, n + 3, 0, 0, -1, 0, 0, 1, 0, 0, 0, 0, 0 >$$
$$\Rightarrow < 0, n + 3, 0, 0, 0, 0, 0, 0, 0, 0, 0, 1, 0 >$$

If the rule $a \rightarrow a; 0$ is fired in the neuron $\sigma_{l_i^{(1)}}$ at the step $t+1$, then the transitions of the module is

$$< \sigma_i, \sigma_r, \sigma_{l_i^{(1)}}, \sigma_{l_i^{(2)}}, \sigma_{l_i^{(3)}}, \sigma_{l_i^{(4)}}, \sigma_{l_i^{(5)}}, \sigma_{l_i^{(6)}}, \sigma_{l_i^{(7)}}, \sigma_{l_i^{(8)}}, \sigma_{l_i^{(9)}}, \sigma_j, \sigma_k >$$
$$\Rightarrow < 1, n+2, 0, 0, 0, 0, 0, 0, 0, 0, 0, 0, 0 >$$
$$\Rightarrow < 0, n+3, 1, 1, 0, 0, 0, 0, 0, 0, 0, 0, 0 >$$
$$\Rightarrow < 0, n+3, 0, 0, 1, 1, 0, 0, 0, 0, 0, 0, 0 >$$
$$\Rightarrow < 0, n+3, 0, 0, 0, 0, 1, 2, 0, 0, 0, 0, 0 >$$
$$\Rightarrow < 0, n+3, 0, 0, 0, 0, 0, 0, 2, 1, 1, 1, 0, 0 >$$
$$\Rightarrow < 0, n+3, 0, 0, 0, 0, 0, 0, 0, 0, 0, 0, 1 >$$

The **SUB module** is the same as the **ADD module**, there are two cases.

$$< \sigma_i, \sigma_r, \sigma_{l_i^{(0)}}, \sigma_{l_i^{(1)}}, \sigma_{l_i^{(2)}}, \sigma_{l_i^{(3)}}, \sigma_{l_i^{(4)}}, \sigma_{l_i^{(5)}}, \sigma_{l_i^{(6)}}, \sigma_{l_i^{(7)}}, \sigma_{l_i^{(8)}}, \sigma_{l_i^{(9)}}, \sigma_j, \sigma_k >$$
$$\Rightarrow < 1, n+2, 0, 0, 0, 0, 0, 0, 0, 0, 0, 0, 0, 0 >$$
$$\Rightarrow < 0, n+2, 1, 1, 1, 0, 0, 0, 0, 0, 0, 0, 0, 0 >$$
$$\Rightarrow < 0, n+1, 0, 0, 0, -1, 1, 1, 0, 0, 0, 0, 0, 0 >$$
$$\Rightarrow < 0, n+1, 0, 0, 0, -1, 0, 0, 1, 0, 0, 0, 0, 0 >$$
$$\Rightarrow < 0, n+1, 0, 0, 0, 0, 0, 0, 0, 0, 0, 0, 0, 1 >$$

or

$$< \sigma_i, \sigma_r, \sigma_{l_i^{(0)}}, \sigma_{l_i^{(1)}}, \sigma_{l_i^{(2)}}, \sigma_{l_i^{(3)}}, \sigma_{l_i^{(4)}}, \sigma_{l_i^{(5)}}, \sigma_{l_i^{(6)}}, \sigma_{l_i^{(7)}}, \sigma_{l_i^{(8)}}, \sigma_{l_i^{(9)}}, \sigma_j, \sigma_k >$$
$$\Rightarrow < 1, n+2, 0, 0, 0, 0, 0, 0, 0, 0, 0, 0, 0, 0 >$$
$$\Rightarrow < 0, n+2, 1, 1, 1, 0, 0, 0, 0, 0, 0, 0, 0, 0 >$$
$$\Rightarrow < 0, n+1, 0, 0, 0, 1, 1, 0, 0, 0, 0, 0, 0, 0 >$$
$$\Rightarrow < 0, n+1, 0, 0, 0, 0, 0, 1, 2, 0, 0, 0, 0, 0 >$$
$$\Rightarrow < 0, n+1, 0, 0, 0, 0, 0, 0, 2, 1, 1, 1, 0, 0 >$$
$$\Rightarrow < 0, n+1, 0, 0, 0, 0, 0, 0, 0, 0, 0, 0, 1, 0 >$$

The transitions of the **FIN module** are as follows:

$$< \sigma_i, \sigma_r, \sigma_{l_h^{(1)}}, \sigma_{l_h^{(2)}}, \sigma_{l_h^{(3)}}, \sigma_{l_h^{(4)}}, \sigma_{l_h^{(5)}}, \sigma_{out} >$$
$$\Rightarrow < 1, n+2, 0, 0, 0, 0, 0, 0 >$$
$$\Rightarrow < 0, n+2, 1, 1, 1, 0, 0, 0 >$$
$$\Rightarrow < 0, n+1, 1, 1, 0, 1, 1, 0 >$$
$$\Rightarrow < 0, n, 1, 1, 0, 1, 0, 1 >$$
$$\Rightarrow < 0, n-1, 1, 1, 0, 1, 0, 0 >$$
$$\Rightarrow \cdots \Rightarrow$$
$$\Rightarrow < 0, 1, 1, 1, 0, 1, 0, 0 >$$
$$\Rightarrow < 0, -1, 1, 0, 0, 0, 0, 1 >$$

During the transitions of outputting the computed result, system Π is reversible.

Therefore, Under the condition of not using the delay rule and forgetting rule, the RASN P system of classifications $(a, \bar{a})$ and (a, a) is reversible.

- Proof of the reversibility of the RASN P systems of classifications $(a, \bar{a})$ and (a, a)

If the number in register r is $n = 0$, the transitions of the **CHE module** is

$$< \sigma_i, \sigma_r, \sigma_{l_i^{(1)}}, \sigma_{l_i^{(2)}}, \sigma_{l_i^{(3)}}, \sigma_{l_i^{(4)}}, \sigma_{l_i^{(5)}}, \sigma_{l_i^{(6)}}, \sigma_{l_i^{(7)}}, \sigma_{l_i^{(8)}}, \sigma_j, \sigma_k >$$
$$\Rightarrow < 1, 0, 0, 0, 0, 0, 0, 0, 0, 0, 0, 0 >$$
$$\Rightarrow < 0, -1, -1, 0, 0, 0, 0, 0, 0, 0, 0, 0 >$$
$$\Rightarrow < 0, 0, 0, 1, 0, 0, 0, 2, 0, 0, 0, 0 >$$
$$\Rightarrow < 0, 0, 0, 0, -1, -1, 0, -1, -1, 0, 0, 0 >$$
$$\Rightarrow < 0, 0, 0, 0, 0, 0, 0, 0, 0, 0, 1, 0 >$$

If the number in register r is $n > 0$

$$< \sigma_i, \sigma_r, \sigma_{l_i^{(1)}}, \sigma_{l_i^{(2)}}, \sigma_{l_i^{(3)}}, \sigma_{l_i^{(4)}}, \sigma_{l_i^{(5)}}, \sigma_{l_i^{(6)}}, \sigma_{l_i^{(7)}}, \sigma_{l_i^{(8)}}, \sigma_j, \sigma_k >$$
$$\Rightarrow < 1, n, 0, 0, 0, 0, 0, 0, 0, 0, 0, 0 >$$
$$\Rightarrow < 0, n-1, -1, 0, 0, 0, 0, 0, 0, 0, 0, 0 >$$
$$\Rightarrow < 0, n-1, 0, 1, 0, 0, 0, 1, 0, 0, 0, 0 >$$
$$\Rightarrow < 0, n-1, 0, 0, -1, 0, 0, 0, 0, 0, 0, 0 >$$
$$\Rightarrow < 0, n-1, 0, 0, 0, 1, 0, 0, 0, 0, 0, 0 >$$
$$\Rightarrow < 0, n-1, 0, 0, 0, 0, -1, 0, 0, -1, 0, 0 >$$
$$\Rightarrow < 0, n, 0, 0, 0, 0, 0, 0, 0, 0, 0, 1 >$$

For the transitions of the **ADD module**, if the rule $\bar{a}^2 \to a$ is fired, then the transitions of the module is

$$< \sigma_i, \sigma_r, \sigma_{l_i^{(1)}}, \sigma_{l_i^{(2)}}, \sigma_{l_i^{(3)}}, \sigma_{l_i^{(4)}}, \sigma_{l_i^{(5)}}, \sigma_{l_i^{(6)}}, \sigma_{l_i^{(7)}}, \sigma_{l_i^{(8)}}, \sigma_{l_i^{(9)}}, \sigma_{l_i^{(10)}}, \sigma_{l_i^{(11)}}, \sigma_{l_i^{(12)}}, \sigma_{l_i^{(13)}}, \sigma_j, \sigma_k >$$
$$\Rightarrow < 1, n, 0, 0, 0, 0, 0, 0, 0, 0, 0, 0, 0, 0, 0, 0, 0 >$$
$$\Rightarrow < 0, n, -1, -1, 0, 0, 0, 0, 0, 0, 0, 0, 0, 0, 0, 0, 0 >$$
$$\Rightarrow < 0, n, 0, 0, 0, 0, -2, -1, 0, 0, 0, 0, 0, 0, 0, 0, 0 >$$
$$\Rightarrow < 0, n, 0, 0, 0, 0, 0, 0, 1, 0, 0, 0, 0, 0, 0, 0, 0 >$$
$$\Rightarrow < 0, n, 0, 0, 0, 0, 0, 0, 0, 0, 0, 0, 0, 1, 0, 0, 0, 0 >$$
$$\Rightarrow < 0, n, 0, 0, 0, 0, 0, 0, 0, 0, 0, 0, 0, 0, 0, 1, 0 >$$

If the rule $\bar{a}^2 \to a$ is fired, then the transitions of the module is

$$< \sigma_i, \sigma_r, \sigma_{l_i^{(1)}}, \sigma_{l_i^{(2)}}, \sigma_{l_i^{(3)}}, \sigma_{l_i^{(4)}}, \sigma_{l_i^{(5)}}, \sigma_{l_i^{(6)}}, \sigma_{l_i^{(7)}}, \sigma_{l_i^{(8)}}, \sigma_{l_i^{(9)}}, \sigma_{l_i^{(10)}}, \sigma_{l_i^{(11)}}, \sigma_{l_i^{(12)}}, \sigma_{l_i^{(13)}}, \sigma_j, \sigma_k >$$
$$\Rightarrow < 1, n, 0, 0, 0, 0, 0, 0, 0, 0, 0, 0, 0, 0, 0, 0, 0 >$$
$$\Rightarrow < 0, n, -1, -1, 0, 0, 0, 0, 0, 0, 0, 0, 0, 0, 0, 0, 0 >$$
$$\Rightarrow < 0, n, 0, 0, 0, 0, -2, -1, 0, 0, 0, 0, 0, 0, 0, 0, 0 >$$
$$\Rightarrow < 0, n, 0, 0, 0, 0, 0, 1, 2, 0, 0, 0, 0, 0, 0, 0, 0 >$$
$$\Rightarrow < 0, n, 0, 0, 0, 0, 0, 0, 2, -1, 0, 0, 0, 0, 0, 0, 0 >$$
$$\Rightarrow < 0, n, 0, 0, 0, 0, 0, 0, 2, 0, 1, 1, 0, 1, 0, 0, 0 >$$
$$\Rightarrow < 0, n, 0, 0, 0, 0, 0, 0, 0, 0, 0, 0, 0, 0, -1, 0, 0 >$$
$$\Rightarrow < 0, n, 0, 0, 0, 0, 0, 0, 0, 0, 0, 0, 0, 0, -1, 0, 0 >$$
$$\Rightarrow < 0, n, 0, 0, 0, 0, 0, 0, 0, 0, 0, 0, 0, 0, 0, 0, 1 >$$

The transitions of the **SUB module** is

$< \sigma_i, \sigma_r, \sigma_{l_i^{(1)}}, \sigma_{l_i^{(2)}}, \sigma_{l_i^{(3)}}, \sigma_{l_i^{(4)}}, \sigma_{l_i^{(5)}}, \sigma_{l_i^{(6)}}, \sigma_{l_i^{(7)}}, \sigma_{l_i^{(8)}}, \sigma_{l_i^{(9)}}, \sigma_{l_i^{(10)}}, \sigma_{l_i^{(11)}}, \sigma_{l_i^{(12)}}, \sigma_j, \sigma_k >$

$\Rightarrow < 1, n, 0, 0, 0, 0, 0, 0, 0, 0, 0, 0, 0, 0, 0, 0 >$

$\Rightarrow < 0, n-1, -1, 0, 0, 0, 0, 0, 0, 0, 0, 0, 0, 0, 0, 0 >$

$\Rightarrow < 0, n-1, 0, 1, 1, 0, 0, 0, 0, 0, 0, 0, 0, 0, 0, 0 >$

$\Rightarrow < 0, n-1, 0, 0, 0, -2, -1, 0, 0, 0, 0, 0, 0, 0, 0, 0 >$

$\Rightarrow < 0, n-1, 0, 0, 0, 0, 0, 1, 0, 0, 0, 0, 0, 0, 0, 0 >$

$\Rightarrow < 0, n-1, 0, 0, 0, 0, 0, 0, 0, 0, 0, 1, 0, 0, 0, 0 >$

$\Rightarrow < 0, n-1, 0, 0, 0, 0, 0, 0, 0, 0, 0, 0, 0, 0, 1, 0 >$

or

$< \sigma_i, \sigma_r, \sigma_{l_i^{(1)}}, \sigma_{l_i^{(2)}}, \sigma_{l_i^{(3)}}, \sigma_{l_i^{(4)}}, \sigma_{l_i^{(5)}}, \sigma_{l_i^{(6)}}, \sigma_{l_i^{(7)}}, \sigma_{l_i^{(8)}}, \sigma_{l_i^{(9)}}, \sigma_{l_i^{(10)}}, \sigma_{l_i^{(11)}}, \sigma_{l_i^{(12)}}, \sigma_j, \sigma_k >$

$\Rightarrow < 1, n, 0, 0, 0, 0, 0, 0, 0, 0, 0, 0, 0, 0, 0, 0 >$

$\Rightarrow < 0, n-1, 0, 1, 1, 0, 0, 0, 0, 0, 0, 0, 0, 0, 0, 0 >$

$\Rightarrow < 0, n-1, 0, 0, 0, -2, -1, 0, 0, 0, 0, 0, 0, 0, 0, 0 >$

$\Rightarrow < 0, n-1, 0, 0, 0, 0, 1, 2, 0, 0, 0, 0, 0, 0, 0, 0 >$

$\Rightarrow < 0, n-1, 0, 0, 0, 0, 0, 2, -1, 0, 0, 0, 0, 0, 0, 0 >$

$\Rightarrow < 0, n-1, 0, 0, 0, 0, 0, 0, 2, 0, 1, 1, 0, 1, 0, 0, 0 >$

$\Rightarrow < 0, n-1, 0, 0, 0, 0, 0, 0, 0, 0, 0, 0, 0, 0, 1, 0, 0 >$

$\Rightarrow < 0, n-1, 0, 0, 0, 0, 0, 0, 0, 0, 0, 0, 0, 0, 0, 1 >$

The transitions of the **FIN module** is

$$< \sigma_i, \sigma_r, \sigma_{l_h^{(1)}}, \sigma_{l_h^{(2)}}, \sigma_{l_h^{(3)}}, \sigma_{l_h^{(4)}}, \sigma_{out} >$$
$$\Rightarrow < 1, n+2, 2, 0, 0, 0, 0 >$$
$$\Rightarrow < 0, n+2, 1, -1, 0, 0, 0 >$$
$$\Rightarrow < 0, n+1, 1, 0, 1, -1, 0 >$$
$$\Rightarrow < 0, n, 1, 0, 1, -1, 0 >$$
$$\Rightarrow < 0, n-1, 1, 0, 0, -1, 0 >$$
$$\Rightarrow \cdots \Rightarrow$$
$$\Rightarrow < 0, 1, 1, 0, 0, -1, 0 >$$
$$\Rightarrow < 0, -1, 0, 0, 0, -2, -1 >$$

During the transitions of outputting the computed result, the system Π is reversible.

Therefore, under the condition of not using the delay rule and forgetting rule, a ASNP system of classifications $(a, \bar{a})$ and $(\bar{a}, a)$ is reversible.

In the above proof, we simulate the reversible register machine to achieve the universality of reversible **SNP** systems.

7   Conclusions and Remarks

In this work, we have proved that RASNP systems with rules on synapses are Turing universal as number generating devices with bounded (or pure) spiking rules and without forgetting rules; Based on these universal results, it can be interpreted that the introduction of the anti-matter can make the non-deterministic selection of traditional spiking neural systems more straightforward; The introduction of the anti-matter can make the traditional reversible SNP system do not use the delay rule and forgetting rule; The research idea of reversible spiking neural membrane system is extended and more kinds of system can be designed. Specifically, the most important is to use the RASN P systems to simulate the reversible register machine, to prove the system is reversible. The systems still have universality and reversibility, without using the forgetting rule and delay rule. This can solve the computation process of unnecessary energy loss.

For further research, a system with fewer neurons could be designed to compensate for the excess of neurons in this system. It is also interesting to design small universal and weakly-small universal reversible SN P systems. Finding more results of reversible SN P systems need to be investigated, especially in the field of application The reversibility in some other variant of P systems, such as tissue-like P systems, also deserves further investigation. Whether other working patterns can be used to build reversible P systems is also a topic worth studying.

Acknowledgments. The work was supported by National Natural Science Foundation of China (61902360, 61772214), and the Foundation of Young Key Teachers from University of Henan Province (2019GGJS131), and Program for Innovative Research Team (in Science and Technology) in University of Henan Province 20IRTSTHN017). The work of Y. Wang was supported by the National Key R and D Program of China for International S and T Cooperation Projects (2017YFE0103900), the Joint Funds of the National Natural Science Foundation of China (U1804262), and the State Key Program of National Natural Science Foundation of China (61632002).

References

1. Păun, G.: Computing with membranes. J. Comput. Syst. Sci. **61**(1), 108–143 (2000)
2. Leporati, A., Manzoni, L., Mauri, G., Porreca, A.E., Zandron, C.: Monodirectional P systems. Nat. Comput. **15**(4), 551–564 (2016)
3. Ionescu, T.Y.M., Păun, G.: Spiking neural P systems. Fundamenta Informaticae **71**(2,3), pp. 279–308 (2006)
4. Păun, G., Mario, J., Rozenberg, G.: Spike trains in spiking neural P systems. Int. J. Found. Comput. Sci. **17**(4), 974–1002 (2006)
5. Chen, H., Freund, R., Ionescu, M.: On string languages generated by spiking neural P systems. Fundamenta Informaticae **75**(1), 141–162 (2008)
6. Zhang, X., Zeng, X., Pan, L.: On string languages generated by spiking neural P systems with exhaustive use of rules. Nat. Comput. **75**(1), 141–162 (2007)
7. Păun, G., Păun, A.: Small universal spiking neural P systems. Biosystems **90**(1), 48–60 (2007)
8. Zeng, X., Pan, L.: Small universal spiking neural P systems working in exhaustive mode. IEEE Trans. Nanobioscience **10**(2), 99–105 (2011)
9. Ishdorj, T., Leporati, A., Pan, L., Zeng, X., Zhang, X.: Deterministic solutions to QSAT and Q3SAT by spiking neural P systems with precomputed resources. Theoret. Comput. Sci. **411**(25), 2345–2358 (2010)

10. Pan, L., Păun, G., Pérez-Jiménez, M.: Spiking neural P systems with neuron division and budding. Sci. China Inf. Sci. **54**(8), 1596–1607 (2011)
11. Zeng, X., Zhang, X., Pan, L.: Homogeneous spiking neural P systems. Fundamenta Informaticae **97**(1), 275–294 (2009)
12. Wang, J., Hoogeboom, H., Pan, L., Paun, G., Pérez-Jiménez, M.: Spiking neural P systems with weights. Neural Comput. **22**(10), 2615–2646 (2010)
13. Pan, L., Zeng, X., Zhang, X.: Time-free spiking neural P systems. Neural Comput. **23**(5), 1320–1342 (2011)
14. Pan, L., Wang, J., Hoogeboom, H.: Spiking neural P systems with astrocytes. Neural Comput. **24**(3), 805–825 (2012)
15. Yu, D.Z.C., Lian, Q., Wu, C.: PAME: evolutionary membrane computing for virtual network embedding. Parallel Distrib. Comput. **111**(2), 136–151 (2018)
16. Orozco-Rosas, O.M.U., Sepúlveda, R.: Mobile robot path planning using membrane evolutionary artificial potential field. Appl. Soft. Comput. **77**(1), 236–251 (2019)
17. Song, T.W.P.Z.M.L.D.W.T., Pan, L., Rodriguez-Paton, A.: Spiking neural P systems with learning functions. IEEE Trans. Nanobiosci. **18**(2), 196–190 (2019)
18. Landauer, R.: Irreversibility and heat generation in the computing process. IBM J. Res. Dev. **5**(3), 183–191 (1961)
19. Bennett, C.: Logical reversibility of computation. IBM J. Res. Dev. **17**(6), 525–532 (1973)
20. Morita, K., Yamaguchi, Y.: A universal reversible turing machine, Computations, and Universality, pp. 90–98 (2007)
21. Priese, L.: On a simple combinatorial structure sufficient for sublying nontrival self-reproduction. J. Cybernet. **6**, 101–137 (1976)
22. Fredkin, E., Toffoli, T.: Conservative logic. Int. J. Theoret. Phys. **21**(3), 219–253 (1982)
23. Toffoli, T., Margolus, N.H.: Invertible cellular automata: a review. Physica D Nonlinear Phenomena **45**(1), 229–253 (1990)
24. Leporati, A., Zandron, C., Mauri, G.: Reversible P systems to simulate Fredkin circuits. Fundamenta Informaticae **74**(4), 529–548 (2006)
25. Tao, S.O.N.G., Xiaolong, S.H.I., Jinbang, X.U.: Reversible spiking neural P systems. Front. Comput. Sci. **7**(3), 350–358 (2013)
26. Rozenberg, G., Salomaa, A.: Handbook of Formal Languages, vol. 1–3. Springer, Berlin (1997)
27. Minsky, M.: Computation: Finite and Infinite Machines. Prentice-Hall, Englewood Cliffs (1967)
28. Song, T., Pan, L., Păun, G.: Spiking neural P systems with rules on synapses. Theoret. Comput. Sci. **529**, 82–95 (2014)

Multi-Objective Algorithm Based on Tissue P System for Solving Tri-objective Grain Dispatching and Transportation

Zhixin He[1] , Kang Zhou[1]([✉]) , Hang Shu[1], Jian Zhou[2], Xinyu Lyu[1] ,
and Guangbin Li[3]

[1] College of Mathematics and Computer Science,
Wuhan Polytechnic University, Wuhan 430023, China
zhoukang65@whpu.edu.cn
[2] School of Food Science and Engineering,
Wuhan Polytechnic University, Wuhan 430023, China
[3] Qianjiang Jujin Rice Industry Co., Ltd.,
Enterprise-School Joint Innovation Center, Hubei, China

Abstract. This paper presents a multi-objective algorithm based on tissue P system(MO TPS for short) for solving the tri-objective grain dispatching and transportation. This problem can be abstracted to solve the tri-objective VRPTW. In the algorithm, the cells of the tissue P system are divided into two groups. The first group, consisting of only one cell, aims at approaching to the Pareto front by the intelligent algorithm with non-domination rule while second group, consisting of six cells, focuses on searching boundaries by the artificial bee colony algorithm with different prioritization rules. The main idea of the MO TPS is about three aspects: search boundaries, approach to the Pareto front and approach to the Pareto front on the premise of preserving the elite boundary. 56 Solomon benchmarks are utilized to test algorithm performance. Experimental results show that on the premise of ensuring accuracy, the proposed approach outperforms compared algorithms in terms of three metrics.

Keywords: Tri-objective VRPTW · Tissue P systerm · Evolutionary Algorithm

1 Introduction

Many real-world problems must be optimized simultaneously on several incommensurable and conflicting objectives. In such a framework, there is no single optimal solution but rather a set of alternative solutions. These problems are called multi-objective problems(MOPs) and are usually solved by finding their maximum or minimum values under certain constrains. In recent years, many scholars around the world have carried out a lot of research work in the field of multi-objective optimization [1–4]. Although many multi-objective algorithms may find some trade-off solutions, the solution still cannot spread along the entire Pareto front. Many optimization problems are non-convex, non-uniform,

© Springer Nature Singapore Pte Ltd. 2021
L. Pan et al. (Eds.): BIC-TA 2020, CCIS 1363, pp. 534–559, 2021.
https://doi.org/10.1007/978-981-16-1354-8_38

discontinuous, and so forth, traditional mathematical methods are very difficult to find Pareto set. As the number of objective functions increases, the pressure in multi-objective evolutionary algorithms to simultaneously obtain optimal solutions which closely approach the Pareto Front and appear better extensibility and distribution increases. Due to these aspects, parallel computing is the key to solve MOPs. It is also the advantage of membrane algorithms but the disadvantage of many evolutionary algorithms.

To the country, people are all-important. To the people, grain is all-important. Our country is a large country with a population of more than 100 million foods, and a great country in food production and consumption. Research on the strategy and efficiency of grain transportation has always been a hot issue in agricultural product logistics management and field. As an effective means to describe practical problems, mathematical models are powerful tools for solving practical problems. This kind of distribution and transportation problem is called combinatorial optimization problem. When considering that the distribution center has multiple vehicles with the same limited capacity, the demand for grain retailers and the time windows for grain retailers to receive, this kind of problem is called vehicle routing problem with time windows(VRPTW). Among many problems of grain dispatching and transportation, this paper abstracts a class of problems that are widely used in actual transportation. Therefore, in this paper, we combine some intelligent optimal algorithms and membrane algorithms to obtain optimal solutions in multi-objective vehicle routing problem with time windows(VRPTW) where they have appeared better extensibility.

The multi-objective optimization problems, such as the VRPTW, are too complex to be solved by exact methods. The VRPTW is a NP-hard problem that can be applied to many distribution systems [5–8], such as grain allocation and supply chain management [9–12]. The VRPTW seeks to determine the optimal number of routes and the optimal sequence of customers(from a geographically dispersed locations that pose a daily demand for deliveries) visited by each vehicle, taking into account constraints imposed by the vehicle capacity, service times and time windows, and defined by the earliest and latest feasible delivery time. In recent years, researchers have proposed various multi-objective evolutionary algorithms for solving VRPTW. In particular, membrane algorithms have some applications to solve optimization problems.

Membrane computing(MC) is one of the recent branches of nature computing, which is inspired by the structure and the function of a single living cell, as well as from the organization of cells in tissue organs, and other higher-order structures [13]. The computational devices in membrane computing are called P system, which consists of three parts: the membrane structure, the objects in the membrane regions, and the evolution rules. Roughly speaking, there are three types of P system, that is, cell-like P systems [14,15], tissue-like P systems [16,17], and spking neural P(SN P) systems [18,19].Recently, there are many new classes P systems have been formulated by researchers.For instance,a natural modification in the architecture of SN P systems has been proposed in [20], namely passing from a neural-like structure (a network of neurons) to a cell-like membrane structure (hierarchical arrangement of membranes). Motivated by the numerical nature of numerical P (NP) systems in the area of membrane computing, Wu et al. [21] proposed a novel class of SN P system named Numerical Spiking Neural P Systems. To get a more flexible syntax in SN P system, [22–24] introduce some new distribution mechanism.

The membrane algorithm, which was introduced by Nishida [25] in 2005, is a membrane computation optimization algorithm. A membrane algorithm is also called a P-based algorithm. Since the first P system was introduced in [13,26], many different variants of P system have been proposed. Tissue P systems are a class of variants of P systems, and cooperation between neurons [27]. In the past years, much attention has been paid to the theoretical aspects, but the applications are worth further discussing, especially for solving real-word MOPs. Evolution algorithms(EAs) are a class of probabilistic search with many advantages such as flexibility, convenient application, and robustness. While MC can provide flexible evolution rules and parallel-distributed framework [28], which is very beneficial to produce the membrane-inspired evolutionary algorithms (MIEAs) [29].

Until now, different kinds of MIEAS have been proposed. In [30], a certain number of nested membrane structures in the skin membrane were combined with EAS for MOPS. A quantum-inspired evolutionary algorithm based on P system(QEPS) was proposed in [31]. It incorporated a one-level membrane structure(OLMS) and a quantum-inspired evolutionary algorithm. In [32], ZhangG discussed a modified QEPS with a local search through analyzing radar emitter signals. In [33], OLMS was integrated with DE and ant colony optimization methods to solve numeric optimization and traveling salesman problems. In [34], a membrane algorithm was proposed with the improvement that the involved parameters can be adaptively chosen to solve some combinatorial optimization problems. Multi-objective numerical optimization problems are solved by combining P system and genetic algorithms [35]. HeJ et al. [36] proposed a hybrid global search algorithm, that belongs to the membrane computing framework for solving the multi-objective multiple traveling salesman problem. These studies clearly illustrate that membrane systems can be used to improve the performance of many metaheuristic search methods and that they sometimes balance exploration and exploitation efficiently [37,38]. In the literature, many heuristic or metaheuristic approaches have been proposed for solving the VRPTW [39]. Applying different metaheuristics to solve the VRPTW can be extensively found in [40–43]. For multi-objective VRPTW, HongS and Park [44] constructed a linear goal programming model for bi-objective VRPTW and proposed a heuristic algorithm to relieve a computational burden. In [45], Pierre proposed the multi-objective genetic algorithm (MOGAs) to solve VRPTW, the results showed that this algorithm can further search an optimal distributed route. In the previous studies of tri-objective VRPTW, Andreas Konstantinidis et al. [46] presented a hybrid multi-objective evolutionary algorithm based on decomposition hybridized with an adaptive local search mechanism (MOEA/D-aLS). It decomposes a multi-objective optimization problem into several scalar optimizations subproblems and optimizes them simultaneously using the LS mechanism. NiuY

et al. [47] proposed an algorithm combined with a tissue-like membrane structure and genetic operators for solving the VRPTW. They also designed a special
improvement strategy to speed up the search process in the subsystem. This work
is motivated by the following observation:

(1) The investigations in [48–50] show that the hybrid algorithms designed by
    applying evolutionary computation and membrane systems outperform their
    counterpart approaches in terms of the quality of solutions. Furthermore,
    [51,52] indicates that the combination of evolutionary computation with
    membrane systems can produce a better algorithm for balancing exploration
    and exploitation. In other words, the combination is helpful for us to study
    the extensibility of the Pareto set.
(2) A tissue membrane system has a network membrane structure consisting of
    several one-membrane cells in a common environment and a certain number
    of channels connecting the cells [53]. The network membrane structure is
    flexible and adaptable to various network topologies. These features are very
    useful in organizing multi-objective intelligent optimal algorithms with some
    certain sorting rules.
(3) Among the various membrane algorithms mentioned above, they are usually
    combined with some other meta-heuristic or heuristic search methodologies.
    In the literature, a detailed process about how the hybrid algorithm to be
    produced from a membrane system is rarely mentioned.

Major contributions of this work are:

(1) We define a new tissue P system considering seven cells divided into two
    groups. The first group including 6 cells aims at approaching the Pareto front
    and the second group consisting of only one cell focuses on searching boundary
    solutions. To the best of our knowledge, this is the first attempt to use a tissue
    P system to properly organize two types of intelligent algorithms to design an
    approximate optimization approach to solve tri-objective VRPTW and also
    the first investigations regarding the structure of tissue P system to descript
    the production process about the hybrid membrane algorithm.
(2) This paper proposed a new multi-objective membrane algorithm by combin-
    ing two evolutionary algorithms. One is the artificial bee colony algorithm
    with prioritization rules, the other one is the intelligent algorithm with non-
    dominated rule. The optimal algorithm with the non-dominated rule insides
    the cell 1 evolves toward finding the boundary, solutions obtained by cell 1
    can be closer to the real Pareto front. The artificial bee colony algorithm
    with different prioritization inside cell 2 to cell 7 independently evolve. The
    six cells are aimed at the distance from solutions obtained toward the Pareto
    front can be measured as small as possible.

The goal of this paper is to search the boundary solution as possible as it
can on the premise of ensuring accuracy, extensibility. All we do is to study
whether the extensibility of solutions gets better and whether the algorithm can
find more boundary solutions while solutions obtained by MO TPS uniformly
distributed and approaches to the boundary of the Pareto set. In the tissue P

system, the channels connecting the seven cells build communication bridges for the two types of algorithms.

The rest of this paper is organized as follows. Section 2 states the problem to be solved and some basic knowledge about the MOPS and tissue P system. In Sect. 3, the hybrid approach, MOTPS, is described in detail. The following section analyzes the experimental results.

2   Basic Theory

In this section, we mainly introduce some basic theories from the following aspects. We first give a general mathematical model of the tri-objective VRPTW. And then some basic concepts about MOPs are mentioned in the Sect. 2.2. Finally, Sect. 2.3 gives a brief description of tissue P system.

2.1   Tri-objective VRPTW

In this paper, the objectives considered are:(1)minimization of the total vehicles and (2)minimization of the total distance cost and (3)minimization of the balance routes. The mathematical model can be defined on an undirected graph $G = (V, E)$,where $V = \{v_i | i = 0, 1, \cdots, N\}$ is a set of vertices,$E = \{e_{ij} | i, j = 1, 2, \cdots, N\}$ is the set of edges between vertices. Vertex v_0 denotes the depot that all vehicles should start from it and back when the tasks are finished. $M = \{1, 2, \cdots m\}$ is a set of vehicles and each vehicle have a limited capacity Q. Each customer must be served by only one vehicle in time window $[T_{si}, T_{ei}]$, where T_{si} and T_{ei} are the earliest and latest service time of customer v_i. However, vehicles might reach their destination before T_{si}, but the customer cannot be served until the time window opens and the vehicle should wait until the time window opens. The vehicle is not permitted to reach its destination after T_{ei}. Assume the following variables:

d_{ij} the distance between v_i and v_j;

q_i the demand of customer v_i;

Q the capacity of a vehicle;

T_{ik} time of the k-th vehicle arrives at customer v_i;

t_{ij} travel time from v_i to v_j;

D_k the distance of the k-th vehicle;

Decision variables:

$$x_{ijk} = \begin{cases} 1 & if\ v_i\ and\ v_j\ are\ sequentially\ visited\ by\ vehicle\ k \\ 0 & otherwise \end{cases} \tag{1}$$

The mathematical model of tri-objective VRPTW is as follows:

$$\min f_1 = \sum_{k \in M} \sum_{j \in N} x_{0jk}$$

$$\min f_2 = \sum_{k \in M} \sum_{i \in N} \sum_{j \in N} d_{ij} x_{ijk} \tag{2}$$

$$\min f_3 = \max_{k \in M} \{D_k\} - \frac{1}{|M|} \sum_{k \in M} D_k$$

$$s.t \begin{cases} \sum_{k \in M} \sum_{j \in N} x_{ijk} = 1, \forall i \in N \\ \sum_{i \in N} (r_i \sum_{j \in N} x_{ijk}) \leq Q, \forall k \in M \\ \sum_{j \in N} x_{0jk} = \sum_{i \in N} x_{i0k} \leq 1, \forall k \in M \\ \sum_{i \in N} x_{ihk} = \sum_{j \in N} x_{hjk}, \forall h \in N, \forall k \in M \\ T_{ik} + t_{ij} - K(1 - x_{ijk}) \leq T_{jk}, \forall i, j \in N, \forall k \in M, K \gg 0 \\ \sum_{k \in M} \sum_{i,j \in D} x_{ijk} \leq |D| - 1, \forall D \subseteq N \\ D_k = \sum_{i \in N} \sum_{j \in N} d_{ij} x_{ijk} \end{cases} \tag{3}$$

Equations (2) denotes the three objectives including the number of vehicles, the total distance cost of all the vehicles and the balance routes that can be measured by the difference between the longest distance and an average distance. Constraint (3) ensures that the quantity of all goods transported in a route does not exceed the capacity of the vehicle, requires that the arrival time at all customers is within their corresponding time window, ensures that each customer vertex is visited by at least one time, and that the total number of vertices visited is equal to the number of customers.

2.2   Consepts of MOPs

The mathematical expression of the multi-objective problem is not only intuitive but also easier to understand. The MOP is described as follows:

$$\begin{cases} \min \; y = F(x) = (f_1(x), f_2(x), \cdots, f_m(x))^T \\ s.t \begin{cases} g_i(x) \leq 0, & i = 1, 2, \cdots, p \\ h_j(x) = 1, & j = 1, 2, \cdots, q \end{cases} \end{cases} \tag{4}$$

where $f_k(x)(k = 1, \cdots, m)$ is the k-th objective, $g_i(x)$ is the i-th constraint equation, $h_j(x)$ is the j-th constraint equation. In order to facilitate our description, we give the following definition.

Definition 1. $X = \{x | x \in R^{''}, g_i(x) \leq 0, h_j(x) = 0, i = 1, 2, \cdots, q, j = 1, 2, \cdots, p\}$ is the feasible region of the above formulas. Assume that there are two feasible solutions $x_a, x_b \in X_f$, x_a is compared with x_b, x_a dominates x_b, if and only if:

$$\forall i \in 1, 2, \cdots, m, f_i(x_a) \leq f_i(x_b) \wedge \exists j \in 1, 2, \cdots, m, f_j(x_a) < f_j(x_b) \tag{5}$$

It can be denoted as $x_a \succ x_b$. A solution $x^* \in X_f$ is the Pareto optimal if and only if:

$$\neg \exists x \in X_f, x \succ x^* \tag{6}$$

Generally, mathematical or nature-based approaches are used to solve such problems. Mathematical approaches may include methods like Goal Programming techniques. The existing literature shows numerous nature-based multi-objective algorithm. The most significant ones among them are NSGA-II, Differential Evolution, SPEA and so on. In brief, the main loop of NSGA-II can be summarized as (1) create a random parent population, (2) sort according to the non-domination, (3) assign fitness to each solution, (4) use binary tournament selection, and mutation operators to create a children population, (5) synthesize parent population and children population. As we all know, NAGA-II is efficient in solving MOPs due to the sorting procedure. Moreover, the fast sorting decreases the complexity. Whether crossover, mutation or a fast non-dominated sorting, the purpose of the algorithm is to get better convergence and maintain diversity of population. Does the algorithm improve the extensibility of the Pareto optimal solutions? This problem needs to be considered.

2.3   Tissue P System

We combine the evolution algorithm and membrane algorithm to propose a specialized multi-objective VRPTW membrane system for solving tri-objective VRPTW, improving the diversity and distribution of Pareto optimal solutions and searching more boundary solutions. In this section, we introduce the basic concepts of the tissue P system.

A general tissue P system is composed of many cells in the common environment and channels connecting these cells. The cell and environment both include objects and multiset of objects. Objects in each cell evolve according to available evolution rules. The cells can communicate with each other through channels between them and all cells can communicate through the environment. For further details regarding this model, here we define a tissue P system adapted to our needs.

A tissue P system of degree m is a construct

$$\Pi = \{O, \sigma_1, \cdots, \sigma_m, syn, i_o\}$$

where
(1) O is a finite non-empty alphabet of objects. From the perspective of P system, objects can be defined by the purpose of what the user want to get applying the P system;
(2) $syn \subseteq \{1, 2, \cdots, m\} \times \{1, 2, \cdots, m\}$ denotes the channels among cells;
(3) $i_0 \in \{1, 2, \cdots, m\}$ indicates the output cell;
(4) $\sigma_1, \sigma_2, \cdots, \sigma_m$ are cells of the form $\sigma_i = (Q_i, s_{i,0}, w_{i,0}, R_i), 1 \leq i \leq m$,
where Q_i is a finite set of objects; $s_{i,0} \in Q_i$ is the initial states; $w_{i,0} \in O^*$ is the initial multiset of objects; O^* is a set of random strings composed by the objects from O. Some objects in O are sorted in a certain order to generate a string.

In different membrane structure, we can design the sort methods according our demands. R_i is a finite set of rules.

3   The Membrane Algorithm for Multi-objectives VRPTW

In this paper, we not only want to get a uniformly distributed and diverse Pareto solutions but also want to explore the true Pareto fronts and a Pareto set with sufficient extensibility. As follows, we explain in detail the overall design idea of the algorithm, the membrane system of tri-objective VRPTW and the membrane algorithm.

3.1   The Tissue P System for Multi-objectives VRPTW

For the tri-objective VRPTW having n customers and m vehicles, the proposed multi-objectives tissue P system is as follow:

$$\Pi = \{O, \sigma_1, \sigma_1, \cdots, \sigma_7, syn, R_0, i_{out}\}$$

where
(1) $O\{x_1, x_2, \cdots, x_{np}\}$ is an alphabet where the objectives $x_i(i = 1, 2, \cdots, NP)$ is an arrangement by customers $1, 2, \cdots, n$. Correspondingly, $x_i(i = 1, 2, \cdots, NP)$ is a set of codes for the tri-objective VRPTW feasible solutions. Therefore, O is a full permutation of integers 1 to n;
(2) $syn = \{(1,2), (1,3), (1,4), (1,5), (1,6), (1,7)\}$ denotes that cell1 communicate with $cell2, cell3, \cdots, cell7$ through the communication rules;
(3) $i_{out} = 1$ indicates that cell1 is the output;
(4) $R_0 = \{(N_{1,0}, N_{2,0}, \cdots, N_{7,0}) \rightarrow (u_{1,0}, u_{2,0}, \cdots, u_{7,0}), (N_{1,t}, N_{2,t}, \cdots, N_{7,t}) \rightarrow (N_{1,t+1}, N_{2,t+1}, \cdots, N_{7,t+1})\}$ is a finite set of the rules for adapting the states of initial cells;
(5) $\sigma_i = (Q_i, s_{i,0}, \omega_{i,0}, R_i)$ indicates cell i,$1 \leq i \leq 7$,
    where
    (a) $Q_i = \{s_{i,0}, s_{i,1}, \cdots, s_{i,t_{max}}\}$,where $s_{i,t}$ is the state of cell i in the configuration t, t_{max} is the maximum configuration in this P system, $i = 1, 2, \cdots, 7, t = 1, 2, \cdots, t_{max}$;
    (b) $s_{i,0} \in Q_i$ is the initial state;
    (c) $\omega_{i,0} = \{u_{i,0}\}$,where $u_{i,0} = x_1^i x_2^i \cdots x_{N_{i,0}}^i$ is the initial string of cell$i$. It corresponds to a population sorted by definition 2. And $x_j^i \in O$ $(j = 1, 2, \cdots, N_{i,0})$,$x_j^i \lhd x_{j+1}^i$ $(j = 1, 2, \cdots, N_{i,0} - 1)$;
    (d) $R_i = \{|u_{i,t}| > 0/s_{i,t}\omega_{i,t} \rightarrow s_{i,t+1}u_{i,t+1}T_{out}^i P_{go}^i, \quad |u_{i,t}| = 0/s_{i,t}\omega_{i,t} \rightarrow s_{i,t+1}\lambda T_{out}^i$ $(t = 1, 2, \cdots, t_{max})$ is a finite set of the rules for cell$i$, where $s_{i,t}, s_{i,t+1} \in Q_i$; $\omega_{i,t}$ is the multiset composed by $u_{i,t}$ and some elements in O;$u_{i,t}, u_{i,t+1} \in O^*$;$T^i, P^i \subseteq O$;$T_{out}^i$ indicates the set T^i generated in cell$i$ and sent to the environment; P_{go}^i indicates the set P^i generated in the cell$i$ and transported to other cells.

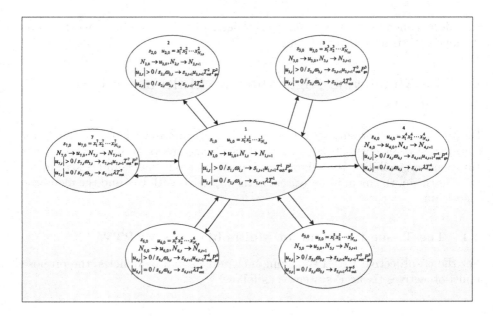

Fig. 1. The framework of the MO TPS.

The framework of the P system mentioned above is shown in Fig. 1.

It can be seen from the informal definition of tissue P systems that the network membrane structure and the ways of communications are flexible due to a variety of connections between cells and consequently various topologies of networks. These features are very useful to organize several distinct DE variants to develop a hybrid approach. Additionally, some concepts, which is listed in Table 1, in tissue P systems can find their corresponding ones in the MO TPS.

Table 1. Corresponding concepts in MO TPS and tissue P systems.

Tissue P system	MO TPS
Object	$1, 2, ..., n$ Customer Number
String	Elements $x_i (i = 1, 2, ..., NP)$
Cell	Cell1, Cell2, Cell3,…,Cell7
Evolution rules	Intelligent optimization operators
Communication rules	Migration

3.2   Rules of the Multi-objectives VRPTW Tissue P System

In the multi-objective VRPTW tissue P system, the evolutionary environments of different cells have differentiation due to the difference of the evolution rules. The environment for cell 1 is configurated by the requirement of the tri-objective optimization while cell 2 to cell 7 is configurated by the requirement of the tri-objective optimization with priority. That is, the elements in cell 1 are sorted by the non-domination and crowding degreed; the elements respectively in cell 2 to cell 7 are sorted by the priority order of each objective.

The sort rules of every strings in cells are given as follows.

Definition 2

(1) The sort rule of $u_{1,t} = x_1^1 x_2^1 \cdots x_{N_{1,t}}^1$ in cell 1 is $1 \leq p,q \leq N_{1,t}$, $x_p^1 \vartriangleleft x_q^1 \Leftrightarrow x_p^1 \succ x_q^1$ where $x_p^1 \succ x_q^1$ means $(x_{prank}^1 < x_{qrank}^1) \vee ((x_{prank}^1 = x_{qrank}^1) \wedge (x_{pdisrance}^1 < x_{qdisrance}^1))$, $x_{prank}^1 < x_{qrank}^1$ denotes the two elements belong to the different fronts, $x_{pdisrance}^1 < x_{qdisrance}^1$ denotes the two elements belong to the same front and the more crowded element dominates the other one.

(2) For the permutations of objective 1,2,3(a,b,c), the rule (a,b,c) of the $u_{i,t} = x_1^i x_2^i \cdots x_{N_{i,t}}^i$ in cell($i = 2, ..., 7$) is $1 \leq p,q \leq N_{i,t}$,

$$x_p^i \vartriangleleft x_q^i \Leftrightarrow$$
$$f_a\left(x_p^i\right) < f_a\left(x_q^i\right) \vee \left(f_a\left(x_p^i\right) = f_a\left(x_q^i\right) \wedge f_b\left(x_p^i\right) < f_b\left(x_q^i\right)\right)$$
$$\vee \left(f_a\left(x_p^i\right) = f_a\left(x_q^i\right) \wedge f_b\left(x_p^i\right) = f_b\left(x_q^i\right) \wedge f_c\left(x_p^i\right) < f_c\left(x_q^i\right)\right)$$

where cell 2 to cell7 respectively adopts the sort rule (1,2,3),(1,3,2),(2,1,3), (2,3,1),(3,1,2),(3,2,1).

Expect for the sort rules, the proposed P system runs in the parallel way through the following rules:

(1) Generation rule of initial configuration $(N_{1,0}, N_{2,0}, \cdots, N_{7,0})$ $\rightarrow$ $(u_{1,0}, u_{2,0}, \cdots, u_{7,0})$

For the initial length vector of strings in each cell, the generated rule $(N_{1,0}, N_{2,0}, \cdots, N_{7,0}) \rightarrow (u_{1,0}, u_{2,0}, \cdots, u_{7,0})$ of initial strings for all cells is given as follows.

Rule 1. $(N_{1,0}, N_{2,0}, \cdots, N_{7,0}) \rightarrow (u_{1,0}, u_{2,0}, \cdots, u_{7,0})$

Begin :
1: For $i = 1$ to   7
   For $j = 1$ to $N_{i,0}$
      $x_j^i = \text{Random}(1, 2, \cdots, n)$
      /random generate the permutation to form the element x_j^i of O/
2: For $i = 1$ to   7
     $\text{Sort}_i(x_1^i, x_2^i, \cdots, x_{N_{i,0}}^i) \rightarrow u_{i,0} = x_1^i x_2^i \cdots x_{N_{i,0}}^i$
     /$x_j^i \vartriangleleft x_{j+1}^i$ $(j = 1, 2, \cdots, N_{i,0} - 1)$/
Retrun.

---

(2) Adaptive rule of the strings' length $(N_{1,t}, N_{2,t}, \cdots, N_{7,t}) \to (N_{1,t+1}, N_{2,t+1}, \cdots, N_{7,t+1})$

At the beginning of the configuration, the string's length should be adaptively adjusted. The rule at t+1 is $(N_{1,t}, N_{2,t}, \cdots, N_{7,t}) \to (N_{1,t+1}, N_{2,t+1}, \cdots, N_{7,t+1})$. Here is the pseudo code.

Rule 2. $(N_{1,t}, N_{2,t}, \cdots, N_{7,t}) \to (N_{1,t+1}, N_{2,t+1}, \cdots, N_{7,t+1})$

Begin :

1: For $i = 2$ to   7

    If $t \leq \left[\frac{t_{\max}}{6}\right]$ then $N_{i,t+1} = N_{i,t}$

    If $\left[\frac{t_{\max}}{6}\right] < t \leq \left[\frac{t_{\max}}{2}\right]$ then $N_{i,t+1} = \max\left\{\left[\frac{3}{2}N_{i,t} - \frac{3t}{5}N_{i,t}\right], 10\right\}$

    If $\left[\frac{t_{\max}}{2}\right] < t \leq t_{\max}$ then $N_{i,t+1} = 0$

2: $N_{1,t+1} = \sum\limits_{i=1}^{7} N_{i,t} - \sum\limits_{i=2}^{7} N_{i,t+1}$

Retrun.

[•]means take the integer.

---

(3) Stopping rule $|u_{i,t}| = 0/s_{i,t}\omega_{i,t} \to s_{i,t+1}\lambda T_{out}^{i}$

At the state $s_{i,t}$, $|u_{i,t}| = 0$ means $u_{i,t} = \lambda$ is an empty string, that is, the set $\omega_{i,t}$ only includes the elements from other cells. When the state is $s_{i,t+1}$, $u_{i,t+1} = \lambda$, the elements in $\omega_{i,t}$ form a set T^{i} are sent to the environment.

(4) For cell 1 , optimization rule $|u_{1,t}| > 0/s_{1,t}\omega_{1,t} \to s_{1,t+1}u_{1,t+1}T_{out}^{1}P_{go}^{1}$

At the states $s_{1,t}$, $s_{1,t}$ includes $u_{1,t} = x_1^1 x_2^1 \cdots x_{N_{1,t}}^1$ and elements of O transported from other cells. These elements form the set $P = \{y_i \,|\, y_i \in O \wedge i = 1, 2 \cdots, m\}$, that is $\omega_{1,t} = \{u_{1,t}, P\}$. The optimization rule of cell 1 is given as follows. Firstly, merge and truncate $u_{1,t}$ and P to optimize $u_{1,t}$; then apply the elitist preservation of genetic operators for the tri-objective optimization to get the new string $u_{1,t+1}$. The specific implementation process is as follows.

Step 1 Get the optimized string $u_{1,t} = x_1^1 x_2^1 \cdots x_{N_{1,t}}^1$. The way how to get the string is to apply the merge-truncation operator. Here is the specific process.

Rule 3.1. The merge-truncation operator for $u_{1,t} = x_1^1 x_2^1 \cdots x_{N_{1,t}}^1$

1: $T_{out}^1 = \phi$

2: For $j = 1$ to m

    If $\exists p \left(x_{p-1}^1 \lhd y_j \lhd x_p^1 \right)$ then $u_{1,t} \leftarrow x_1^1 \cdots x_{p-1}^1 y_j x_p^1 \cdots x_{N_{1,t}-1}^1$

    / optimize the string $u_{1,t}$/

3:   $T_{out}^1 = T_{out}^1 + x_{N_{i,t}}^1$

    Else $T_{out}^1 = T_{out}^1 + y_j$

Step 2 Get the set H. The way how to get the set is to apply the genetic operator for tri-objective.

Select $\left(x_1^1, x_2^1, \cdots, x_{N_{1,t}}^1\right) \to \{x_1, x_1, \cdots, x_{N_{1,t}}\}$.

/selection(tournament strategy and definition 2)/

Crossover $\left(p_c, \{x_1, x_1, \cdots, x_{N_{1,t}}\}\right) \to \{z_1, z_1, \cdots, z_{N_{1,t}}\}$

/crossover(crossover ratep_c)/

Mutation $\left(p_m, \{z_1, z_1, \cdots, z_{N_{1,t}}\}\right) \to H = \{y_1, y_1, \cdots, y_{N_{1,t}}\}$

/mutation(mutation ratep_m/

Step 3 Get the set P_{go}^1. The way how to get the set is to apply the elitist preservation for optimizing the string $u_{1,t}$.

Rule 3.2. The elitist preservation for P_{go}^1

1: $P_{go}^1 = \phi$

2: For $j = 1$ to $N_{1,t}$

$\quad u_{1,t} = x_1^1 x_2^1 \cdots x_{N_{1,t}}^1 = z_1 z_2 \cdots z_n$ /merge-truncation/

3: $\quad$ If $z_{p-1} \lhd y_j \lhd z_p \wedge n < N_{1,t+1}$ then

$\qquad u_{1,t} \leftarrow z_1 \cdots z_{p-1} y_j z_p \cdots z_n; \quad P_{go}^1 = P_{go}^1 + y_j$

$\qquad /N_{1,t} \leq N_{1,t+1}/$

4: $\quad$ If $z_{p-1} \lhd y_j \lhd z_p \wedge n = N_{1,t+1}$ then

$\qquad u_{1,t} \leftarrow z_1 \cdots z_{p-1} y_j z_p \cdots z_{n-1};$

$\qquad P_{go}^1 = P_{go}^1 + y_j;$

$\qquad T_{out}^1 = T_{out}^1 + z_n$

5: $\quad$ Else $T_{out}^1 = T_{out}^1 + y_j$

$\qquad u_{1,t+1} \leftarrow u_{1,t}$

---

where the operator Crossover $\left(p_c, \{x_1, x_2, \cdots, x_{N_{1,t}}\}\right)$ refers to the order crossover in literature[56], the operator Mutation $\left(p_m, \{z_1, z_1, \cdots, z_{N_{1,t}}\}\right)$ refers to the literature [57].

(5) For cell $i(i = 2, 3, \cdots, 7)$, optimization rule $|u_{i,t}| > 0/s_{i,t}\omega_{i,t} \to s_{i,t+1}u_{i,t+1}$

$T_{out}^i P_{go}^i$ $(i = 2, 3, \cdots, 7)$

At the state $s_{i,t}(i = 2, 3, \cdots, 7)$, $\omega_{i,t} = \{u_{i,t}, P\}$, where $u_{i,t} = x_1^i, x_2^i, \cdots, x_{N_{i,t}}^i$ and $P = \{y_i | y_i \in O \wedge i = 1, 2, \cdots, m\}$. The optimization rules of cell $i(i = 2, 3, \cdots, 7)$ are given as follows. Firstly, merge and truncate $u_{i,t}$ and P to optimize $u_{1,t}$; then the bee colony [58] with priority operator for tri-objective optimization is applied to obtain the new string $u_{i,t+1}$. The document string is proposed to store the optimal elements generated in the evolution. Here the initial document string is $d_i = u_{i,0}$.

The specific implementation processes are as follows.

Step 1. Get the optimized string $u_{i,t}$. The way how to get the string is to use the merge-truncation operator. The specific process is shown at Rule 4.1.

Step 2. Get set $H = \{y_1, y_2, \cdots, y_{N_{i,t}}\}$. The way how to get the set is to use the bee colony operator to optimize $U = \{x_1^i, x_2^i, \cdots, x_{N_{i,t}}^i\}$. The specific process is shown at Rule 4.2.

Rule 4.1. The merge-truncation for $u_{i,t}$

1: $T_{\text{out}}^i = \phi$
2: For $j = 1$ to m
3:   If $\exists p\left(x_{p-1}^i \lhd y_j \lhd x_p^i\right)$ then
     $u_{i,t} = x_1^i \cdots x_{p-1}^i y_j x_p^i \cdots x_{N_{i,t}-1}^i;$ $T_{\text{out}}^i = T_{\text{out}}^i + x_{N_{i,t}}^i$
4:   Else $T_{\text{out}}^i = T_{\text{out}}^i + y_j$

Rule 4.2. The bee colony operator for $H = \left\{y_1, y_2, \cdots, y_{N_{i,t}}\right\}$

1: For $j = 1$ to $N_{i,t}$ /optimize the set U/
2:   Neighborhood $\left(x_j^i\right) \to y'_j$
   / perform the neighborhood search to all elements in set U /
3:   If $y'_j \lhd x_j^i$ then
       $T_{\text{out}}^i = T_{\text{out}}^i + x_j^i; x_j^i = y'_j; s_j = 0$
     Else $T_{\text{out}}^i = T_{\text{out}}^i + y'_j; s_j = s_j + 1$
4: Select $(U) \to H = \left\{y_1, y_2, \cdots, y_{N_{i,t}}\right\}$
     /selection(tournament strategy and definition 2)/
5: $T_{\text{out}}^i = T_{\text{out}}^i \cup (U - H)$
6: For $j = 1$ to $N_{i,t}$ / optimize the set U/
     Neighborhood $(y_j) \to y'_j$
7:   If $y'_j \lhd y_j$ then
       $T_{\text{out}}^i = T_{\text{out}}^i + y_j; y_j = y'_j; s_j = 0$
8:   Else $T_{\text{out}}^i = T_{\text{out}}^i + y'_j; s_j = s_j + 1$
9: For $j = 1$ to $N_{i,t}$ / further optimize the set U/
10: If $s_j \geq limit$ then
       $T_{\text{out}}^i = T_{\text{out}}^i + y_j;$ $y_j = \text{Random}\,(1, 2, \cdots, n)\,;$ $s_j = 0$
11: Sort$_i(H) \to x_1^i x_2^i \cdots x_{N_{i,t}}^i$ /for getting the string $u_{i,t+1}$/
12: If $N_{i,t+1} \geq 10$ then /$N_{i,t+1} \leq N_{i,t}$/
       $u_{i,t+1} \leftarrow x_1^i x_2^i \cdots x_{N_{i,t+1}}^i$
13: Else $N_{i,t+1} = 0$ then
       $u_{i,t+1} \leftarrow \lambda$

Step 3 Get the set P_{go}^1. The way how to get the set is to use the set H to optimize the document string $d_i = z_1 z_2 \cdots z_{N_{i,0}}$. The specific process is shown at Rule 4.3.

where the neighborhood search Neighborhood $\left(x_j^i\right)$ adopts the exchange and insertion based on the sort rule . The way of exchange and insertion is referred to the literature [37].

Rule 4.3. Optimize the string $d_i = z_1 z_2 \cdots z_{N_{i,0}}$

1: $P_{go}^1 = \phi$
2: For $j = 1$ to$N_{i,t}$
3:   If $z_{p-1} \lhd y_j \lhd z_p$ then
4:     $d_i = z_1 \cdots z_{p-1} y_j z_p \cdots z_{N_{i,0}-1}$;
$P_{go}^i = P_{go}^i + y_j$;
$T_{out}^i = T_{out}^i + z_{N_{i,0}}$
5:   Else $T_{out}^i = T_{out}^i + y_j$

3.3   The Membrane Algorithm for Tri-objective VRPTW

What the membrane algorithm for tri-objective VRPTW wants to achieve is that we can get a Pareto set with sufficient extensibility on the premise of the uniformly distributed and approaching to the true Pareto front. Thus, the proposed membrane algorithm contains two computation where the two kinds of objectives are not exactly different: (1) find the boundary: the solutions are as close to the boundary of true Pareto front of tri-objective VRPTW as possible; (2)approach to the front: the solutions are close to the Pareto front of tri-objective VRPTW with the optima crowding degreed as possible.

The core of the membrane algorithm for tri-objective VRPTW is that how to allocate the computing resources of membrane system in the best way to achieve the desired effect by utilizing the parallelism of membrane system computing. The proposed membrane algorithm adjusts the computing resources of membrane system according to three stages: the first stage is "mainly based on searching boundaries and partially based on approaching the Pareto font" ; the second stage is gradually changed from "look for the boundary for approaching to the Pareto front" ; in the third stage, carry out the calculation of "approach to the Pareto front on the premise of preserving the elite boundary" with the elitist preservation strategy. The following describes the membrane algorithm for tri-objective VRPTW according to the construction of the initial membrane system and the configuration of the P system.

Step 1 (create P system and initialization)

(1) Create the tissue P system for the multi-objectives VRPTW:

$$\Pi = \{O, \sigma_1, \sigma_1, \cdots, \sigma_7, syn, R_0, i_{out}\}$$

where the sort rule and evolutionary rule of cell 1 are set according to the tri-objective optimization. That is the cell 1 is set up according to the model min $\{f_1, f_2, f_3\}$ and the concrete rules are respectively shown in the definition 2 and 3.2(4). The propose of selecting the elitist preservation for the tri-objective optimization is to ensure that the strings in cell 1 could approach the Pareto front of the tri-objective VRPTW with the optimal crowding degree. The rules of cell $i(i = 2, 3, \cdots, 7)$ are set according to the model of the tri-objective optimization with priority and the concrete rules are respectively shown in definition 2 and 3.2(5). The optimization model of cell 2 is $P_1 : \min f_1; P_2 : \min f_2; P_3 : \min f_3$

that ensures the solutions could achieve the purpose of approaching the Pareto front(tri-objective VRPTW) by focusing on $\min f_1$ and leaning to the $\min f_2$. The model of cell 3 is P_1 : $\min f_1$; P_2 : $\min f_3$; P_3 : $\min f_2$ that achieve the purpose that strings could approach the Pareto front by focusing on $\min f_1$ and leaning to $\min f_3$. The model of cell 4 is P_1 : $\min f_2$; P_2 : $\min f_1$; P_3 : $\min f_3$ which means that strings in cell 4 approach the Pareto front by focusing on $\min f_2$ and leaning to $\min f_1$. The model of cell 5 is P_1 : $\min f_2$; P_2 : $\min f_3$; P_3 : $\min f_1$ that achieve the purpose that strings could approach the Pareto front by focusing on $\min f_2$ and leaning to $\min f_3$. The model of cell 6 is P_1 : $\min f_3$; P_2 : $\min f_1$; P_3 : $\min f_2$ that achieve the purpose that strings could approach the Pareto front by focusing on $\min f_3$ and leaning to $\min f_1$. The model of cell 7 is P_1 : $\min f_3$; P_2 : $\min f_2$; P_3 : $\min f_1$ that achieve the purpose that strings could approach the Pareto front by focusing on $\min f_3$ and leaning to $\min f_2$.

Among them, P_1, P_2, P_3 are object to $P_1 \gg P_2 \gg P_3$. In a word, the environment of cell $i(i = 2, 3, \cdots, 7)$ ensures the MO TPS is close to the six different boundaries of the Pareto front for the tri-objective VRPTW. The communication rules among cell1 and cell $i(i = 2, 3, \cdots, 7)$ require that only the latest optimal elements are transported. The rule ensures that the cell 1 achieves the effect of global search considering the boundary and the cell $i(i = 2, 3, \cdots, 7)$ achieve the effect of optimizing the boundary considering the global layout. Moreover, the rule minimizes the computation.

(2) Set $t = 0$ and the initial strings length of each cell $K_0 = (N_{1,0}, N_{2,0}, \cdots, N_{7,0})$. Perform the generation rule of initial configuration $(N_{1,0}, N_{2,0}, \cdots, N_{7,0}) \rightarrow (u_{1,0}, u_{2,0}, \cdots, u_{7,0})$of the set R_0. The concrete processes are shown in 3.2(1). The initial generated strings in cell i is $u_{i,0} = x_1^i x_2^i \cdots x_{N_{i,0}}^i$. For $\forall i\,(i = 2, 3, \cdots, 7)$, the initial document string of cell i is $d_i = x_1^i x_2^i \cdots x_{N_{i,0}}^i$.

Step 2(terminate condition)

If $t = t_{\max}$, then output the optimal solutions of the tri-objective VRPTW $x_1^1 x_2^1 \cdots x_{N_{1,t_{\max}}}^1$. The algorithm is over.

Step 3(configuration t changes to configuration $t + 1$)

(1) At first, perform the adaptive rule of the strings' length $(N_{1,t}, N_{2,t}, \cdots, N_{7,t}) \rightarrow (N_{1,t+1}, N_{2,t+1}, \cdots, N_{7,t+1})$ of the set R_0. The concrete processes are shown in 3.2(2). Then, the strings' length of cell $i(i = 1, 2, \cdots, 7)$ at the configuration $t + 1$ are $N_{1,t+1}, N_{2,t+1}, \cdots, N_{7,t+1}$, respectively.

It can be seen from the adaptive rule that the configuration of the MO TPS is divided into three stages: in the first stage, we take "find boundary" as the main objective with the computing resources focused on the cell $i(i = 2, 3 \cdots, 7)$; in the second stage, we take the "approach Pareto front" as the main objective with the transition of computing resources from cell $i(i = 2, 3 \cdots, 7)$ to cell 1; in the last stage, we take the "approach the Pareto front on the premise of preserving the elite boundary" as the main objective with the computing resources focused on the cell 1. Because of the second and third stages both contribute to "find boundary" and "approach Pareto front" consumes more computing resources, the total time is allocated to 3 stages according to the proportion of $\frac{1}{6}, \frac{1}{3}, \frac{1}{2}$. In the second stage, the transition is completed by linear change.

(2) Configuration evolution of each cell 1) Perform the optimization rule $|u_{1,t}| > 0/s_{1,t}\omega_{1,t} \rightarrow s_{1,t+1}u_{1,t+1}T_{\text{out}}^1 P_{\text{go}}^1$ of the cell 1.

When the configuration is evolving, the $N_{7,t+1} > 0$ and increases, that is the $|u_{1,t}| > 0$. Perform the rule $s_{1,t}\omega_{1,t} \rightarrow s_{1,t+1}u_{1,t+1}T_{\text{out}}^1 P_{\text{out}}^1$ that the details are shown in 3.2 (2). The execution process is as follows. Firstly, the merge-truncation is performed to optimize the string $u_{1,t}$ in the multiset $\omega_{1,t}$. Then, $u_{1,t}$ is optimized through the elitist preservation of genetic operator for the tri-objective to get the new string $u_{1,t+1}$ which is kept in the multiset $\omega_{1,t+1}$. During the process, the eliminated elements are transported to the environment by the set T^1 and these contributing to the optimization are transported to the $\omega_{i,t+1}$ of cell $i(i = 2, 3, \cdots, 7)$ by the set P^1.

2) For $\forall i\,(i = 2, 3, \cdots, 7)$, the configuration of cell i is shown as follows. At first, determine whether the string $u_{i,t}$ of multiset $\omega_{i,t} = \{u_{i,t}, P\}$ is empty. The stopping rule $s_{i,t}\omega_{i,t} \rightarrow s_{i,t+1}\lambda T_{\text{out}}^i$ shown in the 3.2(2) is used if $u_{i,t}$ is an empty string, $|u_{i,t}| = 0$. Specifically, $\omega_{i,t}$ is transported to the environment through the set T^i. The optimization rules $s_{i,t}\omega_{i,t} \rightarrow s_{i,t+1}u_{i,t+1}T_{\text{out}}^i P_{\text{go}}^i$ shown in the 3.2(5) are used, if $u_{i,t}$ is not empty, $|u_{i,t}| > 0$. The rule specifies that, the merge-truncation operator is utilized to optimize the string $u_{1,t}$ in the multiset $\omega_{i,t}$, then, the bee colony with priority operator for tri-objective optimization is applied to optimize $u_{1,t}$ for getting the mew string $u_{1,t+1}$ which is kept in the multiset $\omega_{i,t+1}$. Finally, the merge-truncation is utilized to optimize the document string d_i. The eliminated elements are transported to the environment by the set T^i and these contributing to optimize d_i are transported to the $\omega_{1,t+1}$ by the set P^i.

It is clearly seen that the function of d_i is that record the $N_{i,0}$ optimal elements while the cell i evolves to the configuration $t + 1$. Use this string to filter out optimal elements that are helpful for optimization of cell 1.

(3) State of each cell at $t + 1$

Step 4. (set $t = t + 1$, turn to step 2)

The Computational Framework of MO TPS is shown in Fig. 2.

4 Experimental Results and Analysis

In this section, we verify the performance of MO TPS by 56 Solomon benchmark instances. First, in order to ensure the fairness of all compared algorithms, the parameters of instances have been tuned to the best. Then, according to the performance index proposed by the reference [59], we compare the extensibility, distribution and the degree to which the non-dominated front of optimal solutions approaches true Pareto front between MO TPS, TSCEA [59]. Then, we compare the accuracy between MO TPS, MOEA/D-aLS [46] solving the tri-objective VRPTW. Finaly, in order to make more compiarisions with other classical algorithm (e.g. FAGA [60]), we adjust the three objectives into the total vehicles, the total distance and the total time balance(the difference between the maximum and minimum of the sum of vehicle run time, waiting time and service time).

State of each cell at $t+1$

1: If $t \leq \left[\frac{t_{\max}}{2}\right]$,

2:　　$\omega_{1,t+1} = \{u_{1,t+1}, P\}$

　　　$u_{1,t+1} = x_1^1 x_2^1 \cdots x_{N_1,t+1}^1, P = \cup_{i=2}^7 P^i$

　　　/the state of cell 1 is $s_{1,t+1}$/

3: Else $t > \left[\frac{t_{\max}}{2}\right]$

　　　$\omega_{1,t+1} = \{u_{1,t+1}\}$

　　　$u_{1,t+1} = x_1^1 x_2^1 \cdots x_{N_1,t+1}^1$

　　　/the state of cell 1 is $s_{1,t+1}$. /

/In this case, the merge-truncation operator of cell 1 can be ignored./

4: For $i = 2$ to 7

　　　$\omega_{i,t+1} = \{P^1\}$

　　　/ the state of cell i is $s_{i,t+1}$/

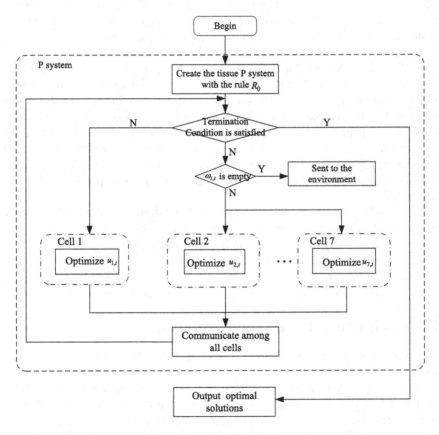

Fig. 2. Computational Framework of MO TPS.

4.1   Parameter Setting

To tune the parameter best, the Solomon benchmarks and the methods of references [54,55] are adopted to get the optimal range of each parameter. The optimal range of the crossover rate Pc is [0.35,0.75], the mutation rate Pm is [0.03, 0.1] and the maximal configuration ua [100, 400]. The string length of cell $i(i = 2, 3, \cdots , 7)$ and cell 1 in the initial configuration ranges from 30 to 50 and 200 to 400. The limit ranges from 1000 to 2000.

4.2   Comparisons with MO TPS and TSCEA

The reference [59] proposed a two-stage multi-objective evolutionary algorithm based on classified population(TSCEA) to solve tri-objective VRPTW and get Pareto solutions with better extendability. The three objectives considered in this paper are the same as our objectives(the number of vehicles, the total distance cost of all vehicles and the balance routes). TSCEA solve the tri-objective VRPTW through classified population which can reduce tri-objective functions to bi-objective functions.

The performance index proposed in the reference [59] considers different characteristics of MOPs mainly including three aspects. The indexes used for evaluating performance are shown in the reference. Let set A demote a solution set of TSCEA and set B denote a solution of MO TPS. MO TPS is a new method to solve the tri-objective VRPTW. Due to the intelligent optimization rules similar to TSCEA are adopted in the P system, these indexes are compared between two algorithms. The instances in Table 1 are randomly chosen.

From the Table 2, the results are gotten by these two algorithms in the same environments (the population size in TSCEA equals to the sum string length of MO TPS) which means the calculation is absolutely fair. In terms of index C, MO TPS outperforms TSCEA in C101, C105, C201, RC101, RC106 and RC201 while TSCEA performs better in R119, R112 and R207. In terms of index S, TSCEA performs better in C101, C109, R109, R112, RC101 while MO TPS outperforms in C105, C201, R207, RC106 and RC201. In terms of index H, MO TPS exhibits better performance than TSCEA except for RC106. It can be seen that Fig. 3 shows the number of solutions in the left graph is more than that in the right graph. Besides, the spatial distribution of the left graph is slightly wider than that of the right. The solutions in the right graphs are relatively concentrated in the space with bigger balance route, but in the space with smaller than 40 balance routes, the number of solutions in the left graph is more than that of right graph. The results show that the distribution and extensibility of MO TPS for tri-objective VRPTW Pareto front better than TSCEA in RC101.

Table 2. Performance comparisons I

Instances	TSCEA			MO TPS		
	C(A, B)	S(A)	H(A)	C(B, A)	S(B)	H(B)
C101	0	**19.33**	0.72	**0.5**	17.61	**0.07**
C105	0	17.25	0.14	**1.11**	**91.34**	**0.10**
C201	0	25.148	0.345	1	**62.89**	**0.16**
R109	**0.57**	**60.839**	0.09	0.09	10.1	**0.37**
R112	**0.41**	82.40	0.16	0.11	14.07	**0.21**
R207	**0.66**	179.48	0.62	0.43	**1064.84**	0.18
RC101	0.20	**26.87**	**0.03**	**0.58**	20.14	0.12
RC106	0.08	20.44	0.09	**0.33**	**36.45**	**0.06**
RC201	0	116.25	0.06	**0.60**	**120.36**	**0.06**

(a)   **(b)**

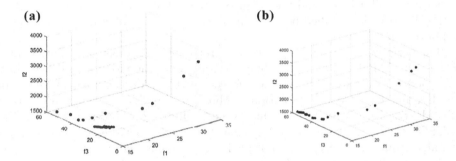

Fig. 3. (a) the spatial distribution of optimal RC101 by MO TPS; (b) the spatial distribution of optimal RC101 by TSCEA

4.3   Comparison with MO TPS and Other Tri-objective Algorithms

MO TPS VS MOEA/D-aLS

In this section, MO TPS is compared with MOEA/D-aLS [46] in terms of three objectives mentioned in previous parts. For the two algorithms, there are the same running environments to ensure fairness. The optimal solution of each objective of MO TPS is compared with that of MOEA/D-aLS, respectively. The experimental results of 56 Solomon's instances are listed in Table 3, 4, 5. In order to clearly understand the difference between them, p_i is used to evaluate the results, where $p_1 = \frac{f_1^{MOEA/D-aLS} - f_1^{MO\ TPS}}{f_1^{MOEA/D-aLS}}$ denotes the percentage difference of the objective f_1, $p_2 = \frac{f_2^{MOEA/D-aLS} - f_2^{MO\ TPS}}{f_2^{MOEA/D-aLS}}$ represents the percentage difference of f_2 and $p_3 = \frac{f_3^{MOEA/D-aLS} - f_3^{MO\ TPS}}{f_3^{MOEA/D-aLS}}$ represents the percentage difference of f_3. $\%p_i = p_i * 100, i = 1, 2, 3$. For the first objective f_1, 45 instances of 56 instances from MO TPs are less than those from MOEA/D-aLS; for the second objective

Table 3. MOEA/D-aLS VS MO TPS

Instances	MOEA/D-aLS			MO TPS			Percentage		
	f_1	f_2	f_3	f_1	f_2	f_3	p_1	p_2	p_3
C101	10.000	828.900	7.200	10.000	828.900	**3.200**	0.000	0.000	0.556
C102	11.000	994.000	5.700	**10.000**	**828.900**	**1.300**	0.090	0.166	0.772
C103	10.000	1148.300	2.500	10.000	**899.300**	**1.400**	0.000	0.217	0.440
C104	10.000	1237.000	0.800	10.000	**913.200**	**0.300**	0.000	0.262	0.625
C105	11.000	956.400	8.300	**10.000**	**828.900**	**0.500**	0.090	0.133	0.940
C106	12.000	1029.400	6.400	**10.000**	**828.900**	**3.400**	0.167	0.195	0.469
C107	10.000	889.300	9.400	10.000	**829.600**	**3.600**	0.000	0.067	0.617
C108	10.000	947.800	3.000	10.000	**828.900**	**2.400**	0.000	0.125	0.200
C109	10.000	992.900	2.200	10.000	**835.600**	**1.500**	0.000	0.158	0.318
Catgegory average							0.039	0.147	0.548
Instances	MOEA/D-aLS			MO TPS			Percentage		
	f1	f2	f3	f1	f2	f3	p1	p2	p3
C201	7.000	954.000	1.500	**3.000**	**591.500**	**0.600**	0.571	0.380	0.600
C202	5.000	838.300	**0.500**	**3.000**	**591.500**	0.800	0.400	0.294	−0.600
C203	5.000	945.100	**0.300**	**3.000**	**630.500**	1.700	0.400	0.333	−4.667
C204	4.000	1095.100	0.100	**3.000**	**617.300**	**0.050**	0.250	0.436	0.500
C205	6.000	854.800	0.500	**3.000**	**588.900**	**0.500**	0.500	0.311	0.000
C206	4.000	763.600	**0.100**	**3.000**	**588.500**	**0.200**	0.250	0.229	−1.000
C207	4.000	858.500	0.300	**3.000**	**588.300**	**0.300**	0.250	0.315	0.000
C208	4.000	711.900	0.300	**3.000**	**588.300**	**0.060**	0.250	0.174	0.800
Catgegory average							0.359	0.309	−0.548

f_2, 55 instance from MO TPS are better than MOEA/D-aLS. It's a pity that, in the third objective f_3, only 18 instances are superior to MOEA/D-aLS and 6 instances equals to MOEA/D-aLS.

It can be seen from the Table 3, 4, 5 that the optimal solutions obtained by MO TPS is obviously better than those of MOEA/D-aLS. Although in the third objective, MOEA/D-aLS performs better than MO TPS in the most instances, there are little difference between the two algorithms. As shown in Table 3, for C1 and C2 problemsMO TPS obtained the optimal solutions on smallest number of used vehicles, lowest total traveled distance and the smallest route balance. It performs well on these two instances of problems. The average % d_1 and % d_2 on C1, C2 problems are no more than 4% on the $f_1 and f_2$. In the objective f_3, the category averages have increased 54.8% in C1 but reduced 54.8% in C2. In $f_1 and f_2$, the averages of % d_1 and % d_2 are no more than 13% on R1 and RC1. For R1 and RC1 in f_3, the averages have reduced 12.4% and 48%. Although the performance of MO TPS on R1 and RC1 problems is not as good as on C1 and C2, the differences between the solutions obtained by MO TPS and MOEA/D-aLS are very small. For R2 and RC2 in the f_1, f_2 have increased no more than

Table 4. MOEA/D-aLS VS MO TPS

Instances	MOEA/D-aLS			MO TPS			Percentage		
	f_1	f_2	f_3	f_1	f_2	f_3	p_1	p_2	p_3
R101	22.000	1789.000	8.000	**20.000**	**1653.100**	**4.700**	0.091	0.076	0.413
R102	19.000	1603.300	3.900	**17.000**	**1480.700**	**2.100**	0.105	0.076	0.462
R103	15.000	1391.600	2.000	**14.000**	**1236.100**	**1.100**	0.067	0.112	0.450
R104	12.000	1216.300	1.900	**10.000**	**998.700**	**1.100**	0.167	0.179	0.421
R105	17.000	1556.800	3.500	**14.000**	**1369.300**	**3.200**	0.176	0.120	0.086
R106	16.000	1437.400	**3.600**	**13.000**	**1267.600**	4.500	0.188	0.118	−0.250
R107	13.000	1268.400	**1.600**	**11.000**	**1086.000**	2.800	0.154	0.144	−0.750
R108	11.000	1085.400	**1.300**	**10.000**	**960.200**	1.700	0.091	0.115	−0.308
R109	14.000	1362.900	**2.700**	**12.000**	**1156.800**	3.800	0.143	0.151	−0.407
R110	13.000	1273.900	**1.500**	**11.000**	**1096.700**	3.300	0.154	0.139	−1.200
R111	13.000	1267.300	3.100	**11.000**	**1071.200**	3.100	0.154	0.155	0.000
R112	11.000	1199.800	**1.700**	**10.000**	**972.800**	2.400	0.091	0.189	−0.412
Catgegory average							0.132	0.131	−0.124
Instances	MOEA/D-aLS			MO TPS			Percentage		
	f1	f2	f3	f1	f2	f3	p1	p2	p3
R201	9.000	1538.000	5.000	**4.000**	**1228.700**	**2.800**	0.556	0.201	0.440
R202	7.000	1368.100	**1.000**	4.000	**1153.000**	3.600	0.429	0.157	−2.600
R203	5.000	1258.600	0.200	**3.000**	**979.900**	0.200	0.400	0.221	0.000
R204	4.000	1024.200	0.200	**3.000**	**801.600**	0.200	0.250	0.217	0.000
R205	5.000	1231.500	0.600	**3.000**	**1018.800**	**0.500**	0.400	0.173	0.167
R206	5.000	1250.300	**0.100**	**3.000**	**963.900**	0.700	0.400	0.229	−6.000
R207	3.000	1120.300	0.300	3.000	**875.800**	0.300	0.000	0.218	0.000
R208	3.000	1095.900	**0.200**	**2.000**	**758.800**	**0.020**	0.333	0.308	0.900
R209	4.000	1167.300	0.200	**3.000**	**920.700**	0.300	0.250	0.211	−0.500
R210	5.000	1274.300	0.300	**3.000**	**970.900**	0.500	0.400	0.238	−0.667
R211	4.000	934.800	0.200	**3.000**	**814.600**	0.200	0.250	0.129	0.000
Catgegory average							0.316	0.192	−0.688

30%. Those on R2 are 31.6 and 19.3 respectively. Those on RC2 are 22.4 and 21.3 respectively.

Through analyzing the experimental results in Table 3, 4 and 5, MO TPS performs well on C1, C2 and R1, but not so well on RC1, R2 and RC2. The results obtained from MO TPS on RC1, RC2 and RC2 are mostly comprising solutions compared with MOEA/D-aLS. Although MO TPS has't achieved all the optimal solutions, it is conmparable to the algorithms obtained the optimal solutions. Generally, the performance such as the accuracy of solutions, the extensibility and the diversity of the algorithm is not poorer than that of traditional algorithms. What the results show that the MO TPS have the effectiveness to solve the tri-objective VRPTW.

Table 5. MOEA/D-aLS VS MO TPS

Instances	MOEA/D-aLS			MO TPS			Percentage		
	f_1	f_2	f_3	f_1	f_2	f_3	p_1	p_2	p_3
RC101	17.000	1879.000	6.400	**15.000**	**1664.000**	**2.700**	0.118	0.114	0.578
RC102	15.000	1651.700	**3.500**	**14.000**	**1489.700**	5.600	0.067	0.098	−0.600
RC103	13.000	1515.100	**1.700**	**12.000**	**1295.600**	2.400	0.077	0.145	−0.412
RC104	12.000	1331.400	**0.900**	**11.000**	**1171.100**	2.100	0.083	0.120	−1.333
RC105	17.000	1727.300	**4.600**	**15.000**	**1558.600**	8.700	0.118	0.098	−0.891
RC106	14.000	1528.900	2.500	**13.000**	**1387.300**	**2.000**	0.071	0.093	0.200
RC107	13.000	1438.200	**2.600**	**12.000**	**1265.700**	5.300	0.077	0.120	−1.038
RC108	13.000	1363.100	**1.500**	**11.000**	**1152.500**	4.900	0.154	0.155	−2.267
Catgegory average							0.096	0.079	−0.480
Instances	MOEA/D-aLS			MO TPS			Percentage		
	f1	f2	f3	f1	f2	f3	p1	p2	p3
RC201	9.000	1535.000	**2.000**	**5.000**	**1392.900**	2.500	0.444	0.093	−0.250
RC202	7.000	1564.700	**1.300**	**4.000**	**1238.900**	2.100	0.429	0.208	−0.615
RC203	6.000	1342.000	0.300	**4.000**	**1044.500**	0.300	0.333	0.222	0.000
RC204	4.000	1263.100	**0.300**	**3.000**	**863.200**	**0.200**	0.250	0.317	0.333
RC205	5.000	1576.700	**0.900**	5.000	**1278.100**	2.100	0.000	0.189	−1.200
RC206	6.000	1530.900	**0.500**	**4.000**	**1120.700**	1.200	0.333	0.268	−1.400
RC207	4.000	1281.700	**0.200**	4.000	**1051.200**	0.500	0.000	0.180	−0.500
RC208	3.000	1117.400	**0.300**	3.000	**859.700**	0.500	0.000	0.231	−0.667
Catgegory average							0.224	0.213	−0.537

MO TPS VS FAGA

This section draws comparison between MO TPS and FAGA [60]. The fitness aggregated genetic algorithm (FAGA for short) is implemented through the fitness aggregation method and dedicated genetic operators to resolve the multi-objective problem.In the reference [60], it takes the total vehicles, the total distance and the sum of vehicle run time, waiting time and service time as three objectives. For the convenience of the comparision, the objectives in MO TPS are adjusted to be the same as the compared algorithm.

In Table 5, the total vehicles is represented by f_1,the total distance is represented by f_2 and the total time balance is represented by f_3. In terms of the three objectives, the results gotten by MO TPS are all smallest than these gotten by FAGA. Because we want to get the minimum value of objectives, the smaller the value is , the better effect the algorithm is.From the accuracy comparisons in Table 5, it can be observed that MO TPS is superior or competitive to FAGA.

Table 6. MO TPS VS FAGA

Instances	FAGA			MO TPS		
	f_1	f_2	f_3	f_1	f_2	f_3
C101	11	1268.70	1165.60	10	828.94	1040.80
C105	11	1299.40	1169.00	10	828.94	1089.46
C106	11	1480.90	1088.80	10	828.94	1026.00
C108	11	1303.80	1056.50	10	828.94	935.45
R102	18	1855.30	220.91	17	1484.74	231.41
R106	14	1685.20	222.74	13	1274.61	197.34
RC105	16	1981.80	236.50	14	1566.21	161.63

5 Conclution

In this paper, we proposed a hybrid optimization method, called multi-objective tissue P system(MOTPS), by combining some intelligent algorithms with a tissue membrane system(also called tissue P system) in a proper way to solve multi-objective VRPTW. In this P system, we use two kinds of cells with different functions. The cell 1 aims at approaching to the Pareto front by the intelligent algorithm with non-domination rule while cell i focus on searching boundaries by the artificial bee colony algorithm with different prioritization rules. These cells evolve during three stages: "mainly based on searching boundaries and partially based on approaching the Pareto font" , "look for the boundary for approaching to the Pareto front" and "approach to the Pareto front on the premise of preserving the elite boundary" . All we do is to optimize the extensibility of solutions getting better while solutions obtained by MO TPS uniformly distributed and approaches to the boundary of the Pareto set. The algorithm was tested in 56 Solomon instances, it was compared with TSCEA and MOEA/D-aLS. Experimental results show that MO TPS has a competitive performance to solve the tri-objective VRPTW and appear better extensibility.

In the future, this paper can be extended from two aspects. On the one hand, the proposed MO TPS, as a general framework, can be extended to solve other variants of multi-objective VRP. On the other hand, the realworld tri-objective VRPTW instances generated in this paper can be seen as benchmarks of many-objective combinatorial problems, which promotes development of new many-objective algorithms for many-objective combinatorial problems.

Acknowledgement. This work is partially supported by subproject of the National Key Research and Development Program of China (Grant No. 2017YFD0401102-02), Key Project of Philosophy and Social Science Research Project of Hubei Provincial Department of Education in 2019(19D59) and Science and Technology Research Project of Hubei Provincial Department of Education (D20191604).

References

1. Meng, W., Ke, L., Kwong, S.: Learning to decompose: a paradigm for decomposition-based multiobjective optimization. IEEE Trans. Evol. Comput. **23**(3), 376–390 (2018)
2. Dbe, K., Hussein, R., Roy, P.C., Toscano, G.: A taxonomy for metamodeling frameworks for evolutionary multiobjective optimization. IEEE Trans. Evol. Comput. **23**(1), 14–116 (2019)
3. He, Z., Gary, G.Y., Zhang, Y.: Robust multiobjective optimization via evolutionary algorithms. IEEE Trans. Evol. Comput. **23**(2), 316–33 (2019)
4. Huang, H.: A hybrid multiobjective particle swarm optimization algorithm based on R2 indicator. IEEE Access. **6**(99), 14710–14721 (2018)
5. Wy, J., Kim, B.I., Kim, S.: The rollon-rolloff waste collection vehicle routing problem with time windows. Eur. J. Oper. Res. **224**(3), 466–476 (2013)
6. Bhusiri, N., Qureshi, A.G., Taniguchi, E.: The tradeoff between fixed vehicle costs and time-dependent arrival penalties in a routing problem. Transp. Res. E: Logist. Transp. Rev. **62**, 1–22 (2014)
7. Amorim, P., Almada-Lobo, B.: The impact of food perishability issues in the vehicle routing problem. Comput. Ind. Eng. **67**(2), 223–233 (2014)
8. Melián-Batista, B., De, S.A., Angelbello, F.: A bi-objective vehicle routing problem with time windows: a real case in Tenerife. Appl. Soft Comput. J. **17**, 140–152 (2014)
9. Eksioglu, B., Vural, A.V., Reisman, A.: The vehicle routing problem: a taxonomic review. Comput. Ind. Eng. **57**(4), 472–1483 (2009)
10. Layani, R., Khemakhem, M., Semet, F.: Rich vehicle routing problems: from a taxonomy to a definition. Eur. J. Oper. Res. **241**(1), 1–14 (2015)
11. Montoya, J.R., Franco, J.L., Isaza, S.N., Jimenez, H.F., Herazo, N.: A literature review on the vehicle routing problem with multiple depots. Comput. Ind. Eng. **79**(1), 115–129 (2015)
12. Dorling, K., Heinrichs, J., Messier, G., Magierowski, S.: Vehicle routing problems for drone delivery. IEEE Trans. Syst. Man Cybern. Syst. **1**–**16** (2016)
13. Paun, G., Rozenberg, G., Salomaa, A.: The Oxford Handbook of Membrane Computing. Oxford University Press, Oxford (2010)
14. Pan, L., Carlos, M.: Solving multidimensional 0–1 knapsack problem by P systems with input and active membranes. J. Parallel Distrib. Comput. **65**(12), 1578–1584 (2005)
15. Pan, L., Daniel, D.P., Marip, J.: Computation of Ramsey numbers by P systems with active membranes. Int. J. Found. Comput. Sci. **22**(1), 29–58 (2011)
16. Martin, C., Pazos, J., Paun, G., Rodriguez, A.: A New Class of Symbolic Abstract Neural Nets: Tissue P Systems. Springer, Heidelberg (2002)
17. Paun, G., Perez-Jimenez, M.J., Riscos-Nunez, A.: Tissue P systems with cell division. Int. J. Comput. Commun. Control **3**(3), 295–303 (2008)
18. Pan, L., Paun, G.: Spiking neural P systems: an improved normal form. Theoret. Comput. Sci. **411**(6), 906–918 (2010)
19. Pan, L., Paun, G., Perez-Jimenez, M.J.: Spiking neural P systems with neuron division and budding. Sci. China Inf. Sci. **54**(8), 1596–1607 (2011)
20. Wu, T., Zhang, Z., Paun, G., Pan, L.: Cell-like spiking neural P systems. Theoret. Comput. Sci. **623**, 180–189 (2016)
21. Wu, T., Pan, L., Yu, Q, Tan, K.C.: Numerical spiking neural P systems. IEEE Trans. Neural Networks Learn Syst. https://doi.org/10.1109/TNNLS.2020.3005538

22. Wu, T.Zhang, L., Pan, L.: Spiking neural P systems with target indications. Theoret. Comput. Sci. https://doi.org/10.1061/j.tcs.2020.07.016
23. Wu, T., Paun, A., Zhang, Z., Pan, L.: Spiking neural P systems with polarizations. IEEE Trans. Neural Networks Learn. Syst. **29**(8), 3349–3360 (2018)
24. Wu, T., Bilbie, F.-D., Paun, A., Pan, L., Neri, F.: Simplified and yet Turing universal spiking nerual P systems with communication on request. Int. J. Neural Syst. **28**(8), 1850013 (2018)
25. Nishida, T.Y.: Membrane algorithm: an approximate algorithm for NP-complete optimization problems exploiting P-systems. In: Proceedings of the 6th International Workshop on Membrane Computing (WMC 2005), Vienna, Austria, pp. 26–43 (2005)
26. Paun, G.: Computing with membranes. J. Comput. Syst. Sci. **61**(1), 108–143 (2000)
27. Martin, C., Pazos, J., Paun, G.: Tissue P systems. Theor. Comput. Sci. **61**(1), 295–326 (2003)
28. Zhang, G., GHeorghe, M., Pan, L., Perez-Jimenez, M.J.: Evolutionary membrane computing: a comprehensive survey and new results. Inform. Sences **279**, 528–551 (2014)
29. Wang, X., Zhang, G., Junbo, Z., Haina, R., Floentin, I., Raluca, L.: A modified membrane-inspired algorithm based on particle swarm optimization for mobile robot path planning. Int. J. Comput. Commun. Control **10**(5), 732–745 (2015)
30. Huang, L., He, X., Wang, N., Yi, X.: P systems based multi-objective optimization algorithm. Progress Natural Sci. Mat. Int. **17**(4), 458–465 (2007)
31. Zhang, G., Gheorghe, M., Wu, C.Z.: A quantum-inspired evolutionary algorithm based on P systems for knapsack problem. Fundamenta Informaticae **87**(1), 93–116 (2008)
32. Zhang, G., Liu, C., Gheorghe, M.: Diversity and convergence analysis of membrane algorithms. In: Proceedings of the 5th IEEE International Conference on Bio-Inspired Computing: Theories and Applications, pp. 596–603 (2010)
33. Zhang, G., Cheng, J., Gheorghe, M., Meng, Q.: A hybrid approach based on differential evolution and tissue membrane systems for solving constrained manufacturing parameter optimization problems. Appl. Soft Comput. J. **13**(3), 1528–1542 (2013)
34. He, J., Xiao, J.: An adaptive membrane algorithm for solving combinatorial optimization problems. Acta Mathematica Scientia **5**, 1377–1394 (2014)
35. Han, M., Liu, C., Xing, J.: An evolutionary membrane algorithm for global numerical optimization problems. Inf. Sci. **276**, 219–241 (2014)
36. He, J., Zhang, K.: A hybrid distribution algorithm based on membrane computing for solving the multiobjective multiple traveling salesman problem. Fundamenta Informaticae **136**(3), 199–208 (2015)
37. Solomon, M.M.: Algorithms for the vehicle routing and scheduling problems with time window constraints. Oper. Res. **35**(2), 254–265 (1987)
38. Orellana-Martín, D., Valencia-Cabrera, L., Riscos-Núñez, A.: Minimal cooperation as a way to achieve the efficiency in cell-like membrane systems. J. Membr. Comput. **1**, 85–92 (2019). https://doi.org/10.1007/s41965-018-00004-9
39. Ullrich, C.A.: Integrated machine scheduling and vehicle routing with time windows. Eur. J. Oper. Res. **227**(1), 152–165 (2013)
40. Yu, S., Ding, C., Zhu, K.: A hybrid GA-TS algorithm for open vehicle routing optimization of coal mines material. Exp. Syst. Appl. **38**, 10568–10573 (2011)
41. Ombuki, B., Ross, B., Hanshar, F.: Multi-objective genetic algorithm for vehicle routing problem with time windows. Appl. Intell. **24**, 17–30 (2006)

42. Tan, K.C., Chew, Y.H., Lee, L.H.: A hybrid multiobjective evolutionary algorithm for solving vehicle routing problem with time windows. Comput. Optim. Appl. **34**(1), 115–151 (2006)
43. Ghoseiri, K., Ghannadpour, F.: Multi-objective vehicle routing problem withtime windows using goal programming and genetic algorithm. Appl. Soft Comput. **4**, 115–151 (2010)
44. Hong, S.C., Park, Y.B.: A heuristic for bi-objective vehicle routing with time window constraints. Int. J. Prod. Econ. **62**(3), 249–258 (1999)
45. Zakaria, N.: Partially optimized cyclic shift crossover for multi-objective genetic algorithms for the multi-objective vehicle routing problem with time-windows. In: 2014 IEEE Symposium on Computational Intelligence in Multi-Criteria Decision-Making (MCDM), pp. 106–115 (2014)
46. Andreas, K., Savvas, P., Christoforos, C.: Adaptive evolutionary algorithm for a multi-objective VRP. Int. J. Eng. Intell. Syst. **22** (2014)
47. Niu, Y., He, J., Wang, Z., Xiao, J.: A P-based hybrid evolutionary algorithm for vehicle routing problem with time windows. Math. Prob. Eng. **2014**, 1–11 (2014)
48. Nishida, T.Y.: Membrane algorithm with Brownian subalgorithm and genetic sub-algorithm. Int. J. Found. Comput. Sci. **18**, 1353–1360 (2007)
49. Huang, L., Suh, I.H., Abraham, H.: Dynamic multi-objective optimization based on membrane computing for control of time-varying unstable plants. Inf. Sci. **181**(18), 2370–2391 (2011)
50. Cheng, J., Zhang, G., Zeng, X.: A novel membrane algorithm based on differential evolution for numerical optimization. Int. J. Unconvent. Comput. **7**(3), 159–183 (2011)
51. Zhang, G., Liu, C., Gheorghe, M.: Diversity and convergence analysis of membrane algorithms. In: Fifth International Conference on Bio-inspired Computing: Theories Applications, pp. 596–603 (2010)
52. Zhang, G., Gheorghe, M., Jixiang, C.: Dynamic behavior analysis of membranealgorithms. In: MATCH Communications in Mathematical and in Computer Chemistry (in press)
53. Martin, C., Paun, G., PAzos, J.: Tissue P systems. Theoret. Comput. Sci. **296**, 295–326 (2003)
54. Eiben, A.E., Smit, S.K.: Parameter tuning for configuring and analyzing evolutionary algorithms. Swarm Evol. Comput. **1**(1), 19–31 (2011)
55. Zhang, W., Lin, L., Gen, M.: Hybrid multiobjective evolutionary algorithm with fast sampling strategy-based global search and route sequence difference based local search for VRPTW. Procedia Comput. Ence **14**(4), 96–101(2012)
56. Davis, L.: Applying adaptive algorithms to epistatic domains. In: Proceedings of the International Joint Conference on Arti®cial Intelligence, pp. 156–166 (1985)
57. Gen, M., Runwei, C.: Genetic Algorithms and Engineering Design. Wiley, New York (1997)
58. Zhang, H., Zhang, Q., Ma, L.: A hybrid ant colony optimization algorithm for a multi-objective vehicle routing problem with flexible time windows. Inf. Sci. (2019)
59. Shu, H., Zhou, K., He, Z., Hu, X.: Two-stage multi-objective evolutionary algorithm based on classified population for the tri-objective VRPTW. Int. J. Unconvent. Comput. **16**, 41–171 (2019)
60. Sivaramkumar, V., Thansekhar, M.R., Saravanan, R.: Demonstrating the importance of using total time balance instead of route balance on a multi-objective vehicle routing problem with time windows. Int. J. Adv. Manufacturing Technol. **98**, 1287–1306 (2018). https://doi.org/10.1007/s00170-018-2346-6

A Multi-objective Algorithm Based on M-MOEA/D Algorithm and Tissue-Like P System for Solving Bi-objective Grain Dispatching and Transportation

Xinyue Hu[1] , Hua Yang[1]([✉]) , Kang Zhou[1] , Hang Shu[1] , Zhixin He[1] ,
Jian Zhou[2], and Guangbin Li[3]

[1] College of Mathematics and Computer Science, Wuhan Polytechnic University,
Wuhan 430023, China
[2] College of Food Science and Engineering,
Wuhan Polytechnic University, Wuhan 430023, China
[3] Qianjiang Jujin Rice Industry Co., Ltd., Enterprise-School Joint Innovation Center,
Hubei, China

Abstract. The vehicle routing problem with time windows (VRPTW) is a classic NP-Hard problem, which has theoretical research value and practical significance. Intelligent optimization algorithms can solve the problem effectively. Among them, the intelligent optimization algorithm based on the membrane computing can combine the parallel computing of the membrane with the precision and efficiency of the intelligent optimization algorithm, and it has become a research hotspot. In this paper, we propose an effective bi-objective optimization algorithm based on M-MOEA/D and tissue-like P system, named TM-MOEA/D, to solve bi-objective VRPTW. It uses the parallel ability of membrane computing to improve the ability of solving VRPTW. So that, non-dominated solutions obtained by TM-MOEA/D evenly distribute and approximate Pareto front. The experimental results show that TM-MOEA/D can obtain the best solutions on the clustered customers data sets, and perform well on the remote customers data sets.

Keywords: M-MOEA/D · Tissue-like P system · VRPTW · Grain dispatching and transportation

1 Introduction

The problem of multi-objective food transportation route planning is widespread in grain dispatching and transportation. During the lockdown period following a COVID-19 outbreak, uniform distribution of food to communities reduces the risk of people gathering to spread the virus. It is particularly important to save time and labor in food transportation. Considering that the time of receiving food in different communities is different, this problem can be regarded as a bi-objective vehicle routing problem with time windows (VRPTW) with single

© Springer Nature Singapore Pte Ltd. 2021
L. Pan et al. (Eds.): BIC-TA 2020, CCIS 1363, pp. 560–581, 2021.
https://doi.org/10.1007/978-981-16-1354-8_39

parking and single vehicle type for the number of used vehicles and the total traveled distance of routings. VRPTW is a multi-objective optimization problems (MOPs). A certain number of customers each has different demand and time window, several vehicles deliver food from a distribution center to each customer and each customer is visited once and only once by exactly one vehicle [1]. The transportation plan needs to meet the needs of customers and achieve objectives such as the minimum number of used vehicles and the shortest total traveled distance of routings subject to certain constraints. Different objectives in MOPs conflict with each other, and there is no way to optimize all objectives at the same time. Therefore, the Pareto set or Pareto front (PF) is usually used to represent the set of optimal solutions obtained after measuring multi-objective in the decision space. The optimal solutions in PF are non-dominate with each other. Therefore, solving MOPs is to find a set of decision vectors (i.e., Pareto set) satisfying all constraints as much as possible.

Savelsbergh had proved that VRPTW is an NP-Hard problem [2]. When the problem is on a large scale, the solving time will increase exponentially. Therefore, how to quickly and accurately solve VRPTW and make solutions evenly distribute and approaches to the boundary of the PF has been the focus of research by scholars for many years. Evolutionary algorithms [3–6] (EAs) are a class of probabilistic search with many advantages such as flexibility, convenient application and robustness. Many EAs have been used to solve MOPs and VRPTW. Such as particle swarm optimization [7] (POS), a fast and elitist multi-objective genetic algorithm [8] (NSGA-II), improving the strength pareto evolutionary algorithm [9] (SPEA2), using goal programming and genetic algorithm for solving a bi-objective VRPTW [10] (MOGP) and multi-objective evolutionary algorithm based on decomposition [11] (MOEA/D). The main advantage of multi-objective evolutionary algorithms [12] (MOEAs) over other algorithms is that they produce a set of temporary optimal solutions from the initial population, and each temporary optimal solution individually iteratively evolves to be closer to the PF. In order to generate a set of solutions evenly distribute and approaches to the boundary of the PF and avoid converging to the local optimal solution, people have studied the distribution of fitness and congestion. MOEA/D is an algorithm based on the allocation of decomposition fitness and maintains the diversity of solutions. Memetic algorithm (MA) is a type of population based meta-heuristics algorithm. It is composed of an evolutionary framework and a set of local search methods that are activated within the generation cycle of the external framework [13]. Three effective local search methods are selected to form a memetic MOEA/D (M-MOEA/D) by Qi [14], and achieved excellent results. Membrane computing [15] as a branch of natural computing, aims to abstract new computing models for living cells. The computational devices in membrane computing are called P system which consist of three parts: the membrane structure, the objects in the membrane regions, and the evolution rules. Roughly speaking, there are three types of P system, that is, cell-like P systems [16], tissue-like P systems [17–19], and neuron-like P systems [20–27]. Among the three types of membrane computing, the rules of membrane splitting, dissolving, creating, merging, and string copying can be used to generate exponentially growing computing space. Therefore, NP-hard problems such as VRPTW can be solved by changing space for time. In tissue-like P systems, transport rules are used to communicate between cells and the environment. Dong [28] had verified its effectiveness on VRPTW. There are three typical tissue-like P systems: basic tissue-like P systems [17,19], population P systems [29] and P-groups [30–32]. Among them, the communication channel between the cells that need to communicate in the basic tissue-like P system is given in advance according to rules. Due to the well performance of P system, researchers designed an effective algorithm based on P system for solving MOPs. The first P system based multi-objective optimization algorithm [33] (PMOA) is used to solve MOPs with bi-objective. PMOA consists of a skin membrane with three subsystems inside. The first two subsystems optimize the two objectives of the problem respectively, and the third subsystem takes charge of both objectives of the problem simultaneously. However, the solutions on the PF obtained by PMOA has the disadvantage of unevenly distribute.

In this paper, in order to solve the bi-objective VRPTW and to make solutions evenly distribute and approaches to the boundary of the PF, we propose an effective multi-objective optimization evolutionary algorithm based on a memetic MOEA/D (M-MOEA/D) and tissue-like P system, named TM-MOEA/D. In order to ensure the accuracy of solutions of bi-objective problem, we adopt the M-MOEA/D with uniform distribution and accuracy. And for the scalability of the PF in bi-objective problems, we adopted the concept of multi-objective planning with priority. Since the problems to be solved have two objectives, we adopt a tissue-like P system that can be calculated in parallel and have dual channels to find a priority solution to expand the boundary of PF.

We designed a tissue-like P system composed of three cell membranes, in which the first two cell membranes optimize the two objectives of the problem separately and transfer solutions to the third cell membrane through the communication channels, and the third cell membrane takes charge of both objectives of the problem simultaneously and transfers solutions to the first two cell membranes through the communication channels. The first two cell membranes work in parallel with the third. The test case is a set of 56 examples proposed by Solomon with 100 customers [34] and the results show that TM-MOEA/D can achieve the best on the clustered customers data sets, and perform well on the remote customers data sets. Solutions obtained by TM-MOEA/D evenly distribute and approaches to the boundary of the Pareto front.

The rest of this paper is organized as follows. Section 2 introduces the mathematical model of bi-objective VRPTW, tissue-like P system and M-MOEA/D. Section 3 describes TM-MOEA/D proposed in this paper in detail. Section 4 introduces the test cases, parameter settings and discusses the experimental results. Section 5 concludes this work.

2   Theory Prerequisites

2.1   Bi-objective VRPTW

The food transportation route planning problems that only considers the number of used vehicles, the total traveled distance and time windows can be abstracted into a bi-objective vehicle routing problem with time windows (VRPTW). VRPTW is a multi-objective optimization problem (MOPs), which refers to a certain number of customers each has different demand and time windows and several vehicles deliver food from a distribution center to each customer and each customer is visited once and only once by exactly one vehicle. The transportation plan needs to meet the needs of customers and achieve objectives such as the minimum number of used vehicles and the shortest total traveled distance subject to certain constraints.

Before presenting the mathematical formulation, some following notations are defined:

- $G = (V, A)$ is a directed graph;
- $V = (N \bigcup \{0\})$ is the set of all points;
- $N = \{1, 2, \cdots, n\}$ is a set of $n\,(n \geq 0)$ customer points, 0 represents the distribution center;
- $A = \{\langle i, j\rangle \,|\, i, j \in V, i \neq j\}$ is the routes set;
- $M = \{1, 2, \cdots, m\}$ is a set of $m\,(m \leq n)$ used vehicles;
- r_i is the demand for goods at $i\,(i \in V)$, $r_0 = 0$;
- T_{ik} is the arriving time of the vehicle $k\,(k \in M)$ to $i\,(i \in V)$;
- $[se_i, sl_i]$ is the time window at $i\,(i \in V)$;
- s_i is the service time at $i\,(i \in V)$, $s_0 = 0$;
- w_i is the waiting time at $i\,(i \in V)$, $w_0 = 0$;
- d_{ij} is the distance from i to $j\,(i, j \in V, j \neq i)$;
- t_{ij} is the traveling time from i to $j\,(i, j \in V, j \neq i)$;
- W is the same maximum load capacity of each vehicle.

decision variables:

$$x_{ijk} = \begin{cases} 1 & \text{if vehicle } k \text{ travels from } i \text{ to } j\,(j \neq i) \\ 0 & \text{otherwise} \end{cases} \tag{1}$$

The optimization model for the VRPTW with the number of used vehicles and the total traveled distance as the bi-objective is as follows:

$$\begin{cases} \min \boldsymbol{F}\,(x) = (f_1, f_2) \\ f_1 = \sum\limits_{k=1}^{m} \sum\limits_{j=1}^{n} x_{0jk} \\ f_2 = \sum\limits_{k=1}^{m} \sum\limits_{i=0}^{n} \sum\limits_{j=0, j\neq i}^{n} d_{ij} x_{ijk} \end{cases} \tag{2}$$

subject to

$$\sum_{j=1}^{n} x_{0jk} = \sum_{i=1}^{n} x_{i0k} = 1, \forall k \in M \tag{3}$$

$$\sum_{i=0, i \neq h}^{n} x_{ihk} = \sum_{j=0, j \neq h}^{n} x_{hjk} \leq 1, \forall h \in N, \forall k \in M \tag{4}$$

$$\sum_{k=1}^{m} \sum_{j=0, j \neq i}^{n} x_{ijk} = 1, \forall i \in N \tag{5}$$

$$\sum_{i=1}^{n} r_i \sum_{j=0, j \neq i}^{n} x_{ijk} \leq W, \forall k \in M \tag{6}$$

$$T_{ik} + w_i + s_i + t_{ij} = T_{jk}, \forall i, j \in V, i \neq j, \forall k \in M, x_{ijk} = 1 \tag{7}$$

$$0 \leq se_i \leq (T_{ik} + w_i) \leq (T_{ik} + w_i + s_i) \leq sl_i, \forall i \in V \tag{8}$$

$$m_i, w_i, s_i \geq 0 \tag{9}$$

Expression (1) defines whether the k-th vehicle travels from i to j. Expression (2) refers to minimizing two objectives, f_1 and f_2, which are the number of used vehicles and the total traveled distance. Constraints (3) and (4) restrict that each used vehicle starts from the distribution center and visits customers one by one and then returns the distribution center. Constraint (5) represents each customer must and only be served by one vehicle. Constraint (6) is the capacity constraint of the vehicles. Constraint (7) describes how the travel time is computed. Constraint (8) defines the time window. Constraint (9) is a non-negative requirement.

2.2 Tissue-Like P System

In order to solve the bi-objective VRPTW and improve the extensibility and accuracy of solutions, we combined M-MOEA/D and the tissue-like P system to design a P system specifically for solving such problems. Therefore, this section introduces the basic concepts of the used tissue-like P system. The tissue-like P system is a mechanism in which multiple cell membranes randomly placed in the same environment cooperate and communicate with each other to complete calculations. The formed membrane structure is a network structure. From reference [36], a tissue-like P system of degree $m\,(m \geq 1)$ is a construct of the form

$$\Pi = (O, \sigma_1, \cdots, \sigma_m, syn, i_o)$$

where

(1) O is the alphabet, its elements are objects. The objects are defined by the user according to the purpose of the P system. In the membrane system of this article, each solution is encoded with a positive integer string, and the length of the string is the number of customers.

(2) $syn \subseteq \{12\cdots, m\} \times \{1, 2, \cdots, m\}$ shows all channels between cells.

(3) $i_o \in \{1, 2, \cdots, m\}$ is the output cell.

(4) σ_i represent the i-th cell. Each cell is of the form

$$\sigma_i = (Q_i, s_{i,0}, w_{i,0}, R_i), 1 \leq i \leq m$$

Q_i is the set of states. $s_{i,0} \in Q_i$ is the initial state. $w_{i,0} \in O^*$ is the initial objects in cell i, object λ shows that there is no object in cell i. R_i is the set of rules in cell i which of the form $sw \rightarrow s'xy_{go}z_{out}$ and $s, s' \in Q_i$, $w, x \in O^*$, $y_{go} \in (O \times \{go\})^*$, $z_{out} \in (O \times \{out\})^*$. $z_{out} = \lambda$ when $i \in \{1, 2, \cdots, m\}$ is different from i_o. s is the cell state before the execution of the rule. s' is the cell state after the execution of the rule. w is the multisets of objects which are consumed by the rule. x, y, z are the multisets of objects which are generated by the rule. Multisets of objects x stay in the current cell, multisets of objects y go to the cells which have channels going from the current cell, and multisets of objects z are sent out of the system.

2.3   M-MOEA/D

MOEA/D is an evolutionary algorithm based on decomposition. It was first systematically proposed in 2007 by Qingfu Zhang et al. [36]. This algorithm decomposes MOP into multiple sub-problems, so that each sub-problems can be optimized to solve MOP. Zhang has proved that Tchebycheff approach is more efficient in solving multi-objective optimization problems among three common decomposition strategies. So M-MOEA/D applies Tchebycheff approach, the scalar optimization problem is in the form

$$\min \; g(x|\lambda, z*) = \max_{1 \leq i \leq m} \{\lambda_i|f_i(x) - z_i * |\}$$

$$subject\ to\ x \in \Omega \tag{10}$$

where Ω is the search space of decision variables. $z* = (z_1*, ..., z_m*)^T$ is the reference point, i.e., $z_i* = \max\{f_i(x)|x \in \Omega\}$ for each $i = 1, ..., m$. For each Pareto optimal point $x*$ there exists a weight vector λ such that $x*$ is the optimal solution of (10) and each optimal solution of (10) is a Pareto optimal solution of (2). Therefore, one is able to obtain different Pareto optimal solution by altering the weight vector.

A memetic MOEA/D [14] (M-MOEA/D) with the Tchebycheff approach and local search algorithms can be used to solve VRPTW. At each generation t, M-MOEA/D maintains:

- A population of N points $x^1, ..., x^N \in \Omega$, where x^i is the current solution to the ith sub-problem. A variable-length chromosome representation for VRPTW which is developed by Tan et al. [35] is employed;
- $FV^1, ..., FV^N$, where FV^i is the F-value of x^i, i.e., $FV^i = F(x^i)$ for each $i = 1, ..., N$;
- $z = (z_1, ..., z_m)^T$, where z_i is the best value found so far for objective f_i;

- An external population (EP), which is used to store non-dominated solutions found during the search. The algorithm works as Algorithm 1.

M-MOEA/D has a one-to-one correspondence evaluation mechanism between each individual in the group and the decomposed sub-problems, which can reduce computational complexity and speed up group convergence.

3   TM-MOEA/D

In this paper, in order to solve the bi-objective VRPTW and to make non-dominated solutions evenly distribute and approaches to PF, we propose an effective multi-objective optimization evolutionary algorithm based on a memetic MOEA/D (M-MOEA/D) and tissue-like P system, named TM-MOEA/D. Then we describe the general framework of TM-MOEA/D and the rules of its tissue-like P system.

3.1   The General Framework of TM-MOEA/D

For the mathematical model constructed in Sect. 2.1, we propose an effective multi-objective optimization evolutionary algorithm based on M-MOEA/D and tissue-like P system, named TM-MOEA/D, to solve bi-objective VRPTW. At the same time, in order to ensure the scalability of the PF in the bi-objective VRPTW, we adopted the concept of multi-objective planning with priority. Since the problem has two objectives, we use a tissue-like P system that can be calculated in parallel and has dual-channel to optimize the solutions with priority to expand the boundary of the PF.

The solutions are sorted according to the concept of priority multi-objective planning. Use (i, j) to represent the objective function (f_1, f_2), and P indicates the priority of bi-objective, which includes P_{ij} and P_{ji}. For example, when the priority is P_{ij}, the priority order of the individuals in the population is i prior to j. That is, solutions with fewer used vehicles is preferred and when the number of used vehicles is equal, solutions with shorter distance is preferred.

The number of membranes in the tissue-like P system is determined according to the number of objectives and the difficulty of the optimization problem. The structure of the tissue-like P system of TM-MOEA/D proposed in this paper is shown in Fig. 1. We design a tissue-like P system composed of four membranes $cel0$, $cel1$, $cel2$, and $cel3$. Membrane $cel0$ collects the non-dominated solutions from $cel1$ as the systemic result. Membrane $cel1$ takes charge of both objectives of the problem simultaneously. Membrane $cel2$ and $cel3$ optimize the two objectives of the problem respectively.

Algorithm 1. Main Framework of M-MOEA/D

Input :

  MO-VRPTW;

  a stopping criterion;

  N: the number of the sub-problems considered in MOEA/D;

  $\lambda^1, ..., \lambda^N$: a uniform spread of N weight vectors;

  T: the number of the weight vectors in the neighborhood of each weight vector;

  Pc: crossover probability;

  Pm: mutation probability.

Output :

  EP: an external population;

1: **Step1 : Initialization**

  Randomly generate an initial population $P = \{X^1, X^2, ..., X^H\}$

2: **Step1.1:** Set $EP = \phi$.

3: **Step 1.2:**

  Compute the Euclidean distances between any two weight vectors and then
  work out the closest weight vectors to each weight vector. For each $i = 1, ..., N$,
  set $B(i) = \{i_1, ..., i_T\}$, where $\lambda^{i_1}, ..., \lambda^{i_T}$ are the T closest weight vectors to λ^i.

4: **Step 1.3:**

  Generate an initial population $x^1, ..., x^N \in \Omega$ randomly or by a problem-specific
  method. Set $FV^i = F(x^i)$.

5: **Step 1.4:**

  Initialize $z = (z_1, ..., z_m)^T$ by a problem-specific method.

6: **Step 2 Update**

  For $i = 1, ..., N$ do

7: **Step 2.1:**

  Reproduction: Randomly select two indexes k, l from $B(i)$, and then generate a
  new solution from x^k and x^l by using genetic operators.

8: **Step 2.2:**

  Improvement: Apply a problem-specific repair/improvement heuristic on y to
  produce y'.

9: **Step 2.3:**

  Optimization of y'. Local search on y' to produce y'', if $g\left(y'' \mid \lambda, z\right) \leq g\left(y' \mid \lambda, z\right)$,
  then set $y' = y'$ and $F\left(y'\right) = F\left(y''\right)$, until can't get a better solution by searching
  for y'.

10: **Step 2.4:**

  Update of z: For each $j = 1, ..., m$, if $z_j < f_j(y')$, then set $z_j = f_j(y')$.

11: **Step 2.5:**

  Update of Neighboring Solutions: For each index $j \in B(i)$, if $g(y' \mid \lambda^j, z) \leq g(x^j \mid \lambda^j, z)$,
  then set $x^j = y'$ and $FV^j = F(y')$.

12: **Step 2.6:**

  Update of EP:

  Remove from EP all the vectors dominated by $F(y')$.

  Add $F(y')$ to EP if no vectors in EP dominate $F(y')$.

13: **Step 3:**

  Stopping Criteria: If stopping criteria is satisfied, then stop and output EP.

  Otherwise, go to Step 2.

The initial population of size N is copied into two populations in membrane
$cel1$ and then sent into membrane $cel2$ and membrane $cel3$ respectively through
the communication channels. Membrane $cel2$ and $cel3$ are responsible for the
single-objective search of the populations in the membrane according to the
priority of P_{ij} and P_{ji} to improve the ductility of the PF, and then return the
population with the optimized PF back to the membrane $cel1$. At this time,
the population size in membrane $cel1$ is $2N$. Membrane $cel1$ is responsible for

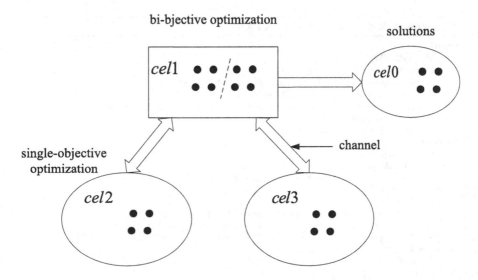

Fig. 1. Tissue-structure of TM-MOEA/D.

solving the bi-objective with the M-MOEA/D and improving the accuracy and distribution of its PF, and truncating the evolved population to ensure that the population size in the membrane is fixed to N. The above is a complete iterative process.

Similar to standard P systems, each membrane evolves respectively with maximal parallel. Therefore, the algorithm should be implemented on a cluster of computers or the evolutions of all membranes are implemented one by one on a computer. One of the strategies is described by following flowchart as Fig. 2.

3.2 The Tissue-Like P System of TM-MOEA/D

For food transportation route planning problems with n customers and m vehicles, the tissue-like P system of TM-MOEA/D is as follows.

$$\Pi = (O, \sigma_0, \sigma_1, \sigma_2, \sigma_3, syn, i_o)$$

where

(1) $O = \{x_1, x_2, \cdots, x_{n!}\}$ is the alphabet, its elements $x_i (i = 1, ..., n!)$ means one order of n customer numbers and corresponds to a feasible solution of bi-objective VRPTW.

(2) $syn = \{(1, 2), (1, 3), (2, 1), (3, 1)(1, 0)\}$ shows all channels between four cells, which respectively indicate that membrane $cel1$ is allowed to transmit solutions to membrane $cel2$, membrane $cel1$ is allowed to transmit solutions to membrane $cel3$, membrane $cel2$ is allowed to transmit solutions to membrane $cel1$, membrane $cel3$ is allowed to transmit solutions to membrane $cel1$, membrane $cel1$ is allowed to transmit solutions to membrane $cel0$, and prohibit the transmission of solutions in other ways.

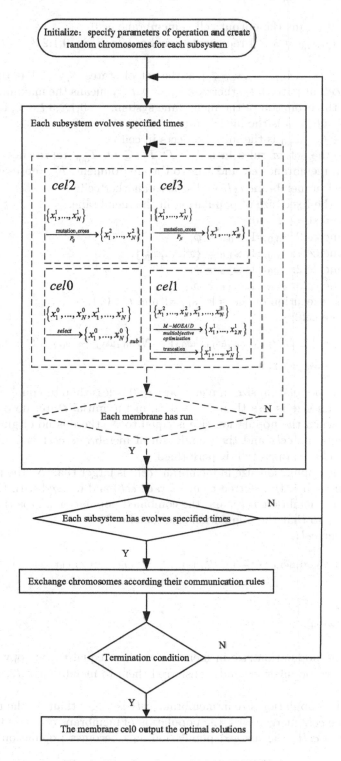

Fig. 2. The flowchart of TM-MOEA/D.

(3) $i_o = 0$ means the output cell is membrane $cel0$.

(4) $\sigma_i = (Q_i, s_{i,0}, \omega_{i,0}, R_i)$ represents membrane $celi$, $i = 0,1,2,3$.

where

(a) $Q_i = \{s_{i,0}, s_{i,1}, \cdots, s_{i,t_{\max}}\}$ is the set of states, $s_{i,t} = 1$ is the state of membrane $celi$ at pattern t, otherwise $s_{i,t} = 0$. $t_{\max}$ means the maximum pattern moment of the evolution of the membrane system. $i = 0,1,2,3$ $t = 0, 1, \cdots, t_{\max}$.

(b) $s_{i,t} \in Q_i$, $s_{i,0}$ is the initial state.

(c) $\omega_{i,t} \in O^*$, $\omega_{i,0}$ is the initial objects in cell i.

(d) R_i is the set of rules in cell i, $T^i, P^i \subseteq O$. T^i_{out} represents the set T^i generated in membrane $celi$ and sent to the environment. P^i_{go} represents the set P^i generated in membrane $celi$ and sent to another cell.

(e) N is the fixed size of population in the membrane.

The initial state, $t = 0$:

membrane $cel0$: $s_{0,0} = 1$, $\omega_{0,0} = \phi$;

membrane $cel1$: $s_{1,0} = 1$, $\omega_{1,0} = \{x_1^1, ..., x_N^1\}$;

membrane $cel2$: $s_{2,0} = 1$, $\omega_{2,0} = \phi$;

membrane $cel3$: $s_{3,0} = 1$, $\omega_{3,0} = \phi$.

After the execution of the rule, $s_{i,t} = 1$ and $t = 0, 1, \cdots, t_{\max}$:

Membrane $cel0$:

$$R_0 = \{|\omega_{0,t}| \leq N/s_{0,t}\omega_{0,t}; |\omega_{0,t}| > N/s_{0,t}\omega_{0,t} \to \omega_{0,t+1}T^0_{\text{out}} \},$$

$$T^0 = \omega_{0,t} - \omega_{0,t+1}.$$

When the population size in membrane $cel0$ is less than or equal to N: when the population size is less than N, that is, in the initial state, no operation is performed; when the population size is equal to N, there is no original population in membrane $cel1$ and the population of membrane $cel1$ is transferred to membrane $cel0$, no operation is performed.

When the population size in membrane $cel0$ is larger than N: the population of membrane $cel1$ is transferred to membrane $cel0$ and merged with the original population in membrane $cel0$, and the combined population $\omega_{0,t}$ is truncated to obtain $\omega_{0,t+1}$ so that the population size remains N.

Membrane $cel1$:

$$R_1 = \{|\omega_{1,t}| = N/s_{1,t}\omega_{1,t} \to (2\omega_{1,t}) P^1_{\text{go}}; |\omega_{1,t}| > N/s_{1,t}\omega_{1,t} \to \omega_{1,t+1} \to \omega_{1,t+2}T^1_{\text{out}}P^{1\,'}_{\text{go}} \},$$

$$P^1 = \omega_{1,t},$$

$$P^{1'} = \omega_{1,t+2},$$

$$T^1 = \omega_{1,t+1} - \omega_{1,t+2}.$$

When the population size in membrane $cel1$ is equal to N: copy the population into two populations and transferred them to membrane $cel2$, membrane $cel3$ respectively.

When the population size in membrane $cel1$ is larger than N: the population of membrane $cel2$ merged with the population of membrane $cel3$ and transferred to membrane $cel1$, the merged population $\omega_{1,t}$ becomes population $\omega_{1,t+1}$ by solving the multi-objective problem, and the truncation operation of population $\omega_{1,t+1}$ is performed to obtain $\omega_{1,t+2}$ so that the population size is maintained at N. Finally, population $\omega_{1,t+2}$ is transferred to membrane $cel0$. P_{go}^1 represents the population P^1 generated in membrane $cel1$ and transported to membrane $cel2$ and membrane $cel3$. $P_{go}^{1'}$ represents the population $P^{1'}$ generated in membrane $cel1$ and transported to membrane $cel0$.

Membrane $cel2$:

$$R_2 = \left\{ |\omega_{2,t}| < N/s_{2,t}\omega_{2,t}; |\omega_{2,t}| = N/s_{2,t}\omega_{2,t} \to \omega_{2,t+1}P_{go}^2 \right\},$$
$$P^2 = \omega_{2,t+1}.$$

When the population size in membrane $cel2$ is less than N, that is in the initial state, no operation is performed.

When the population size in membrane $cel2$ is equal to N, the population of membrane $cel1$ transferred to membrane $cel2$, the merged population $\omega_{2,t}$ becomes population $\omega_{2,t+1}$ by solving the multi-objective problem with P_{ij} as the priority and transferred to membrane $cel1$. P_{go}^2 represents the population P^2 generated in membrane $cel2$ and transported to membrane $cel1$.

Membrane $cel3$:

$$R_3 = \left\{ |\omega_{3,t}| < N/s_{3,t}\omega_{3,t}; |\omega_{3,t}| = N/s_{3,t}\omega_{3,t} \to \omega_{3,t+1}P_{go}^3 \right\},$$
$$P^3 = \omega_{3,t+1}.$$

When the population size in membrane $cel3$ is less than N, that is in the initial state, no operation is performed.

When the population size in membrane $cel3$ is equal to N, the population of membrane $cel1$ transferred to membrane $cel3$, the merged population $\omega_{3,t}$ becomes population $\omega_{3,t+1}$ by solving the multi-objective problem with P_{ji} as the priority and transferred to membrane $cel1$. P_{go}^3 represents the population P^3 generated in membrane $cel3$ and transported to membrane $cel1$.

4   Experimental Results and Analysis

In this section, we used the standard test cases from Solomon database [34] for simulation experiments to test the effectiveness of the proposed TM-MOEA/D. First, set the parameters based on test cases and references. Second, we compare the best solutions obtained by the proposed TM-MOEA/D with the best known solutions to verify the feasibility and effectiveness of TM-MOEA/D. Finally, we compare TM-MOEA/D with three other effective similar algorithms, M-MOEA/D [14], MOGP [10] and MOEA [37], and analyze their non-dominated solutions. The results show that the proposed TM-MOEA/D algorithm has better performance in solving bi-objective VRPTW.

4.1   Test Cases and Parameter Settings

This paper uses the well-known Solomon's benchmark test set to analyze computational performance of the selected algorithm. Solomon's benchmark test set contains 56 examples to represent different problem models. These problems are classified into six categories, namely C1, C2, R1, R2, RC1 and RC2. The customer points in class C data are densely distributed; the customer points in class R data are randomly distributed; in class RC data some customer points are densely distributed, and some customer points are randomly distributed; 1 and 2 represent the width of time windows to be tight and loose respectively.

The experimental environment for all experimental tests: experimental software:VS2013; programming language: C++; processor: Intel(R) Core(TM) i5-5300CPU 2.3GHz, Windows10,64 bits. In order to ensure the fairness of comparison experiments, the program parameters of the selected algorithms are the same as those in reference [14]. In this experimental studies, the maximum number of function evaluations is 50,000, the size of population $N=100$, the crossover probability $P_c=0.8$, the mutation probability $P_m = 0.2$, the neighborhood list size $T = 10$. The experimental results are the average value of 10 independent experiments.

4.2   Comparisons with the Best Known Solutions

In this experiment, we compare the best solutions obtained by the proposed TM-MOEA/D with the best known solutions to verify the feasibility and effectiveness of TM-MOEA/D. The best known solutions are obtained from corresponding literature [14]. TM-MOEA/D is a multi-objective optimization algorithm which minimizes the number of used vehicles and the total traveled distance simultaneously. Hence, we show the best known solutions and the best solutions obtained by TM-MOEA/D with the number of used vehicles and the total traveled distance in Table 1 and Table 2. NV is short for the number of used vehicles, TD means the total traveled distance of routings.

$$\begin{cases} \%NV=(NV\text{-}bestNV)/bestNV \\ \%TD=(TD\text{-}bestTD)/bestTD \end{cases}$$

% NV and %TD are the percentage difference for M-MOEA/D in the number of used vehicles and in the total traveled distance with the best known solutions. The min NV and min TD respectively represent the solutions with smallest NV and lowest TD.

Table 1. Comparisons between the best known solutions and the best solutions obtained by TM-MOEA/D on C1, R1 and RC1 problems.

Problems	min NV						Problems	min TD					
	Best Known		TM-MOEA/D					Best Known		TM-MOEA/D			
	NV	TD	NV	TD	%NV	%TD		NV	TD	NV	TD	%NV	%TD
C101	10	828.94	10	828.94	0.00	0.00	C101	10	828.94	10	828.94	0.00	0.00
C102	10	828.94	10	828.94	0.00	0.00	C102	10	828.94	10	828.94	0.00	0.00
C103	10	828.06	10	828.06	0.00	0.00	C103	10	828.06	10	828.06	0.00	0.00
C104	10	824.78	10	824.78	0.00	0.00	C104	10	824.78	10	824.78	0.00	0.00
C105	10	828.94	10	828.94	0.00	0.00	C105	10	828.94	10	828.94	0.00	0.00
C106	10	828.94	10	828.94	0.00	0.00	C106	10	828.94	10	828.94	0.00	0.00
C107	10	828.94	10	828.94	0.00	0.00	C107	10	828.94	10	828.94	0.00	0.00
C108	10	828.94	10	828.94	0.00	0.00	C108	10	828.94	10	828.94	0.00	0.00
C109	10	828.94	10	828.94	0.00	0.00	C109	10	828.94	10	828.94	0.00	0.00
Catgegory average					0.00	0.00	Catgegory average					0.00	0.00
R101	18	1613.59	19	1655.28	5.56	2.58	R101	18	1613.59	20	1652.05	11.11	2.38
R102	17	1486.12	17	1496.40	0.00	0.69	R102	18	1454.68	18	1481.20	0.00	1.82
R103	13	1292.68	14	1224.81	7.69	−5.25	R103	14	1213.62	14	1224.81	0.00	0.92
R104	9	1007.24	10	991.80	11.11	−1.53	R104	10	974.24	10	991.80	0.00	1.80
R105	14	1377.11	14	1390.59	0.00	0.98	R105	15	1360.78	15	1368.08	0.00	0.54
R106	12	1251.98	12	1265.55	0.00	1.08	R106	13	1240.47	13	1253.52	0.00	1.05
R107	10	1104.66	11	1086.85	10.00	−1.61	R107	11	1073.34	11	1086.85	0.00	1.26
R108	9	960.88	10	958.53	11.11	−0.24	R108	10	947.55	10	958.53	0.00	1.16
R109	11	1194.73	12	1158.53	9.09	−3.03	R109	13	1151.84	12	1158.53	−7.69	0.58
R110	10	1118.59	11	1104.38	10.00	−1.27	R110	12	1072.41	11	1104.38	−8.33	2.98
R111	10	1096.72	11	1067.47	10.00	−2.67	R111	12	1053.50	11	1067.47	−8.33	1.33
R112	9	982.14	10	963.75	11.11	−1.87	R112	10	953.63	10	963.75	0.00	1.06
Catgegory average					7.14	−1.01	Catgegory average					−1.10	1.41
RC101	14	1696.94	15	1672.02	7.14	−1.47	RC101	15	1623.58	16	1654.52	6.67	1.91
RC102	12	1554.75	13	1477.54	8.33	−4.97	RC102	14	1461.23	14	1474.02	0.00	0.88
RC103	11	1261.67	11	1308.18	0.00	3.69	RC103	11	1261.67	12	1301.27	9.09	3.14
RC104	10	1135.48	10	1145.53	0.00	0.89	RC104	10	1135.48	10	1145.53	0.00	0.89
RC105	13	1629.44	14	1578.11	7.69	−3.15	RC105	16	1518.58	15	1543.61	−6.25	1.65
RC106	11	1424.73	13	1396.29	18.18	−2.00	RC106	13	1371.69	13	1396.29	0.00	1.79
RC107	11	1222.10	11	1255.40	0.00	2.72	RC107	12	1212.83	12	1244.91	0.00	2.65
RC108	10	1139.82	11	1139.60	10.00	−0.02	RC108	11	1117.53	11	1139.60	0.00	1.97
Catgegory average					6.42	−0.54	Catgegory average					1.19	1.86

As shown in Table 1 and 2, for C1 and C2 problems, TM-MOEA/D obtained the same solutions as best known. It performs well on these two categories of problems. In min NV, the averages of %NV on R1 and RC1 problems are about 7%, but the averages of %TD on them have reduced about 1%. The averages of %NV and %TD on R1 and RC1 problems are about 1.5% in min TD. In min NV, the averages of %NV and %TD on R2 problems are 16.67% and −0.65% respectively. Those on RC2 problems are 4.17% and 2.75% respectively. For R2 problems and RC2 problems in min TD, the category averages have increased about 6%–9% in %TD, but they have reduced about 20%–30% in %NV. Therefore, most of the solutions obtained by TM-MOEA/D on R2 and RC2 problems are compromising comparing with the best known solutions.

Table 2. Comparisons between the best known solutions and the best solutions obtained by TM-MOEA/D on C2, R2 and RC2 problems.

Problems	min NV						Problems	min TD					
	Best Known		TM-MOEA/D					Best Known		TM-MOEA/D			
	NV	TD	NV	TD	%NV	%TD		NV	TD	NV	TD	%NV	%TD
C201	3	591.56	3	591.56	0.00	0.00	C201	3	591.56	3	591.56	0.00	0.00
C202	3	591.56	3	591.56	0.00	0.00	C202	3	591.56	3	591.56	0.00	0.00
C203	3	591.17	3	591.17	0.00	0.00	C203	3	591.17	3	591.17	0.00	0.00
C204	3	590.60	3	590.60	0.00	0.00	C204	3	590.60	3	590.60	0.00	0.00
C205	3	588.88	3	588.88	0.00	0.00	C205	3	588.88	3	588.88	0.00	0.00
C206	3	588.49	3	588.49	0.00	0.00	C206	3	588.49	3	588.49	0.00	0.00
C207	3	588.29	3	588.29	0.00	0.00	C207	3	588.29	3	588.29	0.00	0.00
C208	3	588.32	3	588.32	0.00	0.00	C208	3	588.32	3	588.32	0.00	0.00
Catgegory average					0.00	0.00	Catgegory average					0.00	0.00
R201	4	1252.37	4	1270.50	0.00	1.45	R201	9	1144.48	5	1224.60	−44.44	7.00
R202	3	1191.70	4	1101.70	33.33	−7.55	R202	8	1034.35	4	1101.70	−50.00	6.51
R203	3	939.54	3	963.34	0.00	2.53	R203	6	874.87	4	944.75	−33.33	7.99
R204	2	825.52	3	790.36	50.00	−4.26	R204	4	736.52	3	790.36	−25.00	7.31
R205	3	994.42	3	1036.25	0.00	4.21	R205	5	954.16	4	1017.45	−20.00	6.63
R206	3	906.14	3	917.85	0.00	1.29	R206	5	879.89	3	917.85	−40.00	4.31
R207	2	837.20	3	828.51	50.00	−1.04	R207	4	799.86	3	828.51	−25.00	3.58
R208	2	726.75	2	734.99	0.00	1.13	R208	4	705.45	2	734.99	−50.00	4.19
R209	3	909.16	3	933.24	0.00	2.65	R209	5	859.39	5	910.16	0.00	5.91
R210	3	938.58	3	965.12	0.00	2.83	R210	5	910.70	3	965.12	−40.00	5.98
R211	2	892.71	3	799.84	50.00	−10.40	R211	4	755.96	3	799.84	−25.00	5.80
Catgegory average					16.67	−0.65	Catgegory average					−32.07	5.93
RC201	4	1406.91	4	1452.29	0.00	3.23	RC201	6	1134.91	5	1360.56	−16.67	19.88
RC202	3	1365.65	4	1213.48	33.33	−11.14	RC202	8	1095.64	5	1160.11	−37.50	5.88
RC203	3	1049.62	3	1091.79	0.00	4.02	RC203	5	928.51	4	1019.41	−20.00	9.79
RC204	3	798.41	3	823.08	0.00	3.09	RC204	4	786.38	3	823.08	−25.00	4.67
RC205	4	1297.19	4	1348.59	0.00	3.96	RC205	7	1157.55	7	1295.27	0.00	11.90
RC206	3	1146.32	3	1295.41	0.00	13.01	RC206	7	1054.61	4	1117.65	−42.86	5.98
RC207	3	1061.14	3	1105.95	0.00	4.22	RC207	6	966.08	4	1026.89	−33.33	6.29
RC208	3	828.14	3	841.63	0.00	1.63	RC208	4	779.31	4	820.64	0.00	5.30
Catgegory average					4.17	2.75	Catgegory average					−21.92	8.71

Although the performance of TM-MOEA/D on R2, RC1, RC2 problems is not as good as on C1, C2 and R1 problems, the differences between the solutions obtained by TM-MOEA/D and the best known solutions are very small. Therefore, most of the solutions obtained by TM-MOEA/D are compromising comparing with the best known solutions.

Table 3. Comparisons of non-dominated solutions by other multi-objective algorithms on C1 and C2.

Problems	TM-MOEA/D		M-MOEA/D		MOGP		MOEA	
	NV	TD	NV	TD	NV	TD	NV	TD
C101	10	828.94	10	828.94	10	828.94	10	828.94
C102	10	828.94	10	828.94	10	828.94	10	828.94
C103	10	828.06	10	828.06	10	828.06	10	828.06
C104	10	824.78	10	824.78	10	824.78	10	824.78
C105	10	828.94	10	828.94	10	828.94	10	828.94
C106	10	828.94	10	828.94	10	828.94	10	828.94
C107	10	828.94	10	828.94	10	828.94	10	828.94
C108	10	828.94	10	828.94	10	828.94	10	828.94
C109	10	828.94	10	828.94	10	828.94	10	828.94
Num. Ns	9		9		9		9	
C201	3	591.56	3	591.56	3	591.56	3	591.56
C202	3	591.56	3	591.56	3	591.56	3	591.56
C203	3	591.17	3	591.17	3	591.17	3	591.17
C204	3	590.60	3	590.60	3	599.96	3	590.60
C205	3	588.88	3	588.88	3	588.88	3	588.88
C206	3	588.49	3	588.49	3	588.88	3	588.49
C207	3	588.29	3	588.29	3	591.56	3	588.29
C208	3	588.32	3	588.32	3	588.32	3	588.32
Num. Ns	8		8		5		8	

4.3 Comparisons with Other Multi-objective Algorithms

In this experiment, the proposed TM-MOEA/D is compared with three other effective similar multi-objective algorithms such as M-MOEA/D [14], MOGP [10] and MOEA [37] in Table 3, Table 4, Table 5 and Table 6. NV and TD have the same meaning as before. Num. Ns is short for the numbers of non-dominated solutions found by the comparing algorithms. The non-dominant solutions among all the solutions in these tables are bolded.

Table 3, Table 4, Table 5 and Table 6 show the comparison results between TM-MOEA/D and the other three comparing algorithms on C1, R1, RC1 and C2, R2, RC2 problems respectively. We can see that TM-MOEA/D performs well on C1 and C2 problems. It obtained the best solutions. TM-MOEA/D performs as well as M-MOEA/D on R1 and RC1 problems, they are better than MOGP but worse than MOEA. For R2 and RC2 problems, the number of the non-dominated solutions found by M-MOEA/D is similar to that of MOGP but smaller than that of MOEA.

Table 4. Comparisons of non-dominated solutions by other multi-objective algorithms on R1.

Problems	TM-MOEA/D		M-MOEA/D		MOGP		MOEA	
	NV	TD	NV	TD	NV	TD	NV	TD
R101	19	1655.28	19	1652.17	19	1677.00	**19**	**1650.80**
	20	1652.05	20	1644.70	20	1651.10	**20**	**1642.88**
R102	17	1496.40	**17**	**1486.12**	18	1511.80	17	1486.12
	18	1481.20	**18**	**1473.73**	19	1494.70	18	1474.19
R103			13	1354.22	14	1287.00	13	1308.28
	14	1224.81	**14**	**1213.62**	15	1264.20	14	1219.37
R104	10	991.80	10	999.31	10	974.24	**10**	**990.79**
			11	991.91			**11**	**984.56**
R105	14	1390.59	14	1410.64	15	1424.60	**14**	**1377.11**
	15	1368.08	15	1366.58	16	1382.50	**15**	**1364.91**
R106	12	1265.55	12	1265.99			**12**	**1261.52**
	13	1253.52	13	1249.22	13	1270.30	**13**	**1241.65**
R107			**10**	**1139.47**			10	1154.38
	11	1086.85	11	1086.22	11	1108.80	**11**	**1083.30**
R108							**9**	**984.75**
	10	**958.53**	10	965.52	10	971.91	10	960.03
R109	12	1158.53	**12**	**1157.44**	12	1212.30	12	1157.76
			13	1155.38	14	1206.70	**13**	**1154.61**
R110	**11**	**1104.38**	11	1110.68			11	1094.75
			12	1106.03	12	1156.50	**12**	**1088.61**
R111	11	1067.47	11	1073.82	11	1111.90	**11**	**1061.37**
R112	**10**	**963.75**	10	981.43	11	1011.50	10	980.83
Num. Ns	3		5		0		15	

Through the simulation experiment on the Solomon standard data sets, it can be shown that TM-MOEA/D has excellent performance in solving VRPTW, especially for the C1 and C2 tests data with clustered customers, it has reached the best known solutions. The distribution and ductility of PF are also very well on the part of the tests data of R1, R2, RC1 and RC2 with random distribution. The results show that the proposed TM-MOEA/D algorithm has better performance in solving bi-objective VRPTW.

Table 5. Comparisons of non-dominated solutions by other multi-objective algorithms on R2.

Problems	TM-MOEA/D		M-MOEA/D		MOGP		MOEA	
	NV	TD	NV	TD	NV	TD	NV	TD
R201	4	1270.50	4	**1253.23**	4	1351.40	4	1254.77
	5	1224.60	5	1196.50			5	**1194.07**
			6	**1185.79**				
R202	4	1101.70	4	**1081.82**	4	1091.22	4	1087.29
			5	**1049.72**			5	1050.41
R203	3	963.34	3	955.70	3	1041.00	3	**950.90**
	4	944.75	4	**904.46**	5	995.80	4	912.24
			5	**889.36**	6	978.50	5	905.34
R204	3	790.36	3	753.32	3	1130.10	3	**752.83**
			4	**745.96**	4	927.70		
			5	**743.29**	5	831.80		
					6	826.20		
R205	3	1036.25	3	**1017.96**	3	1422.30	3	1040.29
	4	1017.45	4	**960.33**	4	1087.80	4	968.09
			5	**954.48**				
R206	3	917.85	3	**915.49**	3	940.12	3	930.58
			4	**887.90**			4	899.83
R207	3	828.51	3	**813.47**	3	904.90	3	818.97
			4	**809.51**				
R208	2	734.99	2	**728.63**			2	736.90
			3	**711.59**	3	774.18	3	712.98
R209	3	933.24	3	**918.82**			3	921.97
	4	917.39	4	**867.47**	4	1008.00	4	878.05
	5	910.16						
R210	3	965.12	3	**952.91**	3	938.58	3	961.36
			4	**928.35**			4	936.68
			5	**920.06**				
R211	3	799.84	3	**774.68**	3	1310.40	3	785.97
			4	**767.10**	4	1101.50		
Num. Ns	0		24		0		3	

Table 6. Comparisons of non-dominated solutions by other multi-objective algorithms on RC1 and RC2.

Problems	TM-MOEA/D		M-MOEA/D		MOGP		MOEA	
	NV	TD	NV	TD	NV	TD	NV	TD
RC101			**14**	**1758.17**				
	15	1672.02	15	1646.81	15	1690.60	**15**	**1625.26**
	16	1654.52	16	1646.65	16	1678.90		
RC102	**13**	**1477.54**	13	1509.18				
	14	**1474.02**	14	1484.89	14	1509.40	14	1480.26
			15	1484.48	15	1493.20		
RC103	11	1308.18	**11**	**1274.85**			11	1278.19
	12	1301.27			12	1331.80		
RC104	10	1145.53	10	1145.79	11	1177.20	**10**	**1144.39**
RC105	14	1578.11	14	1548.43	15	1611.50	**14**	**1540.18**
	15	1543.61	15	1528.61	16	1589.40	**15**	**1519.44**
RC106	13	1396.29	12	1447.84	13	1437.60	**12**	**1395.70**
			13	1399.17	14	1425.30	**13**	**1379.68**
RC107	11	1255.40	11	1254.67	**11**	**1222.10**	11	1234.49
	12	1244.91	12	1235.54			**12**	**1215.06**
RC108			10	1183.85			**10**	**1158.22**
	11	1139.60	11	1138.95	11	1156.50	**11**	**1122.98**
Num. Ns	2		2		1		9	
RC201	4	1452.29	**4**	**1421.88**	4	1423.70	4	1438.43
	5	1360.56	**5**	**1316.61**			5	1329.26
			6	**1297.47**			6	1316.25
			7	**1289.94**			7	1299.58
RC202	4	1213.48	**4**	**1161.29**	4	1369.80	4	1165.57
	5	1160.11	**5**	**1118.66**			5	1120.15
RC203	3	1091.79	3	1097.40			**3**	**1061.47**
	4	1019.41	**4**	**944.50**	4	1060.00	4	954.51
			5	**940.55**	6	1020.10		
RC204	3	823.08	**3**	**801.90**	3	901.46	3	802.71
			4	792.98			**4**	**792.84**
RC205	4	1348.59	4	1327.09	4	1410.30	**4**	**1318.71**
	5	1306.44	**5**	**1245.94**			5	1259.00
	6	1300.60	**6**	**1187.48**			6	1214.49
	7	1295.27					7	1205.06
RC206	3	1295.41	3	1200.92	4	1194.80	**3**	**1191.62**
	4	1117.65	4	1092.70			**4**	**1085.82**
			5	1089.14			**5**	**1077.48**
RC207	**3**	**1105.95**	3	1107.71			3	1133.27
	4	1026.89	**4**	**1000.98**	4	1040.60	4	1001.73
			5	**987.88**			5	1001.51
RC208	3	841.63	**3**	**841.37**	3	898.50	3	844.96
	4	820.64	4	807.83			**4**	**780.07**
Num. Ns	1		14		0		7	

5   Conclusion

In this paper, we propose an effective multi-objective optimization evolutionary algorithm based on M-MOEA/D and tissue-like P system (TM-MOEA/D) for solving bi-objective grain dispatching and transportation. TM-MOEA/D combines the M-MOEA/D with the Tchebycheff approach and local search algorithms and tissue-like P system with parallel computing and dual-channel to make non-dominated solutions evenly distribute and approaches to PF. The experimental results show that TM-MOEA/D can achieve the best on the clustered customers data set, and perform well on the remote customers data set.

In the future research work, we will continue to improve the performance of TM-MOEA/D, and apply it to higher-dimensional multi-objective problems to meet the needs of scientific research and engineering applications and further verify the practicability of it.

Acknowledgement. This work is partially supported by subproject of the National Key Research and Development Program of China (Grant No. 2017YFD0401102-02).

References

1. Lee, L.H., Tan, K.C., Ou, K.: Vehicle capacity planning system: a case study on vehicle routing problem with time windows. IEEE Trans. Syst. Man Cybern. Part A: Syst. Hum. **33**(2), 169–178 (2003)
2. Savelsbergh, M.W.P.: Local search in routing problems with time windows. Ann. Oper. Res. **4**(1), 285–305 (1985)
3. Deb, K.: Multi-Objective Optimization Using Evolutionary Algorithms. Wiley, Chichester (2001)
4. Coello, C.A.C., Veldhuizen, D.A., Lamont, G.B.: Evolutionary Algorithms for Solving Multi-Objective Problems. Kluwer Academic Publishers, Dordrecht (2002)
5. Tan, K.C., Khor, E.F., Lee, T.H.: Multi-objective Evolutionary Algorithms and Applications. Springer, New York (2005)
6. Knowles, J., Corne, D.: Memetic algorithms for multi-objective optimization: issues, methods and prospects. In: Hart, W.E., Smith, J.E., Krasnogor, N. (eds.) Recent Advances in Memetic Algorithms. Studies in Fuzziness and Soft Computing, vol. 166, pp. 313–352. Springer, Heidelberg (2005). https://doi.org/10.1007/3-540-32363-5_14
7. Coello, C.A.C., Pulido, G.T., Lechuga, M.S.: Handling multiple objectives with particle swarm optimization. IEEE Trans. Evol. Comput. **8**(3), 256–279 (2004)
8. Deb, K., Pratap, A., Agarwal, S., Meyarivan, T.: A fast and elitist multiobjective genetic algorithm: NSGA-II. IEEE Trans. Evol. Comput. **6**(2), 182–197 (2002)
9. Zitzler, E., Laumanns, M., Thiele, L.: SPEA2: improving the strength pareto evolutionary algorithm for multi-objective optimization. In: Evolutionary Methods for Design, Optimization and Control with Applications to Industrial Problems. Proceedings of the EUROGEN 2001, September, pp. 19–21. Athens. Greece (2001)
10. Ghoseiri, K., Ghannadpour, S.F.: Multi-objective vehicle routing problem with time windows using goal programming and genetic algorithm. Appl. Soft Comput. **10**(4), 1096–1107 (2010)

11. Zhang, Q., Li, H.: Moea/d: a multi-objective evolutionary algorithm based on decomposition. IEEE Trans. Evol. Comput. **11**(6), 712–731 (2007)
12. Zhou, A., Qu, B.Y., Li, H.: Multiobjective evolutionary algorithms: a survey of the state of the art. Swarm Evol Comput. **1**(1), 32–49 (2011)
13. Neri, F., Cotta, C.: Memetic algorithms and memetic computing optimization: a literature review. Swarm Evol. Comput. **2**, 1–14 (2012)
14. Qi, Y., Hou, Z., Li, H.: A decomposition based memetic algorithm for multiobjective vehicle routing problem with time windows. Comput. Oper. Res. **62**, 61–77 (2015)
15. Păun, Gh., Rozenberg, G., Salomaa, A.: Handbook of Membrane Computing. Oxford University Press, Oxford (2009)
16. Păun, Gh.: Computing with membranes. J. Comput. Syst. Sci. **61**(1), 108–143 (2000)
17. Martin-Vide, C., Păun, Gh., Pazos, J.: Tissue P systems. Theoret. Comput. Sci. **296**(2), 295–326 (2003)
18. Bernardini, F., Gheorghe, M.: Cell communication in tissue P systems: universality results. Soft Comput. **9**(9), 640–649 (2005)
19. Freund, R., Păun, Gh., Perez-Jimenez, M.J.: Tissue P systems with channel states. Theoret. Comput. Sci. **330**(1), 101–116 (2005)
20. Păun, A., Păun, Gh.: Small universal spiking neural P systems. Biosystems **90**(1), 48–60 (2007)
21. Ionescu, M., Păun, Gh., Yokomori, T.: Spiking neural P systems. Fundamenta Informaticae **71**(2), 279–308 (2006)
22. Ibarra, O.H., Woodworth, S.: Characterizations of some restricted spiking neural P systems. In: Hoogeboom, H.J., Păun, G., Rozenberg, G., Salomaa, A. (eds.) WMC 2006. LNCS, vol. 4361, pp. 424–442. Springer, Heidelberg (2006). https://doi.org/10.1007/11963516_27
23. Wu, T., Zhang, Z., Păun, Gh, Pan, L.: Cell-like spiking neural P systems. Theoret. Comput. Sci. **623**, 180–189 (2016)
24. Wu, T., Păun, A., Zhang, Z., Pan, L.: Spiking neural P systems with polarizations. IEEE Trans. Neural Networks Learn. Syst. **29**(8), 3349–3360 (2017)
25. Wu, T., Bîlbîe, F.D., Păun, A., Pan, L., Neri, F.: Simplified and yet Turing universal spiking neural P systems with communication on request. Int. J. Neural Syst. **28**(08), 1850013 (2018)
26. Wu, T., Pan, L., Yu, Q., Tan, K. C.: Numerical spiking neural P systems. IEEE Trans. Neural Networks Learn. Syst. (2020)
27. Wu, T., Zhang, L., Pan, L.: Spiking neural P systems with target indications. Theoret. Comput. Sci. (2020)
28. Dong, W., Zhou, K., Qi, H.: A tissue P system based evolutionary algorithm for multi-objective VRPTW. Swarm Evol. Comput. **39**, 310–322 (2018)
29. Bernardini, F., Gheorghe, M.: Population P systems. J. Universal Comput. Sci. **10**(5), 509–539 (2004)
30. Csuhaj-Varjú, E., Kelemen, J., Kelemenova, A.: Computing with cells in environment: P colonies. J. Multiple Valued Logic Soft Comput. **12**(3), 201–215 (2006)
31. Freund, R., Oswald, M.: P colonies working in the maximally parallel and in the sequential mode. In: Proceedings of 7th International Symposium on Symbolic and Numeric Algorithms for Scientific Computing, Timisoara, Romania, pp. 419–426 (2005)
32. Kelemen, J., Kelemenova, A., Păun, Gh.: On the power of a biochemically inspired simple computing model P colonies. In: Proceedings of the Workshop on Artificial Chemistry and Its Applications, pp. 82–86. ECAL, Boston (2005)

33. Liang, H., Xiongxiong, H., Ning, W.: P systems based multi-objective optimization algorithm. Progress Natural ENCE **17**(4), 458–465 (2007)
34. Solomon, M.M.: Algorithms for the vehicle routing and scheduling problems with time window constraints. Oper. Res. **35**(2), 254–265 (1987)
35. Tan, K.C., Chew, Y.H., Lee, L.H.: A hybrid multi-objective evolutionary algorithm for solving vehicle routing problem with time windows. Comput. Optim. Appl. **34**(1), 115–151 (2006)
36. Zhang, G., Pérez-Jiménez, M.J., Gheorghe, M.: Real-Life Applications with Membrane Computing. Springer, Cham (2017). https://doi.org/10.1007/978-3-319-55989-6
37. Garcia-Najera, A.: Multi-objective evolutionary algorithms for vehicle routing problems. University of Birmingham (2010)

Cell-Like P Systems with Request Rules and Rules Production/Removal

Junrong Li, Yuzhen Zhao(✉), and Xiyu Liu

Shandong Normal University, Jinan 250014, Shandong, China
zhaoyuzhen@sdnu.edu.cn

Abstract. P systems are natural computing models inspired by the architecture and the function of living cells, which have the maximal parallelism characteristic and can improve computational efficiency. This work constructs a new variant of P systems named cell-like P systems with request rules and rules production/removal, which is also called CRQPR P systems for short. The CRQPR P systems use only request rules requesting objects from the parent membrane of a specific membrane. The skin membrane can request objects from the environment. Moreover, new rules can be produced, and existing rules can be removed during the computation. The Turing universality of CRQPR P systems can be achieved. 1) CRQPR P systems with two membranes using request rules of length at most two or one membrane using request rules of length at most three can compute Turing computable natural numbers. 2) CRQPR P systems with two membranes using request rules of length at most three can compute Turing computable functions.

Keywords: Bio-inspired computing · Membrane computing · Cell-like P system · Request rule · Rule production/removal · Universality

1 Introduction

Membrane computing is a branch of natural computing inspired by bio-membranes, proposed by Gheorghe Pun, a member of the Romanian Academy of Sciences, in 1998 [16], opening up a new field of computer science. The purpose of membrane computing is to abstract computing models from the structure and the function of the cells or the interaction of the cell groups, which are called membrane systems or P systems. Up to now, there are three main types of P systems according to different structures: (I) cell-like P systems inspired by the hierarchical structure of membrane in living cells; (II) tissue-like P systems inspired by tissues and (III) neural-like P systems inspired by neural systems [12].

This work was supported in part by the National Natural Science Foundation of China (No. 61806114, 61472231, 61876101, 61602282, 61402187, 61502283, 61802234, 61703251), the China Postdoctoral Science Foundation (No. 2018M642695, 2019T120607), the Funding for Study Abroad Program by the Government of Shandong Province (No. 201801037) and the Natural Science Foundation of Shandong Province (No. ZR2016AQ21).

L. Pan et al. (Eds.): BIC-TA 2020, CCIS 1363, pp. 582–595, 2021.
https://doi.org/10.1007/978-981-16-1354-8_40

In recent years, many pieces of research have been made in membrane computing: (I) Many extension P systems are proposed: For example, Artiom et al. [1] defined three variants of right-hand side randomization. Bogdan et al. [4] defined local time membrane systems inspired by time Petri nets. Song et al. [19] constructed tissue P systems with rule production/removal. Wu et al. [24] considered ASN P systems with rules on synapses, where all neurons contain only spikes or anti-spikes, and the rules are placed on the synapses. Bilbie et al. [3] proposed a variant of SNQ P systems that have weights on synapses, which influence the number of spikes received by the querying neuron. (II) Computing power and complexity of the P system are also investigated: Guo et al. [15] designed a family of P system to judge whether there is a Hamiltonian cycle and find all Hamiltonian cycles in an undirected graph. Daz-Pernil et al. [6] provided an affirmative answer to this question by showing a uniform family of tissue P systems without environment and with proteins on cells which solves the 3-COL problem in linear time. Sun et al. [22] investigated the computational power of weighted SNPSP systems working in maximum spiking strategy. Song et al. [21] proved that axon P systems working in either asynchronous or time-free mode are Turing universal as number generators. (III) Membrane computing has been applied to many fields, such as fuzzy clustering algorithm [14], arithmetic operation [7], and fuzzy reasoning algorithm [23]. (IV) About membrane computational simulation and implementation study. Guo et al. [8] presented a general-purpose P system simulator named UP Simulator for cell-like, tissue-like, and neural-like P systems.

Cell-like P systems are composed of a hierarchical structure of membranes. Each membrane delimits a compartment (also known as a region) with multisets of objects and rules. By using rules, the original objects will be evolved. If the region inside a membrane does not contain other membranes, this membrane is called elementary; otherwise, it is called non-elementary. The outmost membrane is the skin membrane. The outside membrane of the membrane i is called the parent membrane of i recorded as $p(i)$. For the skin membrane, its parent membrane is the environment. There are two forms of rules in cell-like P systems: (I) evolution rules to rewrite objects; and (II) communication rules to exchange objects between different regions.

In standard cell-like P systems, there are three types of rules, evolution rules, communication rules, and rules for handing membranes. Rules never change during the computational process. However, in biological cells, cells need to request energy from the environment. Therefore, request rules are considered in this work. Whats more, the biochemical reactions are influenced by the environment and other substances in the cells. Substances in cells evolve and change over time. Therefore, reactions vary at the same time. Hence, cell-like P systems with dynamic rules, that is, rules production and removal is considered [10].

This work proposes the P systems with only request rules, and the rules can be produced or be removed at any computational step, which is called CRQPR P systems for short. In such P systems, membrane i consumes multisets u and receives multisets v from its parent membrane $p(i)$. At any computational step, new rules can be produced, and existing rules can be removed. With this regulation mechanism, the computational power of CRQPR P systems working in a maximally parallel manner is investigated. Specifically, it is proved that the Turing universality can be achieved for CRQPR P systems. 1) CRQPR P systems with only two membranes, and using request rules of length at most two or only one membrane with request rules of length at most three can compute Turing computable natural numbers. 2) CRQPR P systems with two membranes using request rules of length at most three can compute Turing computable functions.

The contributions of this work are as follows: A new variant called CRQPR P systems is proposed, which is more biologically realistic. The CRQPR P systems are proved still Turing university even if using only request rules.

The rest of this paper is organized as follows. The formal definition of the pro-posed cell-like P systems with request rules and rules production/removal is de-scribed in Sect. 2. Universality results are provided in Sect. 3. Conclusions and future work are given in Sect. 4.

2   CRQPR P Systems

Before introducing the CRQPR P systems, some basic concepts are recalled first. For more details, please refer to [2,13].

For an alphabet Γ, its elements are called symbols. All finite non-empty multisets over Γ are denoted by Γ^*, and $\Gamma^+ = \Gamma^* \backslash \{\lambda\}$. A multiset u over Γ is a finite sequence of symbols from Γ. In u, the number of occurrences of symbols from Γ is called the length of the multiset u, which is denoted by $| u |$. For empty string λ, $| u | = 0$.

A multiset over Γ is a mapping from Γ to N, denoted by $m : \Gamma \to N$, for each $x \in \Gamma$, and N is the set of natural numbers. For two multisets m_1 and m_2 over Γ, the union of them, denoted by $m_1 + m_2$, is the multiset over Γ defined as $(m_1 \cup m_2)(x) = (m_1)(x) + (m_2)(x)$, for each $x \in \Gamma$. The relative complement of m_2 respect to m_1, denoted by $m_2 \subset m_1$ is defined as $\forall x \in \Gamma, (m_1 - m_2)(x) = (m_1)(x) - (m_2)(x)$, otherwise $m_1(x) - m_2(x) = 0$.

NRE indicates the family of recursively enumerable sets of natural numbers.

A register machine is a tuple $M = (m, H, l_0, l_h, I)$, where m is the number of registers; H is a set of labels of instructions, l_0 is the label of the start instruction, l_h is the label of the halting instruction; and I is a set of instructions which expressed in the following forms

- $l_i : (ADD(r), l_j, l_k)$ (add 1 to register r and then non-deterministically go to l_j or l_k);
- $l_i : (SUB(r), l_j, l_k)$ (if register $r \neq 0$, then subtract one from it, and go to l_j; otherwise go to l_k);
- $l_h : HALT$ (the halt instruction).

The definition of CRQPR P systems is given as follows.

Definition 1. *A cell-like P system with request rules and rule production/removal, of degree $q \geq 1$, is*

$$\Pi = (\Gamma, \varepsilon, \mu, M_1, \ldots, M_q, R, i_{in}, i_{out}) \tag{1}$$

where

- Γ *is a finite alphabet of objects and* $\varepsilon \subseteq \Gamma$;
- μ *is a rooted tree with q nodes labelled by* $1, \ldots, q$;
- M_i, $1 \leq i \leq q$, *are finite multisets over* Γ;
- R *is a finite set of rules of the forms:* $(S \mid u^- \leftarrow v, i)$; r; *where* $S \subseteq M_i$, $u \subseteq S, \mathrm{v} \subseteq \Gamma^+$, *and r is a finite set whose elements are of the type* $r \in R$ *or* $-r, r \in R$;
- $l_{in} \in \{1, \ldots, q\}$ *is the label of the input membrane;*
- $l_{out} \in \{1, \ldots, q\}$ *is the label of the output membrane.*

CRQPR P systems of degree $q \geq 1$ contain a set of q membranes labelled by $1, \ldots, q$, arranged in a hierarchical structure of a rooted tree (the root labelled by 1 is the skin membrane), such that: a) M_i express the finite multisets of objects placed in membranes i; b) ε is the set of objects located in the environment of the system. Note that all of these objects have any number of copies; c) R is the finite set of rules, d) i_{in} is a distinguished region encoding the input of the system. The term region $i(1 \leq i \leq q)$ refers to membrane i. e) i_{out} is a distinguished region encoding the output of the system. The term region $i(1 \leq i \leq q)$ refers to membrane i in the case $0 < i \leq q$ and to the environment in the case $i = 0$. For each membrane $i(1 \leq i \leq q)$, $p(i)$ is the parent of it. In the rooted tree, the "parent" of the skin membrane is the environment, denoted by $p(1) = 0$.

Rule $(S \mid u^- \leftarrow v, i)$; r denotes request rules with rules production/removal. S is a multiset over Γ, M_i is a finite multiset in membrane i. When $S \subseteq M_i$, this rule meets the activation condition, which can be activated and applied consuming multiset u, and receiving multiset v from the parent of it at the same time. If $u^- = \lambda$, membrane i consumes no object and receives multiset v only from the region $p(i)$. The vector r consists of two types of multisets r_i and $-r_j$ indicating rule r_i will be produced, and rule r_j will be removed, respectively. If a specific rule $-r_j \in$ r does not exist in membrane i before, this removal operation is skipped. Note that the whole rule takes one step.

An example of a CRQPR P system is

$$\Pi' = (\Gamma, \varepsilon, \mu, M_1, R, i_{in}, i_{out}) \tag{2}$$

where

- $\Gamma = \{a_q \mid 1 \leq q \leq 2\} \cup \{l \mid l \in H\}$;
- $\varepsilon = \{a_q \mid 1 \leq q \leq 2\}$;
- $\mu = []_1$;
- $M_1 = \emptyset$;
- $i_{out} = 1$;

– R:

$$r_{i,1} : \left(l_1 a_1 \mid l_1^- \leftarrow a_2, 1\right) ; -r_{i,1}, r_{i,2}, r_{i,3};$$
$$r_{i,2} : \left(\lambda \mid a_2^- \leftarrow l_j, 1\right) ; r_{j,1}, -r_{i,2}, -r_{i,3};$$
$$r_{i,3} : \left(\lambda \mid a_2^- \leftarrow l_k, 1\right) ; r_{k,1}, -r_{i,2}, -r_{i,3};$$

There is one membrane in the P system. The objects in membrane 1 are stored in M_1. And the multiset ε is the set of objects located in the environment of the system. Note that all of these objects have any number of copies.

If and only if l_i and a_1 exist in membrane 1 at the same time, $r_{i,1}$ can be executed. By using rule $r_{i,1}$, an object l_i in membrane 1 is consumed, and one object a_2 is requested from the environment. At the same time, rules $r_{i,2}, r_{i,3}$ are produced, and $r_{i,1}$ is removed. At the next step, one of rules $r_{i,2}, r_{i,3}$ is chosen to be executed non-deterministically. If rule $r_{i,2}$ (resp. $r_{i,3}$) is executed, object l_j (resp. l_k) is requested from the environment. Simultaneously, rule $r_{j,1}$ (resp. $r_{k,1}$) is produced, and rules $r_{i,2}$ and $r_{i,3}$ are removed.

A configuration of CRQPR P systems is described by all multisets of objects over Γ associated with the regions, and the multiset of objects over $\Gamma \backslash \varepsilon$ associated with the environment at that moment. Note that the objects from ε have an arbitrary number of copies. Hence they are not properly changed along with the computation. The initial configuration is $(M_{10}, \ldots, M_{q0}, \emptyset)$.

Starting from the initial configuration and applying rules as described above, a sequence of configurations can be obtained. Each passage from a configuration to a successor configuration is called a transition. A configuration is a halting configuration if no rule of the system can apply. A sequence of transitions starting from the initial configuration is a computation. Only a halting computation gives a result, encoded by the number of copies of objects present in the output region i_{out}.

The set of natural numbers computed by the CRQPR P system is denoted by $N(\Pi)$. CRQPR P systems with at most m membranes, and using request rules of length at most t, is denoted by $NCP_m^{pr}(req_t)$. If one of the parameters m and t is not bounded, it is replaced with $*$.

3   Universality of CRQPR P Systems

3.1   Turing Universality of CRQPR P Systems as a Number Generator

It is known that the register machine with three registers can generate all sets of numbers and therefore characterizes NRE [11]. Let $M_v = (3, H, l_0, l_h, I)$ be a register machine with 3 registers labeled by 1, 2, and 3, and it generates a number in the following way: at the beginning, all the registers are empty, storing the number zero. The machine starts using l_0, and continues to apply instructions as indicated by the labels (and made possible by the contents of registers); When M_v reaches the halt instruction l_h and stops, the number presented in register 1 at this time is the number generated by it. If the computation does not halt, M_v generates no number.

In this section, CRQPR P systems working in the maximally parallel mode are used to generate any set of Turing computable natural numbers by simulating M_v.

Theorem 1. $NCP_2^{pr}(req_2) = NRE$

Proof. We only prove $NCP_2^{pr}(req_2) = NRE$ because the inclusion of the opposite direction comes from the Church-Turing thesis. A CRQPR system of degree 2 is constructed simulating M_v.

$$\Pi_1 = (\Gamma, \varepsilon, \mu, M_1, M_2, R, i_{out}) \tag{3}$$

where

- $\Gamma = \{a_q \mid 1 \leq q \leq 3\} \cup \{d, e, f, \#\} \cup \{l \mid l \in H\}$
- $\varepsilon = \{a_q \mid 1 \leq q \leq 3\} \cup \{d, e, f, \#\}$
- $\mu = [[\,]_2]_1$
- $M_1 = \emptyset, M_2 = \{e\}$
- $i_{out} = 1$
- R is divided into the following parts:
- For each ADD instruction $l_i : (ADD(r), l_j, l_k)\,(q \neq r)$:

$$r_{i,1} : \left(l_i\,(a_q)^*\,(a_r)^* \mid l_i^- \leftarrow a_r, 1\right); -r_{i,1}, r_{i,2}, r_{i,3};$$
$$r_{i,2} : \left((a_q)^*\,(a_r)^+ \mid \lambda \leftarrow l_j, 1\right); r_{j,1}, -r_{i,2}, -r_{i,3};$$
$$r_{i,3} : \left((a_q)^*\,(a_r)^+ \mid \lambda \leftarrow l_k, 1\right); r_{k,1}, -r_{i,2}, -r_{i,3}$$

Three rules can implement the ADD instruction l_i. Suppose that after a series of calculations, l_i appears activating rule $r_{i,1}$. Object l_i in membrane 1 is consumed, one copy of object a_r is requested from the environment. At the same time, rules $r_{i,2}$ and $r_{i,3}$ are produced, and $r_{i,1}$ is removed. At the next step, one of rules $r_{i,2}, r_{i,3}$ is chosen to be executed non-deterministically. If rule $r_{i,2}$ (resp. $r_{i,3}$) is executed, object l_j (resp. l_k) is requested from the environment. Simultaneously, rule $r_{j,1}$ (resp. $r_{k,1}$) is produced, and rules $r_{i,2}$ and $r_{i,3}$ are removed. Hence, the amount of object a_r membrane 1 adds one indicating that the number stored in register r is increased by one. In this way, instruction l_i of M_v accurately simulated with Π_1, and the system starts to carry out the instruction with label l_j or l_k.

- For each SUB instruction $l_i : (SUB(r), l_i, l_k)\,(q \neq r)$:

$$r_{i,1} : \left(l_i\,(a_q)^*\,(a_r)^* \mid l_i^- \leftarrow d, 1\right); -r_{i,1}, r_{i,2};$$
$$r_{i,2} : \left(d\,(a_q)^*\,(a_r)^* \mid \lambda \leftarrow f, 1\right); -r_{i,2}, r_{i,3}, r_{i,4};$$
$$r_{i,3} : \left(e \mid e^- \leftarrow a_r, 2\right); -r_{i,3}, r_{i,5};$$
$$r_{i,4} : \left(df\,(a_q)^*\,(a_r)^* \mid \lambda \leftarrow e, 1\right); -r_{i,3}, -r_{i,4}, r_{i,6};$$
$$r_{i,5} : \left(a_r \mid a_r^- \leftarrow d, 2\right); -r_{i,5}, -r_{i,6}, r_{i,7}, r_{i,8};$$
$$r_{i,6} : \left(e \mid e^- \leftarrow d, 2\right); -r_{i,6}, r_{i,7}, r_{i,9};$$
$$r_{i,7} : \left(d \mid d^- \leftarrow e, 2\right); -r_{i,7};$$
$$r_{i,8} : \left(f\,(a_q)^*\,(a_r)^* \mid f^- \leftarrow l_j, 1\right); -r_{i,8}, r_{j,1};$$
$$r_{i,9} : \left(f\,(a_q)^* \mid f^- \leftarrow l_k, 1\right); -r_{i,9}, r_{k,1};$$

A SUB instruction l_i is accomplished using the following rules. Suppose that after a series of calculations, l_i appears at step t. Rule $r_{i,1}$ is activated at step $t+1$ consuming this l_i, and requesting one object d from the environment. Meanwhile, rule $r_{i,1}$ is removed, and rule $r_{i,2}$ is generated. At step $t+2$, object f is asked for from the environment, simultaneously, rule $r_{i,2}$ is removed, and rules $r_{i,3}$ and $r_{i,4}$ are created. In what follows, there are two cases.

– The number of copies a_r in membrane 1 is at least 1, which corresponds to the number n in register r meets the condition that $n \neq 0$. In this case, at step $t+3$, rules $r_{i,3}$ and $r_{i,4}$ are enabled. By using rule $r_{i,3}$, an object e in membrane 2 is consumed, and one object a_r is requested from membrane 1. At the same time, rules $r_{i,4}$ is applied. Membrane 1 receives one object e from the environment consuming nothing. With the execution of rules $r_{i,3}$ and $r_{i,4}$, $r_{i,5}$ and $r_{i,6}$ are produced, and $r_{i,3}$ and $r_{i,4}$ are removed. At step $t+4$, by using rule $r_{i,5}$, object d from membrane 1 enters membrane 2, and object a_r is consumed. Meanwhile, rules $r_{i,5}$ and $r_{i,6}$ are removed, and rules $r_{i,7}$ and $r_{i,8}$ are created. Finally, by applying rule $r_{i,7}$, object d is consumed, and membrane 1 sends object e to membrane 2. By using rule $r_{i,8}$, object f is consumed, and object l_j is sent to membrane 1. With the execution of the two rules, rule $r_{j,1}$ is produced, rules $r_{i,7}$ and $r_{i,8}$ are removed. So that, one copy of object a_r is consumed (achieving that the number stored in register r is decreased by one), and the system begins to work in order to run l_j (see that in Table 1).

Table 1. A SUB instruction $l_i : (SUB(r), l_j, l_k)$ with register r is not empty $(n \geq 1)$.

Step	Rules in membrane 1	Rules in membrane 2	M_1	M_2
t	$r_{i,1}$	–	$\{l_i (a_q)^* (a_r)^n\}$	$\{e\}$
$t+1$	$r_{i,2}$	–	$\{(a_q)^* (a_r)^n\} \cup \{d\}$	$\{e\}$
$t+2$	$r_{i,4}$	$r_{i,3}$	$\{(a_q)^* (a_r)^n\} \cup \{d, f\}$	$\{e\}$
$t+3$	–	$r_{i,5}, r_{i,6}$	$\{(a_q)^* (a_r)^{n-1}\} \cup \{d, f, e\}$	$\{a_r\}$
$t+4$	$r_{i,8}$	$r_{i,7}$	$\{(a_q)^* (a_r)^{n-1}\} \cup \{f, e\}$	$\{d\}$
$t+5$	$r_{j,1}$	–	$\{(a_q)^* (a_r)^{n-1}\} \cup \{l_j\}$	$\{e\}$

– There is no object a_r in membrane 1, indicating the condition that the number stored in register r is 0. In this case, at step $t+3$, only rule $r_{i,4}$ in membrane 1 is enabled, receiving one object e from the environment and consuming nothing. At the same time, rules $r_{i,3}$ and $r_{i,4}$ are removed, and $r_{i,6}$ is produced. At step $t+4$, membrane 2 receives an object d from membrane 1 and consumes an object e by using $r_{i,6}$, meanwhile, $r_{i,7}$ and $r_{i,9}$ are produced and $r_{i,6}$ is removed. At step $t+5$, by using rule $r_{i,7}$, object e in membrane 1 is sent to membrane 2, and object d in membrane 2 is consumed simultaneously. By using rule $r_{i,9}$, object f is consumed, and the environment sends l_k to membrane 1. The system then starts to simulate the command l_k (see Table 2).

Table 2. A SUB instruction $l_i : (SUB(r), l_j, l_k)$ with register r is not empty $(n \geq 1)$.

Step	Rules in membrane 1	Rules in membrane 2	M_1	M_2
t	$r_{i,1}$	–	$\{l_i\,(a_q)^*\}$	$\{e\}$
$t+1$	$r_{i,2}$	–	$\{(a_q)^*\} \cup \{d\}$	$\{e\}$
$t+2$	$r_{i,4}$	$r_{i,3}$	$\{(a_q)^*\} \cup \{d, f\}$	$\{e\}$
$t+3$	–	$r_{i,6}$	$\{(a_q)^*\} \cup \{d, f, e\}$	$\{e\}$
$t+4$	$r_{i,9}$	$r_{i,7}$	$\{(a_q)^*\} \cup \{f, e\}$	$\{d\}$
$t+5$	$r_{k,1}$	–	$\{(a_q)^*\} \cup \{l_k\}$	$\{e\}$

- For each HALT instruction l_h:
$r_{h,1} : \left(l_h \mid l_h^- \leftarrow \#, 1\right); -r_{h,1}$

When object l_h appears in membrane 1, rule $r_{h,1}$ is executed, deleting object l_h and introducing object $\#$ showing that the computation has finished. At the same time, rule $r_{h,1}$ is removed, and no rules exist in the system, then the computation halts. The number of copies of object a_1 in membrane 1 corresponds to the result of the computation, hence $N(M_v) = N(\Pi_1)$.

Theorem 2. $NCP_1^{pr}(req_3) = NRE$

Proof. We only prove $NCP_1^{pr}(req_3) = NRE$ by constructing a CRQPR system of degree 1 to simulate M_v

$$\Pi_2 = (\Gamma, \varepsilon, \mu, M, R, i_{out}) \tag{4}$$

where

- $\Gamma = \{a_q \mid 1 \leq q \leq 3\} \cup \{b, c\} \cup \{l \mid l \in H\}$;
- $\varepsilon = \{a_q \mid 1 \leq q \leq 3\} \cup \{b, c\}$;
- $\mu = []_1$;
- $M_1 = \emptyset$;
- $i_{out} = 1$
- R is divided into the following parts:
- For each ADD instruction $l_i : (ADD(r), l_j, l_k)\,(q \neq r)$:

$$r_{i,1} : \left(l_i\,(a_q)^*\,(a_r)^* \mid l_i^- \leftarrow a_r, 1\right); -r_{i,1}, r_{i,2}, r_{i,3};$$
$$r_{i,2} : \left((a_q)^*\,(a_r)^+ \mid \lambda \leftarrow l_j, 1\right); r_{j,1}, -r_{i,2}, -r_{i,3};$$
$$r_{i,3} : \left((a_q)^*\,(a_r)^+ \mid \lambda \leftarrow l_k, 1\right); r_{k,1}, -r_{i,2}, -r_{i,3}$$

The execution process of the rules is the same as that in Theorem 1.

- For each SUB instruction $l_i : (SUB(r), l_j, l_k)\,(q \neq r)$:

$$r_{i,1} : \left(l_i\,(a_q)^*\,(a_r)^* \mid l_i^- \leftarrow b, 1\right); -r_{i,1}, r_{i,2};$$
$$r_{i,2} : \left(b\,(a_q)^*\,(a_r)^* \mid b^- \leftarrow c, 1\right); -r_{i,2}, r_{i,3}, r_{i,4};$$
$$r_{i,3} : \left((a_q)^*\,(a_r)^+ c \mid a_r c^- \leftarrow l_j, 1\right); -r_{i,3}, -r_{i,4}, r_{j,1}$$
$$r_{i,4} : \left((a_q)^* c \mid c^- \leftarrow l_k, 1\right); -r_{i,3}, -r_{i,4}, r_{k,1}$$

In this case, suppose that l_i and $r_{i,1}$ appear in membrane 1 at step t. Then at the next step, by using rule $r_{i,1}$, membrane 1 receives an object b from the environment and consumes l_i. At the same time, rule $r_{i,2}$ is produced and $r_{i,1}$ is removed. At step t+2, membrane 1 gets an object c from the environment and consumes object d by using $r_{i,2}$. Rules $r_{i,3}$ and $r_{i,4}$ are produced, and $r_{i,2}$ is removed. The next step has two cases. If there are some copies of a_r in membrane 1, $r_{i,3}$ is performed, consuming one copy of a_r and object c, introducing one l_j to membrane 1 from the environment, and switching to perform $r_{j,1}$ simulating command l_j. If there is no a_r in membrane 1, $r_{i,4}$ is performed, consuming object c, introducing one l_k to membrane 1, and switching to perform $r_{k,1}$ simulating command l_k.

– For each HALT instruction l_h:

$$r_{h,1} : \left(l_h \mid l_h^- \leftarrow \#, 1 \right) ; -r_{h,1}$$

As mentioned, when rule $r_{h,1}$ is executed, object l_h is consumed, and object $\#$ is introduced showing that the computation has finished. No rule exists in the system at this time, and the computation halts. The number of copies of object a_1 in membrane 1 corresponds to the result of the computation, hence $N(M_v) = N(\Pi_2)$.

We have proved that the CRQPR P system with one membrane use request rules of length at most three can generate any set of Turing computable natural numbers.

3.2   Turing Universality of CRQPR P Systems for Computing Functions

In this section, CRQPR P systems working in the maximally parallel mode are used for computing functions.

A register machine $M = (m, H, l_0, l_h, I)$ can compute a function $f : N^k \to N$ by these steps: Import the parameters to specific registers; The computation starts with the initial instruction l_0 and halts with the instruction l_h; At last, the number stored in a specific register is used as the function value, and other registers are empty.

Let $(\phi_0, \phi_1, \phi_2, \ldots)$ be a fixed admissible enumeration of the set of unary partial recursive functions. We use $M(n_1, n_2, \ldots, n_k)$ to express the partial function computed by the register machine M. A register machine M is universal if there is a recursive function g such for all natural numbers x, y, we have $\phi_x(y) = M(g(x), y)$.

In this study, a specific universal register machine $M_u = (9, H, l_0, l_h, I)$ defined in [9, 20] is used to compute any $\phi_x(y)$. For each recursive function g such that for all $x, y \in N$, we have $\phi_x(y) = M_u(g(x), y)$. In the register machine M_u shown in Fig. 1, there are 9 registers labeled by 1, 2, ..., 9, and 25 instructions, and the last instruction is the halt instruction. As mentioned, $g(x)$ and y are imported in registers 2 and 3, and the result is stored in register 9.

$$l_0 : (SUB(2), l_1, l_2),$$
$$l_1 : (ADD(2), l_0),$$
$$l_2 : (ADD(7), l_3),$$
$$l_3 : (SUB(7), l_2, l_4),$$
$$l_4 : (SUB(7), l_5, l_3),$$
$$l_5 : (ADD(7), l_6),$$
$$l_6 : (SUB(8), l_7, l_8),$$
$$l_7 : (ADD(8), l_4),$$
$$l_8 : (SUB(7), l_9, l_0),$$
$$l_9 : (ADD(7), l_{10}),$$
$$l_{10} : (SUB(5), l_0, l_{11}),$$
$$l_{11} : (SUB(5), l_{12}, l_{13}),$$
$$l_{12} : (SUB(6), l_{14}, l_{15}),$$
$$l_{13} : (SUB(6), l_{18}, l_{19}),$$
$$l_{14} : (SUB(6), l_{16}, l_{17}),$$
$$l_{15} : (SUB(6), l_{18}, l_{20}),$$
$$l_{16} : (ADD(5), l_{11}),$$
$$l_{17} : (ADD(5), l_{21}),$$
$$l_{18} : (SUB(5), l_0),$$
$$l_{19} : (SUB(5), l_0, l_{18}),$$
$$l_{20} : (ADD(1), l_0),$$
$$l_{21} : (ADD(1), l_{18}),$$
$$l_{22} : (SUB(1), l_{23}, l_h),$$
$$l_{23} : (ADD(9), l_{22}),$$
$$l_h : HALT$$

Fig. 1. The universal register machine M_u from [20].

Theorem 3. *CRQPR P systems working in the maximally parallel mode can compute Turing computable set of functions.*

Proof. A CRQPR P system Π_3 is constructed to simulate the computation of the universal register machine M_u, which has ADD, SUB and HALT instructions, and an INPUT module. The INPUT module can read the binary sequence from the environment.

The input arguments $x_1, x_2, \ldots, x_k$ are denoted by binary sequence $z = 10^{x_1-1}10^{x_2-1}1 \ldots 10^{x_k-1}1$. Membrane 1 receives one object b when the bit of z is 1 and receives nothing when the bit of z is 0.

The number of a_r in member 1 corresponds to the number stored in register r of M_u, and the number of a_9 in member 1 indicates the result of M_u. In the initial configuration, all the membranes have no a_q inside. The format definition of the CRQPR P system is as follows.

$$\Pi_3 = (\Gamma, \varepsilon, \mu, M_1, M_2, R, i_{in}, i_{out}),$$

where

- $\Gamma = \{a_q \mid 1 \leq q \leq 9\} \cup \{b, d, e, f, g, \#\} \cup \{l \mid l \in H\}$;
- $\varepsilon = \{a_q \mid 1 \leq q \leq 9\} \cup \{b, d, e, f, g, \#\}$;
- $\mu = [[]_2]_1$;
- $\mathcal{M}_1 = \emptyset, M_2 = \{e\}$;
- $i_{in} = 1$;
- $i_{out} = 1$;
- R :

- For the INPUT module:

$$r_1 : \left(b \mid b^- \leftarrow g, 1\right); -r_1, r_2, r_3;$$
$$r_2 : \left(g(b) * (a_2)^* \mid \lambda \leftarrow a_2, 1\right);$$
$$r_3 : \left(gb\,(a_2)^* \mid gb^- \leftarrow g, 1\right); -r_2, -r_3, r_4, r_5$$
$$r_4 : \left(g(b) * (a_2)^* (a_3)^* \mid \lambda \leftarrow a_3, 1\right);$$
$$r_5 : \left(gb\,(a_2)^* (a_3)^* \mid gb^- \leftarrow l_0, 1\right); -r_4, -r_5, r_1, r_{0,1}$$

First, $g(x)$ and y are imported by the INPUT module. In the initial configuration, membrane 1 has rule r_1, and membrane 2 has one object e. By reading the binary sequence $10^{g(x)-1}10^{y-1}1$, $g(x)$ copies of a_2 and y copies of a_3 enter membrane 1.

At the first step, membrane 1 receives one object b activating rule r_1. One object b in membrane 1 is consumed, and one object g is requested from the environment. At the same time, rules r_2 and r_3 are produced, and rule r_1 is removed. At the next step, rule r_2 is enabled, requesting one object a_2 from the environment consuming nothing. This rule keeps activating until the second b enters membrane 1 at step $g(x) + 1$ activating rule r_3. At the next step, object g and object b are consumed, and object g is requested from the environment by using r_3. With the execution of rules r_3, rules r_4 and r_5 are produced, and rules r_2 and r_3 are removed. At this moment, the amount of a_2 in membrane 1 is $g(x)$.

At step $g(x) + 3$, r_4 is applied requesting one object a_3 from the environment consuming nothing. This rule keeps activating until the third b enters membrane 1 after $y - 1$ steps which activates rule r_5. At the next step, by using rule r_5, object b and object g are consumed, and object l_0 is requested from the environment. At the same time, rules r_4 and r_5 are removed, and rules $r_{0,1}$ and r_1 are produced. At this time, the amount of a_3 in membrane 1 is y.

With object l_0 and rule $r_{0,1}$, the system then starts to simulate the command l_0 of M_u (see that in Table 3).

- For each ADD instruction $l_i : (ADD(r), l_j)\,(q \neq r)$:

$$r_{i,1} : \left(l_i\,(a_q)^* (a_r)^* \mid l_i^- \leftarrow a_r, 1\right); -r_{i,1}, r_{i,2};$$
$$r_{i,2} : \left((a_q)^* (a_r)^+ \mid \lambda \leftarrow l_j, 1\right); -r_{i,2}, r_{j,1}$$

The ADD instruction l_i can be implemented by these two rules. Suppose that at step t, l_i appears activating rule $r_{i,1}$. Object l_i is consumed, one copy of object a_r is requested from the environment. At the same time, rule $r_{i,1}$ is removed, and rule $r_{i,2}$ is produced. At the next step, rule $r_{i,2}$ is executed, requesting object l_j from the environment. Simultaneously, rule $r_{j,1}$ is produced, and rule $r_{i,2}$ is removed. Hence, the amount of object a_r membrane 1 adds one. In this way, instruction l_i of M_u accurately simulated with Π_3, and the system starts to carry out the instruction with label l_j (see that in Table 4).

Table 3. The INPUT module

Step	Rules in membrane 1	Rules in membrane 2	M_1	M_2
0	r_1	–	$\emptyset$	$\{e\}$
1	r_1	–	$\{b\}$	$\{e\}$
2	r_2, r_3	–	$\{g\}$	$\{e\}$
3	r_2, r_3	–	$\{a_2\} \cup \{g\}$	$\{e\}$
4	r_2, r_3	–	$\{(a_2)^2\} \cup \{g\}$	$\{e\}$
...	r_2, r_3	–	...	$\{e\}$
$g(x)$	r_2, r_3	–	$\{(a_2)^{g(x)-2}\} \cup \{g\}$	$\{e\}$
$g(x)+1$	r_2, r_3	–	$\{(a_2)^{g(x)-1}\} \cup \{g,b\}$	$\{e\}$
$g(x)+2$	r_4, r_5	–	$\{(a_2)^{g(x)}\} \cup \{g\}$	$\{e\}$
$g(x)+3$	r_4, r_5	–	$\{(a_2)^{g(x)} a_3\} \cup \{g\}$	$\{e\}$
...	r_4, r_5	–	...	$\{e\}$
$g(x)+y$	r_4, r_5	–	$\{(a_2)^{g(x)} (a_3)^{y-2}\} \cup \{g\}$	$\{e\}$
$g(x)+y+1$	r_4, r_5	–	$\{(a_2)^{g(x)} (a_3)^{y-1}\} \cup \{g,b\}$	$\{e\}$
$g(x)+y+2$	$r_1, r_{0,1}$	–	$\{(a_2)^{g(x)} (a_3)^{y}\} \cup \{l_0\}$	$\{e\}$

Table 4. AN ADD instruction $l_i : (ADD(r), l_j)$.

Step	Rules in membrane 1	Rules in membrane 2	M_1	M_2
t	$r_{i,1}, r_1$	–	$\{l_i (a_q)^* (a_r)^n\}$	$\{e\}$
$t+1$	$r_{i,2}, r_1$	–	$\{(a_q)^* (a_r)^{n+1}\}$	$\{e\}$
$t+2$	$r_{j,1}, r_1$	–	$\{l_j (a_q)^* (a_q)^{n+1}\}$	$\{e\}$

– For each SUB instruction $l_i : (SUB(r), l_j, l_k) \, (q \neq r)$:

$$r_{i,1} : \left(l_i (a_q)^* (a_r)^* \mid l_i^- \leftarrow d, 1\right), -r_{i,1}, r_{i,2};$$
$$r_{i,2} : \left(d (a_q)^* (a_r)^* \mid \lambda \leftarrow f, 1\right); -r_{i,2}, r_{i,3}, r_{i,4};$$
$$r_{i,3} : \left(e \mid e^- \leftarrow a_r, 2\right); -r_{i3}, r_{i,5};$$
$$r_{i,4} : \left(df (a_q)^* (a_r)^* \mid \lambda \leftarrow e, 1\right); -r_{i,3}, -r_{i,4}, r_{i,6};$$
$$r_{i,5} : \left(a_r \mid a_r^- \leftarrow d, 2\right); -r_{i,5}, -r_{i,6}, r_{i,7}, r_{i,8};$$
$$r_{i,6} : \left(e \mid e^- \leftarrow d, 2\right); -r_{i,6}, r_{i,7}, r_{i,9};$$
$$r_{i,7} : \left(d \mid d^- \leftarrow e, 2\right); -r_{i,7};$$
$$r_{i,8} : \left(f (a_q)^* (a_r)^* \mid f^- \leftarrow l_j, 1\right); -r_{i,8}, r_{j,1};$$
$$r_{i,9} : \left(f (a_q)^* \mid f^- \leftarrow l_k, 1\right); -r_{i,9}, r_{k,1}$$

– For the HALT instruction l_h :

$$r_{h,1} : \left(l_h \mid l_h^- \leftarrow \#, 1\right); -r_{h,1}$$

The rules for the SUB and HALT instructions are the same as that in Theorem 1, so the details are not given here.

When the computation halts, the amount of object a_9 in membrane 1 corresponds to the result of the computation.

In this P system, we have used two membranes which only use request rules of length at most three and different types of objects:

- the amount of $a_q (1 \leq q \leq 9)$ for the number in the q-th register,
- object $l_i (i = 0, 1, \ldots, 23, h)$ for 25 instructions labels,
- auxiliary objects b and g for INPUT module,
- auxiliary objects d, e and f for SUB instructions,
- auxiliary object $\#$ for HALT instruction.

4   Conclusion and Discussion

In this work, a new variant called cell-like P systems with request rules and rule production/removal is proposed, and the computational power of such P systems has been investigated. Specifically, it is proved that CRQPR P systems with two membranes only use request rules of length at most two or one membrane with request rules of length at most three can compute Turing computable natural numbers. And CRQPR P systems with two membranes only use request rules of length at most three can compute Turing computable function.

Recently, it has been developing in the field of membrane computing. Song et al. [17] show that with the restrictive condition of monodirectionality, monodirectional tissue P systems with promoters are still computationally powerful. And Song et al. [18] show that monodirectional tissue P systems using two cells are universal. Song et al. proposed Cell-like P systems with evolutional symport/antiport rules and membrane creation [5].

For further research, it is worth studying whether the computational university can be achieved with fewer resources. The idea of rules production/removal can be extended to other types of P systems. It is also meaningful to discuss the application of the CRQPR P systems.

References

1. Artiom, A., Rudolf, F., Sergiu, I.: P systems with randomized right-hand sides of rules. Theor. Comput. Sci. **805**, 144–160 (2020). ISSN 0304-3975, https://doi.org/10.1016/j.tcs.2018.07.016. (https://www.sciencedirect.com/science/article/pii/S0304397518304973)
2. Baranda, A.V., Castellanos, J., Arroyo, F., Luengo, C.: Bio-language for computing with membranes. In: Kelemen, J., Sosík, P. (eds.) ECAL 2001. LNCS (LNAI), vol. 2159, pp. 176–185. Springer, Heidelberg (2001). https://doi.org/10.1007/3-540-44811-X_19
3. Blbe, F.D.: SNQ P systems with weights on synapses. Procedia Comput. Sci. **159**, 1747–1756 (2019)
4. Bogdan, A., Péter, B., Gabriel, C., György, V.: Local time membrane systems and time petri nets. Theor. Comput. **805**, 175–192 (2020). ISSN 0304-3975, https://doi.org/10.1016/j.tcs.2018.06.013. (https://www.sciencedirect.com/science/article/pii/S0304397518304213)

5. Song, B., Li, K., Orellana-Martín, D., Valencia-Cabrera, L., Perez-Jimenez, M.J.: Cell-like p systems with evolutionary symport/antiport rules and membrane creation. Inf. Comput. (2020). https://doi.org/10.1016/j.ic.2020.104542

6. Díaz-Pernil, D., Christinal, H.A., Gutiérrez-Naranjo, M.A.: Solving the 3-COL problem by using tissue p systems without environment and proteins on cells. Inf. Sci. **430**, 240–246 (2016)

7. Frias, T., et al.: A new scalable parallel adder based on spiking neural p systems, dendritic behavior, rules on the synapses and astrocyte-like control to compute multiple signed numbers. Neurocomputing **319**(Nov.30), 176–187 (2018)

8. Guo, P., Quan, C., Ye, L.: Upsimulator: a general p system simulator. Knowl.-Based Syst. **170**, 20–25 (2019). https://doi.org/10.1016/j.knosys.2019.01.013. http://www.sciencedirect.com/science/article/pii/S0950705119300115

9. Korec, I.: Small universal register machines. Theor. Comput. Sci. **168**(2), 267–301 (1996)

10. Linqiang Pan, B.S.: P systems with rule production and removal. Fundam. Informaticae **171**, 313–329 (2020)

11. Minsky, M.L.: Computation: Finite and Infinite Machines (1967)

12. Pan, L.Q., Zhang, X.Y., Zeng, X.X., Wang, J.: Research advances and prospect of spiking neural p systems: research advances and prospect of spiking neural p systems. Chin. J. Comput. **31**(12), 2090–2096 (2009)

13. Paun, G., Rozenberg, G., Salomaa, A.: The Oxford Handbook of Membrane Computing (2010)

14. Peng, H., Wang, J., Pérez-Jiménez, M.J., Riscos-Núñez, A.: An unsupervised learning algorithm for membrane computing. Inf. Sci. **304**, 80–91 (2015)

15. Guo, P., Dai, Y., Chen, H.: A p system for Hamiltonian cycle problem. Optik Int. J. Light Electron Opt. **127**(20), 8461–8468 (2016)

16. Păun, G.: Computing with membranes. J. Comput. Syst. Sci. **61**(1), 108–143 (2000)

17. Song, B., Zeng, X., Jiang, M., Perez-Jimenez, M.J.: Monodirectional tissue p systems with promoters. IEEE Trans. Cybern. **51**(1), 438–450 (2020)

18. Song, B., Zeng, X., Rodríguez-Patón, A.: Monodirectional tissue p systems with channel states. Inf. Sci. **546**, 206–219 (2020)

19. Song, B., Zhang, C., Pan, L.: Tissue-like p systems with evolutional symport/antiport rules. Inf. Sci. **378**, 177–193 (2017). https://doi.org/10.1016/j.ins.2016.10.046

20. Song, T., Pan, L.: Spiking neural p systems with request rules. Neurocomputing **193**(Jun.12), 193–200 (2016)

21. Song, T., Zheng, P., Wong, M.L.D., Jiang, M., Zeng, X.: On the computational power of asynchronous axon membrane systems. IEEE Trans. Emerg. Top. Comput. Intell. **4**(5), 696–704 (2019)

22. Sun, M., Qu, J.: Weighted spiking neural p systems with structural plasticity working in maximum spiking strategy. In: International Conference on Information Technology in Medicine and Education (2017)

23. Wang, J., et al.: Interval-valued fuzzy spiking neural p systems for fault diagnosis of power transmission networks. Eng. Appl. Artif. Intell. **82**(Jun), 102–109 (2019)

24. Wu, T., Wang, Y., Jiang, S., Su, Y., Shi, X.: Spiking neural p systems with rules on synapses and anti-spikes. Theor. Comput. Sci. **724**, 13–27 (2017)

An Editable k-Nearest Neighbor Classifier Based on Tissue-Like P Systems

Juan Hu[1]([✉]), Zhiliang Chen[1], Liping Shi[1], Jiao He[1], Hong Peng[2], and Jun Wang[3]

[1] Department of Information and Communication, Officers College of PAP, Chengdu 610213, China
[2] School of Computer and Software Engineering, Xihua University, Chengdu 610039, China
[3] School of Electrical Engineering and Electronic Information, Xihua University, Chengdu 610039, China

Abstract. In this paper, a new editable k-nearest neighbor classifier evolved by P systems is proposed, called Edit-kNN-P. A tissue-like P system consists of cell-membrance is designed as the computational framework. The tissue-like P system is used to search an optimal editable sample subset from original data set. Each object in the cell is a candidate indictor vector, which represents an editable subset. The discrete velocity-location model is used to evolve the objects in cells. Communication rules are used to share the objects: (i) between cells, (ii) between cell and the environment. Based on the optimal editable sample subset, k-nearest neighbor classifier is used to classify the unknown samples. The effectiveness of the proposed approach is shown on 12 benchmark dataset. The results are also compared with four recently developed kNN algorithms as well as classical kNN algorithm.

Keywords: Membrane computing · P systems · k-nearest neighbor algorithm · Classification

1 Introduction

k-nearest neighbor (kNN) classifier [1] is one of the most famous supervised learning algorithms. The idea is to find k-nearest neighbors in data set for an unknown sample, and then determine the category of unknown sample according to the k neighbors. kNN classifier is a simple and effective classifier, it has been widely used in many fields [2–4], such as data mining, pattern recognition, machine learning, bioinformatics.

The kNN algorithm was first introduced by Cover and Hart [1], and then a lot of variants of kNN algorithms were proposed in the past years. Rhee and Hwang [6] presented a kNN algorithm based on interval type-2 fuzzy sets, known as T2FKNN. Arif et al. [7] proposed a pruning fuzzy k-nearest neighbor classifier for the classification, called PFKNN, which firstly established a series of

© Springer Nature Singapore Pte Ltd. 2021
L. Pan et al. (Eds.): BIC-TA 2020, CCIS 1363, pp. 596–610, 2021.
https://doi.org/10.1007/978-981-16-1354-8_41

prototype data to express the boundary points of different clusters in data set, and then increased the misclassified reference set. In addition, some evolutionary techniques were used to improve the performance of kNN algorithms. Hu and Xie [8] proposed a method that used genetic algorithm to improve the fuzzy kNN algorithm, called GAfuzzy-kNN. Derrac et al. [9] proposed an evolutionary fuzzy k-nearest neighbor algorithm based on interval-valued fuzzy sets, called EF-kNN-IVFS, which used interval-valued fuzzy sets to compute the membership degrees of fuzzy kNN training instances.

The complexity of kNN algorithm is usually related to the number of samples in training set, and the training set is always required for the identification of each unknown sample. The kNN algorithm is sensitive to sample imbalance, noise and outliers etc., the computational efficiency and performance of kNN algorithm can be severely restricted. To overcome the shortcomings, the editable kNN algorithm has received attention in the past years. Wilson [10] presented an editable KNN algorithm. Gil-Pita et al. [11] proposed an evolutionary editable k-nearest neighbor classifier, which obtains an editable sample set by evolutionary techniques and then uses the editable training set to train the kNN algorithm. These editable kNN algorithms can reduce noise data and computing complexity. However, the computation efficiency and performance still needs to further improve.

Membrane computing (as known as P system) is a distributed parallel computing model, inspired by the structure and function of living cells as well as the cooperation of cells in tissues, organs, and biological neural networks [12,13]. In the past years, a lot of variants of P systems have been proposed [14–21], and these were used in a variety of real-world problems. For instance, knowledge representation [22,23], image and signal processing [24–26], fault diagnosis [27], ecology and system biology [28–30].

In recent years, P system applications on machine learning have received great attention, especially on unsupervised learning. Zhao et al. [31] developed an improved clustering algorithm, where the rules in cell-like P systems were applied to achieve k-medoids algorithm. Huang et al. [32] proposed a clustering algorithm in the framework of membrane computing, PSO-MC, which applied the velocity-position model and communication mechanism of objects in cells to determine the cluster centers. Peng et al. [33] developed a fuzzy clustering algorithm based on evolution-communication membrane system. Liu et al. [34] used a cell-like P systems with promoters and inhibitors to develop a k-medoids clustering algorithm. In [35], a membrane clustering algorithm with hybrid evolution mechanism was investigated. In addition, two automatic clustering algorithms using membrane systems were presented in [36] and [37], respectively. Wang et al. [39] discussed a decision tree algorithm induced by membrane systems.

This paper focuses on a supervised learning problem under the framework of membrane computing. We developed an editable kNN algorithm evolved by P system, called Edit-kNN-P. The main motivation behind this work is to overcome the shortcomings of kNN algorithm, and improve the computational efficiency and performance. Under the framework of membrane computing, an optimal

editable training sample set can be obtained by using the evolution and communication mechanisms of P system. The editable set is a subset of original sample
set, and then the kNN algorithm is trained on the optimal editable sample set.
The proposed Edit-kNN-P algorithm has following advantages:

(1) Improvement of classification accuracy.
    The Edit-kNN-P algorithm evolve an optimal editable sample subset with
    the parallelism of P system, it can solve the problem of sample imbalance, the
    noise and outliers are excluded, and then classification accuracy is greatly
    improved.
(2) Robustness. Known as the kNN algorithm performance is relative to the
    parameter k, so we experience on different $k\{3, 5, 7, 9\}$. And we proposed
    Edit-kNN-P has the most number of the best performance on different
    dataset.

2   KNN and Editable kNN Classifiers

2.1   KNN Classifier

k-nearest neighbor (kNN) classifier is one of the most popular classification algorithms. The similarity is used to determine k nearest neighbors for an unknown
sample, and the category with maximum probability (the highest number of
occurrences) is used as its class label.

Table 1. kNN algorithm

Input
Datasets X,test sample y, k value
Output
k nearest neighbors for the test sample y
Begin
for i=1 to len(X)
calculate the similarity between y and x_i
end for
get the top k (according to minimum value)
assign y into the maximum probability category
End

Suppose $D = \{x_1, x_2, \ldots, x_n\}$ is a set of n labeled samples, and y is a sample
with an unknown label. Table 1 gives a classical kNN algorithm.

KNN algorithm is simple and easy to implement. however, kNN algorithm
needs to calculate the distance (or similarity) between the unknown sample and
all the training samples, and correct it properly. The kNN algorithm is sensitive
to sample imbalance, noise and outliers etc. As a result, the performance of the
kNN algorithm is severely limited.

2.2   The Editable kNN Classifier

To overcome the kNN algorithm shortcomings, a editable k nearest neighbor rule is proposed to generate an editable train set, it is a subset of original train set. Note that some train data are excluded, and outliers are removed. The editable train set will be used to train the kNN classifier. Therefore, the classifier performance is imporved, and for classification phases, the reduction of storage space and computation time.

To construct the editable train set, it is often determined by the index of train set. The editable train set is associated with a n-dimensional binary vector z, and n denotes the total number of training samples in original training set. If ith is activated, that is $z[i] = 1$, the ith sample in training set is included in editable subset, $1 \leq i \leq n$. The editable train set S is a reduction set of original training set, $|S| < n$. Generally, the binary vector z is determined by minimizing objective function. In this task, the different optimized technique is used to obtain the optimal vector z.

For optimized process, the objective function is very important. The classification accuracy is often used.

$$F = \frac{1}{n} \sum_{i=1}^{n} h\left(x_i\right) + \alpha z_i \tag{1}$$

where vector $z = (z_1, z_2, \ldots, z_n)$ indicates that current editable subset of $S = \{x_i \mid z_i = 1 \land i \in \{1, 2, \ldots, n\}\}$. We can determine k nearest neighbors of each sample x_i in the subset S by calculating the distance (or similarity), and then estimate the category of sample x_i according to its k nearest neighbors. Usually, $h(x_i)$ is determined as follows: if the actual class of sample x_i is inconsistent with the estimated category (misclassification), then $h(x_i) = 1$, otherwise, $h(x_i) = 0$.

3   The Editable K-Nearest Neighbor Classifier Evolved by the P System

One problem of k-nearest neighbor classifier is sensitive to sample imbalance, noise and outliers etc. This paper proposes a scheme to develop an optimal editable k-nearest neighbor classifier. The proposed scheme uses a P system to determine an optimal editable sample set, it solved the problem of sample imbalance, the noise and outliers are excluded. The kNN classifier classify the unknown samples based on the editable sample set, and the performance of the proposed algorithm has a great improved. In contrast to the original sample set, the cost of computing time(or space) is reduced due to the sample number is reduced.

Figure 1 shows the structure of this scheme, which includes two stages: in the first stage, the P systems are used to evolve an optimal editable sample set from original data set; in the second stage, the kNN classifier is trained on editable sample set (the same with the standard kNN algorithm, as shown in Table 1). The key of this scheme is the first stage, using P system to evolve an optimal editable sample set. Thus we focus on how implemented the first stage is.

Evolution

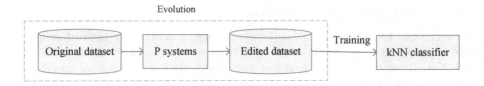

Fig. 1. The structure of the Edit-kNN-P classifier

3.1 Objective Function

To construct an editable sample set from a data set D of n samples. The main idea is to introduce an indicator vector $z = (z_1, z_2, \ldots, z_n)$, where $z_i \in \{0, 1\}$, and n is the number of the original data set. If $z_i = 1$, the ith sample x_i is included in editable data set; otherwise, if $z_i = 0$, the ith sample x_i is not included in editable data set.

In this scheme, we hope that its have a certain optimized criterion. The optimal indicator vector $z = (z_1, z_2, \ldots, z_n)$ can be searched by P system. The sample with $z_i = 1$ is selected into the editable data set, and the sample with $z_i = 0$ is discarded.

To search the optimal indicator vector $z = (z_1, z_2, \ldots, z_n)$ by P system, an optimized criterion is required, that is, the objective function as an optimized function. In this work, a MSE-based function is used as objective function [11]:

$$F = \frac{1}{nc} \sum_{i=1}^{n} \sum_{j=1}^{c} \left(\frac{k_i[j]}{k} - \delta\left[j - c_i\right] \right)^2 \qquad (2)$$

In the MSE-based criterion (2), a kNN classifier is viewed as a system of c outputs (i.e., c classes), each class is seen as one output. For ith sample x_i in original data set, $k_i[j]$ is the number of samples that belong to jth class, according to the k nearest neighbors rule in current subset S. $c_i \in \{1, 2, \ldots, c\}$, it denotes the number of x_i belongs j class. $\delta(\cdot)$ is called Kronecker Delta function: if $c_i = j$, $\delta[j - c_i] = 1$, otherwise, $\delta[j - c_i] = 0$. Note that the current indicator vector $z = (z_1, z_2, \ldots, z_n)$ corresponds to some candidate sample subset $S = \{x_i \mid z_i = 1 \wedge i \in \{1, 2, \ldots, n\}\}$.

Thus, determining the optimal edited sample set can be considered as the following optimization problem:

$$\begin{cases} \min\limits_{z_1, z_2, \ldots, z_n} F(z_1, z_2, \ldots, z_n) = \frac{1}{nc} \sum\limits_{i=1}^{n} \sum\limits_{j=1}^{c} \left(\frac{k_i[j]}{k} - \delta[j - c_i] \right)^2 \\ s.t.\ z_i \in \{0, 1\},\ 1 \le i \le n \end{cases} \qquad (3)$$

3.2 The Designed P System

In this scheme, a tissue-like P system is designed to search the optimal indicator vector $z = (z_1, z_2, \ldots, z_n)$, it corresponds to an optimal editable data set. This tissue-like P system consists of q cells, and each cell contains m objects, shown in Fig. 2. The q cells will cooperatively search for the optimal indicator vector. In Fig. 2, digital "0" labels denotes environment, and there is one object in environment, denoted by z_{best}, which is the best object for the whole system.

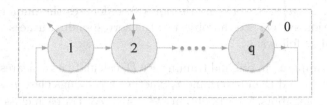

Fig. 2. The designed tissue-like P system.

z_j^i denotes jth object in ith cell, $i = 1, 2, \ldots, q$, $j = 1, 2, \ldots, m$. The arrows in Fig. 2 indicate objects communication. It can be observed from Fig. 2, there are two cases of objects communication: (i) communication between q cells in an unidirectional ring, transferring the current best object to the next cell; (ii) communication between cells and environment, transferring the best current object into the environment. Note that communication is mainly used to update the best object of system between cells and environment, denoted by z_{best}^i.

The environment is also the output region of P system. When system halts, the best object in environment is regarded as the optimal solution. The optimal indicator vector is used to get the optimal editable subset.

3.3 Object Representation

Each object in cells represents a candidate indicator vector, it indicates original data whether included in editable subset. if $z_i = 1$, the editable subset contains the ith sample. Thus, each object in cells is seen as an n-dimensional binary vector.

Each cell uses m objects to complete the search task in parallel. Since the samples in original set is not change, the subscript of each sample can be used to represent it. The integer set $\{1, 2, \ldots, n\}$ denotes training samples $\{x_1, x_2, \ldots, x_n\}$. Each object represents a n-dimensional binary vector, $z = (z_1, z_2, \ldots, z_n)$, where $z_i = 0$ or 1. Each object can be designed as a n-dimensional binary vector: $z = (z_1, z_2, \ldots, z_n)$.

In order to formally describe each object in the P system, denote by z_j^i, the jth object in the ith cell, $i = 1, 2, \ldots, q$, $j = 1, 2, \ldots, m$, and it can be expressed as

$$z_j^i = (z_{j1}^i, z_{j2}^i, \ldots, z_{jn}^i) \tag{4}$$

where $z_{jr}^i = 0$ or 1, $r = 1, 2, \ldots, n$.

A three-dimensional integer array is used to represent all objects in P system.

3.4 Object Evaluation

For each object in P system, $z = (z_1, z_2, \ldots, z_n)$. The scheme uses MSE-based criterion (2) to evaluate it, $f(z) = F|_z$.

Suppose $D = \{x_1, x_2, \ldots, x_n\}$ is original training set. The current object (indicator vector) $z = (z_1, z_2, \ldots, z_n)$ is seen as a candidate subset $S = \{x_i \mid z_i = 1 \wedge i \in \{1, 2, \ldots, n\}\}$, $S \subseteq D$. In criterion (2), c denotes the number of classes for classification system. For an object z, the corresponding fitness value F can be calculated as follows:

(i) For ith sample x_i in original training set D, calculate its k nearest neighbors in subset S, and then determine x_i whether belongings class j according its k nearest neighbors. We can obtain $\frac{k_i[j]}{k} - \delta[j - c_i]$. For each class in c classes, repeat the above steps to compute $F_i = \sum_{j=1}^{c} \left(\frac{k_i[j]}{k} - \delta[j - c_i] \right)^2$.

(ii) Calculating F_i for each sample in original set D. The F value can be obtained by accumulating F_i.

3.5 Evolution Rule

In this scheme, we adopted a n-dimensional binary vector for each object. The n-dimension vector numbers are 0 or 1, so the discrete velocity-position model is used as evolution rules. The discrete velocity-position evolution rule can be get 0 or 1 number. Thus, for the jth object in the ith cell, evolution rules as follows:

$$v_j^i = v_j^i + c_1 r_1 (p_j^i - z_j^i) + c_2 r_2 (z_{ext}^i - z_j^i) + c_3 r_3 (z_{best}^i - z_j^i) \tag{5}$$

$$z_j^i = \begin{cases} 1, & r_4 < g(v_j^i); \\ 0, & \text{otherwise}. \end{cases} \tag{6}$$

where $g\left(v_j^i\right) = \frac{1}{1+exp\left(-v_j^i\right)}$ is the sigmoid function. c is learning rate constant, we set $c_1 = c_2 = c_3 = 0.2$. r_1, r_2 and r_3 are random real numbers in $[0, 1]$. Obviously, $v_j^i >= 0$, that is $-v_j^i <= 0$, that is $0 < exp\left(-v_j^i\right) <= 1$, $\frac{1}{1+exp\left(-v_j^i\right)} >= \frac{1}{2}$, if r_4 is a random reals in $[0, 1]$, at least half of them will be activated ($x = 1$), when we set r_4 is a $[0, 0.8]$ random reals, the algorithm can be accelerate get the optimal editable subset in experiment, and the subset is more reasonalbe. v_j^i and z_j^i are the velocity and position vectors of the jth object in the ith cell. p_j^i is the best position for the jth object in the ith cell so far. z_{ext}^i is an external object, it comes from the best object of other cell by communication rule. z_{best}^i is the best object for the ith cell.

3.6 Communication Rule

The designed tissue-like P system has two type communication rules:

(i) Antiport rule: $< i, a; b, j >$, where a is the object in the ith cell, and b is the object in the jth cell, $i, j = 1, 2, \ldots, q$.

(ii) Symport rule: $< i, a; \lambda, 0 >$, where a is the object in the ith cell and λ denotes the empty object, $i = 1, 2, \ldots, q$.

Antiport rule is used to share and exchange objects between q cells. Symport rule is used to exchange of object between cells and environment, and updating the best object in the environment.

(1) Sharing and exchange of objects between the cells, where each cell transfers the best object to next neighboring cell, and participating cell evolution. The updating formula is as follows:

$$z^i_{exit} = \begin{cases} z_{i-1,best}, & \text{if } i \neq 0; \\ z_{q,best}, & \text{if } i = 0 \end{cases} \tag{7}$$

where z^i_{exit} is the object in the ith cell, which comes from other external cells. $z_{i-1,best}$ is the best object in the $(i-1)$th cell currently. $z_{q,best}$ is the best object in the qth cell currently.

(2) z^i_{best} is the best object in the ith cell, $i = 1, 2, \ldots, q$. The best object is updated as follows.

$$z^i_{best} = \begin{cases} p^i_j, & \text{if } f(p^i_j) < f(z^i_{best}) \\ z^i_{best}, & \text{otherwise} \end{cases} \tag{8}$$

where p^i_j is the best for the jth object in the ith cell so far, and $f(z)$ represents the fitness value of object z.

(3) z_{best} is the best object in the environment. Each cell transports its best object into environment, and updating the best object in the environment.

$$z_{best} = \begin{cases} z^i_{best}, & \text{if } f(z^i_{best}) < f(z_{best}) \\ z_{best}, & \text{otherwise} \end{cases} \tag{9}$$

Note that z^i_{ext}, $z_{i,best}$, z^i_{best} and z_{best} are four n-dimensional binary vectors.

3.7 Termination Condition

A simple halting condition is used in this experiment: the maximum steps(the maximum numbers of iteration), $Maxstep$. Thus, the P system starts at the initial configuration, continuing until the maximum number of iterations, and then halting.

3.8 Output Results

When halting, the best object in the environment is the optimized solution (3), which is a n-dimensional binary vector, corresponding an optimal editable subset. For example, assuming the best object is $z^*_{best} = (z^*_1, z^*_2, \ldots, z^*_n)$ if $z^*_i = 1$, the ith object of original set is included in editable subset S. We can construct the optimal editable subset as follows:

$$S = \{x_i \in D \mid z^*_i = 1 \land i \in \{1, 2, \ldots, n\}\} \tag{10}$$

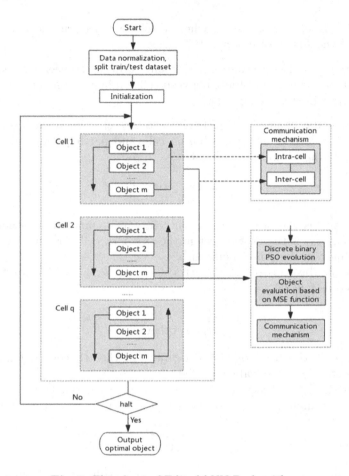

Fig. 3. Flowchart of Edited-kNN-P algorithm.

3.9 Flowchart of the Proposed Algorithm

In this paper, we proposed an editable k-nearest neighbor classifier evolved by P system, which includes two stages: (1) evolving an editable sample subset by P system; (2) using the KNN algorithm on the editable subset. In the first stage, two main mechanisms of P system are used: (i) communication rules: for each cell transporting its best object into environment and next cell; (ii) the discrete binary velocity-position model is used as an evolution mechanism.

The architecture of the proposed algorithm as shown in Fig. 3. There are three cells$(1, 2, q)$ explicitly in Fig. 3. For the 1st cell, giving three objects$(1, 2, m)$ explicitly, currently the best object is communicated to the next near cell 2, and updating the environment best object so far. Each object of cells uses both evolution and communication rules.

Table 2. Data sets considered in experiment

Data set	#Cl.	#At.	#Ins.	Data set	#Cl.	#At.	#Ins.
Balance	3	4	625	Spambase	2	57	4597
Page-blocks	5	10	5472	Spectfheart	2	44	267
Dermatology	6	34	358	Vehicle	4	18	946
Penbased	10	16	10,992	Winequality-red	11	11	1599
Ecoli	8	7	336	Mammographic	2	5	830
Pima	2	8	768	Yeast	10	8	1484

Table 3. Algorithm parameters configuration

Algorithm	Reference	Parameters
kNN	[1]	k value: 7
EF-kNN-IVFS	[9]	k value: 9, population size: 50, evaluation: 500, S_n: 32, m range: [1,4], kInit range: (1,32)
GAfuzzy-kNN	[8]	k value: 5, evaluations: 500, m: 2, Mutation probability: 0.01, crossover probability: 0.8, population size: 50, kInit: 3
IT2FKNN	[6]	k value: 7 , m: 2, kInit: {1,3,5,7,9}
PFKNN	[7]	k value: 9
Edit-kNN-P	-	k value: 9, c: 0.2, $(r_1, r_2, r_3) \in [0, 1]$, $r_4 \in [0, 0.8]$, q: 7, m: 4, Maxstep: 30

4 Experimental Results and Analysis

In order to demonstrate the availability and effectiveness of the proposed scheme, 12 benchmark UCI datasets are used in this experiment. The proposed Edit-kNN-P algorithm is compared with four recently developed kNN algorithms as well as the classical kNN algorithm. Moreover, we also provided the comparison results of these algorithms on different k values.

4.1 Data Sets

Table 2 gives 12 classification datasets in this experiment. In Table 2, we provide three characteristics for each dataset: the numbers of class labels (#Cl), the numbers of instances (#Ins), and the numbers of attributes (#At). And there are no missing values.

4.2 Parameter Setting

Table 3 provides the parameter settings of the proposed and compared algorithms. In experiment, the parameter values of the compared algorithms are derived from the literature [40]. These parameters that all algorithms get the best results on 12 bechemark datasets respectively as shown in Table 4. For our

Table 4. The comparison experiment results of classification accuracy ($k = 3$)

Data sets	Edit-kNN-P	kNN	EF-kNN-IVFS	GAfuzzy-kNN	IT2FKNN	PFKNN
Balance	**87.94**	83.37	84.16	84.01	83.53	73.91
Dermatology	**97.44**	96.90	96.04	96.90	96.90	74.85
Ecoli	**84.82**	80.67	83.07	82.75	82.78	79.77
Mammographic	80.32	80.12	79.16	78.43	78.56	77.72
Page-blocks	95.96	95.91	95.98	**96.07**	96.03	95.45
Penbased	99.33	99.32	**99.34**	99.30	**99.34**	98.85
Pima	**75.56**	72.93	74.36	73.58	74.23	71.62
Spambase	90.03	89.23	**91.26**	90.91	90.97	86.84
Spectfheart	**76.47**	71.20	73.45	74.22	73.45	68.96
Vehicle	70.69	**71.75**	70.21	69.62	70.69	64.54
Winequality-red	63.45	52.41	67.42	67.23	**67.85**	66.79
Yeast	**59.14**	53.17	57.75	56.54	57.82	55.80

Table 5. The comparison experiment results of classification accuracy ($k = 5$)

Data sets	Edit-kNN-P	kNN	EF-kNN-IVFS	GAfuzzy-kNN	IT2FKNN	PFKNN
Balance	**89.42**	86.24	87.84	88.00	87.83	81.13
Dermatology	**97.36**	96.33	96.62	96.35	96.35	74.86
Ecoli	**86.32**	81.27	82.49	82.48	82.17	80.38
Mammographic	**81.82**	81.69	80.12	79.53	80.25	80.37
Page-blocks	95.86	95.83	**96.13**	96.05	95.92	95.83
Penbased	99.24	99.23	**99.37**	99.32	99.25	98.89
Pima	**75.46**	73.06	74.49	74.36	73.58	72.92
Spambase	88.58	89.78	**91.86**	91.26	91.23	88.69
Spectfheart	68.98	71.97	73.11	75.00	73.48	71.60
Vehicle	70.33	**71.75**	69.74	70.33	69.86	66.08
Winequality-red	65.88	54.29	68.23	67.10	**68.35**	68.23
Yeast	59.33	56.74	58.90	57.89	59.50	**59.77**

Edit-kNN-P algorithm, the number of cells is denoted by q, in each cell the number of objects is denoted by m, the maximum iteration numbers is denoted by $maxstep$.

4.3   Experiment Results

In this experiment, classification accuracy is used to evaluate the performance of the proposed and compared algorithms. Note that 4 prior parameters k for the proposed Edit-kNN-P, classical kNN algorithm and four recently developed kNN algorithms are given respectively, $k = 3, 5, 7, 9$. For each dataset, the best experimental results have been highlighted in bold. Table 4, 5, 6 and Table 7 experiment results are discussed as follows.

Table 6. The comparison experiment results of classification accuracy ($k = 7$)

Data sets	Edit-kNN-P	kNN	EF-kNN-IVFS	GAfuzzy-kNN	IT2FKNN	PFKNN
Balance	**90.87**	88.48	88.64	89.28	88.80	85.75
Dermatology	**97.59**	96.34	96.63	95.78	96.34	74.83
Ecoli	**84.48**	82.45	83.07	82.76	82.45	81.57
Mammographic	**81.82**	81.71	79.65	78.33	79.54	80.01
Page-blocks	96.09	95.47	96.16	**96.20**	95.87	95.69
Penbased	99.14	99.13	**99.38**	99.32	99.14	98.81
Pima	**75.11**	72.93	73.84	73.83	73.58	72.67
Spambase	89.87	89.34	**91.65**	91.19	90.93	89.19
Spectfheart	**78.82**	77.58	77.21	78.69	77.55	77.18
Vehicle	71.54	72.34	70.45	71.16	71.16	68.08
Winequality-red	66.89	55.29	**69.29**	67.48	68.73	69.10
Yeast	**60.37**	57.49	59.31	58.29	59.91	60.18

Table 7. The comparison experiment results of classification accuracy ($k = 9$)

Data sets	Edit-kNN-P	kNN	EF-kNN-IVFS	GAfuzzy-kNN	IT2FKNN	PFKNN
Balance	**89.83**	89.44	89.28	89.60	88.95	87.52
Dermatology	**96.26**	95.78	95.78	95.49	96.06	74.27
Ecoli	**84.23**	81.26	83.33	83.92	83.64	83.64
Mammographic	**81.48**	81.23	79.63	79.06	79.29	80.13
Page-blocks	95.94	95.47	**96.22**	96.05	95.85	95.56
Penbased	99.04	99.04	**99.38**	99.33	99.14	98.74
Pima	**75.47**	73.19	73.71	73.18	74.10	72.79
Spambase	89.42	88.88	**91.84**	91.15	90.89	90.30
Spectfheart	**78.75**	76.79	78.30	76.82	78.29	76.81
Vehicle	70.89	**71.40**	70.57	70.81	70.81	66.19
Winequality-red	67.51	55.60	**69.36**	67.35	68.98	69.35
Yeast	59.64	57.62	59.91	57.82	60.25	**60.45**

For the case of $k = 3$, as shown in Table 4. The proposed Edit-kNN-P gets the best result on 6 data sets. Other comparison method get the most numbers of win are EF-kNN-IVFS, it get the best results on 3 datasets. kNN, IF2FKNN, PFKNN three algorithms are get the best result on 1 dataset. GAfuzzy-kNN didn't win once. For the case of $k = 5$, as shown in Table 5. The proposed Edit-kNN-P gets the best result on 5 datasets. For the case of $k = 7$, as shown in Table 6. The proposed Edit-kNN-P obtains the best result on 7 data sets. For the case of $k = 9$, as shown in Table 7. The proposed Edit-kNN-P gets the best result on 6 data sets.

608   J. Hu et al.

5 Conclusions

In this paper, we discussed a novel k-nearest neighbor classifier evolved by P system, called Edit-kNN-P. The classifier consists of two stages: (i) the optimal editable sample subset generated by P system; (ii) k-nearest neighbor algorithm is used on the editable sample subset. Our work is the first stage, it can be seen as an optimization problem. The tissue-like P system is used to determine an editable sample subset, by optimizing a set of binary indictor vectors under the control of evolution-communication mechanism. The compared experiment results demonstrate the availability and effectiveness of the proposed method. Our further work focuses on : the membrane computing characteristics are used as the evolution rules without the help of PSO or other evolutionary algorithms.

Acknowledgement. This work is partially supported by the Research Fund of Sichuan Science and Technology Project (No.2018JY0083), Research Foundation of the Education Department of Sichuan province (No. 17TD0034), and the second batch of Cooperative Education Project between Induastry and University in 2018 (Nos. 201802365003 and 201802295027), China.

References

1. Cover, T.M., Hart, P.E.: Nearest neighbor pattern classification. IEEE Trans. Inf. Theory **13**(1), 21–27 (1967)
2. Papadopoulos, A.N.: Nearest Neighbor Search: A Database Perspective. Springer, Incorporated (2010)
3. Shakhnarovich, G., Darrell, T., Indyk, P.: Nearest-Neighbor Methods in Learning and Vision: Theory and Practice. The MIT Press, Cambridge (2006)
4. Wu, X., Kumar, V.: The Top Ten Algorithms in Data Mining. CRC Press (2009)
5. Kuncheva, L.I.: An intuitionistic fuzzy k-nearest neighbors rule, Notes Intuitionistic Fuzzy Sets, NIFS-**1**(1), 56–60 (1995)
6. Rhee, C.H., Hwang, C.: An interval type-2 fuzzy k-nearest neighbor. The IEEE Int. Conf. Fuzzy Syst. **2**, 802–807 (2003)
7. Arif, M., Akram, M.U., Amir, F.A.: Pruned fuzzy k-nearest neighbor classifier for beat classification. J. Biomed. Sci. Eng. **3**(4), 380–389 (2010)
8. Xie, C., Hu, X.: Improving fuzzy k-nn by using genetic algorithm. J. Comput. Inf. Syst. **1**(2), 203–213 (2005)
9. Chiclana, F., Herrera, F.: Evolutionary fuzzy k-nearest neighbors algorithm using interval-valued fuzzy sets. Inf. Sci. **329**(C), 144–163 (2016)
10. Wilson, D.L.: Asymptotic properties of nearest neighbor rules using edited data. IEEE Trans. Syst. Man Cybern. SMC **2**(3), 408–421 (2007)
11. Gil-Pita, R., Yao, X.: Evolving edited k-nearest neighbor classifiers. Int. J. Neural Syst. **18**(06), 459–467 (2009)
12. Păun, G.: Computing with membranes. J. Comput. Syst. Sci. **61**(1), 108–143 (2000)
13. Păun, G. Rozenberg, G., Salomaa, A.: The Oxford Handbook of Membrane Computing, Oxford University Press Inc (2010)
14. Gheorghe, M., et al.: 3-Col problem modelling using simple kernel P systems. Int. J. Comput. Math. **90**(4), 816–830 (2013)

15. Gh. Păun, M.J. Pérez-Jiménez, Solving problems in a distributed way in membrane computing: dP systems. Int. J. Comput. Commun. Control V(2), 238–250 (2010)
16. Song, B., Zhang, C., Pan, L.: Tissue-like P systems with evolutional symport/antiport rules. Inf. Sci. **378**, 177–193 (2016)
17. Ionescu, M., Păun, Gh, Yokomori, T.: Spiking neural P systems. Fundamenta Informaticae **71**, 279–308 (2006)
18. Peng, H., et al.: Spiking neural P systems with multiple channels. Neural Netw. **95**, 66–71 (2017)
19. Peng, H., et al.: Competitive spiking neural p systems with rules on synapses. IEEE Trans. NanoBioscience **16**(8), 888–895 (2017)
20. Peng, H., Wang, J., Pérez-Jiménez, M.J., Riscos-Núñez, A.: Dynamic threshold neural P systems. Knowl. Based Syst. **163**, 875–884 (2019)
21. Peng, H., Wang, J.: Coupled neural P systems. IEEE Trans. Neural Netw. Learn. Syst. (2018). https://doi.org/10.1109/TNNLS.2018.2872999
22. Peng, H., Wang, J., Pérez-Jiménez, M.J., Wang, H., Shao, J., Wang, T.: Fuzzy reasoning spiking neural P system for fault diagnosis. Inf. Sci. **235**(20), 106–116 (2013)
23. Wang, J., Shi, P., Peng, H., Pérez-Jiménez, M.J., Wang, T.: Weighted fuzzy spiking neural P system. IEEE Trans. Fuzzy Syst. **21**(2), 209–220 (2013)
24. Díaz-Pernil, D., Berciano, A., Peña-Cantillana, F., Gutiérrez-Naranjo, M.A.: Segmenting images with gradient-based edge detection using membrane computing. Pattern Recogn. Lett. **34**(8), 846–855 (2013)
25. Peng, H., Wang, J., Pérez-Jiménez, M.J.: Optimal multi-level thresholding with membrane computing. Digital Signal Process. **37**, 53–64 (2015)
26. Alsalibi, B., Venkat, I., Al-Betar, M.A.: A membrane-inspired bat algorithm to recognize faces in unconstrained scenarios. Eng. Appl. Artif. Intell. **64**, 242–260 (2017)
27. Peng, H., et al.: Fault diagnosis of power systems using intuitionistic fuzzy spiking neural P systems. IEEE Trans. Smart Grid **9**(5), 4777–4784 (2018)
28. Gheorghe, M., Manca, V., Romero-Campero, F.J.: Deterministic and stochastic P systems for modelling cellular processes. Natural Comput. **9**(2), 457–473 (2010)
29. García-Quismondo, M., Levin, M., Lobo-Fernández, D.: Modeling regenerative processes with membrane computing. Inf. Sci. **381**, 229–249 (2017)
30. García-Quismondo, M., Nisbet, I.C.T., Mostello, C.S., Reed, M.J.: Modeling population dynamics of roseate terns (sterna dougallii) in the northwest atlantic ocean. Ecol. Model. **68**, 298–311 (2018)
31. Zhao, Y., Liu, X., Qu, J.: The k-medoids clustering algorithm by a class of p system. J. Inf. Comput. Sci. **9**(18), 5777–5790 (2012)
32. Huang, X., Peng, H., Jiang, Y., Zhang, J., Wang, J.: PSO-MC: a novel pso-based membrane clustering algorithm. ICIC Express Lett. **8**(8), 497–503 (2014)
33. Peng, H., Wang, J., Pérez-Jiménez, M.J., Riscos-Núñez, A.: An unsupervised learning algorithm for membrane computing. Inf. Sci. **304**, 80–91 (2015)
34. Liu, X., Zhao, Y., Sun, W.: K-medoids-based consensus clustering based on cell-like P systems with promoters and inhibitors. In: Gong, M., Pan, L., Song, T., Zhang, G. (eds.) BIC-TA 2016. CCIS, vol. 681, pp. 95–108. Springer, Singapore (2016). https://doi.org/10.1007/978-981-10-3611-8_11
35. Peng, H., Jiang, Y., Wang, J., Pérez-Jiménez, M.J.: Membrane clustering algorithm with hybrid evolutionary mechanisms. J. Softw. **26**(5), 1001–1012 (2015)
36. Peng, H., Wang, J., Shi, P., Riscos-Núñez, A., Pérez-Jiménez, M.J.: An automatic clustering algorithm inspired by membrane computing. Pattern Recogn. Lett. **68**, 34–40 (2015)

37. Peng, H., Wang, J., Shi, P., Pérez-Jiménez, M.J., Riscos-Núñez, A.: An extended membrane system with active membranes to solve automatic fuzzy clustering problems. Int. J. Neural Syst. **26**(03), 1650004, 1–17 (2016)
38. Peng, H., Shi, P., Wang, J., Riscos-Núñez, A., Pérez-Jiménez, M.J.: Multiobjective fuzzy clustering approach based on tissue-like membrane systems. Knowl. Based Syst. **125**, 74–82 (2017)
39. Wang, J., Hu, J., Peng, H., Pérez-Jiménez, M.J., Riscos-Núñez, A.: Decision tree models induced by membrane systems, Romanian. J. Inf. Sci. Technol. **18**(3), 228–239 (2015)
40. Derrac, J., García, S., Herrera, F.: Fuzzy nearest neighbor algorithms: taxonomy, experimental analysis and prospects. Inf. Sci. **260**, 98–119 (2014)

Solving Urban Light Rail Route Planning Based on Probe Machine

Xiang Tian and Xiyu Liu$^{(\boxtimes)}$

Business School, Shandong Normal University, Jinan, China
xyliu@sdnu.edu.cn

Abstract. With economic development and technological progress accelerating, people's demand for urban light rail transportation is becoming more and more urgent. Considering the existence of interchange stations, how to construct the route with the lowest cost is crucial for decision makers. This paper first proposes a practical urban light rail route planning problem, and transforms it into a classic graph model, that is, the minimum spanning tree. Then for this problem, the data library, the probe library and the probe operation graph are defined, respectively. Finally, on the computing platform, only one probe operation is needed to get the true solution of the problem. As a comparison, the solving process of two classic algorithms, i.e., the Prim algorithm and the Kruskal algorithm, are given. Analysis shows that the probe machine significantly outperforms the above two algorithms in terms of computing efficiency.

Keywords: DNA computing · Probe machine · Minimum spanning tree

1 Introduction

With the development of urbanization, traffic congestion is becoming increasingly severe. The existing light rail (including subway) network in developed large cities has been unable to meet people's travel needs, and small and medium-sized cities have also begun to plan and build their own light rail networks. Therefore, how to scientifically and rationally plan the new light rail route to meet people's diversified travel needs, minimize the cost of line construction, and even consider the future development strategy of the city has become the most important and critical issue for decision makers.

Existing literature shows that the minimum spanning tree can effectively solve the problems of route planning and urban layout. Jie et al. [1] applied the Kruskal algorithm of minimum spanning tree to the tourism transportation optimization and tour route designing, and gave the ideal tourism transportation pattern and three theme tour routes. Z. Yang et al. [2] constructed a minimum spanning tree using union-find sets and gave a solution to the urban subway planning problem. Min [3] gave the minimum spanning tree of the connected graph of cities under ideal conditions to provide a solution to urban planning. B. Wu et al. [4] used the Expanded Minimum Spanning Tree (EMST) method to identify local connectivity and patterns of urban buildings from multiple

© Springer Nature Singapore Pte Ltd. 2021
L. Pan et al. (Eds.): BIC-TA 2020, CCIS 1363, pp. 611–623, 2021.
https://doi.org/10.1007/978-981-16-1354-8_42

angles, providing comprehensive and necessary information for urban planning and management.

The characteristics of the minimum spanning tree can be summarized as connecting all nodes, the lowest total cost, and no loops. Based on the above characteristics, the minimum spanning tree also has important applications in other fields. For example, to avoid broadcast storms caused by loop topologies, Spanning Tree Protocol (STP) is used in computer networks to prevent bridge loops and the broadcast radiation that results from them [5]. In the communication network, the minimum spanning tree is used to connect all communication nodes and ensure the minimum total connection cost, which makes the minimum spanning tree widely used in power and communication systems [6–8]. In addition, the minimum spanning tree is also widely used in classification [9], image segmentation [10, 11], and clustering problems [12–14].

Since Adleman [15] successfully used DNA molecular biotechnology to solve the directed Hamilton road problem in 1994, DNA computing has received increasing attentions. Massive parallelism and huge storage capacity are two significant advantages of DNA computing. Parallelism means DNA computing can perform billions of operations simultaneously. The high density of data stored in DNA strands and the ease in duplicating them can make exhaustive searches possible. Adleman-Lipton model [15, 16], the sticker model [17], the self-assembly model [18], the surface-based model [19] and the hairpin model [20] were successively established.

However, the DNA computing models mentioned above have topological limitations, due to the influence of DNA double-stranded thinking, the data bodies can only be connected one-to-one in the direction in which the DNA double-strands are located. This is also the biggest bottleneck encountered by DNA computing, that is, the exponential explosion of the solution space [21]. The proposal of the probe machine model [22] greatly enriches and improves the topology of existing DNA computing models. One-to-many connections can be realized between data bodies through data fibers. Some combinatorial optimization problems based on probe machine are solved, for example, travelling salesman problem [23], working operation problem [24], shortest path problem [25], and so on.

In this paper, a problem of urban light rail route planning with a realistic background is first presented and converted into a graph model of minimum spanning tree. Then the data library, the probe library, and the probe operation graph are respectively defined for this graph model. Finally, only one probe operation is needed to obtain the true solution of the problem on the computing platform. Compared with the traditional Prim algorithm and Kruskal algorithm, the Probe Machine designed in this paper has high parallelism and high efficiency in computing.

The remainder of this paper is organized as follows. Section 2 introduces the probe machine model in detail, gives a description of the actual light rail route planning problem, and the description of model and notations. Section 3 presents the description of model and notations. For comparative analysis, Sect. 4 gives the solving process of the Prim algorithm [26] and Kruskal algorithm [27], as well as the concrete solution procedure of the probe machine. Section 5 shows relevant discussions and analysis. Section 6 concludes this work with a summary and future research directions.

2 Preliminaries

This section is composed of three parts. The first part explains the probe machine, and the second part gives a formal description of the actual light rail route planning problem. Finally, description of model and notations are given.

2.1 Probe Machine

The probe machine is composed of 9 parts, namely data library (X), probe library (Y), data controller ($\sigma 1$), probe controller ($\sigma 2$), probe operation (τ), computing platform (λ), detector (η), true solution storage (Q), and residue collector (C). As shown in Fig. 1, data library X can be composed of multiple data pools (Xi), each of which contains only one type of data xi. Each xi (see Fig. 1(c)) has a data body and different data fibers.

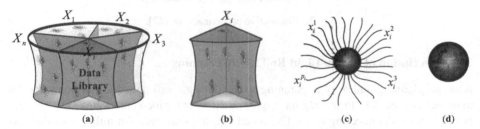

Fig. 1. Composition of the Data Library [22]. (a) Data library. (b) Data pool. (c) one type of data. (d) Data body.

Figure 2 shows the working principle of the probe machine. The data controller and probe controller add the relevant data and probes from the data library and the probe library into the computing platform, respectively, and perform the probe operation. The detector is responsible for detecting the true solution and storing it in the true solution storage. The residue enters the residue collector for recycling.

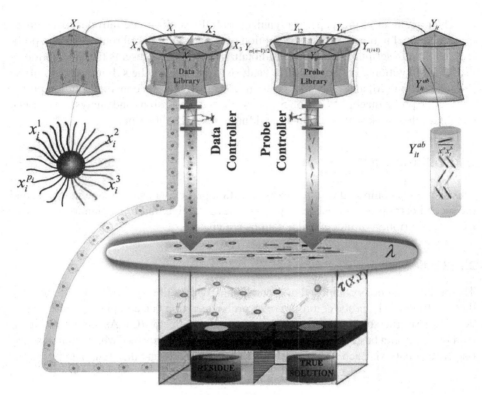

Fig. 2. Connective probe machine [22].

2.2 Description of Urban Light Rail Route Planning

A urban planning authority is planning to build a light rail network that connects the main activity centers in the region. Figure 3 shows the nine centers involved and the possible routes connecting them. Estimated construction costs (in millions of dollars) are also shown on these connections. It should be noted that the relative positions of the nine centers in Fig. 3 do not represent their actual positions, only a compromise to avoid the intersection of line segments.

The final traffic route on the selected background network will be organized into multiple routes with interchange stations. However, decision makers only want to find the background network with the smallest total construction cost, and ensure that there is a path between each of the nine centers. The adjacency matrix corresponding to the

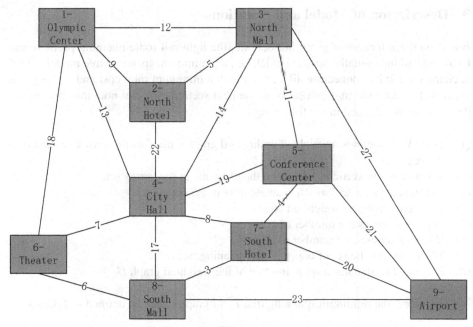

Fig. 3. Nine centers. The weight of the edge represents the construction cost of connecting the two centers.

undirected graph of this problem is expressed as follows.

$$A = \begin{pmatrix}
0 & 9 & 12 & 13 & \infty & 18 & \infty & \infty & \infty \\
9 & 0 & 5 & 22 & \infty & \infty & \infty & \infty & \infty \\
12 & 5 & 0 & 14 & 11 & \infty & \infty & \infty & 27 \\
13 & 22 & 14 & 0 & 19 & 7 & 8 & 17 & \infty \\
\infty & \infty & 11 & 19 & 0 & \infty & 4 & \infty & 21 \\
18 & \infty & \infty & 7 & \infty & 0 & \infty & 6 & \infty \\
\infty & \infty & \infty & 8 & 4 & \infty & 0 & 3 & 20 \\
\infty & \infty & \infty & 17 & \infty & 6 & 3 & 0 & 23 \\
\infty & \infty & 27 & \infty & 21 & \infty & 20 & 23 & 0
\end{pmatrix} \qquad (1)$$

3   Description of Model and Notations

Based on the information given in Sect. 2.2, the light rail route planning problem can be abstracted into a mathematical model, i.e., the minimum spanning tree model, which is characterized by connecting all vertices with a minimum total cost and no loops. In order to facilitate the in-depth study in the next section, relevant notations and model descriptions are defined in the following.

(1) $G = (V, E)$ defines a weighted undirected graph with V as the vertex set and E as the edge set.
(2) u, v denote the vertices, which are the elements in the vertex set.
(3) e represents an edge, which is an element in the edge set.
(4) $w(e)$ represents the weight on edge e.
(5) $|V| = n$ denotes the number of vertices.
(6) $|E| = m$ denotes the number of edges.
(7) TE represents the set of edges in the spanning tree.
(8) $T = (V, TE)$ denotes a spanning tree of the weighted graph G.

Therefore, the minimum spanning tree T^* of graph G can be defined as follows.

$$T^* = \min_{T}\{\sum_{e \in TE} w(e)\} \tag{2}$$

4   Solving the Light Rail Route Planning Problem

After transforming the actual urban light rail route planning problem into a minimum spanning tree, this section will give three different solutions to facilitate the comparative analysis and discussion in Sect. 4.

4.1   Using Prim Algorithm

The set of vertices in the process of generating the minimum spanning tree is denoted by U. The starting vertex u_0 in U can be arbitrarily selected from V. The set t is used to store intermediate variables. The pseudo code of the core part of Prim algorithm is as follows.

Prim Algorithm

Initial: $U = \{u_0\}$, $TE = \{\}$, $t = \{\}$

    For each $u \in U$

        while $|U| \mathrel{!}= |V|$

            For each $v \in (V - U)$

                If $w(u,v) \mathrel{!}= \infty$

                    Add edge (u,v) to set t

                Else PASS

                End If

            $(u',v') = \{(u,v) \mid \min[w(u,v)], (u,v) \in t\}$

            Add edge (u',v') to TE to update TE

            Add vertex u' to U to update U

            Remove v' from $(V - U)$

            Reset $t = \{\}$

    End For

    Return TE

End

It should be noted that in order to avoid the appearance of loops, the two vertices of the newly added edge to TE must be guaranteed to come from U and $(V-U)$, respectively.

Figure 4 is used to help explain the above algorithm process. The blue dashed lines can be regarded as the dividing line between the two vertex sets of U and $(V-U)$ in the algorithm. To connect the 9 points in the graph, 8 edges are needed, so the calculation process is divided into 8 steps. The five blue dashed lines in turn represent the first five steps in the solving process. At each step, the edge with the smallest weight is selected from the edges crossed by the blue dashed line. Three subsequent steps can be deduced by analogy. The number in the circle indicates the corresponding step and is marked on the selected edge. The 8 edges corresponding to the final minimum spanning tree are indicated by bold red lines.

4.2 Using Kruskal Algorithm

Prim's algorithm focuses on the vertices in the graph. In contrast, Kruskal's algorithm is directly concerned with edges in the graph. The pseudo code of the core part of Kruskal's algorithm is as follows.

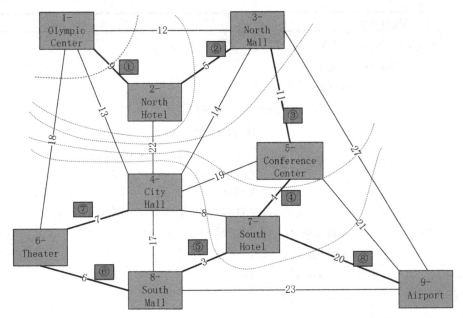

Fig. 4. Schematic diagram of the solving process of Prim algorithm. (Color figure online)

Kruskal Algorithm

Initial: $TE = \{\}$, Sort all the edges in E in ascending order of their weights.

    For each $v \in V$ do

        MAKE-SET(v)

    End For

    For each $(u, v) \in E$ do

        If FIND-SET(u) != FIND-SET(v) then

            Add (u,v) to TE to update

            UNION(FIND-SET(u), FIND-SET(v))

            Remove (u,v) from E

        Else Remove (u,v) from E

        Sort and update E in ascending order of weight

    End For

    Return TE

End

Figure 5 is used to help explain the Kruskal algorithm. Kruskal algorithm first sorts all the weighted edges in graph G in ascending order. On the premise of not forming a loop, each step of the solving process selects the edge with the smallest weight to be added to the set TE. The number in the circle indicates the corresponding step and is marked on the selected edge. The 8 edges corresponding to the final minimum spanning tree are indicated by bold red lines.

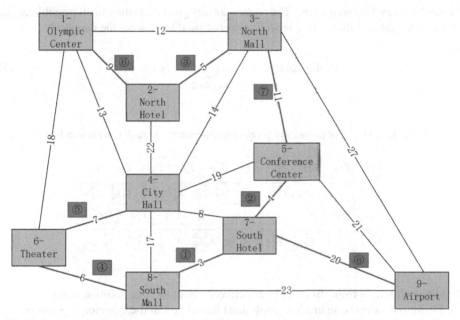

Fig. 5. Schematic diagram of the solving process of Kruskal algorithm. (Color figure online)

4.3 Using Probe Machine

The specific solution procedure using the probe machine is as follows.

Data Library Construction. Considering the practical problems mentioned in Sect. 2.2 and Fig. 3, data library is directly constructed by 9 types of data corresponding to 9 vertices, denoted by $x_1, x_2, ..., x_9$, respectively. For each type of data x_i, its data body is denoted as i, and its data fiber is all possible degrees of the vertex.

For the convenience of true solution detection, the length of the data fiber is proportional to the weight on the corresponding edge. The sets of data fibers of these 9 types of data is shown below.

$$\Im_1 = \{x_1^2, x_1^3, x_1^4, x_1^6\},$$
$$\Im_2 = \{x_2^1, x_2^3, x_2^4\},$$
$$\Im_3 = \{x_3^1, x_3^2, x_3^4, x_3^5, x_3^9\},$$
$$\Im_4 = \{x_4^1, x_4^2, x_4^3, x_4^5, x_4^6, x_4^7, x_4^8\},$$
$$\Im_5 = \{x_5^3, x_5^4, x_5^7, x_5^9\},$$

$$\Im_6 = \{x_6^1, x_6^4, x_6^8\},$$
$$\Im_7 = \{x_7^4, x_7^5, x_7^8, x_7^9\},$$
$$\Im_8 = \{x_8^4, x_8^6, x_8^7, x_8^9\},$$
$$\Im_9 = \{x_9^3, x_9^5, x_9^7, x_9^8\}.$$

Probe Library Construction. The probes are designed according to all possible edges of graph G. Table 1 shows 19 connective probes used to connect the data body.

$$\text{Probe library: } Y = \bigcup_{a=1,b=2}^{a=8,b=9} Y_{ab}, (a < b) \tag{3}$$

Table 1. 19 types of connective probes corresponding to graph G shown in Fig. 3.

Y_{12}	Y_{13}	Y_{14}	Y_{16}	Y_{23}	Y_{24}	Y_{34}	Y_{35}	Y_{39}	Y_{45}
$x_1^2 x_2^1$	$x_1^3 x_3^1$	$x_1^4 x_4^1$	$x_1^6 x_6^1$	$x_2^3 x_3^2$	$x_2^4 x_4^2$	$x_3^4 x_4^3$	$x_3^5 x_5^3$	$x_3^9 x_9^3$	$x_4^5 x_5^4$

Y_{46}	Y_{47}	Y_{48}	Y_{57}	Y_{59}	Y_{68}	Y_{78}	Y_{79}	Y_{89}
$x_4^6 x_6^4$	$x_4^7 x_7^4$	$x_4^8 x_8^4$	$x_5^7 x_7^5$	$x_5^9 x_9^5$	$x_6^8 x_8^6$	$x_7^8 x_8^7$	$x_7^9 x_9^7$	$x_8^9 x_9^8$

Detector Construction. In order to effectively detect the true solution from all generated solutions, a probe operation graph must be defined in the detector. A solution is a true solution if and only if its topology is isomorphic to the probe operation graph.

A probe operation graph of data subset X' and probe subset Y' is denoted as $G^{(X',Y')}$ which is the topological structure of the aggregation of true solutions after probe operation. The vertex set $V(G^{(X',Y')})$ of the probe operation graph $G^{(X',Y')}$ is the set of data in the true solution aggregation. The edge set $E(G^{(X',Y')})$ of the probe operation graph $G^{(X',Y')}$ is the set of probes in the true solution aggregation.

For the problem studied in this work, the probe operation graph $G^{(X',Y')}$ is defined as follows. Since all vertices in the graph G must be connected, let $V(G^{(X',Y')}) = |V| = n$. Because only n-1 edges are needed to connect n vertices, let $E(G^{(X',Y')}) = n-1$. Also the topological structure of the probe operation graph $G^{(X',Y')}$ does not contain any loops. In the final solution, the elements in $E(G^{(X',Y')})$ represent the edge set of the spanning tree. Since the length of the data fiber is designed to be proportional to the weight of the corresponding edge, only a spanning tree with the smallest sum of the lengths of all edges can be regarded as the minimum spanning tree for this problem.

Probe Operation. The data controller and probe controller add the relevant data and probes from the data library and the probe library into the computing platform, respectively, and perform the probe operation. The detector will automatically screen out the true solution that is isomorphic to the probe operation graph and place it in the true solution storage. The remaining residue will be put into the residue collector for recycling and reuse.

After one probe operation, the true solution of the urban light rail route planning problem, that is, the minimum spanning tree corresponding to this problem can be obtained (see Fig. 6).

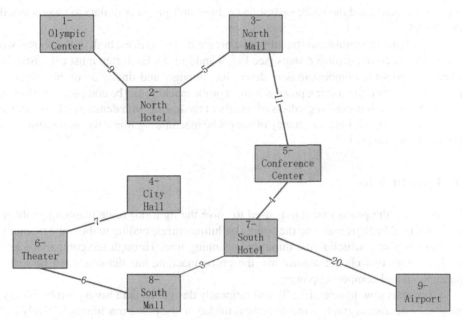

Fig. 6. The minimum spanning tree corresponding to the light rail route planning problem.

5   Results and Discussion

Under the premise of allowing the existence of interchange stations, the minimum spanning tree of the light rail route planning not only ensures the connection of all centers in the city, but also minimizes the total cost of route construction. The results can provide important reference and technical support for decision makers. For example, the seventh center, i.e., the "South Hotel" station, can be used as an interchange station to design two light rail routes. The two recommended routes are 1-2-3-5-7-9 and 4-6-8-7-9.

In spite of the three methods involved in Sect. 3 can achieve the same result, there are essential differences in the solving process and computational efficiency. By observing the pseudo code of the Prim algorithm, it is easy to find that its time complexity is $O(n^2)$. Since its time complexity is only related to the number of vertices n and not to the number of edges m, the Prim algorithm is more suitable for solving dense graphs. In contrast, the Kruskal algorithm pays more attention to the edges in the graph. By observing the pseudo code, it can be easily obtained that its time complexity is $O(m\log m)$. Since its complexity depends on the number of edges m, the Kruskal algorithm is more suitable for solving sparse graphs.

Any algorithm based on Turing machine is subject to linear data placement mode and sequential data processing mode. Therefore, the solving process must be executed step by step. However, the structure of the probe machine breaks through the above two limitations well. The data library of the probe machine defines a non-linear data placement mode, and the probe operation enables multiple pairs of data to be processed in parallel.

For solving the minimum spanning tree problem of 9 vertices, both of the above two algorithms need to perform 8 steps (see Fig. 4 and Fig. 5). Each step must exhaustively search all possible combinations to determine an edge, and finally a complete tree is formed. However, the solving process using a probe machine can be completed with only one probe operation. And regardless of whether it is dealing with dense graphs or sparse graphs, the computational efficiency of the probe machine significantly outperforms the above two algorithms.

6   Conclusions

In this work, the probe machine is used to solve the light rail route planning problem with practical background, and the optimal solution corresponding to the route planning problem is given, which is the minimum spanning tree. Through the comparison and analysis with two classic algorithms, the probe machine has demonstrated powerful parallelism and computing power.

Of course, how to scientifically and rationally design the data library, probe library, and probe operation graph in the detector is the key to the probe machine effectively and efficiently solving complex combination optimization problems. One direction of future works is to explore the possibility of solving the Job Shop Scheduling Problem (JSSP) by using viable biological computational models including the probe machine among others.

Acknowledgments. This work was supported by the National Natural Science Foundation of China (Nos. 61876101, 61802234, 61806114), the Social Science Fund Project of Shandong (Nos. 11CGLJ22, 16BGLJ06), the Natural Science Foundation of the Shandong Province (No. ZR2019QF007), the Youth Fund for Humanities and Social Sciences, Ministry of Education (No. 19YJCZH244), the China Postdoctoral Special Funding Project (No. 2019T120607), and the China Postdoctoral Science Foundation Funded Project (Nos. 2017M612339, 2018M642695).

References

1. Bao, J., Lu, L., Ji, Z.: Tourism transportation optimization and tour route designing of north anhui province based on the kruskal algorithm of graph-theory. Hum. Geogr. **25**(3), 144–148 (2010)
2. Yang, Z., Shi, W., Peng, J.: Application of kruskal algorithm based on union-find sets in subway planning. Comput. Knowl. Technol. **9**(18), 4236–4238 (2013)
3. Pan, M.: Application of minimum spanning tree and kruskal algorithm in city planning. Digit. Technol. Appl. **2017**(08), 132 (2017)

4. Wu, B., et al.: An extended minimum spanning tree method for characterizing local urban patterns. Int. J. Geogr. Inf. Sci. **32**(3), 450–475 (2017)
5. Benvenuti, C.: Bridging: spanning tree protocol. In: Understanding Linux Network Internals. O'Reilly Media, Inc. (2006)
6. Li, C., He, J., Zhang, P., Xu, Y.: A novel sectionalizing method for power system parallel restoration based on minimum spanning tree. Energies **10**(7), 948 (2017)
7. Graaf, M., Boucherie, R.J., Hurink, J.L., van Ommeren, J.-K.: An average case analysis of the minimum spanning tree heuristic for the power assignment problem. Random Struct. Algorithms **55**(1), 89–103 (2019)
8. Ren, Z., Li, H., Liu, Y., Xu, Y., Jin, L., Li, W., et al.: Alterable weight minimum spanning tree method for electrical collector system planning. IEEE Access **7**, 71585–71592 (2019)
9. Guo, H., Liu, L., Chen, J., Xu, Y., Jie, X.: Alzheimer classification using a minimum spanning tree of high-order functional network on fmri dataset. Front. Neurosci. **11**, 639 (2017)
10. Lin, W., Li, Y.: Parallel regional segmentation method of high-resolution remote sensing image based on minimum spanning tree. Remote Sens. **12**(5), 783 (2020)
11. Xu, L., Luo, B., Pei, Z.: Boundary-aware superpixel segmentation based on minimum spanning tree. IEICE Trans. Inf. Syst. **E101.D**(6), 1715–1719 (2018)
12. Huang, J., Xu, R., Cheng, D., Zhang, S., Shang, K.: A novel hybrid clustering algorithm based on minimum spanning tree of natural core points. IEEE Access **7**, 43707–43720 (2019)
13. Mishra, G., Mohanty, S.K.: A fast hybrid clustering technique based on local nearest neighbor using minimum spanning tree. Expert Syst. Appl. **132**, 28–43 (2019)
14. Lv, X., Ma, Y., He, X., Huang, H., Yang, J.: Ccimst: A clustering algorithm based on minimum spanning tree and cluster centers. Math. Prob. Eng. **2018**, 1–14 (2018)
15. Adleman, L.M.: Molecular computation of solutions to combinatorial problems. Science **266**, 1021–1024 (1994)
16. Lipton, R.J.: DNA solution of hard computational problems. Science **268**, 542–545 (1995)
17. Roweis, S., et al.: A sticker-based model for DNA computation. J. Comput. Biol. **5**(4), 615–629 (1998)
18. Winfree, E., Liu, F., Wenzler, L.A., Seeman, N.C.: Design and self-assembly of two-dimensional DNA crystals. Nature **394**(6693), 539–544 (1998)
19. Smith, L.M., et al.: A surface-based approach to DNA computation. J. Comput. Biol. **5**(2), 255–267 (1998)
20. Sakamoto, K., et al.: Molecular computation by DNA hairpin formation. Science **288**(5469), 1223–1226 (2000)
21. Xu, J., Qiang, X., Zhang, K., Zhang, C., Yang, J.: A DNA computing model for the graph vertex coloring problem based on a probe graph. Engineering **4**(1), 61–77 (2018)
22. Xu, J.: Probe machine. IEEE Trans. Neural Netw. Learn. Syst. **27**(7), 1405–1416 (2016)
23. Sha, S., Chen, Y.: Probe model for solving travelling salesman problem. J. Huaibei Normal Univ. Nat. Sci. **37**(2), 36–39 (2016)
24. Yang, J., Yin, Z.: The working operation problem based on probe machine model. In: Gong, M., Pan, L., Song, T., Zhang, G. (eds.) BIC-TA 2016. CCIS, vol. 681, pp. 47–53. Springer, Singapore (2016). https://doi.org/10.1007/978-981-10-3611-8_6
25. Sun, J., Dong, H., Kong, Y., Fang, Y.: Solution to shortest path problem using a connective probe machine. Math. Probl. Eng. **2019**, 1–8 (2019)
26. Prim, R.C.: Shortest connection networks and some generalizations. Bell Syst. Tech. J. **36**(6), 1389–1401 (1957)
27. Kruskal, J.: On the shortest spanning subtree of a graph and the traveling salesman problem. Proc. Am. Math. Soc. **7**(1), 48–50 (1956)

Cortical Neural P Systems

Zhongzheng Fu and Luping Zhang$^{(\boxtimes)}$

Key Laboratory of Image Processing and Intelligent Control of Education Ministry
of China, School of Artificial Intelligence and Automation,
Huazhong University of Science and Technology, Wuhan 430074, China
lpzhang@hust.edu.cn

Abstract. P systems are distributed and parallel computing models inspired from living cells. In this work, a variant of spiking neural P systems, cortical neural P systems, are proposed in the frame work of P systems combining the topology structure of basic P system and information processing style in spiking neurons. The computational power of cortical neural P systems is investigated. It is proved that cortical neural P systems are equivalent to Turing machines as number generators.

Keywords: Membrane computing · Cortical neuron · Weighted channel · University

1 Introduction

P systems initiated by Păun Gh., abstracting computational notions from the structure and function of living cells, have become one of the most attractive fields of computer science [19,21]. In a basic P system, several membranes are hierarchically arranged in the skin membrane, and objects are scattered in the delimited sub-membranes. P systems evolve by using evolution rules associated with according objets and regions. Such systems have been used to solve problems in image processing [5], economic dynamic [26], cryptographic applications [13], etc.

Many variants of P systems have been proposed with biological inspirations or computer science motivation, such as splicing P systems [16], cell-like P systems with evolutional symport/antiport rules and membrane creation [27], tissue P systems with cell division [20], Spiking neural P systems with target indications [32]. Generally, P systems have been classified into three categories [22]: cell-like P systems [15,19], tissue-like P systems [9,10], and neural-like P systems [6,14]. Extensive efforts have been devoted to investigate computational properties of P systems [17,22,24]. The family sets of natural numbers computed by variants of P systems has been compared with that computed by Turing machines [28,34]; the family sets of languages associated with computations in variants of P systems has been compared with Chomsky, Lindenmayer hierarchy, etc. [4,16,29,31]; the computation complexity of variants of P systems has also been widely investigated [1,32].

© Springer Nature Singapore Pte Ltd. 2021
L. Pan et al. (Eds.): BIC-TA 2020, CCIS 1363, pp. 624–638, 2021.
https://doi.org/10.1007/978-981-16-1354-8_43

The biological neocortex consisting of cortical neurons is an intelligent composition involving in various activities in mammalian brains [2,8]. In the neocortex, multi-cortical layers are critical to receive, process, and transmit information through spiking neurons distributed in each layers [7]. Communications between layers are established through activities of neurons in cortical circuits [23], where the stimulus could inspire [3] and inhibit [35] several neurons (a population of neurons) nearby rather than a neuron [11]. In this work, inspired by the above biological characteristic of cortical neurons, we propose a variant of spiking neural P systems, cortical neural P systems, with cell-like structure [33] (corresponding to hierarchical cortical layers in the neocortex) and weighted channels (corresponding to communications between cortical layers).

In a cortical neural P system, there are rules of the form $T_i/c_j \rightarrow (1, tar_{j_1}) \ldots$ $(1, tar_{j_l})$ in a membrane i. If membrane i ($0 \le i \le m$) has exact potential $p_i(t) = T_i$ at step t, then the rule $T_i/c_j \rightarrow (1, tar_{j_1}) \ldots (1, tar_{j_l})$ in membrane i is enabled. If there are several rules enabled, one of the enabled rules are nondeterministically chosen and applied, consuming potential c_j, producing one unit potential and sending it to each of the target membranes tar_{j_k} ($1 \le k \le l$) amplified by the weight of the channel (i, tar_{j_k}). A cortical neural P system evolves by applying rules as the above way and halts when there is no rule enabled. The computation result of a cortical neural P system can be defined in the following two ways. (1) The internal output associated with the potential of specified membrane [33]: when a system halts, the potential of the specified output membrane encodes the number computed. (2) The external output associated with the interval time of the first two potential emitted to the environment [18]: no matter the system halts or not, the time distance between the first two potentials emitted to the environment encodes the number computed.

In this work, the computation power of cortical neural P systems is investigated with both of the internal output and the external output. We prove that cortical neural P systems with both of these two outputs are equivalent to Turing machines as number generating devices.

This work is organized as follows. In the next section, the definition of cortical neural P systems is given. In Sect. 3, several examples of cortical neural P systems are given to show how a cortical neural P system works and the computation results are defined in two different ways. In Sect. 4, we prove that cortical neural P systems are universal as number generator devices. In the final section, conclusions and some open problems are given.

2   Cortical Neural P Systems

We use notions and notations from the handbook of membrane computing and the theory of formal language, and one can refer to [21,22,25] for details. The set of natural numbers is denoted by N.

Definition 1. *A cortical neural P system of degree m ($m \ge 1$) is a construct*

$$\Pi = (\mu, p_0(0), \ldots, p_m(0), R_0, \ldots, R_m, Chan, i_{out}),$$

where

- μ *is the hierarchical membrane structure;*
- $p_i(0)$, $0 \leq i \leq m$, *is the initial potential of membrane* i;
- R_i, $0 \leq i \leq m$, *is the finite set of activation rules in membrane* i, *with the form* $T_i/c_j \rightarrow (1, tar_{j_1}) \ldots (1, tar_{j_l})$, *where* $1 \leq c_j \leq T_i$, $l \geq 1$, $tar_{j_k} \in \{0, \ldots, m\} - \{i\}$ $(1 \leq k \leq l)$;
- $Chan = \{((i, j), w_{(i,j)}) \mid i, j \in \{0, 1, \ldots, m, env\}, i \neq j, w_{(i,j)} \in Z - \{0\}\}$ *is the set of weighted channels, env denotes the environment and the related channel denotes the communication between a membrane and the environment;*
- $i_{out} \in \{0, 1, \ldots m\}$ *is the label for the output membrane.*

By convention, it is assumed that there is a global-clock, and each rule execution takes one step recorded by the global clock. If membrane i has exact potential $p_i(t) = T_i$ at step t, then the rule $T_i/c_j \rightarrow (1, tar_{j_1}) \ldots (1, tar_{j_l})$ in membrane i is enabled. If there are several rules enabled, one of the enabled rules are nondeterministically chosen and applied. The execution of the rule $T_i/c_j \rightarrow (1, tar_{j_1}) \ldots (1, tar_{j_l})$ consumes potential c_j, leaving potential $T_i - c_j$ in membrane i, and produces potential 1 (i.e., one unit potential) sending to each of the target membranes tar_{j_k} $(1 \leq k \leq l)$. Each of the target membranes tar_{j_k} receives potential $w_{(i, tar_{j_k})}$ through the channel (i, tar_{j_k}).

The configuration of system Π at step t is described by the potential distributed in each membrane $C_t = \langle p_0(t), p_1(t), \ldots, p_{m-1}(t) \rangle$, where the $p_i(t)$ $(0 \leq i \leq m - 1)$ is the potential of membrane i at step t. So, the initial configuration is $C_0 = \langle p_0(0), p_1(0), \ldots, p_{m-1}(0) \rangle$. From the initial configuration, by using activation rules, system Π evolves from one configuration to another. A sequence of transition starting from the initial configuration forms a computation. If a computation gets a halting configuration where no rule can be used, then the computation halts.

In this work, we define computation result in the following two ways. (1) The internal output: a membrane is specified as the output membrane; when a system halts, the potential of the specified output membrane encodes the number computed, like [33]. (2) The external output: associated with the interval time between the first two potential emitted to the environment: no matter the system halts or not, the time distance between the first two potentials emitted to the environment encodes the number computed, like [30].

The set of natural numbers generated by the system Π is denoted $N(\Pi)$. The family of the number generated by cortical neural P systems is denoted by $N_\alpha CNP_m$, where m is the degree of the system, when this bound is not specified, then the parameter m is substituted with $*$; the subscript $\alpha = \{in, 2\}$ denotes that the computation results are defined as the internal output or the external output.

3   Examples

In this section, we give three examples to show how a cortical neural P system works and how a computation result is associated with a computation.

Example 1. Consider the cortical neural P system Π_1 of degree 3:

$$\Pi_1 = ([[\ ]_1, [\ ]_2]_0, 1, 0, 0, R_0, R_1, R_2, Chan, 1),$$

where

- $R_0 = \{1/1 \rightarrow (1,1)(1,2)\}$, $R_1 = \{n_1 + 1/1 \rightarrow (1,0)\}$, $R_2 = \{1/1 \rightarrow (1,0)\}$,
  where n_1 is a given constant;

- $Chan = \{((0,1),1), ((0,2),1), ((1,0),1), ((2,0),1)\}$.

The cortical neural P system Π_1 is shown in Fig. 1, where three membranes are respectively denoted by rounded rectangles with labels 0, 1, 2, in which activation rules and the initial potentials are specified. In this example, a computation result of Π_1 is defined as the potential value of membrane 1 at a halting configuration.

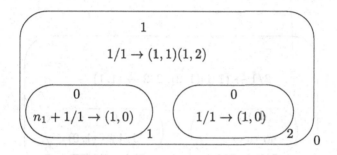

Fig. 1. Cortical neural P system Π_1.

At step $2u - 1$ ($u = 1, \ldots, n_1$), each of the membranes 1 and 2 receives potential 1 through respectively weighted channels $((0,1),1)$ and $((0,2),1)$, by using the rule $1/1 \rightarrow (1,1)(1,2)$ in membrane 0. At step $2u$, membrane 2 uses its enabled rule $1/1 \rightarrow (1,0)$ producing and sending potential 1 to membrane 0 through weighted channel $((1,0),1)$.

Table 1. Distribution of the membrane potential in Π_2 during its evolution.

Membrane	Step					
	1	2	3	...	$2n_1 + 2$	$2n_1 + 3$
0	1	0	1	...	0	2
1	0	1	1	...	$n_1 + 1$	n_1
2	0	1	0	...	1	0

At step $2n_1 + 1$, membrane 1 accumulates potential $n_1 + 1$ with enabled rule $n_1 + 1/1 \rightarrow (1,0)$. At step $2n_1 + 2$, membrane 1 and membrane 2 are simultaneously activated delivering potential 2 to membrane 0. Then, the system gets its halting configuration $C_{2n_1+2} = \langle 2, n_1, 0 \rangle$ with the computing result $N(\Pi_1) = \{n_1\}$. The transitions of configurations are represented in Table 1.

By example 1, we have the following observation.

Proposition 1. *An arbitrary finite number can be generated by a cortical neural P system of degree 3 associated with internal outputs.*

Example 2. The cortical neural P system Π_2 is shown in Fig. 2.

$$\Pi_2 = ([[\ ]_1, [\ ]_2]_0, 2, 0, 0, R_0, R_1, R_2, Chan, 1)$$

- $R_0 = \{2/1 \rightarrow (1,1)(1,2)\} \cup \{2/2 \rightarrow (1,1)\};\ R_1 = \emptyset;\ R_2 = \{1/1 \rightarrow (2,0)\};$

- $Chan = \{((0,1), -1), ((0,2), 1), ((2,0), 1)\}.$

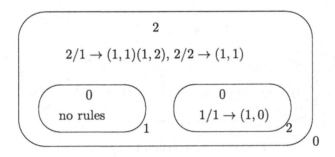

Fig. 2. Cortical neural P system Π_2.

Table 2. Distribution of the membrane potential in Π_2 during its evolution.

Membrane	Step					
	1	2	3	...	$2n-1$	$2n$
0	2	1	2	...	2	0
1	0	-1	-1	...	$-n+1$	$-n$
2	0	1	0	...	0	0

The system Π_2 starts from the initial configuration $C_0 = \langle 2, 0, 0 \rangle$ with the transitions of configurations in Π_2 represented in Table 2. The computation results are defined as the potential value of membrane 1 at the halting configuration.

If membrane 1 initially uses the rule $2/1 \to (1,1)(1,2)$ delivering potential 1 to each of membrane 1 and membrane 2, then membrane 1 can be activated again after membrane 2 using its enabled rule. If membrane 1 having potential 2 uses the enabled rule $2/2 \to (1,1)$ at step $2n-1$ $(n \geq 1)$ when membrane 1 has potential $-n+1$, then membrane 1 accumulates potential $-n$ at the next step. Then, Π_2 halts at the halting configuration $\langle 0, -n, 0 \rangle$. Thus, $N(\Pi_2) = N - \{0\}$.

By Example 2, we have the following observation.

Proposition 2. *A cortical neural P system of degree 3 associated with internal outputs can generate an infinite set of natural numbers.*

Example 3. The cortical neural P system Π_3 of degree 3 is designed (shown in Fig. 3) as follows:

$$\Pi_3 = ([[\ ]_1, [\ ]_2]_0, 6, -n_1, 0, R_0, R_1, R_2, Chan, 0),$$

where

- $R_0 = \{6/1 \to (1,1)(1,2), 5/3 \to (1, env)(1,1)(1,2), 3/1 \to (1,1)(1,2), 4/4 \to (1, env)\}$;
  $R_1 = R_2 = \{1/1 \to (1,0)\}$;
- $Chan = \{((0,1),1), ((0,2),1), ((0, env),1), ((1,0),1), ((2,0),1)\}$.

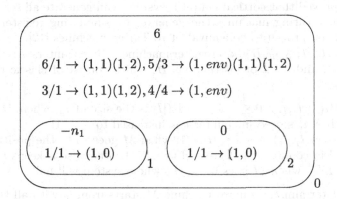

Fig. 3. Cortical neural P system Π_3.

The computation results of system Π_3 is defined by $t_2 - t_1 - 1$, if the interval time of first two potential to the environment is $t_2 - t_1$.

Membrane 0 is activated sending potential 1 to each of the membranes 1 and 2 at step 1 by using the rule $6/1 \to (1,1)(1,2)$. Then, membrane 0 emits the first potential 1 to the environment at step 2 by using the rule $5/3 \to (1, env)(1,1)(1,2)$.

If $n_1 = 0$, then membrane 1 and membrane 2 will be simultaneously activated at step 2, emitting potential 2 to membrane 0. At step 3, membrane 0 is activated by using rule $4/4 \rightarrow (1, env)$ emitting the second potential to the environment, and both of membrane 1 and membrane 2 are activated emitting potential 2 to membrane 0. Then, the system halts at $\langle 2, 0, 0 \rangle$.

If $n_1 > 0$, then only membrane 2 will be activated at step 2 emitting potential 1 to membrane 0. From step 3 to step $n_1 + 1$, membrane 0 is activated by using the rule $3/1 \rightarrow (1,1)(1,2)$, and membrane 2 is simultaneously activated by using the rule $1/1 \rightarrow (1,0)$ in each step. At step $n_1 + 2$, the potential of membrane 1 increases to 1, and both membrane 1 and membrane 2 are activated emitting potential 2 to membrane 0. Meanwhile, membrane 0 is activated by the application of the rule $3/1 \rightarrow (1,1)(1,2)$. At step $n_1 + 3$, membrane 0 is activated by the enabled rule $4/4 \rightarrow (1, env)$ sending the second potential to the environment, and both of membrane 1 and membrane 2 are activated emitting potential 2 to membrane 0. Then, the whole system halts with no rule to be used. Therefore, $N_2(\Pi_3) = (n_1 + 3) - 2 - 1 = n_1 (n_1 \geq 0)$.

By Example 3, we get the following result.

Proposition 3. *A cortical neural P system of degree 3 associated with external outputs can generate an infinite set of natural numbers.*

4   The Computation Power of Cortical Neural P Systems

In this section, we investigate the computation power of cortical neural P systems. It is proved that cortical neural P systems can generate all sets of natural numbers that Turing machines can generate by simulating register machines, which has been proven to be equivalent to Turing machines [12].

Let $M = (q, I, l_0, l_h, H)$ be a register machine with q counters, a set of instruction labels I, and a set of instructions H, which consist of classic three forms instructions.

- $l_i : (ADD(r), l_j, l_k), 0 \leq i \leq |I| - 1$ ($|I|$ is the size of I); when M goes to l_i, the number n_r stored in counter r is increased to $n_r + 1$;
- $l_i : (SUB(r), l_j, l_k), 1 \leq i \leq |I| - 1$; when M goes to l_i, the positive number n_r stored in counter r is decreased to $n_r - 1$, otherwise it keeps $n_r = 0$;
- $l_h : (HALT)$; when M goes to l_h, the whole system will halt.

A non-deterministic counter machine M starts from l_0 with all the counters empty. It proceeds according to the guidance of the instructions and gives the computation results at counter 1 when M gets its halting instruction l_h.

Theorem 1. $N_{in}CNP_* = NRE$.

Proof. We prove the converse inclusion $NRE \subseteq N_{in}CNP_*$ here, as the inclusion $N_{in}CNP_* \subseteq NRE$ can be achieved through Turing thesis.

Let M be a register machine having q registers as described above. Assume that the instruction labels are consecutively listed as $l_0, l_1, \ldots, l_m$. To simulate M, the cortical P system Π of degree $2q + 1$ is constructed as follows:

$$\Pi = ([[~]_1, [~]_2, \ldots, [~]_{2q}]_0, p_0(0), \ldots, p_{2q}(0), R_0, \ldots, R_{2q}, Chan, 1):$$

- $p_0(0) = T$ ($T > m + 2$ is a constant), $p_k(0) = 0$ ($k = 1, 2, \ldots, 2q$);

- $R_0 = \{T + i/T + i - s \rightarrow (1, r)(1, q + 1) \mid r = 1, 2, \ldots, q;\ s = j, k\}$
  $\cup \{T + i/T + i - j \rightarrow (1, q + r) \mid r = 2, 3, \ldots, q\}$
  $\cup \{2T + j/T + j - k \rightarrow (1, env)\},$
  $R_r = \{1/1 \rightarrow (1, 0)\}$ ($r = 1, 2, \ldots, q$),
  $R_{q+1} = \{1/1 \rightarrow (1, 0)\},$
  $R_{q+r} = \{r + 1/r \rightarrow (1, r), 1/1 \rightarrow (1, 0)\}$ ($r = 2, 3, \ldots, q$);
- $Chan = \{((0, q + 1), 1), ((q + 1, 0), T), ((0, env), 1)\}$
  $\cup \{((0, r), -1), ((r, 0), T) \mid r = 1, 2, \ldots, q\}$
  $\cup \{((0, q + r), r + 1), ((q + r, r), 1), ((p + r, 0), T) \mid r = 2, 3, \ldots, q\}.$

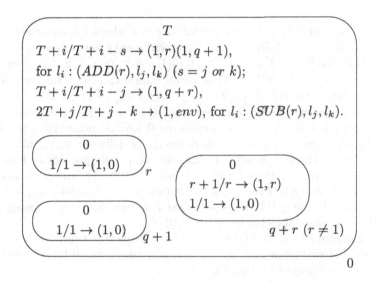

Fig. 4. Cortical P system Π with output membrane 1.

The cortical P system Π is shown in Fig. 4 where membranes are represented by rounded rectangles with corresponding activation rules. The potential of the membrane r ($r = 1, 2, \ldots, q$) is associated with the number stored in register r. To be exact, the potential of the membrane r is $-n_r$ when counter r stores number n_r. The computation results are defined as the absolute value of membrane 1 potential at the halting configuration.

By convention, membrane 1 acting as output membrane is associated with no substraction instruction. Thus, membrane $q + 1$ is the auxiliary membrane designed for simulating the instructions of the form $l_i : (ADD(r), l_j, l_k)$, and each of membrane $q + r$ ($r = 2, 3, \ldots, q$) is the auxiliary membrane designed for simulating the instructions of the form $l_i : (SUB(r), l_j, l_k)$.

Initially, the potential of membrane 0 is T with each of other membranes having potential zero. When the potential of the membrane equals to $T + i$, the system Π starts to simulate the instruction l_i in M. If membrane 0 has potential $T + h$, then Π halts with no applicable rules.

Table 3. Distribution of the membrane potential in Π during the ADD instruction simulation.

Membrane	Step		
	t	$t+1$	$t+2$
0	$T+i$	s	$T+s$
r	$-n_r$	$-n_r - 1$	$-n_r - 1$
$q+1$	0	1	0

Assume that membrane 0 has potential $T + i$ where i is associated with an ADD instruction $l_i : (ADD(r), l_j, l_k)$, and membrane r has potential $-n_r$ at step t. Either the rule $T + i/T + i - j \rightarrow (1, r)(1, q + 1)$ $(r = 1, 2, \ldots, q)$ or the rule $T + i/T + i - k \rightarrow (1, r)(1, q + 1)$ in membrane 0 can be nondeterministically chosen to apply. If the rule $T+i/T+i-j \rightarrow (1, r)(1, q+1)$ (or $T+i/T+i-k \rightarrow (1, r)(1, q + 1)$) in membrane 0 is chosen at step $t + 1$; then potential $T + i - j$ (or $T + i - k$) is consumed from membrane 0 leaving potential j (or k) in it, and produced potential potential 1 is respectively delivered to membrane r and membrane $q + 1$ through weighted channels. Thus, the potential of membrane r decreases to $-n_r - 1$ through the channel $((0, r), -1)$, and the potential of auxiliary membrane $q + 1$ increases to 1 through the channel $((0, q + 1), 1)$. At step $t + 2$, membrane $q + 1$ emits potential T to membrane 0 by using the rule $1/1 \rightarrow (1, 0)$ through the channel $((q + 1, 0), T)$.

The simulation of $l_i : (ADD(r), l_j, l_k)$ is completed: the potential of membrane r is decreased from $-n_r$ to $-n_r - 1$, and membrane 0 has potential $T + s$ ($s = j$ or k) represented in Table 3.

Table 4. Distribution of the membrane potential in Π during the SUB instruction simulation with $n_r > 0$.

Membrane	Step			
	t	$t+1$	$t+2$	$t+3$
0	$T+i$	j	j	$T+j$
r $(r = 1, 2, \ldots, q)$	$-n_r$	$-n_r$	$-n_r + 1$	$-n_r + 1$
$q+1$	0	0	0	0
$q+r$ $(r = 2, \ldots, q)$	0	$r+1$	1	0

Assume that membrane 0 has potential $T + i$ associated with a SUB instruction $l_i : (SUB(r), l_j, l_k)$, and membrane r has potential $-n_r$ at step t. The rule $T+i/T+i-j \rightarrow (1, r)(1, q+1)$ $(r = 1, 2, \ldots, q)$ in the membrane 0 is enabled.

At step $t+1$, membrane 0 consumes potential $T+i-j$ remaining potential j in it, and delivers potential $r+1$ to membrane $q+r$ through channel $((0, q+r), r+1)$ by using the enabled rule in membrane 0. Receiving potential $r+1$, membrane $q+r$ can use the rule $r+1/r \rightarrow (1, r)$ emitting potential 1 to membrane r through weighted channel $((1, r), 1)$ at step $t+2$, increasing the potential of membrane r to $-n_r + 1$.

If $n_r > 0$, then the potential of the membrane r becomes $-n_r + 1 < 1$ receiving one potential from the membrane 0 at step $t+2$. At step $t+3$, the potential of membrane 0 becomes $T + j$, because it only receives potential from membrane $q+r$ which uses the rule $1/1 \rightarrow (1, 0)$. The case of $n_r > 0$ is displayed in Table 4.

Table 5. Distribution of the membrane potential in Π during the SUB instruction simulation with $n_r = 0$.

Membrane	Step				
	t	$t+1$	$t+2$	$t+3$	$t+4$
0	$T+i$	j	j	$2T+j$	$T+k$
r $(r = 1, 2, \ldots, q)$	0	0	1	0	0
$q+1$	0	0	0	0	0
$q+r$ $(r = 1, 2, \ldots, q)$	0	$r+1$	1	0	0

If $n_r = 0$, then the potential of the membrane r becomes 1 at step $t+2$. At step $t+2$, the rule $1/1 \rightarrow (1, 0)$ in membrane r can also be applied besides the rule in membrane $q+1$ with the same form. Hence, the potential of membrane 0 is $2T + k$, for it receives $2T$ units potential from membrane $q+r$ and membrane r at step $t+3$. At step $t+4$, the potential of the membrane 0 becomes $T+k$, as it uses the rule $2T+j/T+j-k \rightarrow (1, env)$ sending potential 1 to the environment. The detailed process is displayed in Table 5.

The simulation of $l_i : (SUB(r), l_j, l_k)$ is completed: the potential of membrane r is increased from $-n_r$ to $-n_r + 1$ when $n_r > 0$, and then membrane 0 has potential $T + j$; membrane r remains potential 0 when $n_r = 0$, and then membrane 0 has potential $T + k$.

When the potential of the skin membrane is $T + h$, there is no rule could be used. Thus, it gets the halting configuration, completing the halting instruction $l_h : HALT$.

As described above, the process of register machines generating numbers can be correctly simulated by Π, and hence $N_{in}CNP_{2q+1} = NRE$. □

The university can also be got from cortical P systems with external outputs.

Theorem 2. $N_2CNP_* = NRE$.

Proof. Let M be a register machine as described above, and T ($T > m + 2$) be a constant. We construct system Π' of degree $2q + 2$ for this Theorem presented in Fig. 5:

$$\Pi' = ([[\ ]_1, [\ ]_2, \ldots, [\ ]_{2q+1}]_0, p_0(0), \ldots, p_{2q+1}(0), R_0, \ldots, R_{2q+1}, Chan, 0) :$$

- $p_0(0) = T$ ($T > m + 2$ is a constant), $p_k(0) = 0$ ($k = 1, 2, \ldots, 2q$);

- $R_0 = \{T + i/T + i - s \rightarrow (1, r)(1, q + 1) \mid r = 1, 2, \ldots, q; \ s = j, k\}$
  $\cup \{T + i/T + i - j \rightarrow (1, q + r), 2T + j/T + j - k \rightarrow (1, env) \mid r = 2, 3, \ldots, q\}$
  $\cup \{T + h/h + 1 \rightarrow (1, 2q + 1), T - 1/1 \rightarrow (1, env)(1, 2q + 1)\}$
  $\cup \{2T - 2/T \rightarrow (1, 2q + 1), 3T - 2/T - 2 \rightarrow (1, env)\},$
  $R_r = \{1/1 \rightarrow (1, 0)\}$ ($r = 1, 2, \ldots, q$),
  $R_{q+1} = \{1/1 \rightarrow (1, 0)\},$
  $R_{q+r} = \{r + 1/r \rightarrow (1, r), 1/1 \rightarrow (1, 0)\}$ ($r = 2, 3, \ldots, q$),
  $R_{2q+1} = \{1/1 \rightarrow (1, 0)(1, 1)\};$

- $Chan = \{((0, q + 1), 1), ((0, 2q + 1), 1), ((q + 1, 0), T), ((0, env), 1)\}$
  $\cup \{((0, r), -1), ((r, 0), T) \mid r = 1, 2, \ldots, q\}$
  $\cup \{((0, q + r), r + 1), ((q + r, r), 1), ((q + r, 0), T) \mid r = 2, 3, \ldots, q\}.$

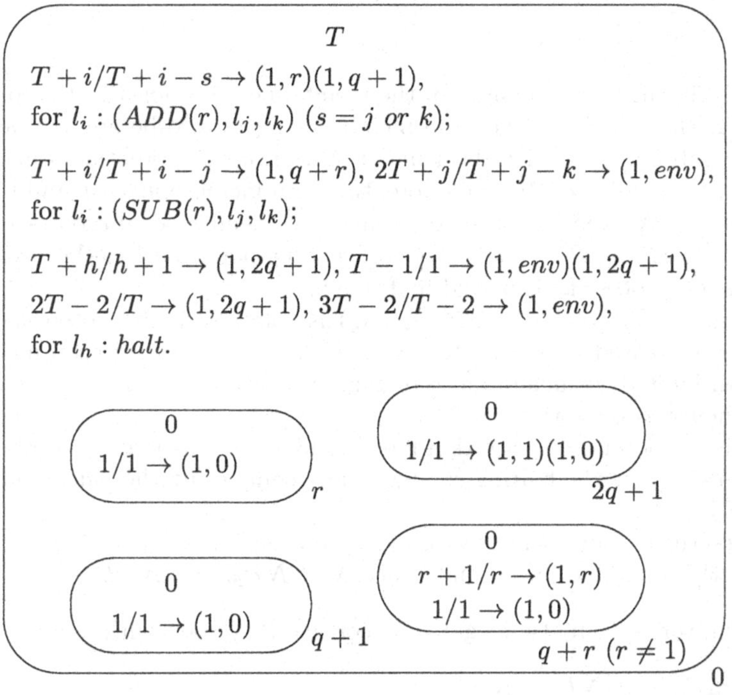

Fig. 5. Cortical P system Π' with output membrane 0.

The proof is based on Theorem 1: the rules for the ADD instructions and SUB instructions in M remain the same with those in Theorem 1, and the repeat simulation of ADD instructions as well as SUB instructions keeping the same with that in Theorem 1 is not shown here; the added four rules and auxiliary membrane $2q + 1$ are used for external computation result.

The computation results of system Π' is here defined by $t_2 - t_1 - 2$, if the interval time of first two potential to the environment is $t_2 - t_1$.

Assume that membrane 0 has potential $T + h$ at step t with membrane 1 having potential $-n_1$. At step $t + 1$, the enabled rule $T + h/h + 1 \rightarrow (1, 2q + 1)$ in membraneoox 0 is applied delivering potential 1 to membrane $2q + 1$ though weighted channel $((1, 2q+1), 1)$. At step $t+2$, the rule $T-1/1 \rightarrow (1, env)(1, 2q+1)$ in membrane 0, the rule $1/1 \rightarrow (1, 0)$ in membrane $q + 1$, and the rule $1/1 \rightarrow (1, 1)(1, 0)$ in membrane $2q + 1$ are applied at the same time emitting the first potential to the environment. The potential of membrane 1 increases to $-n_1 + 1$ at step $t + 2$. From step $t + 3$ to step $t + n_1 + 2$, the rule $2T - 2/T \rightarrow (1, 2q + 1)$ in membrane 0, and the rule $1/1 \rightarrow (1, 1)(1, 0)$ in membrane $2q + 1$ are applied in each step with sustained growth in the potential of membrane 1. At step $t + n_1 + 3$, the rule $1/1 \rightarrow (1, 0)$ in membrane 1 is applied besides the rules in the membrane 0 and membrane $2q + 1$. At step $t + n_1 + 4$, the rule $3T - 2/T - 2 \rightarrow (1, env)$ is applied emitting the second potential to the environment, besides the application of the enabled rules in membrane $2q + 1$ and membrane 1. At step $t + n_1 + 5$, membrane 0 having potential $2T$ receives potential T though the weighted channel $((1, 0), T)$. After the application of the rule $1/1 \rightarrow (1, 0)$ in membrane 1 at step $t + n_1 + 5$, Π' halts with membrane 0 having potential $3T$. The interval time of first two potential to the environment is $(t+n_1+5)-(t+3) = n_1 + 2$, so $N(\Pi') = n_1$, in which n_1 is the computational result of M. Hence, the proof is completed. □

As describe by Theorem 1 and Theorem 2, a cortical neural P system of degree $2q + 1$ with internal outputs or of degree $2q + 2$ with external outputs is enough to simulate a register machine with q register. On the other hand, Minsky have constructed an universal counter machine with only three counters [12]. Hence, the following two equalities are established.

Corollary 1. $N_{in}CNP_7 = NRE$.

Corollary 2. $N_2CNP_8 = NRE$.

5   Conclusion

In this work, inspired by the biological characteristics in the neocortex, we introduce a new type of P systems named cortical neural P systems and investigate the computational power of cortical neural P systems. We prove that both cortical neural P systems whose computation results are associated with two types of outputs are universal as number generator devices.

In this work, each of the activation rule is of the form $T_i/c_j \rightarrow (1, tar_{j_1}) \dots$ $(1, tar_{j_l})$. Some works could be done on the general form of the activation rule. For instance, the activation rule can be extended to the form $(T_{i1}, T_{i2})/c \rightarrow (1, tar_{j_1}) \dots (1, tar_{j_l})$, with $T_{i1} < T_{i2}$, $var = (in_t, in, out, here)$, i.e. membrane i can be activated when its membrane potential is in the interval. It is also interesting to consider incorporating the delay in each activation rule of the form $T_i/c \rightarrow (1, var); d_i$ in cortical P systems, i.e., the produced potential will be delivered to the target membrane after d_i step.

Besides, there are several ways associated computations in P systems with languages [16,29]. It is interesting to investigate the language properties of cortical P systems compared with the classic families of languages, such as the Chomsky hierarchical languages [25].

References

1. Adorna, H.N., Pan, L., Song, B.: On distributed solution to SAT by membrane computing. Int. J. Comput. Commun. Control **13**(3), 303–322 (2018)
2. Aston-Jones, G., Cohen, J.D.: An integrative theory of locus coeruleus-norepinephrine function: adaptive gain and optimal performance. Annual Rev. Neurosci. **28**, 403–450 (2005)
3. Bennett, C., Arroyo, S., Hestrin, S.: Subthreshold mechanisms underlying state-dependent modulation of visual responses. Neuron **80**(2), 350–357 (2013)
4. Bera, S., Pan, L., Song, B., Subramanian, K.G., Zhang, G.: Parallel contextual array P systems. Int. J. Adv. Eng. Sci. Appl. Math. **10**(3), 203–212 (2018). https://doi.org/10.1007/s12572-018-0226-9
5. Díaz-Pernil, D., Gutiérrez-Naranjo, M.A., Peng, H.: Membrane computing and image processing: a short survey. J. Membrane Comput. **1**(1), 58–73 (2019). https://doi.org/10.1007/s41965-018-00002-x
6. Ionescu, M., Păun, Gh., Yokomori, T.: Spiking neural P systems. Fundamenta Informaticae **71**(2,3), 279–308 (2006)
7. Lodato, S., Arlotta, P.: Generating neuronal diversity in the mammalian cerebral cortex. Ann. Rev. Cell Dev. Biol. **31**, 699–720 (2015)
8. Lui, J., Hansen, D., Kriegstein, A.: Development and evolution of the human neocortex. Cell **146**(1), 18–36 (2011)
9. Martín-Vide, C., Păun, Gh., Pazos, J., Rodríguez-Patón, A.: Tissue P systems. Theor. Comput. Sci. **296**(2), 295–326 (2003)
10. Martín-Vide, C., Pazos, J., Păun, Gh., Rodríguez-Patón, A.: A new class of symbolic abstract neural nets: tissue P systems. In: Ibarra, O.H., Zhang, L. (eds.) COCOON 2002. LNCS, vol. 2387, pp. 290–299. Springer, Heidelberg (2002). https://doi.org/10.1007/3-540-45655-4_32
11. McGinley, M.J., David, S.V., McCormick, D.A.: Cortical membrane potential signature of optimal states for sensory signal detection. Neuron **87**(1), 179–192 (2015)
12. Minsky, M.L.: Finite and Infinite Machines. Prentice-Hall Englewood Cliffs (1967)

13. Ochirbat, O., Ishdorj, T.-O., Cichon, G.: An error-tolerant serial binary full-adder via a spiking neural P system using HP/LP basic neurons. J. Membrane Comput. **2**(1), 42–48 (2020). https://doi.org/10.1007/s41965-020-00033-3

14. Pan, L., Păun, Gh., Zhang, G., Neri, F.: Spiking neural P systems with communication on request. Int. J. Neural Syst. **27**(8), 1750042 (2017)

15. Pan, L., Song, B.: P systems with rule production and removal. Fundamenta Informaticae **171**(1–4), 313–329 (2020)

16. Pan, L., Song, B., Nagar, A.K., Subramanian, K.G.: Language generating alphabetic flat splicing P systems. Theoret. Comput. Sci. **724**, 28–34 (2018)

17. Pan, L., Song, B., Valencia-Cabrera, L., Pérez-Jiménez, M.J.: The computational complexity of tissue P systems with evolutional symport/antiport rules. Complexity **2**, 1–21 (2018)

18. Pan, L., Zeng, X., Zhang, X., Jiang, Y.: Spiking neural P systems with weighted synapses. Neural Process. Lett. **35**(1), 13–27 (2012)

19. Păun, Gh.: Computing with membranes. J. Comput. Syst. Sci. **61**(1), 108–143 (2000)

20. Păun, Gh.: Tissue P systems with cell division. Int. J. Comput. Commun. Control **3**(3), 295–303 (2008)

21. Păun, Gh.: Membrane Computing: An Introduction. Springer, Heidelberg (2012). https://doi.org/10.1007/978-3-642-56196-2

22. Păun, Gh., Rozenberg, G.: A guide to membrane computing. Theoret. Comput. Sci. **287**(1), 73–100 (2002)

23. Renart, A., De La Rocha, J., Bartho, P., Hollender, L., Parga, N., Reyes, A., Harris, K.D.: The asynchronous state in cortical circuits. Science **327**(5965), 587–590 (2010)

24. Rong, H., Wu, T., Pan, L., Zhang, G.: Spiking neural P systems: theoretical results and applications. In: Graciani, C., Riscos-Núñez, A., Păun, G., Rozenberg, G., Salomaa, A. (eds.) Enjoying Natural Computing. LNCS, vol. 11270, pp. 256–268. Springer, Cham (2018). https://doi.org/10.1007/978-3-030-00265-7_20

25. Rozenberg, G., Salomaa, A.: Handbook of Formal Languages: Volume 3 Beyond Words. Springer, Heidelberg (2012). https://doi.org/10.1007/978-3-642-59126-6

26. Sánchez-Karhunen, E., Valencia-Cabrera, L.: Modelling complex market interactions using PDP systems. J. Membrane Comput. **1**(1), 40–51 (2019). https://doi.org/10.1007/s41965-019-00008-z

27. Song, B., Li, K., Orellana-Martín, D., Valencia-Cabrera, L., Pérez-Jiménez, M.J.: Cell-like P systems with evolutional symport/antiport rules and membrane creation. Inf. Comput. **275**, 51 (2020)

28. Song, B., Pan, L., Jiang, S., Wang, Y.: The computation power of tissue P systems with flip-flop channel states. Int. J. Adv. Eng. Sci. Appl. Math. **10**(3), 213–220 (2018). https://doi.org/10.1007/s12572-018-0225-x

29. Song, B., Xu, F., Pan, L.: On languages generated by context-free matrix insertion-deletion systems with exo-operations. In: Graciani, C., Riscos-Núñez, A., Păun, G., Rozenberg, G., Salomaa, A. (eds.) Enjoying Natural Computing. LNCS, vol. 11270, pp. 279–290. Springer, Cham (2018). https://doi.org/10.1007/978-3-030-00265-7_22

30. Wang, J., Hoogeboom, H., Pan, L., Păun, Gh., Pérez-Jiménez, M.: Spiking neural P systems with weights. Neural Comput. **22**(10), 2615–2646 (2010)

31. Wu, T., Pan, L., Alhazov, A.: Computation power of asynchronous spiking neural P systems with polarizations. Theor. Comput. Sci. **777**, 474–489 (2019)

32. Wu, T., Zhang, L., Pan, L.: Spiking neural P systems with target indications. Theor. Comput. Sci. (2020)

33. Wu, T., Zhang, Z., Păun, Gh., Pan, L.: Cell-like spiking neural P systems. Theor. Comput. Sci. **623**, 180–189 (2016)
34. Zhang, Z., Wu, T., Păun, A., Pan, L.: Universal enzymatic numerical P systems with small number of enzymatic variables. Sci. China Inf. Sci. **61**(9), 1–12 (2017). https://doi.org/10.1007/s11432-017-9103-5
35. Zhou, M., et al.: Scaling down of balanced excitation and inhibition by active behavioral states in auditory cortex. Nat. Neurosci. **17**(6), 841–850 (2014)

Author Index

Printed in the United States
by Baker & Taylor Publisher Services